Quicken 2009

Bonnie Biafore

POGUE PRESS™
O'REILLY®

Beijing • Cambridge • Farnham • Köln • Sebastopol • Taipei • Tokyo

Quicken 2009: The Missing Manual
by Bonnie Biafore

Published by O'Reilly Media, Inc., 1005 Gravenstein Highway North, Sebastopol, CA 95472.

O'Reilly books may be purchased for educational, business, or sales promotional use. Online editions are also available for most titles (*safari.oreilly.com*). For more information, contact our corporate/institutional sales department: (800) 998-9938 or *corporate@oreilly.com*.

Printing History:

September 2008:   First Edition.

 This book uses RepKover™, a durable and flexible lay-flat binding.

ISBN: 978-0-596-52248-3

[M]

Table of Contents

Part Three: Tuning Your Financial Engine

Part Five: Appendixes

The Missing Credits

About the Author

 **Bonnie Biafore** has put every Quicken feature worth using through its paces since 1990 and has sent innumerable suggestions for improvement to Intuit (many of which can be seen in Quicken 2009). She writes about personal finance, investing, and project management, although she's working on what she hopes will be a best-selling crime novel with movie rights worth oodles of money. As an engineer and project manager, she's thorough and steadfastly attentive to detail but redeems herself by using her sick sense of humor to transform these drool-inducing subjects into entertaining reading. Her *NAIC Stock Selection Handbook* won major awards from the Society of Technical Communication and APEX Awards for Publication Excellence (but the raves she receives from beginning investors mean much more to her).

Bonnie is also the author of O'Reilly's *Online Investing Hacks*, *QuickBooks 2009: The Missing Manual*, and *Microsoft Project 2007: The Missing Manual*. She writes a monthly column called "WebWatch" for Better Investing magazine and is a regular contributor to *www.bankrate.com* and *www.interest.com*. As a consultant, she manages projects for clients and wins accolades for her ability to herd cats.

When not chained to her computer, she hikes and cycles in the mountains, cooks gourmet meals, and practices saying no to additional work assignments. You can learn more at Bonnie's Web site, *http://www.bonniebiafore.com*, or email her at *bonnie.biafore@gmail.com*.

About the Creative Team

Dawn Frausto (editor) is assistant editor for the Missing Manual series. When not working, she plays soccer, beads, and causes trouble. Email: *dawn@oreilly.com*.

Peter Meyers (editor) is the managing editor of O'Reilly Media's Missing Manual series. He lives with his wife, daughter, and cats in New York City. Email: *peter.meyers@oreilly.com*.

Nellie McKesson (production editor) is a graduate of St. John's College in Santa Fe, NM. She currently lives in Jamaica Plain, MA, and spends her spare time making t-shirts for her friends to wear (*mattsaundersbynellie.etsy.com*). Email: *nellie@oreilly.com*.

Jeff Boevingloh (technical reviewer) is an information technology consultant who resides in the Denver area. He has been a dedicated Quicken user since 1994.

Tina Spargo (technical reviewer), her husband (and professional musician) Ed, their toddler Max, their two silly Spaniels, Parker (Clumber), and Piper (Sussex), all share time and space in their suburban Boston home. Tina juggles being an at-home mom with promoting and marketing Ed's musical projects and freelancing as a virtual assistant. Tina has over 15 years' experience supporting top-level executives in a variety of industries. Web site: *www.tinaspargo.com*.

Glenn Court (copy editor) is a freelance manuscript editor in Washington DC who gave up coffee for chai but still tends to meet herself coming and going. She enjoys (in no particular order) digitally enhancing old photographs, behavior watches at the National Zoo, amusing her friends unintentionally, giving tours of the Old Pension Building, walking and hiking, occasional Web design, the beach on and off season, and of course admiring cats. Web site: *www.formandsubstance.com*.

Acknowledgments

My eternal gratitude to everyone who helped make this book what it is today. I am honored and thankful to be part of the O'Reilly community. The folks at O'Reilly have done their usual amazing job: Dawn Frausto for keeping things running smoothly and keeping me company online nights and weekends, Glenn Court for putting the final coat on my words, and Ron Strauss for building an index that helps you find all the information you want (especially important given the complete absence of an index in Quicken Help).

I also want to thank the technical reviewers, Jeff Boevingloh and Tina Spargo, for keeping me honest and providing so many great tips for wrangling Quicken into submission.

The Missing Manual Series

Missing Manuals are witty, superbly written guides to computer products that don't come with printed manuals (which is just about all of them). Each book features a handcrafted index; cross-references to specific pages (not just chapters); and RepKover, a detached-spine binding that lets the book lie perfectly flat without the assistance of weights or cinder blocks.

Recent and upcoming titles include:

Access 2007: The Missing Manual by Matthew MacDonald

AppleScript: The Missing Manual by Adam Goldstein

AppleWorks 6: The Missing Manual by Jim Elferdink and David Reynolds

CSS: The Missing Manual by David Sawyer McFarland

Creating Web Sites: The Missing Manual by Matthew MacDonald

Digital Photography: The Missing Manual by Chris Grover and Barbara Brundage

Dreamweaver 8: The Missing Manual by David Sawyer McFarland

Dreamweaver CS3: The Missing Manual by David Sawyer McFarland

eBay: The Missing Manual by Nancy Conner

Excel 2003: The Missing Manual by Matthew MacDonald

Excel 2007: The Missing Manual by Matthew MacDonald

Facebook: The Missing Manual by E.A. Vander Veer

FileMaker Pro 8: The Missing Manual by Geoff Coffey and Susan Prosser

FileMaker Pro 9: The Missing Manual by Geoff Coffey and Susan Prosser

Flash 8: The Missing Manual by E.A. Vander Veer

Flash CS3: The Missing Manual by E.A. Vander Veer and Chris Grover

FrontPage 2003: The Missing Manual by Jessica Mantaro

Google Apps: The Missing Manual by Nancy Conner

The Internet: The Missing Manual by David Pogue and J.D. Biersdorfer

iMovie 6 & iDVD: The Missing Manual by David Pogue

iMovie '08 & iDVD: The Missing Manual by David Pogue

iPhone: The Missing Manual by David Pogue

iPhoto '08: The Missing Manual by David Pogue

iPod: The Missing Manual, Sixth Edition by J.D. Biersdorfer

JavaScript: The Missing Manual by David Sawyer McFarland

Mac OS X: The Missing Manual, Tiger Edition by David Pogue

Mac OS X Leopard: The Missing Manual, by David Pogue

Microsoft Project 2007: The Missing Manual by Bonnie Biafore

Office 2004 for Macintosh: The Missing Manual by Mark H. Walker and Franklin Tessler

Office 2007: The Missing Manual by Chris Grover, Matthew MacDonald, and E.A. Vander Veer

Office 2008 for Macintosh: The Missing Manual by Jim Elferdink

PCs: The Missing Manual by Andy Rathbone

Photoshop Elements 6: The Missing Manual by Barbara Brundage

Photoshop Elements 6 for Mac: The Missing Manual by Barbara Brundage

Introduction

Like most people who buy Quicken, you're probably looking for help: with credit card receipts, checking account statements, retirement plans, and on and on the list goes. You want Quicken to provide an overview of your financial health, while sparing you the time and tedium of balancing your checkbook and tracking every investment by hand. Quicken 2009 can do all that and more, and this book will show you how. The program's hundreds of features share one purpose: to help manage your personal finances. If you have trouble remembering to transfer extra cash into higher-interest-rate savings, for example, you can set up Quicken to remind you. If budgeting's your downfall, Quicken can help build a budget to achieve your savings goals.

Quicken isn't hard to learn. Using the program as an electronic checkbook isn't much different from recording checks and deposits in a paper register. Features and techniques that you're familiar with from other programs (windows, dialog boxes, drop-down menus, keyboard shortcuts, and so on) work the same way in Quicken. Best of all, once you enter a bit of financial information into Quicken— like a check, deposit, credit card transaction, or loan payment—you never have to type it again. Quicken can use that information over and over to calculate things like what you've spent, how much you still owe, or even your net worth. Every minute you spend learning the program is time well spent.

Your Quicken ambitions may be no bigger than balancing your checkbook. Yet somehow, owning the program might get you thinking about aspects of your personal finances that you were content to completely ignore in the past. As you learn to do more with Quicken, you'll expand your knowledge of—and ideas about— money. Then again, sometimes Quicken seems to raise more questions than it answers: Return of capital from stock—what's that? What does *net worth* actually mean—and why do you need to know yours? Luckily, the book you're holding picks up where Quicken's help resources leave off.

This book begins by telling you how to set up Quicken 2009 to fit *your* needs. It explains the program's basic features and answers questions you're likely to have (but Quicken Help doesn't answer). If speed is your thing, this book shows you the fastest ways to perform financial tasks—like shortcut menus and keyboard short-cuts. It also provides comprehensive discussions and step-by-step tutorials for people who need a bit of handholding. Along the way, you'll discover features and benefits most Quicken owners never knew existed.

Managing Personal Finance with Quicken

Quicken is more than an electronic checkbook—it's a personal finance manage-ment program. Sure, the register you use to record transactions electronically *looks* like your paper register. But by harnessing the power of your PC and the Internet, Quicken opens up new horizons for performing financial tasks more quickly and easily.

Note: This book covers the *Windows* version of Quicken Deluxe 2009, Quicken Premier 2009, and the *personal* finance features of Quicken Home & Business 2009. It also tells you about the investment tools that make Quicken Premier…well, premier. On the other hand, this book doesn't cover Quicken Online or Quicken Starter Edition (page 5), which have radically different features and commands. Similarly, you won't find info on the Mac version of the program, which was developed separately and differs signifi-cantly from the Windows versions. (As of this writing, Quicken Mac 2008 was still not yet available—only Quicken Mac 2007 was.)

What Quicken Does

Perhaps the first benefit you'll come to know and love is that you no longer have to worry about arithmetic. Quicken automatically updates your account balances when you record transactions, calculates the remaining funds when you divvy up a paycheck, matches downloaded transactions with recorded ones, and tells you when you've successfully reconciled your account.

Because Quicken lets you assign transactions to categories, collecting your tax-related information and building a budget are no longer frantic treasure hunts through shoeboxes of paper. Instead, a few quick clicks produce the information you need. You can also feed tax-related data into programs like Turbo Tax and then import your tax return results into Quicken to plan next year's tax strategy.

Quicken doesn't just track what you've done with your money in the past. Whether you spend cash, rack up credit card debt, or salt away savings from each paycheck, the program's planning features help you decide what to do with your money in the future. From simple reminders to pay credit card bills on time to portfolio reports that show you whether your investments are working as well as they could be, Quicken is bursting with tools to improve your financial situation.

What Quicken Doesn't Do

Quicken *isn't* a true bookkeeping or accounting program. Although Quicken Home & Business (page 5) offers features like invoices, accounts receivable, and payroll, it *doesn't* offer ledgers, true double-entry accounting, a chart of accounts, inventory control, or certain financial reports that accountants and the IRS require. For example, because Quicken doesn't include equity accounts, you can't generate a balance sheet like the ones your accountant is used to. (However, Quicken's "Income/Expense by Category" report can pass for a profit-and-loss report or income statement.)

If you have a small business and you *don't* track inventory or generate standard financial reports, you can get by with Quicken Home & Business. But if you work with a bookkeeper or accountant, you've no doubt heard pleas to switch to Quick-Books (Intuit's small-business accounting program)—and it's generally a good idea to listen. Yes, QuickBooks costs a bit more and dumps you unceremoniously into the Scylla and Charybdis of debits and credits. But if you pay your accountant for advice and she's willing to help you get started with QuickBooks, the transition won't be painful. (In fact, your grumbling may decrease as you discover that keeping your books is easier in QuickBooks and that you now have more time to run your business.) If you decide to use QuickBooks, *QuickBooks 2009: The Missing Manual* can help you get started.

Note: If you decide to use QuickBooks for your business, you'll still need Quicken for your personal finances, because QuickBooks doesn't track investments.

Quicken and Accounting

So, though Quicken isn't an accounting program, it does perform *some* accounting tasks. If your financial horizon is no further than your next paycheck, some of Quicken's features may seem like mystical arts. Yet, in a cruel twist, Quicken's accounting features are equally mysterious to those who *are* familiar with accounting. Here's a quick overview of how Quicken accounts for your money:

Accounts vs. categories

Assets are things you own, like checking accounts, certificates of deposit (CDs), brokerage accounts, a house, and your car. Similar to the asset accounts you find in business accounting, Quicken includes several types of accounts for your assets: checking, savings, house, vehicle, and a generic asset account for assets that don't fall under any of the other account types (like the Fabergé egg your Aunt Katrinka left you in her will). Furniture and clothing are assets as well, though most folks don't bother tracking them in Quicken.

Liabilities are what you owe to others, like credit cards, mortgages, and other types of loans. Quicken includes liability accounts to cover every type of debt you carry. The time frame is the only difference between Quicken's liability accounts and the ones you see in business accounting. Businesses keep short-term and long-term liabilities separate. Quicken merely categorizes credit card liability accounts as banking accounts, and mortgages and loans show up in the Net Worth (Property and Debt) center; short-term and long-term liability designations are nowhere to be found.

In business accounting, *income accounts* track money that an organization receives, whether from selling services, selling products, or getting research grants. *Expense accounts* track money the organization spends, like employee salaries, office rent, and accountants' fees. Quicken, by contrast, doesn't have income and expense accounts. Instead, you create income and expense *categories*. When you record a check, charge, or deposit—in fact, any kind of transaction—you assign the money to a category.

Following the money

Business accounting uses *double-entry accounting*, in which every transaction represents a debit in one account and a credit to another account. Although accountants, bookkeepers, and other financial geeks can spot debit entries and credit entries from a mile away, the rest of us don't need that kind of detail.

Quicken takes a more intuitive approach that only partially mimics double-entry accounting. For example, in Quicken, credit card balances act like negative cash, which is an appropriate way to think about it. Whether you spend cash or credit card debt, you're nibbling away at your bottom line. When you pay your credit card bill, Quicken deducts money from your checking account and adds it to the credit card account, decreasing the balance you owe.

Equity

In business accounting, anything worth tracking gets its own separate account, even the difference between the value of your assets and liabilities. An *equity* account is the holding tank for that difference. In business, the financial report called a *balance sheet* gets its name because the total for all the asset accounts equals the total of all the liability accounts and equity accounts.

Quicken doesn't have equity accounts but it can still calculate the difference between your total assets and total liabilities, called your *net worth*. In other words, it's the value of everything you own after you subtract all your debts. Net worth is as important in personal finances as equity is in business. Increasing the value of what you own while decreasing the amount you owe increases your net worth—and helps you achieve all your other goals in life. (Quicken's Account Bar displays your net worth to regularly remind you of your progress.)

Choosing the Right Quicken Edition

You've got five flavors of Quicken 2009 to choose from and this book covers two and a half of them. (It tells you how to use Quicken Deluxe and Quicken Premier. You can also use the book for the home side of Quicken Home & Business.)

Deciding which one suits you is relatively easy. Here's an overview of what each edition does:

- **Quicken Online** ($2.99 per month) is completely Web-based and significantly different from the Quicken editions that run on your PC. It lets you access your accounts (which live online) from a computer or a Web-enabled cellphone. The downside is you can't track anything but income and spending; investing and asset accounts aren't part of this edition.

- **Quicken Starter Edition** ($29.99) is only for first-time Quicken users who are starting from scratch, because you can't import existing Quicken data if you've used the program before. With this edition, you can record your banking deposits and payments, balance your checkbook, reconcile your bank accounts, and see how you spend your money. That's it—and, for many people, that's enough.

- **Quicken Deluxe** ($59.99) handles all the basic personal finance tasks, from tracking spending to paying bills, downloading transactions, budgeting, and tracking your investments. You can even store electronic images of bank statements, receipts, and other financial records. If you plan to use the program to track your spending, gather your tax data, track basic investment information, and do a little planning, Deluxe is all you need.

- **Quicken Premier** ($89.99) is for people who are serious about investing. This edition does everything that Quicken Deluxe does, but throws in additional investment tools. It also offers to help find tax deductions you may have missed.

- The only reason you'd spring for **Quicken Premier Home & Business** ($99.99) is if you run a small business and want to track both your personal and business finances with the program. This edition offers everything that Quicken Premier does and adds payroll, accounts receivable, invoicing, and mileage tracking.

- **Quicken Rental Property Manager** ($149.99) is a new edition that helps you track your personal finances and the rental properties that you manage. This edition is like Quicken Premier on rental-property steroids, with built-in categories for rental income and expenses and other rental-oriented features.

Note: If you track inventory, handle payroll for more than a few employees, or need financial reports formatted to the typical accounting standard, consider forking over the extra cash for QuickBooks. QuickBooks Simple Start is for first-time QuickBooks users and costs $99.95 (about $10 more than Quicken Home & Business). You can test the waters with QuickBooks Simple Start Free Edition, which handles up to 20 customers, employees, or vendors (and it's free). QuickBooks Pro costs $199.95 ($99.95 for upgrades from previous versions) and works for many small businesses.

What's New in Quicken 2009

Most of the time, new Quicken versions come with enhancements, timesaving features, and more online tools to make your work easier and faster. You don't *have* to upgrade every year, but Intuit drops support for versions that are more than 3 years old. With a rebate for existing customers, upgrading every couple of years doesn't cost all that much.

Quicken 2009's changes are more evolutionary than revolutionary, but you may like a few of the additions:

- **Simpler setup.** No more grueling setup interviews. In Quicken 2009, the Setup tab (page 19) is where you choose the features you want to use. When you're ready to expand your financial prowess, simply click the Setup tab and turn on more features. When you do that, Quicken adds navigation tabs (see the next bullet point) and the corresponding menus to the Quicken menu bar.

- **More navigation options.** In Quicken 2009, each of the financial centers (Banking, Investing, and Net Worth) along with screens for setup, paying bills, taxes, planning, and customized views you create are just a click away (page 30)—simply click one of the navigation tabs below the toolbar, shown in Figure I-1.

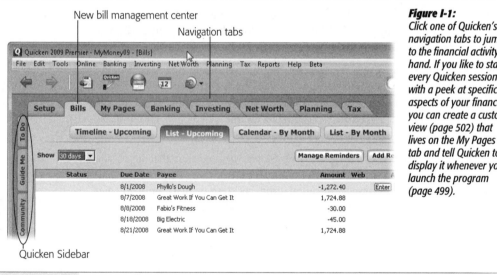

Figure I-1:
Click one of Quicken's navigation tabs to jump to the financial activity at hand. If you like to start every Quicken session with a peek at specific aspects of your finances, you can create a custom view (page 502) that lives on the My Pages tab and tell Quicken to display it whenever you launch the program (page 499).

- **Simplified Account List window.** Before Quicken 2009, you had to click one Account List tab to view accounts and another to manage them. Now, everything about accounts is in one place (page 64): the Account List window (press Ctrl+A to open it). There, you simply select an account and then edit its settings.

- **Bill management center.** If you're constantly juggling funds to stay ahead of your bills, the new bill management center may help. Click the Bills navigation tab (page 30) and you can see what bills are coming up during the next week, the next two weeks, or the next 30 days. When a bill is due, you can enter it right there on the Bills tab.

- **Simplified scheduled transaction dialog box.** The new and improved dialog box for scheduling transactions (called Add Transaction Reminder) puts the fields you fill out in a more logical order (page 186). You start with who you're paying (or receiving money from) and the amount, then you specify the account you're using and the method of payment. If QuickFill (page 88) does its job, it automatically fills in the Category and Tag fields for you. On the schedule side, Quicken automatically sets up a reminder and doesn't set an ending date for the schedule, so you don't have to change those settings unless you want to.

- **Quicken Sidebar.** The tabs hanging off every side of the Quicken screen are beginning to look like a college bulletin board before summer vacation. The new Sidebar (page 33) dangles from the right side of the Quicken main window. Click the To Do tab to see tasks you may need to perform. Guide Me gives you advice about the task at hand. The Community and Services tabs take you to a Quicken Web page with additional assistance. The Tools tab has links to Quicken features that may come in handy for the screen you're looking at, such as Budget when you're on the Banking tab.

About This Book

Despite the many improvements in Quicken over the years, one feature consistently falls short: Intuit's documentation. For a topic as complicated as personal finance, all you get with Quicken is an electronic copy of *Getting Started with Quicken*, which is little more than a list of tasks Quicken performs, with a few step-by-step instructions.

Even if you don't mind reading instructions in one window as you work in another, you'll quickly discover that Quicken Help often isn't worth the screen space it consumes. The help topics usually cover the basic material you already know, but fail to answer the burning questions that made you launch Help in the first place. You have two options for finding help topics: an expandable table of contents and a search feature. There's no index for you to quickly scroll through. In addition, Quicken Help rarely tells you *why* you might want to use any feature. And with onscreen help, underlining key points, jotting hard-earned insights in margins, and reading about Quicken while sitting in the bathtub are out of the question.

Quicken 2009: The Missing Manual is the book that *should* have come with Quicken 2009. Although each version of Quicken introduces new features and enhancements, you'll still find this book useful if you're tracking your finances in an earlier version of Quicken. (Of course, the older your version of the program, the more dissimilarities you'll run across.)

In this book, you'll find step-by-step instructions for using the most popular and useful Quicken features, including those you may not quite understand, let alone know how to do: budgeting (Chapter 11), recording investment transactions (Chapter 12), archiving Quicken data files (page 475), and so on. Along the way, the book helps you evaluate Quicken's features and decide which ones are the most useful to you.

Quicken 2009: The Missing Manual is designed to accommodate readers at every technical level. The primary discussions are written for beginner or intermediate Quicken users. But if you're a first-time Quicken user, special boxes titled "Up To Speed" provide the introductory information you need to understand the topic at hand. Advanced users should watch for similar boxes labeled "Power Users' Clinic," which offer technical tips, tricks, and shortcuts for the experienced Quicken fan.

FREQUENTLY ASKED QUESTION

Importing Data into Quicken

Why can't I import data into Quicken?

One of the biggest changes in recent years (starting with Quicken 2005) is the format that Intuit uses to communicate with financial institutions. The old format was called QIF (Quicken Interchange Format). The new format, called OFX (Open Financial Exchange), makes it much easier to activate accounts for online financial services through Quicken and to download transactions from financial institutions into Quicken accounts.

Unfortunately, OFX eliminates the ability to *import* transactions to Quicken's checking, savings, credit card, 401(k), and brokerage accounts, but you can still import transactions into asset, liability, and cash accounts. (Full details on all these account distinctions await you in the pages ahead.)

Because Quicken 2009 limits the use of the old QIF format, you can no longer import data from other programs (which was helpful if you wanted to convert data from programs other than Microsoft Money which you can convert using a

special tool), from Quicken data files (sometimes helpful with data corruption issues), or from financial institutions that opted not to support Quicken's new OFX format.

To make matters worse, Intuit also dropped support for online financial services that use the old format, rendering Quicken versions prior to 2005 useless for downloading transactions or paying bills online. Express Web Connect is one attempt to lessen the pain. With Express Web Connect, you can use One Step Update to download transactions (page 143) even from financial institutions that don't support direct connections to Quicken.

If you're just getting started with Quicken, all this controversy may seem like a tempest in a teapot. But many Quicken fans consider these changes draconian measures on Intuit's part. Unfortunately, if you want to use the program's online financial services, you have to use Quicken 2005 or later, or choose a different program.

About the Outline

Quicken 2009: The Missing Manual is divided into five parts, each containing several chapters:

- **Part One: Getting Started** (Chapters 1–4) covers how to set up Quicken based on your needs. These chapters explain how to create a Quicken data file, create accounts, and choose categories. It also includes one chapter that takes you through a quick test drive to whet your appetite.

- **Part Two: Getting Down to Business** (Chapters 5–8) follows your money from the moment you earn it to when you reconcile your bank accounts at the end of each month. These chapters describe how to make deposits and pay for expenses, whether you download transactions or record them yourself. You also find out how to rev up your financial work with timesavers like scheduled transactions. Finally, you learn how to reconcile your accounts with your financial institutions' records.

- **Part Three: Tuning Your Financial Engine** (Chapters 9–14) introduces you to some of the features that help you increase your financial success. These chapters explain how to create and use budgets; track property, debt, and investments; plan for the future; and generate Quicken reports to prepare your tax returns or evaluate your financial fitness.

- **Part Four: Quicken Power Tools** (Chapters 15–17) helps you protect your financial information and teaches you how to make Quicken look and act the way you want. These chapters provide care and feeding instructions for your Quicken data files and include the techniques you can use to determine what you see and how Quicken behaves. You'll also learn how to export data from Quicken to other programs and the import options you have.

- **Part Five: Appendixes** is made up of three appendixes that provide a quick review of the most helpful keyboard shortcuts, a guide to Quicken resources, and instructions for installing and upgrading the program, respectively.

The Very Basics

To use this book, and indeed to use Quicken, you need to know a few basics. This book assumes that you're familiar with a few terms and concepts:

- **Clicking.** This book gives you three kinds of instructions that require you to use your computer's mouse or trackpad. To *click* means to point the arrow pointer at something on the screen and then—without moving the pointer at all—press and release the left button on the mouse (or laptop trackpad). To *right-click* means the same thing, but pressing the *right* mouse button instead. Usually, clicking with the left button selects an onscreen element or presses a button onscreen. A right-click usually reveals a *shortcut menu*, which lists several common tasks specific to whatever you're right-clicking. To *double-click*, of course, means to click twice in rapid succession, again without moving the pointer at all. And to *drag* means to move the pointer while holding down the left button the entire time. To *right-drag*, of course, means to do the same thing while holding down the right mouse button.

  When you're told to *Shift-click* something, you click while pressing the Shift key. Related procedures, like *Ctrl-clicking*, work the same way—just click while pressing the corresponding key.

- **Menus.** The *menus* are the words at the top of your screen: File, Edit, and so on. Click one to make a list of commands appear, as though they're written on a window shade you've just pulled down. Some people click to open a menu and then release the mouse button; after reading the menu command choices, they click the command they want. Other people like to press the mouse button continuously as they click the menu title and drag down the list to the desired command; only then do they release the mouse button. Either method works, so choose the one you prefer.

- **Keyboard shortcuts.** Nothing is faster than keeping your fingers on your keyboard, entering data, choosing names, triggering commands—without losing time by grabbing the mouse, carefully positioning it, and then choosing a command or list entry. That's why many experienced Quicken fans prefer to trigger commands by pressing combinations of keys on the keyboard. For example, in most word processors, you can press Ctrl+B to produce a **boldface** word. When you read an instruction like "Press Ctrl+A to open the Account List window," start by pressing the Ctrl key; while it's down, type the letter A and then release both keys.

About → These → Arrows

Throughout this book, and throughout the Missing Manual series, you'll find sentences like this one: "Choose Edit → Preferences → Quicken Program." That's shorthand for a much longer instruction that directs you to navigate three nested menus in sequence, like this: "Choose Edit. On the Edit menu, point to the Preferences menu entry. On the submenu that appears, choose Quicken Program." Figure I-2 shows the menus this sequence opens.

Similarly, this arrow shorthand also simplifies the instructions for opening nested folders, like My Documents → Quicken Data → Backup.

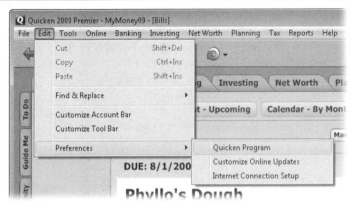

Figure I-2:
Instead of filling pages with long and hard-to-follow instructions for navigating through nested menus and folders, the arrow notations are concise, but just as informative. For example, choosing "Edit → Preferences → Quicken Program" takes you to the menu shown here.

About MissingManuals.com

At *www.missingmanuals.com*, you'll find news, articles, and updates to the books in this series.

But the Web site also offers corrections and updates to this book (to see them, click the book's title and then click Errata). In fact, you're invited and encouraged to submit such corrections and updates yourself. In an effort to keep the book as up to date and accurate as possible, each time we print more copies of this book, we'll make any confirmed corrections you've suggested. We'll also note such changes on the Web site, so that you can mark important corrections into your own copy of the book, if you like.

In the meantime, we'd love to hear your suggestions for new books in the Missing Manual line. There's a place for that on the Web site, too, as well as a place to sign up for free email notification of new titles in the series.

Safari® Books Online

 When you see a Safari® Books Online icon on the cover of your favorite technology book, that means the book is available online through the O'Reilly Network Safari Bookshelf.

Safari offers a solution that's better than eBooks. It's a virtual library that lets you easily search thousands of top tech books, cut and paste code samples, download chapters, and find quick answers when you need the most accurate, current information. Try it free at *http://safari.oreilly.com*.

Part One:
Getting Started

Setting Up Quicken

After you install Quicken (see Appendix C for instructions), you're only a few steps away from reaping the pocketbook-plumping benefits of having the program serve as your personal bookkeeper. Quicken's setup process is a whole lot easier than filling out the paperwork to open an account at your local bank. This chapter takes you through each step.

The first time you launch Quicken, the program offers to help set up your *data file*, an electronic filing cabinet that contains your financial records (the box on page 18 explains what's in this file). If you've used a previous version of Quicken, setup is a snap—a short conversion process preps your existing data file so Quicken 2009 can read it. If this is your first time using Quicken, the program's Setup Center helps you create a new data file, asks a few questions about your finances, and spits out a data file tailored to your basic needs. Either way, you'll have a working file in no time. You'll also learn how to open a Quicken data file, which is helpful if you work with more than one file—for instance, your own and one for your parents.

Launching Quicken

Launching Quicken works the same as pretty much any other program. Figure 1-1 shows the three ways to open Quicken:

- **Windows Quick Launch toolbar.** This is the fastest way to get going. Click the Quicken icon in the lower-left corner of your screen, where Windows tucks a collection of instant-launch icons. (This book covers only Quicken for Windows.) The box on page 17 shows you how to add Quicken to this lineup.

- **Desktop shortcut.** Double-click the Quicken 2009 desktop shortcut that Quicken added to your computer during installation.

- **Start menu.** This tried-and-true approach is great for those who don't use Quicken on a regular basis and want to keep their desktop free of shortcuts. On the Windows taskbar, click Start → All Programs → Quicken 2009 → Quicken 2009. (In Windows Vista, Start is a round button with the Windows logo inside.)

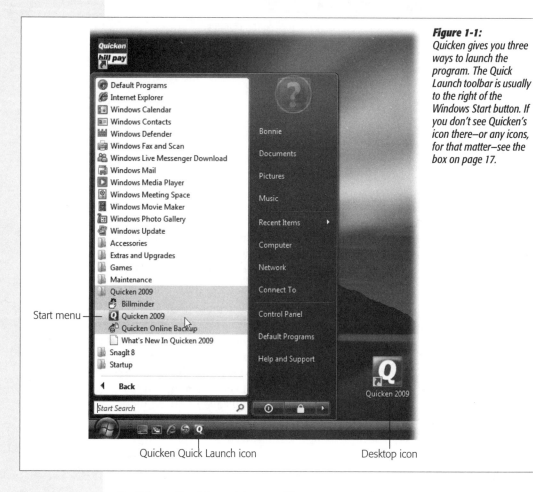

Figure 1-1:
Quicken gives you three ways to launch the program. The Quick Launch toolbar is usually to the right of the Windows Start button. If you don't see Quicken's icon there—or any icons, for that matter—see the box on page 17.

Start menu

Quicken Quick Launch icon   Desktop icon

Setting Up Your Data File

The first time you launch Quicken, the "Get Started with Quicken 2009" window pops up and greets you. If you're new to Quicken, the program guides you through creating and setting up your data file from scratch. If you've used Quicken before, you may not see the Get Started window but the program still helps convert your existing data file so that it works with the new version of the program. This section describes both options.

The Quick Launch Method

Windows' Quick Launch toolbar (no relation to Quicken) gives you a fast way to launch the programs you use most often and keeps your desktop from being overrun with shortcut icons. Unlike the Start menu, the Quick Launch toolbar doesn't display every installed program automatically—you add only the ones you use most often. It's a great timesaver.

The Quick Launch toolbar appears in the Windows taskbar—usually at the bottom left of your screen, as you can see in Figure 1-1. If you don't see the Quick Launch toolbar, turn it on by right-clicking an empty area on the taskbar and then choosing Toolbars → Quick Launch from the shortcut

menu that pops up. The checkmark that appears on the menu next to Quick Launch tells you that you're in business.

To add Quicken to the Quick Launch toolbar, Shift-right-click the Quicken shortcut on the Windows desktop and drag it onto the Quick Launch toolbar. When you release the mouse button, choose Copy Here from the shortcut menu that appears on the toolbar to create a shortcut. (If you're trying to neaten your desktop, choose Move Here instead, to move—rather than copy—the shortcut.) You can also use the Shift-right-click-and-drag technique to copy or move a shortcut from the Start menu or Windows Explorer.

Tip: The "Get Started with Quicken 2009" window isn't your only option when you want to set up or convert a file. If you'd rather create a new data file without the help of the Setup Center, click the Get Started window's Close button and use the commands on the Quicken menu bar, as described on page 481. Whenever you open a data file from an earlier version of the program, Quicken offers to convert the file (page 24).

If You're New to Quicken

For help creating and setting up a brand-new Quicken data file, in the "Get Started with Quicken 2009" window, select the "I am new to Quicken" option and then click Next. The first screen asks, "What do you want to call your data file?" You can let Quicken name your data file and choose its location or you can name the file something meaningful and tell the program where you want to store it. Here's what your options look like:

- **I will use the default file name and location.** Choose this option if you want Quicken to take care of naming and storing your data file. Quicken creates a folder called Quicken in your Documents folder in Windows Vista (My Documents in Windows XP) and puts your new data file in there, with the catchy name *QDATA* (which stands for "Quicken data").

Note: Unless you like to hunt around your hard drive for obscurely named files, choose the second option (described next). If you've already let Quicken name and save a *QDATA* file and need help finding it, see the box on page 21.

- **I want to choose a different file name and location.** This option lets you give your Quicken data file a meaningful name, like *MyMoney* or *Mom's Finances*, and store it in any folder you like. Personalized filenames are essential when you create more than one file—to track your parents' finances, for instance, or manage the income from your child's lawn-mowing sideline.

When you choose the second option and click Next, the Create Quicken File dialog box appears, as you can see in Figure 1-2. Navigate to the folder where you want to store your data file (it should be one you back up regularly). Then, in the "File name" box, type a meaningful name that works in Windows (letters, spaces, and apostrophes are fine). Click OK to create the file.

Figure 1-2:
The choices on the left side of the Create Quicken File dialog box should look familiar if you've saved files in other programs. To store your file within your Windows Vista file folder, click the icon with your username (or click My Documents in Windows XP). Click Computer to access any other hard drives you may have attached to your computer. If you're lucky enough to have a home network, click Network to access a Quicken data file in any shared folder on your network. (In Windows XP, the icons are named My Computer and My Network Places, respectively.)

Quicken creates your data file and then opens the Setup tab to help you customize the file by creating accounts, categories, and other features for tracking your finances. See page 19 to learn what you do next.

If You're a Quicken Veteran

If you have a data file from an earlier version of Quicken or you've just installed the program on a spiffy new computer, you can get started without all the hand-holding. In the "Get Started with Quicken 2009" window, select the "I am already a Quicken user" option and then click Next. The "Select your data file" screen that appears gives you three options:

- **Open a file located on this computer.** If you already have a Quicken data file—for example, one you copied from another computer—choose this option and then click Next. In the Open Quicken File dialog box, navigate to the folder where your data file is saved, select the filename, and then click OK. If the data file is from an earlier version of Quicken, the program helps you convert the file to Quicken 2009, as you'll learn in the section "Converting Existing Data Files" on page 24. (If you're converting an existing data file, you may want to print out parts of it, as described on page 24.)

Tip: You can bypass the "Get Started with Quicken 2009" window entirely by opening an existing data file directly (by double-clicking it in Windows Explorer, for example).

- **Restore a Quicken data file I've backed up to CD or disk.** This option works only with files backed up with Quicken's Backup command, as described in Chapter 15. When you choose this option and click Next, the Restore Quicken File dialog box appears. To restore the backup file, navigate to the folder or CD where the backup file is saved, select the filename, and then click OK. Once the program has reconstituted the backup file into a regular data file, you can choose File → Open to work with it.

- **Start over and create a new data file.** If you've mangled or lost the only copy of your data file in a horrible soda-spilling accident, take a deep breath, make a mental note to back up your data from now on, and then choose this option to tell Quicken to create a brand new file. Click Next and, in the Create Quicken File dialog box that appears, navigate to the folder you use for Quicken data. In the "File name" box, type a name for the new file and then click OK. Quicken creates the data file and displays the Setup tab.

Using the Setup Center

You can't miss Quicken's Setup Center—the program opens the Setup tab as soon as you create a data file. If you know your way around Quicken, you can use menu commands to do everything in the Setup Center. If you're new to Quicken, though, the Setup Center is handy because it pulls together all your options, lets you make your own financial choices, and adds everything you enter to your data file so you can start managing your finances.

Each version of Quicken seems to deliver a revamped setup tool. An earlier rendition was called Quicken Guided Setup, a lengthy process that included confessing your financial goals and spelling out your financial details. Quicken 2008's Express Setup was a shorter step-by-step procedure, but stopping anywhere in the middle could induce feelings of guilt. Quicken 2009's Setup Center places setup tools at your disposal so you can enter information whenever you're ready, as you can see in Figure 1-3. In the Setup tab, you can create *accounts*, electronic twins of your real-world financial accounts. It can also create *categories* to help track the money you spend and organize your budget. For instance, if you tell the Setup Center you're a homeowner, it adds a category for mortgage interest.

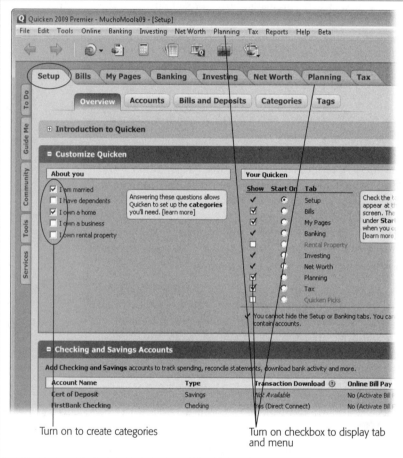

Figure 1-3:
After Quicken creates your data file, it automatically displays the Setup tab. The Overview screen is a long page that lists common setup tasks. (Be sure to scroll down or you'll miss out on some of the fun!) You can also work on specific setup tasks by clicking the buttons near the top of the tab: Accounts, Bills and Deposits, Categories, and Tags. If you want to stop setup for any reason, simply choose a menu command or click a different tab. To return to the Setup Center, click the Setup tab (circled).

Turn on to create categories

Turn on checkbox to display tab and menu

Telling Quicken About Yourself

The Setup Center's Overview screen wants to know a little personal information. Don't worry—it's only to help figure out the categories you'll use to track your finances and which financial features you see. In fact, if you leave the settings as they are, Quicken includes all of its features on tabs and menus and creates basic categories. See the box on page 23 for a quick introduction to categories and why they're so handy. Later on, you can set up more categories (page 74).

FREQUENTLY ASKED QUESTION

Who Moved My Data File?

*I saved my data file in a "special" location and now I can't
find the dang thing. Help!*

For Quicken 2005 and later, Quicken stores data in your
Windows documents folder (*C:\Users\<your username>\
Documents* in Windows Vista, *C:\Documents and settings\
<your username>\My Documents\Quicken* in Windows
XP)—unless you choose a different folder during installation
or move your data file afterward. The advantage of
Quicken's factory-set location is that you'll back up your
Quicken data along with all the other data in your documents folder when you use a backup program like Windows Backup. (Quicken's Backup command, on the other
hand, backs up only the Quicken data file you specify—see
page 463.)

Finding your data files is rarely an issue if you use the folder the
program creates specifically for your Quicken data. But if you
have no idea where you put your data files, you can search for
files ending in the .qdf file extension. Here's what you do:

1. In Quicken, choose File → Find Quicken Files.

2. In the Find Quicken Data File window, keep the All
   Quicken Files option selected. (To find a specific file,

select the Find Quicken Data File Named option and
type the name of the file in the box.)

3. In the "Look in" box, choose where you want to
   search. Quicken automatically enters Local Disk (C:),
   which is usually what you want.

4. Click Find.

5. If you see the file you want in the list, click its name
   and then click Open. Otherwise, choose a different
   location in the "Look in" box (for instance, another
   hard drive on your computer).

By the way, if you already have some Quicken experience
but can't find your data files, don't be embarrassed. Before
Quicken 2005, Quicken tucked your data files in the same
folder as the Quicken software (*C:\Program Files\Quicken*).
But resist the temptation to store it there for old times' sake:
If you use a backup program, it's likely to skip the Program
Files folder because most people don't keep their files and
documents there. (See page 479 for more info on moving
and copying your data file.)

Telling Quicken which categories you want

Quicken automatically adds the most popular categories to your data file without
asking your permission. The "About you" checkboxes on the Overview screen tell
Quicken to create categories for special financial situations, such as separate salary
categories for you and your spouse. Here's what each checkbox does:

- **I am married.** If you're married and want to track categories like income and
  401(k) contributions for each spouse, turn on the "I am married" checkbox to
  set up those categories. (If you *aren't* married but have a living arrangement
  that *looks* like married—say you bought a house together—go ahead and turn
  on the "I am married" checkbox.) Then, each of you will have categories for
  your own income and tax-related items like 401(k) contributions. For money
  that gets mingled in other ways like the expenses for the house you co-own, you
  can run a report at tax time to see the total tax deductions (page 275) and split
  them in whatever percentages you want.

- **I have dependents.** Turn on this checkbox if you have children, parents, or other folks you list as dependents on your tax returns. Quicken creates categories for dependent-related expenses, which you can use to fill out your tax return.

- **I own a home.** Turn on this checkbox if you own a home and want categories for your house, like tax-deductible mortgage interest and home improvements.

- **I own a business.** Although the Quicken Home & Business edition provides special features specific to running a business, you can tell other editions of Quicken to create a few business-related categories by turning on this checkbox.

- **I own rental property.** If you turn on this checkbox, Quicken creates categories to help you track income and expenses for rental property.

Telling Quicken what features you want to use

The Your Quicken section on the right side of the Overview screen lets you turn financial features on and off. Here's what you do:

- **Show.** If you're starting out by tracking your checking account in the program, you can turn off all the checkboxes in the Show column except for Bills and Banking. When you turn off a checkbox, Quicken removes that feature's entry on the Quicken menu bar at the top of the main Quicken window and hides its tab along the top of the screen. Turn a checkbox on to see its menu entry and tab once more, as Figure 1-3 shows.

  When you want to start using other features, click the Setup tab and turn on those features' checkboxes: Investing, Planning, or Tax, for example.

- **Start On.** To tell Quicken which tab you want to see whenever you launch the program, turn on its radio button in the Start On column. If you usually dive right into banking, for example, click the Banking option to make the Banking tab appear front and center when Quicken starts.

Setting Up Accounts

As you scroll down the Overview page, you reach sections for creating different types of accounts (such as checking and savings) and setting up reminders for bills, as well as places to record paychecks and transfers between accounts. The buttons on the Overview page create specific types of accounts: Add Checking Account, Add Savings Account, Add Credit Card, Add Investment Account, and Add Cash Account help you set up accounts in Quicken to mirror your real-world financial accounts (Figure 1-4).

The buttons for creating accounts in the Setup tab don't have superpowers of any kind—they can't magically fill in all your financial data for you. They simply open the Account Setup window and walk you through the same account creation process you use to create accounts anywhere else in Quicken. Chapter 3 explains where you can create accounts in Quicken and steps you through the entire process.

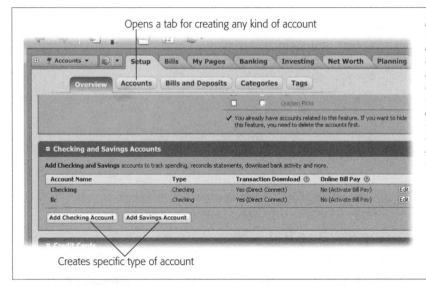

Opens a tab for creating any kind of account

Creates specific type of account

Figure 1-4:
*To create any type of
account without scrolling
through the Overview
screen, click the Accounts
button (next to
Overview). Initially, the
Accounts screen displays
only headings. To add a
new account, click Add
Account at the bottom
right of the screen.*

UP TO SPEED

Categories: The Key to Staying Organized

Categories help you track where your money comes from and where it goes. By assigning Quicken categories to every deposit and payment you make, you can see how you're doing compared to your budget, gather the information you need to prepare your income tax returns, and evaluate your finances in many other ways. For example, when you apply a Charity category to every check you write to bona fide charities, you can run a report at the end of the year that totals your charitable tax deductions for your tax return (page 275).

Categories also let you see how much you spend on certain items to help you cut back—or to build next year's budget (page 291).

Categories are so central to Quicken that the program gets you started with dozens of built-in categories. If your finances are simple, these ready-made categories may do the trick. As your needs change, you can create your own categories, for instance, to watch what you spend on your stamp-collecting hobby. Chapter 4 tells the whole category saga.

Setting Up Bills, Deposits, and Paychecks

Quicken can help keep you out of trouble by reminding you to pay bills before they're due and deposit money so you have funds to cover the checks you write. If you pay bills—and who doesn't—you can add them in the Setup Center and Quicken sets up scheduled transactions (with handy reminders) for credit card payments and other bills you pay. You can also set up your paycheck so the program takes care of your paycheck deposits and all your withholdings and deductions. The Setup tab's Overview screen gives you a chance to cross these important tasks off your to-do list.

On the Overview screen, the Bill Reminders section and the "Income and Transfer Reminders" section have buttons you click to set up *transaction reminders* (which were called *scheduled transactions* in earlier versions of Quicken) that prompt you

---

to enter info about bills and deposits in Quicken—what they're for, how often you pay or receive them, and the account where you withdraw or deposit the money. You can also click the "Bills and Deposits" button (next to Overview and Accounts) to display a screen dedicated to creating transaction reminders and paychecks. Whether you click Add Paycheck on the Overview screen or Set Up Paycheck on the Bills and Deposits screen, Quicken opens the Paycheck Setup wizard (page 192).

When you use the buttons in the Setup tab to add bills, deposits, and paychecks, Quicken launches the same tools you can find elsewhere in the program—the Setup Center just brings them all together to make 'em easy to find. See page 190 in Chapter 7 to learn how to set up transaction reminders for bills and deposits. To set up a paycheck, complete with automatic transfers and payments, see page 192.

Converting Existing Data Files

The first time you open a data file created with an earlier version of Quicken, the program opens the Convert Your Data dialog box. Before you click OK to begin the conversion, it's a good idea to gather key facts from your existing file so you can verify that Quicken converts it correctly. (Problems don't happen that often, but better safe than sorry.)

Here's the information you should have handy: your Account List (page 64), Scheduled Bills and Deposits (page 185), Online Payees (page 149), Category List (page 72), and the information in your Password Vault (page 144). The easiest way to make this comparison is to print these items from the earlier version of Quicken. (It's a good idea to keep the earlier version of Quicken on your computer until you're sure you want to use the new version; the box on page 537 explains how to juggle two versions of the program.) To print such a list, open the appropriate Quicken window—press Ctrl+A to open the Account List window, for example—and then click Print in the window's menu bar.

When you're ready to convert your old data file to Quicken 2009, here's what you do:

1. **In the Convert Your Data dialog box, click OK.**

   Behind the scenes, Quicken creates a subfolder in the folder that holds your old data file (such as *Documents\Quicken*) to store that original file. If you're converting a Quicken 2008 data file, for example, the subfolder is called Q08Files, or Q06Files if you convert a Quicken 2006 file. Before Quicken begins converting, it copies your original data file to that subfolder.

   A message box tells you Quicken is converting your file and shows how many items have been converted so far. As the numbers move into the thousands, congratulate yourself for all the Quicken work you've done over the years. After a few minutes, the conversion finishes and you'll see your data file open in Quicken.

2. **That's it! Start working with your data file immediately.**

   If your data file has business transactions in it, Quicken opens a dialog box asking for information about your business. In the Tell Quicken About Your Business dialog box, click Add. In the Add Business dialog box, type the name of the business, choose the option for who owns it, and then type a name for a business *tag* (see Chapter 4 for more about tags).

After the file conversion, you'll work with the updated Quicken 2009 copy of your data file. Review the Account Bar to make sure that all the accounts are still there and have the same balances they did before the conversion. Also confirm that all the scheduled transactions, online payees, and categories you printed are still present in the converted Quicken file. Should you decide to go back to the earlier version of Quicken, you can always retrieve your pre-conversion data file, saved in the subfolder named Q08Files that Quicken creates in the folder that contains the data file (or Q07Files if you're converting from the 2007 version, and so on).

UP TO SPEED

Converting from Microsoft Money

If you're switching from Microsoft Money 2003 or later, you can download a data converter program from Intuit's Web site to speed up the conversion. The data converter uses a report that you produce in Money to transfer most of your data into Quicken for Windows (versions 2004, 2005, or 2006). If you use a more recent version of Quicken, you then have to open the resulting Quicken data file in your current version of Quicken and then convert it to that version of the program as explained on page 24.

Intuit's data converter can transfer your category list, banking transactions (including split transactions), investment transactions, and a few other lists. It can't convert features, though, such as memorized payees, budgets, tags, online banking connection information, loans, account reconciliation status, and some investment transactions.

To download the data converter, go to *www.quicken.com*. In the Search box in the top-right corner of the page, type "Money data converter", and then click Search. In the list of topics that appears, click the "Quicken Support - How do I convert data from Microsoft Money" link. The answer that appears includes instructions for using the data converter and a "Download the data converter" link. When you click the link, a File Download dialog box opens. Click Run to install the converter on your computer.

After the converter is installed, use Windows Explorer to open the folder where you installed the program. The name of the data converter file is *mny2qdf.exe*. To run it, double-click its filename. Following the instructions on the Intuit Web site, create transactions reports in Microsoft Money. Then close Money, and in the Data Converter dialog box, click "Import into Quicken". When the import finishes, your computer launches Quicken. Be sure to review your data and reconcile your accounts. (Asset and liability accounts appear in the Cash Flow Center. See page 501 for instructions on moving accounts to the Property & Debt Center.)

Now you're ready to start adding new transactions to your Quicken data file.

Opening a Quicken File

To open a data file in Quicken, simply go to File → Open or press Ctrl+O and then select the data file you want to open. After you've opened a data file manually, Quicken obligingly opens that file the next time you launch the program. If, like most people, you have only one Quicken data file, you may never have to choose File → Open again. Even if you jockey between several data files, the File menu makes it easy to open the one you want, as you can see in Figure 1-5.

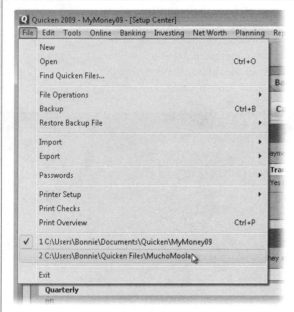

Figure 1-5:
To find and open a Quicken data file, choose File → Open, or press Ctrl+O. The bottom of the File menu lists recently opened data files and adds a checkmark to the one that's currently open (in this case, MyMoney09). Click a filename to open that file.

Taking Quicken for a Test Drive

You might think that trying to get a handle on your finances *and* learn Quicken at the same time is going to push you over the edge. But have faith: With just a bit of up-front work, along with help from this trusty book, you'll have a clear view of your finances in a jiffy. To help keep you motivated, this chapter gives you both a quick tour of the program so you can find your way around and a sneak peek of some of the cool stuff you can do with Quicken. Then you'll learn how to open a Quicken check register, where you record payments and deposits. After that, you'll find out how easy it is to record payments and deposits that occur on a regular schedule, like your rent payment or paycheck, and download transactions if you're an online banking fan. Finally, you'll see a few ways Quicken can give you a quick snapshot of the state of your finances.

Note: If you haven't set up your Quicken data file yet, you can download a sample file from this book's Missing CD page at *www.missingmanuals.com/CDs* that you can use to follow along with this chapter.

Getting Around In Quicken

Your personal finances may start off simple, but they tend to grow more compli-cated over time. Quicken organizes menus, windows, commands, and even your financial accounts into *financial centers* or *tabs* that are dedicated to specific finan-cial activities, so it's easier to accomplish the task at hand. For example, if you're new to the workforce, you want to watch your spending, but investments aren't on your radar yet. Quicken's Banking center and menu can satisfy most of your needs. As your finances get more complicated, you can add more Quicken features to your tool belt, using the Investing tab to monitor your retirement nest egg or the Net Worth tab (called "Property and Debt" in the Account Bar and on the Setup tab) to see just how much you still owe on your car or house.

Quicken gives you several ways to launch the commands you want, from buttons on a tab to shortcut menus waiting to pop into view to the tried and true menu bar along the top of the main Quicken window. This section is your treasure map to Quicken's most useful features.

Quicken's Menu Bar and Tool Bar

Like menu bars in other programs, Quicken's menu bar gives you quick access to the tools you need for different financial activities, as you can see in Figure 2-1. The Online menu contains all sorts of Web-based banking and financial resources. The Banking menu is a concentrated list of commands related to banking activities like writing checks and reconciling bank accounts, and the Investing and Net Worth menus offer commands for handling investments, assets, and loans.

The Quicken Tool Bar, tucked just below the menu bar, comes with a built-in set of icons, such as Update, for downloading transactions from your Web-enabled accounts (page 125). As explained on page 504, you can customize the Tool Bar so that all your favorite commands are readily available. For example, if you don't use add-on services or Quicken.com, you can toss the Services and Quicken.com icons. You can also add icons for commands like the one to work on your budget (page 304) or one that runs reports like "Income/Expense by Category" (page 505), so that they're only one click away.

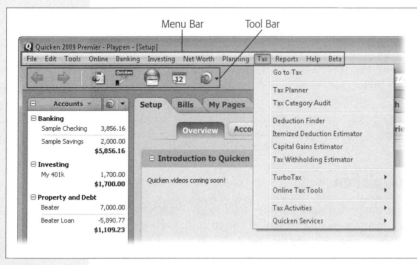

Figure 2-1:
Quicken aficionados use the Quicken menu bar and Tool Bar for fast access to their favorite commands. You can customize the Tool Bar to show the commands and reports you use the most (page 504).

Account Bar

The Quicken Account Bar may be your new best friend. It's the fastest way to open any account's register, and it keeps your financial ups and downs where you can see them. The Account Bar groups your accounts by financial center, as shown in Figure 2-2. Checking, saving, and credit card accounts appear below the Banking heading; IRAs, 401(k) accounts, and other investment accounts show up below Investing; and your house, cars, and loans complete the list below "Property and Debt" (which is an alias for the Net Worth center—page 31).

Here are a few of the things you can do from the Account Bar:

- Click an account's name to open its register.

- Add an account to your data file by clicking the Add Account button at the bottom of the bar.

- Right-click an account's name to bring up a shortcut menu that lists account-related commands like "Edit account".

- Click the gold arrow chasing its tail at the top of the bar to download transactions for your online-enabled accounts (page 125).

- Check the Net Worth at the bottom of the bar to get a sense of what you're worth—financially, that is. (Chapter 9 has more info about net worth.)

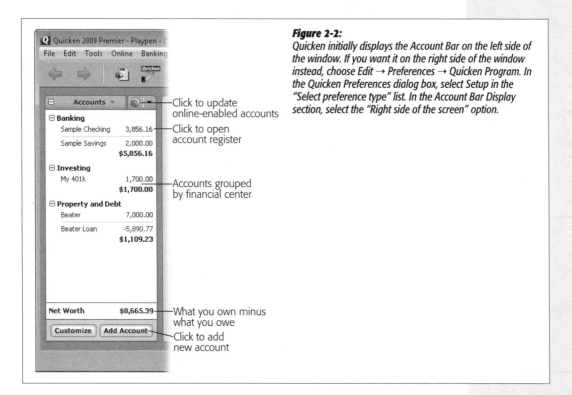

Figure 2-2:
Quicken initially displays the Account Bar on the left side of the window. If you want it on the right side of the window instead, choose Edit → Preferences → Quicken Program. In the Quicken Preferences dialog box, select Setup in the "Select preference type" list. In the Account Bar Display section, select the "Right side of the screen" option.

Navigating with Tabs

Quicken pigeonholes financial management into several buckets (Banking, Investing, Net Worth, and so on) called *financial centers*, each of which merits its own Quicken window, tab, and in some cases, entry on the Quicken menu bar. When you set up Quicken initially, you get to choose the tabs you want to see (page 20) so, for instance, you can focus on bills, banking, and taxes at first, and then graduate to investing and planning later on.

When you click a financial center's tab (just below the menu bar and Tool Bar), the financial center takes charge of the main Quicken window. Each tab comes with a few specialized views of its own. Here's the scoop on each tab:

- You met the **Setup tab** in Chapter 1. When you set up your data file, you can turn on the tabs you plan to use (page 20) and turn the rest off until you need them. Some tabs—like Bills, Banking, and Tax—apply to almost everyone. If you have a 401(k) retirement account, the Investing tab is a must, and a car loan or mortgage makes the Net Worth tab indispensable. In fact, as soon as you create an account related to banking, investing, or your net worth, Quicken automatically turns on the corresponding tabs.

- The **Bills tab,** new in Quicken 2009, provides a snapshot of the bills, paychecks, and scheduled deposits you have coming up. Quicken can't reduce the number of bills you pay or the chunk bills take out of your income, but this tab can help you pay those bills on time so that late fees don't make matters worse. Click the "List - Upcoming" button to see which scheduled transactions are on deck, as shown in Figure 2-3. To see transactions due during a shorter or longer period, in the Show drop-down list, choose the period you want to see (7, 14, or 30 days). You can avoid late fees by taking action as soon as you see the bright-red text that means a payment's overdue. And if a scheduled *deposit* appears in red—meaning the money hasn't shown up—you can investigate why you haven't been paid.

  Click the "List - By Month" button to see which bills and deposits are due during a specific month. To display a different month, click the left or right arrows on either side of the Show button (the label indicates the selected month and year). Quicken displays a green flag with the word *Paid* on the left side of the row for bills that you've already paid.

Note: If you click the "Timeline - Upcoming" button, Quicken shows the next transaction that's due in a huge box, so you can't claim you didn't see the due date, payee, or amount. To record the transaction, click Enter and follow the instructions on page 84. Other bills appear in a timeline, waiting for you to pay them.

- The **Banking tab** is all about what you spend and save. Most of the time, this tab displays the register for the account you've selected. To see an account's attributes like its activated online services or a graph of its balance over time, click the tab's Overview button (Figure 2-4). Click the Transactions button to display the account's register.

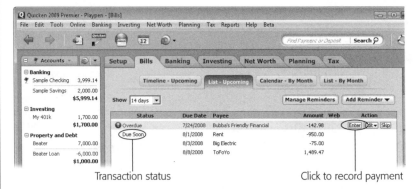

Figure 2-3:
If a bill is overdue, Quicken changes the bill's text to red and displays an exclamation point in a red circle next to the word Overdue at the beginning of the row. To record the bill's scheduled transaction, select it and then click the Enter button that appears on the right side of the row.

Transaction status   Click to record payment

To analyze spending and savings, click the Banking button and then choose one of the options from the drop-down menu. For a hard look at how much you spend and earn each month, choose Cash Flow. Quicken shows how much comes in, how much goes out, and what's left. Page 313 talks about the Cash Flow view in detail. If you choose Analysis & Reports, Quicken displays a page with different reports about your income and spending. (See page 319 for an intro to these financial status features.) Choose Summary to see all your banking accounts and banking alerts like a warning that your balance has dropped below the minimum account balance (page 159).

Note: The Banking menu in the Quicken menu bar has all the banking commands corralled in one place. Chapters 5 and 6 have more on banking activities.

• The **Investing tab** covers investments you make, whether they're earmarked for a down payment on a house, your kids' college education, or your retirement. The Today's Data page lists your investment accounts, their market values, and information about their performance. At the top of the page, click the Performance, Analysis, and Portfolio buttons for closer looks at what your investments are up to. For example, click Portfolio to see each account and investment you own. Then choose a view in the Show drop-down list to look at price quotes, recent performance, tax implications of selling, and so on.

Tip: The Investing menu in the Quicken menu bar gives you access to the program's investing features. Chapter 12 tells the entire investment story.

• The **Net Worth tab** (which, confusingly, corresponds to the "Property and Debt" accounts in the Account Bar) lists the Quicken accounts for what you own and owe: houses, vehicles, other valuable assets, and loans you've taken out. You see your assets in one group and loans in another. In addition to the subtotals of your assets' value and debt, the tab also shows whether you own more than you owe. (The Net Worth menu in the Quicken menu bar has commands for managing your assets and loans. See Chapter 9 for more information.)

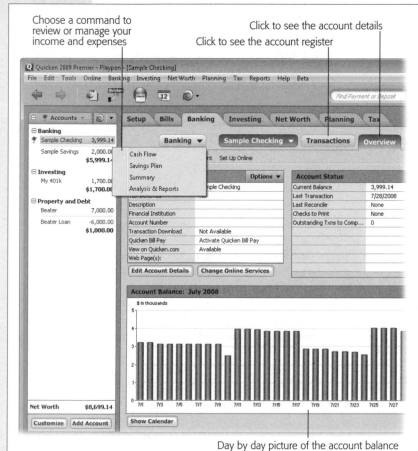

Choose a command to review or manage your income and expenses

Click to see the account register

Click to see the account details

Figure 2-4:
The buttons you see on the Banking tab change depending on which screen you display. When an account register or Overview screen is visible, the first button is Banking, which sports the drop-down menu shown here. The button with an account's name on it (here, it's Sample Checking) has a drop-down menu for choosing another account. If you display a screen like Cash Flow, Quicken sprouts buttons for Savings Plan, Summary, and Analysis & Reports. The button with the account's name takes you back to that account's register.

Day by day picture of the account balance

• The **Planning tab** provides an overview of plans you've set up in Quicken, like a plan for saving for retirement. To set up or modify a plan, in the Quicken menu bar, first choose Planning and then pick a command like Retirement Planner. Chapter 13 explains how to use Quicken's planning tools.

• Thinking about taxes may not be your idea of a good time, but Quicken's tax features—including the ones on the **Tax tab**—can help ease the pain of preparing your tax returns. The tab has a section that estimates the tax you'll owe and a tax calendar to remind you of important tax-related dates. You can run tax reports from the Tax tab, but it's easier to choose Reports → Tax and then the report you want, as you'll learn on page 440.

• In Quicken 2009, the **My Pages tab** is the place to craft your own view of your finances. If you'd like to start every Quicken session with a snapshot of your financial life (such as scheduled transactions, debt, net worth, and investment values), you can create a custom view (page 502) for the My Pages tab, as shown in Figure 2-5, and then tell Quicken to open to that tab every time you launch the program (page 486).

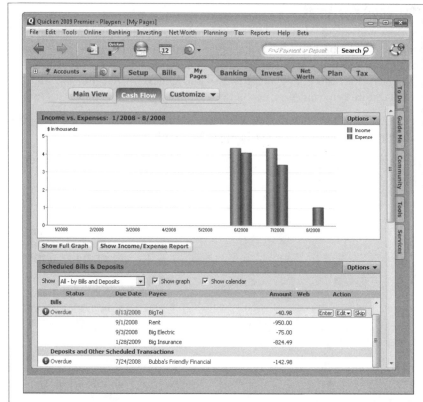

Figure 2-5:
To create a view that summarizes your financial status, click Customize on the My Pages tab. After you choose what you want in the view and save it, a button that displays the view appears, like the Cash Flow button next to Customize, as shown here. You can create as many custom views as you want.

The Quicken Sidebar

Quicken 2009 also has a set of tabs that cascade down the side of the Quicken main window. (If you put the Account Bar on the left—see page 487—the Sidebar appears on the right instead.) The To Do tab lists activities you may want to complete like recording bills that are due or downloading online transactions. The Guide Me tab has instructions for the task at hand. Click Community to go online to Quicken's message boards to find answers. The Tools and Services tabs show you other Quicken features that may help with the financial task you're performing. Page 488 has more information on the Sidebar.

Recording Payments and Deposits

Your finances are nothing more than a series of transactions, from the paychecks you deposit to the checks you write to the credit card charges you make. To get the most out of Quicken, you should record *all* your financial transactions. Fortunately, doing so in Quicken is a snap. You simply open a Quicken account *register* (which is like a paper register on steroids) and either record or download your payments or deposits. The next five sections show you how.

Recording a Payment

Every time you spend money—by writing a check, swiping your credit card, or forking over greenbacks—you're making a payment. Quicken needs to know about all your payments so it can give you an accurate idea of how much money you have left. Recording a payment is easy and Quicken's Account Bar and the QuickFill feature help you every step of the way. Just follow these steps:

1. **In the Account Bar, click the name of the account you want to work with (this example uses an account named Sample Checking).**

   The register for that account appears in the main part of the Quicken window, as shown in Figure 2-6.

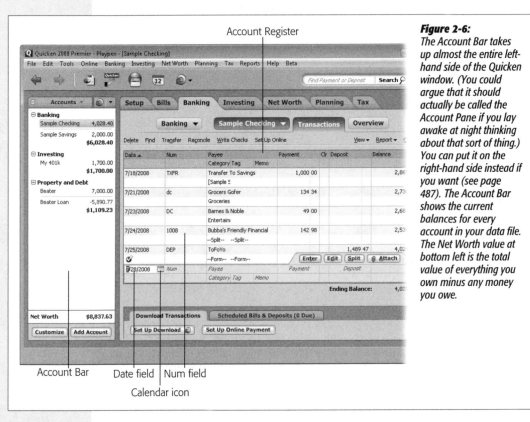

Figure 2-6:
The Account Bar takes up almost the entire left-hand side of the Quicken window. (You could argue that it should actually be called the Account Pane if you lay awake at night thinking about that sort of thing.) You can put it on the right-hand side instead if you want (see page 487). The Account Bar shows the current balances for every account in your data file. The Net Worth value at bottom left is the total value of everything you own minus any money you owe.

2. **To create a new transaction in the register, press Ctrl+N.**

   This takes you to the register's first blank transaction and plunks your cursor in the Date field.

3. **In the Date field, click the calendar icon and choose the date of the transaction (in this case, let's say you've written a check). Then press Tab to move to the Num field.**

Quicken automatically fills in today's date (or the same date as the last transaction you recorded), but you can pick another date. To see a different month in the calendar pop-up box, click the left or right double arrows on either side of the month and year label. If you want a date that's only a few days away, simply press the – key to move back one day at a time, or the + key to advance one day at a time.

4. **In the Num field, type *N* (for Next Check Num) to automatically fill in the next check number in sequence. (If this is the first check you've entered, Quicken fills in 101.) Press Tab to continue.**

When you type *N* in the Num field, Quicken fills in a check number that's one higher than the previous one, as you can see in Figure 2-7, or 101 if there are no previous checks. If the paper check you're filling out has a different check number, type that number in the Num field.

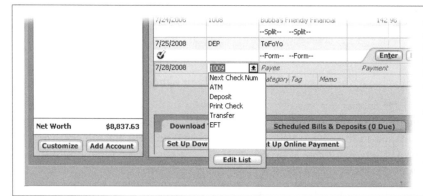

Figure 2-7:
If you're recording something other than a check, choose the type of transaction from the Num dropdown menu. Your choices include ATM, Deposit, Print Check, Transfer, and EFT (which stands for "electronic funds transfer").

5. **In the Payee field, type the name of the person you made the check out to, and then press Tab.**

Every time you record a payment (or deposit), Quicken remembers what you did: the payee, the amount, the category you choose, and more. (Categories are Quicken's transaction-labeling system; page 68 has the full story.) After you've entered a payee once, you just have to type the first few letters of the payee's name. Quicken responds by displaying a drop-down menu of names matching the letters you've typed (see Figure 2-8). Click the name you want and then press Tab to move to the Payment field.

The program has a great timesaving feature called *QuickFill* that automatically fills in all the other transaction fields for you with the information it memorized the last time you entered this payee.

QuickFill may be able to correctly guess what you want in the payee field even if—get this—it's the first time you've used Quicken. That's because the program has a database of commonly used payees, such as major grocery chains, retail stores, and so on. If you type in *Saf*, for example, just select Safeway from the list and then press Tab.

Note: Most people swear by QuickFill (page 88), but you can turn it off if it annoys you. Choose Edit → Preferences → Quicken Program. Under the Register heading, click QuickFill. Turn off the "Complete fields using previous entries" and "Recall memorized payees" checkboxes.

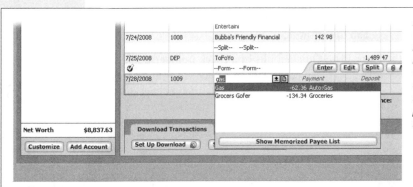

Figure 2-8:
When you enter a payee name that Quicken knows, it fills in the Category field for you, even if this is the first time you've used that payee. Page 68 has the full scoop on categories.

6. **If the value in the Payment field isn't what you want, type the correct amount.**

   If you've entered a payment to this payee before, QuickFill automatically fills in whatever amount you previously used (along with the Category and any text you typed in the Memo field) and then selects the Payment value so you can type a different amount, if necessary. If this is a new payee, the Amount field is blank.

7. **If the values QuickFill proposes are correct, press Enter (or click the onscreen Enter button on the right side of the current transaction) to record the check. If the values aren't correct, fix them and then press or click Enter.**

   Quicken's database of commonly used payees also includes the most likely categories for them. If your payee is Safeway, for example, Quicken pops *Groceries* into the category box.

   When you're just getting started, you may have to choose a category yourself for a local business so the program can memorize it. As you can see in Figure 2-9, the Category drop-down list makes that easy.

Quicken takes care of the math by deducting the amount of your payment from your account balance. Congratulations—you've recorded your first transaction!

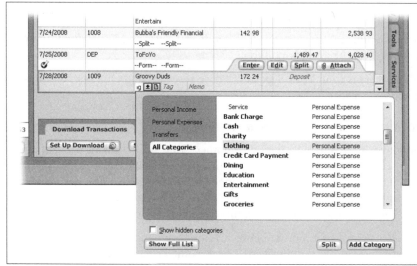

Figure 2-9:
*Just as you did with
payee names, you can
type a few letters and
Quicken tries to pick the
correct category. If it's
wrong, simply select the
category you want.*

Recording a Deposit

Recording a deposit is *almost* identical to recording a check. Follow these steps:

1. **Create a new transaction in the register by pressing Ctrl+N.**

   If the date isn't correct, type or choose the correct date, and then press Tab to move to the Num field.

2. **In the Num field, type *D* for Deposit. Press Tab to get to the Payee field.**

   When you choose Deposit, Quicken knows to jump to the Deposit field after you enter the payor's name instead of the Payment field (like it does with payments).

3. **In the Payee field, type the payor's name, and then press Tab to jump to the Deposit field.**

   Yes, you read that right—you enter the *payor's* name in the *Payee* field. Quicken doesn't change the name of this field. It's just a confusing quirk of Quicken's that you have to accept. Just remember that this field is always used for the name of the person or company giving money *to you* (like a paycheck or a refund).

4. **Enter the deposit amount.**

   When you type a value in the Deposit field, Quicken adds the amount to your account balance.

5. **If the values QuickFill filled in (like the category, tag, and memo) are correct, press Enter or click the onscreen Enter button to record the deposit. If you need to fill in values (if this is your first deposit from this payor) or edit any fields, make your changes and *then* press or click Enter.**

   If you deposit more than one check at the same time, you can split the transaction (page 168) to assign each deposited check to the correct category. For example, you can use a payee called Deposit if you've given a bank teller or an ATM machine a group of checks. Then you can assign each line of the split transaction to a different category like Gift Received, Salary, and Tax Refund. Jump to Chapter 7 for the lowdown on splits.

That's all there is to it. Your deposit has been recorded and Quicken has adjusted your account balance.

Recording a Transfer Between Accounts

If you move cash from one account to another (from your checking account into a savings account where it earns interest, for example) you can record those transfers in Quicken. When you transfer money between Quicken accounts, the programs withdraws the money from one account (checking, say) and deposits it in another Quicken account (savings, in this example).

In Quicken, recording a transfer between accounts is almost like recording a check (page 34). Instead of choosing Next Check Num in the Num field, you choose *Transfer*. Then, you choose an account in the *Category* field to transfer money to that account. The account names that you see in square brackets at the bottom of a Category drop-down list are the ones that you've set up in Quicken. When you choose an account in the Category field, Quicken creates and links transactions in both accounts involved in the transfer (a withdrawal transaction from the account the money is coming out of and a deposit transaction in the account the money is going into).

Here's how to record a transfer in Quicken:

1. **Open the register for the account you're transferring money *from* by clicking the account's name in the Account Bar.**

   For example, if you're transferring extra cash from checking to savings, open the checking account register. When you open a register, Quicken automatically puts your cursor in a blank transaction.

2. **In the Date field, choose the transfer date using the calendar icon (page 35) or by typing the date.**

   Quicken automatically fills in today's date. If the transfer takes place on a different date, choose it or type it in.

3. **In the Num field, type *T* to indicate that you're recording a transfer.**

   When you type *T*, Quicken automatically selects Transfer in the field's dropdown list. When you press Tab, the Num field changes to *TXFR*; the Payee field's label changes to Description; and the Category field's label changes to Xfer Account (short for "transfer account"), as shown in Figure 2-10.

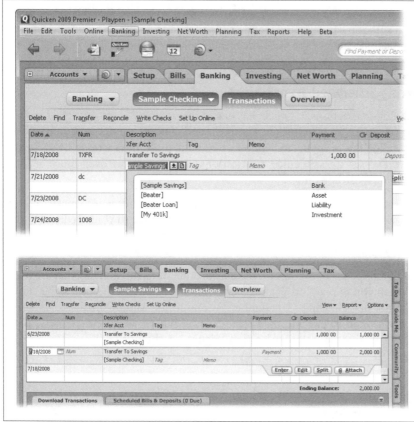

Figure 2-10:

Top: When you choose Transfer in the Num field, Quicken automatically displays accounts in the Category (aka Xfer) drop-down menu. Select the account you're sending the money to.

Bottom: After you record a transfer in the sending account, right-click it and then choose "Go to matching transfer" on the shortcut menu (page 184). You'll see the corresponding transfer transaction in the receiving account as shown here.

4. **In the Description field, type a name for the transfer you're making.**

   Because Quicken memorizes payees, you can use this description to quickly fill in values for this transfer the next time you move money between accounts. For example, the next time you type *Transfer to Savings* in the Description field, Quicken automatically chooses your savings account as the destination and fills in the last amount you transferred (which you can change).

5. **In the Payment field, type the amount you're transferring out of the account.**

6. **In the Xfer Account field, choose the account that receives the money for the transfer.**

   As soon as you press Tab or click in the Xfer Account field, Quicken displays a drop-down menu of accounts, as you can see in the top image in Figure 2-10. You can also quickly choose an account by typing the first character or two of its name (you don't have to type the opening bracket).

7. **Press the Enter key or click the Enter button to record the transfer.**

That's it! You can tell your money has switched to another account because the transaction changes the account balance. In the example in Figure 2-10, the $1,000 transfer into savings increases the savings account's balance by $1,000.

Entering Scheduled Transactions

Scheduling transactions in Quicken is one of the program's best time- and money-saving features. You tell Quicken when bills and deposits are due and then sit back and wait for the program to remind you about those transactions. Even better, after you've set up scheduled transactions, Quicken takes over most of your transaction-recording duties.

When you schedule a payment transaction, Quicken reminds you to make the payment when it's due. If the payment is an automatic charge to your credit card (like your cable bill, say), you can even tell Quicken to record it in your Quicken account without telling you.

The Bills tab (page 30) focuses on the bills that are due soon and any that are overdue. When you're ready to pay bills, click the Bills tab, and then click the "List - Upcoming" or "Timeline - Upcoming" button. In the window that appears, select the bill you want to pay and then click its Enter button. (Figure 2-11 shows a bill on the "Timeline - Upcoming" screen. Figure 2-3 shows the "List - Upcoming" screen.)

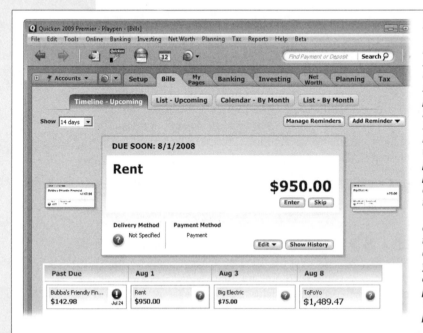

Figure 2-11:
The timeline at the bottom of the screen shows bills in chronological order, starting with any that are past due. Click the Enter button in the big Due Soon box to record that bill. (If your bank works with Quicken's online bill payment feature, you can pay the bill by recording an online payment transaction.) The Enter Transaction dialog box opens, so you can choose the check number or other payment method you used to pay the bill, and the date of the payment. Click Enter Transaction to record the payment or deposit.

Downloading Transactions

Many financial institutions let you download your transactions without ever leaving the comfort of your home. Once you introduce Quicken to your real-world accounts online (page 125), the program can download transactions and fill in most of the transaction fields. If you've already entered a transaction in Quicken, the program matches it with the one you download. Your job is to confirm that the downloaded transactions are correct (and make the changes needed if they aren't).

Most important, you want to make sure that all the downloaded transactions are transactions *you* performed. (If you download an unfamiliar transaction, someone may be using your identify or credit card without your permission.) The amount in the downloaded transaction has to match the amount in your real-world transaction.

Before you can download transactions, you first have to set up your account(s) for online banking (Chapter 6 has the details). Then, follow these steps:

1. **Open the register for the account you want to work with.**

   Click the account's name on the Account Bar to open its register.

2. **On the Downloaded Transactions tab below the register, click Update Transactions.**

   This brings up the dialog box shown in Figure 2-12. Type the password you set up with your bank to access your account online (page 129).

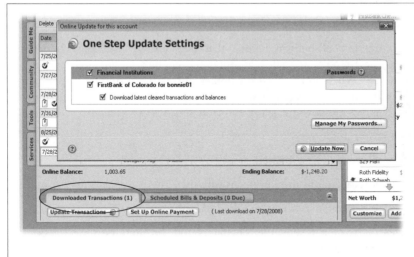

Figure 2-12:
Clicking the Downloaded Transactions tab (circled) brings up this dialog box, where you type your password to access your account online. You can save yourself some typing if you use the Password Vault (page 144) to store all your passwords. Then you simply set a single password to access the vault. That way, all you have to do to access your accounts online is type the Password Vault password and click OK. Quicken then automatically fills in the appropriate passwords so it can download your transactions.

3. To complete the download, click Update Now.

When Quicken and your bank finish talking, your downloaded transactions appear at the bottom of the register window. If the transactions look OK, you can click Accept All below the Downloaded Transactions tab, and Quicken funnels them into the account register. Making sure your records agree with your bank's is called *reconciling,* which you can learn all about in Chapter 8.

You've just experienced the magic that is online banking. Chapter 6 teaches you more about it.

Reviewing Your Finances

Quicken's reporting tools can be a big help in managing your cash. Just knowing how much you have in your bank account—and how little you may have in two weeks—could help you avoid painful bounced check fees. At the same time, seeing how much you're spending in different categories may be enough to coax you toward more frugal living. This section introduces a few of the tools you can use to "follow your money." Chapter 11 tells the whole story of monitoring spending and saving.

Seeing How Much You Earn and Spend

Quicken is teeming with ways to see how much you earn and spend, which you'll learn about in the rest of this book. Here are two of the easiest:

EasyAnswer reports

Quicken has lots of built-in reports that help answer questions about your finances. These reports are called, appropriately enough, EasyAnswer reports. For example, the "Where did I spend my money during the period...?" report shows you how much you earned and spent by category for whatever timeframe you choose. Figure 2-13 shows the graph and table versions of this report.

Here's how to run this report:

1. Choose Reports → EasyAnswer.

The Reports & Graphs window opens with the EasyAnswer category expanded.

2. Click "Where did I spend my money during the period...?"

The entry expands to show the "For the period" box and the Show Report and Show Graph buttons.

3. In the "For the period" drop-down menu, choose the period you want to review ("Last month" in this example).

You can choose a short timeframe like "Month to date" or all the dates in your date file or something in between.

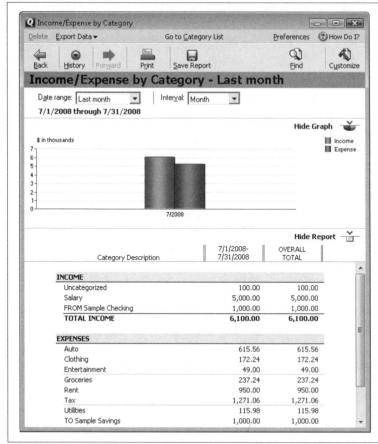

Figure 2-13:
To see the detail behind a bar in the graph, double-click the bar. A pop-up window shows the income or expenses by category. Double-clicking a category in the tabular report displays all the transactions that make up the category's total.

4. **Click Show Report or Show Graph to view the results.**

   If you click Show Report, a tabular report shows your income and expense categories in the rows, and a month's worth of results in each column. If you click Show Graph, the initial bar chart shows two bars: one for income and one for expense.

5. **The report and graph initially show your income and expenses month by month. To see results over a different length of time, in the Interval dropdown menu, choose the time frame you want, like Quarter or Year.**

Monthly cash flow

The Banking tab's Cash Flow page (page 313) shows you how much money comes in, how much goes out, and what's left. It displays info for your spending accounts, which may be only your checking account if you've just set up your data file.

As you add more accounts, spending accounts include cash accounts, savings accounts, and credit card accounts. You can look at the current month, past months, or dates in the future, so this page can show you what you've done in the past and help predict the future.

To see the Cash Flow page (Figure 2-14), click the Banking tab, and then click the Cash Flow button. (If the Cash Flow button isn't visible, click the Banking button and then choose Cash Flow from the drop-down menu.)

The In box shows the money coming in during the month, such as your paycheck (which appears in the Expected Income number) and other unscheduled deposits you made. The Out box shows the money going out during the month. The What's Left box tells you whether you spent more than you earned or vice versa. If your income was more than your expenses, the "Cash Flow difference" value is positive; if you spent more than you made, the value is in red to highlight that the amount is negative. You'll see a red down arrow if your balance dropped over the course of the month or a green up arrow if your balance increased.

Tip: To see what contributes to the values in the In and Out boxes, click any of the blue text in the In, Out, or What's Next boxes. A pop-up mini-report appears, listing the categories and amounts.

The tabs at the bottom of the Cash Flow screen give you different views of your cash flow situation. The Scheduled Bills & Deposits tab shows the scheduled transactions for the month. The Account Balance Graph, shown in Figure 2-14, charts the ups and downs of your checking account throughout the month. If a bar in the graph drops close to zero, you may want to transfer money into the account. (To show the balances for more than one account in the Account Balance Graph, in the Show drop-down list, choose "Multiple accounts" and then, in the Scheduled Bills & Deposits Accounts dialog box, turn on the checkmarks for each account you want to include.) The Spending Graph tab displays pie charts that show the percentages of your expenses that go toward various categories.

Figure 2-14:
You can tell what period you're looking at by the date in the upper-middle part of the screen (here it's July 2008). To change the date, click the right- or left-facing arrow on either side of the date. When you display a month in the past, as shown here, the Cash Flow page shows scheduled bills and deposits as well as the actual payments and deposits. The "Total Available through <date>" value at the bottom of the What's Left box is the actual balance for your spending accounts at the end of that month.

Setting Up Accounts

If you created accounts in Quicken's Setup Center as described in Chapter 1, you already have one or more accounts in Quicken and a basic collection of categories you can use to track your finances. That arrangement is enough to start using Quicken as an electronic checkbook, but it's only the beginning. To make the most of Quicken's planning, tracking, and analysis tools, you'll want to create additional accounts in Quicken to go with all your real-world savings accounts, credit cards, investment accounts, and assets.

This chapter describes Quicken's different account types and shows you how to set up new accounts as well as manage existing ones. It also introduces you to the difference between accounts and *categories* (a handy classification system Quicken uses to help you track different types of income and expenses), so you know how the two work hand in hand. Armed with this knowledge, you can keep your Quicken records up to date as your financial needs change over time. For example, whenever you switch banks, succumb to a fabulous credit card offer, or take out a home equity loan to get your mobile dog-grooming business going, you'll need a new Quicken account. Chapter 4 gives you in-depth coverage of how to set up and get the most out of Quicken categories.

Note: Sometimes, the arrival of a new person or business in your life means you need an additional data file; see the box on page 481 to learn how to create one.

How Accounts and Categories Work Together

As you learned in Chapter 1, a Quicken *account* corresponds to an account you have at a financial institution, like a checking account, savings account, Roth IRA, and so on. You can also create Quicken accounts to keep track of assets you own, like your house or car, and the loans you take out to buy them.

Quicken lets you assign a *category* to each transaction in an account. With categories like Groceries, Auto Insurance, and Poker Winnings, you can see where your money is going (or coming from). Every time you record a deposit, check, or credit card charge, you can assign it a category or split it among several categories (page 168). The payoff comes when you want to find out how much you make and spend to prepare your income tax returns, see if a new hybrid car might save money on gas, or help you curb your shopping habit, for example.

To get a handle on the difference between accounts and categories, consider how one hypothetical couple uses Quicken:

- Tess uses a single Quicken data file to manage both her and her husband Les's finances.

- She and Les share a checking account, savings account, and credit account at 1stBank, each of which Tess manages with corresponding accounts in Quicken.

- Tess assigns categories to every transaction she records to categorize every bit of money coming in and going out. So, for example, she assigns Les's paycheck deposit to the "Salary Les" category, and her paycheck deposit to the "Salary Tess" category. Similarly, the donations she makes to her pals over at the Denver Dumb Friends League get assigned to the "Charity" category, credit card charges at the gas station go to "Gas", and so on.

Figure 3-1 shows you how the checks Tess writes not only affect the checking account balance but also help track how the couple spends money—all thanks to the categories Tess uses.

Choosing Which Account Type to Use

As complicated as personal finances can be in the 21st century, Quicken has an account type for practically every situation. When you create an account, you choose one of the 13 types the program offers, including PayPal (page 58) and 529 college savings plans (also known as "I'm a new parent and I'm freaking out" accounts, page 52).

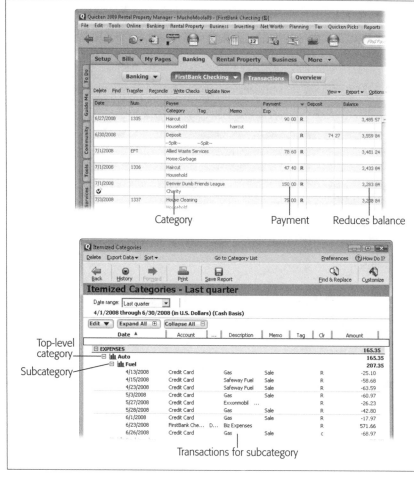

Figure 3-1:
Top: As you can see in the checking account register, checks and other payments Tess records reduce the balance in the Quicken checking account. The categories she assigns appear below the Payee's name.

Bottom: Tess can generate a report (page 439) that uses the assigned categories to see how they spent their money.

As you learned in Chapter 1, Quicken initially divvies account types into the program's financial centers (Banking, Investing, and Net Worth [Quicken sometimes calls that last one "Property and Debt" instead]), as shown in Figure 3-2. You can reassign accounts to a different center later (page 62). This section describes the types of accounts you can create and what most people typically use them for.

Banking Accounts

Use banking accounts when you're dealing with money that flows into and out of your life—checks you write, paycheck deposits, credit card charges, and the wadded-up bills you hand to the cashier at the coffee drive-through. Each type of banking account has slightly different features, based on how you use it. For example, Checking and Savings account registers include a Num field for entering a check number. Credit Card and Cash account registers omit this field, because such transactions aren't typically numbered. (See page 110 for instructions on creating cash accounts.)

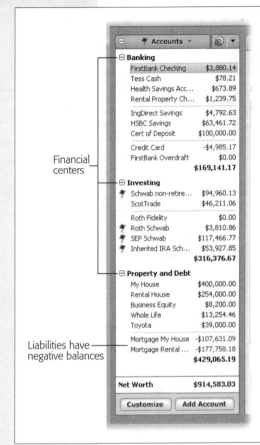

Financial centers

Liabilities have negative balances

Figure 3-2:
Regardless of which financial center houses an account—Banking, Investing, or Net Worth (aka "Property and Debt" in the Account Bar)—every Quicken account is broken down into what you own (assets) and what you owe (loans or liabilities). Assets include money in checking, savings, and investments, as well as more tangible items like your house, car, and autographed books. Liabilities, including credit cards and loans of any kind, show up with negative balances.

Quicken designates the following account types as cash flow accounts:

- **Checking** tracks your real-world checking account(s).

- **Savings** are suited for accounts that pay interest on your deposits, including passbook savings accounts, money market accounts, and certificates of deposit (CDs). You can also use Savings accounts to track money that doesn't earn interest, like the emergency cash hidden under your mattress. Quicken breaks cash flow accounts into subgroups (page 501), so you can keep all the money that's ear-marked for savings together in the Savings subgroup.

- **Credit Card** is for accounts that extend a line of credit to you, including credit cards, store charge cards, and so on. Use this type of account if you can withdraw money (charge) whenever you want and subsequently have to make payments. (By contrast, the loan account type discussed on page 230 is designed for loans that give you a sum of money up front, which you pay back through regularly scheduled payments of principal and interest.)

The Credit Card type is perfect for an overdraft protection feature connected to your checking account. Overdraft lines of credit act like credit card accounts, with credit limits, minimum payments, and interest charged on credit balances. Home equity lines of credit (HELOCs for short) fit the credit card profile, too. If you can make payments toward your HELOC whenever you want and pay interest on the balance, use a Quicken credit card account to track it (page 256).

- **Cash accounts** are useful if you want to track how you spend your money to the penny (or dollar), or to track travel advances you receive and spend. If you write a check to "cash" or withdraw money at the ATM, for example, you can record those transactions as transfers to your cash account. You can then spend the cash any way you like, but the transactions serve as records of how much cash you're spending. (You can see some creative ways of using this type of system on page 111.)

FREQUENTLY ASKED QUESTION

One Quicken Data File or Two?

Do I need another data file?

In Chapter 1, you learned that data files are where Quicken stores all the information about your finances: your bank account, your investments, and all the transactions that go with them. If you take on managing someone *else's* money with Quicken, the first decision to make is whether you need another Quicken data file. And the answer is, "It depends."

Separate tax returns are often a big hint that you should create a separate data file for Party Number Two. For example, suppose you manage your parents' money or keep the books for a local nonprofit organization. Their money isn't your money, and you prepare separate tax returns. Gunking up your Quicken data file with someone else's income and tax deductions is just asking for trouble. The safe route is to create another data file.

Separate tax returns but joint accounts are one exception that may make a single data file the right answer. For example, suppose an unmarried couple files separate tax returns, but pools their money as if they've been married

for years. They have a mixture of joint and individual accounts, from joint checking and taxable investment accounts to their individual 401(k)s and IRAs. Despite the glaring absence of a marriage certificate, these folks look a lot like spouses, making one data file the easiest approach. (As you'll learn in the next chapter, Quicken provides categories for each spouse for tracking tax-related deductions and other spousal spending.)

Although it's easy to transfer funds between *accounts* in the same data file, you can't transfer funds directly from an account in one data file to an account in a *different* data file. For example, if you transfer money between your personal and business checking accounts and use two separate data files, you have to create a check transaction in one checking account to remove the funds. Then, in the other checking account, you create the corresponding deposit. (The Quicken Home & Business edition has features that help you keep the books for a small business—like business-related categories and invoices—but it's still a good idea to separate your personal and business records by using two separate data files.)

Investing Accounts

Use the account types in the Investing Center for every account in which you hold securities—whether it's a retirement-helping 401(k) or a taxable brokerage account earmarked for the trip to Tahiti you're planning for your 20th anniversary.

To learn the details of creating investing accounts, see page 335. Here's a list of Quicken's investing accounts and when you should use them:

- **Standard Brokerage.** Unless your investment account is one of the types that comes with special tax savings (like an IRA, SEP, Keogh, 401(k), 403(b), 529, and so on), this is the investing account type you'll use most often. The Standard Brokerage type handles accounts that hold one or more securities, be they stocks, bonds, mutual funds, annuities, real estate investment trusts—you name it.

- **IRA or Keogh.** Use this type of account for any type of individual retirement account (IRA). In addition to traditional IRAs, this type handles Roth, Simplified Employee Pension (SEP), Keogh plans, SIMPLE (an acronym for the wordy name "Savings Incentive Match Plans for Employees of Small Employers"), and Education IRAs.

- **401(k) or 403(b).** 401(k) and 403(b) accounts are employer-sponsored retirement plans named after the section of the tax code that spawned them. Use this type of account to track your employer-sponsored accounts (including the matching contributions your company makes).

- **529 Plan.** 529 plans are a popular way to save for college education. They defer federal taxes, and, in some cases, state taxes, but they aren't for retirement savings. When you assign a 529 Plan account type, Quicken 2009 handles the tax deferral of income and capital gains correctly without including the account balance in your retirement-related reports and planning. See Chapter 12 for how to create one of these accounts in Quicken.

Net Worth Accounts

The Net Worth account types represent tangible things you own (houses, cars, and so on) and any money you've borrowed. If you want to track your assets, loans, and other liabilities in Quicken (you have to if you want a *truly* accurate picture of your net worth), you can learn how to create net worth accounts on page 229.

Note: Sometimes, you'll see this category of account called Net Worth (for example, on the menu bar and the main tabs). Other times, they're called "Property and Debt", as in the Account Bar and the Setup tab. Fear not. They both represent the same thing.

Here are the account types you can choose from:

- **House.** This type of asset account comes with features unique to property ownership. You can, for example, track your original purchase price and value adjustments for improvements you make. When you create a house account, Quicken also helps you create the corresponding loan account for your mortgage.

- **Vehicle.** This type of asset account includes balance adjustments for reducing the value of a vehicle due to depreciation. Quicken also helps you create the corresponding loan account for a car loan.

- **Asset.** Before you add an asset account for other things you own, consider whether they have any monetary value. For example, your wardrobe may have cost a fortune to buy, but selling all your clothing isn't likely to produce any meaningful cash. On the other hand, if you own the white sequined costume Elvis wore in Las Vegas, the selling price on eBay could cover that Miami retirement timeshare you've been eyeing. You could create an asset account to track the Elvis outfit's value. (As for your other assets, you can keep track of them using techniques described in the box on page 54.)

- **Debt (not including credit cards).** New in Quicken 2009, this type of account is perfect for the gray area between credit cards and loans. For example, say you've borrowed money from a relative and promised to pay the money back by the end of the year, but you don't have to make a minimum payment or pay on a regular schedule. In that case, you can create a debt account for the amount you borrowed. The payments you make reduce the balance on your debt. (Quicken asks if you want to create a loan for this type of account, but you can create a standalone loan account without a debt account to achieve the same result.)

TROUBLESHOOTING MOMENT

Bookkeeping and Quicken

Bookkeepers, certified public accountants, and other financial professionals may balk at Quicken's definition of an account, because it differs from the one they use in the accounting field. (Incidentally, accounting got its name because every flavor of income, expense, asset, and liability gets tossed into a bucket called an account.)

In traditional bookkeeping and accounting, expenses like utilities and advertising reside in expense accounts. Income accounts categorize revenue into different types, like services and products. Other aspects of a business appear in asset, liability, equity, and other types of accounts. Accounts at financial institutions also have their corresponding accounts in bookkeeping and accounting practice. All of these accounts appear under one roof in what's known as the business's *chart of accounts*.

If all that information makes you glad you're not an accountant, good news: Quicken's not an accounting program.

Instead of accounting-style accounts, Quicken uses accounts to represent real-world accounts at financial institutions, and categories to track different types of income and expenses. You won't find the concept of a *ledger*—as in the general ledger that comprises a company's books—in Quicken either. That's the other omission that rattles bookkeeping folks when they start using Quicken.

Quicken Home & Small Business—a separate edition of the program that costs more than Quicken Deluxe or Quicken Premier—has additional features, like estimates and invoices, to help small-business owners manage business as well as personal finances. If your business requires more accounting tools than Quicken Home & Small Business has, or your accountant recommends true accounting software, Intuit also sells QuickBooks, a program specifically for small business accounting. QuickBooks doesn't help you manage personal finances (mainly because it doesn't handle investments), but you can still use Quicken for that.

• **Loan.** This account type tracks how much you owe on a loan. When you create a vehicle asset account for the $20,000 car you just purchased, for example, Quicken helps set up a corresponding loan account to track how much you've borrowed and how much you still owe. Loan accounts don't have to be tied to an asset, though. If Aunt Martha was nice enough to loan you money for college tuition (and smart enough to make you sign a loan agreement), you can set up a loan account to track your progress in paying her back.

Tip: Loans you make to others are *assets* from your perspective, but they're *liabilities* for the people who borrowed money from you.

Creating Banking Accounts

Quicken makes it pretty easy to create accounts for almost any type of bank account you've got. Once you've gone through the steps the first time, you'll get a feel for it and be able to create new accounts in no time. This section walks you through the process from start to finish. The procedures for creating investment accounts, asset accounts, and liability accounts are slightly different. To learn how to create investment accounts, turn to Chapter 12, and to create asset and liability accounts, see Chapter 9.

ORGANIZATION STATION

Tracking Your Possessions

If you look around, you'll see that you probably own a lot more than you've documented in Quicken. Your possessions may be priceless to you, but most of them are worthless, financially speaking, to anyone else. In other words, Quicken asset accounts aren't the answer to tracking your belongings (and their value). For one thing, you can create no more than 512 accounts for each account type, so you'll run out of asset accounts before you document all your possessions. Moreover, creating and maintaining asset accounts as you buy, donate, and throw away items is too much work.

Still, your homeowners' or renters' insurance may cover the cost of these assets should you lose them in a fire or other disaster. It's a good idea to take digital pictures of your belongings to document your insurance claims. You can keep copies of the pictures on your PC, though storing them on a CD in your safety deposit box is the safest approach.

Quicken Home Inventory Manager ($29.99) is a program specifically designed to document your possessions. (There are other programs you can use, like HomeManage, My Stuff Deluxe, and AssetManage Home Edition, but they may cost more and may not have the staying power of an Intuit product.) If you're a technology junkie, you can create a home inventory spreadsheet or database from scratch.

By storing pictures and scanned images of receipts, you can submit insurance claims in a jiffy and speed up your claim payments as well. Home Inventory Manager also lets you identify the beneficiary for each item, one step toward preventing family squabbles after you're gone. You can also use this inventory list to keep track of your belongings when you move or account for the furnishings in a rental property. If you're convinced your belongings have tangible value, you can reflect that value in your net worth by importing the total value from Home Inventory Manager into your Quicken data file.

Note: Chapter 10 explains how to keep track of deposits, expenditures, and reimbursements associated with medical savings accounts offered by employers and health savings accounts connected to health insurance policies.

To create an account, first open the Quicken Account Setup dialog box in any of the following ways:

- **The Account Bar.** If you keep the Account Bar (page 29) visible, as most people do, the simplest way to add any kind of account is to click the Add Account button at the bottom of the Account Bar, shown in Figure 3-3. Or right-click anywhere in the Account Bar and then choose "Add new account" from the shortcut menu, also shown in Figure 3-3.

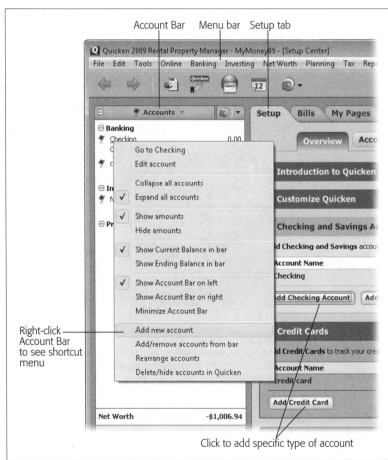

Account Bar   Menu bar   Setup tab

Right-click Account Bar to see shortcut menu

Click to add specific type of account

Figure 3-3:
You can add any kind of account by clicking Add Account at the bottom at the Account Bar (not shown here). Another way to add one of Quicken's banking account types is by clicking the Setup tab and then, on the Overview page, scrolling to the "Checking and Savings Accounts", Credit Cards, or "Wallets, Purses, and other Cash" section. Then click the button to add the type of account you want (Add Checking Account, for example).

- **The Setup Center.** To add a specific type of account, click the Setup tab (page 19) below the Tool Bar, scroll to the section for the type of account you want to add (Checking and Savings Accounts, for instance), and then click the button for the type of account (Add Checking Account or Add Savings Account, in this example).

- **The Quicken menu bar.** If you choose Banking → Banking Accounts → Add Account, the Quicken Account Setup dialog box displays options for checking and savings account types.

- **The Account List.** Open the Account List window (see Figure 3-9 on page 64) by choosing Tools → Account List or by pressing Ctrl+A. At the bottom of the Account List window, click Add Account. If the Account List window disappears, the box below explains how to get it back.

- **Banking Center.** If you display the Banking Center (page 32), click Summary, and then click one of the Add Account buttons to create that type of banking account. The Investing Center and Net Worth Center also have Add Account buttons for creating the types of accounts in those categories. (If you don't see Summary, your Quicken window is too narrow. Click More and then click Summary on the drop-down list.)

- **The File menu.** Traditionalists can choose File → New. In the "Creating new file" dialog box, select the New Quicken Account option, and then click OK.

TROUBLESHOOTING MOMENT

Where Did My Window Go?

If you click anywhere in Quicken's main window while the Account List window is open, the Account List disappears. Don't panic—Quicken's just minimized it so it doesn't block your view. Tucked away at the bottom of the Quicken main window are buttons for each minimized window, as shown in Figure 3-4. To restore any of these windows, simply click its button.

You can restore some windows (like the Account List, Category List, and Scheduled Transaction List) using their keyboard shortcuts: Ctrl+A, Ctrl+C, and Ctrl+J, respectively.

On the other hand, to restore a report window, be sure to click the report button at the bottom of Quicken's main window. If you try to restore a report by choosing Reports and then selecting the name of the report, Quicken creates a *second* report window instead of restoring the first one to view.

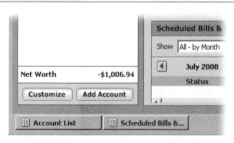

Figure 3-4:
To restore a minimized window to full view, click the window's button or use the keyboard shortcut for opening the window (Ctrl+A to open the Account List window, for example).

Creating a Banking Account: Step by Step

You'll find the steps for creating pretty much any type of banking account refreshingly similar. True, there are a few differences: savings accounts, for example, pay interest, whereas credit card accounts charge interest and limit how much you can spend. But the Quicken Account Setup dialog box streamlines your choices. Just follow these steps:

1. **If you haven't already opened the Account Setup wizard using one of the methods described in the previous section, at the bottom of the Account Bar, click Add Account.**

   You can create an account using any of the methods described, but the Account Bar is a convenient place for most people to start. When you click the Add Account button, the Account Setup dialog box pops up with options for different types of accounts.

2. **To add a banking account, select the account type you want (Checking, Savings, Credit Card, or Cash), and then click Next.**

   If you've already created some accounts, the next screen lists the banks that house your other accounts and asks if the new account is with one of those institutions, as you can see in Figure 3-5.

3. **If the account is at one of the listed banks but requires a different user ID or is at a different bank entirely, select "No, the account is at a different institution or has a different login", and then click Next.**

   The list of already-used financial institutions helps only if the User ID you use for online access is the same as the one you use for an existing account (like a checking and savings account both in your name). If so, then choose "Yes (select from the list below)" and then select your financial institution. Then click Next and jump to step 6.

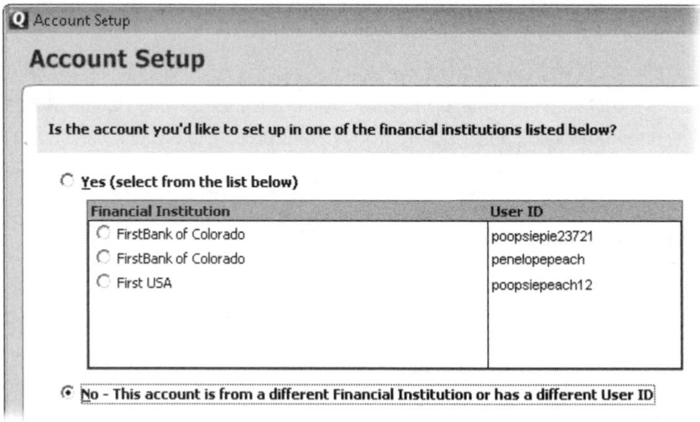

Figure 3-5:
Most of the time, you'll select "No - This account is from a different Financial Institution or has a different User ID", which covers accounts at different banks or one at the same bank that has a different user ID.

4. **If you select "No - This account is from a different Financial Institution or has a different User ID", then you see the "What is the financial institution for this account?" screen. Select the "The account is held at the following institution" option whether or not you have online access to it.**

   The screen includes a reassurance that your data is secure. Nevertheless, if you want to keep the identity of your financial institution to yourself, select the "I do not want to enter my financial institution)" option. The box below explains the consequences of this choice.

   If you don't use Quicken's online option, then you have to give the account a name and tell Quicken the starting date and balance for the account. See page 60 to learn how to set up an account for offline access.

FREQUENTLY ASKED QUESTION

Choosing the Financial Institution

Do I have to specify a financial institution when I set up an account?

You don't *have to*, but you'll probably want to. In days of yore (before the Internet, that is), adding the name of an account's financial institution didn't do much. Today, if you plan to use online services, the name of the financial institution is a necessity: Quicken can't download your transactions if it doesn't know which bank to get them from.

Choosing a financial institution doesn't mean you *have* to use its online services, but you should take a few seconds to set it up now to prepare for the future.

The only time selecting the "I do not want to enter my financial institution" option makes sense is when you create an account that truly isn't connected to a financial institution, like an account you create for the money you keep in your cookie jar.

---

5. **In the text box, start typing the name of the financial institution.**

   As Figure 3-6 shows, Quicken attempts to fill in the full name for you. Although Quicken includes a button for each letter of the alphabet, it's much faster to simply type on your keyboard. On the other hand, clicking "Bank of", "First", or "1st" is a quick way to see banks that begin with these ever-popular prefixes.

Note: To add an account for PayPal, simply select PayPal from Quicken's list of financial institutions. The steps to create a PayPal account are the same as those for creating a regular banking account. After you create the account, you can download transactions from your PayPal account into your Quicken data file just like you do for accounts at other financial institutions.

---

6. **With the name of the institution in place, click Next.**

   If the bank you specified offers online services, you can set those up now, later, or never. Quicken automatically selects the "Yes, Connect to <your financial institution> through Quicken" option, which tells the program to download your account info and transactions. The fastest way to create a new account in Quicken is to leave the Yes option selected, click Next, and then continue with step 7.

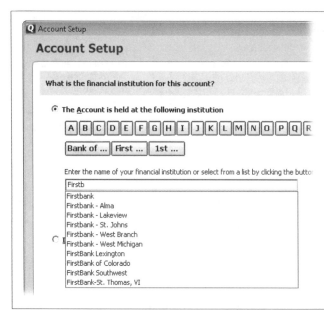

Figure 3-6:
Quicken displays the names of all the financial institutions it knows about that match the letters you've typed so far. For example, typing Firstb displays the banks shown here. If you see the one you want, click it. If your bank isn't in Quicken's database, then you have to type the entire name.

The "No, I'll visit my bank web site to download transactions into Quicken myself" option is a second way to use your financial institution's online services: downloading transactions manually using Web Connect (page 126). If you want to download banking transactions on your own, see page 60 for the rest of the steps.

If you have no intention of using online services and plan to record transactions directly in Quicken, choose the "No I'll enter my transactions into Quicken" option and flip to page 60 to learn what to do next.

7. **If you've set up online banking with your financial institution, in the "<your bank's name> User ID/username", "<your bank's name> password", and "Reenter password" boxes, type the user name and password you use to log into your bank's Web site, and then click Next.**

Quicken automatically selects the "Login using my <your bank's name> ID and Password" option, so you can type in your ID and password. When you click Next, Quicken goes online and finds all the accounts you have with the institution. Quicken automatically selects all the accounts it finds, and displays the account numbers and account types, as shown in Figure 3-7.

If you *haven't* signed up for online banking with your financial institution, select the "I do not have a <your bank's name> user name and password" option. Quicken creates the account, but you can't use any online services until you sign up for them with your bank. Once you sign up and get your username and password, you can activate your account for online banking (page 129) and download transactions.

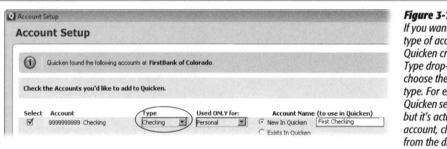

Figure 3-7:
If you want to change the type of account that Quicken creates, in the Type drop-down list, choose the appropriate type. For example, if Quicken selects Checking, but it's actually a savings account, choose Savings from the drop-down list.

Note: See page 125 for the full story on setting up accounts for online services, including activating more than one account at the same financial institution.

---

8. **If the account doesn't exist in your data file, leave the New In Quicken option selected, and type the name you want to use for the account in Quicken, and then click Next.**

The box on page 62 gives you some guidelines for naming accounts.

When you click Next, Quicken goes online and gathers bank info and your transactions.

If you haven't set up a Password Vault yet for your online service passwords, Quicken asks if you want to store your online banking password for the account in Quicken's Password Vault (page 144). If you want to use Password Vault to store your login info, keep the Yes option selected and type your vault password in both the "Password Vault Password" box and the "Re-enter Password" box. Then click Next. If you don't want Password Vault's help, select the "No (I'll enter my financial institution password each time I download transactions.)" option, and then click Next.

9. **When you click Next, the Setup Complete screen shows the account you just added, its connection type, and how many transactions it downloaded. After you finish admiring your handiwork, click Done.**

Quicken opens the account's register and lists all the transactions it downloaded on the Downloaded Transactions tab at the bottom of the screen. To learn how to accept downloaded transactions, see page 137.

Setting Up an Account for Manual Downloads or Offline Access

Some financial institutions aren't on close speaking terms with Quicken. The only way you can download transactions from one of these banks is to save a file from its Web site and then import the info it contains into Quicken. You might also just be uncomfortable with the idea of beaming your financial info across the Internet. Whatever your reason, adding an account that you plan to update with manual downloads or by entering transactions manually starts with steps 1 through 6 on pages 57–59. When you see the screen that asks if you want to download directly from your bank, it's time to take the road less traveled. Here's how to finish setting up an account using manual downloads (Web Connect) or offline data entry:

1. **Select the "No, I'll visit my bank web site to download transactions into Quicken myself" option or the "No, I'll manually enter my transactions into Quicken" option, and then click Next.**

   The "Tell Quicken about this Account" screen asks for a nickname and what the account is used for.

2. **In the Account Name/Nickname box, type whatever you want Quicken to call the account. Click Next.**

   Quicken automatically fills in a generic name for the type of account you're creating, like Checking 1 for a checking account. You can change the generic name to something more descriptive, like ING Savings or My Vacation Treasury. This name appears in the Account Bar, the Account List window, and anywhere else that account names show up.

   Note: If multicurrency support is turned on (page 490), the "Enter the name you'd like to use for this account in Quicken" screen contains a Currency box. When you set up an account for direct online access (page 126), Quicken downloads the account currency with the rest of the info, so you don't see the Currency box. Most of the time, your local currency (U.S. Dollar, for example) is what you want and you can simply click Next. If you're creating a bank account that you opened in another country, choose the appropriate currency for the account in the Currency drop-down list, and then click Next. You can change the currency for the account as long as you haven't entered any transactions in that account.

   ---

3. **On the Statement Date screen, type the ending date of the account's last statement in the Statement Ending Date box.**

   Quicken uses the statement ending date and ending balance (which you'll enter in the next step) to set the account's initial balance in Quicken, so hunt down your most recent bank statement and type in its ending date. If the account is brand new, use today's date and $0 (zero) for the ending balance. If you want your Quicken file to provide complete tax records for a year, use the last statement from the previous year as your starting point and type in that statement's ending date.

4. **In the Statement Ending Balance box, type the ending balance from that statement. Then click Next, and on the Setup Complete screen, click Done.**

   If you selected the "No, I'll visit my bank web site to download transactions into Quicken myself" option in step 1, the Setup Complete screen displays a Go There Now link that you click to open your browser to your bank's Web site, download a file of transactions, and import it into Quicken. (See page 135 for instructions on using Web Connect.) If you selected the "No, I'll manually enter my transactions into Quicken" option in step 1, simply click Done.

Editing Account Information

Once you've created an account, you can edit its details any time you want. You may have set your accounts up perfectly the first time, but the Account Details dialog box is still worth a visit, if only to see the many *other* account characteristics you can document. As you can see in Figure 3-8, in addition to the account name and other info you entered when you set up the account, Quicken gives you both space for comments and a nifty Alerts feature, so you can have the program warn you when your balance reaches certain levels.

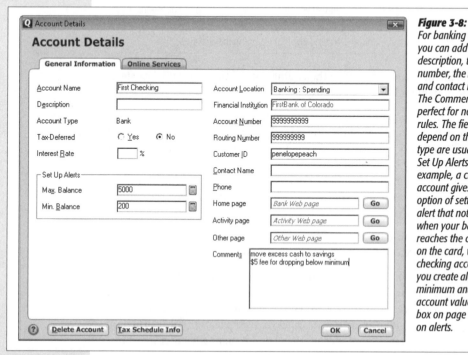

Figure 3-8:
For banking accounts, you can add a description, the account number, the interest rate, and contact information. The Comments box is perfect for noting fees or rules. The fields that depend on the account type are usually in the Set Up Alerts box. For example, a credit card account gives you the option of setting up an alert that notifies you when your balance reaches the credit limit on the card, whereas a checking account lets you create alerts for both minimum and maximum account values. See the box on page 63 for more on alerts.

Note: Just about the only thing you *can't* change about an account is its type. Quicken doesn't let you change a savings account into a checking account, for instance. So make sure you pick the correct type when you set up the account. Otherwise, you'll have to delete the account and recreate it with the correct type.

To edit the details of an account, use either of the following methods:

- In the Account Bar, right-click the name of the account and then choose Edit Account from the shortcut menu.

- In the Account List window, select an account, and then click Edit Details below the account's name.

Note: Investing, asset, loan, and debt accounts have a few fields that are totally different from the ones you see for banking accounts. See Chapter 9 (asset, loan, and debt accounts) and Chapter 12 (investing accounts) to learn about them.

GEM IN THE ROUGH

Staying on Top of Tasks with Alerts

As you'll learn throughout this book, Quicken has *alerts* that can notify you of tasks you should take care of or situations you may want to respond to. For example, the minimum-balance alert is useful if you have a checking account that charges exorbitant fees if your balance drops too low. Conversely, most banks wouldn't dream of telling you that you've deposited too much. But *you* can use the alert for the maximum balance field to see when it's time to move some money into an account that pays a higher interest rate.

You'll probably see some alerts whenever you launch Quicken. Alerts can also appear in the different financial centers, or on the My Pages tab if you customize it to display them (page 502). Here's how to tell Quicken which alerts you want to see:

1. Choose Tools → Set Up Alerts.

2. In the Alerts Center, select the alert you want to use. (You may need to expand the alert category by clicking the + sign to the left of its name.)

3. If you want Quicken to display a message box with an obvious warning the next time that you open the data file after something triggers the alert, select the alert, and then select the "Urgent (pop up dialog box)" option at the bottom of the window.

4. For less critical alerts, like a reminder to reevaluate your mortgage, select the "Text in the alert list" option. This setting displays alerts in the Alerts Center and the Alerts section of each financial center.

Closing Accounts

Over time, you'll probably close some bank accounts: CDs mature, you switch banks, or you finally smarten up and move your credit card balance to one with a single-digit interest rate. In Quicken, you don't delete accounts you no longer use, even if they have a zero balance. That's because deleting an account *deletes all of the transactions in the account*, including transfers to and from other accounts—potentially mangling those accounts.

Fortunately, there's a way of getting those old accounts off your Account Bar and Account List (and out of your hair). When you close a real-world account at a financial institution, enter the final cash transfers out of the account in Quicken and then *hide* the account. Hidden accounts—and their transactions—remain in your data file, but you won't see them in the Account Bar, menus, windows, or drop-down lists.

Here's how to hide an account:

1. **In the Account Bar, right-click any account and choose "Delete/hide accounts in Quicken" from the shortcut menu.**

   Quicken opens the Account List window. In earlier versions of Quicken, the Account List window contained a View Accounts tab and a Manage Accounts tab. Quicken 2009 provides access to all your accounts in a single window.

2. **To hide an account, select the account, and then turn on its "Hide this account in Quicken (lists, menus, reports)" checkbox.**

   Figure 3-9 shows the account checkbox turned on. There's just one more step to hide your account and keep it hidden.

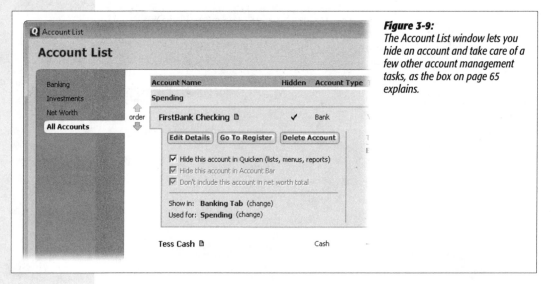

Figure 3-9:
The Account List window lets you hide an account and take care of a few other account management tasks, as the box on page 65 explains.

3. **At the bottom of the Account List window, turn off the "Show hidden accounts" checkbox.**

   The account is now officially hidden.

Other Ways to Manage Accounts

The Accounts List window isn't just for hiding accounts. It also has helpful features even experienced Quicken fans may not know about. Here's what you can do there:

- **Remove an account's balances in Account Bar totals.** Turn on an account's "Don't include this account in net worth total" checkbox if you want to remove its balance from the total for a group of accounts like those in the Banking Center. For instance, you might do this to omit the balances of your medical savings accounts and petty cash from your net worth at the bottom of the Account Bar. (The Account Balances and Net Worth reports include the balances for *all* accounts regardless of their "Don't include this account in net worth total" setting.)

- **Remove an account from the Account Bar.** Quicken automatically displays all your accounts in the Account Bar. As the number of accounts grows, finding an account takes more time and scrolling. If you've got accounts you use daily, and others you open only a few times a year, you may want to remove the more stable accounts from the Account Bar by turning on their "Hide this account in Account Bar" checkboxes. The accounts you remove from the bar are still visible in the Account List window and on the Quicken menu bar (for instance, when you choose Banking → Banking Accounts), and their balances still appear in the total for the group.

- **Change the order of accounts.** Quicken automatically lists accounts in alphabetical order. If you want to see your most frequently used accounts at the top of each section, you can easily change the order that accounts appear in the Account List and Account Bar. Simply click the name of the account you want to move and then click the up or down arrow to the left of the account's name.

- **Change an account's group.** Quicken associates accounts with one of the Quicken Centers, but you can change that, too. Suppose you open a savings account earmarked for a home remodeling project. You can switch that account to the Net Worth group by selecting the account and then clicking "(change)" to the right of the "Show in" label, shown in Figure 3-9. In the Change Account Tab dialog box, choose the new group from the "Show in" drop-down list: Banking, Net Worth, Investing, Business, or Rental Property. Accounts can also have different *uses*, which you can choose from the "Used for" drop-down list. For example, within the Banking group, accounts can be earmarked for Spending or Saving. The Investing group has an Investment use and a Retirement use. Net Worth is broken down into Asset and Liability uses.

- **Display other account information.** To display other information about accounts in the Account List window, click Options. Then click an entry on the shortcut menu that appears, like "Show Current Balance" to add a column for current balances.

Categories and Tags: Tracking Transactions

As you learned in Chapters 1 and 2, Quicken lets you assign *categories* to financial transactions to help you track what you're spending your money on, prepare your tax returns, and so on. If you do a good job of categorizing each entry (and Quicken makes it dead simple), then you're never more than a click or two away from generating reports that answer questions like, "How much did taxis cost me this year?" and "Do I spend more on my Chihuahua or my child?" When you create a new Quicken data file, the program automatically sets you up with a boatload of categories, based on what you tell it during setup (such as your marital status and whether you own a home).

For most of us, our financial needs change as time passes. That apartment you had when you first created your Quicken data file? Gone, replaced by your own home. Or perhaps you're now even renting out condos. You can turn Quicken's built-in categories on and off to track different types of income and spending as changes like these happen.

At the same time, everyone has a personal peccadillo or two. You may have a shoe fetish that warrants tracking how much you spend on footwear, whereas your best friend tracks horse shoes, hay, and vet bills. If Quicken doesn't come with a category you want, creating new ones is easy. The program also includes another feature, called *tags*, to help you slice and dice your information in ways that categories only dream about.

This chapter starts by explaining what categories and tags can do. You'll learn about the types of categories Quicken has, from broad groups for mandatory and discretionary spending to detailed subcategories. Then, if the category list Quicken sets up for you isn't enough, you'll learn how to add built-in Quicken categories to the list or create your own. If you decide to use tags to analyze your income and expenses, you'll learn how to set them up, too.

Tip: Quicken's built-in categories may well be all you need to track your finances. If that's the case, you can safely skip this chapter. You can always come back later if you want to tweak the categories you use.

Understanding Categories and Tags

Quicken has two features to help you organize your financial information:

- **Categories** are like Quicken's own Dewey Decimal system—except a whole lot more intuitive. By assigning plain-English labels (Dining, Groceries, Salary, and so on) to all your transactions, you can use Quicken to easily track how you earn money and what you spend it on. You can apply only one category to each transaction.

- **Tags**, on the other hand, are like keywords. They're flexible enough to cut across categories, letting you track money in ways that would be tedious, if not impossible, with categories. For instance, you can apply the same tag to income and expense categories to determine net profit on a rental property. Or you can apply multiple tags—Ski Houses, Retirement Income, and Idaho—to those same rental property transactions.

Organizing Vertically with Categories

Some people organize their papers so meticulously they can pinpoint the eye doctor's bill from 1997, the telephone bill from last August, or the pay stubs from their last job. For others, two shoeboxes labeled In and Out are enough. In Quicken, categories can support the most careful or cavalier of organizational schemes. Read this section to learn how categories work *before* you start modifying categories en masse. Then, as you think about how you want to track your financial information, you can set up custom categories to match your needs.

Categories break your finances down into ever smaller portions: from basic distinctions like income or expense; to high-level divisions like housing, utilities, and taxes; to subcategories for each utility company you pay. Here's a breakdown of all the levels Quicken provides:

- **Income and expense.** As you'll learn shortly (page 74), when you create a category, you specify whether it represents income or an expense. Income categories are for the money that comes into your personal coffers, like salary, part-time income, and winnings from the gals' bunko game. Expense categories represent the money you spend, including unavoidable expenses like electric service and discretionary expenses like the cost of your skydiving hobby.

Quicken automatically creates a third type of category, **Transfers and Payments,** which works a little differently: Quicken generates categories representing each of your accounts (checking, savings, IRA, and so on). Then, when you transfer money (page 163) from checking to savings or make a mortgage payment, you use these Transfers and Payments categories to show which accounts the money is going into and out of.

- **Category.** Think about filling out an income tax return and you'll quickly see the benefit of using Quicken categories. By categorizing your income and expenses, you can fill out those diabolical tax forms in minutes rather than days. (Chapter 10 explains techniques for making tax forms less, er, taxing.) You can associate categories with tax forms—the Salary category with the W-2 form's "Salary and Wages" line, for example. Once you've applied categories to a year's worth of transactions, Quicken can produce a report with the tax form totals you need (see Figure 4-1), or feed the data to TurboTax for even speedier tax preparation.

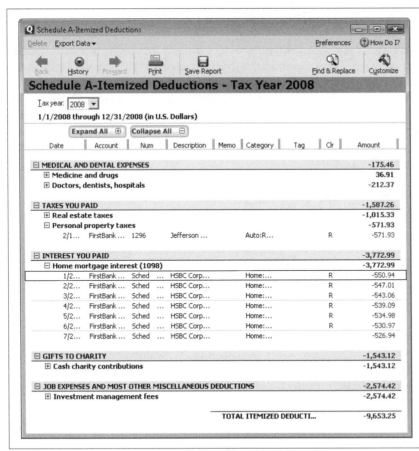

Figure 4-1:
Quicken's built-in Schedule A-Itemized Deductions report is only a few clicks away…if you keep up your end of the bargain and categorize your transactions properly. (Don't fret—it's really easy.) The Tax Summary report (page 275) covers all tax-related categories, including those for Form 1040, Schedule A, Schedule B, Schedule C, and W-2.

Note: Although this book sometimes uses the word *category* to describe any level of category, Quicken reserves the term for top-level categories like Auto and Utilities. Categories below a top-level category are *subcategories*.

- **Subcategory.** As its name implies, a *subcategory* is a category within a category. By lumping several subcategories under one top-level category (as Quicken does with its built-in subcategories for employee benefits), you have the option to look at your spending in detail or more generally. In addition to organizing your category list, subcategories are great for budgeting and tracking. Suppose you set up a category called Food, and then create subcategories for groceries, dining out, and lunch. When you realize you're spending $200 a month on lunch at work (about $10 a day), brown bagging may be easier to swallow.

Tip: Although Quicken lets you create multiple subcategory levels, you usually won't need more than one. If you find you're creating subcategories within subcategories, take a look at your overall category structure. You may be making life too complicated. In some cases, using tags can eliminate additional sub-category levels, as you'll learn in the next section.

- **Category Group.** Quicken also provides *category groups*: high-level categories that encompass broad swaths of individual categories. You can use Quicken for years without needing to use category groups. However, power users find all sorts of uses for them. Out of the box, Quicken includes three category groups: Income, Discretionary, and Mandatory Expenses. If you want to determine how much money you need to cover expenses should you lose your job, for example, you can create a budget (page 291) for only the categories in the Mandatory Expenses group.

Organizing Flexibly with Tags

Categories obey the laws of nature: A dollar can be in only one place (one category) at a time. Tags are more flexible: You can apply the same tag to transactions in different categories, more than one tag to the same transaction, and a tag to both income and expense categories. Here are some examples of what tags can do:

- **Track income and expense together.** Suppose you want to see how much your pottery hobby costs after you deduct what you earn selling your wares. You can set up a tag called Pottery and assign it to any pottery-related transactions, whether they fall into an income or expense category. Then, you can run a report like the built-in "Cash Flow by Tag" report (page 436) to see the net results. You can review income and expense categories together, but you have to customize a report (page 447) to specify the income and expense categories you want to include.

- **Track details with fewer categories.** Tags make it easy to track fine details without creating zillions of categories. Suppose you want to know how much you spend on your kids in *every* category so you can see how much less you'll spend when the little darlings have grown and (you hope) moved away. You can create two tags called Parents and Kids. Then, you can apply the Kids tag to kid-related checks and credit card charges, whether they're for clothing, food, or fun. The built-in "Cash Flow by Tag" report includes a column for each tag, so tag totals are clear, as you can see in Figure 4-2.

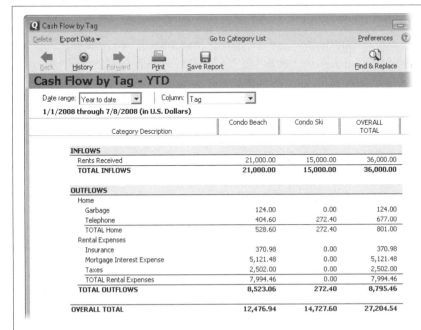

Figure 4-2:
The "Cash Flow by Tag" report includes a column for each tag you create. You can customize the report (page 447) to hide untagged transactions, as is the case with the report shown here. For example, you can hide untagged transactions to see only the income and expenses for rental properties without all the untagged transactions that represent the rest of your financial life.

Note: You might think about creating subcategories to track spending for each family member, but that's not the way to go. For instance, for the Clothing category, you could create subcategories (see page 75) for each member of the family to see the wardrobe costs for an executive mom, a work-at-home dad, and two au courant teenagers. With this approach, you'd have to create family-member subcategories within each category, and that leads to long category lists and lots of scrolling. It's much easier to use tags instead.

- **Track money in multiple ways.** Because you can apply more than one tag to a transaction, you can slice and dice your information in lots of different ways. For example, you can set up tags for each vacation so you can easily find out the total you spent on each one. You could also apply tags for you and your spouse's respective vacation transactions to see how much each of you spent on your separate getaways. Similarly, multiple tags can help you analyze the profit-ability of rental properties in different ways. You could create tags for different types of rental properties—ski versus beach, for example. Then you can review profitability by type of rental property by customizing the "Cash Flow by Tag" report (page 119) to include the Condo Ski and Condo Beach tags, as shown in Figure 4-2.

Adding New Categories

The categories Quicken automatically includes in a newly created data file meet *most* needs for *most* people, but chances are you'll want to make at least a few changes. As you experience life (buy a home, have kids, pay for college, and so on), you'll probably want to track different types of income and spending. Quicken comes with built-in categories for the most common sources of income and expenses, which you can turn on and off as your needs evolve.

But you can also create your own categories from scratch (see page 74). You can even recategorize transactions if you decide to revamp the categories you use.

Whether you want to create one category or several, Quicken makes it easy. Just use one of these methods:

- The Category List window (Figure 4-3) is the best place to make category changes en masse. To open this window, choose Tools → Category List or press Ctrl+C. (If you use the Windows mapping for Ctrl+C, as described on page 488, press Shift+Ctrl+C.)

- Alternatively, if you enter a transaction (say, a credit card charge) and can't find the category you want, you can add a new category then and there: In an account register, when you click a transaction's Category box, a mini-version of the Category List window appears. Click Add Category to open the Set Up Category dialog box, where you can define a brand-new category (page 74).

Tip: If you're hooked on using Ctrl+X, Ctrl+C, and Ctrl+V to cut, copy, and paste, respectively—as is the case in so many Windows programs—don't be alarmed if Quicken doesn't respond the way you expect when you try those keyboard shortcuts. Quicken uses them for its own purposes: Ctrl+X for viewing where transferred money is heading to or coming from, Ctrl+C for opening the Category List window, and Ctrl+V for voiding a transaction. Fortunately, you can tell Quicken to interpret those commands the way you're used to. To do so, choose Edit → Preferences → Quicken Program. In the Quicken Preferences dialog box's "Select preference type" list, click Setup. Under Keyboard Mappings, select the "Windows standard (Undo/Cut/Copy/Paste)" option and then click OK.

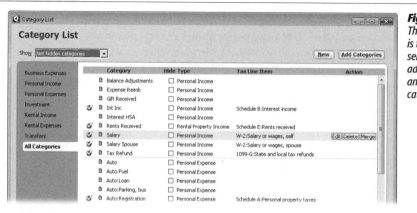

Figure 4-3:
The Category List window is the best place for serious sessions of adding, editing, deleting, and managing categories.

Turning On Quicken's Built-in Categories

The categories you initially see in the Category List window depend on what you told Quicken during setup. But if you have children, buy a house, or get married (not necessarily in that order) after you set up Quicken, you don't have to create categories from scratch just because you don't see them in the drop-down lists in transactions' Category fields. Look through Quicken's built-in categories first to see if the ones you want are there. Built-in categories are more convenient than creating your own because Quicken specifies the tax forms and line items to which they apply. Here's how you find and add built-in categories to your Category List:

1. **In the Category List window (which you open by going to Tools → Category List or pressing Ctrl+C), click Add Categories.**

   Quicken opens the Add Categories dialog box (Figure 4-4).

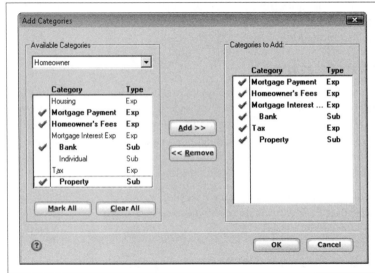

Figure 4-4:
After you select categories and click Add, Quicken moves the categories you selected in the Available Categories list on the left to the "Categories to Add" list on the right. Click OK to make these changes official.

2. **In the Available Categories drop-down menu on the left side of the dialog box, choose the collection of categories you want.**

   For example, if you're the proud new owner of a home, choose Homeowner. In the Available Categories section, you'll see the built-in categories related to the category collection you selected. Some collections correspond to life events, like Married or Children; others apply to special cases like Rentals & Royalties, for types of income and expenses that only some people have.

   By looking at the Type column, you can see whether a category is for income (Inc shown in green) or expenses (Exp in red), or whether it's a subcategory (Sub in the color of the parent category; subcategories are also indented beneath the associated parent category).

3. **To select all the categories that appear, click Mark All.**

   Clicking Mark All is the best approach if you aren't sure which categories you'll need. However, if you want to select specific categories, you can Ctrl+click each category you want. You can also click the first category in a contiguous group and then Shift+click the last one. If you just want to add one category, simply click it.

4. **Click Add to copy the categories over to the "Categories to Add" list.**

   Quicken copies the categories (and their parent categories, if you've selected subcategories) to the "Categories to Add" list, as you can see in Figure 4-4. If you change your mind, you can remove categories from the "Categories to Add" list by selecting them and then clicking Remove.

5. **To actually add the selected categories to the Category List window, click OK.**

   You can remove categories from the Category List one at a time or by selecting several, as explained on page 77. If you remove a parent category, Quicken removes all its subcategories as well.

Creating a New Category

If you want a category that isn't built-in—Aardvark Care, for instance—you can create it in no time. If you add a transaction and the category you want doesn't appear in the transaction's Category drop-down list, you can add a new category without breaking stride. A transaction's Category drop-down list is like a mini Category List window. Click Add Category to open the Set Up Category dialog box, where you can define a new category by following steps 3–7 in the following list.

Planning fans can identify all the new categories they want and create them in one satisfying session. Here's how to create several categories at once:

1. **Choose Tools → Category List or press Ctrl+C to open the Category List window.**

   In addition to creating categories, you can modify or delete categories in the Category list window.

2. **Click New.**

   The Set Up Category dialog box shown in Figure 4-5 appears.

3. **In the Name box, type a name for the new category.**

   Pick a name that identifies the purpose of the category—even if you're creating a subcategory. A subcategory name like *Fees* makes sense when you can see the parent category, but could be obscure in a report or transaction, so use a more descriptive name, like *Condo Fees*.

   You can fill in the Description box as a reminder of what the category represents, but if the category name says it all, feel free to skip this line.

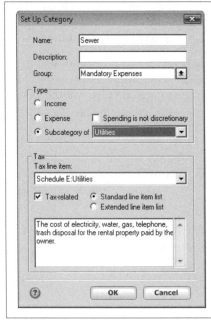

Figure 4-5:
*If you're setting up a subcategory of an existing category, in the
"Subcategory of" drop-down menu, choose the category you want as the
parent. When you do so, Quicken sets the Group field and the "Spending is
not discretionary" checkbox to match that of the parent.*

4. **If you want to assign the category to a high-level category group, in the Group
drop-down menu, choose the appropriate group.**

   For example, most people would choose Discretionary for a category that tracks
   money spent on cappuccinos. But, if you can't function without fancy coffee,
   choose Mandatory Expenses instead. You don't *have* to assign a category group,
   but it takes so little time, there's no reason not to.

5. **Select the type of category.**

   You have three options to choose from. For top-level categories, select either
   the Income or Expense option—the two broadest categories of all. To create a
   subcategory, select the "Subcategory of" option, as shown in Figure 4-5.

   If you select the Mandatory Expenses group, Quicken automatically turns on
   the "Spending is not discretionary" checkbox to indicate that the expense is
   something you need to live like food or rent. If you select the Discretionary
   group, Quicken turns off the "Spending is not discretionary" checkbox.

Tip: Subcategories come in handy when you want to look at your income or spending at different levels.
For example, if you create a parent category called Entertainment with subcategories like Dining Out, Hobbies, and Sports, you can run reports that show your total spending on what you do for fun or drill down
to what you spend on different types of entertainment.

---

6. If the category corresponds to an item on your tax return, turn on the "Tax-related" checkbox. In the "Tax line item" drop-down list, choose the entry that corresponds to the right tax form and the appropriate line on that form.

When you choose a tax line item, Quicken displays a description of that item, but it doesn't guarantee your choice is correct. You can use last year's income tax return to check your line item assignments, or to be sure, ask the IRS or your accountant. Chapter 10 has the full story on setting up Quicken to track taxes.

7. Click OK.

Quicken adds the category to the Category List window, meaning it'll show up in transactions' category drop-down lists. To add another category, simply start back at step 2.

When you're done working on categories, click Done to close the Category List window (or click its Close button, the X at the top-right corner of the window).

Editing Categories

You can modify any aspect of an existing category. For example, you can give it a more meaningful name, change it into a subcategory, assign a tax line item for expenses you joyfully realized qualify for tax deductions, and so on. To change a category's settings, start by opening the Category List window (Tools → Category List or Ctrl+C). Here's what you do next:

1. Right-click the category you want to change, and then click Edit on the shortcut menu that appears.

Or, if your mouse hand needs more exercise, you can click a category and then, on the right end of the category row, click Edit.

The Edit Category dialog box that appears is identical to the Set Up Category dialog box (page 74)—except for its title and the fact that the fields are filled in with the category's current settings.

2. Change the fields you want and then click OK to save your changes.

When you edit a category, the changes you make apply to all transactions in that category.

Removing Categories

You can remove categories from the Category List in two ways. Hiding is a temporary solution, and perfect if you think you'll need the category again in the future; deleting is permanent, meaning you may have to recategorize some transactions. For example, if personal hygiene isn't a priority, you can delete the Personal Care category, which removes the category from the Category List completely. If you

POWER USERS' CLINIC

Tracking Reimbursements

If your company or volunteer association reimburses you for expenses, a category for tracking your reimbursements can help you make sure you receive all the money you're due. Here's how:

1. Create an income category called, say, Business Reimbursements. (You could just as easily use an expense category, but income categories are usually fewer in number and thus easier to spot.)

2. Every time you spend money on reimbursable expenses (like parking), assign the transactions to Business Reimbursements. Then, when you run an Itemized Categories report (page 310), the value for Business Reimbursements shows up as a *negative*

number—your cue that you're still waiting for your reimbursement. In fact, you can use that Itemized Categories report to prepare your expense report. (Creating a customized report [page 447] that shows only the Business Reimbursements category makes it easy to see what you should claim.)

3. When you receive your check for reimbursed expenses, assign the deposit to the Business Reimbursements category as well. You'll know you've been reimbursed for all your expenses when the total for this category is zero or equal to the amount of unreimbursed expenses.

own a home but worry about your spouse kicking you out, you may want to hide the Rent category, so you can restore it if you have to make alternative living arrangements. Here's how to get categories out of your sight:

- **Hiding a category.** In the Category List window, turn on the Hide checkbox for every category you want to hide. To show them again, turn *off* the same checkboxes.

Tip: If you don't see the category you want in the Category List window, check for hidden categories with the Show drop-down menu by choosing either "All categories" or "Hidden categories."

- **Deleting a category.** In the Category List window, click the name of the category you want to delete and then, at the right end of the category row, click Delete. If there are transactions assigned to that category, Quicken asks you to recategorize them, as shown in Figure 4-6. If you don't recategorize transactions, they become *uncategorized* and won't show up in reports (for taxes or actual spending, for example). You can also delete several categories at once. In the Category List window, select all the categories you want to delete. Delete buttons appear at the right end of each selected category's row. Click any one of these Delete buttons to get rid of the selected categories.

Note: If you delete a category that hasn't been used, Quicken displays a dialog box asking you to confirm that you want to delete the category. Although deleting a category is permanent, go ahead and click Yes. It's easy enough to recreate it later.

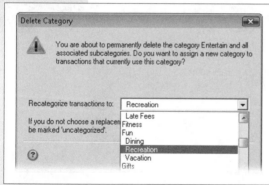

Figure 4-6:
In the "Recategorize transactions to" drop-down menu, choose the existing category you want to reassign transactions to and then click OK. For every transaction that referred to the old category, Quicken switches the category to the new one you selected.

FREQUENTLY ASKED QUESTION

Categories and Budgeting

How do I use Quicken categories to do things like prevent overspending and analyze my income?

Quicken has lots of ways to *track* your spending—but it can't *control* your spending for you. There's no magic button in Quicken to stop you from pulling out your credit card to buy a cobalt blue KitchenAid mixer at Nordstrom.

But tracking is the first step to understanding your financial situation, and ultimately, to controlling it. To track income and spending, you assign categories to your transactions—the paychecks you deposit, the mortgage payments you make, and the checks you write. For example, if you work

full-time during the day and earn freelance income as a superhero at night, you can create two income categories: Salary and Skeeter Boy Donations. To reserve your tax expense categories for the taxes you pay, you can create an income category for Tax Refund.

To build a budget in Quicken (page 291), you specify the maximum amount you want to spend for a category. Then, when you generate a report that shows your budgeted amounts compared to your actual spending (page 311), you can see where you've done well and where spending has gone horribly awry. That report may act as your conscience the next time you reach for your plastic.

Organizing Categories

The Category List window gives you plenty of tools to help review and organize the categories you're working with:

- **Show.** To inspect a portion of the Category List (and filter out the others), in the Show drop-down menu, choose a type of category. For instance, choose "Tax-related categories" to check whether you've assigned your tax categories to tax line items correctly (see page 76).

- **Category types.** Quicken breaks income, expense, and transfer types into fine-grained classifications. For example, to see only personal expense categories, on the left side of the Category List window, click the Personal Expenses tab. (This hides expenses related to investments and rental property, for example.)

- **Options.** Click Options at the bottom of the window to choose what you want to see in the window. For example, you can show or hide category descriptions, category groups, the type of category (income, expense, or sub), and the tax line assignment. To assign a category group, choose Options → "Assign category groups". The Assign Category Groups dialog box is a one-stop shop for assigning category groups. The steps to assign a category group are helpfully located at the top of the dialog box. See page 70 to learn more about category groups.

Tip: At some point, you may decide to organize your categories differently, for example, to map your medical expenses categories to specific line items on the Schedule A federal tax form. After you set up your new categories, you can reassign existing transactions to them (see page 179) by going to the Quicken menu bar and choosing Edit → Find & Replace → Recategorize.

Setting Up Tags

With Quicken's built-in categories and the custom ones you create, you may never need tags. However, if you want to take advantage of the special powers that tags have (page 70), they're a cinch to set up. (You'll learn how to *apply* tags on page 118.)

Creating a Tag

Unlike categories, Quicken doesn't create any tags automatically (unless you use Quicken Home & Business—page 5—in which case the program sets up business tags to help you track your business income and expenses.) You have to create any tags you want to use. Here's how:

1. **Choose Tools → Tag List or press Ctrl+L.**

   The Tag List window opens.

2. **Click the New button at the top of the Tag List window.**

   The New Tag dialog box opens.

3. **In the Name box, type a name that clearly describes the tag, like Kids or Parents (for tracking your kids' expenses versus your own), and then click OK.**

   If you want to describe the tag in more detail, type a description in the Description box. You fill in the "Copy number" box only in a few situations, as the box on page 80 describes.

4. **Click OK.**

   Quicken creates your new tag, and it appears in the Tag List window, ready for you to use.

Tracking Rental Properties

When you create a tag, you fill in the "Copy number" box only if you track your rental properties in Quicken *and* you want to export your rental income and expenses to TurboTax. The IRS requires a separate Schedule E tax form for each rental property you own. In Quicken and TurboTax, the combination of a tag and a copy number uniquely identifies a rental property so you can generate its Schedule E.

For example, say you own a ski condo and a beach condo. First, set up a tag, such as Ski Condo, and fill in the "Copy number" box with the number 1. Then, create a second tag, called Beach Condo, and set its "Copy number" box to 2. When you assign these tags to rental condo-related transactions, Quicken can export each property's rental income and expenses to TurboTax, which in turn generates a Schedule E form for each condo.

Editing a Tag

If you want to edit a tag—to rename it, say—in the Tag List window (choose Tools → Tag List or press Ctrl+L), click the tag and then click Edit at the right end of the tag row. The Edit Tag dialog box that appears is almost identical to the New Tag dialog box, except the boxes are filled in with the tag's current values. Make the changes you want and then click OK. Any transactions using the tag automatically reflect the changes you made.

Hiding and Deleting Tags

Like categories, tags are willing to hide or go away permanently. Hiding tags is perfect if you want to clean up your Tag List, but keep tags around if you might use them in the future. For example, if your kids have a habit of moving back home, you can hide the Kids tag until your empty nest fills up again. To hide a tag, in the Tag List window, turn on the tag's Hide checkbox; restore it to view by turning *off* the same checkbox.

Deleting a tag is permanent. Quicken removes the tag from the Tag list and also deletes the tag in the Tag field of any transactions using it. If you delete the Kids tag and then decide you want to run one more report of children's expenses, you're out of luck. To delete a tag, in the Tag List window, select the tag, click Delete at the right end of the tag row, and then click OK.

Part Two:
Getting Down to
Business

2

Recording Banking Transactions

Underneath Quicken's fancy exterior—its number-crunching features, its tracking and reporting tools, and its reminder system—lies a database. Like any database, there's not much it can do until you start feeding it data. Quicken's main meal is all your daily transactions: the credit cards you swipe, the bills you pay, and the cash you hand over. Your job is to tell Quicken each time one of these things happens; that's what this chapter is all about. Fortunately, Quicken is loaded with timesaving tools that make data entry easy—and, some might even argue, fun.

Note: You can take even more work off your plate by letting Quicken automatically record some of your transactions. Chapter 7 shows you how to set up scheduled transactions, so you don't have to remember when bills or deposits are due. You'll also learn how to set up a paycheck in Quicken, which records every paycheck you deposit and meticulously splits it into various categories for your income and all the deductions. Quicken can also help you keep track of the bewildering array of transactions in the world of health insurance and taxes—as long as you're careful about the categories and accounts you use. To learn how to master these tricky transactions, see Chapter 10.

Transaction Basics

Before you can record transactions, you first need to open the account *register* you want to work on. Quicken's registers are the spreadsheet trackers for each of your accounts; they function just like paper registers (like the one in your checkbook)—except that Quicken packs nifty shortcuts into every field.

Getting to the Register

The Account Bar, shown in Figure 5-1, is the fastest way to open up any register—simply click the name of the account whose register you want to open.

Quicken also gives you a few other options: To open a banking account register from the Quicken menu bar, go to Banking → Banking Accounts, and then choose the account name. To open an investing account or property and debt account register, choose Investing → Investing Accounts or Net Worth → Net Worth Accounts, respectively.

Click account name in either location to open register

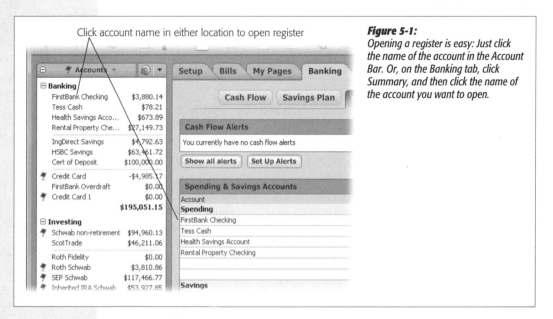

Figure 5-1:
Opening a register is easy: Just click the name of the account in the Account Bar. Or, on the Banking tab, click Summary, and then click the name of the account you want to open.

Entering Transactions

Okay, so you're ready to get down to business. Here's a look at the three main ways to record your transactions in Quicken, along with some advice on when to use each method:

- **Register window.** A Quicken account register makes quick work of recording all kinds of transactions, and it's the only game in town for cash transactions. A register is also good for entering checks you've written by hand (page 86); setting up online payments (page 151); and manually entering credit card charges, debit card charges, and transfers (page 106). Downloading transactions (described next) may be convenient, but entering transactions in Quicken *before* you download them is a good security precaution. Because financial institutions set a time limit for reporting card theft or suspicious charges, comparing the transactions you enter to the ones you download is a great way to catch transactions you don't recognize.

- **Downloading transactions.** The fastest way to get transactions into Quicken is to download them, as Chapter 6 (page 121) explains in detail. Once you've created a connection between Quicken and your real-world accounts, Quicken can download transactions and fill in most, if not all, of the transaction fields. If you've already entered a transaction in Quicken, the program matches downloaded transactions to the ones in the register; it marks the matched downloads as accepted (page 137) so you don't end up with duplicates. If you haven't entered transactions, you can edit the downloaded transactions if necessary (for example, to change the payee name or category), and then accept them. Either way, your job is to confirm that the transactions Quicken downloads are correct.

- **Write Checks window.** If you plan to print checks using Quicken, you can record them in the Write Checks window. Then, simply click the window's Print button to print all the checks in the queue (see page 95). Open the Write Checks window by choosing Banking → Write Checks or by pressing Ctrl+W.

Navigating Between Transactions

To make recording transactions as fast as possible, use these keyboard shortcuts to move through transaction fields faster than grain through a goose:

- **Move to a new transaction.** In the register, press Ctrl+N or Ctrl+End to jump to the first blank row in the register. You're ready to record a new transaction.

- **Move to the next field.** Whether you're creating a transaction directly in the register or using a dialog box like Write Checks, press Tab to move to the next field and display its QuickFill options (page 88). You can skip fields by pressing Tab or by clicking the next field you want to fill in.

- **Record a transaction.** As soon as you've plugged in all your values, click the transaction's Enter button or press Enter (or Ctrl+Enter) to record the transaction. The box on page 86 explains when to use each option. Keyboard shortcut mavens can press Alt+T to record a transaction at any time.

Tip: For a list of additional keyboard shortcuts, see Appendix A.

Recording Checks

With the popularity of swiping credit or debit cards and paying bills online, writing checks is almost as quaint as playing vinyl records. Yet even leading-edge technology buffs write checks every now and then. This section shows how easy it is to record the checks you write by hand. In addition to recording handwritten checks, you can record *and print* dozens of checks in no time. All it takes is some setup to tell Quicken how you want to print checks.

To Tab or to Enter

Out of the box, Quicken is set up so that you press Tab to move between transaction fields and Enter to record the transaction. The advantage of this method is that you can press Enter as soon as the transaction fields are filled in—which can be almost immediately if QuickFill features and memorized payees (page 202) do their jobs.

You can change this behavior, though, so that you press Enter to move through every field and then press it one more time to record the transaction. This way, you don't have to jockey between Tab on the left side of the keyboard and Enter on the right. The drawback to this approach is

that the Enter key no longer provides a shortcut to accepting QuickFill entries in one fell swoop. To record the transaction, you either have to press Enter through every field, click the Enter button in the second row, press Ctrl+Enter, or press Alt+T.

If you want to switch to using the Enter key to move through fields, choose Edit → Preferences → Quicken Program. In the "Select preference type" list, click QuickFill. Turn on the "Use enter key to move between fields" checkbox and you're all set.

Recording Handwritten Checks in the Register

With a combination of keyboard shortcuts, clicks, and the occasional typed character, you can make short work of recording checks in the register. Remember to press Tab (or Enter, as explained in the box above) to move to the next field.

Here are the steps:

1. **Open the appropriate register (see page 84).**

2. **Create a new transaction in the register by pressing Ctrl+N.**

   If you've been scrolling through old transactions, pressing Ctrl+N takes you to the end of the register and places the pointer in a blank transaction. You can also jump to a new transaction by pressing Ctrl+End.

3. **In the Date field, enter the date you want listed for the check.**

   Quicken automatically fills in today's date. If you want a date that's only a few days away, press the minus key (–) to move back one day at a time, or the + key to advance one day at a time. For dates other than today's, Quicken assumes you want the current year, so you can type just the month, a slash (/), and the day: *12/20*, for example. (Take care when you enter transactions at the *beginning* of a new year. Typing *12/20* right after New Year's creates a transaction dated several months in the future.)

   If you're overwriting an existing date, you don't have to type any slashes. As you type numbers, Quicken automatically moves to the month, day, and then year. For example, to change the date to November 15, 2009, you can type *111509*. Appendix A lists additional keyboard shortcuts for selecting dates.

Note: The Quicken calendar icon is the most foolproof method for entering dates, though it's slower than typing them by hand. Click a Date field and then click the Calendar icon that appears to the field's right. A small calendar pops into view. To switch months, click the right or left arrows at the top of the calendar. When the month you want is visible, click the specific day, and Quicken fills in the Date field for you.

4. **In the Num field, type N (for Next Check Num) to automatically fill in the next check number in sequence, as long as you've recorded at least one check. To record a printed check, type P for Printed check (page 95).**

   When you type N or choose Next Check Num in the Num field drop-down menu, Quicken fills in a check number that's one higher than the previous one, as shown in Figure 5-2. If the number Quicken fills in doesn't match the one on your paper check, don't panic. Simply type the number that's on the paper check.

   If you're recording something other than a check, the Num field drop-down menu is where you tell Quicken what type of transaction you want to create. To record the checks you'll print on preprinted checks (see page 98), choose Print Check; to set up a transfer between two accounts (page 163), choose Transfer. With your cursor in the Num field, you only need to type the first letter of the transaction type to select it: *A* for ATM withdrawal, *D* for Deposit, *T* for Transfer, *E* for Electronic fund transfer. You can also create your own transaction types as the box on page 88 explains.

Tip: If details like missing check numbers drive you mad, choose Reports → Banking → Missing Checks to produce a report of the check numbers that don't appear in your Quicken data file. The report lists *all* your transactions, but you'll also see bolded entries like ***** Missing Check 2452 *****.

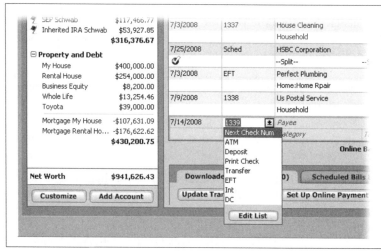

Figure 5-2:
In the Num field's drop-down menu, type the first letter of a transaction type to select it. For example, type N to fill in the next check number in sequence.

POWER USERS' CLINIC

Creating Your Own Transaction Types

Quicken's built-in transaction types each have their own superpowers. Next Check Num automatically fills in a check number one higher than the last one you recorded. Deposit automatically puts your cursor in the Deposit field. Transfer changes the label in the category field to Xfer Acct to remind you that you have to specify the account you're transferring money to. Print Check queues the check up for printing. And ATM (automated teller machine) and EFT (electronic fund transfer) create check-like transactions but without check numbers.

But you don't have to stick with the transaction types that Quicken offers. By creating your own transaction types, you can identify special kinds of transactions, that function like the built-in ATM type (page 109). For example, if you earn interest in several accounts, you can create a type called Int, as shown in Figure 5-2, to flag all your interest deposits. You might also want to create a transaction type for payments you make with a debit card.

Here's how you create your own transaction type:

1. Click a transaction's Num field.

2. In the Num field's drop-down list, click the Edit List button.

3. In the Edit Num List dialog box that appears, click New.

4. In the Add New Num/Ref dialog box, type a name for your new transaction type (up to nine characters). By starting the name with a letter that doesn't match any of the existing types, you can select this type in the list simply by typing the first letter.

5. Click OK to close the Add New Num/Ref dialog box and then click Done to close the Edit Num List dialog box.

Voilà—you've got yourself a new transaction type.

5. **In the Payee field, start typing the payee's name.**

If this is your first transaction with this payee, you may have to type the entire name if Quicken doesn't have the payee in its database. Otherwise, as you type, Quicken scans the names in your Memorized Payee List, Address Book, and Online Payees List, and the QuickFill feature displays a drop-down menu of names that match the letters you've typed so far, as the box on page 89 explains. As soon as the program selects the one you want or you click the payee's name, press Tab (or Enter) to move to the Payment field.

Tip: If the name highlighted in the Payee list is *close* to the correct entry, either type a few more letters or press the up or down arrow key (or the + or – key) to move up or down in the list.

6. **If the value in the Payment field isn't what you want, change the amount by typing the correct value.**

QuickFill automatically fills in the last values you used for that payee (amount, category, tag, memo—whatever fields you filled in last time). When you move to the Payment field, Quicken selects the payment value so you can type a different amount. You can enter numbers using the number keys along the top of your keyboard or the numeric keys on the keypad on the right end of your keyboard. (Apparently, Intuit is optimistic about its customers' financial status, because the maximum amount for a transaction in Quicken is $9,999,999.99.)

Quicken's Quicker with QuickFill

Quicken works hard to do as much of your transaction data entry as it can, and most of the time it does an outstanding job. Every time you create a transaction, Quicken remembers what you did so it can automatically fill in your next transaction for the same payee. In no time, you can add transactions by choosing the date and typing a few letters of the payee's name; Quicken takes care of the rest.

The first time you record a transaction for a payee, Quicken adds almost everything about it to the Memorized Payee List (page 202): the payee, amount, categories, and memo text. For new transactions, you still have to fill in the date, and, for check transactions, the check number. Then, when you record a new transaction and choose a payee, the

QuickFill feature (page 88) automatically fills in all the other transaction fields for you, as you can see in Figure 5-3.

If you've assigned different categories to different transactions for the same payee, Quicken memorizes each variation. For example, you may purchase groceries on one visit, health supplies another time, and, later, tires for your car. When Quicken displays the payee in the Payee field, it shows all the memorized variations, as the three Costco entries in Figure 5-3 show. Press the up or down arrow key (or click the up or down arrow on the right side of the drop-down list) to select the transaction with the category matching your current purchase.

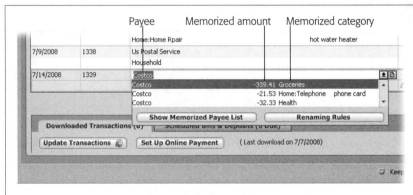

Figure 5-3:
As you type letters in the Payee field, QuickFill displays all the matching payee names it finds in the Memorized Payee List. The drop-down menu also shows you the memorized category and transaction amount. You can modify field values—for instance, to enter a different amount—before completing the transaction.

If the amount is the same each time and QuickFill already filled in the other fields, you can press the Enter key or click the onscreen Enter button to record the check. If you travel the globe, you can tell Quicken to record a transaction in another currency, such as euros, as the box on page 90 explains.

You don't have to precede the value with a dollar sign ($), but you do have to include a decimal point to separate dollars and cents (or corresponding denominations in other currencies, as described on page 490). If you like to keep your fingers on number keys, you can tell Quicken to insert the decimal point automatically: Choose Edit → Preferences → Quicken Program and, in the "Select preference type" list, choose Register. Turn on the "Automatically place decimal point" checkbox, and from now on Quicken inserts a decimal point before the last two digits of the number you enter.

UP TO SPEED

Dollars and Dinero

Quicken can handle multiple currencies at several different levels. You can pick an overall currency for Quicken to use, called your *home currency*, which means the program works in that currency unless you tell it otherwise. You can also designate a currency for an account, like a checking account you opened in Toronto for your Canadian business travel expenses (page 61).

You can even assign a currency to an individual transaction so you can type the amount you spent or received *in the foreign currency*. When you choose the currency for the transaction, Quicken takes care of converting the amount into U.S. dollars (or whatever your home currency is).

Here are the not-so-elegant steps for assigning a currency to a single transaction:

1. First, turn on Quicken's multicurrency support, as described on page 490.

2. In the account register, create a new transaction.

3. In the Amount field, type the transaction amount in the foreign currency, like *10* if your lunch cost $10 Canadian. Don't leave the Amount field just yet.

4. Press Ctrl+Q or choose Tools → Currency List to open the Currency List window.

5. In the Currency List window, right-click the currency you want (Canadian dollars, in this case), and choose Edit on the shortcut menu that appears.

6. In the Edit Currency dialog box, type the exchange rate that was current at the time of the transaction in one of the exchange rate boxes. If you know the exchange rate of Canadian dollars to U.S. dollars, type the exchange rate in the "C$ per $" box, and then click OK.

7. Back in the Currency List window, select the currency again, and then, in the menu bar at the top of the window, click Use. Quicken converts the value in the account register's Amount field to the currency you selected. For example, if the exchange rate is 1.0222 Canadian dollars per U.S. dollar, the amount changes to $9.78 U.S.

To find exchange rates for a given date, go to *www.xe.com/ict*.

Sometimes, you can't finalize a transaction that uses an exchange rate until you receive your bank statement or view transactions online, for example, if your receipt shows only the foreign currency. In that case, you can estimate the dollar amount and then edit the transaction when you find out what exchange rate your bank used.

7. **If the rest of the values QuickFill plugged in are correct, you're done. Simply press the Enter key or click the onscreen Enter button to record the check.**

   If you use Enter to move between fields, press Alt+T or Ctrl+Enter to record the check (see the box on page 86).

   If you want to change any of the other fields, continue with step 8.

8. **If the Category field doesn't show the right category, click the field and begin typing the category you want.**

   You can click this field and *choose* a category, but you rarely have to. QuickFill automatically fills in the last category you used for the payee you've chosen. Quicken even has a database of commonly used payees and the most likely categories for them. The first time you type one of these payees (Safeway, for example), Quicken fills in the category as well (Groceries).

If QuickFill doesn't take care of picking the category, type a few letters until Quicken chooses the right one—or at least gets close. You can press the up or down arrow keys (or + or – keys) to move up or down in the list. If Quicken doesn't have a category that suits your needs, you can create your own, as described on page 74. (See Chapter 4 for more on categories.)

Tip: Sometimes, transactions apply to more than one category. Say you're recording a check for your local coffee shop, but part of your bean order is a gift. At the bottom of the drop-down category menu, click Split, and follow the instructions on page 168.

---

9. **If you use tags (page 70) to further categorize income and expenses, in the Tag field, choose the tag you want to apply to the transaction.**

10. **To add a reminder about what the check is for, type a brief description in the Memo field.**

   For many transactions, you can skip the Memo field entirely. (See the box on page 92 to learn how to hide the Memo field.) The date of the check and the payee usually tell the whole story, like a check to Qwest on June 20 for the May telephone bill.

   On the other hand, the Memo field can hold up to 63 characters, so you can record important details about purchases or payments. For example, you can store the brand, model, and serial number of major purchases in the Memo field. You can also use Quicken's Find feature (page 175) to search for Memo text when you're trying to find a specific payment. For instance, search for "Panasonic" if you need to locate the check you wrote for that widescreen TV.

Tip: You can attach longer notes, reminders, and even images to transactions, as described on page 112.

---

11. **Press Enter (or click the onscreen Enter button) to record the check.**

   You're done! Quicken deducts the amount of the check from your bank balance.

Quicken calculates the new account balance to reflect the check you wrote and—if sounds are turned on—makes a cash register sound to indicate success. (If all this racket scares the cat off the windowsill, see the box on page 93 to learn how to turn sounds off.)

Note: When you create transactions, Quicken skips over the Clr field, which shows the status of a transaction as uncleared, cleared, or reconciled. Reconciling (Chapter 8) and downloading transactions (Chapter 6) change the Clr value automatically. The rest of the time, you're better off leaving this field alone. To learn why you might want to change this value and how to do so, see the box on page 219.

Changing Your Register View

Out of the box, Quicken uses two lines of the register to show each transaction. The date, check number, payee, and amount show up on the first line, and the category, tag, and memo entries appear on the second line. If you'd rather see more transactions (and rarely refer to the Memo field anyway), you can make the register show just one line per transaction.

To switch to one-line view, on the right side of the Register menu bar just above the register, choose View → "One-line display". This places a checkmark in front of the option and displays a much denser version of the register. To switch back to a roomier view or to see memos again, choose View → "One-line display" once more.

The standard sort order for transactions—first by date, then by amount—isn't all that helpful. Sorting by cleared status (View → "Sort by cleared status") keeps you focused on transactions that aren't yet cleared or reconciled. This sort order displays reconciled transactions first, followed by cleared ones, and finally uncleared. That makes it easy to spot things like an older check that hasn't cleared, so you can follow up to see if the payee received your payment.

You can troubleshoot by temporarily switching to other sort orders; just choose the one you want from the View menu. For example, to look for missing or duplicate check numbers, sort by check number. Or, to spot missing monthly payments, sort by payee. To change the field Quicken sorts by *without* using the View menu, simply click a column heading above the register.

Recording Checks You Want Quicken to Print

Paying bills can be tedious if you handwrite each check in one long session at the end of the month. One boredom-slaying solution: Delegate check writing to Quicken. Simply record all the checks you want to print and sit back while your printer spits them out.

If you're printing a lot of checks at once, you can have Quicken automatically put them in the *printer queue* (a virtual holding pen so you can print checks in batches). When you choose Banking → Write Checks (or, if you're keyboard shortcut savvy, press Ctrl+W), the Write Checks window appears. Not surprisingly, it looks like a paper check, as you can see in Figure 5-4. You can choose the checking account, fill in check fields (pressing Tab to move from field to field), and then click Record Check to add it to the list of checks waiting to print. When you've recorded all the checks, click Print to send them to a printer that you've loaded with preprinted checks. (Full printing instructions begin on page 95.)

Using the Write Checks window not only tells Quicken what to print on each check, it also enters the transaction in the register for you. (If you can't see the register, drag the Write Checks window off to the side or minimize it.) You can also record the checks you want to print right in the register by choosing Print Check in the Num field and then filling in the rest of the fields as you would any other transaction.

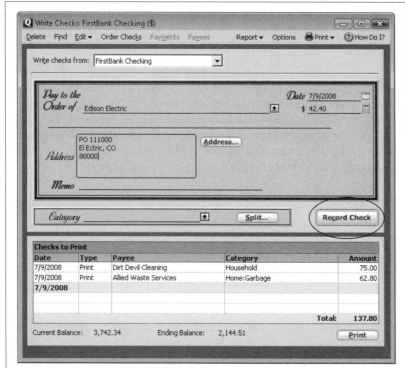

Figure 5-4:
When you click Record Check (circled), Quicken adds the check to the list of checks waiting to print (at the bottom of the window). Once all your checks are ready to go, click Print to send them to the printer (page 95).

WORKAROUND WORKSHOP

Stop That Ka-Ching!

Software developers don't seem to feel their job's done until they've endowed their creations with an assortment of bells and whistles—literally—and Quicken is no exception. If you create several checks in quick succession, the cacophony of cash register noises sounds like a mariachi band imprisoned in your computer.

Other sounds are tucked away here and there, firing off when you perform various tasks. If you don't want Quicken to make noise, choose Edit → Preferences → Quicken Program. In the "Select preference type" list, click Setup, and then turn off the "Turn on Quicken Sounds" checkbox.

Choosing the checking account

You create a check in the top half of the Write Checks window much as you would write a check by hand. The one important difference is that the Write Check dialog box doesn't belong to any particular account, so the first choice you have to make is in the "Write checks from" drop-down menu.

If you've got only one checking account, Quicken automatically selects it. However, if you write checks from a checking account most of the time and a money market account every once in a while, you'll need to choose the correct account for the checks you're about to write.

Filling in check fields

As in the register, you can press Tab to move from field to field in the Write Checks window, entering the date, payee, and so on. QuickFill and other data entry shortcuts also work exactly as in the register.

The one field you *don't* see in the Write Checks window is the check number. Printed check forms are prenumbered because banks can't process stop-payment requests properly without preprinted numbers. Unprinted checks appear in the Quicken check register with the word *Print* in the Num field. Later, when you send the checks to your printer, you tell Quicken what the first preprinted check number is, and *then* the program adds check numbers to the transactions.

Choosing categories

QuickFill usually takes care of filling in the category. If the Category field is still blank after you've chosen the payee, move to the Category field and start typing the name of the category. When Quicken chooses the category you want, click Record Check.

Mailing addresses

Quicken can print mailing addresses on checks, which is a real timesaver if you use window envelopes to mail your checks. Type a mailing address the first time you write a check to a payee or open the Address Book to add several mailing addresses at once. When you print checks, Quicken prints the address on the check to show through the window on the envelope. Page 100 gives the lowdown on entering mailing addresses and other contact information in Quicken's address book.

Reviewing the checks to print

At the bottom of the Write Checks window, Quicken lists the checks you've queued up to print. *Before* you send these checks to the printer and use up several preprinted check forms, review your checks for accuracy. The "Checks to Print" table shows the date, payee, category, and amount. Simply look over the values in the table (scroll if you have several checks queued up).

If you find a mistake in the "Checks to Print" list, click anywhere in the row for the check with the error. Quicken displays the check in the top half of the dialog box. Correct your mistake and then click Record Check to record the revised transaction.

Tip: If you created a check by mistake but haven't yet printed it, you can remove the check completely by clicking the check in the list at the bottom of the Write Checks window and then choosing Delete in the Write Checks menu bar. If you've already printed a check and notice a mistake or decide not to send it, you have to void it *in the register* as described on page 167.

When you're working in the register, Quicken updates the running account balance as you add transactions. If you see your balance dropping dangerously low, you can transfer money from savings or delay making some payments. In the Write Checks window, you have to look a little harder to find your current balance. The crucial numbers are at the bottom of the window:

- **Total of queued checks.** Below the Amount column, Quicken displays the total amount for all the checks you've queued up to print (see Figure 5-4).

- **Current account balance.** Under the list of checks, Current Balance is the balance in the account as of today, without factoring in the checks.

- **Ending account balance.** Ending Balance is the final balance after deducting all the queued up checks and any other transactions you've already recorded that occur in the future. If the Ending Balance is negative, you may need to deposit or transfer money into the account to cover your checks.

Printing Checks

If you write dozens of checks each month, printing your checks saves both time and your writing hand. The box on page 96 tells you a few places where you can buy Quicken-friendly preprinted checks. You have to do some setup work the first time around, but from then on, you simply load the checks into your printer and press a few keys.

Setting up Quicken to print checks

The first step to a successful check-printing session is telling Quicken what type of preprinted checks you use and whether you want to print partial pages of checks. For example, if you use checks that come three to a sheet, one check run may use only one or two of the checks on the last sheet. You can make use of every check on a sheet by starting your *next* print run with the partial sheet of checks left over from your *last* print run. The program remembers these settings, so you only have to go through this process once. After you've specified your check printing settings, Quicken fills them in automatically in the Print dialog box. (You can always edit these options before you print.)

Here's how you set up Quicken to print checks:

1. **Choose File → Printer Setup → For Printing Checks.**

   The Check Printer Setup dialog box appears (Figure 5-5), providing all the settings you need to match Quicken's printer options with the checks you've bought.

2. **In the Printer box, choose the printer you want to use for checks.**

   The Printer drop-down menu lists all the printers connected to your PC. If you use a laser or inkjet printer, Quicken automatically selects the Page-oriented option to feed one sheet at a time to the printer. If you use a printer that feeds paper from a roll, the program chooses the Continuous option.

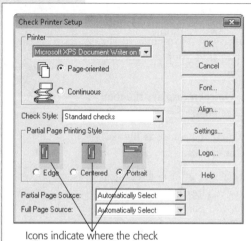

Figure 5-5:
Once you've bought preprinted checks, or if you want to start using a new type of preprinted check, open the Check Printer Setup dialog box to set up Quicken to work with your checks.

Icons indicate where the check
will appear on the printed page

FREQUENTLY ASKED QUESTION

Buying Quicken-Friendly Checks

Do I have to order preprinted checks from Intuit?

Intuit sells checks that work with Quicken, but you can buy them from your bank or a business form company like Clarke (*www.clarkeamerican.com*) or Deluxe (*www. deluxe.com*) just as easily. Banking regulations require the company you order checks from to preprint your bank account number, bank routing number, and the check number. When you print checks in Quicken, the program prints the payment-specific information like date, payee, address, and amount.

Although you don't *have* to buy from Intuit, their pre-printed checks have a few advantages:

*   Quicken reminds you when you're running low on checks.

*   You can order from within the program.

*   Not surprisingly, Intuit's checks work perfectly with Quicken.

*   The price is about the same as from other sources.

To order Intuit checks, choose Banking → Quicken Services → Order Checks & Supplies. Or, if the Write Checks window is open, in the menu bar, click Order Checks. Another option is to point your Web browser to *http://intuitmarket. intuit.com*.

If you order your checks from anywhere else, be sure to tell the vendor that you use Quicken. The checks you buy need to have fields positioned to match where Quicken prints data.

Note: If you print checks on continuous-feed paper, the alignment of the paper in the printer is critical. You can save time and a lot of wasted checks by aligning the paper *before* you print batches of checks, as described in the box on page 98.

3. **In the Check Style drop-down menu, choose the style of checks you purchased.**

Quicken chooses "Standard checks", meaning plain checks without a voucher or extra stub. Standard checks are popular because they use the smallest amount of paper. (The transaction in your Quicken data file serves as a record of your check.)

"Voucher checks" are forms with a check and a detachable voucher (like most paychecks) that shows complete check information including category and class. Pick this check style if you want a record beyond the electronic one in your Quicken data file. Furthermore, because voucher checks come one to a page, you don't have to bother with feeding partial pages of checks as described in step 4. "Wallet checks" print complete check information on a stub on the page's left side.

4. **For page-oriented printers (which print one sheet at a time) loaded with either standard or wallet checks, choose how you want to feed partial pages of checks.**

Quicken chooses the Portrait option automatically, meaning you need to feed the *top* edge of a check into the printer first. (Whether you feed pages with the printed side up or down depends on your printer, so you'll have to experiment.) The Portrait option shows a check oriented as you would have it to write it by hand. The check image is at the top of the Portrait icon to indicate that you feed the top edge of the sheet into the printer. The dialog box shows an example of how to feed the check, as you can see in Figure 5-5. It's always a good idea to set up a sample printed check and test your print settings.

You won't use the Edge or Centered options very often. However, if the Portrait option doesn't do the trick, you can try these options. Edge lets you feed a partial page of checks end-first, with the page aligned with the left edge of the feeder. The Edge icon shows a check rotated counterclockwise and pushed over to the left edge to indicate how you feed the paper. The Centered option is even less useful, because you have to center a partial page of checks in the feeder, which can be tricky. The Centered icon shows the check rotated vertically and the end of the check centered in the feeder.

Note: For printers with multiple feed mechanisms or trays, you can choose which feeder to use in the Partial Page Source and Full Page Source drop-down lists. For example, you can feed full pages of checks through the regular feed tray. But when you print partial pages, you can specify Manual Feed to use the sheet you insert into the manual feed slot.

---

5. **Click OK to save your check-printing settings.**

Now you're ready to actually print your checks, which the next section explains how to do.

Aligning Checks

The slightest difference between what Quicken prints and the corresponding field on a preprinted check can mean lots of wasted paper. Unfortunately, printers and preprinted forms sometimes need a little nudge before they play well together. Before you print a big batch of checks, it's a good idea to check the alignment of your preprinted check forms with a test page. If the test page doesn't print quite right, you can adjust the alignment in the Align Checks dialog box.

If you're using a page-oriented printer, in the Check Printer Setup dialog box, click Align. In the Align Checks dialog box, click "Full Page of Checks". In the Fine Alignment dialog box, type distances in the Vertical and Horizontal boxes to tweak where Quicken prints vertically and horizontally. The numbers in Vertical and Horizontal boxes represent hundredths of an inch. So, to realign printing 1/10 of an inch

down and to the right on the checks, for instance, type *10* in both boxes. Click Print Sample to test the alignment. Lather, rinse, and repeat until Quicken prints values in the right spot on the preprinted form.

The method for aligning forms in continuous-feed printers varies depending on how much the alignment is off. The first step is the same: In the Check Printer Setup dialog box, click Align. With the Continuous option set, the dialog box that opens includes a Coarse button and a Fine button. If your checks are off by more than one line of text, click Coarse. After the sample form prints, you see instructions on the screen for adjusting the coarse alignment. Once the vertical alignment is closed, click Fine to display the same Fine Alignment dialog box you see for page-oriented printers.

Printing to preprinted checks

With your print settings in place and a list of checks waiting to print, you're finally ready to pull the print trigger. Here's what you do:

1. **Load your printer with preprinted checks.**

   Loading checks into continuous feed printers is easy: Line up the holes in the paper with the pins in the printer and make sure the preprinted side of the check faces up. If you use a page-oriented printer, you may have to experiment a bit if you've never loaded preprinted forms into your printer's tray. The printer's manual should include instructions for loading paper so it prints correctly.

   Tip: Once you figure out the direction to load paper in a page-oriented printer (for example, printed side down with the top of the page nearest to you), jot down those instructions and tape them to the printer. That way, you won't have to sacrifice additional preprinted forms to figure out how to load preprinted checks in the future.

2. **To print the checks-in-waiting, press Ctrl+W to open the Write Checks window, and then click Print.**

   You can also print checks without opening the Write Checks window (if you record printed checks directly in the register, for example) by pressing Ctrl+P or choosing File → Print Checks. Quicken opens the "Select Checks to Print" dialog box. As you can see in Figure 5-6, Quicken displays the name of the checking account you're using at the top of the window (in the figure, the account is FirstBank Checking).

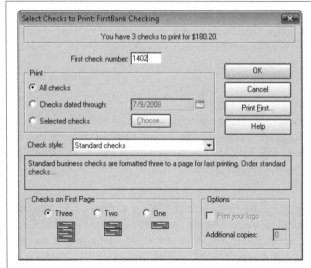

Note: If you messed up and the checks should be written from a different account, click Cancel, delete the checks in the Write Checks window, and recreate the checks with the correct account.

3. **In the "First check number" box, type the number that's on the first pre-printed check you're using.**

   Quicken uses this number to fill in the Num fields on this batch of checks.

4. **Tell Quicken which checks you want to print.**

   Quicken automatically selects the "All checks" option, which prints all the checks in the queue regardless of their dates. If you tend to queue checks long before you want to pay them, select the "Checks dated through" option and specify the check date. The "Selected checks" option lets you choose individual checks to print, so you can do things like hold off printing a credit card payment check until your next paycheck has cleared.

5. **Make sure the "Check style" matches the checks you've loaded in your printer.**

   Quicken automatically uses the check style you set in the Check Printer Setup dialog box (page 97). If you've changed check styles, choose the new style here.

6. **For page-oriented printers, choose the option for the number of checks on the first page.**

   Quicken automatically selects Three, which represents a full page of checks. If the first page has only one or two checks, choose the corresponding option.

> ***Note:*** If you use the "Voucher checks" style, you can type a number in the Additional Copies box if you want Quicken to print extra copies of the voucher. Those copies come in handy if someone you've paid claims your check was incorrect. You can review the information on your voucher copy to resolve the problem.

7. **Click OK or Print First.**

   To print all the checks, click OK. To print only the first partial page of checks, click Print First. After Quicken prints the checks on a partial page, it updates the number in the First Check number box and changes the "Checks on First Page" option to Three. Now, you can click OK to print the remaining full pages of checks.

   Quicken sends the checks to the printer and displays a dialog box that asks whether the checks printed correctly. Before you click OK, inspect the checks coming off the printer. If something didn't work right—a paper jam, a mis-alignment, or no toner, for example—in the First Incorrectly Printed Check box, type the number of the first check that didn't print correctly, and then click OK to try again.

8. **If your checks printed correctly, click OK and you're done.**

   Quicken adds the check numbers for the printed checks to the transactions in the checking account register. Now all you have to do is sign the checks, stuff them in envelopes, and get them in the mail.

Storing Addresses

Quicken comes with an address book, and is happy to store all kinds of info about payees from essential facts like mailing addresses and phone numbers to the touchy-feely stuff like anniversary dates and children's names. The Address Book can be a real timesaver if you print checks. When you enter a payee for a check you're going to print, Quicken checks the Address Book for the payee's name, and if it recognizes the name, adds the mailing address to the check. Stuff the printed check in a windowed envelope, add a stamp, and that puppy is ready to mail.

Sadly, Quicken's Address Book has some painful limitations. In Quicken Deluxe and Quicken Premier, *typing* is the only way to get contact info into the Address Book. (If you use the Quicken Home & Business Edition—page 5—you can import addresses from comma- or tab-delimited files created by programs like Microsoft Outlook.) So unless you like typing practice, it's probably only worth storing contact info for printed-check payees in the Quicken Address Book.

You can add mailing addresses to the Address Book one at a time as you write checks. Or, you can spend some time in the Address Book window, adding payees one after the other. This section tells you how to do both.

Adding Addresses from the Write Checks Window

If a payee's mailing address is the only info you want to store in the Address Book, the fastest method is to type the address directly in the Address area of the Write Checks window. Here's how:

1. **Choose Banking → Write Checks or press Ctrl+W.**

   The Write Checks window opens.

2. **In the Payee drop-down list, choose the payee for the check.**

   If this is a new payee, type the payee's name in the Payee field instead.

3. **Click in the Address box.**

   Although the Address box doesn't look editable, you can click it and start typing.

4. **Type the address as you want it to appear on the check, and then click the Address button to open the Edit Address Book Record dialog box.**

   Quicken is quite clever at mapping the address you enter to the fields in the Address Book, as you can see in Figure 5-7. If the info in the Edit Address Book Record dialog box looks good, click OK to close it. If you notice a mistake, fix it and then click OK.

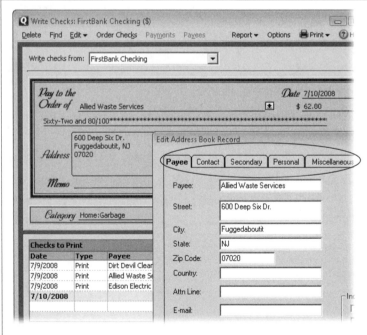

Figure 5-7:
To add more information about a payee, click Address in the Write Checks window. In the Edit Address Book Record dialog box that appears, click one of the tabs (circled) to display more contact fields. Fill in as many as you want, and then click OK to save the updated address record.

5. **Back in the Write Checks window, click Record Check.**

   Quicken adds the check to the print queue and the address to the Address Book.

Note: Changes you make to the Address Book *don't* update the Online Payees list. The box on page 151 explains how to edit online payees.

Adding Addresses in the Address Book

Not surprisingly, the Address Book window is the perfect place for adding, editing, deleting, and looking for payees, as the following sections explain. Here's how you add several payees at once:

1. **Choose Tools → Address Book.**

   The Address Book window opens, displaying all the payees whose addresses you've recorded so far, as shown in Figure 5-8.

Figure 5-8:
To display different address fields in the Address Book window, choose an entry in the Column Sets drop-down list. (Your choices correspond to the various tabs in the Edit Address Book Record dialog box.)

2. **On the Address Book's menu bar, click New.**

   The Edit Address Book Record dialog box opens to the Payee tab. The empty address boxes are your clue that you're adding a new record.

3. **On the Payee tab, type the payee's name and address in the appropriate fields.**

   If you're adding a payee only for check-printing, you can skip the other tabs. But if you've got other information about the payee that you want to record, click the appropriate tab and fill it in.

Note: You can create your own set of fields by choosing <New>. In the Customize Column Sets dialog box that appears, click New, and then type a name for the new set of fields, such as "My favs". In the Available Columns list, select the fields you want to see in the Address Book, and then click Add to copy them to the Displayed Columns list. Click OK, and Quicken displays your new set of fields in the Address Book.

---

4. **To add the payee to the Quicken's QuickFill list, turn on the lower-right QuickFill List checkbox.**

   From now on, as you type the first letters of the payee's name in a transaction, Quicken will select the payee in the QuickFill List.

5. **Click OK.**

   Quicken stores the payee and address in the Address Book.

Editing Addresses

You edit addresses in the aptly named Edit Address Book Record dialog box, which you can get to from the Write Checks window, the Address Book window, or by editing a memorized payee or scheduled transaction. Regardless of where you edit an address, the changes appear in the Address Book, the Memorized Payee list, and the Scheduled Bills & Deposits list.

Here's how to open the Edit Address Book Record dialog box in each location:

- In the **Write Checks window** (press Ctrl+W to open it), select the check for the payee in the table of queued-up checks and then click Address.

- In the **Address Book window** (Tools → Address Book), select the payee and then, in the window's menu bar, click Edit.

- In the **Memorized Payee List** (Tools → Memorized Payee List, or press Ctrl+T), select the memorized payee, and then in the menu bar, click Edit. Then, in the Edit Memorized Payee dialog box, click Address.

- In the **Scheduled Bills & Deposits List** (Tools → Scheduled Bills & Deposits List, or press Ctrl+J), click the Edit button in the scheduled transaction's row. Then, in the Edit Transaction Reminder window, click Address.

In the Edit Address Book Record dialog box, make your changes, and then click OK.

Tip: If you change a payee's name, when you click OK, Quicken asks whether you want to create a new payee record or replace the existing one. Click Yes to create a new record using the new payee name, or click No to update the existing record with the new payee name.

Deleting Addresses

Deleting a payee's address record in the Address Book simply deletes the payee's contact info—it doesn't delete the payee from any transactions. If you delete a payee's address record and then write a check to that payee, you have to re-enter the payee's mailing address.

To delete an address, head to the Address Book window (Tools → Address Book) and click anywhere in the payee's row. Then, in the window's menu bar, click Delete. Quicken warns that you're about to delete the address. Click Yes to delete it or Cancel to keep it.

Modifying Addresses

The Address Book window has a few tricks up its sleeve. You can swap fields in address records (to switch the payee's name and organization, or primary and secondary addresses), or tell Quicken how to arrange fields on a printed check. And you can modify a single record or several at once. Here's how:

1. **Choose Tools → Address Book.**

   The Address Book window opens.

2. **Select the address records you want to change.**

   In the window's menu bar, choose Modify → "Select all" to select them all. Choose Modify → "Select none" to clear the selection and start over.

   To select several adjacent addresses, Shift-click the first and last address. To select non-adjacent addresses, Ctrl-click each one.

3. **To swap the values in the First Name and Last Name fields with the value in the Organization field, choose Modify → "Switch Names and Organization".**

   Swapping these values comes in handy if you were confused about what info to enter where. If the name in the Organization field is two words, Quicken moves the first word to the First Name field and the second word to the Last Name field.

4. **To switch the primary and secondary addresses, choose Modify → "Switch Payee & Secondary addresses".**

   Quicken swaps the Payee and Secondary values.

Tip: To view primary addresses in the Address Book window, choose Payee in the Column Sets drop-down list. To view secondary addresses, choose Secondary in the Column Sets drop-down list.

---

5. **To tell Quicken how to display addresses on a printed check, choose Modify → "Format address".**

   Up pops the Format Print Check Address dialog box. Here, you can specify where you want Quicken to put the attention line (the line that identifies the recipient within the organization); whether to show the payee, a salutation, or the country; and whether to place the city and state on separate lines. The checkboxes in the Add Blank Line section let you add a blank line before the address (in case you want to adjust the address position in the envelope window), before the street (to make the recipient stand out), or after the address.

Note: If you use another program for contacts and don't have that many payees in the Address Book, groups aren't all that useful. When you assign payees to groups, you can filter the Address List to show only the payees in a group (in the Group drop-down list, choose the group). However, if your Address Book is long, you can categorize payees by selecting them, choosing Modify → "Assign to Groups", and then choosing a group. For example, you can assign payees to groups like Friends, Family, and Work, or create your own group by choosing <New> in the Group drop-down list.

Sorting Addresses

You can sort the addresses in the Address Book by any field. For example, you might sort by last name to find the address for one of your friends or sort by organization to find a company that notified you of an address change. Here's what you do:

1. **In the Address Book window's menu bar, choose Sort, and then choose the field you want to sort by.**

   The drop-down menu includes commonly used fields: payee, last name, first name, organization, city, zip code, and birthday. To sort by a field not listed on the drop-down menu, choose "Sort by other", select the field you want, and then click OK.

2. **To change the sort order, choose Sort, and then pick "Ascending sort" or "Descending sort".**

   Ascending sort lists names from A to Z, or numbers from lowest to highest. Descending sort goes from Z to A, or from the highest number to the lowest.

Recording Deposits

Recording a deposit into an account is *almost* identical to recording a check. Follow the steps starting on page 86, but with the following adjustments:

- In the Num field, choose Deposit (or type *D*) instead of entering a check number. When you do that, Quicken changes the order you Tab through fields to match the task at hand. The program automatically jumps to the Deposit field instead of the Payment field, preventing you from accidentally recording money that's coming *into* your account as money going out.

- In the Deposit field, enter how much money you're depositing.

- If you deposit more than one check at a time, you can split the Quicken transaction (page 168) and assign each deposited check to the correct category. For example, you can use a payee called Deposit to indicate a multicheck deposit. Then you can assign each line of the split transaction to a different category like Gift Received, Other Income, and Tax Refund.

The Quicken Calculator

If your deposit includes more than one item, turn your attention to the Quicken Calculator icon on the right side of the Deposit field. This feature isn't a data entry shortcut or a replacement for your business calculator, but it's still quite handy. You'll use it most often to add up several checks you're depositing for the same category, because it automatically fills in the Deposit field with the result when you're done.

The Quicken calculator does the same simple calculations as the Windows calculator or the calculator keys on your computer: addition, subtraction, multiplication, division, and percentages. When your cursor is in a transaction's Payment or Deposit field, you can start pressing the calculator keys on your keyboard and Quicken automatically launches its calculator for you. As you press number keys, the digits appear in the Payment or Deposit field. And if you press +, -, *, or /, the Quicken calculator keypad appears immediately below the field and shows the results of your keystrokes.

Recording Credit Card Charges

Credit cards have become many people's favorite way to pay. Some folks like the convenience of swiping a card out at the gas pump and avoiding the junk food inside the station. Others like the airline miles or cash back they receive. In Quicken, you can track your credit card charges either by recording just the single monthly payments to the credit card company, or by recording each credit card charge. As you'll see in this section, though, tracking each credit card charge individually has so many advantages, it's almost a no-brainer.

Tracking Credit Card Charges

The best way to track what you charge to your credit card is to record individual charges every few days and assign each charge to a category in Quicken. Then, when your credit card statement arrives, you can reconcile the account (see Chapter 8) and record the check or online payment you use to pay your credit card bill (see page 86). This approach has several huge advantages:

- **Complete spending records.** If you pay for a lot of things with your credit card, you can assign every charge to one or more categories and know exactly how you spend your money. With doctors, dentists, and just about everyone else accepting credit cards these days, you'll also have complete records of your tax deductions.

- **Spending red flags.** If you feel as if credit card charges somehow don't use *real* money, tracking individual charges as you make them keeps the cash you owe in plain sight. Swiping your card at the store is still incredibly easy, but the alarming increase in your credit card balance may diminish your yearning for that five-way massage chair. (For more tips on keeping charges under control, see the box on page 109.)

• **Security.** If you set up your credit card for online downloads, manually recording each purchase (using your charge slips as references) is a great way to catch
erroneous or fraudulent charges. For example, after entering your charges manually, you can download the charges from your credit card company (page 133).
Quicken matches the charges you record with the ones you download and turns
each matched duo into a single cleared charge in the register. If you see extra
charges that don't match the ones you entered, either you forgot to record a
charge or someone's buying stuff with your card. If you check your charges
every few days, you can report the activity to your credit card company before
the thieves have too much fun at your expense.

Entering Credit Card Transactions

Recording credit card charges is similar to recording checks and deposits in other
accounts. The basic steps are described on pages 86–91. You specify the date,
payee, amount, category, and (optionally) a memo. A credit card register, though,
has a Ref (for "reference") field instead of a Num field. Quicken includes this field
on the off chance you want to type the terribly long identification strings you see
on your credit card statement (they're usually around 20 characters). Just press
Tab to move past the Ref field and choose the payee.

Credit card transactions come in a few different flavors. Figure 5-9 and the list that
follows show how you handle each one:

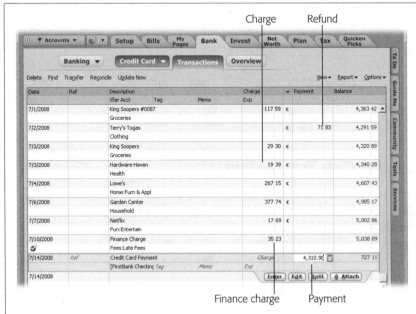

Figure 5-9:
*In a credit card register,
charges go, naturally
enough, in the Charge
field. Payments, whether
for credits or payments,
go in the Payment field.
Finance charges are like
other charges but are
assigned to a category,
like Fees:Late Fees.
Payment transactions
appear in the account
register when you write a
check to your credit card
company (transferring
the money to the credit
card account in
Quicken).*

- **Charges.** Here's how you actually record the money you spend. The merchant who accepted your credit card is the payee, and the amount you spent goes in the Charge column.

- **Payments.** Typically, you'll create a credit card payment by recording a check in your checking account. In the check transaction's Category field, you assign the Xfer Acct (the account you're transferring the funds *to*, as described on page 39) to your credit card account. Quicken automatically records the payment in your checking account register. At the same time, the transaction shows the payment amount as a deposit in your credit card register.

- **Credits and Refunds.** If you return that Vespa scooter you bought (those bugs in your teeth were getting annoying), the dealer might post a credit to your credit card account. To record a credit or refund, fill in all the fields as you would for a charge, except for the amount field. Type the refund amount in the *Payment* field instead of the Charge field. That way, the refund *reduces* your credit card balance.

- **Finance charges and fees.** If you don't pay your balance each month, the credit card company charges you interest—and usually lots of it. For a finance charge transaction, type the name of the credit card company (or a generic name like Finance Charge) in the Payee field, and then choose a category like Int Paid or Fees:Late Fees.

- **Credit card rebates.** If you use a credit card that pays some sort of rebate, the technique for recording the rebate depends on the type of rebate and your preference. For example, if the credit card company sends you a check, you can record the deposit as you would any other. One way to categorize the rebate is to use an income category, perhaps one dedicated to rebates.

  If the card pays a rebate on specific types of purchases, you can record the deposit against the corresponding category. For example, if you receive a rebate for gas, you can use the Auto:Fuel category for your deposit, reducing your total fuel expenses.

Recording Cash Transactions

It's amazing how easy it is to withdraw money from an ATM and spend it all within a few hours. It's much harder to remember what you spent it on, and where. Unfortunately, Quicken won't help improve your memory. But this section gives you a few cash-tracking methods to choose from, covering everyone from the memory-challenged to memory champions.

If Your Memory Is Like a Sieve

If remembering how you spent your cash is a lost cause or you use cash very rarely, you can take a simple approach in Quicken: Treat your wallet like a payee instead of creating a separate cash flow account. In other words, treat your cash withdrawals

Putting the Brakes on Charging

If you've charged ahead once too often, Quicken alerts can raise a red flag before you get into trouble. A credit card account in Quicken includes a Credit Limit field, which you can set so Quicken displays an alert when you've exceeded your limit. With credit cards, you don't want to exceed your credit limit, because that can result in embarrassing rejections from waiters, not to mention dates.

Instead of filling in the Credit Limit field with the *actual* credit limit on your card, use a value a few thousand dollars *below* your limit. Better yet, fill in the Credit Limit field with a limit *you* set to ensure you can afford to pay the balance off each month.

The fastest way to change the credit limit on a credit card account is in the Account Bar. Right-click the credit card account and, on the shortcut menu that appears, click "Edit account" to open the Account Details dialog box. In the Credit Limit text box, type the value at which you want Quicken to alert you, and then click OK.

Here's how you set up an alert for when you near your credit limit:

1. Choose Tools → Set Up Alerts.

2. In the Alerts Center window, click the + sign to the left of Cash Flow to expand the Cash Flow alert category.

3. Turn on the "Credit card limits" checkbox.

4. In the "Enter Values for credit card limits" table, click the credit card's Remind Me At field. Type the value at which you want Quicken to alert you the first time. For example, if your credit card limit is $10,000, set Remind Me At to $8,000. The program reminds you a second time when you actually exceed the limit.

5. To see a pop-up box the next time you open the data file after you exceed your credit limit, select the Urgent option at the bottom of the window.

6. In the "Keep the alert in the list for" drop-down list, choose the length of time you want the alert to remain in the alert list after it's been triggered. For example, to make sure you see the alert, choose "One week" or "One month".

7. Click OK and your alert is all set.

The only downside to this alert feature is that Quicken is subtle with its warnings. Alerts pop up in the middle of the window when you first launch Quicken. After that, you can see bank account alerts you've triggered if you open the Banking Center (click the Banking tab and then click Summary). Page 508 provides complete instructions on setting up alerts.

like checks made out to cash. The withdrawal transaction in Quicken says you took out so many dollars and the category is simply "Cash". Then, tracking cash consists of the following two tasks:

1. **When you withdraw spending money from a bank account, record the transaction as an ATM withdrawal.**

   Choose ATM in the Num field (where the check number goes). Name the payee something like My Cash or Mad Money. Quicken automatically adds a category called Cash to new data files, which is perfect for a cash withdrawal's category, but you can set up your own category if you want (page 74).

2. **At the end of the year, run a "How much did I spend on...?" EasyAnswer report for the Cash category to see how much cash you spent.**

To run this report, choose Reports → Easy Answer. On the left side of the Reports & Graphs window that appears, in the Easy Answer category, click "How much did I spend on...?" In the "Show spending on" drop-down list, choose Cash, and then click Show Report.

If your unaccounted spending exceeds the gross national product of a small nation, you might consider saving all your receipts or capturing cash spending in a notebook or PDA, and then recording cash transactions in Quicken, as described next.

Creating a Pocket Money Account

If you remember every dime you've spent since the first grade *and* you want to track your cash expenditures, you first have to create a cash flow account to go along with the cash in your wallet. Here's how:

1. **Right-click the Account Bar, and choose "Add new account" from the shortcut menu.**

If you create a new account by choosing File → New instead, be sure to select the New Quicken Account option. Otherwise, Quicken creates a new *data file*.

2. **In the first screen of the Account Setup window, select Cash, and then click Next.**

The "Tell Quicken about this Cash Account" screen appears.

3. **In the "Name this account" box, type a name for your pocket money account, and then click Next.**

Quicken fills in the "Name this account" box with *Cash Account*, which is a great name as long as you have only one cash account. You don't have to specify a financial institution, because Quicken knows that a cash account doesn't have one.

4. **In the "Current Cash Balance for Cash Account" screen, set the starting date and the starting balance. Click Next and then click Done.**

Pull out your wallet, count your cold cash, and type the total into the "Amount of cash you currently have" box. Quicken sets the "Date you want to start tracking" box to today's date, which is exactly what you want.

That's it. You're ready to track your cash spending.

Cash Tracking for Photographic Memories

After you create an account for your cash, you can start recording your cash transactions in it. Here's the rigorous way to track cash spending:

1. **When you withdraw money from the ATM, the drive-through window, or even inside at a teller window, record the withdrawal as a transfer (page 164) to your Quicken cash account.**

   The transfer reduces the balance in your checking or savings account and increases the amount of money in the cash account, as the first transaction in Figure 5-10 shows.

2. **Every few days, record transactions in the cash account to reflect what you've purchased—cappuccinos, video rentals, or that tasteful tattoo.**

   When the balance in the Quicken cash account matches the amount of money in your wallet, you're all set.

Figure 5-10:
The Ref field (circled) in a cash transaction is optional. You can use it for receipt numbers or other identifiers.

Note: You can even *reconcile* your cash account in Quicken to the cash you have in your wallet (see the box on page 477). If you actually do that, though, you may need counseling for obsessive financial tracking.

No matter how closely your habits resemble Felix Unger's, you *will* forget how you spent cash every now and then. Don't panic. Just assign the money to a category like Cash. Likewise, you probably don't care enough to create a transaction each time you use some change to buy a newspaper or chewing gum. When you compare your cash on hand to your Quicken cash account balance, simply create one catch-all transaction assigned to the Cash category to square things up.

Editing Transactions

If you notice a mistake in a transaction (the wrong amount, the wrong payee, or a check you wrote for dog food assigned to the Telephone category), you can simply go back to the transaction and change those details, as described in this section.

You can freely edit any field, including the amount, as long as you haven't yet reconciled the transaction. Quicken doesn't stop you from editing a reconciled transaction, but you should proceed with caution or your next account reconciliation might be fraught with problems. See the box below for what to watch out for.

Editing a transaction in the account register is easy: Simply click the field with the mistake, correct the information, and then click Enter. If you click another transaction without first clicking Enter, Quicken displays a message box asking if you want to save the changes. Click Yes to save, or No to discard them. If you were distracted by a phone call and can't remember which transaction you were working on, it's probably best to click Cancel until you remember what you were doing.

Tip: If you want to replace many occurrences of a value in transactions, try using the Find/Replace command, described on page 177.

WORKAROUND WORKSHOP

Editing After Reconciling

Once you've reconciled a transaction (indicated by an *R* in the Clr field), you shouldn't change its amount unless you're looking for a mindbender of a problem to solve. If you realize you assigned the wrong category, used the same check number twice, or selected the wrong payee, you can click the Category, Num, or Payee field of a reconciled transaction, and ever so carefully change *only* the incorrect value. Then, click Enter to save the change.

Changing the amount of a reconciled transaction means the numbers for your next reconciliation won't balance. Because Quicken doesn't tell you which transaction you edited after reconciliation, correcting the error usually requires digging out last month's statement and reviewing discrepancies carefully. To use Quicken's reconciliation report to find errors, choose Reports → Banking → Reconciliation (see page 439 for details).

Reminders, Notes, and Attachments

If you want to add more information to a transaction than the 63-character Memo field can handle, a transaction's Attach button may provide just what you need.

When you select a transaction in a register, an Attach button appears at the right end of the transaction along with the Enter, Edit, and Split buttons. You can create a reminder to follow up, add detailed notes about the transaction, or attach an image like a receipt or cancelled check.

Note: If you don't see the Attach button after you select a transaction, you may have turned off Attach buttons in Quicken's preferences. To turn them back on, choose Edit → Preferences → Quicken Program. In the Quicken Preferences dialog box, click Register. In the "Register appearance" section, turn on the "Show Attach button" checkbox.

Suppose you call your credit card company to dispute a charge. In the Quicken credit card register, you can store information about the dispute with the transaction. For example, you can set up a reminder for the following month when the next statement arrives to check that the charge was reversed. You can also add your notes from the conversation you had with the customer service employee including the person's name, extension, and what you talked about. Finally, you can attach images to the transaction, like a photograph of the mangled DVD player you received in the mail, the receipt for your purchase, or the warranty. The following sections explain all your options.

Attaching Reminders and Notes

When you click Attach, the drop-down menu includes "Add follow-up flag" and "Add note" options. The "Add follow-up flag" option is your best choice, because it lets you do everything the "Add note" option does, and more.

Here's how you add reminders and notes to a transaction:

1. **In the appropriate register, select the transaction you want to annotate, click Attach, and then choose "Add follow-up flag".**

   Quicken opens the "Transaction Notes and Flags" dialog box, shown in Figure 5-11. The Notes box is where you type detailed notes.

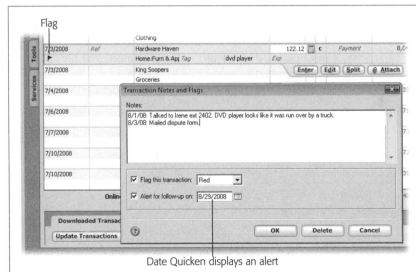

Flag

Date Quicken displays an alert

Figure 5-11:
The "Flag this transaction" checkbox is turned on automatically, and tells Quicken to display a colored flag below the transaction's date in the register. The "Alert for follow-up on" checkbox is initially turned off, but you can turn it on and choose the date you want to be alerted.

   If you choose "Add note" from the Attach drop-down menu instead, the "Flag this transaction" checkbox is turned off and the "Alert for follow-up on" checkbox is grayed out. If you turn on the "Flag this transaction" checkbox, the "Alert for follow-up on" checkbox comes to life and you can type notes, flag the transaction, and set up a reminder.

2. **Type notes about the transaction in the Notes box.**

   If your customer service adventure drags on, Quicken adds more lines to the Notes box as you need them.

3. **If you want Quicken to remind you to follow up, turn on the "Alert for follow-up on" checkbox, and then choose a date in its date box.**

   A reminder is perfect when you want to make sure that a problem is resolved, but the solution may take some time. When the date you selected for the alert arrives, you'll see an alert in the Cash Flow Alerts section of the Banking Center Summary tab. Although the alert says something vague like "A transaction in account First Checking is flagged for follow-up", you can click the word *transaction* to jump to the flagged transaction in the register.

4. **Click OK to add the note and reminder to the transaction.**

   If you get additional information about the transaction later on, you can add to the existing note. Simply select the transaction, click Attach, and choose "Add follow-up flag". Quicken opens the "Transaction Notes and Flags" dialog box filled with the existing notes. You can type more text in the Notes box or change the date for the alert.

Working with Attached Images

You can attach as many images as you want to Quicken accounts or to transactions within Quicken accounts. Bank statements, setup documents, or loan agreements are all good things to attach to accounts. For transactions, you might attach receipts and cancelled checks to document a tax deduction or purchase date for a product warranty. You can also attach images of bills, invoices, and product warranties, so they're at your fingertips whenever you look at the transaction in Quicken. You can even attach a digital picture of what you bought.

Tip: Keeping copies of cancelled checks in Quicken can be a lifesaver if your bank doesn't send you your cancelled checks. An attached image of a bank statement showing cancelled checks may be the only thing between you and a huge tax penalty. The IRS, for example, can surprise you with an audit years after the fact–possibly after your bank deletes its electronic images of your checks.

Attaching images to transactions

Quicken includes several categories for images: Check, Receipt/bill, Invoice, Warranty, and "Other file". Quicken can't tell what an image represents, so you can choose any category you want. For instance, if you attach just a few images, you may prefer to store them all together in the "Other file" category.

Here's how to attach an image to a transaction:

1. **Select the transaction and click Attach. Choose "Add electronic image", and then choose the category you want.**

   The Transaction Attachments window shown in Figure 5-12 opens.

Figure 5-12:
The Transaction Attachments window displays thumbnails of attached images on the left. When you select a thumbnail, a larger version of the image appears on the right. To see the image at its actual size, in the Transaction Attachments menu bar, chose View → "Actual size".

2. **To change the image category, click the down arrow next to the "Attach new" box and choose the category you want.**

    After you attach the first image to a transaction, the label changes to "Attach another", as you can see in Figure 5-12.

3. **To attach the image, click File, Scanner, or Clipboard.**

    If the image is already stored on your computer, click File. The Select Attachment File dialog box is like an Open File dialog box: You navigate to the folder where the image file is saved and then double-click the filename to attach it to the transaction.

    If you want to scan a document directly into Quicken, click Scanner. In the Select Source dialog box, select the scanner and then click Select to start scanning the document.

    If the image is in the Windows Clipboard (for example, if you used Print Screen to capture an image), simply click Clipboard. Quicken adds the contents of the Clipboard as an image.

4. **Make sure the image is attached to the transaction.**

    When the image is attached, Quicken displays it in the Transaction Attachments window. In the register, an image attachment icon appears below the transaction date (or to the left of the date if the register displays transactions in one line). The icon looks like a piece of paper with a paperclip.

5. **When you're sure the image is attached, click Done to close the Transaction Attachments dialog box.**

To view an attached image later, click the image attachment icon. The Transaction Attachments window opens. You can manage image attachments in this window as described in the box on page 117.

Attaching images to accounts

You might want to attach your monthly statements to an account, but you can also attach other images like the agreement you sign for a home equity loan or the fees the bank charges for services. Attaching an image to an account is similar to attaching an image to a transaction. Here's what you do:

1. **Open the account you want to attach an image to.**

   In the Account Bar, click the account's name. If one of the centers is open (like the Banking center), click Summary, and then click the account's name.

2. **If the Overview page doesn't appear automatically, click Overview.**

   The Account Attachments section is at the bottom of the Overview page, as shown in Figure 5-13. If you don't see the section, scroll to the bottom of the page.

3. **Below the left end of the Account Attachments section, click Add.**

   The Add Attachment dialog box opens.

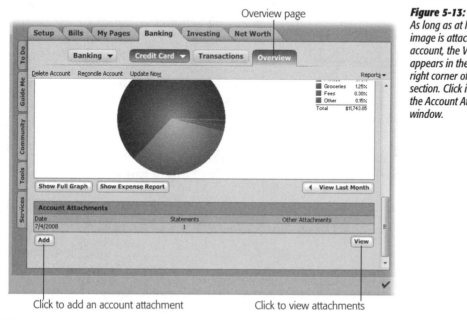

Overview page

Figure 5-13:
As long as at least one image is attached to the account, the View button appears in the lower-right corner of the section. Click it to open the Account Attachments window.

Click to add an account attachment

Click to view attachments

4. **Select either Statement or "Other attachment" depending on the type of image you want to attach, then select a date to identify the image.**

For statements, your choice is easy: Choose the ending date on the statement. (You can attach as many statements to the account as you want.) For other attachments, choose any significant date.

5. **Click OK.**

The Account Attachments window opens; it's identical to the Transaction Attachments window (Figure 5-12) except for the title.

6. **Select the image you want to attach, as you would for a transaction attachment (page 114), and then click Done.**

The attachment appears in the Account Attachments section of the Overview page, sorted by date. To view an attachment, click View to reopen the Account Attachments window.

UP TO SPEED

Managing Images

The Transaction Attachments window and the Account Attachments window both let you manage the images you attach. You can print attachments to provide documentation to the IRS, delete attachments you no longer need (like the receipt for a dead stereo), encrypt attachments so they *can't* be viewed outside Quicken, or save attachments so they *can* be viewed outside Quicken. Here's how:

• **Print an attachment.** Select the attachment in either attachment window, and then click the lower-left Print icon.

• **Delete an attachment.** Select it and then click Delete in the lower-right corner of the window. Click Yes to confirm you want to delete the image, and it's gone.

• **Encrypt an attachment.** Quicken creates a sub-folder called Attach in the folder that contains your data file. When you attach an image to a transaction or account, the program creates several additional subfolders, but the image attachment is stored in the lowest subfolder. If you don't encrypt the attachment, you can navigate to the subfolder in Windows Explorer and double-click the file to view it. Encrypting an attachment means you can view the image file only within Quicken. The image is protected only if you make sure to delete any other (unencrypted) copies of the file on your hard drive. To encrypt an attachment, select it and then, in the window's menu bar, choose Options → "Encrypt attachment". You can reverse the encryption by choosing Options → "Unencrypt attachment".

• **Save an attachment.** If you added an attachment directly from the Clipboard, you can save a copy to view outside Quicken. Select the attachment you want to save and then click the lower-left Export button. The Export Attachment File dialog box is merely an undercover Save As dialog box. Specify the folder, filename, and file type you want and then click Save.

Tagging Transactions

As you learned in Chapter 4, Quicken tags are a flexible way to categorize your transactions. You can apply one or more tags to a transaction to cut across categories, whether they're for different rental properties you own, different family members, or whatever. For example, consider a pair of lovebirds who live together but haven't pooled their money. If they keep track of their finances in one Quicken data file, even if they use separate bank accounts in the real world, tags for each person can show how much they each spend in every joint category. By viewing their total contributions to shared expenses, they can settle any inequity. This section uses Irv and Irene as an example of how to tag transactions and analyze the results. (To learn how to create tags, see page 79.)

Assigning Tags to Transactions

Assigning a single tag to a transaction is similar to assigning a category. You click the Tag field and then type the tag you want or choose it from the Tag drop-down menu. You can even add more than one tag to a transaction. Here's how:

1. **In the account register, create or select the transaction you want to tag, and then click the Tag field.**

   The Tag field is to the right of the Category field, as shown in Figure 5-14.

Note: If you don't see the Tag field in transactions, Tag fields may be turned off. To get them back, choose Edit → Preferences → Quicken Program. In the "Select preference type" list, click Register, and make sure the "Show Tag field" checkbox is turned on.

---

2. **To apply one tag to the transaction, type the tag's name, or click the down arrow in the Tag field and choose the tag in the drop-down menu.**

   You can also apply a tag to a transaction by appending a slash (/) and the tag's name to the end of the category in the Category field, like *Groceries/Irene*, for example.

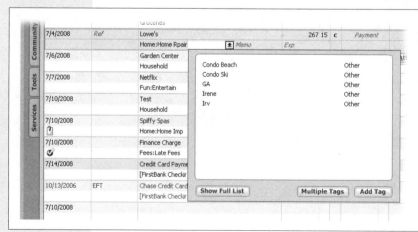

Figure 5-14:
As shown here, the Category field is already assigned to Home:Home Rpair. Click the down arrow to the right of the Tag field to see the Tag drop-down list, and then, click the tag you want to assign.

3. **If you want to apply more than one tag to the transaction, click the Tag field's down arrow. In the drop-down menu, click Multiple Tags.**

   The Tag drop-down menu adds checkboxes in front of each tag. Turn on the checkboxes for all the tags you want to apply. For example, if you want to tag a transaction for a family member and a specific rental property, you could turn on both the Irene and Condo Beach checkboxes.

4. **Fill in the transaction's other fields and then press Enter.**

   You've got yourself a tagged transaction.

Note: If you split a transaction over several categories, you can apply the same tag or different tags to each split item (page 168). In the Split Transaction dialog box, simply choose the tag you want in the Tag field of a split line.

Changing Applied Tags

If you applied the wrong tag to a transaction, you can edit the tag just like you edit other transaction fields. Click the Tag field in the transaction you want to change. Type the name of the new tag, or click the down arrow and choose the new tag from the Tag drop-down menu.

Reviewing Tag Results

You can view income and expenses according to how they're tagged in two ways: one tag at a time, or by comparing multiple tags. For instance, if you own rental properties and you want to see your income and expenses for one property, a tag mini-report is the answer. Quicken also has a built-in report showing all tags at the same time.

To view the results for a single tag, choose Tools → Tag List. In the Tag List window, click the mini-report icon to the left of the tag (the icon looks like a piece of paper with a dog-eared corner). Quicken generates a report showing all the transactions (or split transaction items) marked with that tag.

You can customize a report to show income and expenses for only certain tags, as shown in Figure 5-15. Here's how:

1. **Choose Reports → Banking → "Cash Flow by Tag".**

   Quicken generates the "Cash Flow by Tag" report, which shows income and expenses by category, with columns for each tag.

2. **At the top right of the "Cash Flow by Tag" window, click Customize.**

   The "Customize Cash Flow by Tag" dialog box opens.

3. **Click the Tags tab.**

   The Select Tags section lists all the tags you've created (page 79).

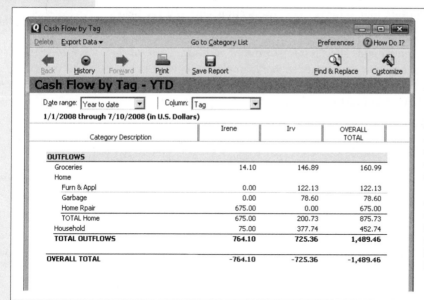

Figure 5-15:
When you display specific tags, the Overall Total column is the total amount for the tags included in the report. In this example, the Overall Total ($1,489.46) is the total of shared expenses. Irene and Irv can calculate the average contribution by dividing the overall total in half ($744.73). Then, Irv can make amends by paying Irene the difference between what he contributed so far and the average ($744.73– $725.36, or $19.37).

4. **To remove tags from the report, turn off their checkboxes.**

   You can turn all tags on or off by clicking Mark All or Clear All, respectively.

5. **Click OK.**

   The report displays columns for each tag you included in the report.

Chapter 14 gives the full story on customizing reports.

Quicken and the Web: Online Banking

Before online banking, your bank balance was like the surprise ending of a cinematic thriller: You had to wait until your bank statement arrived by snail mail to discover how much money you had on hand, which checks and deposits had cleared, and whether you were overdrawn. But now that Quicken and most financial institutions offer online banking services, you can view your bank balances and transactions any time, download them into your Quicken data file, and take evasive action to avoid fees for bounced checks and low balances.

You can also pay bills online without having to write checks, lick stamps, or drive to the post office. For the ultimate in convenience, you can set up recurring online payments so you can go on a long vacation without worrying about missing your mortgage payment or other bills.

Before you can take advantage of all the spiffy stuff you can do online, though, you've got to do some setup. (There had to be a catch.) You need to sign up for your bank's online services and instruct Quicken how to connect to them. This chapter explains how these services work and shows you step-by-step how to link them to Quicken. With these connections in place, you're ready to download transactions and make online payments. You'll also learn how to compare downloaded transactions with ones you recorded yourself (and correct any discrepancies).

Note: If you prefer paper checks and brick-and-mortar banks, simply skip this chapter. Quicken lets you manage all aspects of your personal finances without ever dipping a toe in the Internet.

What Quicken Can Do Online

Online services boil down to three electronic tasks, listed below. Although Quicken can handle all three, not all banks offer them. Bank services vary widely, so contact yours directly to get all the details. If your bank doesn't provide a certain service—online bill payment, say—you can purchase that option directly from Intuit (see the box on page 123).

- **Online account access.** Knowing what your money is doing at any given time is the reason online account access is so popular. While sitting at your computer in your jammies, you can download all the deposits, payments, and transfers that have cleared at your bank or the investment transactions from your investment accounts. In the past, you recorded transactions in Quicken and then, when the bank sent your paper statement, you checked off the transactions to reconcile the program's records with your bank's. You can still manually record your transactions in Quicken (which is one way to catch mistakes or unauthorized activities). However, when you download transactions from the bank, Quicken can either record the new transactions or match the ones you've entered. To reconcile your data with the bank's records you simply accept the downloaded transactions, as you'll learn shortly.

  Once you set up an account in Quicken for online access—a checking account, credit card, investment account, and so on—you can download transactions that have cleared in that account and update your account balances. If you have *two* accounts at the same financial institution set up for online access (checking and savings, for example), you can electronically transfer funds between accounts from within Quicken.

  Quicken online account access works only if your bank supports it. You can find out by checking Quicken's list of participating financial institutions, as discussed on page 127. If you use a bank that doesn't support Quicken online account access, you may still be able to see what's going on with your account through the bank's Web site. (You can learn how to do that on page 133.)

Note: You can download credit card transactions the same way as checking transactions—as long as you set up your credit card in Quicken as a Credit Card account and record individual credit card charges. (Setting up a credit card as a payee and entering only the monthly bill payment won't work.)

- **Online bill payment.** Paying bills with Quicken takes only a few mouse clicks. Your days of writing checks, stuffing envelopes, digging out stamps, and dropping payments in mailboxes are over. You record a transaction in Quicken, and then send the instructions to your online bill payment service and let it do the grunt work. Perhaps the most addictive aspect of online bill payment is automatic repeating payments (page 153). You can sit back and relax without firing a single neuron over the bills that are due. Quicken takes care of sending online payments on the schedule you set.

If your bank doesn't work with Quicken's online bill payment features, you may still be able to pay your bills online. You can sign up for online bill payment directly with your financial institution and set up electronic payments on its Web site. Most banks with Web-based bill payment let you make single payments or payments that repeat on a set schedule. If you use this approach, you can create the corresponding transactions in Quicken or simply download them from your bank with your other transactions. For financial institutions that haven't leapt onto the online bandwagon, you can use Intuit's online services, as described in the box on page 128.

- **Other online features.** Online banking aside, Quicken can do plenty of other things online: update your version of the program, show you information about financial services, convey feedback to Intuit, and connect you to support options like the Quicken Community Forums (see Appendix B).

- **Shopping for personal finance services.** Quicken includes dozens of links to Web sites providing personal financial services. If you want more assistance than Quicken provides, these sites can help you research and comparison shop for loans, insurance, financial institutions, and even financial planners.

Tip: The links in Quicken take you to the Web sites of Intuit partners, but this doesn't mean their services are the best or least expensive—they just ponied up for a placement deal with Intuit. To research all your options, surf the Internet on your own.

WORD TO THE WISE

Paying for Online Services

Whether you pay for online services depends on your financial institution. Some banks give you free online account access—perhaps because downloading transactions and transferring funds electronically saves them from having to hire staff to handle face-to-face transactions.

However, many banks charge for their online bill payment services, like Intuit does for its Quicken Bill Pay service. The fees can exceed $10 a month. Before you scoff at a monthly fee for online bill payment, consider how much money you spend on stamps, envelopes, and printed checks, and the priceless time you spend paying bills each month. For example, paying 15 bills electronically saves $6.30 in stamps alone (and eliminates 15 samplings of foul-tasting envelope glue).

Quicken Bill Pay service and banks' online bill payment services that work with Quicken do the same thing. There are two situations where it makes sense to use the Quicken Bill Pay service: if your bank doesn't have online bill payment or if Quicken Bill Pay costs less than what your bank charges. On the other hand, if your bank has a Web site for paying bills online instead of a service that works with Quicken, you don't have to sign up for Quicken Bill Pay. You can go to your bank's Web site and pay your bills there. Then, you simply download those bill payments into Quicken along with your other transactions. Page 158 describes another way to pay bills online at no charge.

Connecting Quicken to the Internet

Chances are that Quicken figured out what kind of Internet connection you use when you installed the program. (This may seem like magic, but it's actually just a process only geeks can understand.) If the program can't identify your type of connection, you have to give it some additional information. That's what this section is all about.

If Quicken isn't already going online, start by choosing Edit → Preferences → Internet Connection Setup to launch the Internet Connection Setup wizard. The first screen of the wizard has three options, covering all possibilities for Internet access, as shown in Figure 6-1.

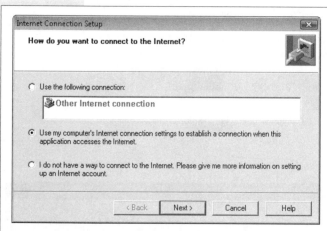

Figure 6-1:
When you first set up Quicken to go online, you tell it which connection you want it to use. If you have several ways to connect, you'll see them all listed here. If you don't have an Internet connection, click Cancel and get your PC online before launching the Internet Connection Setup wizard again. (The third option listed here isn't very helpful—you still have to get an Internet connection on your own.)

- **Use the following connection.** The entries listed here show all your PC's different dial-up or network connections. (If you have more than one and don't see them all listed here, see the box on page 125 for advice.) Select this option if you use a dial-up connection: Quicken dials your ISP (or runs your ISP's connection program) when it wants to go online.

    You can also select this option to change the Internet connection Quicken uses or if Quicken is having trouble detecting a connection.

- **Use my computer's Internet connection settings to establish a connection when this application accesses the Internet.** Select this option if you have an Internet connection that's always available, like DSL, WiFi, or cable modem. Despite its lengthy label, this option is the easiest to use. You're telling Quicken to use the Internet connection that's already running whenever it needs to go online.

Note: *Selecting this option is easy* only if *you have a running Internet connection. If Quicken tries to go online and can't find a connection, the screen in Figure 6-1 reappears, and you're back to square one.*

• **I do not have a way to connect to the Internet. Please give me more information on setting up an Internet account.** This option oversells the help it actually provides. Truth be told, if you don't have Internet access, you're not ready for the Internet Connection Setup wizard. Click Cancel, find an Internet Service Provider, and subscribe to its Internet service. When you're online, return to this wizard and choose one of the other two options.

After you choose a connection option, click Next to finish up. Testing your connection is as simple as launching one of the helpful features that takes you to a Web site. For example, choose Help → "Ask a Quicken User" to see if the program reaches the Quicken Community Web site (*www.quickencommunity.com*).

Tip: If Quicken can't connect to the Internet, you have to determine whether the problem is with the program or your Internet connection. To answer this question, check for email or open your Web browser. If those programs can connect, launch the Internet Connection Setup wizard again and check your settings.

TROUBLESHOOTING MOMENT

When Connections Don't Appear

The connections you've configured for your computer *outside* Quicken should appear in the "Use the following connection" box that's displayed when you launch the Internet Connection Setup wizard. If they don't, click Cancel to close the wizard. Launch your connection to the Internet as if you were planning to check email. While the connection's running, reopen the Internet Connection Setup wizard (Edit → Preferences → Internet Connection Setup), which should now list the connection you're using. Choose that connection and then click Done.

If Quicken doesn't recognize your connection no matter what you do, don't panic. You can always choose the "Use my computer's Internet connection settings…" option. With this option, you have to connect to the Internet outside Quicken before you perform any Quicken task that requires Internet access. If you try to use one of the online features before connecting to the Internet, the program reminds you to connect to the Internet first.

Setting Up an Account for Online Services

Connecting your real-world accounts to your Quicken accounts is more like matchmaking than personal finance. First you have to prepare both participants for the relationship and then introduce them. When you first create an account (page 47), Quicken asks you for the name of the institution that holds the account and whether you want to set up the account for online services. If you took care of setting up your account at that point, you can skip to "Downloading Transactions" on page 133. If not (or the matchmaking didn't work at that time), then read on.

Before connecting your account with online services, first confirm that your institution works with Quicken's services. For accounts listed in the Banking Center (including checking, savings, and credit cards), the account Overview tab is the fastest way to do this. In the Account Bar, click the account name. If the account's Overview page doesn't appear, click the Overview button at the top right of the account page. Figure 6-2 shows how to tell which online services are available.

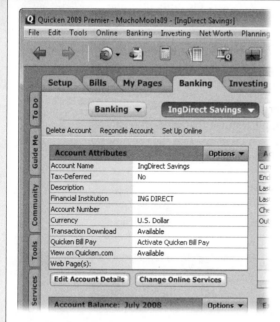

Figure 6-2:
The word Available appears next to the names of services like Transaction Download and Online Payment if your financial institution's services are Quicken-friendly. If the box reads Not Available, you're out of luck. If you see Online Payment (not shown here), your bank can pay bills directly through Quicken. (In the figure, the list item Quicken Bill Pay is your clue that the bank doesn't offer Quicken-friendly online bill payment.) Although investment accounts don't have an Overview page, you can tell they handle online services if you see a Set Up Download button at the bottom of the register window.

Note: If the dreaded words Not Available appear next to an online service you want to use, all may not be lost. For example, you can use Quicken's bill payment service (see the box on page 128) to pay bills from that account. Another alternative is to use your bank's online bill payment service to schedule payments from the bank's Web site.

Your financial institution takes the lead in how it communicates with Quicken: It decides whether it has a direct connection, Web Connect, or no connection at all. Firms using direct connections can do more than those using Web Connect (explained next). As a result, you do less work to link accounts with direct connections to Quicken. The next section tells you how to find out what kind of connection your bank has with Quicken. Here are the connection possibilities:

- **Direct connection,** the most convenient option, is a secure Internet connection linking Quicken directly to your online accounts. With this type of connection, you can download your bank statements and transactions directly into your data file, transfer funds between accounts, pay bills online, and email your bank. (You can learn more about direct connections on page 135.)

- **Web Connect** uses a secure connection to your bank's Web site to download your statement information, but, unlike with a direct connection, Quicken doesn't automatically load the downloaded information. With Web Connect, you have to take the extra step of importing the downloaded information into Quicken.

- **Express Web Connect** is more like a direct connection than Web Connect. Because you don't have to log into your financial institution's Web site to download transactions, you can update accounts as part of One Step Update (page 141). What you *can't* do with Express Web Connect is send instructions from Quicken to your bank; that is, you can't set up bill payments or transfers between accounts from Quicken. PayPal is one of the better-known financial institutions using Express Web Connect.

Finding Participating Institutions

Many, but not all, financial institutions can work with Quicken's online features. If your bank is behind the times, you may want to shop around. Whether you're on the prowl for a new bank or want to apply for online services with your current one, Quicken provides a list of participating institutions so you can see—and apply for—the services they offer. As long as you've registered your copy of Quicken (page 539), the program updates the list when you go online.

To view the list, choose Online → Participating Financial Institutions. When the "Apply for Online Financial Services" window appears, you can filter the list for institutions that support different types of online financial services. As shown in Figure 6-3, finding a financial institution is a snap.

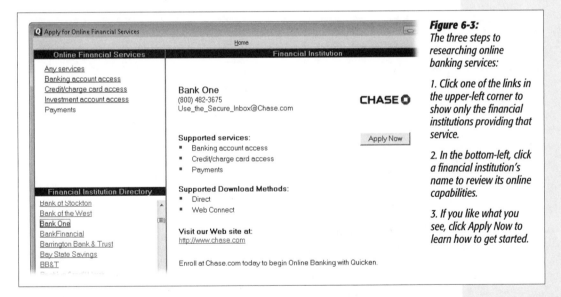

Figure 6-3:
The three steps to researching online banking services:

1. Click one of the links in the upper-left corner to show only the financial institutions providing that service.

2. In the bottom-left, click a financial institution's name to review its online capabilities.

3. If you like what you see, click Apply Now to learn how to get started.

If you're not shopping for a new bank, you can use the "Apply for Online Financial Services" window to sign up for additional services with your current institution. Here's what you can search for:

- **Any services.** The least common denominator: displays financial institutions supporting at least one of Quicken's online financial services.

- **Banking account access.** This service lets you download transactions from your bank account into Quicken.

- **Credit/charge card access.** With this service, you can download your credit card transactions into Quicken.

- **Investment account access.** This service lets you download transactions from your investment account into Quicken.

- **Payments.** With this service, you can set up online bill payments in Quicken and send them to your bank to pay from your account (though you usually pay for the privilege).

To find a bank that supports all the services you want, click each link and make sure the company's name appears each time. If you know which institution you want to use, it's much easier to choose its name in the list and review the info Quicken displays, as shown in Figure 6-3.

Tip: Before you go through the hassle of moving your accounts to another bank, give your current financial institution a call to see if it's planning to provide online services. If online bill payment is a service your bank doesn't have, you can keep your account where it is and sign up for Quicken's Bill Pay service instead (see the box below).

Using Intuit Online Financial Services

If your bank doesn't offer Quicken-based online bill payment or credit card access, Intuit's happy to take more of your business. The company offers Quicken Bill Pay and a Quicken Credit Card—but these add-ons aren't free. (At least Intuit gives you one month free to try things out.)

In the Online Financial Services section of the "Apply for Online Financial Services" window (choose Online → Participating Financial Institutions), click Payments. On the Financial Institution side of the "Apply for Online Financial Services" window that appears, click the Quicken Bill Pay link to sign up for Intuit's bill payment service. Click the Quicken Credit Card link to apply for a credit card through

Intuit. You can also sign up for these services by choosing Tools → Quicken Services and then, in the Services & Add-Ons section, clicking the appropriate link.

Lest you forget about them, Intuit does its fair share of marketing for these features. Every now and then, a message box pops up asking if you want more information about a personal finance service related to the task you're performing. (No, there's no way to turn them off.) In addition, in the bottom-right corner of the Quicken main window, you'll find a link that rotates between these services, including Quicken Bill Pay or downloading credit card transactions.

Applying for Online Services

The first step in a budding online relationship between Quicken and your bank accounts is applying for online banking services at your financial institution. If you've already started the application ball rolling, you can skip this section. If you haven't, choose Online → Participating Financial Institutions to open the "Apply for Online Financial Services" window.

Look through the Financial Institution Directory to find your bank or institution, and then click its name. When the company's details appear in the right pane, simply click the big Apply Now button to start the process. One of two things happens, depending on whether the firm has an online application:

- **No online application.** A window opens thanking you for your interest in online services...and telling you to contact your financial institution. How helpful. In the menu bar, click Home to return to the "Apply for Online Financial Services" window, which includes the telephone number to call.

- **Online application.** Quicken displays the institution's Web site for Quicken folks, as you can see in Figure 6-4.

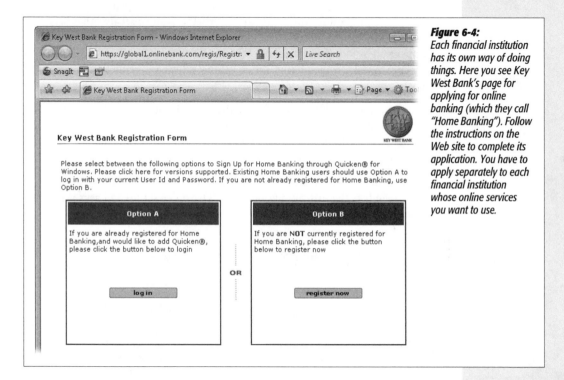

Figure 6-4:
Each financial institution has its own way of doing things. Here you see Key West Bank's page for applying for online banking (which they call "Home Banking"). Follow the instructions on the Web site to complete its application. You have to apply separately to each financial institution whose online services you want to use.

After you complete the application process, your bank will send you confirmation information, a PIN (personal identification number) or password, and so on. Check to make sure your account number and other information is correct. Now you're ready to activate your account for online services in Quicken, as described next.

Activating Online Services

A week to ten days after you apply for online services, you should have gotten a confirmation letter from your bank with your new customer ID and password.

To start banking online, all you have to do is activate the corresponding account in Quicken. Here's how:

1. **In the Account Bar, select the account you want to activate.**

   The screen that appears is either the register or the Overview tab, depending on which one you opened last. Either way, the menu bar immediately above the register or overview includes the Set Up Online command (for banking accounts) or the Set Up Download button (for investment accounts). After you activate your online service, this command changes to Update Now.

2. **Click Set Up Online or Set Up Download.**

   The screen you see when the Account Setup dialog box opens depends on the type of account you're working with and whether you've set up other accounts with the same financial institution. In some cases, the Account Setup dialog box jumps straight to the screen asking for your ID and password. (Why? It's a mystery known only to the folks at Intuit.) If that's the case, rejoice and proceed to step 7.

   If this account is the first one you've activated with this financial institution and it supports direct communication with Quicken, the Account Setup dialog box automatically selects the "Yes, connect to <your bank name> through Quicken" option. Click Next and jump to the step 7.

   If you've already set up some accounts with the same financial institution, the next screen lists the institutions and User IDs you've set up and asks if the new account is with one of them, as shown in Figure 6-5.

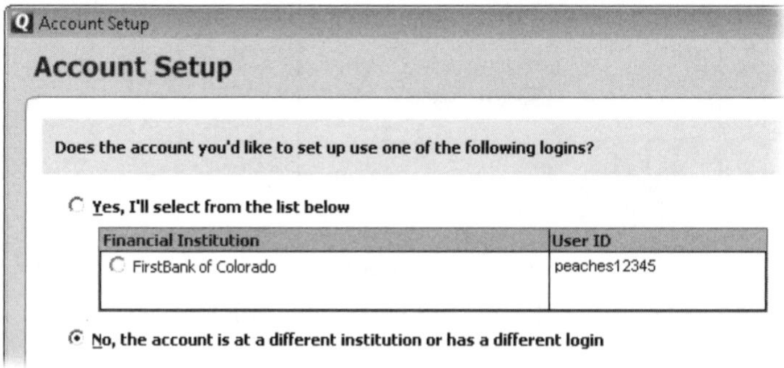

Figure 6-5:
You can choose "Yes, I'll select from the list below" if the account you're activating is at the same bank and uses the same login. If the account uses a different login (for example, a checking account for your business), choose "No, the account is at a different institution or has a different login".

3. **If the account is at the same bank as another account you've set up but requires a different user ID, or the account is at a different bank entirely, select "No, the account is at a different institution or has a different login", and then click Next.**

   The list of financial institutions you already use helps only if the ID you need for online access is the same as one for an account you've already set up (for example, a checking account and savings account that you opened). In that situation, choose "Yes, I'll select from the list below" and then select your bank. Click Next to hop to step 8.

4. **If you select the No option, you see the "What is the financial institution for this account?" screen. Select the "The account is held at the following institution" option.**

   The screen includes the "I do not want to enter my financial institution" option, which isn't what you want when you're trying to set up an account for online access.

5. **In the text box, type the name of your institution, and then click Next.**

   Typing on your keyboard is much quicker than using the letter buttons Quicken displays, though clicking "Bank of", First", or "1st" is a handy way to see banks that begin with these popular prefixes. When you start typing, Quicken attempts to fill in the full name for you.

6. **When you see the screen with the "Yes, Connect to <your bank name> through Quicken" option selected, click Next.**

   The "No, I'll visit my bank web site to download activity and import it into Quicken myself" option represents a second method for using your financial institution's online service: Web Connect (page 135). If you want to download banking transactions on your own, see page 134 for the rest of the steps.

7. **In the "<your bank name> User ID/username", "<your bank name> password", and "Reenter password" boxes, type the ID and password you use to log into your bank's Web site and then click Next.**

   Quicken automatically selects the "Login using my <your bank name> ID and Password" option, so you can type in your ID and password. When you click Next, Quicken goes online and finds all the accounts you have with that institution. It automatically selects all the accounts it finds, and displays the account numbers and account types (in Figure 6-6 you'd see the account number instead of the text "<acct num>").

8. **Select the Exists In Quicken option and choose the Quicken account from the drop-down list. Then click Next.**

   Quicken automatically selects all the accounts at that institution that use the same ID so you can activate them all at once. For each account, select the appropriate Type option (page 48). Then, choose either New In Quicken or Exists In Quicken. If you choose the New option, Quicken prompts you to type a name for the account. If you choose Exists In Quicken, choose the account from the drop-down list. To activate only the account you're working on, turn off the Select checkboxes for the other accounts.

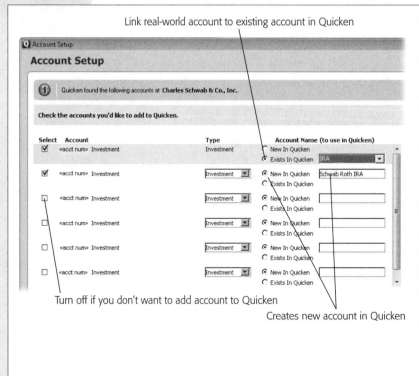

Link real-world account to existing account in Quicken

Turn off if you don't want to add account to Quicken

Creates new account in Quicken

Figure 6-6:
*If you have several
accounts that you access
using the same ID,
Quicken selects them all.
To activate only the
account you're working
on, turn off the Select
checkboxes for the other
accounts in the list. To
link the real-world
account to an existing
Quicken account, select
the Exists In Quicken
option and then choose
the account from the
drop-down list. To set up
a new Quicken account
to go with the real-world
account in the list, select
the New In Quicken
option, and then type the
name that you want
Quicken to use for the
account. Quicken has
already downloaded the
info it needs about the
account, so the Quicken
account name is the only
thing you have to tell it.*

9. In the "Keep your financial institution password in Quicken's secure Password Vault" screen, keep the Yes option selected, and type your vault password in the "Password Vault Password" box and the "Re-enter Password" box. Then click Next.

   If you don't want Password Vault's help, select the "No (I'll enter my financial institution password each time I download transactions)" option, and then click Next.

10. The Setup Complete screen appears, showing the account you just added, its connection type (page 124), and how many transactions Quicken downloaded from that account. Click Done.

    Quicken opens the account's register and lists all the transactions it downloaded on the Downloaded Transactions tab at the bottom of the screen. To learn how to accept downloaded transactions, see page 137.

Tip: If you have trouble getting your account linked up with Quicken, don't even think about calling Intuit's technical support line. First, they charge an exorbitant fee per minute. More important, your financial institution's online support team is more likely to know what it takes to get their service to play well with Quicken, so call them instead.

Deactivating Online Services

Online banking is so convenient, you're not likely to want to quit once you get started. But at some point you may want to turn off online services in Quicken, perhaps just temporarily. For example, if you're switching banks, you can deactivate the online services associated with your Quicken account before you close the real-world account. Or, if your bank changes its name, you have to deactivate online services in Quicken before you can tell the program the new name.

Here are the steps for deactivating online services:

1. **In the Account Bar, select the account you want to deactivate.**

   Quicken displays the Banking tab, which shows either that account's register or an overview of the account.

2. **If you don't see the register, click the Transactions button. Then accept (page 137) any downloaded transactions you haven't accepted yet.**

   You can't deactivate online services for an account if it has any downloaded transactions still waiting to be accepted.

3. **On the Banking tab, click the Overview button.**

   The Overview screen's Account Attributes section shows the services you've activated. For example, if you download transactions, the Transaction Download field says Activated.

4. **Click Change Online Services.**

   The Account Details dialog box opens and displays the Online Services tab.

5. **Click "Remove from One Step Update" and then click OK.**

   That's it—you can no longer access that account online through Quicken unless you reactivate the account. You can change the name of the financial institution when you reactivate online services by choosing a different institution name during the setup procedure (page 130).

Downloading Transactions

Most financial institutions offer some kind of transaction-downloading feature. With a direct or Express Web Connect connection (page 127) you can download records with a single click. Using Web Connect (page 126) takes a few more steps, but you still get the goods long before a paper statement arrives. Getting downloaded transactions directly from your bank into Quicken is a three step process:

1. **Download transactions from your bank.**

   The transactions you see are all the new ones that have cleared at your bank.

2. **Review the downloaded transactions.**

   If the downloaded transactions have values matching transactions you recorded manually (amount and check number, for instance), Quicken links them so you end up with only one cleared transaction in the register for each matched pair. If Quicken doesn't find a match, you should review the downloaded transactions to make sure you authorized them and that the values are correct. (You can still manually record your transactions in Quicken even if you download them. Matching downloaded transactions to the ones you record is a great way to catch mistakes or unauthorized activities.)

3. **Accept the downloaded transactions.**

   In this step, Quicken either records new transactions or disposes of the downloaded transactions if you've already recorded them in the register. In both cases, Quicken marks the transactions as cleared (page 137).

This section explains how to download transactions, whether you use direct connections or Web Connect.

Downloading Transactions Directly

If your financial institution supports direct connections (or Express Web Connect; see pages 126–127 for explanations of both), you never have to leave Quicken to download your transactions. When you display an account's register, it lists transactions in the top half of the window, and tabs for downloaded and scheduled transactions in the bottom half. To download transactions, follow these steps:

1. **On the register's Downloaded Transactions tab, click Update Transactions.**

   If you use the Password Vault (a great, timesaving tool for storing all your passwords—see page 144), the Vault Password dialog box appears. Type the password you set to unlock the Password Vault and then click OK. The "Online Update for this account" dialog box (Figure 6-7) opens. If you use the Password Vault, Quicken automatically fills in your password (using asterisks to hide your actual password) and turns on the checkboxes to download your transactions. If you don't use the Password Vault, go ahead and type your password in the Password box.

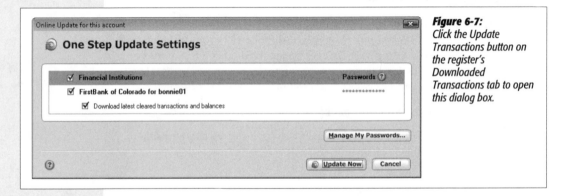

Figure 6-7:
*Click the Update
Transactions button on
the register's
Downloaded
Transactions tab to open
this dialog box.*

2. **To complete the download, click Update Now.**

A dialog box displays the status of the communication between Quicken and your financial institution. When the two finish talking, your downloaded transactions appear at the bottom of the register window, as shown in Figure 6-8.

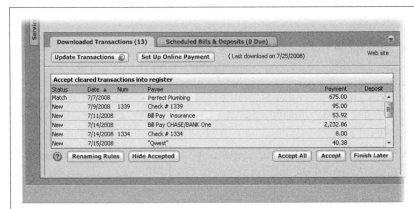

Figure 6-8:
Depending on your financial institution's limits, you can download transactions that are up to several months old. See page 137 to learn how to accept downloaded transactions into the register.

Downloading Statements with Web Connect

The register window looks the same whether your account uses a direct connection, Express Web Connect, or Web Connect. You still see a Downloaded Transactions tab with an Update Transactions button. The big difference comes when you click that button. For banks using Web Connect, clicking Update Transactions opens a browser window, which in turn displays the Web site for your financial institution.

Unfortunately, Quicken can't help you find the button or link on your bank's Web page that downloads transactions because each institution's site is different. A link labeled "Download into Quicken" is a likely candidate, but your financial institution may call it something else. For example, some banks use a Download link that displays a separate Web page for downloading. On that page, you may have to click a Quicken or Money (for Microsoft Money) button to tell the Web page what format you want your transactions in. If you can't find the link, call your bank's customer support number for assistance.

Once you find and click the appropriate link, your browser launches Quicken (if it isn't running already) and downloads the transactions into your data file. When the program finishes downloading the file, you can review and accept the downloaded transactions as you would for direct connect downloads, which begins in the next section.

Reviewing and Incorporating Downloaded Transactions

If you've done the grunt work of manually recording transactions in the account register, once you download transactions, you can then incorporate them into your data file in seconds. Quicken matches up most of the transactions you entered with the transactions you downloaded. You simply match up any others yourself, correcting the discrepancies that prevented Quicken from correctly identifying them.

On the other hand, if you don't record transactions in the register—whether due to laziness, a trusting nature, or a bad memory—you should review each downloaded transaction one by one, changing the payee name to something meaningful and filling in category or other fields that QuickFill (page 88) hasn't already completed. You can accept downloaded transactions one by one or tell Quicken to accept them all at once (accepting transactions is explained in the next section).

As you can see in Figure 6-9, the Status column tells you whether Quicken has matched a downloaded transaction to one you've previously entered. Here's what each status value means:

- **Match.** Quicken found a transaction in the register matching the one it downloaded. You have to make sure Quicken matched the *correct* transaction, as described on page 137. Then you accept the transaction and your work is done.

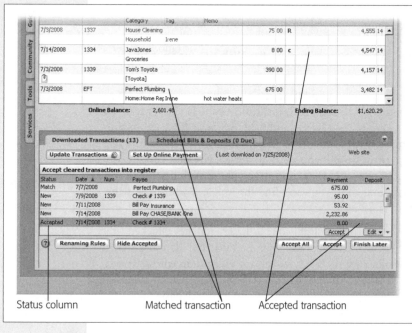

Figure 6-9:
If Quicken matches a downloaded transaction to one you've recorded manually, it changes the Status column to "Match". Unmatched transactions have a status of "New". When you accept a transaction, its status changes to (you guessed it) "Accepted".

Status column   Matched transaction   Accepted transaction

- **New.** The register doesn't contain a transaction matching the one Quicken downloaded. Maybe you forgot to record it, or the one you recorded differs from the one the program downloaded. (Incorrect check numbers and transposed digits are the most common culprits. Page 139 explains how to correct these problems.) Downloaded checks come with the check number, the payment amount, and the date that the check cleared. For checks you haven't already recorded, click the downloaded transaction to add it to the register. In the register, choose the payee name in the Payee drop-down menu so that QuickFill completes the category for you. Now, you're ready to accept the transaction as explained in the next section.

- **Accepted.** You've accepted the transaction (as explained in the next section) either by matching it to an existing transaction or adding a new one to the register.

Accepting Transactions

When the stars are aligned, Quicken matches every downloaded transaction with one you've previously entered—and you agree with the program's judgment. In that case, in the bottom-right corner of the Downloaded Transactions tab, simply click Accept All. Quicken responds by adding the transactions to the register and marks them as cleared.

If you forgot to record a few transactions—or you let Quicken download transactions directly into the register—Accept All is *not* a good idea. You might accept bank errors (they do happen) or even fraudulent charges (which happen often enough that you want to watch for them). If you see any downloaded transactions with a New status, review them carefully before accepting them: Find the corresponding receipts, the entries in your paper register, or simply think about whether the transactions are yours.

In the Downloaded Transactions tab, clicking anywhere in a transaction row displays Accept and Edit buttons immediately below the right end of the transaction row. You can click these buttons to work on the selected transaction. Here's what you can do:

- **Accept a matched transaction.** When you click Accept for a transaction Quicken has matched to one in your register (its status column says Match), the program adds a lowercase *c* to the Clr field in the register to indicate that your financial institution cleared the transaction. If you accept a transaction by mistake, see the box on page 140 for ways to recover.

- **Accept a new transaction.** If you click a downloaded transaction whose status is New, Quicken automatically adds the transaction to the register with the information it knows—the date, the amount, and in many cases, the payee. If Quick-Fill can figure out the category, it fills in that field as well.

Note: If the transaction is fraudulent or incorrect due to a bank error, leave its status as New. Contact your bank to correct the problem. (See the box on page 139 to learn about emailing your bank.) When your bank gets rid of the transaction, you can click the Edit button at the right end of the downloaded transaction's row and then choose Delete, as described on page 141.

In the register, fill in blank fields or correct any values (for instance, replace *Check #1339* in a downloaded transaction with the actual payee name, or change an incorrect category, as Figure 6-10 shows). When the new transaction is complete, click Enter in the register, or click Accept in the Downloaded Transactions tab.

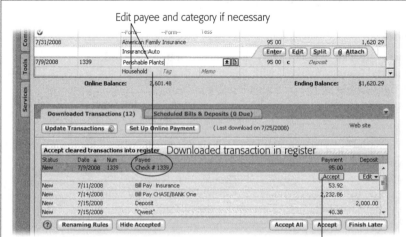

Edit payee and category if necessary

Downloaded transaction in register

Click to accept transaction and mark as cleared in register

Figure 6-10:
If you click a downloaded transaction whose status is New, Quicken creates a new transaction in the register. It fills in the date the transaction cleared at the bank, the amount, the payee that the bank provided (which could be something like Barnes & Noble 1234 or Check # 1119), and the category if QuickFill can figure it out based on the payee name.

- **Edit a downloaded transaction.** Sometimes you need to edit a transaction you download—to make it match the transaction you manually entered in the register, for example. To do this, select the transaction in the Downloaded Transactions tab and then click the Edit button that appears at the right end of the transaction's row. The next section explains reasons why you might want to edit downloaded transactions and how to do so.

When all the downloaded transactions have a status of Accepted, the Finish Later button changes to Done. Click Done to clear the accepted transactions from the Downloaded Transactions tab.

Tip: If you don't have time to finish reviewing and accepting transactions, or if you found a problem you want to resolve before you finish, click Finish Later (below the table of downloaded transactions). Quicken saves the work you've done so far. The transactions will still be there with the same status the next time you open the account register.

Exchanging Emails with Your Bank

When you set up your account for online services, your bank may send you email messages along with the transactions you download. You can read and reply to these messages in the Quicken Online Center, which you access by choosing Online → Online Center. If your bank sends emails with transactions, click the E-mail tab that appears. (You won't see the E-mail tab if your bank or brokerage doesn't send messages this way.)

If you've received a message, the label of the E-mail tab shows how many messages are waiting. For example, if you have one message, the tab says E-mail(1). Click the E-mail tab, select the message you want to read and then click Read. A dialog box opens and displays the message.

If you want to send a message to your financial institution, here's what you do:

1. Click Create and the Create dialog box opens, which looks a lot like email composition windows in other mail programs.

2. Fill in the To, From, and Subject boxes as you would for an email you send from your regular email program. Quicken automatically fills in the "Regarding account" box with the name you gave the account in Quicken.

3. In the Message box, type the note you want to send and then click OK. Quicken adds the message to a queue to send.

4. To actually send the message, click Update/Send.

When Quicken Doesn't Match Transactions Correctly

If you see a downloaded transaction that *should* match one in the register but Quicken hasn't spotted the match, chances are a small mistake in the transaction *you* recorded is the culprit. Discrepancies between recorded transactions and downloaded transactions come in several forms, like values you typed incorrectly or transactions you recorded individually that your bank consolidated into one. Regardless where the disagreement lies, you can correct your transactions or the ones you downloaded to make them agree. Here are various ways you can correct mismatch issues:

- **Mismatched values.** You may have assigned the wrong check number in your Quicken register or typed, say, a *3* instead of an *8* in the payment amount. If you know you recorded the transaction in Quicken before you downloaded the one from the bank), try scrolling in the account register until you spot the transaction you entered. If it's there but the amount is different than the bank's (*$14.49* instead of *$14.59,* for example), click the transaction's amount field (Payment, Charge, or Deposit) and edit the amount to match the bank's value. When you click Enter in the register's transaction row, Quicken automatically matches it to the downloaded transaction, which changes its status to Match.

- **Mismatched dates.** Quicken doesn't match a transaction you recorded if you set its transaction date *later* than the date it cleared the bank (but earlier dates are OK). For example, if you recorded a transaction with a date of March 6 and the bank cleared it on March 1, change the transaction's date in the account register to March 1. Quicken changes the status for the downloaded transaction to Match.

• **Multiple transactions.** You may have recorded several individual checks you deposited as separate deposits, but your bank bundles all the checks you deposit on the same day into one transaction. When the number of transactions doesn't match, you can manually match several of your transactions to one you downloaded.

To do the matching yourself, select the downloaded transaction and click the Edit button that appears in the downloaded transaction's row (Figure 6-11). Then, on the drop-down menu, choose Match Manually. The Manually Match Transactions dialog box, also shown in Figure 6-11, appears. Turn on the checkbox for each register transaction you want to match to the selected downloaded transaction. Click Accept to complete the match.

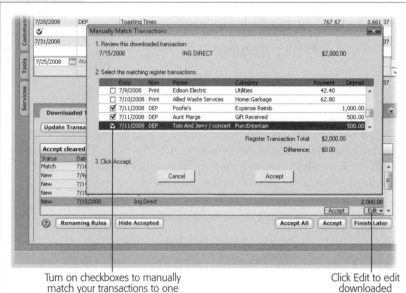

Figure 6-11:
In the Manually Match Transactions dialog box, Quicken adds up the amounts for each register transaction you turn on. When the total of those transactions equals the amount of the downloaded transaction, the Difference value becomes $0.00, indicating a match.

Turn on checkboxes to manually match your transactions to one you downloaded

Click Edit to edit downloaded transactions

Note: If you match more than one transaction to a downloaded transaction, Quicken creates a Split entry (page 168) for each matching transaction from the register.

- **Similar transactions.** Quicken sometimes matches the wrong transactions. For example, if you have two $100 ATM withdrawals in your register, Quicken's standard behavior is to match the newer one—leaving the older one abandoned and unmatched. If you want Quicken to find another matching transaction (the earlier of your two ATM withdrawals, say), select the downloaded transaction and then click the Edit button that appears in the transaction's row. On the drop-down menu, choose Unmatch. If the program finds a new match, it changes the status to Match. If the new match is correct, click Accept. If it doesn't find a match, the transaction's status changes to New.

- **Already reconciled transactions.** Once in a while, you want to delete a downloaded transaction. For example, say you impatiently reconciled your account before going online to download the most recent transactions. The box on page 142 tells you how to get out of this mess. To remove a transaction from the downloaded transaction list, you have to delete it. Click the Edit button for the downloaded transaction and, on the drop-down menu, choose Delete. In the confirmation dialog box that appears, click Yes. Quicken removes the downloaded transaction without adding it to the account register.

Note: You can force Quicken to create a new transaction by choosing Make New on a downloaded transaction's Edit menu (click the transaction and then click its Edit button). You might want to do this if, say, Quicken matched a similar transaction but you haven't manually recorded the one you want. Instead of looking for matching transactions, the program changes the status of the downloaded transaction to New. Click Accept to create a new transaction in your register. If you don't like the way Quicken matched your downloaded transactions, select any downloaded transaction, click its Edit button, and then choose Make All New. This command resets all transactions with a Match status to New. Then, you can step through each transaction and match them the way you want.

Updating All Accounts: One Step Update

Banking online is all about making your life easier, so why download transactions and send payment instructions one account at a time? Quicken's One Step Update automatically downloads transactions and sends payment instructions for every account you've set up for online services. Even with One Step Update in place, you can still download transactions for only one account, if you want to quickly check whether a certain deposit cleared, or you want to get a snapshot of your checking account balance.

Setting Up One Step Update

To set up One Step Update, choose Online → One Step Update to open the dialog box shown in Figure 6-12.

WORKAROUND WORKSHOP

Deleting Downloaded Transactions

Every now and then, your downloaded transactions are out of sync with what's in your register. For example, if you've just activated online services for an account you've reconciled manually, Quicken downloads transactions that you've already reconciled. The program doesn't check reconciled transactions for matches, so older transactions come in with a New status. At that point, you don't need to accept the downloaded transactions, because they duplicate the ones you've already reconciled.

Downloading transactions from both checking accounts and credit card accounts creates a different kind of duplication. Say you pay your credit card bill by writing a check. Quicken downloads the check into your checking account and downloads a second transaction for the payment in your credit card account. Instead of these two transactions,

what you want is a transfer in Quicken from your checking account to your credit card account. To turn a check you've written into a transfer to another account, in your Quicken checking account register, click the check transaction's Category field. In the Category drop-down menu, choose the name of the destination account—in this example, the credit card account. When you record the transaction, the check transaction now represents a transfer of money to the credit card account.

To delete duplicate downloaded transactions from any source, simply select the downloaded transaction in the Downloaded Transactions tab, click Edit and then choose Delete from the drop-down menu. (You have to delete downloaded transactions one at a time.)

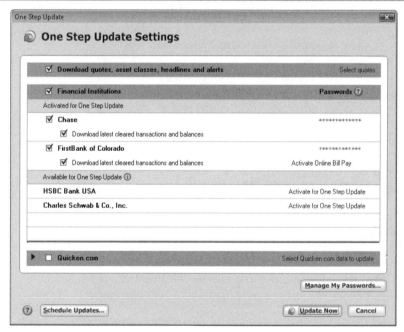

Figure 6-12:
One Step Update downloads bank transactions, investment transactions, and investment price quotes in one fell swoop; it can also automatically enter your account passwords (represented by asterisks in this figure).

One Step Update can perform all or some of the following tasks:

- **Download quotes, asset classes, headlines, and alerts.** To download information about your investments, turn on this checkbox. Quicken automatically gets price quotes, your investments' asset classes (page 347), headlines about your investments, and alerts about things like gut-wrenching price drops. To specify which quotes to download, click the "Select quotes" link on the right side of the dialog box. (See Chapter 12 to learn about working with investments in Quicken.)

- **Financial institutions.** Quicken lists all the financial institutions you've set up for online services. The checkboxes you see depend on the online services you've activated. If you've also set up online bill payment, that account has a second checkbox labeled "Bring my payment information up to date".

  The "Available for One Step Update" section of the One Step Update window shows the Quicken accounts you haven't set up for online services; to activate any of these, click its "Activate for One Step Update" link and then follow the instructions.

- **Quicken.com.** Uploading your records to Quicken.com (it's free) lets you manage your money online, which comes in handy if you're traveling. The downside is that your sensitive financial data is stored at Quicken.com. If that makes you squeamish, turn off this checkbox. To upload only specific data to Quicken.com, click the "Select Quicken.com data to update" link.

Running One Step Update

After you tell One Step Update what you want it to do, it runs the same updates every time. (You can always change the settings later by turning account checkboxes on or off the next time the One Step Update dialog box opens.) To go ahead and actually run One Step Update, follow these steps:

1. **In the Account Bar title bar, click the One Step Update icon, which looks like an orange arrow chasing its tail.**

   Or choose Online → One Step Update. In either case, the One Step Update dialog box appears.

2. **Click the Update Now button.**

   Quicken starts updating, but its visual hints are subtle. The best place to watch for signs of updating is in the Account Bar. When Quicken connects with one of your financial institutions, an orange One Step Update arrow enthusiastically chases its tail to the left of that financial institution's accounts. Accounts that One Step Update hasn't yet updated have a light blue One Step Update arrow to the left of their names. After One Step Update finishes updating an account, a red flag appears to the left of the account's name if that account has new downloaded transactions.

If you watch the account register or Downloaded Transactions tab, you'll notice downloaded transactions starting to appear. At the same time, your cursor may waver between a pointer and an hourglass shape.

3. **When the One Step Update Summary window (Figure 6-13) opens, review each account to see if the update went okay.**

   You can tell Quicken to open the Summary window only if there's a problem. Before you click Close, turn on the "Show this dialog only if there is an error" checkbox (at the bottom left).

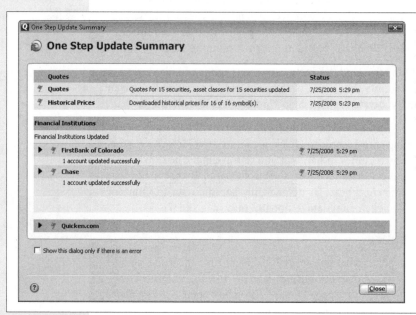

Figure 6-13:
Quicken pops up the One Step Update Summary window when it's finished updating your accounts. To see an account's current balance and the number of downloaded transactions, click the black triangle to the left of the account's name.

Tip: The only time you're likely to pay any attention to the One Step Update Summary window is when an update didn't succeed. You can tell this window to stay hidden unless there's a problem by turning on the "Show this dialog only if there is an error" checkbox in the window's bottom-left corner.

Storing Passwords

The Quicken Password Vault belongs in the Convenience Hall of Fame. Using this service, you can launch online sessions without having to retype your login info each time. All you have to do is type the password to the Vault. One Step Update (or other commands that use this tool) can then grab customer IDs and passwords for all your online-activated accounts and complete the connection automatically.

Tip: Quicken uses encryption and passwords to protect your data file, as explained on page 469. But the Password Vault holds the keys to *all* your financial accounts. So, as an added precaution, you might want to set up *another* level of password protection using some of Windows built-in tools. For example, if you use a screensaver, set it to require a password before anyone can resume working on your PC. If you haven't set up a password for your Windows account, do that now. (If you need help, choose Start → "Help and Support". In the "Help and Support Center" window, search for *set password*.)

Although Quicken creates the Password Vault automatically, you can also set it up yourself (for instance, if you deleted the Vault and want to create a new one). Here are the steps:

1. **Choose Online → Password Vault → Set Up. When the Password Vault Setup wizard appears, click Next.**

   The wizard displays the EasyStep tab and fills in the Financial Institution box with the first financial institution (in alphabetical order) that's set up for online services. Click Next.

2. **In the "Enter the password" screen, fill in the Password and Re-enter boxes and then click Next.**

   You don't have to fill in your ID for the account, since the Password Vault stores only passwords.

   The "Enter additional passwords?" screen asks if you want to add passwords for other financial institutions.

3. **If you want to add passwords for other financial institutions, leave Yes selected and then click Next.**

   In the "Select the financial institution" screen, choose another bank or brokerage from the drop-down list.

4. **Repeat steps 2 and 3 for each institution you want to include in One Step Update.**

5. **When you're done storing passwords, on the "Enter additional passwords?" screen, select No, and then click Next.**

   The wizard displays the "Enter a password to protect your Password Vault" screen.

6. **Fill in the Password and Re-enter boxes with the vault password you want to use, and then click Next.**

   Pick a password that's different than your data file password (page 472); that puts a separate lock on your Quicken data file and your bank account info. When you see the Summary screen, make sure that you've stored passwords for all your accounts and then click Done.

If you ever need to modify the Vault's contents, you can add or remove financial institutions or change login names, passwords, and so on by choosing Online → Password Vault → Edit. Then do one of the following:

- **Add a password.** To add a password for an account that doesn't have one assigned, select the financial institution and then click Add Password.

- **Change a password.** Underneath a financial institution's entry, click the row containing the customer ID and password, and then click Change Password.

- **Remove a password.** If you no longer want to store a password, click the row containing the customer ID and password, and then click Delete Password.

- **Change the vault password.** To change the password to the Vault itself, click Change Vault Password at the top of the dialog box.

Renaming Payees

One drawback to downloading transactions is the incomprehensible payee names that often show up in your Quicken accounts. A simple transfer between your checking and savings account may show up as *INTERNET PYMT TO TXSA 472GP952*. Gee, thanks. Or a gas-station credit card charge downloads with the station's ID number—*Conoco #00092372918027*. You want payee names that make sense, like *Savings Transfer* or *Gasoline*, or are at least consistent, like *Safeway #121* and *Conoco*. Quicken understands: Its *renaming rules* feature lets you replace downloaded payee names with something short, sweet, and meaningful.

Out of the box, Quicken comes with its "Downloaded transactions" preferences set so Quicken automatically creates renaming rules if it sees that you've changed the payee name for a downloaded transaction. Quicken's gotten smarter in recent years: The renaming rules it creates are more flexible than the ones created by earlier versions of the program.

For example, the renaming rule in Figure 6-14 is one that Quicken created automatically. As you can see in the figure, if you change a downloaded payee named *King Soopers #02270* to *King Soopers*, the program creates a renaming rule that looks for a payee name that contains *King Soopers*. The next month, when you charge some groceries at King Soopers #03082, the renaming rule will catch it.

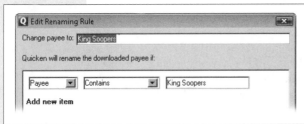

Figure 6-14:
Quicken creates renaming rules that look for text anywhere in a payee's name.

To train Quicken to set up and apply renaming rules the way you want, choose Edit → Preferences → Quicken Program and modify the following settings:

- **Apply renaming rules to downloaded transactions.** In the "Select preference type" list, select "Downloaded transactions". The "Apply renaming rules to downloaded transactions" checkbox is automatically turned on, which is usually what you want. If you turn this checkbox off, Quicken won't rename any of the downloaded payees, regardless how many rules you've defined. If you open the "Renaming Rules for Downloaded Transactions" dialog box (choose Online → Renaming Rules), you can turn this setting on or off by selecting the "Use renaming rules to downloaded transactions" setting's On or Off option.

- **Automatically create renaming rules.** In the "Select preference type" list, select "Downloaded transactions". The "Automatically create rules when manually renaming" checkbox is also turned on automatically, for good reason. This setting tells Quicken to create a new renaming rule whenever you change the payee name for a downloaded transaction. In the "Renaming Rules for Downloaded Transactions" dialog box (Online → Renaming Rules), you can turn this setting on or off by selecting the "Let Quicken create renaming rules during downloading" setting's On or Off option.

- **Don't display a message when renaming.** This checkbox is turned off initially, and tells Quicken to alert you when it creates a rule. If you want to rename payees without interruptions, turn this checkbox on.

Tip: It's a good idea to review the existing renaming rules. If you find rules that are too rigid, you can edit them so they catch more downloaded payees.

Managing Renaming Rules

In the "Renaming Rules for Downloaded Transactions" dialog box, you can create your own renaming rules, edit existing rules, or delete rules for payees you no longer use. To open the dialog box, choose Online → Renaming Rules or, at the bottom of the Downloaded Transactions tab below the register click the Renaming Rules button.

To edit a renaming rule, do the following:

1. **In the "Renaming Rules for Downloaded Transactions" dialog box, select the name of the payee you want to edit and then click Edit.**

   The Edit Renaming Rule dialog box opens, as shown in Figure 6-15.

2. **In the "Change Payee to" box, type the payee name you want Quicken to use in place of the downloaded name.**

   You can use a company name like Conoco or Safeway. Another alternative: use a category like Gas or Groceries. Then you can set up multiple rules for the same payee name, as described in step 6. You might want, for example, to change all downloaded payees containing *Safeway, King Soopers,* or *Albertsons* to *Groceries* so that you can easily track your grocery store purchases.

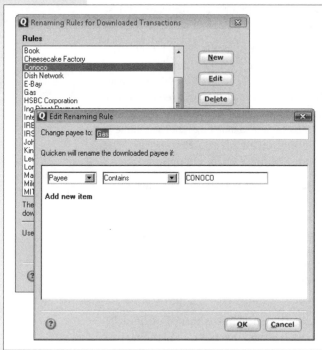

3. **If your bank downloads transactions with the payee name in the Memo field instead of the Payee field, in the box that says Payee, click the down arrow and then choose Memo from the drop-down menu.**

   Quicken automatically fills in Payee because most financial institutions put the payee name in the Payee field, but yours may not.

4. **In the middle drop-down menu, choose the test you want to use.**

   Choosing Contains tells Quicken to look for the text you enter in the third box anywhere in the downloaded payee name, which helps the program find a payee regardless of how the downloaded name is formatted. Start With tells it to look for a payee name starting with the text in the third box. Is Equal To is the least flexible: It tells Quicken to look for the exact payee name.

5. **In the third box, edit the text to what you want the program to look for.**

   The most flexible tests look for a small part of the name, like *Safeway*.

6. **Click OK to save the rule.**

   If you want to set up an additional rule for the same payee name, click "Add new item" below the first row of boxes. Quicken adds another row of boxes for the field, test, and downloaded text value (Figure 6-16). Repeat steps 3 through 5 to define the additional rule and then click OK.

Figure 6-16:
If you change several different downloaded payees in a specific category to the same payee name, like Gas or Groceries, you can easily see your fuel or grocery store purchases.

Paying Bills Online

Whether you use the Quicken Bill Pay service or your bank's, Quicken is your control center for all your online bill paying. Inside Quicken you decide things like who gets paid, how much to pay them, and when. Best of all are recurring payments (like your monthly mortgage or rent), which Quicken is happy to send off on a repeat basis. This section explains all.

Note: Not all banks can accept bill payment instructions from Quicken, because that requires information that goes from Quicken to the bank. (Downloading transactions is a one-way trip with information going from your bank into Quicken.) If you use your bank's Web site to set up bill payments, you can't use the instructions in this section. Instead, you have to either record those transactions manually in the Quicken account register or download the bill payments along with other transactions from your bank.

Setting Up Online Payees

Before you can send online payments from Quicken, you have to tell it who to pay, where to send the payments, and how the payee will know who the payment's from. Quicken's Online Payee List stores all of this information. Just follow these steps:

1. **Choose Online → Online Payee List.**

   The Online Payee List window opens.

2. **In the window's menu bar, choose New.**

   The Set Up Online Payee dialog box opens, as shown in Figure 6-17.

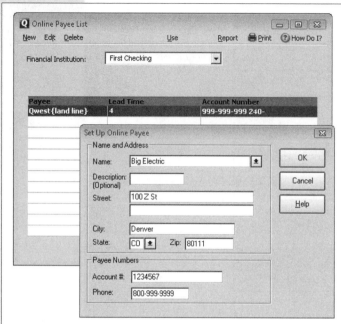

Figure 6-17:
In the Online Payee List window (background), you can create, edit, or delete online payees. If you click Use in the menu bar, you can create a new payment to the selected payee. In the Set Up Online Payee dialog box (foreground), choose a payee from the Memorized Payee List by clicking the down arrow to the right of the Name box.

3. **In the Name box, either type the payee name as it appears on your bill or choose a payee from the drop-down menu.**

   The drop-down menu lists all the entries in your Memorized Payee List (page 202).

4. **Fill in the Street, City, State, and Zip text boxes with the address from your bill.**

   Use the address where you would normally send a paper check.

5. **In the "Account #" text box, type your account number for that payee.**

   If you don't have an account number, you can type any kind of reference information, like your last name.

6. **In the Phone box, type the payee's phone number and then click OK.**

   Quicken doesn't use this phone number for automatic dialing, so the number format doesn't matter, but do type the full number with area code. The number is for reference in case a problem arises with the payment.

7. **A dialog box appears, showing you the values you entered. Quicken isn't trying to be annoying. If you don't specify the correct address and account number, your payment may not make it to the payee or may be credited to the wrong account. Carefully review the values and then click Accept.**

   When you do so, Quicken adds the payee to the list.

Note: The lead time shown for each payee in the Online Payee list is based on the number of days your financial institution sets and is part of the information Quicken downloads from your bank.

Once you've added an online payee, you're ready to send money to that company. But keep in mind that Quicken won't automatically update the payee information if, say, the company moves. Be sure to update this information as necessary, as discussed in the box below.

WORD TO THE WISE

Keeping Online Payees Up to Date

When a bill comes in, it's always a good idea to scan for changes to the company's address and account number. If a payee's address changes, you need to edit your online payee to match, or your payments may not reach their destination. In the Online Payee List window, select the payee and then click Edit in the menu bar.

Account numbers are tougher to change because you can't change them by editing the online payee. You have no choice (bummer) but to delete the existing online payee and create a new one with the new account number.

Creating the Payment Request

Next up: entering the payment details. In this step, you're not actually sending out the money—you're just filling in the payment's particulars. Choose one of the following options based on how you prefer to record payments.

- **Account register window.** If you usually record payments in your checking account register, there's no reason to change. In the Num field, choosing Send Online Payment turns a transaction into an online payment. (If you haven't activated online bill payment or your bank doesn't offer it, Send Online Payment won't appear as one of the choices in the drop-down menu.)

- **Write Checks.** In the Write Checks window (page 101), turn on the Online Payment checkbox to tell Quicken that the check is actually an online bill payment.

- **Scheduled Bills & Deposits.** You can also schedule online bill payments, which are perfect for monthly payments whose amounts change each month. Press Ctrl+J to open the Scheduled Bills & Deposits window. In the menu bar, choose Create New, and then choose "Scheduled Bill or Deposit". In the Add Transaction Reminder dialog box that opens, select the online payee from the Payee drop-down menu. In the "Payment method" drop-down menu, choose "Online Payment from Quicken" (page 153).

Filling in the information required for an online payment is almost exactly the same as making a regular payment. If you want to enter the amount for each payment, leave the Amount box blank. The biggest difference is the "Delivery date", which should be a few days before the payment is due to ensure that it arrives on time. If you select a date that doesn't give your bill payment service enough time to process your payment (usually five days), Quicken tells you and changes the date to the first feasible date.

• **Online Center.** In the account register on the Downloaded Transactions tab, click the Set Up Online Payment button. In the Online Center window that appears, click the Payments tab. At the top of the Payments tab, fill in the text boxes as you would any payment transaction.

Fill in the Delivery date text box with the date you want the payee to receive the payment. You don't have to worry about filling in the "Processing date" field. In most cases, your bank sets that date based on the delivery date you specify.

Tip: If the bill's due date is coming up, you can also choose the ASAP option to tell your bank to process the payment as quickly as it can.

Sending Payments

Payee set up? Check. Payment info entered? Check. Now, finally, you're ready for liftoff. Except for—sigh—one more little thing: You need to tell Quicken to send the payments you've set up to your online bill payment service. Think of it as sending email. Recording a check in Quicken and choosing the Send Online Payment transaction type (or turning on the Online Payment checkbox in the Write Checks window) is the same as writing the contents of an email message. But just as you sometimes find an email message that you forgot to send, you have to tell Quicken to send those payments to your online service.

Here are the steps for sending the online payments you've created:

1. **On the account register's Downloaded Transactions tab, click the Set Up Online Payment button.**

   The Online Center window opens.

2. **Click the Update/Send button, as shown in Figure 6-18.**

   When you click Update/Send, a dialog box appears listing your payment instructions (new payments, edited payments, and even cancelled payments).

3. **Unless you use the Password Vault, type your password for online access to your bank. Click Update Now to transmit your instructions to your online bill payment service (again, that might be the Quicken Bill Pay service or your bank).**

   In the account register, the Num field for your online payments now reads Sent (or the check number that Quicken Bill Pay assigns).

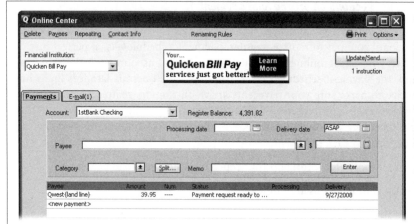

Figure 6-18:
The Online Center is your one-stop shop for online tasks. You can set up online payees (in the menu bar, choose Payees) and create, edit, delete, send, or cancel online bill payments, including repeating online payments. You can even read emails from your bank by clicking on the E-mail tab (page 139).

Setting Up Repeating Online Payments

For fixed-amount payments you make on a regular schedule, good news. Repeating online payments are possibly Quicken's most convenient feature. You tell Quicken who to pay, how much, and how often, and the program sets up a repeat payment with whatever bill payment service you use. Because the instructions reside with the bill payment service, you could go for months without launching Quicken, and the payments would still arrive on time. Not bad.

Note: You can't use repeating online payments for regularly scheduled payments whose amounts change from month to month. For payments like these, you can set up a Quicken scheduled transaction (page 186) to use an online payment and tell the program to remind you to enter it. When the reminder appears, you fill in the amount and send off the online payment.

Repeating online payments come in two flavors and you set each one up a bit differently. For payments that happen on a regular schedule for the same amount each time, you specify the schedule and the amount of the payment. For loan payments, you set up an online repeating payment and then link it to the loan it pays off.

Creating repeating online payments

Creating a recurring payment is almost exactly the same as setting up a scheduled transaction, described on page 186. In the Add Transaction Reminder dialog box, you choose "Online Payment from Quicken" in the Method box, as you would for a one-time online payment. The essential difference is that you have to also turn on the "This is a repeating online payment" checkbox.

Once you've specified the details of the payment, click OK. Quicken adds the payment to the transactions in the Scheduled Bills & Deposits window. You can identify repeating payments by the value "Rept-Send" in the Method field.

Setting up repeating amortized loan payments

Making payments on amortized loans—mortgage payments, car loans, or any other loan you pay off on a regular payment schedule—is a perfect use for Quicken's repeating online payments. The payment amounts are the same each period, the payment schedule doesn't vary, and the onerous late fees are a huge incentive to make sure your payments arrive on time no matter what. Moreover, though you set up a repeating online payment to handle every payment in the loan's schedule, Quicken automatically allocates the amount of principal and interest you pay each time.

Here are the steps for setting up your repeating amortized loan payment:

1. **Set up your lender as an online payee.**

   This step's no different than setting up any other online payee (full instructions start on page 149).

2. **Press Ctrl+J to open the Scheduled Bills & Deposits window.**

   You can also choose Tools → Scheduled Bills & Deposits List.

3. **In the Scheduled Bills & Deposits window's menu bar, choose Create New → "Scheduled Bill or Deposit".**

   Quicken opens the Add Transaction Reminder dialog box (Figure 6-19).

4. **Set up the transaction as you would a regular scheduled payment.**

   In the Payee drop-down menu, choose your lender. Choose the account you use to make your payments. Choose "Online Payment from Quicken" for the transaction method.

5. **In the Category drop-down menu, choose the loan account for your loan or mortgage.**

   Your accounts appear at the bottom of the Category drop-down menu and have square brackets around them. Your loan account, for example, may look something like *[Mortgage]*.

6. **Click OK to save the repeating online payment.**

   You don't have to specify the amount or the schedule before you click OK; Quicken grabs this info when you link the repeating payment to the loan.

7. **Press Ctrl+H to open the View Loans window.**

   You can also choose Property & Debt → Loans.

8. **In the View Loans window's menu bar, select Choose Loan. In the drop-down menu, choose the loan you want to pay.**

   The View Loans window displays the overall information about the loan, like the loan amount, interest rate, payment, and current balance (page 258).

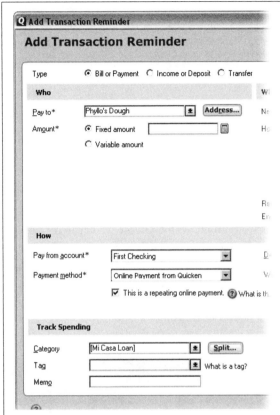

Figure 6-19:
Two settings work together to produce a repeating online payment: In the "Payment method" drop-down menu, choose "Online Payment from Quicken" and turn on the "This is a repeating online payment" checkbox just below the Method box.

9. **Click Edit Payment.**

   The Edit Loan Payment dialog box appears. For a refresher on editing loans, see page 257.

10. **In the Transaction section, click Payment Method.**

    The Select Payment Method dialog box opens, as shown in Figure 6-20.

11. **In the Payment Type section, select the "Repeating online payment" option.**

    Quicken immediately displays the For Repeating Payments section.

12. **In the Repeating Payment box, choose the payment you created for your loan from the drop-down menu. Click OK.**

    The Select Payment Method dialog box closes. Back in the Edit Loan Payment dialog box, the Type field now shows Repeating Pmt.

13. **Click OK to save the payment.**

    If you ever need to change any part of this setup—for example, to adjust the escrow amounts in your payment—see the box on page 156.

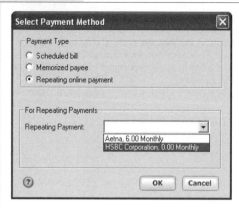

Figure 6-20:
When you select the "Repeating online payment" option, the Repeating Payment drop-down list displays all the repeating online payments you've set up in Quicken. Choose the one you created for your loan and then click OK.

The repeating online payment is ready to go. In the Online Center, remember to click Update/Send to send the new instructions to your online bill payment service.

About a month before a payment is due, the bill payment service records the pending payment using the next scheduled date. The next time you download transactions, Quicken automatically downloads these payments along with your checks, deposits, and transfers. When the delivery date comes around, your payee gets its payment with no effort on your part.

TROUBLESHOOTING MOMENT

Editing a Loan's Repeating Online Payment

Repeating online payments are great for mortgages, but they can generate serious head scratching if you have to change the payment in any way. For example, suppose your escrow amount changes and you want to update your payment to reflect your new total. There are several steps involved in making this change and you have to perform them in the correct order:

1. Cancel any pending loan payments with your bill payment service and then click Update/Send to send the cancellation instructions.

2. In the View Loans window, edit the loan to change its payment method to a scheduled transaction and make it a regular payment instead of an online payment.

3. In the Scheduled Bills & Deposits window, delete the repeating online payment for the loan.

4. Create a new repeating online payment for the loan.

5. Edit the loan payment to the new amount and set the Payment Method back to repeating online payment (choosing the repeating online payment you just created).

6. Finally, send the new instructions to your bill payment service by clicking Update/Send in the Online Center window (Online → Online Center).

Canceling Payments

Suppose you've been sending online payments to your cable company but now think a library card is a more cost-effective way to entertain yourself. With enough lead time, you can cancel an online payment. Unlike paper checks, which require a stop payment from your bank (at an additional cost), canceling an online payment doesn't cost you a dime.

How much lead time you need depends on your bank. In general, you can cancel any time before the online payment's Processing date. To find out whether an online payment arrived, or to see if you have time to cancel a payment, select the transaction in the register. Below the Num field, you see a Status link, which you can click to view the payment, including its processing and delivery dates, as shown in Figure 6-21.

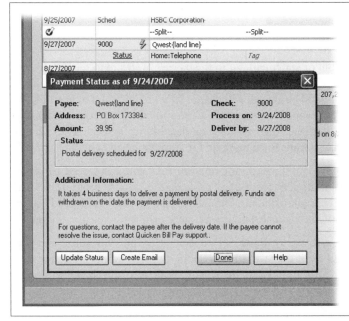

Figure 6-21:
This window shows you the status of the online payment you've selected in the register. As long as today's date is earlier than the "Process on" date, you usually have time to cancel the payment.

How you cancel a payment depends on what type of online payment it is. Regardless of which type of payment you cancel, you have to click Update/Send to send the cancellation instructions to your financial institution. Here are your options:

• **A single online payment.** To cancel a one-time payment or one instance of a repeating online payment, select the transaction in the register and then click the transaction's Edit button. Choose Cancel Payment on the shortcut menu. In the confirmation dialog box, click Yes. You'll see Cancel in the Status column.

• **A repeating online payment.** To cancel the entire series of a repeating online payment, press Ctrl+J to open the Scheduled Bills & Deposits window. Select the repeating online payment you want to stop, and then, in the window's menu bar, choose Delete. In the confirmation dialog box, click Delete.

Note: If the repeating online payment is linked to a loan, you have to break that link *before* you can cancel the payment. See the box on page 156 for advice on editing repeating online payments for loans.

Letting Payees Come and Get Their Payments

Doing your own online transactions, manually downloading them into Quicken, and then trying to match them with your own entries is a lot of work...but maybe you just don't want to pay for an online banking service. Take heart: You can automate payments for many of your bills without a bill payment service or bank-initiated payments—and it's free. You can take advantage of payees who offer their own automatic bill payment by either electronically retrieving their payment from your bank account or charging your credit card. Using this approach, you can still keep things simple in Quicken by setting up scheduled transactions that reflect these recurring bills. This section explains how to pay payees who are willing to come get their money.

Payee setup

When you receive a bill or statement, go to the payee's Web site to see if they have an automatic payment option. Many companies can take money straight from your checking account and almost all will charge your credit card. For example, on the Qwest Web site (*www.qwest.com*), in the Customer Service section under payment options, you'll find the "Sign up for paperless billing" option. You can also check your bill for instructions for signing up for automatic payments.

Sign up for the automatic billing routine only for bills you don't need to review before you pay. Telephone service, utilities, cable, and insurance premiums are all candidates for automatic bill payment. Should you set up your credit card bill for automatic payment, be sure you also review the statement for suspicious charges.

To make sure your system is working, set up only a few bills for automatic payment each month and see if they work properly. If you don't want to wait for your statement to arrive, you can go to the bank's or credit card's Web site to inspect the posted transactions.

Quicken setup

In Quicken, set up scheduled transactions using the "Automatically enter" option (page 195) so that the program records the payment in your Quicken checking or credit card account without your help. You can set up scheduled transactions for all recurring bills, even if they happen only once a year.

Tip: For bills whose amounts vary, set up the scheduled transactions with estimated amounts. You can edit those amounts later.

To prevent bounced payments or minimum balance fees, apply a minimum balance alert to your checking account in Quicken. (In the Account Bar, right-click the account name and then choose Edit Account from the shortcut menu. In the Set Up Alerts section, in the Min. Balance box, type the minimum balance you want to keep in the account.) Give yourself a cushion beyond the minimum balance the bank sets. For example, if you have to keep $1,000 in your account to avoid monthly service fees, set the Quicken alert to $2,000. Quicken examines your upcoming scheduled transactions and displays a warning message box if you're approaching the minimum.

Don't wait until the last minute to move money into your checking account to cover your bills, particularly if you're transferring money from a different financial institution, like a mutual fund company. New banking rules let financial institutions yank money from your account immediately but still allow banks to drag their feet when it comes to making your deposits available. Transfer money into your checking account at least three days ahead of time if you use online transfers—a week or more ahead if you use snail mail.

Tip: If you frequently withdraw cash from your checking account, consider increasing the cushion you keep there. Similarly, if you write a large check that *isn't* a scheduled transaction, check your estimated balance when automatic bills are going to hit your account to see if you should transfer money in.

Paying an Occasional Bill Online

A payee's Web site is also handy for paying bills you don't pay automatically. The same Web page that lets you set up automatic payments usually includes an option to make a one-time payment by transferring money from your checking account or charging your credit card. In Quicken, record the transaction in the appropriate account register so you know how much money you have in your account.

It's a good idea to set a scheduled transaction to remind you in advance about the bill so that you have some breathing room in case the company's Web site is down. For example, set the due date for bills you pay manually to 7 to 10 days before the bill is due. You can set these transactions up as scheduled transactions (page 186), except that you use the Remind Me setting instead of "Automatically enter". This way, for example, you have time to transfer money to your checking account or to make sure your credit card isn't maxed out.

Coordinating Bill Payments with Quicken

Here are the steps to coordinating payee-initiated bill payments (the ones described on page 158) with your Quicken data:

1. **Record every credit card charge, check, withdrawal, and deposit as they happen.**

   This is the best way to know how much money you actually have in the bank and what you'll owe when the credit card bill arrives.

---

2. **When you receive a bill whose amount varies from month to month, like utility bills, edit the scheduled transaction in Quicken to reflect the new payment amount.**

   If it's an automatically paid bill, simply file the original in your filing cabinet. When the bill's due, the payee pulls the money from your checking account (or charges your credit card) and Quicken records the scheduled transaction.

Tip: If you have a scheduled transaction set up for a bill, let Quicken record that transaction instead of making a manual entry. Otherwise, you miss out on the convenience of recording scheduled transactions *and* create the extra work of telling Quicken to skip one occurrence of the scheduled transactions.

---

3. **For bills you don't pay automatically, record the scheduled transaction in the Scheduled Bills & Deposits window.**

   To do this, press Ctrl+J to open the Scheduled Bills & Deposits window. Select the scheduled transaction and then, in the transaction's row, click Enter. In the Enter Transaction dialog box that appears, change fields to match the bill and then click Enter Transaction.

4. **When you receive your checking account and credit card statements, reconcile your accounts.**

   If you forgot to enter a check or credit card charge, reconciling Quicken accounts to statements shows your omission. You have to keep your Quicken accounts in sync with your financial institution's records if you want your balances to be correct.

This approach takes a bit more work on your part to record transactions, but it doesn't cost a dime, and it works even with financial institutions that don't do business with Quicken services.

Setting Up Online Transfers

You can set up online fund transfers in Quicken as long as both accounts are at the same financial institution—Quicken can't transfer funds electronically between banks. Also, you need to set up both Quicken accounts (checking and savings, say) for online services, as described on page 125.

The register is the easiest place to record an online transfer. Here are the steps:

1. **In the register for the account holding the money you're going to transfer (your savings account, for example), create a new transaction by pressing Ctrl+N.**

2. **In the Num field, select Oxfr (Online Transfer).**

   This option appears only if you have two accounts at the same financial institution that are both set up for online services.

3. **In the Xfer Acct drop-down menu, select the account that'll receive the money you're transferring (your checking account, for example).**

   The source account is the one whose register is open.

4. **In the Payment field, enter the amount you want to transfer between the accounts.**

   If you type the amount in the Deposit field instead, the transfer brings the money in from the account you set in the Xfer Acct field. So, in this example, *100* in the Deposit field would transfer $100 from your checking account into your savings account, whereas typing *100* in the Payment field would transfer $100 from your savings account into your checking account.

5. **In the register immediately below the transaction, click Enter.**

   Quicken completes the transaction in the register, but you're not done yet. Don't forget to open the Online Center (page 152) by choosing Online → Online Center and click Update/Send to send the transfer instructions to your financial institution.

Transaction Timesavers

Chapter 5 taught you transaction basics, like how to record checks and deposits. But Quicken gives you the power to do a whole lot more. For example, you can search for specific transactions, change previously assigned categories, or allocate money in a single payment to several categories. Even better, you can reduce your record-keeping chores by automating transactions in Quicken. That way you don't have to remember when bills or deposits are due—Quicken reminds you and does most of the grunt work. Automating transactions requires a bit of setup, but the time you save down the road makes it all worthwhile.

This chapter guides you through all these transaction tasks, and more. You'll find out what each command on the Transaction Edit menu does—though you may use some of those commands only once in a blue moon. Finally, you'll learn how to manage memorized payees so QuickFill can live up to its name.

Tip: Automating your paycheck in Quicken may be the granddaddy of timesavers. You can tell Quicken about your income, payroll tax withholdings, and other paycheck deductions, as well as the tax-form lines to which each applies—and reduce recording each paycheck to a click or two. The real payoff, though, comes at tax time, when Quicken totals the paycheck numbers you need to complete your tax return. You can learn about automating paychecks starting on page 192.

Transferring Money Between Accounts

Chances are that you transfer money between accounts all the time. Maybe you keep your cash in a savings or money market account where it earns interest, and transfer it to your checking account only when it's time to pay the plumber.

(What are those pipes made out of, anyway—*gold?*) To record the movement of money between accounts, you use a Quicken *transfer* transaction.

When you tell Quicken to transfer money from savings to checking, the program withdraws the money from your Quicken savings account and deposits it in your Quicken checking account. (Of course, you have to set up the corresponding transfer between your real-world savings and checking accounts, too.) With Quicken transfers, you create a transaction in one account (the account the money is being moved *from*, for example). Then, you assign the Category field to the account you're transferring money *to*, instead of to a category like Groceries. When you record the transaction, the program automatically creates the companion transaction to show the money going into the other account. (Alternately, you can record the transaction in the account the money is being deposited into, and Quicken will create the corresponding withdrawal transaction in the account the money is coming from.) This section shows you how the whole process works.

Note: To create a transfer, you choose an *account* from the Category drop-down list; Quicken calls these *transfer categories,* and they're at the bottom of the Category drop-down list in square brackets. The transfer categories you see are the same as the accounts that you've set up in Quicken. When you choose one in the Category field, Quicken creates linked transactions in the accounts at each end of the transfer.

Recording a Transfer Between Accounts

Recording transfers between accounts is like recording checks (page 34), with a few minor differences, as you'll see. You can use Quicken's Transfer dialog box, which provides some handholding and is great for first-timers. (In the menu bar immediately above an account register, click Transfer to get started.) The Transfer dialog box includes boxes for the from and to accounts, the date, and the amount of money you're transferring. But you'll quickly graduate to the quickest way to record a transfer, which is directly in the account register. Don't worry—the process is pretty simple:

1. **Open the register for the account you're transferring money *from*.**

   For example, if you're moving money from checking to savings, open the checking account register. When you open a register, Quicken automatically puts your cursor in a blank transaction.

2. **In the Date field, enter the date for the transfer using the calendar icon (page 87) or by typing the date.**

   Quicken automatically fills in today's date. If your financial institution has rules about when transfers happen, you can keep your account balances more accurate by using the actual date when the money will move between accounts.

3. **In the Num field, type *T* to indicate that the transaction is a Transfer.**

   As soon as you choose Transfer in the Num field, Quicken changes the name of the Payee field to Description and the Category field to Xfer Account (short for "transfer account") as shown in Figure 7-1.

Tip: If you use Quicken's standard keyboard shortcuts (page 488), simply press Ctrl+X to jump to the other end of a transfer (from the account the money is coming *from* to the account it's going *into*, or vice versa).

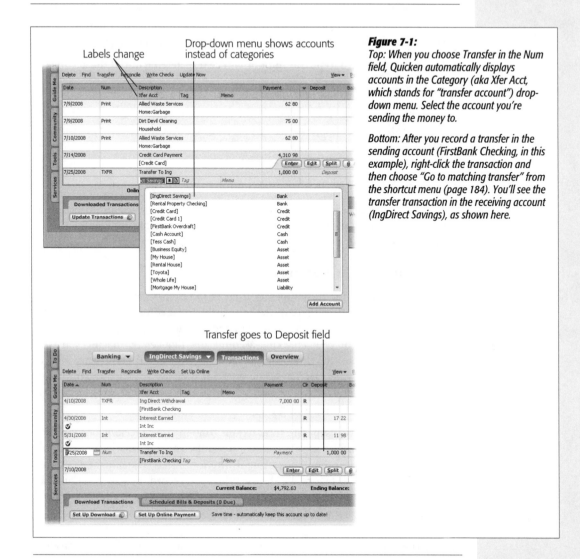

Figure 7-1:

Top: When you choose Transfer in the Num field, Quicken automatically displays accounts in the Category (aka Xfer Acct, which stands for "transfer account") drop-down menu. Select the account you're sending the money to.

Bottom: After you record a transfer in the sending account (FirstBank Checking, in this example), right-click the transaction and then choose "Go to matching transfer" from the shortcut menu (page 184). You'll see the transfer transaction in the receiving account (IngDirect Savings), as shown here.

Tip: Most people think of transfers as moving money *out of* one account and into another. But it's perfectly fine to do it the other way: That is, you can create the transaction in the register of the *receiving* account in which case you'd type the transfer amount in the *Deposit* field. The result is the same either way. (For example, the transfer into savings shown at the bottom of Figure 7-1 shows the amount in the Payment field in one account and the Deposit field in the other.)

4. **In the Description field, type a name for the transfer you're making.**

Because Quicken memorizes payees, you can use this description to call up the values for this transfer the next time you move money between accounts. For example, the next time you type *Transfer to Savings* in the Description field, Quicken automatically chooses your savings account as the destination (it also starts you off with the last transfer amount, which you can change, of course).

5. **In the Payment field, type the amount you're transferring out of the account.**

6. **In the Xfer Account field, choose the account that's receiving the money.**

As soon as you press Tab or click in the Xfer Account field, Quicken displays a drop-down menu of accounts, as you can see in Figure 7-1. You can also quickly choose an account by typing the first character or two of the name— you don't have to type the opening bracket.

7. **Press the Enter key or click the Enter button to record the transfer.**

That's it! You can tell your money has switched to another account because the transaction changes the account balance. In the example in Figure 7-1, the $1,000 transfer into savings increases the savings balance by $1,000.

Turning Checks into Transfers

Sometimes, checks you write act like transfers in Quicken. Consider the check you write to pay your credit card bill. In the real world, the credit card company cashes your check and credits your account with the payment. In Quicken, the check transfers money out of your checking account and reduces the balance on your credit card account (see the box on page 168 if you're curious about why both of these show up as Payments). The same goes for a check you deposit into your money market account: it transfers money *from* your Quicken checking account *to* your Quicken money market account.

Instead of recording two separate transactions (one in your checking account and one in your credit card or money market account), you can save time by simply recording the check and then converting it into a transfer. Transforming a check into a transfer is easy, as Figure 7-2 shows: When you record the check in Quicken, simply choose the appropriate *account* in the Category field (instead of a standard *category* like Groceries or Gas).

Tip: In your real-world accounts, transfers show up as two separate transactions, like the check you send to the credit card company and the payment that the credit card company credits to your account. If you download transactions from both accounts, you can end up with duplicate and unlinked transactions in each account. To prevent these duplicates, record transfers in Quicken *first*. Then, when you download transactions, Quicken matches them with the linked transactions in your data file, as described on page 136.

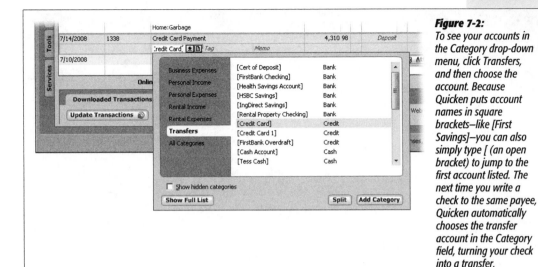

Figure 7-2:
To see your accounts in the Category drop-down menu, click Transfers, and then choose the account. Because Quicken puts account names in square brackets—like [First Savings]—you can also simply type [(an open bracket) to jump to the first account listed. The next time you write a check to the same payee, Quicken automatically chooses the transfer account in the Category field, turning your check into a transfer.

Voiding Transactions

Sometimes you need to cancel a transaction but still want to keep a record of it in Quicken. That's when Quicken's *void* feature comes in handy. For instance, say you fill out a paper check with the wrong payee. You can't edit it the way you do in Quicken, so you have to tear up the check and try again. If you delete the transaction from Quicken, you won't have any record of it. In a couple of months, you might wonder if you accidentally dropped that check in the street. But if you void the transaction, you'll still see the transaction and the check number, so you'll be able to remember what happened. (To document *why* you voided the transaction, type a note in the transaction's Memo field.) Voiding a check in Quicken changes the transaction amount to zero so that it doesn't affect your account balance.

The quickest way to void a transaction is to right-click the transaction in the register and then, on the shortcut menu that appears, choose "Void transaction(s)". If you use Quicken's Standard keyboard shortcuts (page 523), you can also void a transaction by selecting it and then pressing Ctrl+V.

When you void a transaction, Quicken makes the following changes to it:

- Adds **Void** to the beginning of the name in the Payee field.

- Changes the field containing the transaction amount to zero and the values for any categories and splits to zero.

- Changes the transaction's status to cleared, indicated by a lowercase *c* in the Clr field.

One Payment, Two Payment Fields, Lots of Confusion

When I pay my monthly credit card bill, the amount paid shows up in the Payment field of both my checking account and my credit card account registers. What gives?

When you write a check to pay your credit card bill, you enter the amount in the check register's Payment field. However, if you look at the other end of the transaction, that same amount shows up in the credit card account's Payment field. Huh? How can both accounts show the transaction as a Payment?

The reason both accounts use the Payment field is that credit card accounts represent money you owe (called *liability accounts*), whereas *asset accounts* (like checking accounts) represent money that belongs to you. The term *payment* means something different in each context. Here's what's going on:

When you write a check to pay your credit card bill, you're making a payment *from* your checking account; the transfer amount appears in the check's Payment field, which reduces your checking account balance (in other words, it reduces the amount of money you *own*). For a liability account like a credit card, you make a payment *to* your credit card company to reduce the balance that you *owe*; so the transfer transaction in the credit card account appears in the Payment field and reduces the credit card account balance. If you start out with $4,000 in checking and owe $3,000 on your credit card, you have a net amount of $1,000. If you then make a $3,000 payment to the credit card company, you'll have $1,000 in checking and owe nothing to the credit card company—so you'll still have a total of $1,000. The best part? None of this will be on the test.

When you sort your register by cleared status (page 506), all your voided (and thus cleared) transactions huddle between the transactions you've reconciled and the ones you just recorded.

Those voided transactions build up like barnacles, making you scroll past them to see the reconciled transactions you want. To move voided transactions out of view, change their status to reconciled (you'll see an *R* in the Clr field). The voided transactions move backward in the register and appear in chronological order alongside all the other reconciled transactions. To reconcile a voided transaction, right-click it and then choose Reconcile → Reconciled from the shortcut menu that appears. Because its amounts are zero, changing it to reconciled won't affect account reconciliation.

Tip: You can get rid of a transaction completely if, for example, you need to remove a duplicate deposit that makes your account balance look much better than it really is. In the register, right-click the transaction and then, on the shortcut menu that appears, choose Delete. You can also press Ctrl+D.

Splitting Transactions

Most of the time, a single category is enough for each check or a credit card charge you record. Life is simple: You create the transaction, pick the category, and Quicken tracks how you spent that money. But, more often than you might think, a transaction actually applies to *more than one* category. Say you deposit a fistful of checks all at once—your paycheck, a health insurance reimbursement, and a birthday present from your favorite aunt. Your bank probably records this as a single deposit, but you, on the other hand, want to keep track of each type of income you receive. Similarly, the popularity of galaxy-sized supermarkets means that one credit card charge can cover groceries, auto supplies, running shoes, and baby photos, but you want to know what you spent in each category. Finally, the typical mortgage payment doles your money out to principal, interest, and the mortgage escrow account (page 247). Quicken handles these multipurpose payments with *splits*—transactions you divide among several categories.

Tip: Another use for split transactions is when you want to deposit only *part* of a check into the bank and take the rest in cash. Simply record the check deposit with one split going into the bank account and the second to your Quicken cash account (page 51).

Here's how to split a payment among several categories:

1. **In the register, create the transaction as you normally would, by typing the payee name and the amount (see page 34 for a refresher on entering transactions).**

   Or select the existing transaction you want to split by clicking anywhere in the transaction.

2. **Click the Split button, or press Ctrl+S.**

   The Split Transaction dialog box (Figure 7-3) opens with the cursor in the first Category cell. (You can also open the dialog box from the Category field by clicking the down arrow and then, at the bottom of the Category drop-down menu, clicking the Split button.)

   If you selected a paycheck transaction, the Edit Current Paycheck dialog box opens instead (page 201).

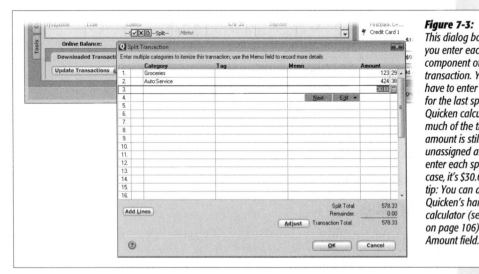

Figure 7-3:
This dialog box is where you enter each component of a split transaction. You don't have to enter the amount for the last split, because Quicken calculates how much of the transaction amount is still unassigned after you enter each split (in this case, it's $30.66). Another tip: You can also use Quicken's handy built-in calculator (see the box on page 106) in the Amount field.

3. **In the Category field, choose the category you want.**

   The Category fields in the Split Transaction dialog box work the same way as the Category fields for transactions. Type the first few letters of a category name and Quicken fills in the category. Or scroll through the Category drop-down menu to choose the one you want. You can also apply a different tag (page 68) to each split by pressing Tab to move to the Tag field and then choosing the Tag from the drop-down menu.

Tip: If you want to add a memo about the split, press Tab until the Memo field is active, and then type your notes. If you decide to add a memo later, simply click the Memo field you want and type away.

---

4. **Press Tab to move to the Amount field, and then type the amount that belongs in this category.**

   When you press Tab after typing the amount, Quicken moves to the next row and automatically subtracts the category's amount from the total transaction amount and puts the amount that's left in the new row's Amount field, as you can see in Figure 7-3.

5. **If the amount for the next category doesn't equal the remaining unassigned amount, double-click the Amount field and type the correct value.**

   Fill in the Category, Tag, and Memo fields, and then press Tab to move to the next row.

6. **Repeat steps 3 through 5 for each additional category.**

   For the last category, the amount Quicken fills in should match the amount intended for that category, if you did your math right.

Tip: If the amount for the last category doesn't match because the Transaction Total is incorrect, simply click the Adjust button (page 172). Quicken changes the Transaction Total to match the split amounts you've entered so far.

---

7. **To save the splits, click OK.**

   Back in the register, in the transaction's Category field, you see "--Split--", but you're not quite done.

8. **Click Enter to record the transaction.**

   Now you're done.

Editing Splits

When you see "--Split--" in a transaction's Category field, it means that the transaction is split among several categories. Quicken also displays two new buttons, circled in Figure 7-4, which you can use to view or edit the splits:

- **Green checkmark.** Click this button to open the Split Transaction dialog box, where you can review and edit the splits.

- **Red X.** Click this button to clear all split categories and values from the selected transaction. If you confirm that you want to remove the splits (by clicking Yes in the confirmation box that appears), Quicken removes all split categories and values, leaving the transaction's Category field blank. For example, suppose Quicken memorized a payee as a split transaction. If you now want to assign that payee to only *one* category, click the red X to clear the splits, and then choose the category you want and memorize the payee again (page 183).

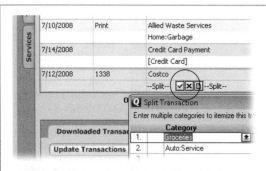

Figure 7-4:
You can view a transaction's splits without opening the Split Transactions dialog box. Just position your cursor over the transaction's Category field, and Quicken displays a pop-up box right next to the Category field. You can't edit the values in the box—you have to click the green checkmark button (circled) to do that.

POWER USERS' CLINIC

Using Split Transactions to Calculate Deposits

If you've got a pile of checks you plan to deposit and you're a bit clumsy with a calculator, you can use the Split Transaction dialog box to figure out your total deposit. The Quicken calculator is fine if you're adding up several checks in the same category. To create a deposit transaction that assigns each check to a different category, though, splits are the way to go.

To use the split feature as a calculator, *don't* fill in a value in the transaction's Deposit field. Instead, click the Split button to open the Split Transaction dialog box. The Transaction Total at the bottom of the dialog box starts at 0.00. As you enter checks in the split rows, the Transaction Total updates the total to include the checks you've entered so far. When you've accounted for all your checks, click OK to save the splits. In the register, Quicken fills in the transaction's Deposit field with the total of all the checks.

Handling Remaining Amounts

Every once in a while, the transaction amount you enter in the register doesn't agree with the total that Quicken calculates from all your splits. For example, suppose you're about to head to the bank with three deposits, all in the same envelope and destined for the ATM. Before heading out, you fire up Quicken to record the transaction and create a deposit transaction with *500* in the Deposit field. In the Split Transaction dialog box, you then enter each check you're going to deposit. As Quicken sums them up, you see they total only $490. As you can see in Figure 7-5, top, you're left with a $10 remainder. Uh-oh.

When the Remainder value isn't zero, you have two choices:

- **Adjust the transaction total.** If all your split values are correct and the transaction total is wrong, click Adjust in the Split Transaction dialog box. Quicken keeps your splits as they are and changes the value for the transaction, as you can see at the bottom of Figure 7-5.

- **Correct the split values.** If you're missing a category—perhaps the total actually *is* $500 and you forgot to enter a $10 check from your neighbor—or the split values are incorrect, make the changes until the Remainder equals 0.00. Then click OK to save the splits, and click Enter on the register to record the transaction.

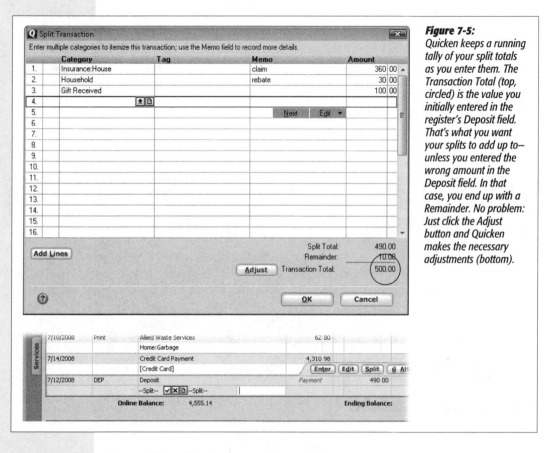

Figure 7-5:
Quicken keeps a running tally of your split totals as you enter them. The Transaction Total (top, circled) is the value you initially entered in the register's Deposit field. That's what you want your splits to add up to—unless you entered the wrong amount in the Deposit field. In that case, you end up with a Remainder. No problem: Just click the Adjust button and Quicken makes the necessary adjustments (bottom).

Searching for Transactions

Before you know it, your Quicken registers will be teeming with transactions. To find a particular transaction, you can scroll through a register or press the Page Up and Page Down keys until your fingers turn blue. Fortunately, Quicken gives you some better options.

Finding Similar Transactions with One Click

When you select a Payee or Category field in a new or existing register transaction, a button with a tiny icon (it looks like a dog-eared piece of paper) appears to the right of the field's drop-down arrow. Click this button to review transactions for the same payee or category across *all* of your accounts. For instance, you can find out how much your son spent on gadgets this summer by looking at all the transactions you assigned to the Electronics category. Figure 7-6 shows this thrill-inducing concept in action.

The pop-up transaction list lets you view similar transactions in different ways and over different lengths of time. Here are your options:

- **Change the period.** The selected period appears immediately below the payee or category name ("Last 3 years" is the default). To change the period, click the down arrow to the right of the time frame and choose another period. Your choices range from the last 30 days to the last 3 years.

- **See more detail.** The pop-up transaction list shows only dates and amounts. To see *everything* about these transactions—payee, account, check number, and so on—click the Show Report button. Quicken generates a report showing the transactions for the selected payee or category for the last 12 months.

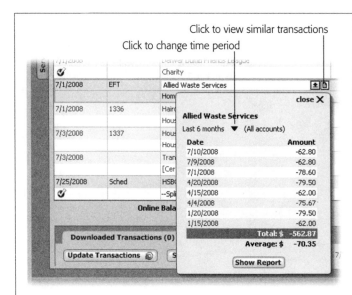

Figure 7-6:
This pop-up box calculates the average of your recent transactions. You can compare recent transactions to the average, for instance, to see if your lunch budget is working. The average can also help if you want to adjust your Quicken budget to reflect higher heating costs: Simply check the average of your recent energy bills before editing your budget (page 291).

Finding All Matching Transactions

Suppose you venture into your basement and find six inches of icky water lapping around your ankles. You want to get in touch with that ace plumber you used a few years ago, but don't remember his name or how you paid him. To search for payments or deposits regardless of which account they're in, use the text box and Search button in the upper-right corner of Quicken's main window (Figure 7-7).

To track down transactions anywhere in your data file, just follow these steps:

1. **In the Search text box, type what you're looking for, like the category** *Home Repair,* **and then click the Search button.**

   The Search Results window lists all the matching transactions, which could be quite a few if you're searching by category. Quicken searches all transactions in all accounts, except for investment transactions involving securities, like mutual fund purchases.

Note: Although the instructions in the Search box initially say "Find Payment or Deposit", you can actually search for payees, categories, amounts, dates, or check numbers. For example, if you're sure the plumber's company name included the word "puddles," type *puddles* into the box, and then click Search. Quicken looks for the search text in any transaction field.

---

2. **To narrow your search, head back to the Search text box, and type more of the text or value you want to find.**

   Or if Quicken didn't find any matching results, you can broaden the search by choosing a higher-level category or typing just a portion of the text or value you're looking for.

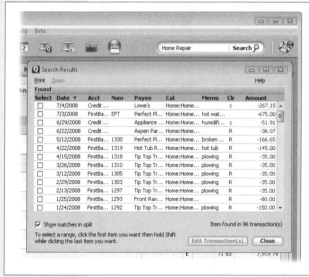

Figure 7-7:
You can sort search results by clicking the column headings in the Search Results dialog box. Click the Date heading, for example, to sort transactions from oldest to newest. Click the same heading again to reverse the order from newest to oldest.

If you want to change a value in one or more transactions (say you noticed a typo in a payee name), turn on their Select checkboxes (on the left side of the list) and then click Edit Transaction(s). The "Find and Replace" dialog box opens. Page 177 has the full scoop on replacing values.

Finding Specific Transactions

If you're sure the transaction you're looking for is in the register you're working in, you can limit your search to that register by using the Find feature. Quicken's Find feature isn't particularly sophisticated, but you'll quickly learn how to hunt down the transactions you're looking for.

Here's what you do:

1. **If you can, give Quicken a head start by clicking a transaction field that has the value you're looking for.**

   That way, when you open the Quicken Find dialog box (which you'll do in the next step), the Search box contains the value of whatever field you clicked, as shown in Figure 7-8. So if you click, say, the Payee field in a check written to Allied Waste Services, Quicken sets the Search field to Payee and the Find field reads *Allied Waste Services*. If you can't find a relevant transaction, you can always just start in an empty transaction with the next step.

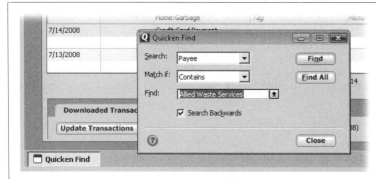

Figure 7-8:
Once you've made your selections from the three drop-down menus, click the Find button to begin searching the account you're in. (Click Find All to search all accounts.) If you want to search the oldest transactions first, turn off the Search Backwards checkbox.

Tip: Quicken automatically turns on the Search Backwards checkbox because you're usually looking for recent transactions. This setting tells Quicken to start with the most recent transactions and work its way back in time. Searching forward is handy if you want to search from a specific date through today. Suppose you want to find your fuel purchases since you started your new job. To move to the first transaction for that time frame, press Ctrl+G to bring up the Go To Date dialog box. Type your hire date, and then click OK. Back in the Quicken Find dialog box, turn off the Search Backwards checkbox and search for the Auto:Fuel category. Quicken starts at your hire date and works up to today.

---

2. **Press Ctrl+F to open the Quicken Find dialog box.**

   You can also choose Edit → Find & Replace → Find, or click Find in the register's menu bar.

3. **In the Search drop-down menu, choose the field you want to search.**

   If you want to search for a value in *all* transaction fields instead of just one, choose "All fields". This option is incredibly helpful if you know that the transaction you want includes a word, like "*market*," but you can't remember the field where it appears.

4. **If you want to broaden or narrow the search, in the "Match if" drop-down menu, choose how precisely the results have to match the value in the Find box.**

   Quicken automatically chooses Contains, which is the most relaxed match. Contains means the value you're looking for appears somewhere in the result. For example, if you type *Bank* in the Find box, Quicken finds Citibank, Bank One, and Douglas Fairbanks.

   At the other end of the spectrum, choosing Exact tells Quicken to return only transactions that exactly match the value in the Find box.

   Starts With and Ends With are ideal choices if you're looking for text at the very beginning or very end of an entry. For numbers, you can also choose Greater, "Greater or equal", Less, or "Less or equal", which work just like they did in math class. (To learn how to use wildcards to determine a match, see the box on page 177.)

5. **In the Find box, type the value you're looking for, or choose it from the drop-down menu.**

   If you choose the transaction field in the Search drop-down menu first, Quicken automatically fills the Find drop-down menu with appropriate choices. For example, if you choose Payee in the Search box, the Find drop-down menu includes your payee names. Choosing Category in the Search box fills the Find drop-down menu with the entries in your Quicken Category List.

6. **Click Find.**

   Quicken finds the first matching transaction, scrolls to it in the register, and highlights it.

7. **To find the next matching transaction, click Find again.**

   Click Find as many times as it takes to find the transaction you want. If you click Find All, you can scan the Search Results dialog box for the transaction (see Figure 7-7).

The aptly named Find Next command looks for the next matching transaction. You can blast through several matching transactions with the Find Next keyboard shortcut, Shift+Ctrl+F. You can also choose Edit → Find & Replace → Find Next.

Using Wildcards to Find Transactions

The Find dialog box's "Match if" options may not be enough if you're looking for something precise. For example, suppose you want to find all the interest you've both paid and received, so you want to search for the Interest Paid *and* Interest Earned categories. You can use wildcards in the Find box to specify the exact value you're looking for. Here are the wildcards and what they do:

- **.. (two periods)** represent any number of characters at the beginning, middle, or end of the field. For example, *Interest..* finds Interest Earned and Interest Paid.

- **? (question mark)** acts as a wildcard for a single character. For example, a search for *b?d beer* finds bud beer, bgd beer, and bad beer.

- **~ (tilde)** excludes matching values from the results. By typing a tilde followed by before your search text, Quicken finds all the transactions that *do not* match your search criteria. For example, searching for *~Bud's Ferrari Repair* returns all transactions *except* those for Bud's fine automotive service work.

Finding and Replacing Values

Sometimes, you want to find transactions that you need to change. Suppose you've brought shame on the family by mistakenly entering several transactions with the payee Aunt Large, when it should be Aunt Marge. Although your aunt isn't likely to see your Quicken data file, you can use Quicken's Find/Replace feature to correct this gaffe in a jiffy. Find/Replace finds every occurrence of the specified value in all your accounts so you can replace it with another.

Tip: Although you can use Find/Replace to replace transactions you've categorized incorrectly, the Recategorize feature (page 178) gives you a more streamlined way to do that.

Here's how you use Find/Replace:

1. **Choose Edit → Find & Replace → Find/Replace.**

   Quicken opens the "Find and Replace" dialog box (Figure 7-9) which looks like the Quicken Find dialog box stacked on top of the Search Results window.

2. **Fill in the "Look in", "Match if", and Find boxes with your search criteria.**

   The "Look in" box is where you tell Quicken which field to search.

3. **Click Find All.**

   In the Found section, Quicken displays all matching transactions. Quicken automatically turns on the "Show matches in split" checkbox in the lower-left corner of the dialog box. This setting searches for matches in every category of split transactions, which is important if you're searching for text in Memo fields or categories.

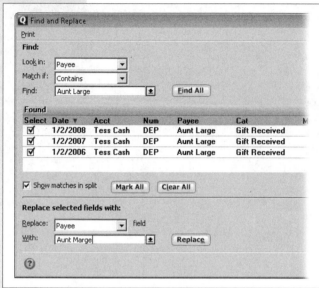

Figure 7-9:
The boxes at the top of the "Find and Replace" dialog box are the same as the ones in the Quicken Find dialog box (page 175), only with slightly different names. The boxes at the bottom—under "Replace selected fields with"—are grayed out (unclickable) until you select at least one matching transaction in the Found section.

GEM IN THE ROUGH

Categorizing the Uncategorized

Even with a helping hand from QuickFill, the most meticulous record keepers can slip up and create a transaction without assigning a category. Once in a while, it's a good idea to look for uncategorized transactions and fill in the appropriate categories, like before you run tax deduction reports (page 276).

The Find command gives you an easy way to locate and recategorize all transactions that don't have assigned categories. You can't use Quicken's Recategorize command to perform this task, because you have to choose an *already assigned* category to look for. Here's how you assign categories to orphaned transactions:

1. Press Ctrl+F to open the Find dialog box.

2. In the Search box, choose Category/Tag.

3. In the Find box, type a space, and then click Find All.

4. In the Search Results window, you see all your uncategorized transactions. Turn on the Select checkboxes for all the transactions you want to put in one category, and then click Edit Transaction(s).

5. In the "Find and Replace" dialog box, in the Replace drop-down menu, choose Category/Tag.

6. In the With drop-down menu, choose the category you want to assign.

7. Click Replace to assign the category to the selected transactions.

The transactions remain in the Search Results dialog box, but the category column displays the newly assigned category. The dialog box remains open, so you can select another batch of transactions to assign to a different category. When you're finished, click Done to close the dialog box.

---

4. **Turn on the Select checkboxes for the transactions you want to change.**

If you accidentally select a transaction, just click the checkbox again to unselect it. To select all the transactions that Quicken found, click the Mark All button below the Found section.

5. **In the Replace box, choose the field you want to replace.**

   Although you can *search* for a value in any transaction field, you can *replace* that value in only one field at a time. If you chose All Fields in the Search drop-down menu to find the value "Aunt Large" in every transaction field, you'll have to repeat the replace operation, choosing a different transaction field each time. For example, you'll replace it in the Payee field first and then in the Memo field.

6. **In the With box, type the replacement value.**

   For instance, if you searched the Payee field for "Aunt Large," typing *Aunt Marge* in the With box replaces all occurrences of *Aunt Large* with *Aunt Marge*.

7. **Click Replace.**

   You immediately see the changes in the transactions listed in the dialog box.

8. **Click Done to close the dialog box.**

   The "Find and Replace" dialog box stays open after it replaces a value. If you want to perform another find and replace, repeat steps 2 through 7.

TROUBLESHOOTING MOMENT

Find Isn't Finding My Transaction

If the Find feature (page 175) doesn't locate a transaction that you *know* is out there, the problem could be a small error in the transaction. Just after New Year's Day, for instance, you may create transactions in the wrong year. If your first search isn't successful, broaden your search. For example, try searching for a longer date range, a small portion of the payee name, or for the category.

If you've had your Quicken data file for a while, small errors can creep in and lead to odd behaviors—like not finding a transaction you know exists. If broadening your search with the Find command doesn't help, you can validate your data file and have Quicken try to repair any problems it finds. Page 482 has the details on validation.

Recategorizing Transactions

The day may come when you realize that your Category List isn't quite what you need. For example, you start with Medical:Doctor and Medical:Medicine categories, but at tax time you see that you can declare deductions for doctor visits, medicines, dentistry, eyeglasses, and more. You dive in and create several new categories only to discover that your reports for tax-deductible expenses don't look any different. Quicken isn't a mind reader. You have to reassign your *existing* transactions to the *new* categories. Fortunately, the Recategorize command does just what you want. Here's how you put it to work:

1. **If a category you want to use doesn't exist, create it before using the Recategorize command.**

   The Recategorize command doesn't include an option to add a category. You have to create all the new categories (as described on page 74) you want to reassign transactions to *before* you open the Recategorize dialog box.

---

2. Choose Edit → Find & Replace → Recategorize.

   The Recategorize dialog box opens. The "Look in" field is set to Transactions, which searches all transactions in all accounts. To limit the search to payees you use frequently, try choosing Memorized Payee. You can also limit the search to scheduled transactions, for example, to find all instances of a scheduled transaction that you miscategorized when you set it up last year.

3. In the "Find category" drop-down menu, choose the category you want to change.

   Choose a category even if you're planning to change only *some* of the transactions in that category. For example, to change some of your medical expenses into dental expenses, in the "Find category" drop-down menu, choose Medical: Expenses.

4. Click Find All.

   Quicken displays all the transactions assigned to the category you chose and activates the "Recategorize selected transaction(s) with" box at the bottom of the dialog box.

5. To select the transactions to recategorize, turn on their Select checkboxes in the leftmost column, as shown in Figure 7-10.

   Click a Select checkbox to toggle between selecting and deselecting a transaction. To reassign all the transactions in the list, click the Mark All button.

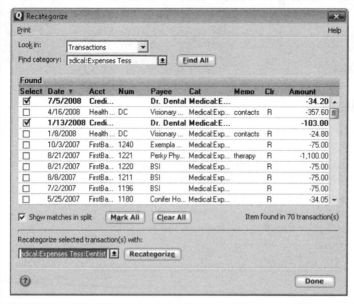

Figure 7-10:
Quicken automatically turns on the "Show matches in split" checkbox in the lower-left corner of the dialog box, which is the best way to ensure that you recategorize everything you want. If you split transactions among several categories, this setting finds every use of a category, even when it's buried in the Split Transactions dialog box.

6. In the "Recategorize selected transaction(s) with" drop-down menu, choose the new category you want to use.

   For example, to change some of your medical expenses into dentist's expenses, in the "Recategorize selected transaction(s) with" drop-down menu, choose a category you created, such as Medical:Expenses:Dentist.

7. Click Recategorize.

   Quicken immediately changes the category fields for the transactions you selected in the dialog box. Unless your category names are super short, you may not notice the change in the Found section. Position your cursor over a category to make Quicken reveal its full name.

8. If you want to recategorize another category, repeat steps 3 through 7.

   The Recategorize dialog box remains open after you replace a category, so you can recategorize something else. (Be sure to clear any selected transactions from the last time around before you do.)

9. When you're finished, click Done.

The Transaction Edit Menu

You can perform just about any transaction-related task from the Transaction Edit menu, shown in Figure 7-11. To call it up, right-click a transaction or click its Edit button. Many of the commands on this menu are covered elsewhere in this book. Think of this section as a cheat sheet. The following list explains what each command does and where you can find out more about it.

- **Enter.** Records the active transaction. Does the same thing as clicking the Enter button in the transaction row or pressing Enter.

- **Restore transaction.** Lets you change values in a transaction if you change your mind about what you've just done. It undoes any changes you've made *as long as* you haven't yet clicked Enter. Another way to undo changes is to click in another transaction; when the dialog box appears asking if you want to save the changed transaction, click No.

- **Split.** Opens the Split Transaction dialog box (page 169) for the current transaction. Does the same thing as clicking the transaction's Split button or pressing Ctrl+S.

- **Notes and flags.** Attaches notes and reminders to transactions (page 112). For example, when you record a payment for a magazine subscription renewal, you can add a note indicating when it'll be time to renew so you can ignore premature requests. Or you can add a reminder to check that your credit card company reversed the late charges it levied.

- **Attachments.** Opens the Transaction Attachments window (page 115). Does the same thing as clicking a transaction's Attach button.

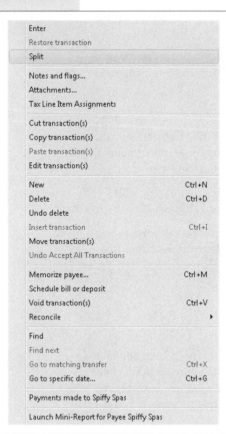

Figure 7-11:
You can display the Transaction Edit menu by either right-clicking a transaction in the register or by selecting a transaction and then clicking its Edit button. The menu options that are active depend on which transaction field you right-click.

- **Tax Line Item Assignments.** Lets you assign a tax form and line to a transaction. See page 76 for more on tax assignments.

- **Cut transaction(s).** Removes the transaction(s) you've selected and places them on the Windows Clipboard. It's like pressing Ctrl+X in most other programs. If you want to remove several transactions from a register, use this command instead of Delete, which deletes only the *current* transaction. Once the transactions are on the Clipboard, you can paste them into another register (for instance, if you recorded transactions in the wrong Quicken account).

Tip: If you want to move one or more transactions from one account to another, you can also choose "Move transaction(s)", as described on page 183.

- **Copy transaction(s).** Copies one or more transactions. For example, you can quickly add this month's transactions by duplicating several from last month. Quicken leaves the originals in the register but places copies on the Windows Clipboard. To add the copies to the register, follow this command with "Paste transaction(s)".

- **Paste transaction(s).** Pastes any transactions currently on the Windows Clipboard into the register.

- **Edit transaction(s).** Lets you make changes in current transaction. To edit one or more transactions in the "Find and Replace" dialog box (page 178), select the transactions, right-click them, and then choose this command.

- **New.** Starts a new transaction. If you're far from the bottom of the register but can't remember any keyboard shortcuts, choosing this command places your cursor in a fresh blank transaction at the bottom of the register. It's just like pressing Ctrl+N.

- **Delete.** Removes all traces of a transaction from your Quicken data file. You can also press Ctrl+D. This command is perfect if you inadvertently created a duplicate of an existing transaction. If you want to eliminate a transaction but keep a record of it, choose "Void transaction(s)" instead (see page 184).

- **Undo delete.** Lets you restore a transaction you've deleted. With the Delete command right below the New command, inadvertently deleting a transaction is almost inevitable. You can recover the deleted transaction by choosing "Undo delete" *immediately*. (That is, before you issue any other commands. Once you issue another command, the deleted transaction is gone for good and you'll have to recreate it from scratch.)

- **Insert transaction.** Adds a blank transaction below the selected transaction, with the same date. Note the difference from the New command, which places you at the bottom of the register and automatically selects today's date. With "Insert transaction," you can easily go back and fill in a transaction you missed.

Note: If the "Insert transaction" command is grayed out, you may have to change the sort order you use in your register. "Insert transaction" isn't available if you sort transactions by the order entered or cleared status.

- **Move transaction(s).** Lets you correct putting a transaction (or several) in the wrong account—if you deposited money in the wrong savings account, say. Simply select the misplaced transactions, right-click them, and then choose "Move transaction(s)". In the dialog box that appears, in the "Move to account" drop-down menu, choose the correct account, and then click OK.

- **Undo Accept All Transactions.** Lets you change your mind after downloading transactions. If you choose Accept All, select this command immediately (without issuing any other commands in between) to return the transactions to their original downloaded state, as described on page 140.

- **Memorize payee.** Gives you the option to memorize a payee. Quicken comes with the "Automatically memorize new payees" feature turned on, so it memorizes every new payee you enter. If you prefer to handpick the payees you add to the Memorized Payee List (page 202), turn off the automatic memorization

---

(page 204). Then, when you're entering a transaction that's for a payee you'll do business with again, choose "Memorize payee" to add the payee to the Memorized Payee List (it's the same as pressing Ctrl+M).

- **Schedule bill or deposit.** Lets you schedule the selected transaction to repeat in the future or recur on a set schedule (see page 186 for detailed instructions).

- **Void transaction(s).** Lets you eliminate a transaction but keep a record of it (see page 167).

- **Reconcile.** Lets you change the status of a transaction. If a transaction's status isn't correct—Unreconciled, Cleared, or Reconciled—choose this command, and then choose a different status from the submenu.

Warning: Be careful when you change the status of a transaction outside of the Quicken reconciliation process. If you accidentally change an item's status to one that doesn't match your bank's records, your accounts won't reconcile. (For full details on reconciling accounts, see Chapter 8.)

- **Find.** Opens the Find dialog box, described in detail on page 175. You can also press Ctrl+F.

- **Find next.** Finds the next occurrence of the current search criteria.

- **Go to matching transfer.** If the selected transaction is a transfer, moves you to the *other* end of the transfer. For example, if you're in your checking account register and the selected transaction is a transfer from checking to savings, choosing this command opens the register for the savings account and selects the corresponding deposit.

- **Go to specific date.** Delivers you to the first transaction in the current register for any date you specify. Choose this command and, in the Go To Date dialog box, select the date you want. When you click OK, Quicken jumps to the first transaction that took place on that date and highlights it. This command comes in handy for things like reviewing your end-of-the-year tax activity.

Tip: Keyboard mavens can also press Ctrl+G to open the Go To Date dialog box.

- **Payments made to <payee>.** Opens a Payee Report window that shows all the payments made to this payee.

- **Launch Mini-Report for <payee>.** Does the same thing as clicking the mini-report icon in the transaction's Payee field (the icon looks like a dog-eared piece of paper). Quicken displays a pop-up box showing recent transactions for that payee.

Scheduling Transactions

Bills are usually due at the same time every month, and many are even for the same amount. For example, your electric bill is due the 19th of the month, but the amount varies each time. On the other hand, your mortgage is due on the 5th, and it's the same amount month after month. Likewise, monthly interest from a certificate of deposit arrives on the last day of each month and is always the same amount. Quicken's Scheduled Bills & Deposits feature, which creates automated transactions, is perfect for payments, deposits, and transfers like these. You set up scheduled transactions the same way you record checks, but you also tell Quicken the *schedule*—when and how often you make this payment, deposit, or transfer.

Not only can the program create future transactions, but, unlike us mere mortals, Quicken also doesn't forget that they're due. When it's time to make a payment or deposit, Quicken reminds you—so you can say goodbye to late fees!

If the amount due is fixed, Quicken can even create the transaction without your assistance. That maneuver requires a little bit of extra work—namely, scheduling an automatic online payment. Start by following the steps in this section for scheduling the transaction in Quicken, and then flip back to page 149 for the details on how to set up the actual payment.

You can also schedule a transaction to happen just once—perhaps for the big tax refund you hope to receive by April 30. But scheduled transactions truly shine when it comes to financial obligations that happen repeatedly. The garbage bill, your monthly contribution to your savings account, a disability benefit you receive, you name it. In fact, unless you have a scheduled transaction for every transaction you make regularly, you're cheating yourself out of Quicken's most timesaving—and potentially money-saving—feature.

The Scheduled Bills & Deposits window is a one-stop shop for working with scheduled transactions. Whether you want to set up, edit, delete, or record scheduled transactions, press Ctrl+J or choose Tools → Scheduled Bills & Deposits List to open the window shown in Figure 7-12.

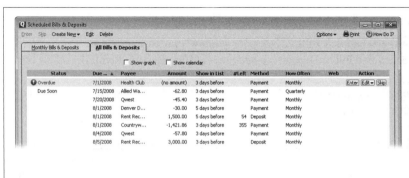

Figure 7-12:
In the Scheduled Bills & Deposits window, you can do all kinds of things with scheduled transactions: set up new ones (by choosing Create New in the window's menu bar), edit or delete existing ones, or record them. Transactions with an Overdue status, like the one at the top of the list in this figure, appear in red.

Setting Up a Scheduled Transaction

When you create a scheduled transaction, the Add Transaction Reminder dialog box (called the "Schedule a Bill or Deposit" dialog box in Quicken 2008) may seem daunting at first. As you can see in Figure 7-13, the left side is nothing more than the same fields you fill in when you record a check in an account register. The right side is where you set up the schedule. This section explains how to use each section to its fullest.

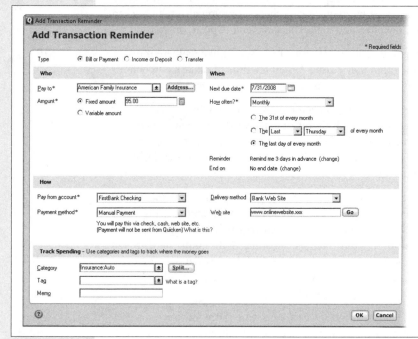

Figure 7-13:
The labels and fields change depending on whether you're scheduling a payment, deposit, or transfer. For example, the dialog box contains "Pay to" and "Pay from account" fields when you create a scheduled payment. The labels change to "Receive from" and "Add to" for a deposit.

Here's how to get started with a scheduled transaction:

1. **Press Ctrl+J to open the Scheduled Bills & Deposits window.**

   Or choose Tools → Scheduled Bills & Deposits List.

2. **In the Scheduled Bills & Deposits window's menu bar, choose Create New → "Scheduled Bill or Deposit" to open the Add Transaction Reminder dialog box.**

Note: The other command on the Create New menu is Paycheck, which helps you set up and schedule your paychecks (see page 192).

If you're puttering around in the Banking Center, you can open this dialog box by selecting the Summary tab, scrolling to the bottom of the page, and then clicking Add Reminder. On the shortcut menu that appears, choose Bill,

Income, Paycheck, or Transfer to specify the type of scheduled transaction you want to create. When the Add Transaction Reminder dialog box opens, it displays labels that correspond to that type of transaction.

You can also get to the Add Transaction Reminder dialog box from the Setup Center Overview screen (page 20), which has separate buttons for bills, deposits, transfers, and paychecks. In the Bill Reminders section (scroll down), click Add Bill. In the "Income and Transfer Reminders" section, click Add Paycheck, Add Other Income, or Add Transfer.

3. **If you opened the Add Transaction Reminder dialog box directly from the Scheduled Bills & Deposits window, at the top of the dialog box, select the type of transaction you want to create.**

"Bill or Payment" is for money headed out the door, "Income or Deposit" is for money coming in, and Transfer is for money moving between two of your accounts. When you select one of these options, the labels in the rest of the dialog box change to reflect the transaction type. Red asterisks mark the fields you have to fill in. The following sections explain how to fill in each part of the dialog box.

Who and how much

The Who section at the top left of the dialog box sticks to the basic 411—who you're paying or receiving money from and the amount:

- **"Pay to", "Receive from", or Payee/Payer.** This field is labeled "Pay to" for a bill or payment, "Receive from" for a deposit, and Payee/Payer for a transfer. It works the same as the Payee field in a register transaction. Click the down arrow to choose a name from the memorized payee list. This field is required—you can't create a transaction without filling it in.

- **Address.** Clicking the Address button opens the Edit Address Book Record dialog box (page 103), which lets you edit the existing address for your payee or enter a new one.

- **Amount.** The Amount section includes two options: Fixed or Variable. Quicken automatically selects "Fixed amount", which you use when you pay (or receive) the same amount each time. Select the "Variable amount" option when the payment is different each time.

  If you select "Variable amount", you'll see the message "No estimate given", which makes sense because Quicken doesn't have anything to base an estimate on because you're setting up a new reminder. To record the scheduled transaction, simply fill in the amount for that occurrence. You can edit the amount when you record the occurrence of the scheduled transaction. If you want to, you can set an estimated amount by clicking the "change" link to the right of the "No estimate given" label; this brings up a version of the Change Reminder Options dialog box. Although you edit the scheduled transaction to record the actual amount, an estimated amount helps you forecast your future cash flow (page 318). However, as with any estimate, chances are you'll have to edit the amount each time you record the scheduled transactions.

In the dialog box, select "Estimated amount" to specify a value for the scheduled transaction, which is handy when the amount is *almost* always the same. (If it's exactly the same each time, you should be using the "Fixed Amount" option instead.) Quicken uses the value you enter in the "Estimated amount" text box to fill in the amount when you record an occurrence of the scheduled transaction, so you only have to edit the scheduled transaction when the amount differs. "Estimate from the last _ _ payments" sets the value to an average of the number of payments you specify. This option isn't all that helpful because few companies offer this kind of payment plan, but it may help if you calculate your credit card payments based on what you've paid in the past. "Estimate from last year at this time" is handy for estimating seasonal expenses, such as heating oil and electricity.

How you pay or receive money

The How section tells Quicken about the account you want to use and how you want to pay:

- **"Pay from" account, "Add to" account, or From account.** This field's label depends on what kind of transaction you're creating. Choose the account you want to make the payment from or receive the deposit into. For a transfer, choose the account in which you start the transfer, whether it's the one that money's coming out of or going into. This is another required field—Quicken needs to know which account will be involved in the transaction.

- **Payment method.** You'll see this field only if you're creating a bill or payment transaction. The choices you see in this drop-down menu depend on the type of transaction you're creating and whether you use online bill payment (page 122). Your choices are Manual Payment (writing a check by hand), "Print Check with Quicken", and, (if you pay bills online) "Online Payment or Online Payment from Quicken". This is another required field.

- **Delivery method.** This field is optional. It simply gives you a place to record how you plan to deliver a payment, make a deposit, or transfer money. For example, you can choose Bank Web Site if you pay your bills from your bank's bill payment Web page, Payee Web Site if you set up your payment on the payee's Web site, Mail if you send it by regular post, or In Person if you hand the payment over directly. If the transaction occurs without any effort on your part (if your cable TV bill is charged to your credit card automatically, for example), you can choose Automatic. Page 190 explains how you can coax Quicken into automatically recording the transaction.

If you're creating a deposit, you have different choices: At Bank Branch works when you go to your bank, Direct Deposit is for deposits wired directly into your account (like maybe your paycheck), and Mail is for spiffy bank-by-mail envelopes. If you want to differentiate between depositing money at an ATM and handing a check and deposit slip to a bank teller, you can choose Bank Branch to indicate the ATM transaction and In Person for the bank teller. If you're sending deposits via carrier pigeon, choose Other.

- **Web site.** This is another optional field, but it can be quite handy. If you type a Web site address in this box, the word *Go* appears in the Scheduled Bills & Deposits window's Web column. You can click the Go link to go to the biller's Web site (to see what your next payment is if you don't receive a paper statement, for instance). You have to log in to the Web site, though.

What it's for

The Track Spending section includes the same fields you use for categorizing transactions in an account register, all of which are optional:

- **Category.** This drop-down menu lists all categories. Although it's optional, Quicken is most helpful when you assign a category to every transaction.

- **Split.** Click the Split button to divide a scheduled transaction among categories (page 168).

- **Tag.** This drop-down menu lists all tags.

- **Memo.** You can include the same note with every future transaction by typing text in the Memo box.

When

Next up: scheduling the transaction. Among the many advantages of scheduled transactions are that they let you record transactions ahead of time and set reminders based on how often you use Quicken. They also help ensure that you record transactions and make the correct number of payments—no more, no less.

The top-right corner of the Add Transaction Reminder dialog box looks awfully busy, as you can see in Figure 7-13, but it boils down to four ways to control your transaction schedule:

- **When to start.** In the "Next due date" box, choose the date for the future transaction (or the first of many recurring transactions). This field is required, because Quicken needs to know when to start the schedule.

- **How often.** In the "How often" drop-down menu (another required field), choose Only Once for a one-time payment or deposit. This option is perfect when you want to be sure to make a crucial payment or deposit. To set up a recurring transaction, choose one of the time frames, like Weekly or Yearly. There's even an Estimated Tax choice for setting up estimated tax payments on the 15th of January, April, June, and September.

The radio button options that appear in the "How often" section depend on the time frame you choose in the drop-down menu. For many time frames, like "Every four weeks", you don't get any options at all; Quicken picks the day of the week based on the starting date you choose. For monthly schedules, you can specify a day of the month, the last day of the month, or a specific weekday, as shown in Figure 7-13. For example, if your investment club meets on the second Tuesday of each month, you can schedule your contribution to match.

- **Reminder.** Quicken automatically sets a reminder for three days before the transaction is due. To change the advance warning schedule, click the "change" link to the right of the reminder text. The Change Reminder Option dialog box, shown in Figure 7-14, opens. Choose the schedule you want and then click OK.

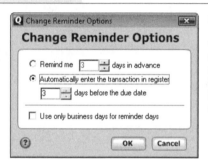

Figure 7-14:
Your ideal reminder schedule depends on how addicted you are to Quicken. If you launch Quicken every day without fail, you can set the number of days somewhere between 1 and 5. If you use Quicken occasionally, you should pick a higher number so that you're more likely to see the reminder before it's too late. To see reminders only on weekdays, turn on the "Use only business days for reminder days" checkbox.

If the transaction amounts are the same each month, you can select the "Automatically enter the transaction in register" option and specify the number of days in advance, and let Quicken add the transactions without any effort on your part. When you select one of these totally automated scheduled transactions in the Scheduled Bills & Deposits window, the Enter button is missing in the Action column, and "(Auto)" appears in its place.

- **When to end.** Quicken automatically keeps the scheduled transaction going like the Energizer bunny—until you delete it (page 191) or tell Quicken to stop. To tell Quicken when the transaction schedule ends, click the "change" link to the right of "No end date". In the End Reminders dialog box, select the "End on" option and specify the date to stop the scheduled transaction. The "End after _ reminders" option is ideal for payments that take place a specific number of times. For example, you can choose "End after _ reminders" and type 360 in the box to set up 30 years worth of mortgage payments.

Once you've filled out the Add Transaction Reminder dialog box, click the OK button to create the reminder.

Editing and Deleting Scheduled Transactions

You can edit a scheduled transaction at any time. Say you just turned 45 and, depressingly, your disability insurance premium increased. You can edit your scheduled payment to change the amount you pay.

Here are the steps for editing a scheduled transaction:

1. **In the Scheduled Bills & Deposits window, click anywhere in the transaction's row.**

   The Enter, Edit, and Skip buttons appear in the Action column.

2. **Click the transaction's Edit button, and then choose either "Only this instance" or "This and all future reminders".**

   If you choose "Only this instance", the abbreviated Edit Reminder dialog box opens, where you can change the amount and the due date. All other future transactions keep your original settings.

   Choosing "This and all future reminders" opens the Edit Transaction Reminder dialog box, which lists all the same fields and options as the Add Transaction Reminder dialog box. The only difference is that the changes you make affect the current *and* future occurrences of this scheduled transaction.

3. **Click OK to save your changes.**

   The changes appear in the Scheduled Bills & Deposits List.

Tip: Say you take a temporary assignment in Katmandu and put your cable service, ISP, and garbage pickup on hold indefinitely. To keep scheduled transactions in the Scheduled Bills & Deposits List without receiving reminders about them, simply edit the transactions and set the next due date to a date a few years in the future. Then, when you're ready to resume your transactions, edit the next due date once more.

If you no longer want to use a scheduled transaction, simply delete it. To do so, in the Scheduled Bills & Deposits window, click the transaction you want to delete, and then, in the window's menu bar, click Delete. A message box warns you that you're about to delete a scheduled transaction. Click OK to delete it, or click Cancel to give it another chance. Just be careful: If you use this method, the scheduled transaction is gone for good, so if you delete the wrong one by mistake, you'll have to set it up again.

Paying and Skipping Scheduled Transactions

You can wait until Quicken reminds you to pay a scheduled transaction, but you can also pay a scheduled transaction *before* its scheduled time. This second option is especially handy if you're leaving for an extended vacation and don't want your car repossessed while you're away. Here's how you pay ahead of time or skip transactions:

- **Manually record a scheduled transaction regardless of when it's due.** In the Scheduled Bills & Deposits List window (press Ctrl+J to open it), click the Enter button in the transaction's row.

- **Skip scheduled transactions.** If you forget that you have a scheduled transaction set up for your telephone bill and manually record a check for one month's bill, you'll want to skip your scheduled payment. To skip one transaction of the schedule, in the Scheduled Bills & Deposits window, click the Skip button on the right end of the transaction's row.

Automatically Recording Paycheck Deposits

Paychecks seem to grow more complicated every year, what with pre-tax medical and retirement deductions, taxes, and after-tax deductions. Whether you're content to let your employer summarize your payroll on a W-2 each year or you want to track your paycheck to the penny, the Paycheck Setup tool helps simplify your record-keeping. It takes all the nitty-gritty details of your paycheck and spits out a scheduled deposit transaction. This section explains how to set up and record paychecks.

Getting Started with Paycheck Setup

Quicken makes it easy to set up paychecks using the Paycheck Setup wizard, a series of screens that guide you from start to finish. You can launch the wizard by choosing Banking → Banking Activities → Set Up Paycheck. Or, in the Scheduled Bills & Deposits window's (press Ctrl+J) menu bar, choose Create New → Paycheck. Then simply follow these steps:

1. **On the first screen of the Paycheck Setup wizard, you can read about all the great things Quicken can do with your paycheck…or just click Next to get started.**

2. **On the "Tell Quicken about this paycheck" screen, select the option for your or your spouse's paycheck.**

   If you didn't turn on the "I am married" setting (page 21), you won't see an option to select. The option you choose depends on who you view as the owner of the data file. The "This is my paycheck" option goes with the primary person on the data file (usually the person who created the data file and does most of the Quicken work). The "This is my spouse's paycheck" option goes with the primary person's better half.

3. **In the Company Name text box, type the name of the employer, and then click Next to continue.**

   You don't need the full legal name of the company. What you type in the Company Name box is what you'll see when you create a paycheck transaction, so you can make it short—but recognizable. If you and your spouse work for the same company, you can type the company name followed by your initials to help differentiate between the two paychecks.

4. On the "How much of your paycheck do you want to track?" screen, choose the option for the level of detail you want to track.

Quicken automatically selects the "I want to track all earnings, taxes, and deductions" option. If you want Quicken's help minimizing the taxes you pay or tracking company benefits, this is the option you want. With this level of detail, you'll know how much money you've earned so far this year, how much has been withheld for taxes, and what's available in your flexible spending account. And your deductions like FICA and state taxes go into separate categories that you'll then see on Quicken's tax reports (page 402) when you're ready to fill out your tax return.

For folks who just want to know how much money goes into the checking account to pay bills, the "I want to track net deposits only" option (page 200) is a better choice. You don't get the benefits of tracking all paycheck deductions, but the setup is much simpler. If you choose this option, you'll use the W-2 that your employer provides at the end of the year to fill out your tax return.

5. Click Next to begin the paycheck setup in earnest.

The specific Set Up Paycheck dialog box that appears depends on the level of detail you chose. The "I want to track net deposits only" option opens a compact dialog box with a few boxes where you enter the net deposit and how often the paycheck arrives. If you see a Set Up Paycheck dialog box that stretches from the top of your screen to the bottom, you know you're about to track full detail. See the next section to learn how to complete paycheck setup.

WORD TO THE WISE

When Paycheck Values Vary

If the amounts on your paycheck are never the same—say you're paid by the hour and work different hours each week—the Set Up Paycheck dialog box may not seem all that useful. Why set up a paycheck if you have to edit the numbers each time?

Filling in the Set Up Paycheck dialog box *without* dollar values still saves you quite a bit of effort. When Quicken creates

a paycheck transaction, it creates category splits for every paycheck item you add in the Set Up Paycheck dialog box, but leaves the split values blank. That way, when you go to record a paycheck, you don't have to spend time choosing paycheck categories. You can proceed directly to entering the numbers for your current paycheck.

Setting Up Paycheck Details

If you choose the "I want to track all earnings, taxes, and deductions" option, the Set Up Paycheck dialog box sprouts sections, boxes, and buttons you can use to specify every last item on your pay stub. Quicken makes adding and editing earnings, tax, and other deductions simple—a real boon when your paycheck seems to have more entries than the local phone book. The Set Up Paycheck dialog box automatically adds the most common paycheck items, including Salary, Federal Tax, State Tax, Social Security (FICA), and Medicare Tax. If your pay stub stops there, all you have to do is fill in the amounts. If your paycheck includes other items, you add them in the corresponding parts of the Set Up Paycheck dialog box, described in the following sections.

Although Figure 7-15 shows only a portion of this behemoth of a dialog box, filling it out breaks down into three basic steps:

- **Set a schedule.** In the Scheduling section, specify how often you or your spouse receive the paycheck. Setting this schedule is even easier than setting the schedule for a regular scheduled transaction (page 189).

- **Set up paycheck items.** For each entry on your pay stub, click one of the "Add" buttons (Add Earning, Add Pre-Tax Deduction, and so on) and choose the type of earning, tax, deduction, or payment. For each item you add, a small dialog box opens with a few text boxes like Name and Category, many of which Quicken fills in for you.

- **Bring your pay information up to date.** After you've added all the items on your pay stub, click Done, and Quicken opens the Enter Year-to-Date Information dialog box. The program automatically selects the "I want to enter the year-to-date information" option, which is the only logical choice if you want complete tax records at the end of the year. If you leave this option selected and click OK, Quicken opens the Paycheck Year-to-Date Amounts dialog box. The "Year to Date" column is initially filled with zeros. The values don't look editable, but you can click them to display an edit box. Use the year-to-date amounts from your most recent pay stub to fill in the values for each item and then click Enter when you're done.

If you don't care about tax records, select the "I do not want to enter this information" option and then click OK. The dialog box closes and you're back in the Scheduled Bills & Deposits window.

Setting up the paycheck account and schedule

At the very top of the Set Up Paycheck dialog box, Quicken fills in the "Company name" box with the name you typed earlier in the wizard. (You can change it if you notice a typo or your company changes its name.) Your initial task is to choose the account where you deposit your paycheck and then set the paycheck schedule.

Here's how you set up the paycheck basics:

1. **In the Account drop-down list, choose the account where you deposit your paycheck.**

   If you've set up automatic contributions to a savings account or another type of payment, see page 196 to learn how to add those to your Quicken paycheck transaction.

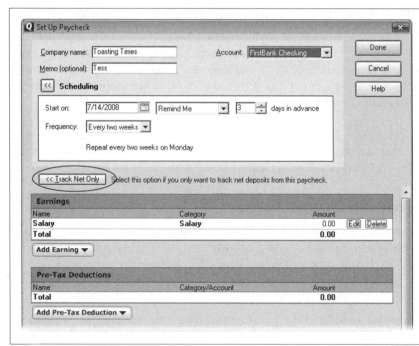

Figure 7-15:
If the sheer magnitude of the Set Up Paycheck dialog box intimidates you, you can click Track Net Only (just below the Scheduling section, circled). Quicken switches to the less detailed version of the Set Up Paycheck dialog box.

2. **In the "Start on" box, choose the next date you'll receive a paycheck.**

   The Scheduling section is an abbreviated version of the when and how often options you set for a regular scheduled transaction. If you want to fill in your data from the beginning of the year, you can choose the first payday of the current year. You don't have to tell Quicken the day of the week; it figures it out from the "Start on" date you choose.

3. **Choose a setting in the box to the right of the "Start on date".**

   Your choices are Remind Me and Automatically Enter. The Remind Me setting reminds you to enter your paycheck transaction several days in advance. When you see the reminder, you can make any necessary adjustments to match your pay stub.

   If you're one of those folks whose paycheck is always for the same amount, choose Automatically Enter to tell Quicken to add the paycheck transaction without asking for permission.

4. **In the "days in advance" box, choose when you want to record your paycheck.**

   Quicken sets this box to 3, mainly because employers often hand out pay stubs a few days before the pay date. If you like to plan your cash flow in advance, you can choose a higher number to add your paycheck transaction to the register earlier. (Although the transaction shows up in the register earlier, the transaction date is still based on your "Start on" date and the frequency.)

5. **In the Frequency Box, choose how often you receive your paycheck.**

Quicken can handle almost any paycheck schedule, unless your employer pays you whenever there's enough cash to cover payroll. Choose from Only Once, Weekly, "Every two weeks", "Twice a month", and so on. You don't have to choose an end date or number of recurrences—Quicken optimistically assumes you'll receive this paycheck indefinitely.

Tip: Once you set up a paycheck, you can hide the Scheduling section by clicking the button to the left of the Scheduling label. The button sports two left-facing arrows when the section is visible. After you click the button, it changes to two right-facing arrows to indicate that you can click it to expand the section.

An introduction to adding paycheck items

When you choose one of the paycheck items from one of the drop-down menus, a small dialog box opens for setting up that item, such as the Add dialog box in Figure 7-16. If you click an existing item's Edit button, the corresponding Edit dialog box appears. Either dialog box will contain some (or all) of these basic fields, depending on the specific item:

• **Name.** Quicken fills in the Name box with its name for the type of paycheck item you're adding. You can change the name to something that makes sense to you. For example, the Quicken name for a 401(k) deduction is *Employee Contribution Transfer*, but you can rename it *401k Spouse* if you like.

• **Category or Account.** The program automatically chooses a category to go with the item, such as Salary or Bonus. Quicken fills in Category boxes with one of its built-in categories. For example, the Federal Tax item uses Quicken's federal tax category. If you don't like the category Quicken chooses, simply select the one you want. If Quicken doesn't have a category for one of your items, click the Category down arrow. Then click Add Category to create a new one.

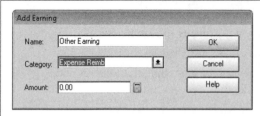

Figure 7-16:
If the amount you receive varies from paycheck to paycheck, leave the Amount field equal to zero; you'll fill that in whenever a paycheck includes that item.

Other items represent a transfer to another account, in which case you choose an account instead of a category. For example, for a 401(k) contribution, you choose your 401(k) account. If you haven't created the account yet, at the top of the Account drop-down menu, choose <Add New Account>, and the Quicken Account Setup dialog box (page 57) opens.

• **Amount or Contribution.** Type the specific amount for this item from your most recent pay stub.

Some items create their own accounts. For instance, in the Pre-Tax Deductions section, adding a Flex Spending item opens the Quicken Account Setup dialog box so you can create a Quicken account (page 47) to go with your employer's flexible spending account. (See page 278 to learn how to track contributions and withdrawals from health and flexible spending accounts.) After you complete the account setup, Quicken opens the dialog box for specifying an item amount like the one in Figure 7-16, except that the program automatically fills in the newly created account's name in the Account box. When you record your paycheck in Quicken, some of your paycheck transfers into the flexible spending account, which you can then use to pay for medical and other expenses.

Adding earnings

The first section of paycheck items is for earnings, and, sadly, these are usually the fewest in number. Quicken automatically adds the Salary item, though the amount is zero. To add a new item that represents money paid to you, click the Add Earnings button and then choose one of the following:

• **Salary.** Quicken assigns this paycheck item to the built-in Salary category, which appears in the tax reports you can generate (page 402). If you're setting up a paycheck for your spouse, you can edit the Salary item that Quicken added to use the Salary:Spouse category. (There's no reason to have two salary items on the same paycheck.)

• **Bonus.** Although bonuses are often paid once at the end of the year, you can add this item to your paycheck, so that it's ready when you receive that windfall.

• **Profit Sharing.** If your company pays out some of its profit in a profit-sharing plan, add this item to your paycheck.

• **Vacation, Holiday, or Sick Pay.** The only time you'd add one of these items to your paycheck is when your company pays you money in exchange for time off that you don't take.

• **Other Earning.** If you receive travel reimbursements in your paycheck, choose this item, and change the name to something like *Travel* or *Reimbursements*. If you use a category to track your reimbursable business expenses (page 77), choose that category in the Category field. (That way, the reimbursements reduce the amount in that category, so you can tell how much your company still owes you.) This item also works for other categories of income, like nontaxable payments for housing. To include nontaxable income, simply choose a category for that income and make sure that you've set the category up as nontaxable.

Adding pre-tax deductions

Pre-tax deductions are the handy contributions you can make before taxes are taken out of that income, such as 401(k), 403(b), and SEP retirement plans; flex spending accounts; and medical, dental, and vision insurance. To add a new item, click Add Pre-Tax Deduction, and then choose it from the list. Pre-tax deductions items come in two flavors: deductions you make to a Quicken category and those you contribute to a tax-advantaged account:

- The **Medical Insurance, Dental Insurance,** and **Vision Insurance** items open a basic dialog box with Name, Category, and Amount boxes like the one for adding earnings to your paycheck.

- If you add one of the other items for retirement plans and spending accounts, the Quicken Account Setup wizard (page 57) launches. For example, if you contribute to a flex spending account, you can create an account to hold your contributions. (See page 278 to learn how to track contributions and withdrawals from health spending accounts.) You step through the wizard to create a new account, which Quicken automatically sets up as tax-deferred.

Note: The Add 401(k) Deduction dialog box that opens when you choose the 401(k)/403(b)/457 pre-tax deduction (click Pre-Tax Deduction and then choose 401(k)/403(b)/457 from the drop-down menu) has an additional text box labeled Employer Match. If your employer is generous enough to match some of your contributions, fill in the amount of the match.

Adding taxes

Quicken automatically adds all the predefined tax items to a new paycheck—Federal Tax, State Tax, Social Security (FICA), and Medicare Tax, as shown in Figure 7-17. If you work in a tax-happy city, click Add Tax Item, and then choose Other Tax from the drop-down menu. In the Name box, type a name like *Silly City Tax*. If you've set up a special category for that tax, choose it in the Category drop-down list. (Otherwise, click the Category down arrow and then click Add Category to create a new one.) Type the Amount in the Amount box. See the box on page 202 to learn how to handle tax withholdings that don't happen on every paycheck.

Adding after-tax deductions

This classification includes stock purchase programs, where your company deducts money from your check and invests it in the company's stock. These items open a dialog box with Name, Account, and Amount boxes. If you haven't created an account for these deductions, you can create one on the fly by choosing <Add New Account> at the top of the Account drop-down menu.

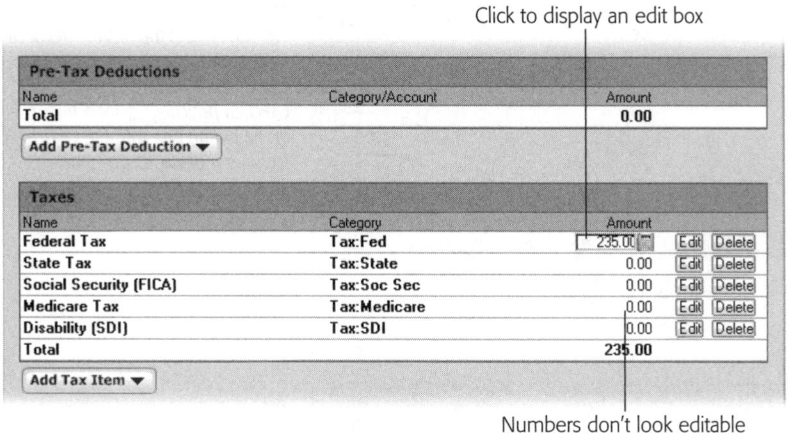

Click to display an edit box

Figure 7-17:
*After you've added an
item to your paycheck,
the amount doesn't look
editable. However, you
can edit the amount at
any time by clicking the
item's value, and then
typing the new amount.*

Numbers don't look editable

Adding transfers to other accounts

Initially, your checking account appears in the Deposit Accounts section with the net amount from your paycheck (after all the deductions). When you record a paycheck, that net amount shows up as a deposit in your checking account.

As the box on page 201 explains, frugal folks can set up additional deductions through their employers to transfer money to other bank accounts, like a savings account, for example. For these automatic transfers, click Add Deposit Account. Choose the account and the amount, and then click OK. Quicken subtracts the amount you transfer from the amount deposited to your primary account. For less dependable people, this paycheck item also works if a government agency garnishes wages.

Entering Year-to-Date Information

If you're setting up your paycheck midyear, you want to give Quicken complete tax information so it can help you come tax season. After you add all the items to your paycheck and click Done, the Enter Year-to-Date Information dialog box appears. Leave the "I want to enter the year-to-date information" option selected and click OK. Up pops the Paycheck Year-to-Date Amounts dialog box, shown in Figure 7-18, which lists the categories and accounts that appear on your pay stub. Click each value and type the year-to-date amount from your pay stub, and then click Enter.

Note: Your other option is "I do not want to enter this information". If you select this option, you don't enter your year-to-date information, so clicking OK completes your paycheck setup. The downside is your Quicken data for the year won't have all the info you need to prepare your tax return.

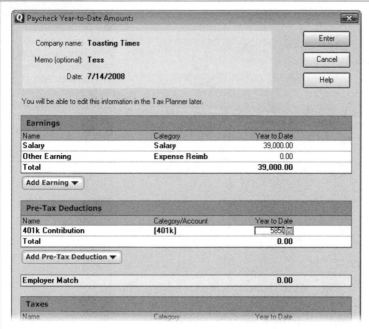

Figure 7-18:
The date at the top of the Paycheck Year-to-Date Amounts dialog box shows the date of your first Quicken paycheck transaction. Fill in the dialog box with the values from your previous pay stub.

Paycheck Tracking Made Easy

If you choose the "I want to track net deposits only" option in the Paycheck Setup wizard (page 193) and click Next, the Set Up Paycheck dialog box is refreshingly brief. The top of the dialog box has the same fields to specify when and how often you get paid as its exhaustive sibling. The only difference is the Amount box—you fill in this box with the net amount on your paycheck, that is, the amount you deposit into your checking account.

This option is easy to set up, but it doesn't give you the sort of information you need if you want Quicken to help with tax-related tasks—one of the main benefits of using Quicken. If you decide that you want more detail, you can click Track Deductions at the bottom of the dialog box to switch to the full-blown version of Set Up Paycheck.

Managing Paychecks

Because life is rarely simple, the meticulous paycheck setup you've just gone through won't last forever. Even minor changes in your family or job situation can affect the numbers on your paycheck. A new job or a new spouse means new paychecks to set up in Quicken and old paychecks to delete.

At least Quicken makes the necessary adjustments easy—far easier than changing jobs or getting married. If you have one or more paychecks set up, you can open

Automatic Transfers to Savings

"Out of sight, out of mind" is an adage that still applies when it comes to saving money. One of the least painful ways to save money is to have money deducted from your paycheck and deposited to your savings account. After all, you're less likely to spend money you forgot you had. Quicken's Set Up Paycheck dialog box can handle this deduction as easily as any other. Of course, you have to fill out the paperwork from your employer to set up this transfer to your real-world account.

After you set up these additional transfers with your employer, here's what you do in Quicken:

1. Near the bottom of the Set Up Paycheck dialog box, click Add Deposit Account.

2. In the Add Deposit Account dialog box's Account drop-down menu, select your savings account.

3. In the Amount box, type how much you want to transfer to savings from each paycheck.

4. Click OK.

Quicken automatically transfers this amount to your savings account. What's left of your paycheck (after your deductions and this transfer) goes into your primary deposit account.

the Manage Paychecks dialog box by choosing Banking → Banking Activities → Set Up Paycheck or, in the Scheduled Bills & Deposits window, Create New → Paycheck. Here's what you can do in that dialog box:

- **New.** To create a new paycheck—for that second job you've taken on, say—click New. Quicken opens the Sep Up Paycheck dialog box. See page 192 for the step-by-step details.

- **Edit.** Select one of the paychecks in the list and then click this button to open the Edit Future Paychecks dialog box. It's the same as the Paycheck Setup dialog box except that it makes changes only to future paychecks.

- **Delete.** If you quit a job and no longer receive a scheduled paycheck, select the paycheck in the list, and then click Delete.

Recording a Paycheck

As you can see from the scheduling options in the Set Up Paycheck dialog box (page 195), Quicken sets up your paycheck as a scheduled transaction (page 185), which means you'll receive a reminder to enter your paycheck. Recording scheduled paycheck transactions takes only a couple of clicks.

If you want to review the paycheck before you record it, press Ctrl+J to open the Scheduled Bills & Deposits window. On the All Bills & Deposits tab, click anywhere in the paycheck row and then click the Enter button that appears. The "Edit Current Paycheck and Enter into Register" dialog box opens. If your pay stub shows values different from the ones you entered when you set up your paycheck, make those changes first and then click Enter to record the paycheck. If you find minor changes in a few items from paycheck to paycheck, read the box on page 202 for a possible solution.

Tip: After you've entered the first paycheck, the easiest way to record another is to start a new transaction in your checking account register and then type your company's name in a transaction's Payee field. Quicken fills in the rest of the transaction's fields with the paycheck values it memorized from the first paycheck.

Every so often, you'll catch a mistake after you've recorded a paycheck and it's already a transaction in your checking account register. Although a paycheck is split among several categories, the Category field displays "--Form--" instead of "--Split--". That's Quicken's way of saying that the Edit Current Paycheck form will open if you click the transaction's Split button. The dialog box looks exactly like the Set Up Paycheck dialog box, except that it affects only the selected paycheck. Click the amount you want to change, make your changes, and then click Enter to record the revised paycheck.

Managing Memorized Payees

Quicken's QuickFill feature usually does a fine job filling in transaction information for you, almost as if the program had ESP. As explained in the box on page 89, though, there's no magic involved, just a list of values stored in Quicken's electronic brain—the Memorized Payee List. All the program does is find matches based on your first few keystrokes, which is something the software does really well, and really fast.

Of course, even Quicken's ESP isn't perfect. Sometimes the information it memorizes is incorrect, outdated, or just not what you want—like when Quicken memorizes "RBROS7537-2XX-CANL" instead of "Rasta Brothers Market (Canal St)." With a little human input, you can make QuickFill even better. By performing some electronic brain surgery, so to speak, you'll improve Quicken's psychic abilities and free up its brain cells for more important information. All you have to do is open the Memorized Payee List and edit away. This section shows you how.

One downside to this automatic memorization is that Quicken can be overly enthusiastic about memorizing payees. Before you know it, the program has memorized every Tom, Dick, and Harry—and Sally, Teresa, and Bubba. You can end up with more than one entry for the same payee. For instance, Quicken memorizes one payee for your grocery store when you create a transaction assigned to the Groceries category. Then, if you record additional transactions with your grocery store split among several categories, Quicken memorizes *another* payee for your store. Pick up a prescription at the grocery store pharmacy or buy gas at the grocery store pumps and you're on your way to a fistful of memorized payees for your grocery store alone.

Depending on the size of your transactions (splits are larger than their one-category cousins and memos take up space, too), the Memorized Payee List can hold between 1,000 and 2,000 entries. Quicken tells you that it's turning off automatic memorization when the list is half full. If you continue to add memorized payees manually until the list is full, you can't memorize any more until you delete some of the existing entries. If your Memorized Payee List has bloated to a startling degree, you've got three options:

- Tell Quicken which payees to remember by manually adding memorized payees (instead of automatically memorizing *every* payee).

- Limit how long Quicken remembers memorized payees (page 206).

- Delete memorized payees you no longer need (page 205).

The following sections explain all these options in detail.

GEM IN THE ROUGH

Quicken's Many Payee Lists

When you're trying to edit the info Quicken uses to auto-fill transaction fields, remember that Quicken grabs payee information from several places: the Memorized Payee List, the Address Book, and the list of online payees. If you don't find a payee in the Memorized Payee List, check the other lists as well.

Quicken's Address Book is where it stores the addresses it prints on checks. To open the Address Book so you can add

or edit payees and their addresses, choose Tools → Address Book. (See page 102 for more details.)

You may also have an Online Payee list, if you use Quicken for online bill payment. Choose Online → Online Payee List to see the companies you pay electronically. You can create online payees and specify the payee's address in the Set Up Online Payees dialog box (page 150).

Adding Memorized Payees Manually

One way to keep your Memorized Payee List lean is to prevent Quicken from memorizing one-hit wonders and other unimportant payees. You do this by telling Quicken to *not* memorize any payees, and then telling it which specific payees you want to add to the list. This method is more work for you, but it gives you the most control over the Memorized Payee List.

A Quicken preference tells the program whether to memorize payees. Choose Edit → Preferences → Quicken Program. In the Quicken Preferences dialog box, in the "Select preference type" list, click QuickFill, and then turn off the "Automatically memorize new payees" checkbox.

When automatic memorization is turned off and you enter a transaction that uses a payee you want to memorize, simply press Ctrl+M (or right-click the transaction and choose "Memorize payee" from the shortcut menu) and Quicken adds the payee to its Memorized Payee List.

Tip: When Quicken memorizes a payee, it memorizes *everything* about a transaction including its Cleared status. To make a memorized payee more useful, make sure the transaction includes information you want (like the category) and *doesn't* include information you don't want (like a Cleared or Reconciled status). Of course, you can memorize the payee as is and then edit the memorized payee (page 206) in the Memorized Payee List to fine-tune it.

You can also build a memorized payee from scratch. Here's how:

1. **Choose Tools → Memorized Payee List or press Ctrl+T to open the Memorized Payee List.**

2. **In the Memorized Payee List window's menu bar, click New.**

    The Create Memorized Payee dialog box opens, shown in Figure 7-19.

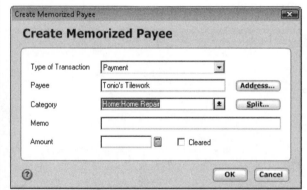

Figure 7-19:
To set up a payee that always uses the same set of splits, click Split instead of choosing a category in the Category drop-down menu. The Split Transaction dialog box opens. Define the splits you want as you would for a regular transaction (see page 168 for a refresher), and then click OK when you're done. Leave the values blank if you want to fill them in each time.

3. **In the "Type of Transaction" drop-down menu, choose Payment, Deposit, Print Check, or Online Pmt.**

    The type of transaction tells Quicken whether to create a check or deposit transaction for the payee, set up a check to print, or generate an online payment to send.

4. Type the payee's name in the Payee box.

   Memorized payees keep your payee names consistent, which can help you find all your transactions with a certain company. For example, if you've typed *Lowes*, *Lowe's*, and *Lowes'* for the same home-improvement store, a quick search (page 179) may not catch all your different spellings. See page 146 to learn how to use renaming rules to make downloaded payee names consistent.

5. Choose the category you want to use.

6. If you want to include the same memo every time, type the text in the Memo box.

7. In the Amount box, type the amount you want Quicken to fill in every time.

   If the amount is the same each time, type that value in the Amount box. If the amount varies, leave this box empty. Remember, you can edit the value in a transaction after QuickFill fills in all the fields. If you want to mark every transaction as cleared, turn on the Cleared checkbox.

8. When you're done, click OK to save the payee.

Removing Payees from the Memorized Payee List

For a Memorized Payee List that's already overfed, removing payees is the only option. Quicken has two ways to remove payees: You can delete memorized payees yourself or delegate the job to Quicken. Don't worry—deleting memorized payees doesn't remove them from recorded transactions.

Deleting memorized payees

If your Memorized Payee List is cluttered with names you never want to see again, you can excise these entries from the list:

1. Open the Memorized Payee List by pressing Ctrl+T or choosing Tools → Memorized Payee List.

2. Select one or more payees.

   You don't have to delete only one memorized payee at a time. You can click one entry and then Shift-click another entry several rows down to also select all the payees in between. To select payees scattered around the list, Ctrl-click each one you want to trash.

3. In the Memorized Payee List menu bar, choose Delete (or click the Delete button at the bottom of the window).

   Quicken displays a confirmation box (Figure 7-20) asking if you're sure you want to delete the selected payees. Click OK and they're history.

Figure 7-20:
This confirmation box shows you how many payees you've selected. Click OK to delete, or click Cancel to spare them.

Limiting the length of Quicken's memory

The easiest way to keep your Memorized Payee List under control is with a Quicken Register preference (page 493). You simply tell Quicken how long to keep memorized payees in the Memorized Payee List. If you don't use a memorized payee within that time frame, Quicken deletes it.

Choose Edit → Preferences → Quicken Program, and then click Register. By turning on the "Remove memorized payees not used in last" checkbox and typing a number (in months), you tell Quicken to continually review your Memorized Payee List and toss out any payees you haven't used in that time frame.

Tip: If you have companies you pay once a year, like your insurance company or the septic tank cleaner, type, say, *14* in the months box. By giving yourself a few extra months, Quicken won't remove memorized payees before you've had a chance to reuse them.

Editing Memorized Payees

You can change any aspect of a memorized payee at any time. The changes you make appear the next time you use that payee. In the Memorized Payee List window, select the payee you want to change, and then use one of the following methods to edit that payee:

• **Modify a memorized payee.** In the window's menu bar, click Edit (or click the Edit button at the bottom of the window). The Edit Memorized Payee dialog box opens with all the same fields as the Create Memorized Payee dialog box (Figure 7-19). Change any value you want and then click OK.

• **Rename a memorized payee.** If you just want to change the *name* of a memorized payee, click the Rename button at the bottom of the window.

- **Show payees on the Quicken Calendar.** Quicken automatically sets memorized payees to appear on the Quicken Calendar (page 316) on the date of the transaction you memorized. In the Memorized Payee List window, a calendar icon appears in the "Show on Calendar" column indicates that the payee appears in the Calendar; otherwise, the cell is blank. If you don't want the calendar to fill up with one-time payments, click the payee's "Show on Calendar" cell to toggle it off.

Note: The Memorized Payee List window's menu bar includes the command "Go to Find and Replace", which opens the standard "Find and Replace" dialog box (page 178). The command doesn't, however, fill in any values.

Locking Memorized Payees

When Quicken memorizes payees, it stores them in an *unlocked* state, which means that Quicken overwrites that memorized payee's values when you create a new transaction. For example, if your electric bill is different every month, each time you create a new transaction, the amount of the *previous* month's payment appears in the Payment field the next time you pay your electric bill. That's because Quicken memorizes the payment amount each time you enter a new value.

If you want to keep a memorized payee the same, regardless of what you do with it in a new transaction, you can *lock* the entry so that the Memorized Payee List remembers the same value no matter what. For example, suppose you have a memorized payee for your cable TV bill. Every month, you pay $36.95 for the privilege of surfing through 150 channels of reruns, so you lock the entry at that amount. One month your bill is only $20 because you received a credit for a week's service outage, so you edit the amount for that transaction. But when you create the payment the next month, the regular amount of $36.95 pops up again.

The fastest way to lock a payee is to head to the Memorized Payee List window and click the Lock cell in the payee's row. You'll know that an entry is locked by the gold padlock in the Lock column. To unlock an entry, simply click its padlock icon.

Tip: If you want to lock several entries at once, select all the entries, and then click the button with the picture of the padlock on it in the bottom-right corner of the window.

Reconciling: Making Sure Quicken and Your Bank Agree

Admit it: Your least favorite part of having a checking account is the monthly struggle to make your handwritten register agree with your bank's balance. (The technical term for this is *reconciling*.) No matter how carefully you record every check, debit card withdrawal, and ATM fee, the numbers never seem to match. Tracking down the error is an exercise in frustration: Did the bank make an error, or do you have to redo your math yet *again?* And though you probably don't keep a handwritten register for your credit card, it's a good idea to reconcile your Quicken credit card account, too, by comparing it to the monthly statement you get from your credit card company.

Note: If you've never experienced the pleasures of reconciliation firsthand, the process (at least in theory) is pretty simple. You simply review each transaction listed on your monthly bank statement, and then make sure there's a corresponding entry in your own records (a paper checkbook, Quicken, or whatever you use).

Don't despair—Quicken takes the agony out of reconciliation. If you download transactions from your bank (or credit card company), you may be able to reconcile with as little as a single click because your register and the bank will almost always agree on which checks have cleared. If you accidentally transpose numbers or forget to record an ATM withdrawal, Quicken has tools to help you find the problem. And here's the best part: Quicken does the math for you, error-free.

With Quicken, reconciliation is so easy, there's no excuse for *not* doing it. And it happens to come with loads of benefits: Never again will you bounce a check because you thought you had more funds available. You may even get lucky and discover you accidentally recorded the same payment twice, so you have *more* money than you thought—ka-ching! And when you reconcile regularly, you're more likely to catch transactions you *didn't* make—and catch some con artist using your credit card to build up his Pez dispenser collection.

Prep Time: Reviewing Your Account

Statements you receive from your bank and credit card company have the info you need to reconcile your accounts. So, *when* you reconcile depends on *when* you receive your statements. Most firms send monthly statements, which means you reconcile each account once a month. As you'll learn on page 221, Quicken can dispense with the monthly reconciliation chore—if you download transactions, it can automatically reconcile your transactions every time you go online.

Part of Quicken's charm is that it doesn't care if you create, edit, or delete transactions right in the middle of a reconciliation. This flexibility means you can correct mistakes as you reconcile. But the trade-off is that you're constantly flipping back and forth: a little bit of reconciling, then back to the register to fix an entry. A little more reconciling, then back to the register to fill in a missing transaction. And so on. You're better off taking a moment *before* you reconcile to make sure you've properly entered all your transactions. That way you can reconcile your account in mere seconds. Here's the prep work you should always take care of first:

- **Checks.** Missing check numbers are a tip-off that you wrote a paper check and didn't record it in Quicken. If you fill out a paper register with checks as you run errands, look through it to see if you can spot any of the check transactions missing from Quicken. To look for missing checks in your Quicken data file, choose Reports → Banking → Missing Checks. The Missing Checks report inserts entries in bold text and bracketed with asterisks to show check numbers that aren't in your Quicken banking accounts, as shown in Figure 8-1.

    If you notice checks missing from Quicken (page 87) *and* your paper register, review the bank statement you just received (or look at recent transactions on your bank's Web site) to figure out what happened to those checks.

- **Charges.** If you have credit card receipts scattered across your desk, gather them up and make sure you've recorded them all in your Quicken credit card account. (And if you're not in the habit of saving your receipts, it's worth starting: It's really the best way to make sure some thief isn't using your card, and that waiters input the correct tip amount that you wrote on the receipt.)

- **Transfers and withdrawals.** Don't forget to record transfers and ATM withdrawals.

- **Deposits.** If you're like most people, you don't forget to deposit checks you receive. Just make sure you've recorded those deposits in Quicken as well.

- **Online transactions.** For accounts you've set up to use online banking, download transactions (page 133) *before* reconciling your account. (This step is so useful that Quicken reminds you to do so as soon as you begin reconciliation.)

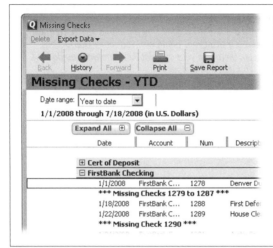

Figure 8-1:
You may be surprised to see that the Missing Checks report lists all your transactions for all your banking accounts (checking, savings, credit cards, and cash). After all, you won't see missing checks in savings, credit card, or cash accounts. Quicken inserts bolded entries for the check numbers it didn't find in your sequence of checks within each account. To keep the Missing Checks report on target, you can customize the report to include only your checking accounts (page 447) and then save it (page 455).

Tip: If several months have gone by since you last reconciled your account, don't try to make up time by reconciling multiple months at once—you'll just find it harder to spot discrepancies and trace problems to their source. Put your bank statements in chronological order, and then walk through the reconciliation process for each statement. With Quicken, each one takes only a few minutes.

First Steps: Telling Quicken What to Compare

Reconciling an account involves two simple, distinct steps. First, choose the account you want to reconcile and tell Quicken some basic facts about that account (like the starting and ending balance for the month you're reviewing). Second, perform the actual reconciliation: the transaction-by-transaction matchmaking of your records to the bank's records. The steps for reconciling offline accounts and those set up for online access are basically the same, but what you see is a little different. The sections that follow describe the process for online and offline accounts.

First Steps for Online Accounts

Before you compare your Quicken transactions to the ones from your bank, you have to set the stage for the review. In effect, you tell Quicken, "Here's how much my bank says I *started* with this month, and how much I *ended* with."

Here's how to get an account set up for online access ready for reconciliation (see page 125 to learn how to turn on online access):

1. **Start by going to the Account Bar, and then clicking the account you want to reconcile. Then, in the register's menu bar, choose Reconcile.**

   The Reconcile Online Account dialog box (Figure 8-2) opens.

Figure 8-2:
When you use online banking, you download service charges and interest transactions along with your other transactions. You accept them into your account the same way you do checks, charges, and deposits.

Tip: If the account is set up for online access and you haven't downloaded transactions today, you see a dialog box warning you that your downloaded transactions don't appear up to date. Click Yes to cancel the reconciliation, and then go ahead and download your transactions. (You want those downloaded transactions up to date, because they're often the very transactions you're going to reconcile!) When your account is up to date, choose Reconcile once more.

2. **To reconcile downloaded transactions to your paper statement, leave the Paper Statement option selected.**

   When you set up an account to download transactions, you can choose whether to reconcile to your paper statement when it arrives (the Paper Statement option), or reconcile to your online balance every time you go online (the Online Balance option). As you tick off transactions on a paper statement, you have a chance to catch fraudulent checks, charges, or withdrawals. If you record transactions manually in Quicken and catch those types of problems when you match downloaded transactions (page 134) with the ones you record, then you may want to forego reconciling to the paper statement. See page 221 to learn how to reconcile faster and more frequently.

3. **In the Ending Statement Date box, type or choose the ending date that appears on your paper statement.**

   The statement ending date determines the period that the reconciliation covers. Quicken starts you off with a date one month after the previous reconciliation (or today's date if this is your first reconciliation for this account). Because financial institutions sometimes schedule statements on a specific day of the week, you may have to adjust this date to match the ending date on your paper statement.

Note: The first time you reconcile a checking or savings account, Quicken fills in the Opening Balance with whatever balance you entered when you first created the account. From then on, the program uses the ending balance from the previous reconciliation. If the Opening Balance doesn't match the beginning balance on your bank statement, click Cancel, and then turn to page 217 to learn how to correct the problem. (The Opening Balance box doesn't appear for a credit card account.)

4. **For a credit card account, fill in the "Charges, Cash Advances" box with the total of the charges, cash advances, and debits from your current statement. Fill in the "Payments, Credits" box with the total credited to your account.**

   "Charges, Cash Advances" is the total for purchase charges, cash advances you withdraw, and other debits such as the annual fee or interest you pay. "Payments, Credits" is the total amount credited to your account, including payments you make and credits you receive from returning what you bought.

5. **In the Ending Balance box, type the ending balance from your paper statement.**

   After you've entered this info, click OK to proceed to the second part of reconciliation, described on page 215.

First Steps for Offline Accounts

As you do for online accounts, you have to tell Quicken how much your bank says you had at the beginning of the statement period and how much you had at the end.

Here are the steps for setting up a reconciliation for an account you update manually:

1. **In the Account Bar, choose the account you want to reconcile. Then, in the register's menu bar, choose Reconcile.**

   The Statement Summary dialog box shown in Figure 8-3 appears. Quicken fills in the Opening Balance box automatically. (You won't see the Opening Balance box if you're working with a credit card account.) For the first reconciliation, the Opening Balance is the balance you entered when you created the account. From then on, the Opening Balance is the ending balance from the previous reconciliation.

   If the Opening Balance box and your bank statement's beginning balance don't agree, click Cancel, and see page 217 to learn how to correct the problem.

2. **For a credit card account, fill in the "Charges, Cash Advances" and the "Payments, Credits" boxes with the values from your statement.**

   "Charges, Cash Advances" is the total of charges you make for purchases, cash advances you withdraw, and other debits such as the annual fee you pay. "Payments, Credits" is the total amount credited to your account, including payments you make and credits you receive from returning purchases.

3. **In the Ending Balance box, type the ending balance from your paper statement.**

   Whether you're reconciling a checking, savings, or credit card account, you fill in the Ending Balance box with the ending balance on your paper statement.

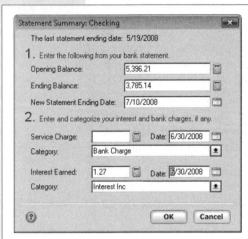

Figure 8-3:
The boxes you see in the Statement Summary dialog box depend on the type of account you're reconciling. For checking and savings accounts like the one shown here, specify the opening and ending balances, the statement date, and any service charges or interest earned. With credit accounts, specify the ending statement date, charges, payments or credits, and the ending balance.

4. **In the New Statement Ending Date box, type or choose the ending date that appears on your paper statement.**

   The statement ending date is the last date of the period that the reconciliation covers. Quicken automatically sets the date to one month after the previous reconciliation (or today's date, if this is the first time you've reconciled this account). You may have to adjust this date to match the ending date on your paper statement if your bank doesn't follow a one-month schedule.

5. **Fill in the Service Charge box (or Finance Charges box, if this is a credit card account) with the amount that your bank charges you each month.**

   The service charge is the monthly service charge for this statement, which may include a regular charge, bounced check charges, or fees for dropping below the minimum balance. In the Date box, choose the date when the service charge was levied. In the Category box, select the category you want to assign the charge to (Bank Charge or Fees, for example). Quicken uses this information to create a service charge transaction for you.

   For credit card accounts, the box is labeled Finance Charges, which represents interest and finance charges you have to pay if you don't pay your balance off in full each month.

Note: You don't see this box for online accounts, because you download these fees along with the rest of your transactions.

After your first reconciliation, Quicken automatically fills in the date and category for service charges and interest earned. You have to enter these values only if you've changed categories or Quicken's date is significantly different than the actual date.

6. If your account pays interest, enter that value in the Interest Earned boxes.

As you did for service charges, specify the date and category you use to track this interest. You can skip the Interest Earned boxes if your account doesn't pay interest.

After you've entered this information, click OK to proceed to the second part of reconciliation, described next.

Reconciliation: The Actual Review

When you click OK in the Statement Summary dialog box (or the Reconcile Online Account dialog box for online accounts), Quicken opens a large window, which lists the money that flows into and out of your account. For checking and savings accounts, this window is titled Statement Summary; money flowing out appears in the "Payments and Checks" column, and money flowing in appears in the Deposits column. (For online-enabled credit accounts, the window is titled Reconcile, and the columns are labeled Charges and Payments, respectively.)

Reconciling Online Accounts

If you download transactions from your financial institution and match them to the transactions in Quicken, there's not much for you to do besides click Finished. (The bank isn't likely to disagree with itself, and you've already cleared most transactions during your downloads, as described on page 137.) Now wasn't that easy?

Every so often, though, an online reconciliation doesn't line up perfectly. For example, say you accidentally turned off the Clr field for a cleared transaction. In that case, Quicken opens the full-blown Statement Summary window when you click OK in the Reconcile Online Account dialog box. To track down the problem and complete your reconciliation, follow the steps in the next section, as though you were dealing with an offline account.

Reconciling Offline Accounts

If you record transactions in Quicken yourself, you have to mark the cleared transactions in Quicken to reconcile them to the paper statement. But even that's pretty painless. Figure 8-4 and the following steps explain how the process works:

1. **Review each transaction in your bank statement. If the corresponding entry in the Statement Summary or Reconcile (for credit card accounts) window is for the same amount, then click it to let Quicken know that transaction is cleared.**

Clicking a transaction toggles its Clr checkmark on and off. Check the transaction off on the paper statement, too, so you know you've reviewed it. If you get to the end and the Difference hasn't reached zero, an unchecked transaction in either place is probably the culprit. (If you *can't* track down the problem and are desperate to stop searching for that stray $1.50, see the box on page 217. If you find a discrepancy, see page 217 to learn how to correct it.)

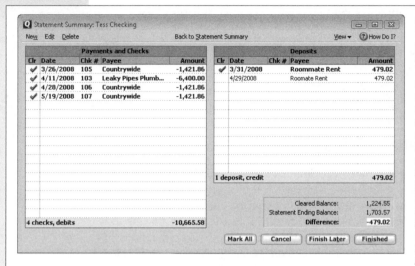

Figure 8-4:
To reconcile an account, click transactions to mark them as cleared. That's your way of saying, "Yep, I recognize and agree with this amount." Quicken sticks a checkmark next to any item you've OK'd, and keeps a running tally of all your cleared items next to the Cleared Balance label (bottom-right corner). The Statement Ending Balance displays whatever you entered from your bank statement. You're trying to get the Difference amount to equal zero: It's the amount separating your cleared balance from the statement ending balance. When Difference equals zero, Quicken and your bank agree. Click Finished and bask in the glory of a perfect reconciliation.

2. **When the Difference value equals zero, click Finished.**

Quicken displays the Reconciliation Complete dialog box, and asks if you want to create a reconciliation report, which shows the totals for cleared and uncleared transactions, along with the ending balance from your bank statement and the one in your Quicken register. If you use Quicken only for personal finances and generally breeze through reconciling without problems, click No, the most popular choice by far. If you want a record, whether to resolve potential problems in the future or for the paper trail that accountants and bookkeepers need, click Yes.

Even if you reconcile your statements every month without a hitch, your accounts aren't necessarily error-free. For example, you may notice that there are a few transactions from 4 months ago languishing uncleared. When you examine these transactions closely, you'll probably find a charge you made on a different credit card got entered in the wrong account, or that it's a duplicate charge you forgot to delete, or some other minor problem. This error could also happen because a check didn't make it to the vendor, or your deposit never made it to the bank. Either way, it's worth researching these old, uncleared transactions every once in a while. If you find a transaction that doesn't belong, select it, and then, in the

Statement Summary or Reconcile (for credit card accounts) window's menu bar, choose Delete to remove the transaction from the account register. To move a transaction to the correct account, right-click it and then choose Move Transaction(s) from the shortcut menu (page 183).

Modifying Transactions During Reconciliation

Even if your Quicken register is rife with errors and omissions, getting through reconciliation is surprisingly painless. Quicken immediately updates the Statement Summary or Reconcile (page 215) window with changes you make in the account register window, so you can jump to the register window and make your changes. When you return to the Statement Summary or Reconcile window, the changes are there—ready for you to mark as cleared.

WORKAROUND WORKSHOP

Adjusting an Account That Won't Reconcile

When the Difference value in the Statement Summary or Reconcile (page 215) window refuses to change to 0.00, reconciling *without* finding the problem is an option. Before you give up, though, see page 219.

If your reconciliation has hit a roadblock and you don't see any way around it, you can add an adjustment to force your statement and your Quicken records to see eye to eye. In the Statement Summary or Reconcile window, simply click Finished. If you have a Difference value other than zero, Quicken automatically opens the Adjust Balance dialog box. This box tells you what you already know: There's an unresolved difference between the total for the items you cleared in Quicken and the total on your bank or credit card statement. If you decide to give the problem one last look, click Cancel to return to reconciling.

To create an adjustment transaction, change the Adjustment Date text box to the date you want for the adjustment (for example, the ending date for the statement you're trying to reconcile). Then click Adjust, and Quicken creates a transaction in the register to make up the difference.

If you create an adjustment transaction and then later stumble across the source of the discrepancy, you can edit the balance adjustment transaction to turn it into the missing transaction you discovered. Although the transaction is marked as reconciled, you can edit the payee name and the category to the values for the missing transaction.

When you work in the register window during reconciliation, you'll see an extra button—"Return to Reconcile"—to the left of the Enter, Edit, Split, and Attach buttons, as shown in Figure 8-5. After you add, edit, and delete the transactions, you can click "Return to Reconcile" to jump back to the Statement Summary (or Reconcile) window.

Here's how you make changes while reconciling:

- **Adding transactions.** If a transaction appears on your bank statement but isn't in Quicken, in the Statement Summary or Reconcile window's menu bar, choose New. Quicken jumps to a blank transaction in the account's register window.

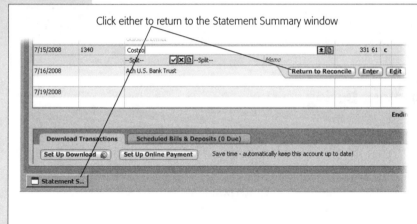

Click either to return to the Statement Summary window

Figure 8-5:
As long as you're in the middle of reconciliation, any transactions you select in the register include a "Return to Reconcile" button, which pops you back into the Statement Summary or Reconcile window. Alternatively, at the bottom of the Quicken main window, you can click Statement Summary, which restores the minimized Statement Summary window (or Reconcile to restore the Reconcile window).

Note: In the Statement Summary or Reconcile window, double-clicking any transaction takes you to that transaction in the register. Once you're in the register, you can record as many forgotten transactions as you want. To get back to the Statement Summary or Reconcile window, click the active transaction's "Return to Reconcile" button.

- **Deleting transactions.** If you find a duplicate transaction, select it and, in the Statement Summary or Reconcile window's menu bar, choose Delete. You have to click Yes to confirm your decision before Quicken deletes the transaction, but then it's history.

- **Editing transactions.** If you notice an error in a transaction, select it, and then, from the Statement Summary or Reconcile window's menu bar, choose Edit. Quicken jumps to that transaction in the account register. Correct the mistake, record the transaction by clicking Enter, and then click "Return to Reconcile".

Stopping and Restarting a Reconciliation

The Statement Summary or Reconcile window includes a Finish Later button for saving your reconciliation work without completing it. You're likely to click this button only when you've run into a discrepancy that requires some research. Say you're relaxing on Sunday by reconciling your checking account, and notice a questionable bank charge. You can click Finish Later, and return to your reconciliation after you've talked to your bank on Monday morning.

In the Statement Summary or Reconcile window, when you click Finish Later, Quicken closes the window, but remembers the balances you entered and what you've cleared. In the register, you'll see a lowercase *c* in the Clr column for each transaction that you've marked, which indicates that the transaction is only *tentatively* cleared.

When you're armed with fresh information and a strong dose of caffeine, choose Reconcile in the register's menu bar. The Statement Summary (Figure 8-3) or Reconcile Online Account window (Figure 8-2) opens, containing the summary values you typed in on your first attempt. If they're still correct, click OK to open the second Statement Summary (or Reconcile) window (Figure 8-4) for another try. This second Statement Summary (or Reconcile) window opens with previously cleared transactions still checked, so you're ready to pick up where you left off.

When Your Records Don't Agree with Your Bank's

When you try to modify a transaction that you've already reconciled, it would be great if Quicken set off flashing lights and sirens to warn you about the havoc you're about to wreak. After all, the transaction appeared on your bank statement because it was a done deal, and changing it in Quicken doesn't change it in the real world. But, unfortunately, Quicken lets you change or delete reconciled transactions with nothing more than a mild message box asking if you're sure you know what you're doing.

But make no mistake: Making changes to reconciled transactions is the quickest way to create mayhem in your accounts. For example, in the register window, deleting a reconciled transaction subtracts that amount from the Opening Balance the next time you try to reconcile the account. And *that* means that the Opening Balance won't match the beginning balance on your paper bank statement (which is one reason you might be reading this section). You can change a reconciled transaction in a few ways to correct a problem without messing up future reconciliations, as the box below explains.

POWER USERS' CLINIC

Changing Reconciled Transactions

Occasionally, you'll find a reason to change a reconciled transaction. For example, maybe you reconcile your checking account, and then realize that Quicken matched one of the monthly $100 payments you made to the wrong transaction (the May payment instead of the April payment, say). The easiest way to switch the transaction mismatch is to change the reconciled status of the two transactions. Here's what you do:

1. Right-click the first transaction that was reconciled incorrectly.

2. On the shortcut menu that appears, choose Reconcile → Not Reconciled. Quicken turns off the Clr field

for the $100 transaction to show that it hasn't cleared at the bank. Click Enter to save the change.

3. Right-click the other transaction that *did* clear at your bank.

4. On the shortcut menu, choose Reconcile → Reconciled. Quicken fills in the Clr field with *R* to show that the transaction cleared at the bank and has been reconciled. Click Enter to save the change.

That's it! You still have one reconciled transaction and one uncleared transaction, so your next reconciliation will work like a charm.

Sometimes, subtle errors, missing transactions, or an errant click on an uncleared check can foul up your attempts to reconcile an account. Here are some techniques to help bring your records back into balance:

- **Look for transactions cleared or uncleared by mistake.** Go through your bank statement again, checking off each transaction you've marked in Quicken. Look for the telltale missing checkmark on your paper statement—which indicates a transaction that you haven't marked in Quicken—and then mark the unchecked transaction in Quicken. Then, make sure that every transaction on the bank statement is marked in the Statement Summary or Reconcile window, and that no additional transactions are marked. If you want to start over, unmark all the transactions in Quicken, and then begin checking them one by one.

Note: If the Difference value in the Statement Summary or Reconcile window is positive, that means you and Quicken think you have *more* money than the bank says you do. Chances are you forgot to record a check you wrote or an ATM withdrawal, or you recorded a transaction twice. If the Difference value is negative, you may have forgotten to record a deposit.

- **Look for duplicate transactions.** If you both download transactions and create some manually in Quicken, duplicate transactions are often to blame for reconciliation discrepancies. Scan the register for multiple transactions with the same date, payee, and amount.

  Here's a trick for ferreting out duplicate transactions: Count the number of transactions on your bank statement, and then compare that number to the number of cleared transactions displayed at the bottom of the Statement Summary or Reconcile window (illustrated in Figure 8-4, back on page 216). Unfortunately, this trick doesn't help if you enter transactions in Quicken differently from the way they appear on your bank statement. If you record every deposit individually, say, but your bank shows one deposit for every business day, your transaction counts won't match.

- **Look for a transaction equal to the amount of the difference.** This approach helps you find a single transaction that you marked or unmarked by mistake, or a duplicate transaction that you marked as cleared. Use Quicken's Find command (page 175) to look in Amount fields for such transactions.

- **Look for a transaction equal to half the difference.** This technique helps you find transactions that you recorded the wrong way around. For example, if a $500 check becomes a $500 deposit by mistake, your reconciliation will be off by $1,000 ($500 because a check is missing, and another $500 because you have an extra deposit).

- **Review transactions for transposed numbers.** It's easy to type $95.40 when you meant $94.50. Before you examine every transaction amount for these hard-to-spot errors, divide the Difference value by 9. If the result is a whole number of dollars or cents, such as $5 or 10 cents, chances are you've transposed numbers.

For example, say you have a difference of .90, or 90 cents. Dividing by 9 results in .1—that is, 10 cents. If the result is something like 1.52 or .523 (52.3 cents), transposed numbers are not to blame.

Note: For extra credit, here's why this trick works: Transposing two numbers changes the order of 10 that each digit is multiplied by. Take the numbers 87 and 78, for example. In 87, the number 8 is multiplied by 10 and the number 7 is multiplied by 1. The opposite is true for the number 78. Substituting a for 8 and b for 7, the arithmetic looks like this: $(a \times 10) + (b \times 1) - (b \times 10) - (a \times 1)$. That's the equivalent of $10a + b - 10b - a$, or $9a - 9b$. Divide by 9 and you have a whole number!

WORD TO THE WISE

When Your Bank Makes a Mistake

Banks do make mistakes: Digits get transposed or amounts are flat wrong. When this happens, you can't ignore the difference. In Quicken, you can add an adjustment transaction to make up the difference, as described in the box on page 217, but be sure to tell your bank about the mistake.

When you receive your *next* statement, check that the bank made an adjustment to correct its mistake. Delete the adjustment transaction you created and then reconcile as you normally would.

Reconciling Automatically

No, Quicken doesn't automatically email apologies when you've had a fight with your girlfriend. But if you use online banking, the Online Balance option in the Reconcile Online Account dialog box does something almost as useful. When you choose this option, you don't have to fill in the Opening Balance, Ending Balance, or Ending Statement Date boxes. Quicken takes the Opening Balance from the last reconciliation, and it goes online and gets the current balance as of the most recent banking day.

In the Reconcile Online Account dialog box, when you select the Online Balance option, Quicken turns on the "Auto reconcile after compare to register" checkbox, and takes on the chore of reconciling. Every time you download transactions, you accept them as you would normally. Then, as long as the Quicken balance and your bank account's online balance agree, Quicken automatically reconciles the account. Whether you write checks by hand, pay bills online, or have payees pull money from your account, most of the time, all you do is click OK, and Quicken reconciles your account up through your most recent downloaded transactions. If the balances don't match, then the Statement Summary window opens so you can resolve the discrepancies, as described on page 215.

Anytime after you've activated online access for a Quicken account (page 129), you can switch the account to reconcile automatically. From then on, Quicken reconciles

---

the account every time you go online. To turn on Quicken's automatic reconciliation, do the following:

1. **Open the register for the account.**

   In the Account Bar, click the account's name. You can also open the register by choosing Banking → Banking Accounts, and then selecting the name of the account you want to reconcile.

2. **In the register's menu bar, click Reconcile.**

   The Reconcile Online Account dialog box opens.

3. **Select the Online Balance option, as shown in Figure 8-6, and then click OK.**

   Quicken turns on the "Auto reconcile after compare to register" checkbox, which is what you want. This setting tells the program to automatically reconcile downloaded transactions that match those already in the register. If you haven't downloaded transactions recently and you try to reconcile the account, the program asks you if you want to download transactions first. Click Yes to do just that.

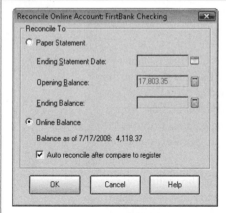

Figure 8-6:
Below the Online Balance option, the "Balance as of" line shows the date that Quicken obtained the online balance and the balance itself. If the date isn't today's, cancel the reconciliation and download your recent transactions. Otherwise, you may have to resolve needless discrepancies.

The next time you download transactions, Quicken reconciles your account automatically. The program fills in the Clr field for accepted downloaded transactions with an "R" (for reconcile), and you're done. If Quicken can't reconcile the account balance and the online balance, the Statement Summary window (or the Reconcile window for credit accounts) opens, so you can find and correct the discrepancy. For example, the two balances won't reconcile if you accidentally duplicated a deposit or payment in your Quicken account. The program automatically reconciles the first transaction, but can't reconcile the duplicate. In this case, you simply delete the duplicate transaction. See page 219 for other hints on resolving reconciliation errors.

Switching Back to Manual Reconciliation

You can turn automatic reconciliation off if you prefer to inspect each transaction closely when your bank statement arrives. (When you switch back to paper reconciliation, you reconcile from the last automatic reconciliation to the ending date of your most recent bank statement.) Here's how:

1. **To revert to paper reconciliation, open the register, and then, in the register's menu bar, click Reconcile.**

   The Reconcile Online Account dialog box opens with the Online Balance option selected.

2. **In the Reconcile Online Account dialog box, select the Paper Statement option.**

   The Ending Statement Date, Opening Balance, and Ending Balance boxes become active.

3. **Fill in the Opening Balance box with the balance as of the last automatically reconciled transaction in your Quicken register, as shown in Figure 8-7.**

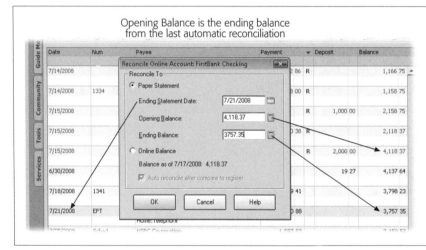

Figure 8-7:
Fill in the Ending Statement Date and Ending Balance boxes with the ending date and ending balance from your paper bank statement, as you would for a normal paper reconciliation. Click OK and complete the reconciliation as described on page 215.

3

Part Three: Tuning Your Financial Engine

Tracking Property and Debt

As you learned in Chapter 3, you use *asset accounts* to track the things you own (property) and *loan or debt accounts* to track what you owe (debt, also known as liabilities). You don't have to monitor every last penny in Quicken, but the more you do, the more benefits you'll reap. For example, set up a mortgage account, and the program automatically reminds you when it's payment time. So you can say goodbye to those pesky late fees and, more important, measure your progress in that long journey toward actually owning your house. And, with a clear picture of assets and liabilities, Quicken can do things like calculate your *net worth* (the value of your assets minus whatever you owe)—a good way to check your financial health.

This chapter shows you how to set up Quicken to track assets and debts. Once you've done that, you can spend your time thinking about more exciting things— like what to do with all that money Quicken saved you in late fees.

Property and Debt: An Introduction

To make the most of Quicken's property- and debt-tracking features, it helps to understand a few basic concepts:

- **Assets** are things you own that have value: your house, car, appliances, and that baseball signed by Mickey Mantle. By tracking the value of your assets in Quicken, you're on your way to figuring out how much you're really worth.

Quicken's asset, loan, and debt accounts have registers—just like checking accounts. As you can see in Figure 9-1, transactions you record reflect changes in asset value: paying off mortgage principal, depreciation, and home improvements.

Quicken has specialized asset accounts for houses and cars. If you have other items of value (like jewelry, artwork, and so on) that you'd like Quicken to include in your net worth, you can create asset accounts for them as well.

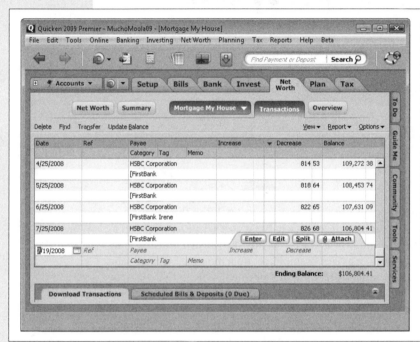

Figure 9-1:
An asset or liability account's register lists transactions that increase or decrease the balance in the account. For example, the principal that you pay off each month with your mortgage payment decreases the balance in your mortgage loan account (hallelujah!). If you finish renovating your basement, then you can add a transaction to your house asset account to reflect its increased value (page 263).

Tip: There's no need to create separate asset accounts for every last item you own, even if you want Quicken to track the value of your personal property. You can create a *single* asset account that includes your estimated value of things like furniture, clothes, tools, and so on.

- **Liabilities** represent money you owe, whether for an asset, like a house or car, or something less tangible but no less important, like your college education. In Quicken, you create loan or debt accounts for the money you borrow.

If you borrow money to buy a car, purchase your home, and pay for your child's college education, you create a *loan* account for each debt (whether or not it's secured by an asset that you own). New in Quicken 2009, *debt* accounts represent money you've borrowed but don't have to pay back on a regular schedule—like a loan from a generous relative. The payments you make reduce the balance on your debt. (When you create a debt account [page 256], Quicken asks if you want to create a loan for it. If the debt has a regular payment schedule, which is what a loan account is for, it's easier to create a loan account than a debt account.)

- **Loans.** When you borrow money, the loan is your legal commitment to pay that money back. If you've purchased a house, you already know the mountains of paperwork involved. One crucial item is the loan document, which describes the amount being borrowed (the *principal*), the interest rate, the length of the loan, the number of payments, and how much principal and interest you fork over with each payment.

  Most loans *amortize* your payoff: The monthly payment remains fixed, but the ratio of principal to interest changes. Early in the loan's life, your payments are mostly interest and very little principal—which is great for tax deductions. By the end, your payments go almost entirely toward paying off principal. Constantly changing allocations sound like a tracking nightmare, but Quicken easily handles amortized payments. It calculates your loan amortization schedule, assigns the principal and interest in each payment to the appropriate categories or accounts, and even handles escrow payments (the amounts that your mortgage company collects in advance to pay property taxes and property insurance premiums when they come due), so you can conserve your brain power for more interesting things.

- **Equity and net worth.** The *equity* you hold in an asset is the asset's value minus the balance you owe. For example, if your house is worth $200,000, and the balance on your mortgage is $125,000, you have $75,000 in equity in your home.

  Net worth is the big picture of equity—the value of all your assets minus the balance of all the money you owe. Net worth is a key measure of your financial health. Say you own houses, cars, boats, and other toys that are worth $4,000,000. But if you borrowed $3,950,000 to buy them, you're still a financial pauper with a net worth of only $50,000. On the other hand, a couple who have a house, car, and retirement fund with a combined value of $850,000, and a mortgage balance of only $25,000 are well on their way to millionaire status with a healthy net worth of $825,000.

  By linking loans in Quicken to the corresponding asset accounts (linking your mortgage with the asset account for your home, for example), you can see how much equity you have in each asset, as well as your net worth.

Setting up Asset and Liability Accounts

Quicken makes it easy to create asset and liability accounts. For example, if you create a vehicle asset account for the new car you bought with the help of a car loan, then the program asks if you want to set up a loan account to go with it. This section teaches you how to set up various kinds of asset accounts and loan accounts—whether or not the loans correspond to your assets.

Types of Asset and Liability Accounts

Quicken has three types of accounts for your assets, and two for liabilities:

- A **house** account can represent any type of real estate (house, condo, whatever), whether you have a mortgage or own it free and clear. When you create a house account, you specify the original purchase price and the current value. Quicken asks if you want to set up a mortgage to go with the house. As time passes, you can adjust the account's balance to reflect the house's increase in market value or improvements you make—like that commercial-quality kitchen with the six-burner stove and trash compactor.

- A **vehicle** account works much like a house account: You specify the car's original purchase price and an estimate of the current value. (You can tell Quicken the make, model, and year, if you want.) The program asks if you want to set up a corresponding loan for the vehicle; page 237 has the details. As time passes, you can adjust the vehicle account's balance (sadly, unlike houses, vehicles usually *decrease* in value).

- An **asset** account is the one to use for all other types of possessions—from the tchotchkes that clutter your house to your signed Ansel Adams photographs. As with house and vehicle accounts, Quicken asks if you want to set up a loan account to go along with your asset. You can adjust the asset account's balance to increase its value (for example, if your pristine Grateful Dead albums are suddenly worth a ton) or to decrease its value (if you drink the wine in your wine cellar without replenishing it).

Tip: If you convert a Quicken data file from a version of the program that didn't have house and car accounts (Quicken 2005 or earlier), you can convert an asset account to a house or car account, as the box on page 232 explains.

- A **loan** account represents money you borrow and then pay back on a set schedule, whether for a mortgage on a house, a car loan, or something else. Quicken wants to know a lot about loans so that it can calculate the amortization schedule accurately: when the loan starts, how long it lasts, the interest rate, how often you make loan payments, and so on.

- A **debt** account is for money you borrow without a fixed payment schedule, such as a personal loan from Aunt Marge. Because the payment schedule is flexible, you don't have to tell the program much: when and how much you borrowed will do.

Creating an Asset Account

You can create an asset account *without* a loan—for instance, to include the value of your wine collection in your net worth (assuming you didn't borrow money to buy the bottles). If you're flush enough to buy a valuable asset without borrowing

UP TO SPEED

When Loans Are Assets

Most of the time, the loans you create in Quicken represent liabilities—the money you owe a financial institution or an individual. But when you think about it, loans are actually two-way agreements. On one side, someone is *borrowing* money (and therefore creating a liability). Then there's the other side of the fence: the party that's *lending* the money. From the lender's point of view, the loan is an asset.

This dual definition doesn't bother Quicken at all. In fact, when you create a new loan, as described on page 237, the first thing the program asks is whether you're borrowing or lending money. If you're borrowing, then it creates a loan account. If you're lending (page 239), then it creates an asset account to show how much the other person owes you.

money, create an asset account for your purchase. Then, when you record the check you wrote and choose the asset account in the Category field, Quicken shows the amount you paid as the asset's value, as the box on page 238 explains.

Most of the time, though, you borrow money to buy assets valuable enough to track. In Quicken, it's easy to create a house, vehicle, or asset account and a corresponding loan account to track the loan.

You can create an asset account in Quicken in several ways. Choose whichever one you like best:

- **Net Worth menu.** This is the quickest route to a new asset account. Choose Net Worth → Net Worth Accounts. In the Account Setup wizard that appears, select the type of asset account you want to create.

- **Account Bar.** Click the Add Account button at the bottom of the Account Bar to open the Account Setup wizard. Select the Asset option and then select the option for the type of asset account.

- **Account List window.** If you intend to add several different types of accounts in one productive session, press Ctrl+A to open the Account List window. Then click the Add Account button at the bottom left of the Account List window to launch the Account Setup wizard. Because the Account List window includes every type of account you can create, this method gives you more account type options than you have when creating an asset account from the Net Worth menu.

- **File → New.** If you choose File → New, Quicken automatically selects the New Quicken File option, which creates a new *data* file. If you want to create an *account* instead, be sure to select the New Quicken Account option before you click OK.

Whatever way you start creating an account, you'll find detailed instructions on how to complete it in the following sections.

UP TO SPEED

Converting an Asset into a House or Vehicle

In older versions of Quicken (2005 and earlier), the program offered only asset accounts. Starting with Quicken 2006, you could set up accounts specifically for houses and vehicles, and the generic asset account is still around for anything else of value that you own.

Quicken can't magically transform your Beanie Baby collection directly into a house you can live in. But if you're a long-time Quicken user, you can convert a Quicken asset account that represents a house you own into a house account (or into a vehicle account if the asset is a car, motorcycle, boat, and so on). Here's how:

1. In the Account Bar, click the asset account you want to convert.

2. If the Overview tab for the account doesn't appear, click the Overview button below the Net Worth tab. On the right side of the screen in the Account Status section, Quicken asks if this asset is a house or a car, as shown in Figure 9-2.

3. To convert the asset account to a house account, click the word *house,* which is blue to indicate that it's a link. To convert the account to a vehicle account, click the word *car.*

4. When a message appears that warns you that you can't undo the conversion, click Yes to convert the account, or click No to leave the generic asset account as it is.

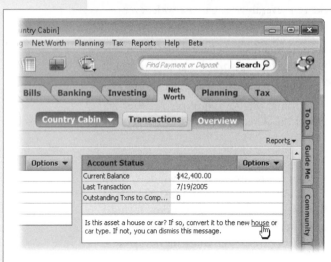

Figure 9-2:
When you position your cursor over the word house or car, the pointer changes to a pointing hand and the word gets underlined, to indicate that it's a link.

Creating a vehicle account

Here are the steps for creating a vehicle account:

1. **In the Account Bar, click the lower-right Add Account button.**

   The Account Setup wizard opens, letting you add any type of Quicken account. You can also open this dialog box by choosing Net Worth → Net Worth Accounts → Add Account, which gives you options for creating each type of asset and liability account.

2. Select the Asset option, and then select the Vehicle option.

   Options for the three types of asset accounts appear, as you can see in Figure 9-3. Select Vehicle and then click Next.

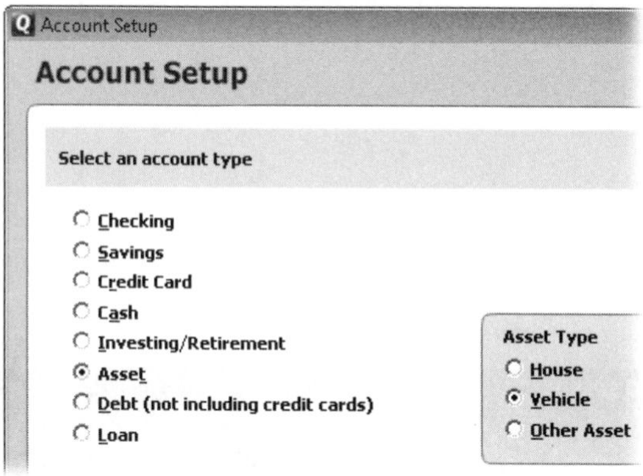

Figure 9-3:
Instead of adding an asset account first, you can also add one later by creating a loan and having Quicken generate the asset account that goes with it. The only downside to this approach is that the program doesn't let you specify the type of asset account—it creates a plain vanilla asset account, not a house or vehicle account.

3. In the Account Name/Nickname box, type a descriptive name for the account, and then click Next.

   Quicken fills in the Account Name/Nickname box with *Car* for a vehicle account. Change the name to something meaningful like *02 Forerunner*.

Note: If you turned on the setting to use more than one currency (page 490), the Currency box appears below the Account Name/Nickname box. The box is set to the home currency you chose for your data file (page 90). To use another currency, click the down arrow in the Currency box, and then choose the currency.

---

4. In the "Tell Quicken about the vehicle you'd like to track" screen (Figure 9-4), enter the date you bought the vehicle, its purchase price, and its current estimated value. Then click Next.

   If you don't have your purchase paperwork close at hand, fill in your best guesses; you can change the values later (page 261). See the box on page 234 for advice on estimating house, vehicle, and other asset values.

5. In the "Is there a loan on this vehicle?" screen, choose the option that matches your loan situation.

   You may think there are only two choices: yes or no. But in Quicken, you actually have *four* choices. The most common situation is when you have a loan but haven't yet created the loan account in Quicken. In this case, leave the Yes option selected, and then select the "I'd like to track this loan in Quicken. Set up a new account for this" option.

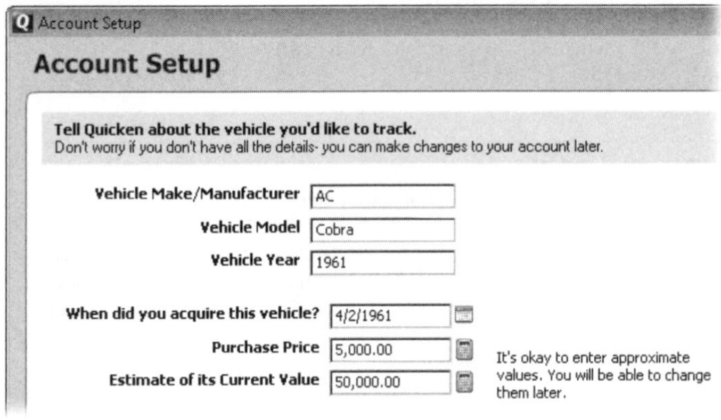

Figure 9-4:
The "Tell Quicken about the vehicle you'd like to track" screen includes text boxes where you can enter the make, model, and year of the vehicle, if you want.

Estimating Asset Values

If you think you paid a fair price for your house, the purchase price and your estimate of its current value may be identical. For hard bargainers who don't buy *anything* unless it's a good deal, the estimated value may be higher than the purchase price.

Vehicles are a different story. If you buy a new car, its value drops by 10 to 15 percent as soon as you drive it off the lot—that first tenth of a mile turns your new car into a used car. Used car dealers, of course, make their money by buying used cars for less and selling them for more. In fact, if you were to buy a used car from a dealer and try to sell it back the very next day, the price could drop by a few thousand dollars!

Other types of assets are even harder to estimate, because value is in the eye of the beholder. In fact, you might have to *pay* someone to haul away the magenta bathroom fixtures you paid extra for.

If you're having trouble coming up with an estimated value for an asset, try searching for similar items on the Internet before you shell out for a professional appraisal. Here are a few Web sites that can help estimate the value of your property:

- *http://www.zillow.com*, *http://www.propertyshark.com*, *http://www.cyberhomes.com*, or *http://www.tulia.com*. Enter an address on one of these Web sites to find out the estimated value for a house and others nearby.

- *http://www.edmunds.com* or *http://www.kbb.com*. Select the make, model, and year of your car along with your Zip code and the condition of the vehicle. Both sites then tell you how much it's worth if you sell it to a private individual or trade it in at a dealer. You can also use these Web sites to find the going price for a used car you want to buy.

- *http://www.eBay.com*. You can estimate the value of all sorts of items by watching auctions for similar items on eBay.

For a loan that already exists in your data file, choose the "I'm already tracking the loan in Quicken" option. In the Select Existing Account drop-down menu, choose the loan account. If you've been tracking the vehicle loan in Quicken, but never tracked the vehicle value, this is the option to choose.

You can make loan payments on a car without tracking the loan in Quicken, though you won't know how much is left to pay on the loan. You simply assign your payment transaction to a category like Car Payment. For this situation, select the "I do not want to track the loan in Quicken" option

If you bought the asset with cash or have already paid off the loan, choose the No option.

6. **Click Next.**

If you don't owe any money on the asset, or you already have a loan set up in Quicken, click Done to seal the deal. Quicken creates the asset account and, if the loan exists, links the asset and the loan.

If you told Quicken to create a loan account, the Loan Setup wizard shown in Figure 9-7 (page 240) opens. You don't get to click Done until you finish setting up the loan and loan payment. Jump to page 237 to learn how to set up a loan account.

Your new vehicle account appears in the Account Bar and other account lists in Quicken.

Creating a house account

Creating a house account is a lot like creating a vehicle account, except that the text boxes have different labels. Here are the steps for creating a house account:

1. **In the Account Bar, click Add Account. In the Account Setup wizard, select the Asset option, and then select the House option. Then click Next.**

   Quicken displays the "Enter the name you'd like to use for this account in Quicken" screen.

2. **In the Account Name/Nickname box, type a descriptive name for the account, and then click Next.**

   Quicken fills in the Account Name/Nickname box with *House*. Change the name to something meaningful like *900 5th Ave*.

   If you turned on the setting to use more than one currency (page 490), you'll see the Currency box, where you can specify the currency for this account; for example, if the house is a Jamaican waterfront bungalow.

3. **In the "Tell Quicken about the house you'd like to track" screen, enter the date you bought the house, its purchase price, and its current estimated value. Then click Next.**

   The fields on this screen are the same as the ones for a vehicle (Figure 9-4). (Quicken doesn't bother asking you about other details like the color of the house or the type of roof shingles.) See the box on page 234 for a list of Web sites that can help you estimate the value of your home.

4. **In the "Is there a mortgage on this house?" screen, choose the option that matches your mortgage situation.**

Much like it does for car loans, Quicken provides four choices for mortgages. To set up a mortgage account in Quicken, leave the Yes option selected, and then select the "I'd like to track this mortgage in Quicken. Set up a new account for this" option.

Because tracking a house and mortgage together in Quicken is so helpful, you won't choose the "I'm already tracking the mortgage in Quicken" option very often. But if you already have a loan account for your mortgage in Quicken, choose this option, and then, in the Select Existing Account drop-down menu, choose the loan account.

When you track a mortgage in Quicken, the program calculates the proportions of principal and interest in each payment, tells you how much you've paid, and shows how much more you have to pay. Moreover, Quicken can tell you how much tax-deductible interest you've paid and how much equity you have in your home. To forego all those benefits, select the "I do not want to track the mortgage in Quicken" option.

If you've paid off your mortgage (you lucky person, you), choose the No option.

5. **Click Next.**

If you don't owe any money on the house, or you already have a loan set up in Quicken, click Done to close the Account Setup wizard. Quicken creates the house account and, if the loan exists, links the house account and the loan.

If you told Quicken to create a loan account, the Loan Setup wizard shown in Figure 9-7 (page 240) opens. Jump to page 237 to learn how to set up a loan account. When you finish setting up the loan and loan payment, you're ready to click Done in the Account Setup wizard.

Your new house account appears in the Account Bar and other account lists in Quicken.

Creating a generic asset account

Creating a plain ol' asset account is simpler than setting up vehicle or house accounts, but the process is similar. Here are the steps:

1. **In the Account Bar, click Add Account. In the Account Setup wizard, select the Asset option, and then choose Other Asset. Then click Next.**

A screen appears that asks you to name the account.

2. **In the Account Name/Nickname box, type a descriptive name for the account, and then click Next.**

Quicken fills in the Account Name/Nickname box with *Asset*. Change the name to something meaningful like *Wine Cellar*.

3. In the "Enter the ending date from your latest statement (or the date you want to start tracking this asset)" screen (Figure 9-5), enter the date to start tracking the asset and its current estimated value. Then click Next.

   Quicken fills in today's date, which is perfect if you simply want to start tracking the asset now. If you want to document several purchases, such as additions to your wine cellar, choose the earliest date you want, the date of your last full inventory, say. In the Asset Value box, type the estimated value.

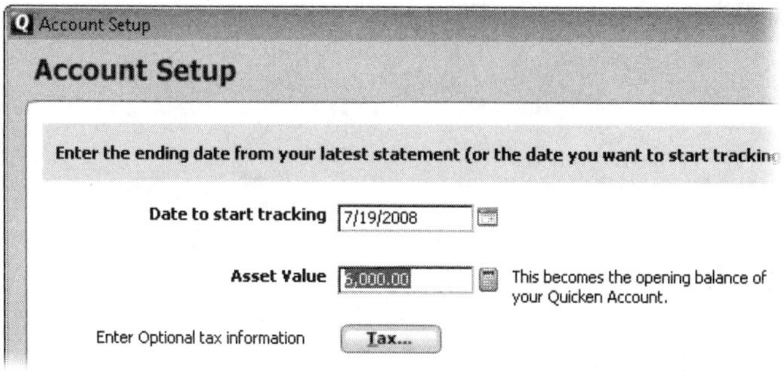

Figure 9-5:
If the asset has tax advantages or consequences, you can choose tax schedules for transfers in or out of an asset account by clicking the Tax button. See page 272 to learn how to assign tax schedules to transfers.

4. In the "Is there a loan on this asset?" screen, choose the option that matches your loan situation.

   See step 5 on page 233 to learn about your options.

5. Click Next.

   If you don't owe any money on the asset, or you already have a loan set up in Quicken, you're done. Click Done to close the dialog box.

   If you told Quicken to create a loan account, the Loan Setup wizard shown in Figure 9-7 opens. The next section tells you how to set up a loan.

   Your new asset account appears in the Account Bar and other account lists in Quicken.

Setting Up Loan Accounts

In Quicken 2009, a loan account (called a *liability account* in earlier versions of the program) is all you need to track any kind of loan. Quicken needs quite a bit of information about a loan to correctly calculate its *amortization schedule* (the allocation of principal and interest in each payment), but it's worth feeding Quicken all this info because the program can then report the interest you've paid come tax time, how much principal you've paid back, and the balance you've got left to go. Setting up a loan in Quicken requires lots of steps, but fear not: Each step is easy and the process is surprisingly quick.

Buying Without Borrowing

If you write a check or use a credit card to pay for a lawn tractor or diamond anniversary ring, create the asset account *before* you record the transaction in your Quicken checking or credit card account. That way, when you record your check or charge, you can transfer the amount you paid into the asset account as the initial value of the asset. If you already have an asset account (for your jewelry, say), start at step 3. Here are the basic steps:

1. Create the asset account, and then, in the "As of Date" box, enter the date that you bought the item.

2. Leave the Value box set to 0.00, and then click Done.

3. Open your checking account or credit card register (depending on how you paid for the item).

4. Record the check or credit card charge for your purchase by filling in the date, payee, and amount as you would for a regular purchase.

5. In the Category box, click the down arrow, and then, from the drop-down menu, choose the new asset account. (If you don't see the account in the menu, then on the left side of the menu, select Transfers to display only your Quicken accounts.) If your purchase includes sales tax, you can split the transaction between the asset account and a sales tax category, as shown in Figure 9-6.

6. Press Enter or click the Enter button to record the transaction.

Quicken deducts the payment from the balance in your checking account (or adds the credit card charge to your credit card balance), and the purchase value shows up as the balance in the asset account. Pretty spiffy, huh?

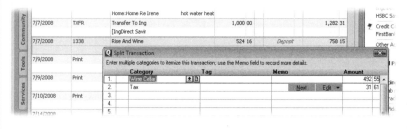

Figure 9-6:
In the transaction row, click the Split button to open the Split Transaction dialog box (top). Enter one split to transfer the value of the item to the asset account, and a second split for the sales tax category. The check or charge transaction shows the full amount you paid, but the value in the asset account equals the purchase price of the item minus any tax you paid (bottom).

Before you begin, gather up all your loan documents. Quicken wants plenty of details, as you'll soon see. If you create an account to track a house, vehicle, or other major asset, the easiest way to set up the corresponding loan account is to let Quicken walk you through these steps as soon as you're done setting up the asset account. However, you can set up a loan account without an associated asset account. Say, for example, you want to use Quicken to track the student loan you took out to finance your college education. Or, if you're rolling in dough, you may want to track the money you lend to other people. The Setup Loan wizard is your one-stop-shop for setting up any kind of loan.

Note: If you have a loan that corresponds to an asset you purchased, create the asset account first. That way, you can tell Quicken to create a loan account while you set up the asset (for a vehicle, create the loan starting with step 5 on page 233; for a house, start with step 4 on page 236; and for an asset, start with step 4 on page 237). Then, when you click Next in the Account Setup wizard, the Loan Setup wizard appears. Now you can jump to step 2 of the following list to create the loan.

Here's how you create a loan account:

1. **In the Account Bar, click Add Account. In the Account Setup wizard that appears, select the Loan option, and then click Next.**

   When you launch the Loan Setup wizard this way, the only kind of account you can associate with the loan is an Asset account. So if you want to set up a loan for a house or car, it's easiest to create a house or vehicle asset account (page 235 or page 232, respectively) and then, when Quicken opens the Loan Setup wizard, choose the house or vehicle account you just created. You can also convert the asset account to a house account or vehicle account later, as explained in the box on page 232. The other solution is to set up the loan without a corresponding asset account and then link it to a house or vehicle account (page 249).

Tip: You can also launch the Loan Setup wizard by clicking the Setup tab and then clicking the Overview button. Scroll down to the "Property and Debt" section, and then click the Add Loan button.

---

2. **In the Loan Setup wizard, click the Summary tab.**

   The Loan Setup wizard launches with the EasyStep tab selected. Save yourself some time and click the Summary tab (Figure 9-7), which lets you answer several questions at a time (as opposed to EasyStep's one-question-per-screen format).

3. **In the Loan Type section, indicate whether you're borrowing or lending money.**

   The choice you make determines whether the loan is a liability or an asset *for you* (remember that the person on the other end of the loan views it the opposite way—every loan is an asset for one party and a liability for the other party).

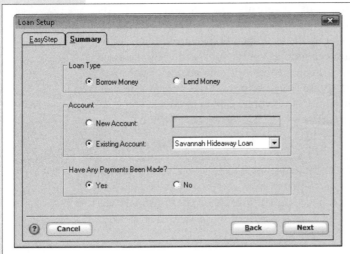

Figure 9-7:
The Summary tab in the Loan Setup dialog box is the fastest way to give Quicken all the info it needs about your loan. If you've just created an asset account (Savannah Hideaway, in this example) and then told Quicken to create a loan account to go with it, the program creates the loan account, selects the Existing Account option, and fills in the Existing Account box with the new loan account name (Savannah Hideaway Loan).

If you select the Borrow Money option, Quicken creates a *loan* account, because you have an obligation to repay the balance. If you select the Lend Money option, Quicken sets up an *asset* account because the money you lend is still your money, plus you'll receive interest from the borrower.

4. **In the Account section, specify the loan account you want to use.**

   If the Loan Setup wizard opened because you asked Quicken to set up a loan to go with a new asset you created, the program creates the loan account and names it by appending the word *Loan* to the end of the asset account's name. For example, if you create a house account called *Savannah Hideaway*, Quicken names the loan account *Savannah Hideaway Loan*. Quicken selects the Existing Account option and fills in the Existing Account box with the new loan account's name.

   On the other hand, when you launch the wizard on its own, it selects the New Account option. To create a new account, type a name for it in the New Account text box. If the loan account exists, select the Existing Account option, and choose the account in the Existing Account drop-down list (for example, if you created a debt account and want to link a loan to it).

   Adding *Loan* or *Mortgage* to the account name helps differentiate your loan account from the associated asset account. For example, if your car's asset account is named *02 Forerunner*, name the loan account *02 Forerunner Loan* (letters, numbers, and punctuation are all fair game).

5. **In the "Have Any Payments Been Made?" section, select Yes or No, and then click Next.**

   If you choose Yes, you'll have a chance to tell the wizard how much you've paid off before you're done (in step 12).

When you click Next, the summary screen displays a new batch of fields Quicken needs you to fill in (Figure 9-8).

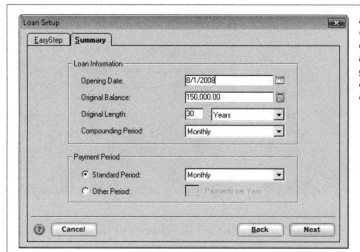

Figure 9-8:
Quicken automatically sets the loan's opening date to whenever it thinks you bought the asset—but the program often guesses wrong. Your loan documents have all the info you need to fill in the boxes shown here.

6. **In the Opening Date box, choose the date when you took out the loan.**

   If you're creating a loan to go with an asset, Quicken automatically fills in the date you said you acquired the asset. Otherwise, it fills in the current date. But don't assume that either of these choices is correct. Choosing the correct date is key, because the program uses the opening date to calculate accrued interest. (You can ask the lender for the date that interest began to accrue, but if you have a hard time getting that info, read the box on page 242 for tips on figuring out the correct date.)

7. **In the Original Balance box, type the amount you borrowed when you opened the loan.**

   If you're creating a loan in Quicken for a real-world loan you've had for a while, be sure to enter the original amount you borrowed. Later, you'll have a chance to tell Quicken the current balance. For loans associated with an asset, Quicken fills in the Opening Balance box with the purchase price. If you made a down payment on the asset, change the Opening Balance value to the original balance of the loan.

8. **In the Original Length boxes, enter the loan's duration—for instance, *4* and *years.***

   Most car loans last 4 years, though some run 5 years. Mortgages come in many different lengths, from 3 years or more for balloon mortgages (described in step 11) to 15, 20, and 30 years. Quicken doesn't care if you define the loan's length in years, months, or even weeks—as long as you specify the correct number of time periods. For example, though you know the duration of a 30-year mortgage in years, you could also tell Quicken that the mortgage length is 360 months, to match the number of payments you'll make.

Finding a Loan's Opening Date

How do I find the opening date for my loan?

Many mortgages and loans are set up so that each check you write pays off the interest accrued in the previous month (or whatever your payment period is). You might sign loan papers on December 10, 2008, that show your first payment isn't due until February 1, 2009. Somewhere in between those two dates is the loan's opening date—but which one is it?

To keep things simple, most lenders set up loans and mortgages so the opening date is one payment period prior to your first payment. For example, if you pay monthly and your first payment is due February 1, the opening date for the loan is most likely January 1. For a mortgage, you can confirm this date by checking the Uniform Settlement Statement (one of the many pieces of paper you got when you took out the loan). Line 901 represents the interest you have to pay up front; this interest is what accrues between the time you sign the papers and the loan's opening date. So if line 901 shows interest from December 10 through January 1, you can be sure that January 1 is your loan's opening date.

If you have a balloon mortgage, set the Original Length boxes to whenever the mortgage comes due. For example, enter *7* and select *years* for a 7-year balloon mortgage.

9. **In the Compounding Period box, choose the unit of time the financial institution uses to calculate compounding interest.**

Quicken automatically chooses Monthly because that's the most common compounding period. Check with your lender to be sure. Daily racks up the most interest because the bank compounds interest on what you owe every day. Semi-Annually means you pay less interest because the bank calculates compounded interest only twice a year.

10. **In the Payment Period section, choose the Standard Period option, and then choose from the drop-down menu. Then click Next to continue.**

Quicken's standard payment periods cover most periods that lenders use—from Weekly and Bi-Weekly up to Annually, with lots of others in between. If you've borrowed money from your eccentric cousin who goes by the Mayan calendar and you have an unusual payment schedule, you can choose the Other Period option, and then, in the "Payments per Year" box, type the number of payments you make in a year.

11. **If the loan includes a *balloon payment*—the loan industry's name for a whopper of a payment that pays off the loan balance after only a few years—in the Balloon Information section (shown in figure Figure 9-9), tell Quicken about its characteristics.**

Balloon loans amortize the loan over a period of time—30 years for a mortgage, for example—but don't actually last that long. Instead, you have to pay off the balance in full before then, often after 5 or 7 years. Balloon loans are great if you know that your company will relocate you in a few years or you want a short-term mortgage to hold you over until interest rates come down. If you aren't planning to move, a balloon loan means you have the hassle of refinancing when the loan comes due.

Quicken selects the No Balloon Payment option automatically. If your loan includes a balloon payment, select the Amortized Length option and fill in the boxes for the number and length of the periods. For example, if a 7-year balloon loan is amortized over 30 years, in the number text box, type *30*, and in the period drop-down menu, choose *Years*.

12. **If you've already made payments on the loan, the Current Balance section appears below the Balloon Information section. Enter the amount you currently owe, and the date when that balance applies.**

You can easily find your current balance by looking at your last loan statement. Look for an entry called something like Current Balance or Current Principal Balance. Fill in the Current Balance box with that value, and then fill in the "as of" box with the date of your most recent payment.

13. **In the Payment section, select the "Payment Amount (P+I)" option, and then type the amount of your payment and the next due date, as shown in Figure 9-9.**

Your loan documents show the payment amount including principal and interest (aka P+I). For a mortgage, be sure to include only the principal and interest—not other amounts, like escrow payments or private mortgage insurance premiums. You add those amounts when you set up your loan payments (page 245).

For a new loan, in the "due on" text box, choose the date when your first payment is due. For a loan that you've *already* made payments on, choose the date your *next* payment is due.

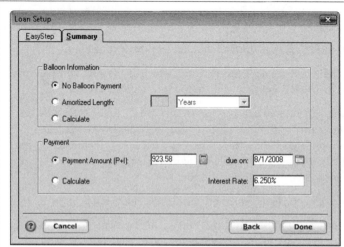

Figure 9-9:
Quicken can calculate your payment for you, if you select the Calculate option and then, in the box on the bottom right, provide the interest rate for your loan. But if you make a mistake when setting up the loan, Quicken calculates the wrong payment amount, which can cause big problems. Because your loan documents include the payment the lender expects, you're better off just entering that value in the "Payment Amount (P+I)" field.

Note: Loans come in all shapes and sizes, such as interest-only loans, negative amortization loans, and loans you make to others. The box below explains how to handle special loan cases like these.

Setting Up Special Loan Terms

Although some loans sound complicated or scary (like negative amortization loans), you can still set them up with the Loan Setup wizard. Quicken can even help you track loans you've made to other people. It's simply a matter of knowing how to tell Quicken about the special terms of your loan.

A *negative amortization loan* means that your payment doesn't cover the principal and interest you owe, so you actually owe *more* rather than less as time passes. (If that sounds like a bad deal, you're absolutely right. Instead, buy a house at a price that you can afford.) To set up a loan with negative amortization, fill in the boxes as you would for a regular loan, including the loan's interest rate. In the "Payment Amount (P+I)" box, type the payment you make. Because this payment doesn't cover the interest on the loan, the payment schedule (page 250) shows your loan balance increase at the end of the payment period.

With a negative amortization loan, you eventually (often after 5 years) have to make higher payments to pay back the principal and the additional interest you accrued. When your payment changes, you can enter the new amount in the Loan Rate Changes window (page 259).

Interest-only loans start with payments that cover only the interest on the borrowed amount, so the balance on the loan remains the same. Like negative amortization loans, this deal lasts only so long and then you have to start paying the principal and interest. Set up an interest-only loan as you would a regular loan. In the "Payment Amount (P+I)" box, type the payment you make. When your payment increases to start paying off principal, you can enter the new amount in the Loan Rate Changes window (page 259).

If you loan someone money and receive loan payments from them, Quicken can calculate the loan amortization for you. The key is to select the Lend Money option during loan setup (see step 3 on page 239). Quicken creates an asset account for the money you lent. Then, when you set up the loan payment, Quicken automatically sets the payment type to deposit (because you're receiving money), the payee name to the borrower's name, and the Category for Interest to an income category. Quicken schedules a loan deposit transaction for the payments you receive. The balance in the asset account shows how much the borrower still owes you.

---

14. **In the Interest Rate box, type the annual interest rate of your loan.**

    Banks usually advertise a loan's annual rate, which is the rate you pay on the amount you borrowed. Enter this value in the Interest Rate box.

    To find out the *real* rate you're paying—often called the *effective rate*, or the *annual percentage rate* (APR), check out your loan disclosure agreement. The APR is always a bit higher than the annual rate because it includes origination fees and points you pay up front to get the mortgage, prepaid mortgage interest, mortgage insurance premiums, and other fees.

15. **Once you've got all your loan information entered, click Done.**

    The Loan Setup wizard closes, and the Edit Loan Payment dialog box opens. This box is where you set up and schedule your loan payments. Scheduled loan payments are one of the best things about Quicken; the next section explains how to take advantage of this helpful feature.

Receiving a Check from a Lender

When you buy a house, the mortgage lender doesn't write you a check for hundreds of thousands of dollars to hand over to the seller. Instead, the title agent or attorney orchestrating the transaction makes sure the money gets where it needs to go.

For some smaller loans, on the other hand, the lender may actually write you a check to deposit in your checking account. Then you write your own check to pay for the car or other purchase. Here's how to handle this kind of transaction in Quicken:

1. Create the loan as you would normally, setting its opening balance to the amount you borrowed (page 237).

2. When you create the asset account, set the asset value to 0.

3. Link the loan and the asset account, as described on page 249.

4. In the loan's account register, select the transaction that has the words Opening Balance in the Description field. In the Category field, you see the name of the loan account, like *02 Forerunner Loan*.

5. In the Category field, choose your checking account (in Figure 9-10, top, it's FirstBank Checking). When you do this, Quicken transfers the money you've borrowed into your checking account. (In the real world, you have to deposit the check you received from the lender into your checking account.)

6. Write a check for your purchase, and then record it in your Quicken checking account (Figure 9-10, bottom). In the category field, select the asset account (in the figure, it's Toyota). When you do this, Quicken makes the value of the asset you bought equal to the amount of the check.

Voilà! The money shows up in all the right accounts.

Setting Up a Loan Payment

Unless you borrow money from a good, rich friend, chances are that you'll get slapped with a hefty late fee if you don't make payments on time. Lucky for you, you've got Quicken, which is great at keeping you on track. In just a few steps, you can create a scheduled transaction for your loan payments. Then, Quicken can remind you to make your payment on time or even process the payment automatically with a repeating online payment (see Chapter 6). Either way, Quicken is great at helping you stay on top of your payments and avoid those painful late fees. This section walks you through everything you need to do.

As soon as you finish setting up a loan in Quicken, the program opens the Edit Loan Payment dialog box (Figure 9-11). Quicken fills in a few of the boxes in the Payment section with information from your loan:

- The **Current Interest Rate** box shows the interest rate you specified for the loan in step 14 on page 244.

- The **"Principal and Interest"** box has the value you provided in the "Payment Amount (P+I)" text box in step 13 on page 243.

- The **Next Payment Date** box contains the next payment date you set for the loan in step 13 on page 243.

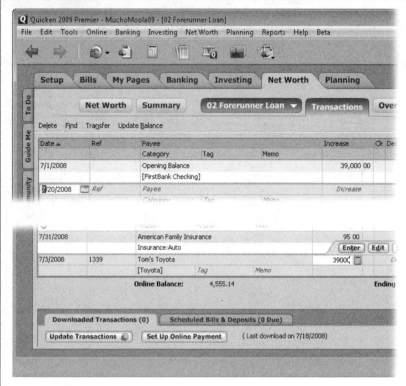

Figure 9-10:
You can modify a loan's Opening Balance to transfer the money you've borrowed into your checking account. Then, when you write a check for your purchase, select the asset account in the category field, which sets the value of the asset you bought equal to the amount of the check.

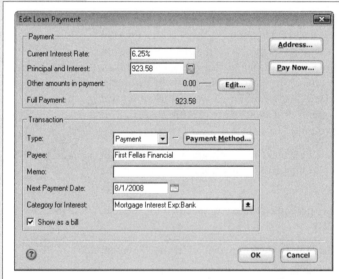

Figure 9-11:
Quicken automatically fills in the Current Interest Rate, "Principal and Interest", and Next Payment Date boxes with values you provided while setting up the loan. You can add other amounts (such as escrow) to your payment, tell Quicken about the loan payment, and decide which category to use to track interest. For example, interest you pay on a mortgage for the home you live in is tax deductible; interest you pay on a car loan isn't.

Tip: Compare the values in these three text boxes with the values from your loan document (for a new loan) or your last statement (for an existing loan). If the numbers don't jibe, the amortization that Quicken calculates will be off as well. If the loan values are amiss, click Cancel to skip the loan payment setup for now. Edit the loan to correct the discrepancies (page 257), and then set up your loan payment, as described on page 251.

To complete the loan payment setup, you have to tell Quicken whom to pay, and what payment method to use. Also, if your payment includes more than principal and interest—like property tax or homeowners' insurance escrow, for instance—you can add those items here, too.

Here's how to reap the benefits of a scheduled loan payment:

1. **If the Edit Loan Payment dialog box isn't open, press Ctrl+H to open the View Loans window. In the window's menu bar, click Choose Loan, and then, in the drop-down menu, pick the loan you want to modify. Then click Edit Payment.**

   The Edit Loan Payment dialog box opens.

2. **If your loan payment includes more than principal and interest, click the Edit button to the right of the "Other amounts in payment" label.**

   Quicken opens the Split Transaction dialog box (Figure 9-12), which you first saw in Chapter 7. Mortgage payments usually have additional amounts, like escrow payments for property taxes and homeowners' insurance (see the box on page 250), or premiums for private mortgage insurance. For each additional amount in the payment, choose a category, and then type the amount. When you've added all the extra amounts, click OK to add the total to the "Other amounts in payment" line.

3. **If you want to print loan payment checks or make payments electronically, in the Type drop-down menu, choose Print Check or Online Pmt, respectively.**

   Quicken automatically chooses Payment in the Type field, which sets your loan payment up as a scheduled transaction (page 186). If you create this kind of transaction, then the program reminds you a few days before your payment is due, so you can make sure you have enough money in your account to cover the payment and remember to *make* the payment, too.

   Online Pmt appears on the drop-down menu only if you have a bank account set up for online bill payments. This option sets the payment to transmit electronically.

4. **If you want to check the settings for your payment, click the Payment Method button. In the Select Payment Method dialog box that appears, specify the details for the payment method.**

   Quicken automatically selects the "Scheduled bill" option, which sets up a reminder for the payment. If you use online bill payment, you can select "Repeating online payment" for an automatic payment. You can also choose the account to use, and how many days in advance to process the payment.

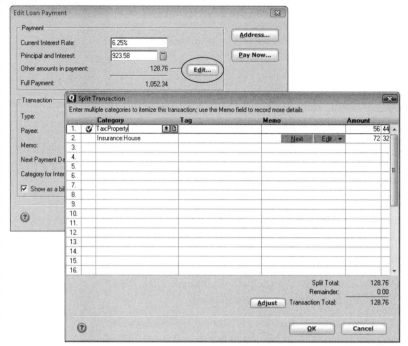

Figure 9-12:
When you click Edit (top, circled), the Split Transaction dialog box (bottom) opens. In the dialog box, enter each separate escrow or additional amount. When you click OK, Quicken adds the total from the Split Transaction dialog box to the principal and interest payment to calculate the total payment you make.

Note: If you want your online bill pay service to send the payments without *any* action on your part, you need to set up a repeating online payment. Set up your payment with Payment as the payment method for now. Next, set up a repeating online payment to your mortgage company for the full amount of your mortgage payment. Page 153 takes you through all the steps.

5. **In the Payee text box, type the name of the lender.**

   If you're printing your loan payment checks, click the Address button, and then enter the payee's mailing address (page 100).

6. **If Quicken hasn't picked the right category for your loan interest, in the "Category for Interest" drop-down menu, choose the correct category.**

   For mortgage interest, which is tax deductible, choose a category like Quicken's built-in Mortgage Interest Exp:Bank to assign the interest to the correct tax form and line. For interest on other loans, choose a category like the built-in Interest Exp category, which doesn't link to a tax form.

7. **Click OK.**

   Quicken adds your loan payment to the Scheduled Bills & Deposits list, as you can see in Figure 9-13.

If you set up a loan to go with an asset you created, the Account Setup wizard is still open, waiting for you to click Done to complete the asset account setup.

If you set up a loan on its own, Quicken asks if you want to create an asset account to go along with this loan. For houses and vehicles, you've probably already set up the asset account in Quicken, as explained on pages 232–236, in which case, click No to complete the payment setup. Click No for loans that pay for things that *aren't* assets, like school loans or debt consolidation loans.

If you need to create the corresponding asset account, click Yes. The program opens the Account Setup wizard for an asset account. Follow the steps on page 230 to create the account.

When you're done, you can check out your payment schedule, as described in the box on page 250.

Figure 9-13:
If you want to change your scheduled loan payment (so that you get reminders sooner or to change it to an online payment, for example), press Ctrl+J to open the Scheduled Bills & Deposits window. On the All Bills & Deposits tab, select the loan payment you want to edit, and then, in the window's menu bar, click Edit. The Edit Loan Payment dialog box opens, where you can change the payment method, the account you use, or the reminder schedule.

Linking an Asset and a Loan

Most big-ticket items like cars and houses need to be linked to the loans that helped pay for them. For example, if you buy a house by taking out a mortgage, linking the asset (the house) and the loan (the mortgage) means that Quicken can tell you how much equity you have in your home. And if you take out a *second* mortgage on your house, you also need to link this second loan to the same house asset account to keep track of your home equity. With Quicken, linking assets and loans is a snap.

Tracking Escrow Amounts

With Quicken, you can make escrow tracking amazingly simple. (Escrow payments are extra monthly amounts you pay for things like property taxes and homeowners' insurance.) The easiest way is to create a single Quicken category for it (see page 74) called something catchy like *Escrow* or *Other Property Costs*. Then, when you click the "Other amounts in payment" line's Edit button (see step 2 on page 247), enter a split under this category for the total escrow amount in each payment. Quicken then adds this amount to the Principal and Interest value to calculate your Full Payment amount (see Figure 9-12). With this method, Quicken doesn't know how much you pay for different escrow items, but that's not a problem, since your lender summarizes those expenses for tax reporting at the end of the year.

You can also easily handle escrow by calculating the average amounts for each item, and then creating a split for each one. For example, if your escrow payment is based on property taxes of $3,600 a year and an annual homeowners'

insurance premium of $900, you can enter a $300 split for property taxes and a $75 split for insurance. Although your monthly numbers aren't necessarily accurate, the totals at the end of the year should be.

Finally, if you're a stickler for accuracy (or like to do things the hard way), you can create an asset account for the escrow you pay, and then choose this escrow account for the split that represents your escrow in the payment. (It's an asset account because the money is still yours until it's time to pay the insurance, property taxes, or other items.) When you make a loan payment in Quicken, the split transfers the escrow amount to your escrow asset account. If you go this route, you'll have to keep an eye on your loan statements: When your lender pays property taxes or insurance premiums, you record the corresponding payment transactions in your escrow asset account. Later on, when you close the loan, the balance in the escrow account shows the escrow refund you should receive from the mortgage company.

Note: Assets that you own free and clear (like that yacht you bought after you won the lottery) don't have corresponding loans. Similarly, loans that pay for intangible items (like your college education) don't have corresponding assets. In either case, you don't need to do any asset-loan linking.

Viewing Payment Schedules and Graphs

The View Loans window has a lot of useful information, organized into three tabs. The Loan Summary tab shows the loan's vital statistics: starting date, original amount, payment amount, interest rate, length, payment frequency, current balance, remaining payments, and—the sign that there's an end in sight—the final payment date. The other two tabs tend to sit lonely and unclicked most of the time, but they come in handy if you're thinking about big loan changes, like refinancing or paying off early.

When you click the Payment Schedule tab, you see a full amortization schedule for your loan: the principal and interest

allocation for each payment and the remaining balance after each payment.

The Payment Graph tab (Figure 9-14) shows that amortized loan payments begin by paying mostly interest and very little principal, but near the end, the payment involves very little interest and lots of principal. One reason to consult this graph is to see whether it makes sense to pay off a loan. If you've already paid most of the price of borrowing the money (the interest), you may as well use the lender's money for the life of the loan.

Current balance

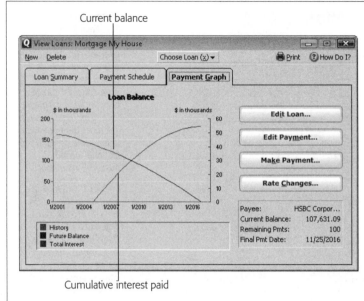

Figure 9-14:
The Payment Graph tab shows you how much principal you owe and how much you've paid in interest. If you've paid most of the interest for the loan, (the curve showing cumulative interest has flattened out) paying the balance off won't save you much.

Cumulative interest paid

Here are the steps for linking a loan to an asset:

1. **In the Account Bar, choose the loan account you want to link to an asset (for example, choose the second mortgage you want to link to your house). Then, above the loan account's register, click Overview.**

   The Overview page shows basic account attributes, like the current loan balance and equity.

2. **Below the Account Attributes section, click Edit Account Details.**

   The Account Details dialog box opens. Here you can add or edit account details, like the asset account to which this loan account is linked, as shown in Figure 9-15.

3. **In the Linked Asset Account drop-down menu, choose the asset account you want to link the loan to, and then click OK.**

   The Linked Asset Account drop-down menu lists all the asset accounts in your data file.

That's it! The loan is linked to the asset.

Making a Loan Payment

If you dutifully performed each step on pages 239–244 when you set up your loan, you should already have a scheduled loan payment in place. If you do, you can clean house, play cards, or carve voodoo dolls until Quicken reminds you it's time to make a loan payment. Then you pay your loan just as you would any other

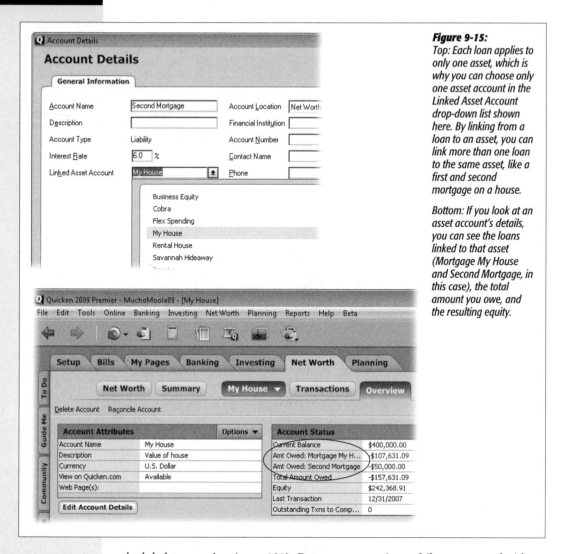

Figure 9-15:
Top: Each loan applies to only one asset, which is why you can choose only one asset account in the Linked Asset Account drop-down list shown here. By linking from a loan to an asset, you can link more than one loan to the same asset, like a first and second mortgage on a house.

Bottom: If you look at an asset account's details, you can see the loans linked to that asset (Mortgage My House and Second Mortgage, in this case), the total amount you owe, and the resulting equity.

scheduled transaction (page 191). But, every once in a while, you may decide to make an extra payment or pay your mortgage a little early. This section describes how to make loan payments, whether you're making a regularly scheduled payment, paying on a different date than usual, or making an extra payment.

Quicken splits loan payment transactions into principal, interest, and other payments. Here are the program's ground rules for loan payment splits:

- **Interest.** Quicken assigns interest payments to categories dedicated to interest expense; you select the category you want to use, as explained on page 248. For example, there's a built-in category called Mortgage Interest Exp:Bank that's associated with IRS Schedule A.

- **Principal.** Quicken assigns the principal you pay to the loan account, which reduces the balance you owe on the loan.

- **Other amounts.** Other payment amounts go to splits assigned to the categories you chose when you set up the loan payment, like property taxes and property insurance. See the box on page 250 to learn about setting up these other amounts.

Note: Loan payments don't have any effect on the value of the linked asset account, if one exists. The balance of an asset account simply indicates the current value of the asset—and making a loan payment doesn't change that.

Making a Regular Payment

If you set up a loan payment as a scheduled transaction, it's hard to miss the reminders that Quicken gives you. Whenever you launch the program, a message box tells you about any scheduled transactions that are due. On the Banking Center Summary screen, your scheduled payments show up in the Cash Flow Alerts list. And, if you somehow miss these notices and forget to make a payment, when you view the register for the account that you use to pay your loan, the Scheduled Bills & Deposits tab at the bottom of the window shows overdue payments in red text with the word *Overdue!* in the Status column.

To keep Quicken happy, take its advice and make loan payments before they're overdue. Here's how:

1. **Press Ctrl+J at any time to open the Scheduled Bills & Deposits window.**

   Your scheduled payments appear on the Monthly Bills & Deposits tab. Click the All Bills & Deposits tab to see all your scheduled transactions.

2. **In the row for the payment you want to make, click the Enter button.**

   The Enter Transaction dialog box appears.

3. **If you want to make the payment early, in the Date box, choose the new date for the payment.**

   Quicken automatically fills in the Date box with the date as defined by the schedule you set up, but you can make the payment earlier or later. You may want to make a loan payment early, perhaps to squeeze an extra mortgage payment into the tax year to increase your deductions. If you're postponing a payment, be sure to check the grace period that your lender allows, unless you don't mind handing over your first-born puppy in addition to the principal and interest.

4. **To record the payment, click Enter Transaction.**

   Unless you're using an online payment, don't forget to write or print the check (page 95) and mail it to the lender.

Downloading Scheduled Transactions

Downloading transactions can save you lots of time—as long as you remember what you need to do to keep your Quicken register in sync with your bank's records. If you download transactions from your bank (page 133), make sure to record the scheduled transactions for your loans in your Quicken register *before* you download them. The scheduled transaction includes the correct allocations to principal, interest, and other amounts. When you download the transaction, Quicken simply matches it with your register transaction, so the cleared transaction has all your payment splits in place.

If you download a loan payment that you haven't recorded in your Quicken register, then Quicken creates the transaction in the register—no splits, no link to your loan, no reduction in loan balance. Though it's possible to clean this mess up (as you'll see in a moment), you're better off preventing the problem in the first place by making sure you record scheduled transactions before you download them.

If you're unlucky enough to have a mess to clean up (that is, a cleared loan payment transaction in the register with no loan information associated with it), here's how to replace it with a well-mannered loan payment:

1. In the checking account register, select the downloaded (and cleared) payment, and then press Ctrl+D to delete it.

2. Record your scheduled loan payment (page 253).

3. Right-click the scheduled loan payment you just recorded, and then, on the shortcut menu that appears, choose Reconcile → Cleared.

You've just replaced the downloaded and cleared transaction with your scheduled transaction that's marked as cleared, so you won't run into any problems when you reconcile your account (page 215).

Making an Extra Payment

If you decide to make an *extra* loan payment—to use a holiday bonus to pay off additional principal, for instance—the View Loans window is the place to go. Here's the drill:

1. **Open the View Loans window by pressing Ctrl+H (or by choosing Net Worth → Loans).**

   The window's title includes the name of the loan that's selected. If the loan you want to pay isn't visible, in the window's menu bar, click Choose Loan, and then, in the drop-down menu, select the loan you want. The Loan Summary tab displays the basic values for the loan.

2. **Click Make Payment.**

   The Loan Payment message box appears, asking if you want to make a regular or extra payment.

3. **Click Extra.**

   Quicken opens the Make Extra Payment dialog box. Because the payment isn't part of the loan payment schedule, you can pay any amount you want, so Quicken leaves the Amount text box blank. Fill in or edit the boxes to fit the payment you're making, as shown in Figure 9-16.

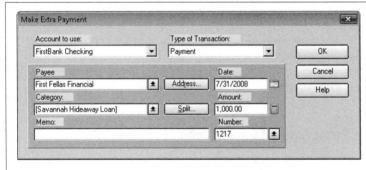

Figure 9-16:
For an extra payment, you have to tell Quicken how much you want to pay, and when you want to pay it. The program automatically chooses the loan account in the Category box so that the payment pays off loan principal. Change the category to something more appropriate if you're making an extra payment to satisfy the loan company's escrow minimum, for example.

4. **In the Date text box, choose the date that you plan to make the payment.**

   Quicken automatically sets the date to today, but you can choose something else.

5. **If you're paying toward something other than principal, choose it in the Category box.**

   Most of the time, extra payments pay off principal (a smart thing to do because it reduces the length of your loan and the total interest you pay). Quicken automatically sets the Category text box to the loan account, which transfers the payment amount into the account, thus reducing the outstanding balance. But you can change the category to Escrow, for example, if the extra payment is to satisfy your lender's minimum escrow balance.

6. **In the Amount text box, type the payment amount.**

   If you're making an extra payment to reduce your principal, you get to choose the payment amount. If your lender is asking for more money to make up for a shortfall in escrow, type that amount.

7. **In the Number drop-down menu, choose how you plan to pay, just like a regular transaction in an account register (page 35).**

   Next Check Num, Print Check, Send Online Payment, and EFT are the likely choices.

8. **Click OK.**

   Quicken adds the transaction to the register of the account from which you paid.

If you're paying off principal, the payment acts as a transfer to reduce the balance in the loan account.

Working with Other Kinds of Debt

Although amortized loans (page 237) and credit card debt (page 238) make up the lion's share of borrowed money, you can borrow in other ways. A home equity line of credit (affectionately known as a HELOC) is money you borrow against the

---

equity you have in your home (the value minus what you owe on your mortgage). HELOCs act a lot like credit card accounts, which is exactly how you set them up in Quicken. For any other kind of debt, Quicken's Debt accounts are indispensable. For example, if you borrow money from a generous relative with a promise to pay the money back next year, with no interest charge and no set schedule, a Debt account keeps track of how much you owe. This section shows you how to set up these types of debt in Quicken.

Setting Up a Home Equity Line of Credit

A HELOC lets you borrow money against the equity you have in your house. You can write checks at any time to withdraw money from your home equity line of credit, and you can deposit money whenever you want to pay back what you've borrowed. When you receive your monthly statement, it lists the interest accrued and the minimum payment you have to make. If that sounds like a credit card account, you're right—and you use a credit card type of account to track them in Quicken.

Here's how you use a Quicken credit card account to track a HELOC:

- First, **set up a credit card account** (page 50) for your HELOC. Fill in the Opening Balance field with zero, and the Credit Limit field with the maximum amount of credit your bank is extending to you.

- **When you withdraw money** from your line of credit, record that transaction in the credit card account register. If you use checks, type the check number in the Ref field; if you have a debit card, leave the Ref field blank or type *DC* for "debit card". The withdrawal increases the balance you owe.

- **When you make a deposit,** record it as a payment in the credit card register. Recording the interest you pay on your HELOC is similar to recording interest payments on a credit card (page 108). The only difference is that you use a tax-deductible category for interest, like Mortgage Interest Exp:Bank. Then, all your house-related interest payments show up as deductions in your Quicken tax reports (page 402).

Setting Up a Debt Account

If your kindhearted uncle Jimmy agrees to lend you money for that sound system you're dying to buy and tells you to pay it back whenever you can, interest free, Quicken can help make sure you repay him in full. Simply record the loan as a quicken Debt account, which represents debt without pesky borrowing constraints like payment schedules, so you can set one up in a jiffy. Here's how:

1. **In the Account Bar, click the Add Account button. In the Account Setup wizard that appears, select the "Debt (not including credit cards)" option, and then click Next.**

    The first screen asks you to name the account.

2. **In the Account Name/Nickname box, type a descriptive name for the account, and then click Next.**

Quicken fills in the Account Name/Nickname box with *Liability*. Change the name to something meaningful like *Aunt Marge College Loan*.

3. **In the "Date to start tracking" field, enter the date you want to begin tracking the debt. In the Liability Amount field, enter the current balance, then click Next.**

Quicken fills in today's date, which is perfect if you want to start tracking the debt now. Otherwise, fill in the date when you received the money.

4. **In the "Is there a loan on this liability?" screen, select No, and then click Next.**

Unlike with a formal loan, you don't need to specify an interest rate or payment schedule. You just want to track the amount of principal you have left to pay.

Note: If the debt *does* have an interest rate and payment schedule, set it up as a loan account instead. Click Cancel to close the Account Setup wizard, and then, follow the instructions on page 237.

---

5. **Click Done.**

That's it! The Debt account appears in your Account Bar and the other account lists in Quicken.

If you write a check from your checking account to pay back some of the money you owe, choose the Debt account in the Category field. That way, Quicken transfers the amount of the check to the Debt account, which reduces the amount you owe.

Editing a Loan

Loans can change over time. For example, if you have an adjustable-rate mortgage, the interest rate changes every so often. And each year, your escrow payment increases as property taxes and homeowners' insurance premiums go up. Or maybe you need to correct a small error you made when you initially set up the loan in Quicken. Regardless of the reason, the View Loans window is the place to make all these changes.

The fastest way to open the View Loans window (Figure 9-17) is to press Ctrl+H. If keyboard shortcuts aren't your thing, choose Net Worth → Loans.

Changing Loan and Payment Details

The most common reason to change loan details is to adjust values you initially set up. Suppose you chose the No Balloon option when setting up a loan because you didn't know the details of your balloon payment, and now you want to fill in the amortized length. Or perhaps you provided the wrong opening date and want to correct that. Quicken makes it easy to change these aspects of your loans.

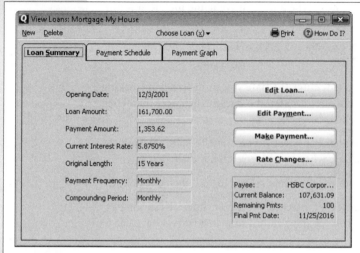

Figure 9-17:
Before you make any changes, make sure you're looking at the right loan. (The loan's name appears in the title of the dialog box; here, it's Mortgage My House.) In the View Loans window's menu bar, click Choose Loan, and then, from the drop-down menu, select the loan you want to edit. The Loan Summary tab shows you basic info about the original loan, and how much you have left to pay off.

The most common reason to edit a loan payment is to adjust the escrow for a mortgage. Mortgage lenders usually demand an escrow payment for property taxes and homeowners' insurance, because their money's on the line and they don't want a local government seizing the property because they haven't paid their taxes. Property taxes and insurance premiums seem to increase constantly, so lenders usually review your escrow account once a year, and adjust the escrow amount accordingly.

Changing your payment method is another reason to edit a payment in Quicken. For example, say you want to switch from a scheduled transaction to a repeating *online* payment. Or, if you're really lucky, you might need to *decrease* your payment amount. (One reason your payment might drop is if the equity in your home has increased to the point where you no longer need private mortgage insurance.)

Whatever the reason, open the View Loans window by pressing Ctrl+H or choosing Net Worth → Loans. Then, do the following to edit the loan or payment:

- Click Edit Loan to open the Edit Loan dialog box. The fields you can change are identical to those you set when you created the loan.

- Click Edit Payment to open the Edit Loan Payment dialog box. The steps for changing the values in this dialog box should be familiar—they're identical to adding values in the first place (page 245).

Adjusting a Loan's Interest Rate

Much as you might want to lower the 8.5 percent rate on your 30-year fixed-rate mortgage, using the Rate Changes button is appropriate only if you borrowed money with an adjustable-rate loan. When the interest rate changes on one of these loans, the payment changes along with it. (The *potential* for a smaller payment is one of the charms of an adjustable-rate loan, though payments can go *up*, too.) With Quicken, you don't have to do any fancy calculations; just tell the program the new rate, and it automatically calculates your new payment amount.

Here's how to change the interest rate and figure out your new payment:

1. **In the View Loans window (press Ctrl+H, or choose Net Worth → Loans), make sure the loan whose rate you want to change is visible, and then click Rate Changes.**

   Quicken opens the Loan Rate Changes window, which lists the current and previous rates for the loan. If the interest rate adjusts, add a new rate with the date it becomes effective, as shown in Figure 9-18.

Warning: Quicken lets you enter a new rate for any loan. If you make changes to a fixed-rate loan, your payments won't match what the lender expects. So be sure you're looking at the right loan in the View Loans window before you click Rate Changes.

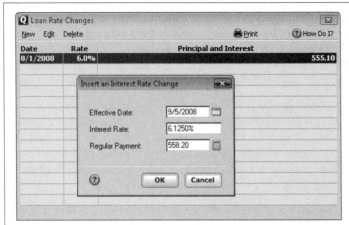

Figure 9-18:
The Loan Rate Changes window lists all the rates you create, but the only one that matters is the one you're currently paying. You can leave old rates in to see the ups and downs of an adjustable-rate mortgage over time. In the window's menu bar, click Edit to change a rate that's incorrect or has the wrong effective date. If the list of rates has grown long, you can highlight the row for an older rate that no longer applies, and then click Delete to remove it.

2. **In the Loan Rate Changes window's menu bar, choose New.**

   The "Insert an Interest Rate Change" dialog box shown in Figure 9-18 appears, with boxes for the critical values: the date the change goes into effect, the new interest rate, and the new amount that you'll have to pay.

3. **In the Effective Date box, choose the date when the new rate goes into effect.**

   Adjustable-rate loans don't change their rates any old time. Some do so in as little as a month, though loans that adjust once a year are the most common. The lender will tell you what day the interest rate takes effect.

4. **In the Interest Rate text box, type the new interest rate.**

   The Regular Payment text box is empty until you press Enter or click away from the Interest Rate text box. Quicken calculates the new payment and fills in the box, as you can see in Figure 9-18. If the value that Quicken calculates isn't correct, simply type the payment amount your lender specified.

Tip: If you have an interest-only mortgage or a negative-amortization loan, you eventually have to start paying off the balance you owe. When that time comes, the "Insert an Interest Rate Change" dialog box is where you specify your new payment, even though the interest rate hasn't changed. After Quicken calculates the Regular Payment value, type the payment the lender requires. Quicken applies part of the payment to interest based on the interest rate. Any amount left over goes to pay off the balance.

5. **Click OK.**

   Quicken not only adds the interest rate to the Loan Rate Changes list, it also modifies the loan payment to reflect the new amount, beginning with the first payment after the rate's effective date.

Refinancing a Loan

When you refinance a loan or mortgage, you use money from a new loan to pay off the balance of the old one and you also have to pay a few other fees. The balance on the old loan drops to zero. In Quicken, the new loan should be linked to the asset it's paying for. If the thought of getting all these changes straight makes you sweat, relax. All you have to do is follow the money, and Quicken makes that easy.

First, create a loan account for the new loan as you would for any other (page 237). You'll have an opening balance transaction in this new loan account that's equal to the amount you've borrowed with the new loan. All you have to do is split this opening balance transaction to account for the items that the new loan covers: paying off the old loan, closing costs, and any accrued interest. Figure 9-19 shows you how.

If you roll the closing costs and payoff interest into the new loan, then the split transaction includes three entries, as you see in Figure 9-19:

- **Pay off old loan balance.** To pay off the balance on the old loan, in the Category field, choose the liability account for the old loan (in the figure, it's *Mortgage Rental House*). In the Amount field, type the balance of the old loan. This transfer reduces the balance on the old loan to zero.

- **Closing costs.** To allocate some of the new loan to pay its closing costs (that's right, you pay closing costs when you open a new loan), choose a category like Fees. In the Amount field, type the value of the closing fees.

- **Pay off interest.** When you close out an old loan, you typically have to pay some interest that accrued after the last payment you made. In the Category field, choose the category you use to track deductible interest expense, such as Quicken's built-in Mortgage Interest Exp:Bank category.

Click OK to save the splits, and then click the Enter button to save the changes to the Opening Balance transaction.

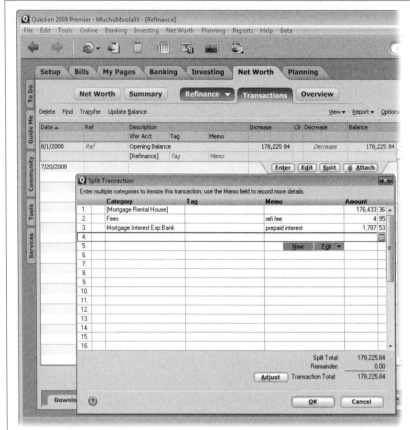

Figure 9-19:
The Category field for a loan's opening balance transaction is initially set to the transaction's liability account. To allocate the new loan to your refinance costs, click the opening balance transaction's Split button. In The Split Transaction dialog box (shown here), create a split for each item the new loan covers, such as paying off the old mortgage, closing costs, and financing the upfront points for your mortgage.

Changing the Value of an Asset

The things you own change in value over time. When you buy a car, it loses value as soon as you drive it off the lot, and it continues to *depreciate* (that is, lose value) year after year. But if the model is destined to be collectible and you take good care of it, the car's value may increase again someday. In fact, any collectible item can change in value due to market supply and demand, and a house's value may increase when you make improvements, like finishing a basement. If you use Quicken to track your net worth, you can adjust the value of your Quicken asset accounts, but how you do that depends on *why* the value changed. This section explains the three most common approaches.

Changing Market Value

Suppose real estate in Barbados gets hot and the market value of your air-conditioned bungalow near the beach soars from $50,000 to $220,000, and you want Quicken to reflect this increase in value. On the other hand, real estate values can take a fall, too. Either way, all you have to do is update the balance in your Quicken asset account. Here's how:

1. **In the Account Bar, click the asset account you want to update.**

   Quicken displays the register for that account.

2. **In the register's menu bar, choose Update Balance.**

   The Update Account Balance dialog box opens. The name of the selected asset account appears at the end of the dialog box title to help you avoid updating the value of the wrong asset, as you can see in Figure 9-20 (in this case, it's *Savannah Hideaway*).

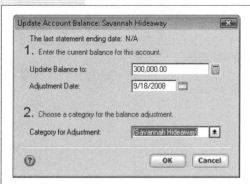

Figure 9-20:
When you update the value of an asset, fill in your estimate of its value and the date of the change. The value of an asset account has no effect on the balance in a linked liability account: You still owe the same amount on your mortgage or loan. But the equity you have in the asset increases, which is a good thing.

3. **In the "Update Balance to" text box, type your estimate of the asset's value.**

   You don't know the real value of something you own until you sell it. The "Update Balance to" text box is for your best guess of the present value.

4. **In the Adjustment Date text box, type the date for the change in value.**

   The adjustment date isn't that important. If you had an asset appraised by a professional, use the appraisal date. Otherwise, use the date when you checked the asset's value (by looking up the Blue Book value of your car, for example).

5. **In the "Category for Adjustment" drop-down menu, choose the asset account.**

   By choosing the account whose balance you're updating, your balance update doesn't show up in a category or other account; it simply changes the value of your asset account with no side effects.

   Out of the box, Quicken automatically chooses the Misc category (a built-in catchall category for expenses) If you accept that suggestion, though, a big increase or decrease in asset value makes your income and expense reports look better or worse than they really are, kind of like Enron accounting. That's because Quicken's built-in reports include the Misc category. So a $20,000 drop in value assigned to the Misc category shows up as $20,000 in expenses in an income and expense report. But you didn't actually spend $20,000. Likewise, a $20,000 increase in house value assigned to the Misc category makes it *look like* you spent $20,000 less in expenses.

6. **Click OK.**

If you set the "Category for Adjustment" to the asset account, as recommended in the previous step, you may see a warning about transferring into the same account. Just click OK again.

Quicken changes the balance in the asset account, as shown in Figure 9-21.

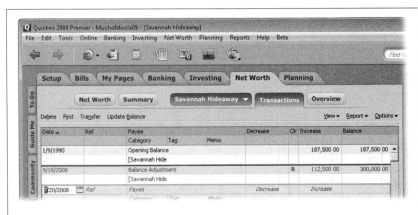

Figure 9-21:
If you set the "Category for Adjustment" in the Update Balance dialog box to the asset account whose balance you're updating, then the decrease doesn't affect income and expense reports or other accounts, because the money isn't going anywhere. The same goes for increases in value.

Depreciation

Depreciation is an accounting technique that reduces the value of an asset, which businesses like because it's a tax-deductible expense. If you *don't* use your assets for business, stop right here—any decrease in asset value doesn't generate a tax deduction so there's no reason to track depreciation. For assets not used for business, you can update the balance in the asset account to reflect the lower value, as described in the previous section.

If you use an asset for business and plan to take a tax deduction for depreciation, you can use the Update Account Balance dialog box to track depreciation. Before you follow the steps in the previous section, create a category like Business:Depreciation. Then, in the Update Account Balance dialog box, choose that category for the decrease in value transaction. That way, at the end of the year, you can run a report to total your depreciation for the year.

Improvements

If you spend money on improvements that increase the value of your home, then you can update the asset account balance as part of recording your expenditures. For example, when you renovate your kitchen, the value of your house usually increases. When you enter the check or credit card purchase for the kitchen materials, in the Category field, choose the asset account for your house. As you can see in Figure 9-22, the transaction changes the balance in your checking or credit card account, decreasing your checking account balance or increasing the amount you owe on your credit card. But the transaction also transfers the value of your purchase to your home asset account, where it *increases* the value.

Note: Some honey-do projects don't increase the value of your home, like repainting it or fixing the leaky roof. In fact, the increase in your home's value usually doesn't match the money you've put into a home improvement project; the $25,000 kitchen may increase the value by $20,000, say. To keep track of home maintenance expenses, assign transactions to a category like Home:Maintenance. For those big home improvement projects, you can split the transaction to assign part of the cost to Home:Maintenance and part to the house asset account to increase its value.

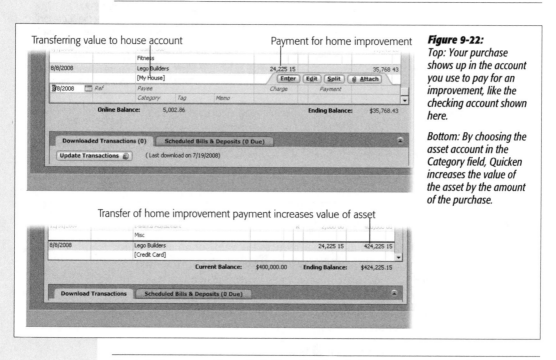

Transferring value to house account   Payment for home improvement

Transfer of home improvement payment increases value of asset

Figure 9-22:
Top: Your purchase shows up in the account you use to pay for an improvement, like the checking account shown here.

Bottom: By choosing the asset account in the Category field, Quicken increases the value of the asset by the amount of the purchase.

Tip: In the improvement transaction's Memo field, type the improvement you made. If you want to find the transaction later, it's easier to remember "new carpet" than "Sears." Even better, attach images (page 114) of receipts to your home improvement purchases. Then, the documentation you need is readily available in case the IRS questions your tax return.

Acquiring and Disposing of Assets

Every time you buy something, you're acquiring an asset. You usually have to spend money to acquire assets, unless you get them as gifts—or bribes. Likewise, if you sell an asset to someone (like that collection of 1920s hubcaps you've suddenly grown tired of), you probably receive a check or cash that you can put in the bank. Quicken can help you you track the shifting value of your assets and the money flowing into and out of your accounts as a result.

Much like when you make home improvements to increase your home's value (page 263), you can change the value of an asset account as you record your purchase or deposit transaction in Quicken. For example, if you sell your '63 Mustang, when you deposit the check for $50,000 into your checking account, in the transaction's Category field, choose the asset account for the Mustang.

In addition to *increasing* the checking account balance, the deposit transaction *decreases* the asset account balance by $50,000. It makes sense for the asset's value to decrease to zero when you sell it because you no longer own the asset. However, if you sold an asset for more or less than the value in the Quicken asset account, the account balance won't equal zero. Say you valued the Mustang at $45,000, but sold it for $50,000; you'd still have a $5,000 balance on the asset account. To correct this discrepancy, choose Update Balance, and then set the new balance to zero. That's all there is to it.

Tip: If you purchase a new asset, create the asset account *first*, and set the balance to zero. Then, when you create the banking transaction that pays for the purchase, in the Category field, choose the asset account, as described in the box on on page 238.

Taxes and Insurance

Taxes and insurance are stunningly complicated systems. They're also unavoidable, unless you want the taxman in hot pursuit or heaps of medical bills to pay. Quicken can't make these systems any simpler, but it *can* keep track of the taxes you owe or the refunds you're due, as well as the numerous types of insurance transactions you make, such as funding a flexible spending account, paying for medical expenses, and depositing reimbursement checks.

As you learned in Chapters 3 and 4, Quicken's powers come mainly from accounts and categories. These two features are also your foundation for tracking tax and insurance transactions. Quicken sets up several types of accounts like IRAs with the tax-related settings you need to track your nontaxable income and tax deductions. With these settings in place, Quicken knows which accounts to include in the tax reports you run.

You can also assign Quicken categories to specific lines on tax forms and schedules. As long as you assign tax-related transactions to the appropriate categories, you can whip out reports of your taxable income and tax deductions in no time. Quicken even has tools you can use to plan your finances so that you pay the least amount of tax (legally) possible and find all the deductions you qualify for.

Following money through the insurance maze can seem like a shell game. Contributions to pretax savings accounts and insurance premiums here, payments for reimbursable expenses there, reimbursement checks if you're lucky—and these transactions have tax ramifications, too. But if you use the right Quicken account and category tax settings, you can keep track of your pretax funds from start to finish.

This chapter describes how to set up categories to track tax-related transactions. You'll also learn how to run Quicken tax reports and get an introduction to the program's tax planning tools.

Then you'll learn how to combine account and category tax settings to manage the money in *flexible spending accounts* and *health savings accounts* (accounts that let you pay for health, medical, and a few other types of expenses with pretax dollars). This chapter walks you through the transactions from contributing to one of these accounts, to paying for qualified expenses, to depositing reimbursement checks, so you can get the money to the right place each step of the way without frying your brain.

Setting Quicken Up to Help with Taxes

Enlisting Quicken's help with your taxes is all about categories and accounts. You assign the appropriate tax form and tax line to a Quicken category (or in the case of built-in categories, let Quicken do it for you). Then you apply these tax-related categories to your transactions. If you designate an account as tax-deferred, Quicken ignores some or all of its transactions (page 272) in the tax reports you run to add up your taxable income and tax deductions. This section tells you how to set up categories to track all your tax-related transactions.

Turning on Built-in Categories

Quicken comes with several sets of categories that cover most common financial situations and life events, like owning a home or business, getting married, and starting a family. When you first create a data file, Quicken adds all the built-in categories in the Standard category. You can tell Quicken to add other sets of categories during setup by simply turning on checkboxes in the Setup tab's "About you" section (page 20). As your situation changes, you can return to the Setup tab and turn on other checkboxes.

If you don't see the categories you want in either the Category List or the drop-down lists in transaction Category fields, look through Quicken's built-in categories. To see the full Category List, choose Tools → Category List or press Ctrl+C if you use Quicken's keyboard mapping (page 488). Built-in categories are better than ones you create from scratch because Quicken takes care of assigning the appropriate tax forms and line items, as shown in Figure 10-1. (See Chapter 4 for the full story on categories.)

A Guide to Quicken's Built-in Categories

Here are the types of built-in categories that Quicken offers:

- **Standard.** These are basic categories that most people use. Quicken automatically adds all these categories to your Category List when you create a data file. To see the categories in this set, in the Add Categories dialog box's Available Categories drop-down list (shown in Figure 10-2), choose Standard.

Red checkmark indicates that a
category has a tax line assignment

Click to add or remove
built-in categories

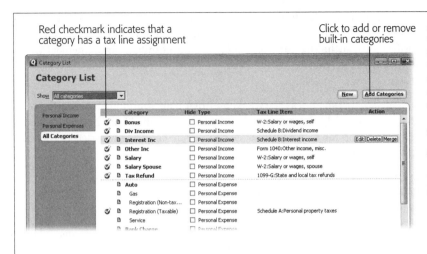

Figure 10-1:
Quicken puts a red checkmark to the left of categories assigned to tax lines. You can look for categories with missing tax line assignments by skimming the Category List for tax-related categories that don't have a red checkmark. (If you don't see the Tax Line Item column in the list, at the bottom of the window, click Options and then choose Show Tax Line Item.)

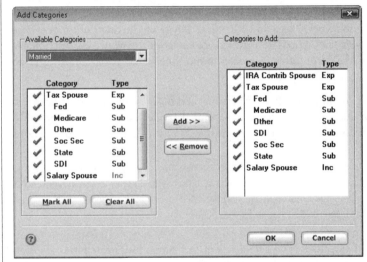

Figure 10-2:
The Type column shows whether a category is for income (Inc shown in green), expenses (Exp in red), or is a subcategory (Sub in the color of the parent category). Subcategories are indented beneath the associated parent category.

Tax-related categories in this collection include Salary (assigned to the tax form and line item "W-2:Salary or wages, self"), Interest Inc (assigned to "Schedule B:Interest income"), Div Income (assigned to "Schedule B:Dividend income"), and so on.

The Standard set also contains tax-related expense categories. Charity is assigned to "Schedule A:Cash charity contributions" and IRA Contrib is assigned to "Form 1040:IRA contribution, self". You'll also see the top-level Tax category, which has several subcategories, like Fed, State, Soc Sec, and Medicare, which are all assigned to their corresponding W-2 tax lines.

Quicken isn't infallible, though. For example, it assigns the Medical category to "Schedule A:Medicine and drugs" even though Schedule A has several medical classifications, including "doctors, dentists, and hospitals" and "medical travel and lodging". Fortunately, you can add your own categories and assign tax lines to them, as page 74 explains.

- **Married.** This set includes salary, tax, and IRA contribution categories for your spouse. You can add these categories by turning on the "I am married" checkbox in the Setup tab's "About you" section or by choosing Married in the Add Categories dialog box's Available Categories drop-down list.

- **Dependents** or **Children.** This set isn't really a set, it's just one lonely category—Childcare—which you'll see if you turn on the "I have children" checkbox on the Setup tab or choose Children in the Add Categories dialog box.

- **Homeowner.** Home ownership gives you a number of tax deductions, including mortgage interest and property taxes. Quicken's Homeowner set includes categories with tax line assignments, such as Mortgage Interest Exp:Bank ("Schedule A:Home mortgage interest (1098)") and Tax:Property ("Schedule A: Real estate taxes"). The set also includes a few categories that aren't tax-related, such as Homeowner's Fees and Mortgage Payment (in case you track a mortgage that isn't tax deductible). Add these categories to your data file either by turning on the Setup tab's "I own a home" checkbox or by choosing Homeowner in the Add Categories dialog box.

- **Business.** If you intermingle your personal and business finances in Quicken, you can add business-related categories to your data file. Turn on the Setup tab's "I own a business" checkbox or choose Business in the Add Categories dialog box.

Tip: Keeping your personal and business finances separate makes it easier to track each part of your financial life and could be a lifesaver if the IRS audits your tax return. One way to keep business finances separate is to create a second data file (page 481) dedicated to your business and to open a real-world checking account and credit card specifically for your business.

- **Rentals and Royalties.** The categories in this set includes categories associated with line items for Schedule E, which covers income and losses from rental real estate, royalties, partnerships, S corporations, estates, trusts, and the like. For example, Rents Received is assigned to "Schedule E:Rents received", "Cleaning and Maintenance" is assigned to "Schedule E:Cleaning and maintenance", and so on. To add all these categories, turn on the Setup tab's "I own rental property" checkbox, and Quicken adds them at the top level of the Category List. If you want to gather them all into one place, create a top-level category (for example, Rentals) and then edit the built-in categories to make them subcategories (page 76).

Note: Although turning on an "About you" checkbox on the Setup tab *adds* categories to the Category List, turning the same checkbox off *doesn't remove* those categories. To remove them, you have to delete or hide them individually (page 77).

Fine-Tuning Quicken Tax Categories

If you have tax-related income and expenses that Quicken's built-in categories can't handle (like Schedule A's assortment of medical classifications and the ones you'll learn about later in this chapter for tracking flexible spending accounts), the good news is you can create your own categories or edit existing ones to assign them to the appropriate tax schedules and line items. The bad news is that Quicken is no help at picking the *right* tax schedule and line item. For that assistance, you can ask your trusty accountant or (horrors!) the IRS. Go to *www.irs.gov* to get tax forms and instructions or find a contact phone number.

Creating or editing tax-related categories is similar to working with other categories. First, open the Category List window (Ctrl+C or Tools → Category List). Then do one of the following:

- To create a new category, click New. The Set Up Category dialog box opens.

- To edit a category, in the Category List, click anywhere in the category's row and then click the Edit button that appears on the right end of the row. The Edit Category dialog box opens.

With either the Set Up Category dialog box or Edit Category dialog box open, in the "Tax line item" drop-down list, choose the entry that corresponds to the appropriate tax form and line on that form, as shown in Figure 10-3.

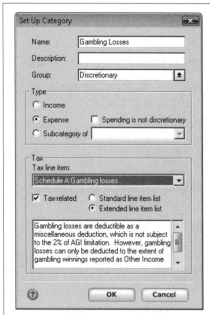

Figure 10-3:
Quicken automatically selects the "Standard line item list" option, which shows you the most common tax forms and line items. If you don't see the line item you want, select the "Extended line item list" option (as shown here) to expand the list of choices in the "Tax Line item" drop-down list. For example, the extended list tacks on choices for Schedule F and Form 4835, which relate to farm income and expenses.

One way to identify the appropriate tax form and line item is to check your income tax return from last year. If you filled in your gambling losses on Schedule A Line 28 (Other Miscellaneous Deductions) and you're still gambling, for example, you can choose "Schedule A:Gambling losses" from the "Tax line item" drop-down menu.

Quicken tries to help you get tax-line assignments right, but it only goes so far. Choose Tax → Tax Category Audit. In the Tax Category Audit window that appears, Quicken lists built-in categories and, in some cases, custom categories you've created that may not be assigned to the correct line item. To change a category's tax-line assignment, click Change in the category's Action column. Click Ignore to leave things as they are.

Setting Up Account's Tax Features

In the real world, you have to fill out applications to open specific types of tax-advantaged accounts. Then the financial institution that holds the account sends you reports at the end of the year to help you fill out your tax return. In Quicken, getting the right tax settings is sometimes as easy as creating a specific type of account. For example, Quicken's IRA, 401(k), and 529 Plan accounts come with the tax features you need. If you create one of these types of accounts and then run Quicken's built-in "Schedule D-Capital Gains and Losses" report, the report automatically *includes* your taxable investment accounts and *excludes* your tax-advantaged investment accounts like IRAs, Roth IRAs, and 401(k)s.

If the tax settings that Quicken applies to an account don't suit your needs, you can change its status to tax-deferred any time you want. Here's how:

1. **In the Account Bar, click the account whose tax status you want to change.**

   Quicken selects the tab where the account lives (Banking, Investing, or Net Worth) and opens the account's register or overview screen.

2. **If Quicken displays the account's register, click the Overview button above the register and then click the Edit Account Details button (Figure 10-4).**

   The Account Details dialog box opens.

3. **To the right of the Tax-Deferred label, select the Yes option and then click OK to close the dialog box.**

   This setting tells Quicken to ignore income-related transactions like stock sales or dividends earned in its tax reports.

4. **In the Overview screen's Account Attributes section, choose Options → "Set tax attributes".**

   The Tax Schedule Information dialog box shown in Figure 10-4 opens.

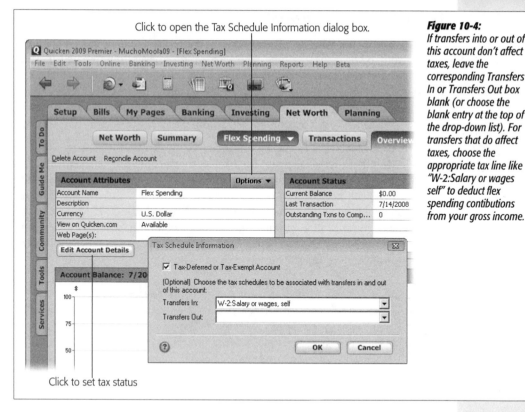

Click to open the Tax Schedule Information dialog box.

Figure 10-4:
If transfers into or out of this account don't affect taxes, leave the corresponding Transfers In or Transfers Out box blank (or choose the blank entry at the top of the drop-down list). For transfers that do affect taxes, choose the appropriate tax line like "W-2:Salary or wages self" to deduct flex spending contibutions from your gross income.

Click to set tax status

5. **In the Transfers In drop-down list, choose the tax schedule and tax line that applies to money you transfer into the account.**

   For example, money you contribute to a flexible spending account isn't taxed, so you can choose "W-2:Salary or wages, self" to subtract your contribution from your gross income. Choose "Form 1040:IRA Contribution, self" to subtract an IRA contribution from your gross income.

6. **In the Transfers Out drop-down list, choose the tax schedule and tax line that applies to money you transfer out of the account.**

   For example, if money you withdraw from your IRA is taxable, you'd choose "Form 1040:Other income, misc" to add that to your taxable income.

7. **Click OK.**

   The Tax Schedule Information dialog box closes and your account has its tax features in place.

Gathering Tax Information

Whether you fill out your tax returns with someone else's help or bravely fill them out on your own, come tax time you need to know everything related to your taxes. Quicken has tax reports for individual tax schedules, but the Tax Schedule report is even better: It assembles all your tax-related info into one handy report. The Tax Summary report is another great tax-preparation tool, especially if you fill out the tax organizer your accountant sends you each year.

If you link your tax-related Quicken categories to lines on tax forms (page 76), and you've diligently entered all your tax-related transactions in Quicken, the Tax Schedule report can be a huge timesaver. Simply run the report, and Quicken spits out the figures you need to start working on your return, schedule by schedule, tax line by tax line. If you set up Quicken categories to match the classifications in the tax organizer your accountant sent you, run the Tax Summary report to see your tax figures grouped by Quicken category. The box on page 276 tells you how to make sure you've recorded all your tax-related transactions.

Note: If you use TurboTax (Intuit's tax-preparation program) and Quicken, TurboTax can reuse data you've already recorded in Quicken. You don't have to do anything in Quicken to get data over to TurboTax: When you launch TurboTax, you simply tell it to import your Quicken data and it pulls the numbers out of your data file. But keep in mind that TurboTax isn't perfect. No matter how meticulously you set up Quicken for taxes, you'll probably have to make some adjustments to your data in TurboTax to reflect your tax situation accurately.

To run the Tax Schedule report, choose Reports → Tax → Tax Schedule. Here are some of the changes you can make to the Tax Schedule report to see the information you want:

- **Dates.** To produce a report for your annual tax return, in the "Date range" drop-down list, choose Yearly. In the second drop-down list, choose the year for your tax return (2008, for example).

- **Expand categories.** To see every transaction in every category, below the "Date range" box, click Expand All. (This can help you make sure that you've caught every last deduction.) Click the – sign to the left of a category's name to collapse that category.

- **Collapse categories.** To see only category totals in the Tax Schedule report, first click Collapse All. The report then shows only the forms and schedules that have associated transactions—without any totals. To see the totals for each tax-related category, as shown in Figure 10-5, click either the + sign to the left of the form or the schedule's name.

If you want to look at specific tax-related transactions, other reports provide more targeted views. Here are Quicken's other tax reports and what they show:

When you click the + sign, the form or schedule expands.
Click the − sign to collapse the form or schedule.

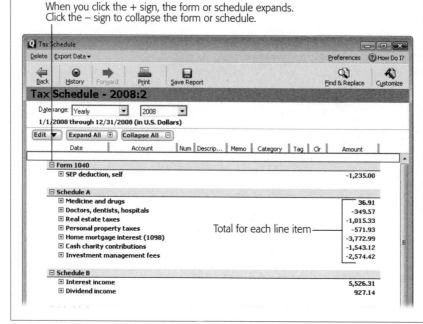

- **Capital Gains.** When you first run this report, Quicken organizes capital gains–related transactions into short-term and long-term groups, which the IRS taxes at different rates.

- **Schedule A–Itemized Deductions.** This report includes all the categories associated with Schedule A. You can expand each category to see individual transactions or collapse categories to see only the total for that line item.

- **Schedule B–Interest and Dividends.** You can generate this report to see your taxable interest and dividends.

- **Schedule D–Capital Gains and Losses.** As its name suggests, this report shows your capital gains and losses you can use to offset those gains.

- **Tax Summary.** This report includes all tax-related categories, but groups them by income and expense categories, rather than by forms and schedules, as on the Tax Schedule report.

Planning for Taxes

Quicken has several wizards that can help you pay the right amount of taxes—no more, no less. Whether you want to find deductions you may have missed, pay estimated taxes during the year to avoid a big bill at tax time, or figure out which investments to sell to minimize capital gains, the Tax menu has the tools you need.

Finding Missing Tax Transactions

To double-check that you've recorded all monthly and quarterly tax-related transactions, you can run an itemized category report that covers the past year. Then make sure you see 12 transactions for monthly payments and four transactions for quarterly payments. Here's how to customize a report to see your tax transactions:

1. Choose Reports → Spending → Itemized Categories.

2. In the Itemized Categories window's toolbar, click Customize.

3. In the Customize Itemized Categories dialog box, click the Advanced tab.

4. Turn on the "Tax-related transactions only" checkbox. This setting tells Quicken to include transactions only for categories whose "Tax-related" checkboxes are turned on (page 76).

5. Click OK to close the Customize Itemized Categories dialog box.

6. Take a look at the report to make sure it lists all the tax-related transactions you're looking for.

If you want to save the report, in the Itemized Categories report window's toolbar, click Save Report (page 455).

Here's a quick overview of Quicken's tax-planning tools and what they do:

- **Deduction Finder.** When you choose Tax → Deduction Finder, Quicken launches the Deduction Finder wizard. In the Deduction Finder window, choose a type of deduction, like Homeowner, as shown in Figure 10-6. Quicken lists deductions you might qualify for and asks you questions about them. To answer a question, turn on its Y or N checkbox. After you step through all the deductions and dutifully answer all the questions, click the Action Plan tab to find out what to do to earn additional tax deductions.

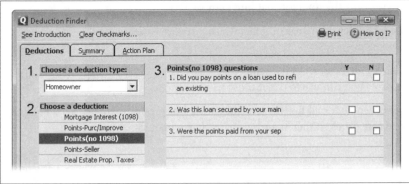

Figure 10-6:
If an entry in the "Choose a deduction type" drop-down list doesn't apply to you, you don't have to answer questions about it.

- **Itemized Deduction Estimator.** This wizard (which you launch by going to Tax → Itemized Deduction Estimator) helps you maximize your deductions by taking into account the thresholds you must exceed. For example, if your medical expenses are close to 7.5 percent of your adjusted gross income, you can fill in amounts for items like miles driven to and from appointments to see if you qualify.

- **Capital Gains Estimator.** After you tell this wizard which accounts you want to analyze and your tax rates, Quicken recommends what investments you should sell (for instance) to maximize your gains or minimize taxes. You launch this wizard by choosing Tax → Capital Gains Estimator.

- **Tax Withholding Estimator.** This wizard (which you launch by going to Tax → Tax Withholding Estimator) looks at your income and deductions and then estimates whether you're under- or over-withholding from your paycheck.

Working with Insurance Transactions

A *flexible spending account* (FSA) is an employer-offered plan that lets you set aside pretax income to pay for medical expenses, dependent care, and other qualifying expenses. With an FSA, you have to spend the money you contribute within that calendar year or you lose it. A *health savings account* (HSA) is available to anyone who enrolls in a high-deductible health insurance plan. Not only can you contribute pretax dollars to an HSA, you can also roll unspent funds over from year to year, accumulating money to pay for future expenses. An HSA account can even be a brokerage account invested in securities, though this option makes sense only when the balance is relatively high.

The tax deductions you earn from these types of accounts are worth cheering about. When your inner cheerleader quiets down, though, you'll realize that the price you pay is the headache caused by trying to track the darned things in Quicken. The program doesn't automate the process and doesn't give you any guidance, not even in its Help files. But never fear: This section explains how to make Quicken track these tax-advantaged accounts.

An Overview of Pretax Spending Accounts

The big attraction to FSAs and HSAs is the upfront tax deduction. The money you contribute to these accounts reduces your gross income and thus the taxes you pay. If your employer deducts these contributions from your paycheck, your net pay doesn't drop that much, because the pretax contribution decreases the amount your withholdings are based on.

Quicken's Paycheck Setup wizard makes it easy to tell the program about contributions you make through paycheck deductions. If you're self-employed, you can make your contributions to an account by writing a check and recording it in Quicken. The wizard even walks you through creating an account with all the tax settings you need, as the next section explains.

Once you have money in the tax-advantaged account, you can pay for qualifying expenses in one of two ways:

- **Paying directly from the account** is an option if you get checks or a debit card for that purpose. In some cases, your employer may deduct expenses like your health insurance premium from the FSA automatically. In Quicken, you can record these transactions as you would other checks and debit charges (see page 34 for the details).

- **Paying out of pocket and submitting expenses for reimbursement** isn't as simple, but many FSAs work this way. You write checks or charge your expenses and then fill out a reimbursement request that you give to your account administrator. You deposit the reimbursement checks you receive in your checking account.

As you pay for medical expenses out of pocket, the biggest challenge is tracking how much money is available in your account and how much you've submitted for reimbursement. The best way to track both the money available in your FSA or HSA and the submittable expenses you've paid is to create a second Quicken account. This second asset account keeps track of your submittable expenses and what's been reimbursed. See page 282 for the full story.

When you receive reimbursements, you have to document how much your FSA or HSA covered and how much falls back into your medical expense category as a potential Schedule A tax deduction. Tracking these gyrations in Quicken takes some fancy footwork. Page 283 shows you the right moves.

FSAs have a few additional wrinkles that appear at the end of the year and when you switch jobs. On the one hand, if you don't spend all the money you've contributed within the same calendar year, you forfeit it. On the other hand, if you spend more than you've deposited and then quit your job, you don't have to pay that windfall back—your employer eats the difference. In either case, you need to change the FSA balance in Quicken to zero (page 286 tells you how).

Setting Up an FSA or HSA in Quicken

If you set up your paycheck with the Paycheck Setup wizard (page 192) and tell it about your FSA, the program creates an account for your FSA with the tax settings you need. If you've already set up your paycheck and forgot to tell Quicken about the FSA, you can edit your Quicken paycheck to add the pretax deduction and FSA account. (Even if you don't receive a paycheck, you can trick the wizard into creating an account for you, as explained in the following list.) But it's easy to set up an FSA or HSA account on your own, too. In fact, if your HSA is an investment account, you *have to* set up the account manually so that you can choose an investment account. This section describes both approaches.

Method #1: Using the Paycheck Setup wizard

When you add a pretax deduction for an FSA to your paycheck, Quicken asks if you want to create an account. If you say yes, Quicken automatically applies the correct tax-deferred status and assigns transfers into the account to the correct tax schedule and tax line. Pretty nifty, huh?

Here's how you create an FSA or HSA account with the help of the Paycheck Setup wizard:

1. **Launch the Paycheck Setup wizard to create a new paycheck, as described on page 192.**

   If you're creating a new paycheck, you have to specify a company name and then click Next to open the Set Up Paycheck dialog box. Once that dialog box is open, proceed to step 2.

   If you already have a paycheck set up, you can edit the paycheck (page 201) to open the Edit Future Paychecks dialog box. You're ready for step 2.

2. **In the Set Up Paycheck dialog box or the Edit Future Paychecks dialog box (Figure 10-7), click the Add Pre-Tax Deduction button and then choose Flex Spending from the drop-down menu.**

   The Quicken Account Setup dialog box opens.

Note: You pick the Flex Spending option whether you're setting up an FSA or an HSA. You can specify the type of account when you name it.

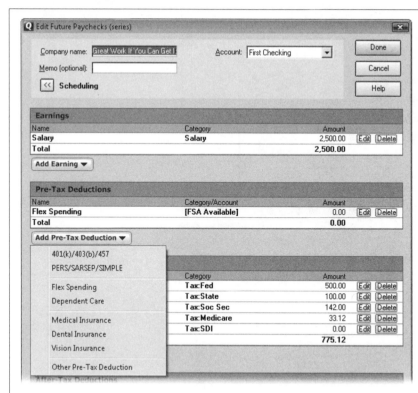

Figure 10-7:
The Medical Insurance, Dental Insurance, and Vision Insurance entries on the Add Pre-Tax Deduction drop-down menu are for insurance premiums your employer deducts from your paycheck. You want to choose the Flex Spending option instead.

3. **In the Quicken Account Setup dialog box, type a name in the "Name this
account" box and then click Next.**

Quicken automatically names the account *Flex Spending*. You can keep this
name or change it to something like *FSA Available* (or *HSA Available* for a
health savings account) to track how much money you have for expenses.

4. **Fill in the "As of Date" and Value boxes as you would for any account (page
61).**

Quicken fills in today's date and *0.00*, which are perfect for a brand-new FSA or
HSA. The program also sets Transfers In to the correct schedule and tax line, as
Figure 10-8 shows.

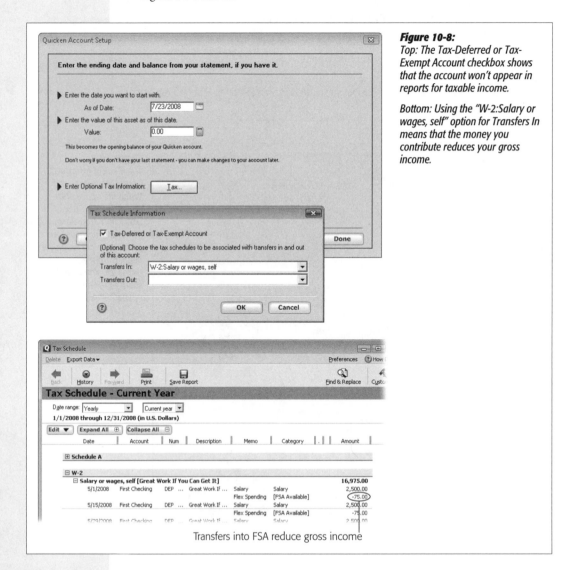

Figure 10-8:
*Top: The Tax-Deferred or Tax-
Exempt Account checkbox shows
that the account won't appear in
reports for taxable income.*

*Bottom: Using the "W-2:Salary or
wages, self" option for Transfers In
means that the money you
contribute reduces your gross
income.*

Transfers into FSA reduce gross income

5. **Click Done.**

The Add Pre-Tax Deduction dialog box opens. If you're setting up a real pay-check transaction, in the Amount box, type the amount your employer deducts from each paycheck to deposit into your FSA. Click OK to close the dialog box and continue setting up your paycheck. When you're finished, click Done to close the Set Up Paycheck wizard.

Tip: If you created a paycheck simply to add the FSA or HSA account, you can stop here. Click OK to close the Add Pre-Tax Deduction dialog box and then click Cancel to close the Set Up Paycheck wizard without creating a scheduled paycheck.

The new FSA or HSA account (which is an asset account—see page 230) appears in the "Property and Debt" section of the Account Bar and the Net Worth tab.

Method #2: Manually Setting Up an Account

When you create an FSA or HSA account manually, you choose the type of account you want. An asset account works perfectly for an FSA or an HSA that acts like an interest-bearing checking account. If your HSA is an investment account, however, you can set up an IRA-type account.

Here's how you create your own FSA or HSA account:

1. **In the Account Bar, click Add Account.**

   The Account Setup dialog box opens.

2. **Select the type of account you want to create.**

   For most FSA and HSA accounts, select the Asset option and then—in the Asset Type section that appears—select Other Asset Type (page 236).

   If your HSA is an investment account, select Investing/Retirement and then select "IRA or Keogh Plan".

3. **Complete the rest of the steps to create the account.**

   See page 236 to learn how to create a generic asset account. Page 335 explains how to create an investment account.

4. **Set the tax status for the account to tax-deferred and assign each of your con-tributions to the appropriate tax schedule and line item.**

   Choose "W-2:Salary and wages, self" to subtract FSA or HSA contributions from your gross income.

The new FSA or HSA account appears either in the "Property and Debt" section of the Account Bar and on the Net Worth tab or, for an investment HSA, in the Investing section of the Account Bar.

Tracking Qualifying Expenses

If you pay for medical expenses out of pocket and then submit reimbursement requests, it's a good idea to keep track of your submittable expenses and which ones have been reimbursed. Simply create a plain asset account (page 236) and call it something like *FSA Submittable.* You don't have to worry about tax settings because this account simply stores medical expenses you've paid but haven't yet been reimbursed for.

Setting Up a Medical Category

When you pay medical or other qualifying expenses with funds in an FSA or HSA, those expenses don't qualify for the medical expense deduction on Schedule A (page 284). So you need to create a new category for FSA/HSA expenses that isn't assigned to a tax schedule or tax line. That way, Quicken's Schedule A report will *omit* expenses paid from your FSA or HSA but *include* other medical expenses that you paid out of pocket without reimbursement.

To create such a category, follow the steps for creating a typical category (page 74) and name it something like *Medical HSA* or *Medical FSA.* In the Set Up Category dialog box, make sure the Tax-related checkbox is turned off. Fill in any other necessary fields and then click OK to create the category. Now you can apply that category to any expense that you pay for with your FSA or HSA, as described on page 283.

Funding an FSA or HSA

In addition to giving you two ways to setting up an FSA or HSA account in the first place (page 278), Quicken also gives you two ways to deposit funds into that account. Here are your options:

- **Using a scheduled paycheck.** When you set up a paycheck with Quicken's Paycheck Setup wizard and include a pretax deduction for you FSA or HSA, simply record your paycheck. Quicken takes care of the rest, as you can see in the report at the bottom of Figure 10-8.

- **Writing a check.** If you write checks to contribute money to your account (which is more common with HSAs than FSAs), you can record the check as a transfer to your HSA account. To do that, type the name of the financial institution that holds the HSA in the Payee field and the amount in the Payment field. Then, in the Category drop-down list, choose your HSA account. If you don't see your account in the Category drop-down list, click Transfers and then click the account's name. Quicken transfers the money from your Quicken checking account to your Quicken HSA and subtracts the contribution from your reportable income.

Recording Qualifying Expenses

As explained above, depending on your particular FSA or HSA account, you'll either pay for medical and other qualifying expenses directly from your account or pay out of pocket and then request reimbursement. Occasionally, you'll pay out of pocket for expenses that aren't covered by your FSA or HSA. You need to record all these transactions in Quicken, and each one requires a different process. This section describes the steps for each method.

Paying directly from an FSA or HSA

This approach is the easiest by far. If you have printed checks or a debit card for your account, simply write a check or hand the debit card to the checkout clerk. In real life, the money comes out of your account to pay the vendor. In Quicken, recording these kinds of checks or debits is similar to recording other checks and debit charges (see Chapter 5 for a refresher). Fill in the Payee field with the doctor's name, store name, and so on. Then fill in the Decrease field with the amount you spent. In the Category field, choose the Medical FSA or Medical HSA category to indicate that you paid for the expense with your pretax dollars. Figure 10-9 shows how the expense reduces the balance in your FSA.

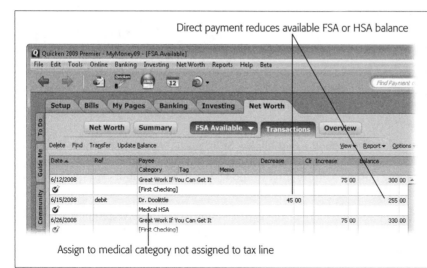

Direct payment reduces available FSA or HSA balance

Assign to medical category not assigned to tax line

Figure 10-9:
In an FSA or HSA register, contributions to the account increase the account balance and payments you make to doctors, pharmacies, and so on decrease it. Reimbursements you receive are paid from your FSA or HSA so they also decrease the balance (not shown here).

Requesting reimbursements

Because requesting expense reimbursements involves several parties (you, your account administrator, and the doctor or company you paid), this approach requires additional steps, but each one is easy. Here's how to tell Quicken about expenses you've paid out of pocket and reimbursements you've requested:

1. **Open the register for the Quicken account you used to pay the expense.**

   Your checking, credit card, and cash accounts are the likely suspects.

2. Record the expense as a transfer to the account you use to track submittable expenses (page 38).

In the Category field, choose FSA Submittable or HSA Submittable, or whatever you named the account. Type the payee in the Payee field and the amount in the Payment field (for a checking account) or Charge field (for a credit card account).

By assigning the transaction to the submittable asset account, Quicken increases that account's balance, as you can see in Figure 10-10. The balance in the submittable asset account is the amount you should ask to have reimbursed.

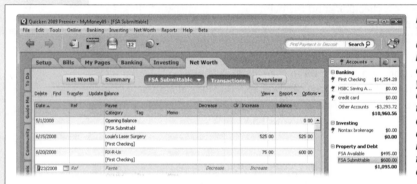

Figure 10-10:
Your out-of-pocket expenses reduce the balance in your checking account or increase what you owe on your credit card. When you transfer these expenses to an FSA asset account, the account's balance is how much you should request from your account administrator.

3. When you receive your reimbursement or explanation of benefits (see below), in the *FSA Submittable* or *HSA Submittable* account, record a transaction (page 37) to assign the reimbursed expenses to the correct tax-related category (Figure 10-11).

This transaction assigns reimbursed expenses to your nontax-related Medical FSA (or Medical HSA) category (page 282). Because you've already received a tax deduction for contributing to the FSA or HSA, reimbursed expenses don't qualify for the Schedule A medical expense tax line.

If your plan denied any of the expenses you asked to have reimbursed, you'll receive an *explanation of benefits* that tells you why. In this situation, in Quicken, record a split transaction to assign the reimbursed expenses to your nontax-related Medical FSA (or Medical HSA) category and the unreimbursed expenses to a second split assigned to your regular medical category (page 270), which *is* assigned to the Schedule A medical expense tax line.

4. Finally, record a transaction to show that you've deposited the reimbursement check into your checking account, as explained on page 37.

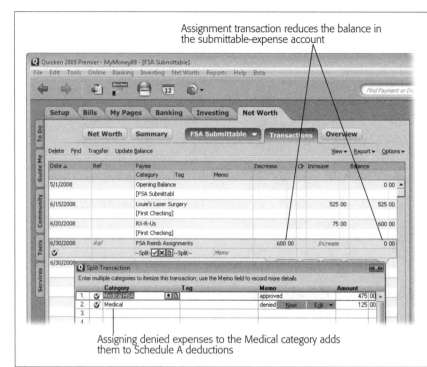

Assignment transaction reduces the balance in the submittable-expense account

Assigning denied expenses to the Medical category adds them to Schedule A deductions

Figure 10-11:
When you record your reimbursement, the balance in your submittable-expense account should change to zero to show that you've been reimbursed for all the expenses you've submitted. If any of your expenses were denied, the split transaction assigns these expenses to your Schedule A medical category so that you can get a tax deduction for them (if you exceed the IRS threshold).

Paying for nonqualifying expenses

If you have medical-related expenses that don't qualify for your FSA or HSA or you've already exceeded your annual contribution, you can record those expenses directly to a Quicken medical category assigned to Schedule A (page 284). Simply record the check or credit card charge in Quicken and choose a category like Medical or Medical:Dentist in the transaction Category field. That way, when you run one of Quicken's tax reports, that expense appears in the Schedule A (Figure 10-5).

Depositing Reimbursement Checks

The last step in the reimbursement process is recording the reimbursement check you deposited (Hallelujah!). This transaction reduces the balance in your FSA Available or HSA Available account to show how much of your funds you've used (Figure 10-12) and increases your checking account balance.

When you record the deposit (page 37), name the payee something like *FSA Reimb Deposit* or include the name of the bank that holds your FSA or HSA account. To increase your checking account balance and reduce your available FSA or HSA funds, choose FSA Available or HSA Available from the Category drop-down list. Congratulations! You've successfully tracked your medical expense from beginning to bitter end. (If the reimbursement check isn't reward enough, get a massage and charge it to your FSA or HSA.)

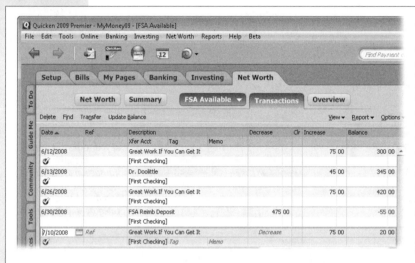

Figure 10-12:
When you deposit the reimbursement check in your checking account—ka-ching!—and assign it to the appropriate account, the transfer reduces your FSA or HSA account balance. If the balance is negative, you've spent more than you've contributed so far, but future contributions can make up this shortfall. See page 278 to find out what happens if you quit your job before you make your full contribution.

Cleaning Up Your FSA Account

With an FSA, you choose the amount you want to contribute annually (up to the regulatory limit) and then your employer deducts money from each paycheck until you reach that amount. If New Year's Eve rolls around and you haven't spent all the money for that year, you're out of luck. The money simply goes away and you start the next year with a zero balance. But in that situation, your Quicken FSA account will still show the previous year's balance, so you have to clear it manually at the end of each year.

If, on the other hand, you spend the entire annual amount in the first week of the year to cover the bills for a mysterious "illness" that strikes on New Year's Day, your real-world account won't have the funds, but your employer will cover the amount you've agreed to contribute. If you then quit your job in February, you don't have to make up the difference: You walk away and your employer foots the bill. In this case, your Quicken FSA account shows a negative balance, which you also need to clear out.

In both cases, you simply use Quicken's Update Balance feature and you're all set. Here's what you do to clear a balance in an FSA account:

1. **In the Account Bar, click the FSA account to open its register.**

   If the Overview screen appears, click the Transactions button to view the register.

2. **In the menu bar above the register, choose Update Balance.**

   The Update Account Balance dialog box opens.

3. **In the "Update Balance to" box, type *0* (zero).**

   Typing *0* resets the account balance, giving you a clean state.

4. In the Adjustment Date box, type *12/31/* followed by the current year.

Choosing the last day of the year tells Quicken to start your FSA out fresh (meaning with zero dollars) on January 1.

5. In the "Category for Adjustment" drop-down list, choose the FSA account and then click OK.

If you don't see the account in the drop-down list, click Transfers and then choose the FSA account. By choosing the account, you change the account's balance without assigning the amount to a Quicken category.

Your FSA balance is now zero and ready for the new year. You don't have to reset your account again until next year.

Let Quicken Remember

If the insurance-transaction money trail makes you think of hard-to-follow bread crumbs, Quicken's memorized payees (page 204) can help. With memorized payee, you record a transaction correctly once, and Quicken handles the transfers or category assignments from then on.

Here are the different types of FSA and HSA transactions and how you make Quicken memorize them:

- **Paycheck with FSA or HSA contribution.** If you set up a paycheck with the Paycheck Setup wizard, then you don't have to memorize the transaction. You simply record the paycheck every time you receive one and Quicken transfers your contribution to your FSA or HSA account.

- **Contribution made by check.** When you write your first check to contribute to an FSA or HSA, fill in the payee (the bank that holds the account, say) and choose the *FSA Available* or *HSA Available* account from the Category drop-down list. Then press Ctrl+M to memorize the transaction without the amount filled in. Then each time you record a contribution check, you need to fill in only the amount. If you contribute the same amount every time, you can memorize the transaction with the amount filled in.

- **Payment for an expense you submit for reimbursement.** If you paid with a check, create a transaction in your checking account register named something like *Submittable Expense* and leave the amount field blank. Choose the *FSA Submittable* or *HSA Submittable* account (page 278) from the Category drop-down list. Then press Ctrl+M to memorize the transaction. (You can also have Quicken memorize a separate transaction for submittable expenses you pay for with a credit card.) When you record a check for a submittable expense, begin typing *Submittable Expense* in the Payee field. QuickFill

selects the Submittable Expense payee and automatically fills in the Category field with your *FSA Submittable* or *HSA Submittable* account. Change the Payee field to reflect the vendor you paid and fill in the amount.

- **Payment directly from FSA or HSA account.** You don't have to memorize a transaction for this kind of payment. When you record the check or debit in the appropriate account register, Quicken deducts the expense from your available balance.

- **Reimbursement or denial of expenses.** If you submit expenses for reimbursement, the account administrator may accept your expenses, deny them, or do a little of both. To assign your expenses to the correct medical category, memorize a split transaction named something like *Medical Expense Assignments*. Add your regular Medical category (the one assigned to Schedule A) as the first split and the Medical FSA or Medical HSA category that you created as the second split. Then memorize the transaction by pressing Ctrl+M. When you receive your statement or explanation of benefits from the account administrator, enter the amount that was denied in the Medical split and the amount that was approved and reimbursed in the Medical FSA or Medical HSA split.

- **Deposit of reimbursement check.** When you receive a reimbursement check, record the deposit to your checking account (or whatever account you deposited the check into). In the Category drop-down list, choose the FSA Available or HSA Available account. In the Payee field, type something like *HSA Reimbursement Deposit* and then memorize the transaction (Ctrl+M.). When you record your next reimbursement deposit, all you have to do is fill in the amount.

Monitoring Spending and Saving

The word *budget* makes most people think of severe spending restrictions, like giving up the little treats that help them get through the day (goodbye, morning
lattes!). But a budget is nothing more than a plan for spending and saving your
money—and it can even include those lattes. Whether you create your budget in
Quicken or on a piece of paper, it can give you a sense of freedom that comes from
knowing you have a plan to make ends meet. The only requirement is that your
budget works *for you*. If you come up with a way to spend $5,000 a year on shoes
and *still* save enough for retirement, then your budget's working.

Quicken has a bunch of features that help you estimate how much money you'll
make, how much money you'll spend, and from there, how much money is available for saving or investing. Ideally, you base your budget on how much money
you want to save, whether your goal is buying a house, having a comfy retirement,
or paying for your kid's college education. With your income and savings goals as
the bookends, you can play with the expense categories in your budget until the
numbers add up. On the other hand, if you're a compulsive shopper, your first
crack at a budget may reveal that your expenses outweigh your income. Armed
with that knowledge, you can focus on scaling back spending—or look for a second job to help pay for all your purchases.

You can create budgets for special purposes, like estimating your annual retirement expenses so you can calculate how much you need to squirrel away. Or you
can create a budget of mandatory expenses to see how much you need in emergency funds if your job moves to Guam—and you don't.

After you've made a plan for spending and saving, Quicken's tools can help you monitor your performance. Whether you want to know how much you earn, spend, and save; how these numbers compare to the budget you set; or whether your checking account balance can get you through the month, Quicken reports and graphs have the answers. For a timetable of financial events, look at the Quicken Calendar, which shows when deposits and payments are scheduled and what your checking account balance may be each day.

If you're trying to save for a short-term goal (next year's vacation, say), Quicken's Savings Goals are ideal. The program tells you how much you need to save each month to reach that goal and shows your progress toward it. Quicken's Savings Plan feature helps you stay on top of your spending weaknesses. But this feature has its drawbacks, as you'll learn on page 321, so it's best reserved only for the categories you want to monitor closely.

Watching your projected cash flow is yet another way to manage your spending and saving. Cash flow adds the element of time to your income and expenses, so you can see what goes in and out of your cash accounts, and what's left over each month. In this chapter, you'll learn how to use all these tools to better manage your money and make saving for financial goals easier.

UP TO SPEED

What Quicken Budgeting Can and Can't Do

Some folks hate the idea of tracking their spending and limiting it to a target amount. But others want to control their (or their partner's) spending with an iron hand, divvying up paychecks into buckets of money for different purposes.

Budgeting in Quicken is more laissez-faire than the control-freak approach, but it can still be an effective tool for controlling where your money goes. The basic idea is to estimate how much you'll earn and spend in different categories—from your salary and earned interest to groceries, utilities, and music. *You* decide how detailed you want to be and how often you check in. Most people work with monthly budgets, because they can check their progress frequently and spot spending problems early, but you can budget by the week or year if you prefer.

Creating a budget and then comparing it to your actual spending is something of an art because your estimates rarely match what you spend. Unless the electric utility puts

you on a monthly program, your electric bill goes up and down each month; sometimes it's a little more than your budget and sometimes less. These small fluctuations are nothing to worry about, even if you're a stickler for detail.

What you're looking for is trends in over- or underspending. For example, if you budget $50 a month for dining out but find that you're spending $100 or more, you should reevaluate your budget. Can you afford twice your budgeted amount for dining out? Or do you want to cut back so you can save more for retirement?

If you insist on more control, a Quicken Savings Plan can help. You can allocate each buck to a corresponding category bucket. Then, as you spend money, the Savings Plan shows what you allocated, what you spent, and what's left over (or how much you overspent). You can even roll over allocated dollars that you didn't spend to the next month. See page 320 for more on setting up and using a Savings Plan.

Creating a Budget in Quicken

In Quicken, a budget is the most thorough way to track your income, expenses, and savings. If you want, you can include just a few categories in your budget, but the typical budget covers *all* your income and expense categories as well as some transfers, like the money you put in savings each month. The box on page 290 explains what a budget can do for you—and what it can't.

If you're new to Quicken, you don't have any existing info in your data file to use as a basis for a budget, so you have to build a budget from scratch with your best guesses in each category. But if you've got several months of transactions already in Quicken, you have a record of your actual spending and income, which the program can use to build a budget. Once you discover all the benefits of budgets and decide you can't live without them, you can copy existing budgets to create new ones.

Regardless of how much financial data you have available, you start budgeting by choosing Planning → Budget. In the Budget window, click the Setup tab to see the three budget-building methods Quicken offers:

- **Automatic.** If you have at least several months' worth of data in Quicken, the fastest way to build a budget is using your actual income and expenses. Once Quicken builds a budget from existing transactions, editing the values you want to change is a breeze. The program bases a new budget on the values from the previous calendar year, but you can change the dates Quicken uses to the period that best reflects your income and spending (see page 293).

- **Manual.** Although this method is the most tedious, it's your only option when you don't have existing data to use. You do have to type in all the numbers. Fortunately, though, you have to take this approach only for your first budget. And Quicken has shortcuts to make it as painless as possible. See page 297 for more info.

- **Copy current.** If you've already created a budget in Quicken, you can use it as the basis for next year's budget or a frugal budget in case you lose your job. Although many of your numbers may change, copying a budget is still faster than starting from scratch. See page 295 to learn how to copy a budget.

Creating a Budget Automatically

If you have several months of transactions in Quicken, you're in luck: The program can generate a budget for you based on your actual spending. How's that for simple? The closer you are to having 12 months' worth of transactions, the more accurately this budget will reflect what you actually make and spend. Fewer than 3 months' worth of transactions and the resulting budget won't be very useful.

Alas, what you earn and spend doesn't necessarily generate a *good* budget, particularly if you can't pass up a great price on a houseboat on eBay, but that's not Quicken's fault. So you'll probably have to tweak the budget Quicken generates.

Choosing the Right Planning Tool for the Job

As you can see if you go to Quicken's menu bar and open the Planning menu, Quicken comes with several planning tools for life events like college and retirement, along with several others that are hard to make heads or tails of: My Savings Plan, Budget, Cash Flow Forecast, and Savings Goals. Here's what you can do with each of these:

- **Life event planners.** From the Retirement Planner to the Special Purchase Planner, Quicken has tools to help you achieve financial goals, big and small. These planners are powerful, flexible wizards (sets of guided question screens). You tell the planner what you want to achieve, how much you plan to save, the investment return you expect, and so on, and Quicken tells you whether your plan works. If it doesn't, you can also create what-if scenarios to test different assumptions, like how much you'll have to save each year if you want to put a down payment on a house in 4 years instead of 5. Chapter 13 shows you how to use Quicken's Planners.

- **My Savings Plan.** A Quicken Savings Plan is a detailed planning tool that can help you save for a specific expense or control your spending. With a Savings Plan, you set up spending targets for a few key categories and monitor them month by month to help keep your spending under control. You can also use a Savings Plan to help save for big bills that arrive infrequently, like car insurance. Unlike the other planning tools, you can create only one Savings Plan, though your Plan can handle multiple spending categories. You'll learn how later in this chapter (page 320).

- **Budget.** You use a budget to spell out your plan for income, spending, and savings for a year, broken down by month or quarter. Once you've created this plan (page 291), you can compare it to your actual income, spending, and savings to see if you need to make any changes. You can create more than one budget in Quicken—like one to plan for emergencies, and one for the next year—but you choose one of those budgets to compare to your actual income and spending. (When a new year rolls around or you want to edit a budget, you can make a different budget the active one.)

- **Cash Flow Forecast.** A Quicken Cash Flow Forecast (page 318) isn't really a plan. It just tells you about income and expenses over a period of time, up to 2 years. You can set up different forecast scenarios to include different accounts or use different budgets to help figure out how much you can save each month, and how much you could have in your accounts as time passes.

- **Savings Goals.** This feature helps you earmark the money you save for different goals. Suppose you're saving for a down payment on a house, a vacation, and the starter cash for a small business. You sock away a ton of money each month, but it just shows up as one big balance in your savings account. With Savings Goals, you can tell Quicken how much of each month's savings goes toward each goal (page 327), so you can keep tabs on how close you are to having the money you need.

For example, you may want to rein in your spending in categories you can do without, increase budgeted amounts for categories you expect to go up, or earmark leftover cash for transfers to savings.

Here's how to create a budget automatically:

1. **Choose Planning → Budget.**

   The Budget window opens to the Setup tab unless you already have a budget set up (then it opens to the Summary tab).

2. **Click the Setup tab.**

Quicken automatically selects the Automatic option, as shown in Figure 11-1, so you're ready to create your new budget.

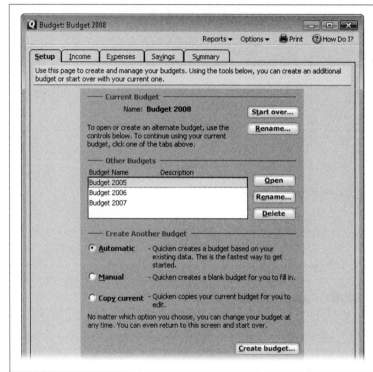

3. **Click "Create budget".**

The Create Budget: Automatic dialog box asks for a bit more information, as you can see in Figure 11-2.

4. **In the Name text box, type a meaningful name for the budget.**

The Name box appears only if you have at least one budget. If this is your first budget, the first box you see is "Choose date range to scan". Quicken automatically fills in a generic name, such as *Budget 2,* but you should change the name to something more meaningful. You can name a budget by calendar year— *Budget 2009,* for example—or, for a budget with a special purpose, give it a name like *Retirement Budget* or *Unemployment Budget.*

5. **In the "Choose date range to scan" section, in the From and To text boxes, type the dates you want the budget to be based on.**

Quicken automatically fills in the dates for the most recent 12 months. For example, if you create the budget in January of 2009, the From box is set to

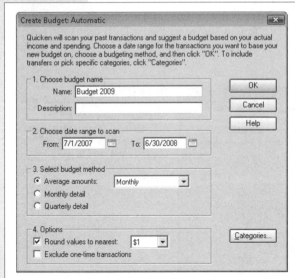

Figure 11-2:
The Create Budget: Automatic dialog box has several options to help make your first pass at a budget more accurate. The settings Quicken automatically picks work well for most folks. But you can fine-tune an automatically generated budget to match your goals.

1/1/2008, and the To box is set to 12/31/2008. (Remember, at this stage of the game, Quicken is looking at your transaction *history* to create a budget for you. So that's why it suggests having a look at the previous year.) You can choose other dates if they give a more accurate picture of annual income and expenditures. For example, if you were out of work for the first 3 months of the date range, change the From date to the day you started your new job.

6. **In the "Select budget method" section, leave the "Average amounts" option selected. If you want to budget over something other than months, select the duration in the drop-down menu.**

   Quicken automatically selects the "Average amounts" option and sets the frequency to Monthly. Using average amounts is the easiest approach and works well for all but the most fastidious budgeters. With this option selected, Quicken calculates monthly averages in each category by dividing the total you spent during the date range by the number of months in the range.

   Choose the "Monthly detail" option to use your actual monthly values as your budgeted monthly values. For most categories—like Groceries—monthly detail is overkill, because the amount you spend doesn't change much from month to month. But monthly detail is a great way to catch infrequent income and expenses (like tax refunds and auto registration fees), or expenses that vary by season (like your gas and electric bill). One way to compromise is to choose "Quarterly detail", which turns actual quarterly totals into your budgeted quarterly totals. Or you can switch individual categories to show monthly detail— see page 302 to learn how.

7. **If you want nice round budget numbers, in the "Round values to nearest" text box, choose the number of dollars to use for rounding.**

   Because budgeting isn't an exact science, consider having Quicken round your budget amounts to the nearest $10. If your money is really tight, you can keep the rounding value at $1. On the other hand, Bill Gates might set rounding to the nearest $100.

8. **To keep one-time transactions in Quicken's calculation, leave the "Exclude one-time transactions" checkbox turned off.**

   Plenty of one-time transactions *belong* in your budget, like annual home-owner's insurance premiums or auto registration. You're better off keeping one-time transactions initially. You can remove the ones you don't want when you fine-tune the budget (page 297).

   Suppose you received a whopping refund from the IRS in April and bought a motorcycle in May to celebrate. With the "Exclude one-time transactions" checkbox turned off (as Quicken sets it initially), your generated budget shows a large chunk of income in April for your tax refund as well as a large expenditure in an expense category (or vehicle asset account) in May. Unless you expect that kind of windfall every year, excluding these one-time transactions will give you a more accurate budget. To ignore one-time transactions in Quicken's budget calculation, turn on the "Exclude one-time transactions" checkbox.

Note: Quicken automatically includes *all* its categories in your budget, whether you've used them or not. If you want to choose specific categories for budgeting, click the Categories button and then turn category checkboxes on or off.

---

9. **Click OK.**

   Quicken displays a message box telling you that it created your new budget, and the Budget window displays the Income tab, as shown in Figure 11-3. Click OK to dismiss the message box and then skip to page 297 to learn how to edit your new budget.

Copying the Current Budget

If next year's budget is almost identical to this year's, copying this year's budget and changing a few numbers is the fastest and easiest way to generate your new budget. For that matter, once you have one budget in Quicken, it's almost always easier to copy an existing budget than to create one from scratch.

Here's how you copy a budget:

1. **Choose Planning → Budgets and then, in the Budget window, click the Setup tab.**

   Immediately below the Current Budget heading, you see the name of the current budget. Any other existing budgets appear under the Other Budgets heading.

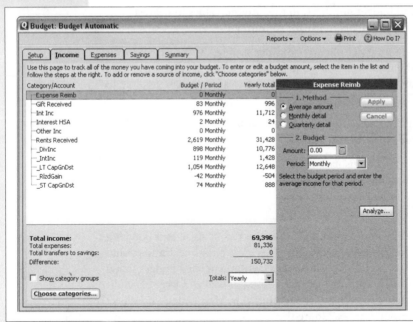

Figure 11-3:
Below the income categories, Quicken shows your total income, total expenses, total transfers to savings, and the difference. If the Difference figure is negative, your expenses are greater than your income, so you know you have some budgeting work to do (page 319).

2. **Make sure the budget you want to copy is the current budget.**

   If you have only one budget, it's already current, so skip this step. If the budget you want isn't current, then in the Other Budgets list, select it and then click Open. The Income tab appears with the values from the budget you opened. Click the Setup tab once more. The name of the budget you opened appears under the Current Budget heading.

3. **In the Create Another Budget section, select the "Copy current" option and then click "Create budget".**

   The Budget Name dialog box appears so you can give your budget a new name and description.

4. **In the Name text box, type a name that indicates what you plan to use the budget for.**

   Quicken's names (*Budget 2, Budget 3,* and so on) won't help you remember which budget is which. Replace Quicken's names with more meaningful ones, like *Budget 2009* or *Budget for a Kept Man.*

Note: If you want more detailed notes on the budget than you can fit in the Name text box, fill in the Description box. For example, type something like "Includes only mandatory categories," or whatever you want to remember about this budget. To read this description later when your memory fails you, in the Budget window (Planning → Budgets), click the Setup tab. The Other Budgets list shows budget names and descriptions.

---

5. Click OK.

Quicken displays a message box telling you that it successfully created the budget. In the background, you can see the Income tab with the income values for the new budget. Click OK to close the dialog box.

You're ready to start tweaking your budget values, as described below.

Creating a Budget Manually

Creating a budget from scratch is far more work than either building one from existing data or copying one you've already created. But if you're new to Quicken, your only option is to start from scratch. You need to indicate the categories you want to budget, as well as your estimated values for each category. On the bright side, this process forces you to think about how much you expect to spend in each category and where you can show more restraint. And Quicken does its best to make the process of manual budget creation as painless as possible.

Here are the basic steps to creating a budget manually:

1. **In the Budget window (Planning → Budgets), click the Setup tab.**

   If this is your first Quicken budget, the Setup tab displays only the Automatic and Manual options, and the "Create budget" button.

2. **Select the Manual option and then click "Create budget".**

   The Budget Name dialog box asks for a name and an optional description.

3. **Name the budget and (if you want) type a description and then click OK.**

   A manual budget in Quicken is truly blank—it doesn't even have categories, as you can see in the background of Figure 11-4.

4. **To add categories to your budget, click the "Choose categories" button and then select the categories and accounts to include in the budget.**

   You can Ctrl-click to select individual categories or Shift-click to select several contiguous categories. Page 305 explains how to add or remove income, expense, and savings categories in your budget. With categories in place, you're finally ready to add some budget numbers, as described in the next section.

Filling In Budget Values

Entering budget numbers in Quicken is the same regardless of whether your budget is completely empty or full of numbers that need changing. Quicken gives you several ways to add and adjust numbers, all of which are described in this section.

Before you get started, make sure that the budget you want to edit is the current budget. The name of the budget you want should appear in the Budget window's title, as shown in Figure 11-5 (where the budget is named *Budget 2009*). To learn how to change the current budget, see page 304.

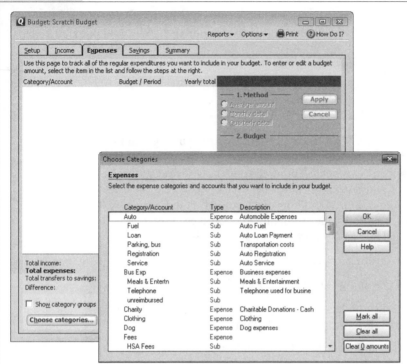

Figure 11-4:
In the Choose Categories dialog box, you can select as few or as many categories as you want. If you're dipping your baby toe into budgeting, you can start by clicking just a few categories to select them. If you're ready to dive in headfirst, you can click "Mark all" to budget every category.

In the Budget window, you can (and should) change how Quicken displays your categories to get the best overview of your situation:

- **All-in-one view.** If you want to budget all income, expense, and transfer categories on a single tab (labeled Budget), choose Options → Combined View. Quicken lists categories starting with Income categories, followed by Expense categories and finally Transfers at the bottom of the list.

- **No savings view.** If you live from paycheck to paycheck, you can choose Options → Income/Expense View to hide the Savings tab altogether. The Budget window includes the Setup, Income, Expenses, and Summary tabs.

- **Separate view.** To see income categories separate from expenses and transfers, as shown in Figure 11-5, choose Options → Separate View.

At the bottom of the Budget window, you can see whether your budget works. The values for "Total income", "Total expenses", "Total transfers to savings", and Difference tell you whether you make more money than you spend or need to tighten your belt a bit. Here's what each value tells you:

- **Total income** is how much money you expect to make over the course of a year.

- **Total expenses** represent how much you've budgeted for spending during a year.

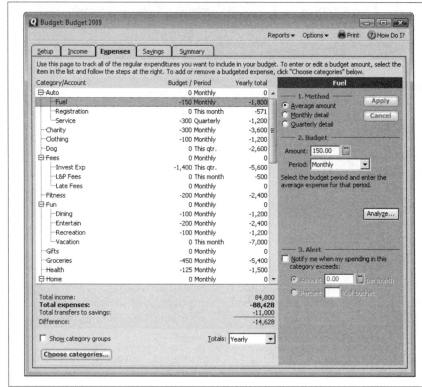

Figure 11-5:
The pane on the Budget window's right side includes options and text boxes for setting the budget values for a category. Here, the selected category is Fuel.

- **Total transfers to savings** shows how much you're planning on socking away. For example, this amount may include your monthly contribution to a 401(k) account, a weekly deposit in a savings account, or the bonus you invest every December.

- **Difference** is how to tell whether your budget is a success. If this value is positive, you've got money left over. If this value is negative, you're heading for trouble.

Tip: Quicken automatically displays yearly budget totals. But you can see monthly or quarterly totals by choosing a different value in the Totals drop-down menu, in the bottom-center part of the window, as you can see in Figure 11-5 (where it says "Yearly").

Average Budget Values

Average values are the fastest and easiest approach to budgeting—and they're quite effective for most categories. For example, say your grocery bill comes in at $260 this month, $282 the next, and goes over $400 when you throw your annual Bastille Day party. Overall, the monthly average is about $300. Instead of trying to anticipate the actual monthly figures, you're better off setting the monthly budget value to $300 and letting the actual costs average out over the course of a year. The box on page 300 provides some tips for successful averaging.

How the Budget Balances

As budgeting aficionados know, regardless of the numbers in a budget, you'll spend more than the average in some months and less in others. If your salary is constant, sometimes you'll have money to spare and other times you'll raid the piggy bank.

The key to success, whether you make a budget or not, is to not spend that spare cash on frivolities. Otherwise, you may not have enough to pay the electric bill when expenses peak. Suppose you pay $1,200 twice a year for auto insurance.

If you don't sock away $200 a month for that expense, chances are you won't have the $1,200 for the premium when it's due.

As you'll learn in this section, you can add budget values to specific months to represent these infrequent but painfully large payments so you'll be prepared when they come due. You can also look at your cash flow forecast (page 318) to see whether you're stockpiling enough cash to cover upcoming expenses.

Here are the steps for using an average value for a budget category:

1. **In the Category/Account column, click the category you want to edit.**

   When you select a category, on the right side of the Budget window you see a pane for setting the budget values for that category, as shown in Figure 11-5. Quicken automatically selects the "Average amount" option unless you've previously chosen a different option for that category.

2. **In the Method section, select the "Average amount" option (if it isn't already selected).**

   The heading on that section is "1. Method", which is a hint that selecting the method you want to use is the first step in the process of setting up budget values. Depending on the Method option you choose, you see different text boxes underneath the heading "2. Budget".

3. **In the Amount box, type the average value you want to use. In the Period box, choose the period to which the average amount applies.**

   Between the amount and a period, you can create any type of average you want. For a category like Groceries, it's easy enough to type in the typical amount you spend in a month and then, in the Period drop-down menu, choose Monthly.

   But Quicken offers lots of choices for period: daily, weekly, every two weeks, twice a month, monthly, every two months, quarterly, twice a year, and yearly. If your garbage pickup costs $60 every quarter, for example, type in *60* and then choose Quarterly. When you click Apply, the "Yearly total" for your garbage category on the left side of the Budget window changes to $240.

   If you don't know what a realistic average is but you've tracked your finances in Quicken for at least a few months, the Analyze button can help. Click it to see a pop-up window with your actual values during the previous year (or however long you've been tracking your finances) and an average value using the period you've chosen, as you can see in Figure 11-6. If the average value from the past is very different from the average you entered, consider typing a new value into the Amount box.

Tip: If you don't see the Analysis section on the right side of the Budget window, the window isn't tall enough. You can either click the Analyze button to pop up the graph in another window or resize the Budget window to make it taller. (As you drag the corner of the window, the graph appears as soon as the window is tall enough.)

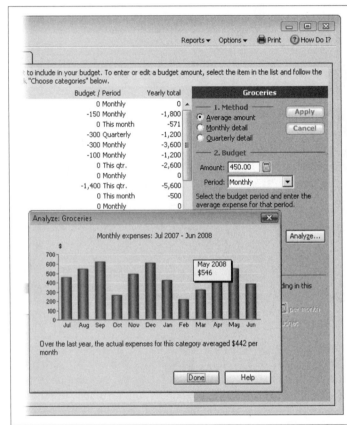

Figure 11-6:
The Analyze bar graph shows values for the previous year organized by the period that you selected in the "2. Budget" section (in this case, they're organized by month). If the values in the bar graph change dramatically from period to period, you may want to switch to detailed budgeting (page 302). To see the actual value for a period, hover your cursor over the appropriate bar. After a couple of seconds, the time period and the value appear in a pop-up box (here, the box reads "May 2008 $546").

4. **Click Apply.**

   Quicken adds the amount and period to the columns on the left side of the Budget window (Quicken has added the $450 per month from Figure 11-6 to the Groceries category, as shown in Figure 11-7). If you'd like Quicken to warn you when you're outspending your budget, you can set up budget alerts in this window's Alert section, as described in the box on page 302.

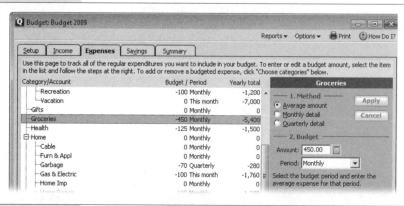

Figure 11-7:
For each category in the Budget window, Quicken shows the budgeted amount, and the period to which that amount applies. The "Yearly total" column lists the budgeted amount for an entire year regardless of how you define your budget numbers (weekly, monthly, quarterly, or whatever).

POWER USERS' CLINIC

Setting Up Budget Alerts

Quicken can't stop you from handing a sales clerk your credit card, but it can remind you that you're spending more than you had planned. When you add budget values, you can also create an alert that pops up if you exceed a specific dollar amount or percentage of your budget value.

In the Budget window's Alert section, shown in the bottom-right part of Figure 11-5, turn on the "Notify me when my spending in this category exceeds" checkbox. For a category that uses average values, choose the Percent option and set a percentage of the budget. If you want to see an alert

before you exceed your budget, then set the Percent text box to *90*. If you want a warning only when you've gone too far, then set the value to *110*.

For some categories with monthly or quarterly detail, you may not bother with alerts given that you can't change your car insurance premium. If you have some control over the amounts (like lowering the heating oil bills by turning down the thermostat), you can use the Amount option to specify a dollar amount for that period, but it requires regular updating if your budget values change each year.

Detailed Budget Values

If you want more detail in a category than you can see with average budget numbers, then, in the Budget window's Method section, you can opt for "Monthly detail" or "Quarterly detail". These options are perfect when you have large payments that take place in the same month each year, like auto insurance premiums, or payments that vary from season to season, like your heating bill. So rather than seeing, say, a value of $1,400 for your budgeted auto insurance, you see that you need to come up with $700 in April and October. If you add the $3,000 you expect to owe the IRS on April 15, you can see that you need to save up for your April expenses. Each category can use a different option: an average, monthly detail, or quarterly detail.

When you select the "Monthly detail" option, Quicken displays a text box for each month (or for each quarter for the "Quarterly detail" option). The next time you look at that category, the program selects the same option, and displays the same text boxes.

As you can see in Figure 11-8, to set a value for a given period, all you have to do is click the text box for that period and then type in a value. The Analysis graph in the bottom right of the window (or the Analyze window, which appears when you click Analyze) is particularly helpful for figuring out when these erratic amounts show up and how much they are. To see the average amount you spent in a specific period, hover your cursor over the appropriate bar.

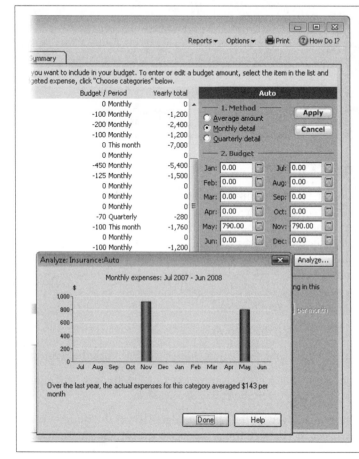

Figure 11-8:
Click a value box in the Budget section and then type in the budget value for that period (here, the periods are months). Press Tab to move to the next box. To see the value of a past period, click Analyze and then in the Analyze pop-up window, hover your cursor over a bar.

Resetting detailed values

If you use an average value for a category and switch to the "Monthly detail" option, then Quicken fills in every month's box with the average monthly value. Instead of editing every month's value by hand, here's a shortcut for clearing out values in the month boxes:

1. **With the "Average amount" option selected in the Method section, change the value in the Budget section's Amount box to zero and then click Apply.**

   The value in every period changes to zero.

---

2. Select the "Monthly detail" or "Quarterly detail" option.

All the month or quarter boxes are set to zero, so you can enter budget values only in the months or quarters when you have income or expenses.

Budgeting at Different Levels of Detail

If you use parent categories and subcategories to break down your income and expenses, then you can budget some categories in detail, and others at a higher level. For example, you may set a budget value for every subcategory within the Auto category. By doing that, you can compare your spending on repairs and fuel to your budget. (Maybe you'll decide to buy a more dependable car or one that's less fuel-hungry.)

On the other hand, you can assign a budget value to the Fun category and leave out budget numbers for the subcategories (Vacation, Recreation, Entertainment and Hobbies, for example). Then, you can track your overall spending on fun without worrying about whether the money was spent on hobbies or recreation. (Because you assign transactions to the subcategories, you can still see how much you spent in each one.)

Making a Budget Current

After you create your first budget, you can create as many other budgets as you want. But you can work with only one budget at a time—the *current* budget. Any changes you make to budgeted values on the Income, Expenses, or Savings tabs apply to this budget. Quicken also uses the current budget when you choose the "Copy current" option to create a new budget, as you learned on page 295. Perhaps most importantly, the program uses the current budget when you generate reports that compare your budget to actual spending, so it's essential that you summon the budget you really want to work on.

To change the current budget, do the following:

1. **Choose Planning → Budgets and then, in the Budget window, click the Setup tab.**

   Check the budget name that appears under the Current Budget heading. In Figure 11-1 (page 293), the current budget is *Budget 2008*.

2. **To change the current budget, in the Other Budgets list in the middle of the Budget window, select the budget you want to work with and then click the Open button.**

   Quicken makes the budget you selected the current budget, and displays the Income tab that shows the current budget's numbers. The program also adds the budget name to the window title. For example, the Budget window's title changes to something like Budget: *Budget 2008*.

3. **Click the Setup tab once more.**

   The name of the budget you opened appears under the Current Budget heading. Now you can edit any of its values by clicking the appropriate tab: Income, Expenses, or Savings. If you want to use this budget as the basis for a new one, choose the "Copy current" option and then follow steps 3–5 on pages 296–297.

Saving or Restoring a Budget

Quicken automatically saves the changes you make to any budget when you close the Budget window or switch over to a different budget. If you've worked on your budget for a while and want to make sure you don't lose your changes to a computer crash or power outage, then, in the Budget window's menu bar, choose Options → Save Budget.

On the other hand, if you've made changes that are a total bust, you can choose Options → Restore Budget to replace the values from your current editing session with the previously saved ones.

Choosing Budget Categories

Quicken doesn't make you include every income or spending category in all the budgets you create. For example, if you want to create a budget for your retirement spending, it makes sense to omit categories for payroll taxes, commuting, and business lunches. Similarly, you'll probably want to add categories for things like long-term care insurance, greens fees, and Florida road maps. Quicken makes it easy to add, change, or delete categories from any budget. If you create a budget manually, you have to start by adding categories before you can budget anything, but you can change these categories later if you change your mind. This section describes how to choose income and expense categories, and how to categorize transfers to savings that you include in your budget.

Choosing Income and Expense Categories

The Income and Expenses tabs have buttons for choosing which categories to include in your budget. Clicking the "Choose categories" button found at the bottom left of each tab displays either income categories or expense categories (Figure 11-9). Because the Savings tab is for transfers to other accounts, the button at the bottom left of the Savings tab reads "Choose accounts".

Note: Although transfers to savings appear on the Savings tab, the Expenses tab is where you find the transfers to loan accounts or credit card accounts that reduce the balance you owe. Scroll to the bottom of the Category/Account list, and you'll see an entry for each loan you've created in Quicken. The label looks something like "TO Mortgage My House", as shown in the background of Figure 11-9.

Here are various ways to add or remove categories from a budget:

- **Click individual entries.** Clicking an unchecked entry adds it to the budget and displays a green checkmark to show that it's included. Click a checkmarked category to remove it from the budget (which also removes the checkmark). You can select several adjacent entries by clicking the first category and then Shift-clicking the last category in the group. You can also Ctrl-click entries to select multiple non-sequential entries.

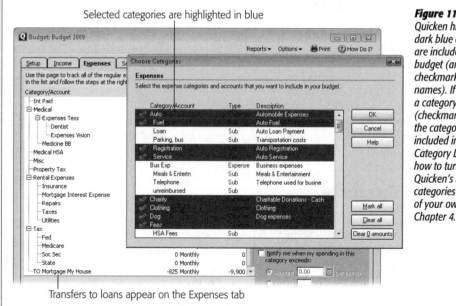

Selected categories are highlighted in blue

Transfers to loans appear on the Expenses tab

Figure 11-9:
Quicken highlights in dark blue categories that are included in the budget (and places a checkmark next to their names). If you don't see a category you want (checkmarked or not), the category isn't included in your Category List. To learn how to turn on one of Quicken's built-in categories or create one of your own, see Chapter 4.

Note: Clicking a high-level category (like Auto) *doesn't* automatically select all the subcategories underneath it (Auto Loan, Fuel, and so on). You have to select the subcategories you want, even if you've already selected their parent category.

- **Mark all.** The fastest way to add categories is to click "Mark all", which adds *all* the categories in the list (income categories from the Income tab or expense categories from the Expenses tab).

- **Clear all.** If you've hopelessly mangled the categories in your budget and want to start afresh, click "Clear all" to turn off all of the categories shown. You can then click individual categories to turn them back on.

- **Clear 0 amounts.** This button is particularly helpful if you've created a budget from your existing data. When you click "Clear 0 amounts", Quicken automatically turns off the categories that didn't have any actual transactions assigned to them. If you click this button, it's a good idea to review the category list to make sure that you haven't turned off any categories you want to keep. You may not have gone on vacation last year, but you still want to budget for some fun this year.

Choosing Accounts for Transfers to Savings

The most effective way to save money is to squirrel it away in savings before you get the urge to spend it. By budgeting for transfers to savings, you're halfway to making those transfers a reality. As long as you stick to your budgeted income and expense values, you'll have enough money to make your budgeted transfers to savings, too.

Tip: If you're interested in setting up regular savings transfers, Quicken provides a feature called a Savings Goal that helps you track how much you've saved, as described in the box on page 292.

To add a savings transfer to your budget, follow these steps:

1. **On the Budget window's Savings tab, click the "Choose accounts" button in the bottom-left corner. (If you don't see the Savings tab, in the Budget window's menu bar, choose Options → Separate View.)**

   Sure enough, the Choose Accounts dialog box appears showing your bank accounts, asset accounts, and investment accounts. (Liability accounts don't appear in the list, because you add transfers to loan and credit card accounts on the Budget window's Expenses tab [page 305] instead.)

2. **In the Choose Accounts dialog box, turn on the accounts you transfer money to and from and then click OK.**

   Be sure to include accounts that you might transfer money *out* of, such as CDs that mature or investment accounts that provide your retirement income. The accounts you select appear on the Savings tab.

Tip: You don't want to click "Mark all" in the Choose Accounts dialog box, because you'll just fill up your budget with transfers that never see any action. Instead, turn on the individual accounts that you transfer money to regularly, like your 401(k) or vacation club savings account. The interest that CDs and other savings accounts pay is already covered by an Income category such as Interest Income.

3. **To budget a savings transfer, select the account that receives the funds.**

   The name of the account appears at the top of the right-hand pane, as shown in Figure 11-10 (where the selected account is *SEP Schwab*).

4. **In the Method section, select the "Average amount" or "Monthly detail" option.**

   If you plan to set aside some money each month, choose "Average amount". For example, you could add your 401(k) contribution using an average value set to the "Every two weeks" period to match your paycheck. On the other hand, if you transfer money to your brokerage account in December when you receive that year-end bonus, you can select "Monthly detail" and then type the value you plan to invest in December.

5. **In the budget value pane on the right side of the Budget window, type the amount you want to transfer to savings, like the *3,000.00* in Figure 11-10.**

   When you look at the "Yearly total" column on the left side of the Budget window, the transfer to savings shows up as a negative number. That's because the transfer comes out of your income, so Quicken subtracts it to see whether your budget balances.

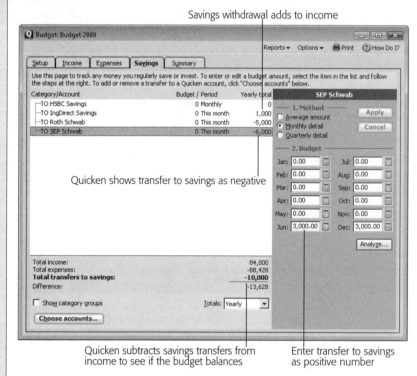

Savings withdrawal adds to income

Figure 11-10:
To budget for withdrawals from savings, such as a required distribution from an IRA, type a – sign before the number you enter in the budget values pane. On the left side of the Budget window, that withdrawal from savings becomes a positive number because it adds to your income.

Quicken shows transfer to savings as negative

Quicken subtracts savings transfers from income to see if the budget balances

Enter transfer to savings as positive number

6. **Click Apply.**

   The Budget window's left-hand pane shows the budgeted amount and the period, along with the yearly total. (Quicken adds up the "Total income", "Total expenses", and "Total transfers to savings" to see whether you have any money left over at the end of the year.)

Now that you've *budgeted for* regular transfers to savings, all you have to do is transfer the money. To make these transfers as easy as possible, you can set up regularly scheduled transfers to savings (see the box on page 201 for details).

Reviewing Spending and Saving

Sometimes, you need a laser-like focus on what you've spent, for example, to see just how much you spent at fast-food restaurants last month. Other times, the big picture is enough to tell you whether you're living within your means. If a few red flags are waving in your financial picture, you can review your finances in different ways to find the problems and come up with solutions. Many of Quicken's windows and tabs include shortcuts to reports and graphs that may answer the questions you're asking. You can also generate any Quicken report you want from the Reports & Graphs Center. If you customize reports (page 447), you can save them for future use. This section walks you through reports, graphs, and other tools that help you monitor your income, spending, and saving. (Chapter 14 has the full scoop on reports.)

How Much Did You Spend?

Every so often, you have specific questions about your spending. Say your neighbor wants to know how much your spiffy gas grill cost. Or you just dented your car *again* and want to know what the repairs cost last time. Or maybe the cost to fill up your Hummer is downright scary and you want to know how much you spent on gas last month. Quicken has several ready-made reports for these types of questions. Here are the reports you can use to find out how much you've spent and where to find them in Quicken:

- **How much did I spend on…?** This EasyAnswer report (page 434) tells you how much you spent in a category over a specific period. You choose a category and a period, and Quicken customizes the Itemized Categories report (page 310) for you. To run this report, choose Reports → EasyAnswer. In the Reports & Graphs window that appears, click "How much did I spend on…?" In the "Show spending on" drop-down list, choose the category you want to see. In the "For the period" drop-down list, choose the timeframe (page 449), for instance, "Last month".

Tip: If you don't see any transactions, click the + sign to the left of the category's name to expand it so you can see the transactions assigned to it. If the category has subcategories, click the + to the left of a subcategory's name to display its transactions.

- **How much did I pay to…?** This report shows what you paid to a specific payee. It's perfect for finding transactions when you know who you paid or for payments that you're sure you made, but the payee claims you didn't. Choose Reports → EasyAnswer. In the Reports & Graphs window that appears, click "How much did I pay to…?" In the "Show payments to" drop-down list, choose the payee and, in the "For the period" drop-down list, choose the timeframe.

How Are You Doing Overall?

What you spend doesn't tell the whole story. If you're a college student scraping by on waiting table tips, spending $2,000 a month could break the bank. On the other hand, if your tech company just went public, spending only $5,000 a month may seem like unnecessary restraint. Quicken has two flavors of reports for reviewing your income and spending, depending on whether you want a high-level overview or want to peruse itemized transactions. Here are the built-in reports you can use to look at income and expenses:

- **The big picture.** Quicken's "Where did I spend my money during the period…?" EasyAnswer report is the same as the built-in "Income/Expense by Category" report. It summarizes how much you earned and spent by category over a given period. You can drill down to transactions in this report by double-clicking a value in the report, which opens a QuickZoom report window (page 434). All you have to choose is the period, which you can change in the report window at any time, as Figure 11-11 shows. Choose Reports → EasyAnswer. In the Reports & Graphs window that appears, click "Where did I spend my money during the period...?" In the "For the period" drop-down list, choose a timeframe (page 449), for instance, "Year to date".

Note: Another way to launch the "Income/Expense by Category" report is by choosing Reports → Spending → "Income and Expense by Category".

Choose the time period for the entire report

Choose the interval shown in each column

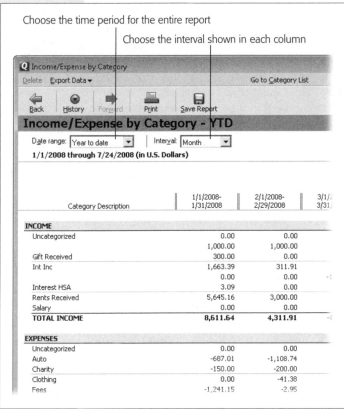

Figure 11-11:
To change the time frame covered by the report, in the "Date range" drop-down list, choose an overall period, such as "Last year". To change the interval that each column represents, in the Interval drop-down list, choose a period, such as Month, Quarter, or Year.

- **Income and expense detail.** If you want to scan through all your transactions grouped by category, the Itemized Categories report is what you want. This report shows the same numbers as the "Income/Expense by Category" report, but you can expand each category to see the transactions that make up the category's total. Because transaction reports like this one contain columns for transactions fields, you can't create additional columns for time intervals.

Tip: If you don't want to see all your categories in the "Income/Expense by Category" report or the Itemized Categories report, you can customize these reports to show only the categories you want. In the report window's toolbar, click Customize. In the Customize dialog box that appears, click the Categories tab and then turn off the checkboxes for categories you don't want to see. Page 453 gives the full story about choosing report categories in reports.

How Are You Doing Compared to Your Budget?

Reviewing your income and expenses tells you whether you're living within your means. However, if you're trying to live frugally so you can buy a house or put three kids through college, you probably want to know how your income and expenses are doing compared to the budget you prepared (page 291). A personal budget isn't like a corporate or government budget, which cuts off spending when it reaches the budgeted values (at least that's how those budgets are *supposed* to work). Instead, your budget is a target. Still, it would be nice if Quicken gave you a little help figuring out whether you're actually sticking to your plan. Good news: You can generate a budget *report*, which includes how much you budgeted, how much you actually earned or spent, and the difference between the two.

Note: Budget reports are columns of numbers, which tend to blur together. To help you spot potential problems, Quicken uses red text for income that's *less* than you budgeted and expenses that are *more* than you budgeted.

Quicken gives you three ways to compare your budget to your actual spending, all of which you can tweak to see exactly what you're interested in:

- **Monthly Budget Report.** Despite the emphasis on *budget* in its name, this report shows actual values, budgeted values, and the difference between the two for each month of the date range you choose. This report is the best for spotting categories where you regularly overspend. However, if income or expenses don't happen exactly when you planned, this report can raise red flags needlessly. If you budgeted your car insurance payment for March but paid it in February, for example, the report shows that you overspent on car insurance in February and underspent in March. The last three columns in this report cover the entire date range, so you can see whether your budget is working over a longer period.

- **Budget Report.** This tabular report starts with three columns (actual values, budgeted values, and the difference between the two) showing your income and expenses for the year to date, which is ideal for a sneak peek at whether your budget is generally working. (The report pictured in Figure 11-12 is a Budget Report.) To change this report into a *Monthly* Budget Report (or any other period), pick a different period from the Column drop-down list.

- **Budget Graph.** For more visual folks, this bar graph provides an overview that shows whether you ran short of your budget or had money left over. The graph displays two bars for each category. The bars for budgeted expenses are blue. Actual values show up as green bars if your actual spending was *less* than you budgeted, and as red bars if your actual spending was *more* than you budgeted.

Here are the steps for generating and fine-tuning a budget report—and for saving that report so you don't have to customize it over and over:

1. **Choose Reports → Spending and then choose either Budget or Monthly Budget.**

   A report window opens, and displays the report you selected. The window's title is the name of the report (Budget or Monthly Budget).

Note: To see all the available reports, in the Quicken Tool Bar, click Reports (or choose Reports → Reports & Graphs Center). To run a budget report from the Reports & Graphs Center, expand the Spending section and then click Budget or Monthly Budget. See Chapter 14 for more information on working with reports.

---

2. **Quicken initially runs these reports for the current year to date. To see a different date range, like "Last month" or "Last 12 months", in the Date range drop-down menu, choose a period.**

   Quicken displays three columns for each period, as you see in Figure 11-12.

Tip: To view a bar graph of your performance, choose Reports → Graphs and then choose either Budget or Monthly Budget.

---

3. **If you want to see intermediate results within the date range—to show your budget and actuals for each quarter within the year, for example—in the Column drop-down menu, choose a period like Month, Quarter, or Year.**

   The Monthly Budget Report already has columns for each month, so it doesn't have a Column drop-down menu.

4. **To customize the report in other ways, at the right end of the report window's toolbar, click Customize. (The Customize icon looks like a hammer in front of a piece of paper.)**

   You can tweak budget reports to inspect specific aspects of your income and expenses. For example, you can choose categories and tags (page 68) to evaluate your budget for a rental property. See Chapter 14 for the full scoop.

5. **To save this report to re-run in the future, in the report window's toolbar, click Save Report (the disc icon).**

   The Save Report dialog box opens. In the "Report name" box, type a descriptive name for the report, like *Quarterly Budget Prior 12 Months*. Quicken automatically sets the "Save in" value to "None (My Saved Reports)", which means

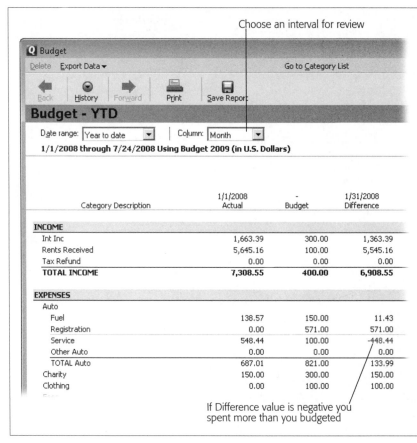

Choose an interval for review

If Difference value is negative you spent more than you budgeted

Figure 11-12:
If a value in a Difference column is negative (Quicken displays negative values in red text), you've spent more than you budgeted in that category, or earned less than you budgeted, if it's an income category. Before you take corrective action, scroll to the bottom of the report to see the total for the period. If the Overall Total is positive, your total income for the period was greater than your total spending. The box on page 314 has more hints for evaluating your actual performance.

you're saving the report to the My Saved Reports folder, not a subfolder. To keep your customized reports organized, click Create Folder to make a folder where you'll store your reports. For example, you may want to keep all budget reports in a folder named Budgets. Then you'd save a report to that folder by changing the "Save in" value to Budgets. Or you could create one folder for spending reports and a second folder for investing reports. Use whatever filing system makes sense to you. See page 455 for instructions on saving reports to folders.

To generate your customized report at a later date, choose Reports → My Saved Reports & Graphs and then choose the name of the report. Quicken generates your custom report with the current values in your data file.

How's Your Cash Flow?

If your checking account has ever run dry between paychecks (and whose hasn't?), you understand how important cash flow is. (*Cash flow* is the amount of money you have left over after you take your income and spending into account.) Although your annual budget may show plenty of income to cover your expenses,

WORD TO THE WISE

Budget Course Corrections

Because the amount you spend from month to month often varies, comparing the budgeted and actual numbers for a single month is bound to make you a little nervous. Perhaps you hit Costco on March 1 and March 31 instead of your budgeted once a month, so it looks like you spent twice as much on groceries as you planned. Here are a few tips for evaluating your performance, and suggestions of what to do if things go awry:

- **Report over longer periods.** Change your budget report to show numbers quarter by quarter or for the year to date, rather than for each month. By comparing longer periods, you'll smooth out any month-to-month variations. As long as your income for the year to date is greater than your expenses (and savings) for the same period, you're OK.

- **Check actual income.** If you didn't receive that bonus you counted on or an illness cut into your billable hours, you may want to adjust the expense categories in your budget for the rest of the year to reduce future spending.

- **Don't sweat the small stuff.** Don't worry about expenses that come in slightly over budget. Yes, they're negative and show up in red, begging for you to do something, but you don't need to fret about spending $5 more than you planned in a given category. Instead, watch for a steady trend of overspending and then review the transactions in that category to see if there's any way to spend less in the future. (See Chapter 14 to learn how to create transaction reports to help you with this review process.)

- **Keep an emergency fund.** If you set money aside in a readily accessible savings account, you don't have to worry about the occasional month when you spend more than you earn. You can always transfer the money you need from savings to checking. Just be sure to transfer money back from checking to savings in the months when you have more income than expenses!

an unexpected expense like a new water heater could require more money than you have on hand. Quicken gives you several ways to keep an eye on your cash flow. The Banking tab is the place to start. You can also call on built-in reports to see whether your cash stream is running freely.

Projecting your income and expenses during different periods can help identify when cash may be tight. Quicken uses scheduled bills and deposits to forecast expenses and income, so its cash flow features are only as helpful as you let them be—for the most accurate cash flow forecasts, set up your paycheck and other scheduled deposits in Quicken so the program knows about the money that comes in. Same goes for expenses: Set up as many of them as you can stand as scheduled bills, so the program knows when and how much money goes out.

Expenses like groceries, which are less regular than things like rent or mortgage payments, and unexpected expenses (like that darned water heater) make it tough to accurately forecast how much money you'll have on hand at any given time. Quicken's Cash Flow Forecast feature uses your budget to help you spot trouble before it hits.

Tip: Stashing some extra cash in a savings account is the best way to avoid a cash flow crunch. When your bills temporarily exceed your income, you can move some of that money into your checking account. The trick is to keep adding money to that savings account each month to replenish what you withdraw.

Watching your account balance

The Account Balance Graph is the best place to spot a potential cash crunch. The colored bars in the graph (sadly, they're a uniform gray in Figure 11-13) show the actual or projected balance for the selected account for the selected month. If you see a bar that's close to zero (or below zero), you can take action before that date arrives. To view this graph, click the Banking tab and then click the Cash Flow button. (If an account register is open, click the Banking button and then click Cash Flow on the drop-down list.) At the bottom of the Cash Flow screen, click the Account Balance Graph tab. The box on page 316 tells you another way to view your account balances.

Initially, the Account Balance Graph shows the balance for your checking account. When the graph represents a single account (as in Figure 11-13), the green bar on the graph indicates today's date. (The graph changes months as you click the left and right date arrows at the top of the page.)

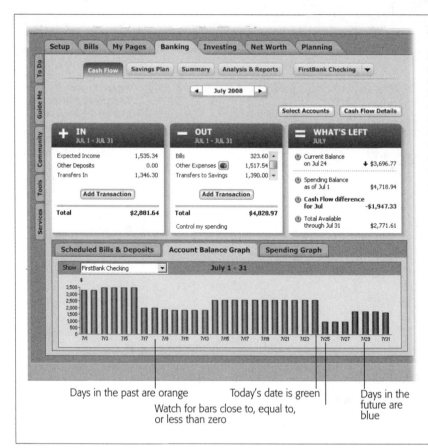

Days in the past are orange   Today's date is green   Days in the future are blue

Watch for bars close to, equal to, or less than zero

Figure 11-13:
You can use this graph to monitor several different accounts at once. On the left side of the tab, in the Show list, choose the account or accounts you want to review. If you include multiple accounts, each bar has a different color, one for each account. (A legend maps the colors to accounts.)

Reviewing Your Financial Calendar

The Quicken Calendar (Figure 11-14) isn't a report per se, but some people swear by it for tracking current banking activities. To display the Quicken Calendar, choose Banking → Calendar (or press Ctrl+K). Each date box shows transactions for that date, color-coded as follows:

- **Transactions recorded in the register** have gray shading.

- **Overdue payments** have brick-red shading.

- **Scheduled bills that are due soon** are shaded with light orange.

- **Scheduled deposits (income you expect soon)** are shaded in money green.

At the bottom of each date box, you initially see the total balance for *all* your spending accounts as of that date (based on your account balances and scheduled transactions). That total balance *doesn't* help you spot when your checking account is getting low, but you can change the calendar to show only the balance in your checking account:

1. In the Calendar window's menu bar, choose Options → "Select calendar accounts".

2. Click Clear All. Then click your checking account to turn on its checkmark and then click OK.

Now the calendar helps warn you when your checking account might be empty—just look for negative numbers displayed in red text in a date box's bottom-right corner.

Figure 11-14:
To display a past month, click the left arrow next to the month and year box near the top of the page. If you look at a month in the future (click the right arrow instead), you see projected values that are based on your scheduled deposits, bills, and paychecks.

Viewing monthly cash flow

The top of the Cash Flow page gives you an overview of your cash flow during any given month. Click the Banking tab and then click the Cash Flow button (see Figure 11-13) to get to the Cash Flow page. If an account register is open, click the Banking button and then, in the drop-down list, click Cash Flow. You can see how much money comes in, how much goes out, and what's left. Most important, you can see what your balance will be in the account you use to pay bills. If that balance is predicted to drop dangerously low, you can plan ahead and transfer some money into the account or figure out how to defer some of your expenses.

The Cash Flow page shows cash flow for your spending accounts, which are initially your checking and cash accounts. If you use other types of accounts, like a credit card, to pay for expenses, you need to tell Quicken that you use the account for spending. (See page 501 to learn how to change an account's "used for" setting.)

When you use the Cash Flow page to look at a month that's already passed, you see your scheduled bills and deposits as well as the actual deposits and expenses you incurred—a full accounting of what you earned and spent during the month. If you spent more than you made, the What's Left box shows how much you overspent. If you spent less than you made, it shows how much you have left over. The Total Available at the bottom of the What's Left box is the actual balance for your spending accounts at the end of the month.

Note: When you first open the Cash Flow page, the In, Out, and What's Left boxes show your actual and projected income and expenses for the current month. If you display a past month (by clicking the left arrow next to the month and year box near the top of the page), you see the *actual* values for that month. If you look at a month in the future (click the right arrow instead), you see *projected* values that are based on your scheduled deposits, bills, and paychecks.

Here's a guide to the Cash Flow page's boxes:

- **Monthly income.** The In box shows the money that you make during the month. The Expected Income value represents your paycheck (if you set it up in Quicken), and any other scheduled deposits you've defined (page 186). The Other Deposits value shows actual income for the month not accounted for by scheduled transactions, like an insurance claim or birthday money. (When you look at a month in the future, the Other Deposits value is zero, because no actual transactions have taken place, as you can see in Figure 11-13.)

- **Monthly expenses.** The Out box shows the money you spend during the month. The value on the Bills line represents all your scheduled bill payments. The Other Expenses value shows actual expenses that weren't scheduled. If you're looking at a month in the future, this value is zero because you haven't actually spent any money in that month yet.

Tip: To keep the Cash Flow page up to date, you can add transactions without leaving the page. In the In or Out box, click the Add Transaction button. In the Add Transaction dialog box that appears, select Yes if you want to set up a new *scheduled* transaction. (Quicken automatically selects No, which sets the new transaction up for one time only.) The rest of the boxes are similar to the ones in the Add Transaction Reminder dialog box (page 155).

- **What's left.** The What's Left box subtracts the money going out from the money coming in, and tells you whether you spent more than you earned or vice versa. The first number in the box is the total starting balance of your spending accounts at the beginning of the month. If the "Cash flow difference" value is negative (and displayed in eye-catching red), you know you spent more than you made. The "Total Available through <last day of month>" is the value of your spending accounts on the last day of the month. You see a red down arrow if your balance dropped over the course of the month, or a green up arrow if your balance increased.

Tip: To see what contributes to the values in the In and Out boxes, click any of the blue text in the In, Out, or What's Left boxes (Expected Income, Transfers In, Bills, Other Expenses, and "Transfers to Savings"). A pop-up minireport (page 432) appears, listing the categories and amounts. To see all the cash flow transactions for the month, click the Cash Flow Details button above the What's Left box. The Cash Flow Details window lists deposits, paid bills, and other expense transactions.

Quicken's Lowest Balance Forecast feature can also help you figure out whether you're going to run out of money any time soon. It shows the lowest balance for the current account based on the scheduled bills and deposits that will happen during the period you choose. To see the projected low balance for an account, open its register and then click the Scheduled Bills & Deposits tab (below the register). At the bottom right, the "Lowest Balance Forecast before" link tells you the end date for the period and the lowest account balance before that date. For example, if you see "Lowest Forecast Balance before 8/23/2009: 25.12", you know that your account will be almost dry on August 23.

To change the date range for the lowest balance, click the "Lowest Balance Forecast before" link. In the Forecast Lowest Balance dialog box that appears, you can set options to specify a period of time, a date, or the lowest balance before your next paycheck. Click OK, and the link displays the lowest balance in the time period you've chosen.

Note: Quicken also includes a Cash Flow report, but it doesn't help you manage your cash flow. It simply reports your actual income and expenses (without any transfers between accounts) over a given period.

Forecasting cash flow

Instead of using scheduled transactions to predict your financial future, a Cash Flow Forecast uses one of the budgets you've set up to estimate how much you'll save (or lose) over a period of up to 2 years. In the Cash Flow Forecast window, shown in Figure 11-15, you can choose a length of time to cover, specify the income and expense items to include, and so on.

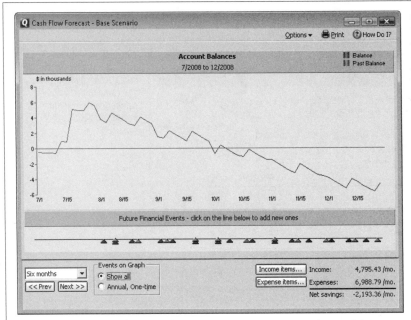

Figure 11-15:
Quicken's Cash Flow Forecast window. To set up an alternative scenario (say with a tighter budget), choose Options → Manage Scenarios. You can change the budget on which Quicken bases the forecast by choosing Options → Update Budget.

Looking for Ways to Cut Costs

Spending money always seems easier than making it. If you're spending more than you make, Quicken reports can help you find places to cut corners. Here are some of the reports and graphs that show spending, as well as some advice on how you can use them to cut costs:

- **Discretionary categories.** When you create categories, you can assign them to category groups (page 70), such as Mandatory or Discretionary. Discretionary categories should be the first place you look to find expenses you can give up or cut back on. As long as you've assigned categories to the Discretionary group, filtering a report to show only those categories is easy. Choose Reports → "Income/Expense by Category". In the report window's toolbar, click Customize. In the Customize dialog box, click the Category Groups tab. Click Clear All and then click Discretionary to turn on its checkbox. Click OK, and you see a report like the one in Figure 11-16.

Tip: If cutting costs is a regular activity, you can save your custom report that shows only discretionary categories. Page 455 tells you how.

- **Expenses graph.** A pie chart of your spending by category is a good place to start when you're looking for ways to spend less. The categories that show up as big slices of pie could provide big savings if you find less expensive places to shop. If groceries are a big part of your monthly expenses, for example, switching to a warehouse store or clipping coupons may help. To see this chart,

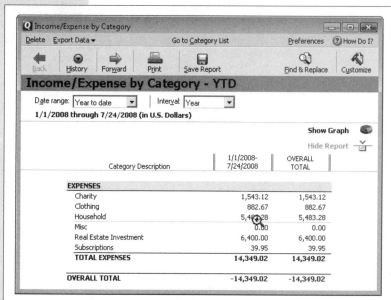

Figure 11-16:
*When you position your
cursor over a category, the
cursor changes to a
magnifying glass (as shown
here), which indicates that
you can double-click a
category to see all the
transactions within that
category.*

click the Banking tab and then click the Analysis & Reports button. The
Expenses pie chart is at the top of the page that appears.

- **Out of budget categories.** If you scroll down to the bottom of the Analysis &
  Reports page, the "Top out-of-budget categories" list shows the categories
  where your spending (or income) is the furthest off your budget. For example, if the
  Household category shows up in this list, you can run the "How much did I spend
  on…?" EasyAnswer report (page 434) to see the transactions for that category.

- **Spending trends.** If you want to see how your spending has changed, for example, to see the effect of paying $4 a gallon for gas, the "Has my spending
  changed in this category?" EasyAnswer report fits the bill. You choose a category, a period, and a comparison period ("Year to date" and "Prior year
  period", for example).

Savings Plans: Iron-Handed Spending Control

If you're like most people, you have a weakness or three that makes it hard to save
money. Quicken's Savings Plan is Intuit's attempt to help you spotlight and contain these trouble areas. For example, if *most* of your spending is under control but
you're a sucker for sushi and shoes, you can create a Savings Plan to keep a closer
eye on your Footwear and Dining Out categories. You define how much you'd like
to spend in each category, and the Savings Plan's bar graph and value boxes tell
you whether you're on the mark (see Figure 11-17).

A Savings Plan highlights your spending in each category you include, so you can see whether you've spent all the money you budgeted for a given category (Figure 11-18). If you haven't, then the Savings Plan sets those dollars aside for the future. Say you go out to dinner twice a month most of the year, but this increases to four times a month in November and December. If you set up a spending target in a Savings Plan, you can reserve the money you *don't* spend in that category from January through October so it's available during the holidays.

Savings Plans are a good idea in theory, but their care and feeding is probably more than you bargained for. Truth be told, using a Savings Plan may help you control your spending mainly because you're too busy managing it to go shopping. You set up your plan and then move money between categories, taking money you didn't spend on groceries to cover the additional money you spent on clothes. However, if your spending in one area is completely out of control and you're desperate for help, keep reading. Otherwise, skip this section and stick to using a budget (page 291) and setting aside a cash buffer (see the box on page 201) instead.

Unlike with a budget, which tracks most (if not all) your categories, you set up a Savings Plan to keep only certain categories under the microscope. Then you can watch your spending in those categories (and use the reserves you've built up in the Rollover Reserve column) to cover the months with higher spending, or transfer money in one category's rollover reserve to cover overspending in another category.

Setting Up a Savings Plan

It's better to use a Savings Plan to focus on a few problem areas rather than applying it to every dollar you spend. Quicken initially fills out a Savings Plan with information from your data file: your paycheck, scheduled transactions, and existing categorized transactions for the month. You can adjust the target values to what you want to spend. Then, as time passes, you can continue with the same plan or change its values or categories.

Note: Because Savings Plans track spending by category, be sure to categorize all your transactions if you want to use one. Savings Plans automatically include scheduled bills, so if you use scheduled transfers to move money into savings, then you don't have to set up savings targets in your Savings Plan—those transfers already appear in the Scheduled Bills section.

Here's how to set up a Savings Plan:

1. **Make sure the accounts you use to pay for things are assigned to the Spending or Credit "Used for" designation (called *groups* in earlier editions of Quicken).**

   A Savings Plan works with accounts in the Quicken Spending and Credit Card "Used for" designations (checking accounts, credit cards, and cash accounts, as described on page 501). If you make payments from an account in the Savings group, like a money market fund, move it to the Spending group. See page 501 to learn how.

2. **Choose Planning → Savings Plan.**

   Quicken switches to the Banking tab and displays the Savings Plan page. (Don't be concerned if you see values in the plan even if you haven't set one up yet—Quicken fills in the plan with your existing data. You'll edit the plan in the steps that follow.) The graph on the top shows the status of your plan. The table below is where you set up your spending and saving targets.

3. **To define the total amount of money you want to track with the plan each month, click the Edit button to the right of the Expected Income label (shown in Figure 11-17).**

   Quicken automatically includes your paycheck (if you've set it up in the program) and even figures out the equivalent monthly income, if you're paid every 2 weeks. Using your total monthly income makes it easy to see how much you're spending compared to what you earn. If you expect a windfall one month like a bonus or tax refund, you can edit the Expected Income amount to reflect that increase. When you edit the amount, the label changes to Total Monthly Allocation.

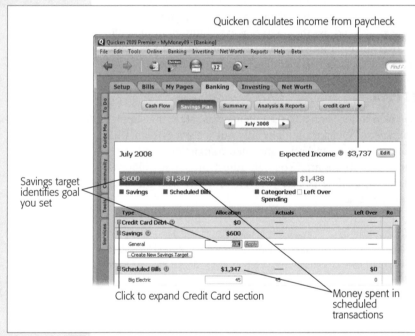

Quicken calculates income from paycheck

Savings target identifies goal you set

Click to expand Credit Card section

Money spent in scheduled transactions

Figure 11-17:
At the top of the Savings Plan page, you see the total amount you're tracking for the month ($3,737 in this case). The horizontal bar right below the Expected Income figure compares your spending so far this month to the allocated amount and how much is left over. This plan shows $600 earmarked for saving, $1,347 for scheduled bills, $352 in categorized transactions, and $1,438 not yet spent.

4. If you carry balances on your credit cards and want to designate a monthly amount to pay off those balances, expand the Credit Card Debt section by clicking the + sign to the left of that section (Figure 11-17). Then, in the Allocation box, type how much of your credit card balances you want to pay off each month.

   If you plan to pay $100 a month toward your credit card balances, type *100* and then click Apply. The amount you allocate is the total you plan to pay off on *all* cards with outstanding balances—you can't track them separately.

The Credit Card Debt section is only for *balances* on your credit cards. Credit card *charges* show up in the Categorized Spending section, because you choose a category when you record those transactions.

Tip: Because credit cards often levy onerous fees and charge exorbitant interest rates on balances, you're better off paying off your credit card debt before you add to your savings. Say you deposit $1,000 in a savings account that pays 3 percent a year. You'll earn $2.50 in interest in one month. However, if you instead use that $1,000 to reduce your balance on a credit card balance that charges 12 percent interest, you pay $10 less in interest that month.

---

5. **If you want to set aside money for savings, expand the Savings section (it's expanded in Figure 11-17) and then allocate funds toward savings targets.**

   Quicken automatically includes one savings target called General, which you can use to set aside a total monthly savings amount. If you want to allocate savings toward a specific goal, however, such as a down payment on a house, click the Create New Savings Target button. Then name the target, and specify the amount.

6. **Keep the scheduled transactions that Quicken adds in the Savings Plan. (If you don't want to include one for some reason, expand the Scheduled Bills section and then set the allocation values for the entry to zero.)**

   Including big bills that arrive infrequently helps you set aside the money you'll need when the bill comes due. Each month you *don't* pay the bill, the monthly amount you set aside goes into the bill's rollover reserve. For scheduled bills that don't occur on a monthly schedule (like car insurance payments), Quicken calculates the equivalent monthly payment and makes that the monthly allocation in the Savings Plan. If you pay $675 for car insurance twice a year, for example, Quicken allocates $113 a month. Each month that you don't pay car insurance, Quicken adds $113 to the car insurance category's rollover reserve. Then, when your insurance payment is due, you can transfer the money from the rollover reserve into that category (page 326).

7. **To include specific categories in the plan, click the "Choose Categories to Watch" button and then turn on the checkboxes for the categories you want.**

   In the Choose Categories dialog box, you can include parent categories and subcategories independently—turning on the checkbox for a parent category doesn't automatically turn on the subcategories. Click OK to add the categories to the Categorized Spending section, as shown in Figure 11-18.

8. **In each category's Allocation box, type the amount you want to allocate. Click Apply.**

   When you specify how much you want to spend in a category, the Categorized Spending section displays outlined bars for each category you track. The length of the bars corresponds to the amount you've allocated to each category. As you spend money in that category, Quicken fills the bar in to show your status (Figure 11-17).

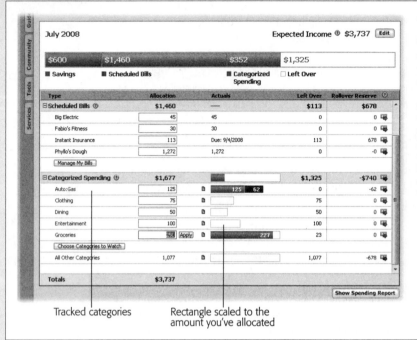

Figure 11-18:
The table that fills most of the Savings Plan page lists each category you're tracking. This plan tracks five expense categories (Auto:Gas, Clothing, Dining, Entertainment, and Groceries). Choose only the categories that you want to watch closely. Quicken totals the remaining categories in the All Other Categories row.

Tracked categories

Rectangle scaled to the amount you've allocated

Reviewing Spending with a Savings Plan

A Savings Plan shows you a snapshot of your income and spending for a specific month. But the Rollover Reserve column (Figure 11-19) also shows how much you've stockpiled in previous months, either for a big bill that you pay once or twice a year or for a category that varies by season. This section explains how to review your Savings Plan for potential problems—and solutions.

- **Overall status.** The status bar across the top of the Savings Plan page (see Figure 11-17) shows how much you've spent of the monthly income you've allocated. If you see dollars in the Left Over section, congratulations—you haven't spent your full monthly allotment.

  If your spending surpasses the monthly allocation, then Quicken displays a message warning you that you've overspent. Because some expenses hit only a few times a year, an overallocation warning isn't the end of the world. The month you're looking at may be the time that you call in the rollover reserves you've been stockpiling. See page 326 to learn how to apply these reserves to an overspent category.

- **Category status.** The Categorized Spending section displays outlined bars for each category you track. The length of the bars corresponds to the amount you've allocated to each category. If you haven't spent the full amount, a green progress bar fills in part of the outlined bar to indicate the amount you've spent so far, as shown in Figure 11-19. If you've overspent, a red progress bar extends past the right side of the outlined bar. The progress bar inside the outlined bar is yellow if you've exceeded the monthly allocation, but haven't used up the rollover reserve.

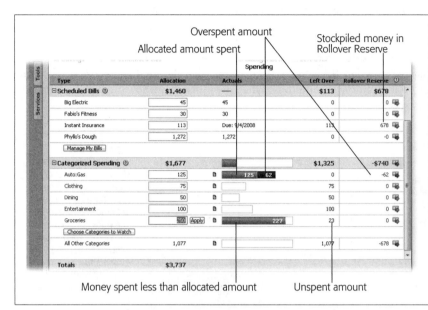

Overspent amount
Allocated amount spent
Stockpiled money in Rollover Reserve

Figure 11-19:
You can build up reserves of money in categories where you've underspent and then move that money to categories where you've overspent. If you see red bars in the table, you've overspent your monthly amount for that category. Now's the time to call in that rollover reserve. Page 326 tells you how.

Money spent less than allocated amount   Unspent amount

Managing Spending with a Savings Plan

When you overspend in a category in one month, you can resolve this problem in a couple of ways. One is to use the money salted away in the category's rollover reserve to cover this month's shortfall. Applying the rollover reserve is perfect for an occasional big payment like car insurance. You can also use money you've allocated to one category to cover overspending in another category.

Here's how to manage your spending with your Savings Plan:

- **Using rollover reserve.** If the monthly allocation doesn't cover the amount you've spent, you can apply money from the category's rollover reserve to cover the shortfall. If you pay $1,350 per year for car insurance, Quicken allocates $113 a month to your car insurance category (The Instant Insurance scheduled bill in Figure 11-19). When your biannual insurance payment is due, Quicken automatically applies the money from the rollover reserve to cover it. Similarly, if the Dining category has a rollover reserve when the holidays roll around, Quicken automatically applies those reserve dollars to cover overspending on holiday social events.

- **Changing the reserve amount.** You can change the reserve amount for a category, for example, to set up a reserve for a bill you've been saving for. In the Rollover Reserve cell for the category you want to change, click the icon that looks like an arrow in front of a dollar bill (shown in Figure 11-20). In the Edit

Rollover Reserve dialog box that appears, select the Change Amount option and then, in the value box, type the new reserve amount. The overall value of the Savings Plan doesn't change.

- **Moving money between categories.** If you want to move the reserve from one category to another—to use money that you allocated but didn't spend on clothing to cover unexpected fuel expenses, say—click the Rollover Reserve icon for the category with the excess reserve. Then, in the Edit Rollover Reserve dialog box, select the Move To option and then choose the category you want to move it to. In the amount box, type how much you want to transfer to the new category.

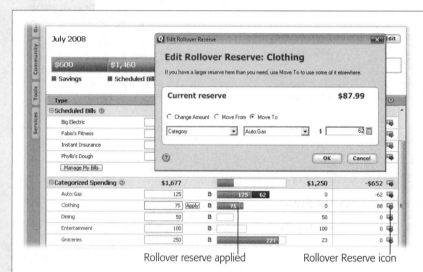

Rollover reserve applied   Rollover Reserve icon

Figure 11-20:
The Left Over column shows the amount of money that hasn't been spent for each category in the selected month. The value is zero if you've exceeded your allocated amount. To see a spending mini-report of what's contributed to the overspending, click the category's name (like Clothing or Groceries).

Saving for Short-Term Goals

Quicken includes a feature called a *Savings Goal*, which tries to help you plan for purchases like a car, a down payment on a house, or that liposuction you've always wanted. You specify how much you want to save, and when you'll need the money, and Quicken calculates how much you have to contribute each month to reach your goal.

A Savings Goal helps hide the money you've earmarked for your purchase. You simply flag money in an existing bank account as belonging to a Savings Goal. Although the money stays in that bank account (so it doesn't interfere with reconciling your account), the Account Bar reduces the balance that you see by the amount you've contributed to the goal. For example, if you have $5,000 in your savings account and earmark $2,000 of it toward a down payment on a car, then the Account Bar shows a balance of only $3,000.

Tip: For really big-ticket items, Savings Goals fall short, because they don't take into account interest you might earn. If you're planning to save over decades (for retirement, say), a Quicken Savings Goal significantly overestimates how much you need to save each month, because it ignores the dividends, capital gains, and interest you'd earn on your investments. For long-term planning, turn to the program's planning wizards like the Retirement Planner or College Planner (see Chapter 13).

Creating a Savings Goal

To set up a Savings Goal, follow these steps:

1. **Choose Planning → Savings Goals. In the Savings Goals window's menu bar, click New.**

   The Create New Savings Goal dialog box opens.

2. **In the Goal Name box, type a name for the goal.**

   Use a descriptive name like *Vacation 2009* and *New Car*.

3. **In the Goal Amount box, type the total amount you want to save.**

   Savings Goals are simple: They don't take into account inflation, interest, or other earnings. If you think your new car will cost $25,000 two years from now, type *25,000* in the Goal Amount box.

4. **In the Finish Date box, type or choose the date when you want to have that money saved up, and then click OK.**

   Quicken calculates how much you need to contribute each month to reach your goal by the finish date, as Figure 11-21 shows.

Earmarking Money for a Savings Goal

A Savings Goal simply tags some of your money for a future purpose. When you contribute money toward a Savings Goal, those funds don't leave your bank account. But Quicken keeps track of the progress you've made and recalculates your future monthly contributions.

Here's how you contribute money from an account to a savings goal:

1. **In the Savings Goals window's menu bar, click Contribute.**

   Don't be misled by the command's name: Contribute. You aren't really moving any money. You're simply marking some money as belonging to that goal. The Contribute To Goal dialog box opens.

2. **In the From Account drop-down list, choose the account with the money.**

   Savings accounts are so named for a reason: It's easier to set aside money in a savings account because you don't deposit or withdraw money from it as frequently as you do in a checking account.

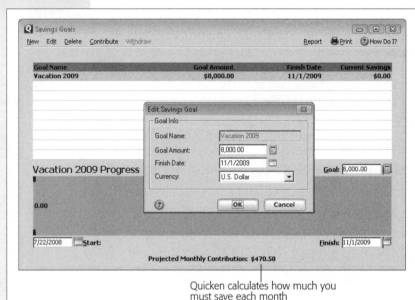

Figure 11-21:
The Savings Goals window shows each goal you've created, the amount you want to save, when you want the money, and how much you've saved so far.

Quicken calculates how much you must save each month

3. **In the Date box, select the date of the contribution.**

Because money doesn't actually move between accounts, this date isn't crucial. Quicken uses the date to recalculate your projected monthly contributions.

4. **In the Amount box, type the amount and then click OK.**

The Savings Goals window shows a progress bar for your savings and the Quicken Account Bar reduces the account balance by the amount of the contribution (Figure 11-22).

Tip: You can hide earmarked Savings Goal money so you aren't tempted to spend it. Open the register for the bank account from which you've contributed money. In the register's menu bar, choose View → Hide Savings Goals. The balance in the register remains the same, but the account's balance in the Account Bar hides the amount you've set aside for the goal. To see your true balance in the Account Bar, choose View → Hide Savings Goals once more.

Withdrawing Money from a Savings Goal

Sometimes, stuff gets in the way of your plans. An emergency root canal, say, requires cash you've stashed in a Savings Goal. The root canal and the withdrawal may be painful, but recording that withdrawal isn't. In the Savings Goals window (Planning → Savings Goals), select the goal and then, in the window's menu bar, click Withdraw. The Withdraw From Goal dialog box looks like the "Contribute to Goal" dialog box. Choose the account, fill in the amount and the date, and then click OK. Quicken removes the flag from that amount and recalculates your projected monthly contribution.

Savings goal funds hidden in Account Bar

Actual account balance in register

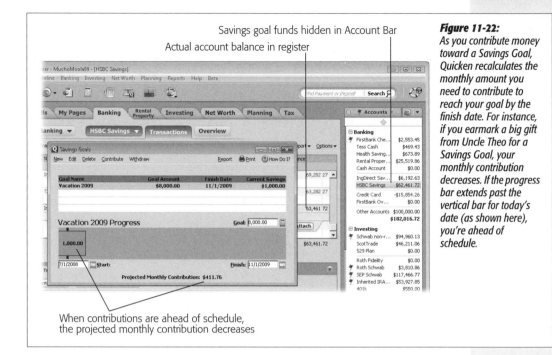

When contributions are ahead of schedule, the projected monthly contribution decreases

Figure 11-22:
As you contribute money toward a Savings Goal, Quicken recalculates the monthly amount you need to contribute to reach your goal by the finish date. For instance, if you earmark a big gift from Uncle Theo for a Savings Goal, your monthly contribution decreases. If the progress bar extends past the vertical bar for today's date (as shown here), you're ahead of schedule.

Investments

Doing investment calculations probably isn't your idea of a good time. Sure, you like raking in the dough when your mutual funds grow, but keeping an eye on what's up and what's down can be pretty tedious. Fortunately, Quicken's just as good at tracking your investments as it is your checks, charges, and ATM withdrawals.

You have lots of reasons to track your investments in Quicken. At tax time you can generate reports that show your taxable interest and dividends, as well as gains and losses on sales. If you've ever sold a mutual fund that you've owned and reinvested distributions into for decades, you *know* how painful capital-gain calculations can be. Quicken, though, can instantly spit out the numbers you need. And with Quicken's tools for reviewing your portfolio, you can tell whether you're putting too many nest-eggs in one basket.

This chapter starts by explaining when it makes sense to track the details of your investments in Quicken—and when an overview may be enough. You'll learn how to create investment accounts, set up your investments, and record transactions. Once you've entered (or downloaded) all the numbers, you can review your portfolio's performance and get a good sense of whether you've distributed your moolah in a way that makes sense. Using Quicken may not turn you into a Certified Financial Planner, but it'll sure give you a better picture of your long-term finances than that overstuffed folder you keep dumping statements into.

Note: Like it or not, investments come with a slew of concepts and terminology: dividend, capital gain, 401(k), and so on. You have to learn a little bit about these terms both to fill out your tax returns and to make sure your investments perform as well as they can. To learn more about investing, check out *Online Investing Hacks* (Biafore, O'Reilly, 2004) and *Stock Selection Handbook* (Biafore, National Association of Investors Corp., 2003).

Quicken Investment Tracking: Details or Overview?

If you're generating investment income (capital gains, dividends, or interest) that the IRS wants to know about, or if you're juggling lots of stocks and mutual funds, tracking every last investment transaction (purchases, sales, reinvested dividends, and so on) in Quicken can be a huge help. Come tax time, you can whip up reports about your taxable investment results, like dividends you've earned or capital gains from investments you've sold. Keeping investment minutiae in Quicken also lets you look at how well your investments are doing and how your nest egg is allocated to different types of investments (which helps keep your portfolio chugging along in good times and bad). With so many institutions offering online services, tracking the details can be almost painless.

That said, you may be content with keeping an eye on the overall value of your investment accounts (so you know how much you're worth overall), and leaving the details to someone else. Here are some examples of when you might want to skip detailed investment tracking in Quicken and what you can do instead:

- **You invest only in your 401(k).** If your investments are limited to your 401(k) or 403(b) account (page 52), and your account statements are nice and simple, you probably want to track the details for these accounts in Quicken only if you want help managing the investments purchased with your contributions or tracking your 401(k) performance. Otherwise, the Track 401(k) wizard and Update 401(k) Holdings command (page 391) make it easy to update your account balance each time you receive a statement and know how much you've socked away for your golden years. (Quicken finds out about your tax-deductible 401(k) contributions when you enter your paycheck in the program.)

Tip: Because employer-sponsored retirement accounts like 401(k)s and 403(b)s typically offer limited selections of mutual funds, you can get annual performance figures from the plan administrator (ask your HR department whom to call) if the funds aren't publicly traded. That way, you can evaluate your choices, and decide whether to switch to different funds. *Online Investing Hacks* (Biafore, O'Reilly, 2004) tells you how.

- **Your financial institution provides the tax info you need.** As long as your financial institution sends clear and easy-to-read statements of your taxable investment transactions (like taxable dividends and capital gains you've earned from selling investments), you can use those statements to prepare your taxes and skip tracking that info in Quicken. To see your net worth in Quicken, simply update your account balances to reflect their new values every time you receive statements.

- **You use another program to manage your portfolio.** There are lots of programs out there that can help you analyze investments (see the box on page 406). If you've decided to use one of them, you're free to bypass Quicken's investment features completely.

- **You track nothing but net worth.** To keep track of your net worth in Quicken, you need to know the value of your assets—including all your investment accounts. But you can keep your investment account balances up to date without tracking every single investment transaction. If you don't care about taxes or performance calculations, simply adjust your account balances manually (page 389) when you want to update the value of your net worth.

Whether you want to track the details or just update account balances, the rest of this chapter tells you how to use Quicken's investment-tracking features.

Choosing the Right Type of Account

Quicken offers four types of investment-specific accounts to track your investment holdings (mutual funds, stocks, bonds, and so on). But depending on what you invest in, you may actually find one of the cash- or asset-oriented account types a better fit. Here's a quick overview of all your options, along with some advice on which account types work best for which investments. Figure 12-1 shows the Account Setup window—your starting point for creating any investment account.

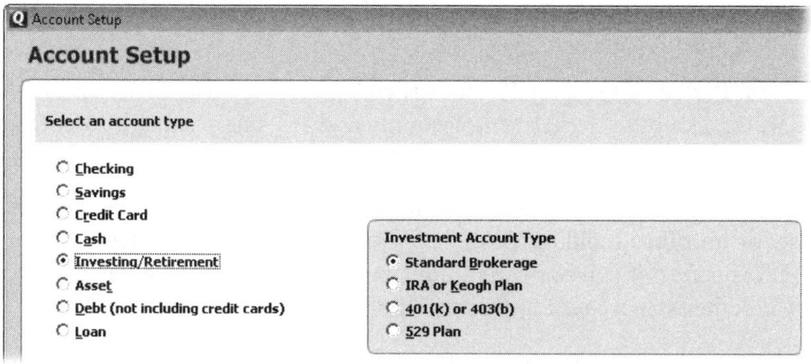

Figure 12-1:
The fastest way to create an investment account is to click Add Account in the Account Bar. In the Account Setup window that appears, select the Investing/Retirement option, and then select the specific investment account type you want to create.

- **Standard Brokerage.** Despite its pole position in the Account Setup dialog box, this account type is actually a catch-all for investments that don't fit any of the other account types. A brokerage account holds one or more securities of any type that Quicken supports—stocks, bonds, mutual funds, real estate investment trusts (REITs), options, and investment cash. You might use a Savings account for a single certificate of deposit (CD), but you could just as easily keep several CDs from the same bank in one Quicken brokerage account.

Note: Earlier versions of Quicken included the Single Mutual Fund account, which did only one thing: track a single mutual fund. Now that this account type is gone, simply use the Standard Brokerage account type instead. If you don't add any securities to the account when you create it, the Account Setup wizard asks if it's an account for one mutual fund.

- **IRA or Keogh Plan.** Not a lot of ambiguity here. Use this account type for your individual retirement account options—IRAs (traditional, Roth, Simplified Employee Pension [SEP], and Education), SIMPLE plans, and Keogh plans.

Note: For an acronym run amok, it doesn't get any better than SIMPLE: Savings Incentive Match Plans for Employees of Small Employers. Gets a laugh at bean-counter cocktail parties every time.

- **401(k) or 403(b) Plan.** Named after the sections of the tax code that created them, these are the well-known retirement plans you can sign up for at work. Choosing this account type lets Quicken handle the details of these employer-sponsored accounts, including any matching contributions that your employer makes, loans you can withdraw, and the tax advantages you get.

  Financial institutions vary in how much detail they provide on 401(k) statements. In Quicken, the 401(k)/403(b) account type can track just the dollar values of your account balances and contributions if that's what your 401(k) statement provides. But if your statement tells the entire story of share purchases and reinvestments of dividends, Quicken's happy to track the actual shares you own with how much they're worth, perfect for seeing exactly where your retirement investments stand.

- **529 Plan.** Parents know that 529 means college savings. The 529 Plan account type works like other investment accounts and it's smart enough to correctly handle the tax implications of a 529 plan (page 52).

- **Asset/House.** To track real estate you purchased as an investment (like land, a house, or an office building), use the Asset or House account type. A House account is perfect if you borrowed money to buy the property, because you can easily link the asset account to the corresponding loan account (page 249).

- **Savings.** CDs and money market funds sometimes count as investments. If you set up a separate money market bank account or use CDs for cash you'll need sooner rather than later, Quicken savings accounts are ideal. Be sure to give the account a descriptive name (see the box on page 62 for advice on naming accounts). Many brokerage accounts include a linked money market fund for holding cash. Instead of setting up a separate Quicken savings account for those money market funds, you can create a brokerage account with a built-in linked cash account, as described in the box on page 341.

Tip: You can move a savings account from Quicken's Banking center to the Investing center, if you view that savings account as money you're socking away for the future rather than as easy-access cash. That way, the account shows up in the Investing section of the Account Bar and in investing reports you run. To make this move, you edit the account's details to change where the account lives (see page 501). This doesn't change the type of account, only the center to which the account (and its balance) belongs.

Creating an Investment Account

In Quicken, setting up an investment account isn't all that different from setting up a banking account. You fill in text boxes, choose options, and click Next until the Account Setup screen displays the Done button. (See page 54 for all the details.) You just have to answer a few more questions that Quicken doesn't ask when you're setting up a banking account. This section walks you through the basic questions you have to answer to create a brokerage, IRA, or 401(k)/403(b) account. (A 529 Plan is a beast unto itself, as page 52 explains.) Then, the remaining sections explain how to answer the extra questions for specific types of investment accounts.

To create an investment account, follow these steps:

1. **Choose Investing → Investing Accounts → Add Account.**

   This approach displays a specialized version of the Account Setup dialog box that shows only the options for the four types of investment accounts. A faster way to open the Account Setup dialog box is to click Add Account in the Account Bar. (If you use this method, the dialog box displays all Quicken's account types.)

2. **In the Account Setup dialog box, select the option for the type of investment account you want to create and then click Next.**

   If you open the Account Setup dialog box from the Investing menu, you can choose one of the four types of investment accounts (Standard Brokerage, "IRA or Keogh Plan", "401(k) or 403(b)", and 529 Plan). If you click Add Account in the Account Bar, select the Investing/Retirement option and then select the specific account type you want.

3. **In the "What is the financial institution for this account?" screen, specify the institution that holds your account and then click Next.**

   You have to fill in the institution's name if you want to use online services. Luckily, Quicken makes it easy to choose an institution (page 131).

   If you're creating a 401(k) or 403(b) account, the 401(k)/403(b) Setup dialog box appears when you click Next. Jump to page 336 for the remaining steps.

4. **For brokerage and IRA accounts, on the next screen, choose the Yes option to connect to your financial institution and download your account information. Then click Next.**

Page 125 provides more detailed steps on setting up an account for online access. If you'd rather connect later (or never), choose No. (See page 60 for setting up an account for manual download or offline access.) If you create an investment account without downloading info from the institution, you provide other information, like the account number and contact information when you edit the account, as described on page 62.

After you've chosen a type of investment account and clicked Next, Quicken poses some questions that pertain to the account type you chose. Read on to learn how to respond to the rest of Quicken's interrogation.

Creating a 401(k) or 403(b) Account

Everyone knows they should start saving for retirement by the time they turn 12—or at least as soon as they start a job that offers an employer-sponsored retirement account. But even if you do enroll in your company's 401(k) or 403(b) program, tracking your investment can be confusing, or at best tedious. Quicken can help. The first step is to set up your retirement account in Quicken.

Choosing the "401(k) or 403(b)" option in the Account Setup dialog box (Figure 12-1) creates an account for your employer-sponsored retirement plan. After you choose the financial institution as described in step 3 on page 335, the 401(k)/403(b) Setup dialog box opens, as you can see in Figure 12-2. It's no surprise that you have to answer some questions about your employer and the features that its plan offers.

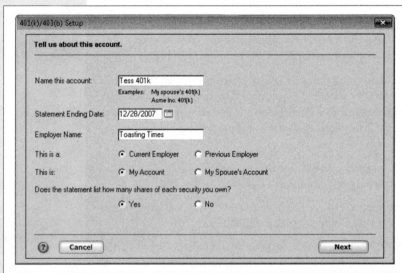

Figure 12-2:
If you're married, you have to specify whether the account belongs to you or your spouse, so Quicken can track your tax info correctly. If the account is with your current employer, you can set up your paycheck (page 192) in Quicken to transfer your 401(k) or 403(b) paycheck deduction to this account.

Here are the steps and additional info you need to provide to create 401(k) and
403(b) accounts:

1. **In the "Tell us about this account" screen, fill in the "Name this account" box
   with whatever you want to call the account in Quicken.**

   For example, include the employer name and *401k* or *403b*.

2. **In the aptly named Employer Name text box, type the name of the employer
   that provides this retirement account.**

   As long as the employer who offers this account still signs your paycheck, leave
   the Current Employer option selected. If you still have a 401(k) with a previous
   employer and are just getting around to creating the account in Quicken, select
   the Previous Employer option.

3. **If the account belongs to you, leave the My Account option selected. Otherwise, select the My Spouse's Account option.**

   This choice can be tricky if you and your spouse take an egalitarian approach to
   Quicken duties. The "me" and "my spouse" designations depend on how you
   set up your data file and how you file your taxes. Your choices here have to
   match the main taxpayer and spouse on your tax returns—especially if you use
   your Quicken data to do your returns in TurboTax.

4. **If your statement shows the shares you own, leave the "Does the statement list
   how many shares of each security you own?" setting's Yes option selected. Otherwise, select No. Then click Next.**

   Dig out the last statement you received from the 401(k) or 403(b) administrator. If the statement tells you how many shares you own of each mutual fund
   (or other security), select Yes. If the statement simply tells you dollar values,
   select No.

5. **In the "Would you like to track loans against this account?" screen, select Yes
   or No depending on whether you plan to borrow against your retirement
   account.**

   401(k) and 403(b) accounts let you borrow money from yourself, so the 401(k)/
   403(b) Setup dialog box asks if you'd like to track loans you've taken against the
   account. If you haven't borrowed against the account, select the No option. You
   can add a loan later, if need be, by creating a loan associated with your retirement account (page 391).

   If you've borrowed against the account, select the Yes option. In the "How
   many?" text box, type the number of loans you've taken. If you tell Quicken
   that you have loans, when you click Next, the program displays an additional
   screen for each loan asking for info about each one: a description, the current
   balance, and the original loan amount.

6. In the "What securities are in this account?" screen (which appears if you told Quicken that your statement shows the number of shares), type the ticker symbol for each holding, as shown in Figure 12-3. Then click Next.

Fill in these boxes to tell Quicken about the securities (aka investments or holdings) you keep in the account. You see this screen no matter what type of investment account you create. If you don't know the ticker symbol, click Ticker Symbol Lookup to go online to find it. Click Add More if you own more than five securities. If you don't connect to the Internet or your investments don't have ticker symbols (like privately held securities and many 401(k) mutual funds), you can tell Quicken everything about your investments, as described in the box on page 346.

After you type the ticker symbols and click Next, Quicken goes online and double-checks that you've entered the symbols correctly. The program also collects info about your investments, like whether they're stocks, mutual funds, or other types of securities.

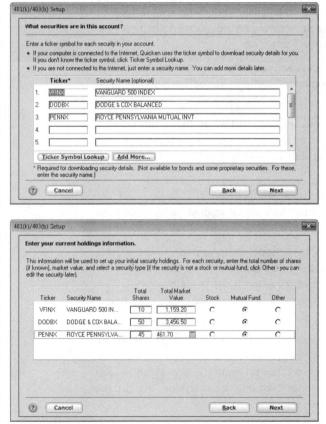

Figure 12-3:
Top: Type the ticker symbol for each security you own in the account. When you click Next, Quicken goes online to check the ticker symbols, and gathers information about those securities.

Bottom: After Quicken downloads info about the securities, fill in the total value of each security from your statement. If you told Quicken that your statement shows how many shares you own, fill in the Total Shares boxes with the number of shares.

Tip: If you're ready for a break, you can leave this screen blank and add the securities to the account after setup. Quicken pops up a message box asking if you're sure you want to create the account without securities. Click Yes, and then take your well-deserved break.

---

7. **In the "Enter your current holdings information" screen, type the value of the securities from your statement (and number of shares, if you know it), and then click Next.**

   Use the numbers on your last statement. When you click Next, the Summary screen shows the securities you own and the button you've been waiting for—Done.

8. **Click Done.**

   Quicken adds the account to the Account Bar and its other account lists.

If you haven't set up your paycheck using the Set Up Paycheck feature, take a moment now to set it up and include your 401(k) or 403(b) paycheck deduction as a pretax deduction (see page 198).

Creating a Brokerage Account

The Standard Brokerage account type is Quicken's catch-all for investments that don't fit into any other type of Quicken account. And, fortunately, the questions Quicken asks when you set up this type of account are simple. If you set the account up for online access, you can follow the steps on page 57. Otherwise, you tell the program the date of the statement on which you're basing your answers and provide the following info:

- **Cash.** In the Cash text box, type the cash balance in your account.

- **Money Market Fund.** For brokerage accounts that come with what's called a *sweep fund* (which holds cash from sales or interest), in the Money Market Fund text box, type the balance of your sweep fund. (See the box on page 341 to learn about different options for tracking sweep funds.)

- **Securities.** As described in the previous section, you see a screen (Figure 12-3) where you can type the ticker symbols for the securities you own. If you'd rather add the securities later, leave the boxes blank and click Next.

Creating an IRA Account

In Quicken, an IRA account is simply a brokerage account with tax advantages, so the questions you answer to create one are almost identical to those for a brokerage account, described in the previous section. Here's the other information you have to provide for an IRA account:

- **Who owns this IRA?** Choose either the Myself or the My Spouse option. Your choice has to match the main taxpayer and spouse on your tax returns.

- **What type of IRA is this?** IRAs come in as many flavors as Starbucks lattes. Choose the type of IRA from the list shown in Figure 12-4. If you don't know what type of IRA you own, ask your financial institution.

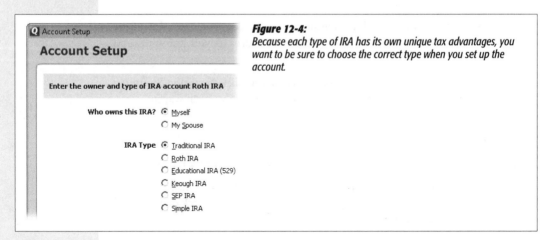

Figure 12-4:
Because each type of IRA has its own unique tax advantages, you want to be sure to choose the correct type when you set up the account.

Creating a 529 Account

When you select the 529 Plan option, Quicken asks you to name the account. Then you fill in the statement date, cash balance, money-market balance if the account uses a sweep fund (page 341), and securities in the account, as you would for a brokerage account.

Setting Up and Tracking Securities

Investments like bonds, mutual funds, and stocks are officially called *securities*, but you may see them called *holdings* or simply *investments*. Whatever you call them, if you typed in ticker symbols when you created your investment account (page 338), your existing securities are already in Quicken, and you may not have to set up a new one for some time. If you skipped that step, now's the time to set up the securities you own. At some point, you'll probably decide to switch mutual funds in your 401(k) account or buy a new stock in your taxable brokerage account. This section explains how to track your securities and add new securities to the list of ones you already own.

This section introduces a few lists you can use to categorize your investments by type (stocks, bonds, and so on), investing goals (like growth or income), and asset class (see the box on page 350 for details). Smart investors know there's no such thing as a free lunch on Wall Street. So investments that offer higher returns almost always come with higher risk. Categorizing your investments in Quicken helps you evaluate whether the risks you take with your investments are paying off—making *you* one of those smart investors.

Sweeping Money into Accounts

Many brokerages offer checking accounts to go along with their investment accounts. Most of those checking accounts sweep their cash balances into money market funds that pay dividends, so they're known as *sweep funds*. You can track sweep funds a couple of ways. Here are your options, along with the pros and cons of each:

- **Pretend the sweep fund doesn't exist.** You can treat the money in the sweep fund like cash in your investment account. The upside to doing this is that you don't have a gazillion transactions moving cash back and forth between your investment account and the money market fund. If you don't download transactions, this is the easiest option. You can record the dividends that the money market fund pays as interest in your investment account (see page 362 for instructions on recording income). The downside is that you have to forever ignore Quicken's offers to synchronize your Quicken investment account with your brokerage holdings.

- **Create a linked cash account.** To set up scheduled transactions that use your sweep fund, set up your investment account with a checking account linked to it. You can then create scheduled bill payments or even online bill payments from that linked checking account. To add a linked checking account to your investment account, press Ctrl+A to open

the Accounts List window. Right-click the investment account, and then, from the shortcut menu, choose Edit. In the Account Details dialog box, select the Yes option that goes with the "Show cash in a checking account" label.

- **Leave your investment account as it is.** This is the easiest option, if you download transactions. Quicken downloads all the transactions for buying and selling shares in the money market fund. If you write a check, you see one transaction for the check you write, and a second one that sells enough shares of the money market fund to cover the check. The sale of money market shares increases the cash balance in the linked checking account, and the check you write spends that money.

Quicken includes investment transaction types that cover cash transactions. When you click Enter Transactions above an investment account register (page 353), a dialog box appears. Its "Enter transaction" drop-down menu includes the options Write Check (for writing a check in your account), Deposit (for depositing money into the account), Withdraw (for pulling money out of the account using an ATM), Online Payment (for making an online payment from the account), and Other Cash Transaction (for transactions that don't fit the other choices).

When it comes to working with securities, whether you're setting one up, editing its characteristics, or reviewing its price history, the Security List window is the place to start. Press Ctrl+Y or choose Investing → Security List, and the window in Figure 12-5 appears.

Adding Securities

You can add securities to your Security List when you create an investment account (page 335) or when you record a purchase transaction (page 354). Either way, your main task is to provide the ticker symbol or security name so that Quicken can download information about the security.

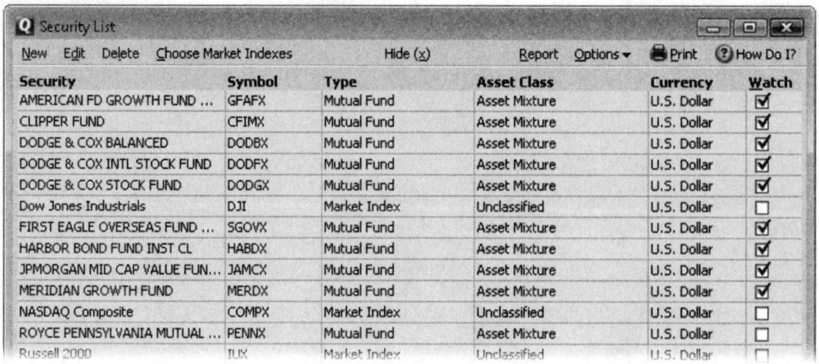

Figure 12-5:
In the Security List window, you can add, edit, delete, and hide securities. To open the Security Detail View for a specific investment, double-click its name in the list. The last column in this window indicates whether the security is on your watch list (page 394). Turning on the Watch checkbox for a security tells Quicken that you want to download price quotes and other information about it.

Just follow these steps to add a security:

1. **Press Ctrl+Y (or choose Tools → Security List).**

   The Security List window opens. If you're a Quicken veteran, in the Security List window, turn on hidden securities (see the box on page 344) so that you can see if the security you want to add is already on the list (maybe you've owned it in the past, for example). In the Security List window's menu bar, choose Options → "View hidden securities".

   If the security exists but is hidden, a hand icon appears to the right of its name. To unhide the security, click anywhere in the security's row and then, in the window's menu bar, click Hide. The hand icon disappears. (The box on page 344 explains in more detail how to hide securities and restore them to view in both the Security List and throughout Quicken.)

2. **In the Security List window's menu bar, choose New.**

   The "Add Security to Quicken" dialog box appears, as shown in Figure 12-6.

3. **In the Ticker Symbol text box, type the security's ticker symbol and then click Next.**

   Although the screen asks for the ticker symbol *and* name, you can type just one and let Quicken fill in the other. Quicken automatically goes online to retrieve the security info when you click Next.

   If you don't know the ticker symbol, type part or all of the security name in the Name box and then click Look Up. A browser window opens to Quicken.com's ticker search Web page. The most likely matches for the name you typed appear at the top of the list. Select the correct ticker symbol and then press Ctrl+C to copy it. Switch back to the Quicken window, click the Ticker Symbol text box,

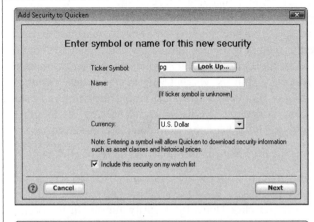

Figure 12-6:
Top: The quickest way to retrieve security information is to type the ticker symbol. If you type the security's name, Quicken takes you online to pick the ticker symbol.

Bottom: When you click Next in the "Add Security to Quicken" dialog box, the Quicken One Step Update Status dialog box appears and connects to the Internet to retrieve info about the security. When it's done, the program replaces the text boxes with the downloaded info, as shown here.

and then press Shift+Ctrl+V (or Ctrl+V if you set Quicken's keyboard mapping to Windows standard [page 488]) to paste in the ticker symbol. See the box on page 346 to learn how to handle securities without ticker symbols.

Quicken initially turns on the "Include this security on my watch list" checkbox, which means you can keep an eye on what the investment is doing by looking at the watch list section of the Portfolio page (page 394). If you're adding a security to your list, you usually want to know its current price, and the watch list is a good way to keep track of this. If you're adding a security that isn't traded on an exchange (a privately held investment, say), turn off the watch list checkbox before you click Next.

Note: You can add or remove securities from the watch list at any time: In the Security List window, turn off the security's Watch checkbox. Taking a security off the watch list after you sell it is a good idea so you don't have to feel your heart sink when its price goes *up*. If you repurchase a security later on, you can turn its Watch checkbox on to download quotes again.

If you typed in a ticker symbol that doesn't exist, the "No data found for <*ticker*>" screen appears. Quicken automatically selects the "Correct ticker symbol and try again" option, so you can retype the ticker symbol and go online again. If you're sure the symbol is correct, choose the "Add manually" option. You have to tell Quicken the security type and provide the other information, but at least Quicken doesn't spin its wheels trying to find a ticker symbol it doesn't have in its database. (Quicken's database lists securities from most stock exchanges, like the New York Stock Exchange and NASDAQ. It doesn't list securities that aren't publicly traded and therefore don't have ticker symbols.)

4. **Once Quicken retrieves the information for the correct security, click Done.**

If the ticker you typed is valid, but not the one you wanted, the last screen of the "Add Security to Quicken" doesn't show the security you want to add. Click Back to try again. When you click Done, the security appears in the Security List. If it doesn't, read the box below.

TROUBLESHOOTING MOMENT

Where's My Security?

Suppose you complete the steps for adding a security but don't see it in the Security List. What gives? Hidden securities could be to blame. If you're like most people, you have investments you used to own but don't any more. You have to keep them around for your tax returns and investment reports, but you don't want to see them in drop-down lists or in reports for your current portfolio. By hiding securities in Quicken, you can still see the transactions that use them, but your Security List, drop-down lists, and other investment windows stay neat and clean with only the securities you currently own. If you already have the security in your Security List but it's hidden, adding it again doesn't change anything: The security is still in the Security List *and* it's still hidden. (The good news is that Quicken doesn't create a second entry for a security if you add one that's already there.)

Before you pull out your hair, do this:

1. Open the Security List window, if it isn't already open (press Ctrl+Y).

2. In the window's menu bar, choose Options → "View hidden securities". Quicken lists all the securities you've set up in your data file, whether they're hidden or not.

3. Scroll to the security's name (they're listed alphabetically). If the security is hidden, you see a hand symbol to the right of the name.

4. Select the security and then, in the window's menu bar, click Hide to toggle that security's hidden setting to display it. Quicken shows that it's no longer a hidden security by turning off the hand icon to the right of its name.

5. Now that you've reset that security's hidden setting, you can tell the Security List to stop displaying hidden securities. To do this, choose Options → "View hidden securities". All the hidden securities go back into hiding, but the security that you unhid remains visible.

Working with Securities

Whether you want to view, edit, or update a security in Quicken, the Security Detail View window is the place to go. As you can see in Figure 12-7, this window has all kinds of details about the security, like its type and asset class, its transaction history, info about the shares you own (number, market value, cost basis, and

so on), a current price quote, and a price chart. To open this window, choose
Investing → Security Detail View. The window displays the info for the security
you viewed the last time you opened the window. In the security name drop-down
menu in the window's upper-left corner (which reads Meridian Growth Fund in
Figure 12-7), choose the security you want to see.

Figure 12-7:
*The Security Detaild View
window isn't tied to a
specific account. If you
own the same security in
more than one account
(your IRA and your
husband's, for example),
then transactions from
both accounts appear in
the Transaction History.
The Account column
shows the investment
account each transaction
belongs to.*

Here's what you can do in the Security Detail View window:

• **Edit the security type, asset class, and other details.** To change any of the security's details, click Edit Security Details (in the Security Details section or in the
menu bar). See page 347 for the items you might want to change.

• **Download security information.** Quicken retrieves information about securities when you add them to the Security List. But once securities are in your data
file, you download security info from time to time to make sure that values like
asset class or security type are still correct. In the window's menu bar, click
Update and then, on the drop-down menu, choose Download Asset Classes.

• **Review price and price history.** The price chart shows the security's historical
prices, which by itself isn't enough to say buy, sell, or hold. Click More Chart-
ing to go online and generate price charts that are more helpful, like ones that
compare your mutual fund's price performance to the index it mirrors. See
page 386 to learn how to download price quotes and price histories.

WORKAROUND WORKSHOP

Tackling Securities Without Tickers

In addition to publicly-traded securities that Quicken doesn't have in its database, you may run into investments that simply don't have ticker symbols—like investments that aren't traded on public exchanges. And 401(k) plans are renowned for setting their own share prices, even for supposedly public mutual funds. These special share prices take into account the 401(k) administrator's management fees that are deducted before calculating the investment returns you see on your statements. For example, spouses who work at different companies that both use the same 401(k) plan administrator may see different share prices for the same investment if the administrator charges higher management fees for smaller employers.

If an investment doesn't have a ticker symbol or comes with a customized share price, simply create a security *without* a ticker symbol. In step 3 on page 342, fill in the Name box with a name for the security (like *Vanguard 500 MyEmployer*), leave the Ticker Symbol box blank, and then click Next. When the "No data found for *<ticker>*" screen appears, choose the "Add manually" option. Then you tell Quicken whether it's a stock, mutual fund, option, or whatever. You can then manually update the security's price (page 390) using the prices on the statements you receive.

- **Check the value of your holdings.** The Holdings section shows how many shares of the security you own, and its market value, cost basis, and the gain or loss by dollars and percentage. To see these values for *all* your investments, check out the Portfolio page (see page 394).

- **Review the most recent price quote.** When you download price quotes (page 386), the Quote section displays the 411 from the most recent quote. The date and price are listed first. As you work down the list, you can see the 52-week high and low prices, volume, and other security quote tidbits.

- **Review transactions.** In the Transaction History section, you can scroll through all the security's transactions. This is handy if, for example, you're trying to find a transaction because your Quicken records don't match your broker's statement. Scan the Shares or Amount column for numbers that match the discrepancy, which means there's a duplicate transaction. You can also review each transaction and look for a missing reinvested dividend that you forgot to record.

Tip: In the Security Detail View menu bar, the Online Research command looks tempting. Its drop-down menu takes you to Web sites with in-depth info about the security you're looking at: quotes, news, charts, and research. You can also set up alerts that tell you when the security's price hits certain levels by choosing "Set up Alerts".

But you don't have to limit yourself to the links that Quicken provides. Tons of Web sites (that you may like better than Quicken's) can keep you on top of your investments, like *http://money.msn.com*, *http://finance.yahoo.com*, or *http://investor.reuters.com*. They're only a click away when you save them as bookmarks in your browser.

Editing a Security

Quicken uses your Internet connection to download information about securities when you first create them (page 342). When you open the Edit Security Details dialog box, the program reminds you of this by turning on the "Matched with online security" checkbox, shown in Figure 12-8. But things change. Every now and then, you still need to edit a security's details to keep them up to date. You can update things like the *backload* on a mutual fund (which is the fee a fund charges for selling), how you want Quicken to calculate your capital gains when you sell the security, or the specific investing goal the investment helps you achieve.

To edit these details, in the Security List window (Ctrl+Y), select the security you want to change and then, in the window's menu bar or in the Security Details section, click Edit Security Details. The Edit Security Details dialog box shown in Figure 12-8 appears.

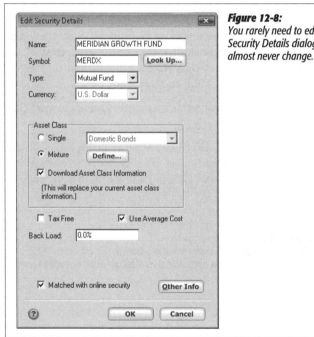

Figure 12-8:
You rarely need to edit the three text boxes at the top of the Edit Security Details dialog box, because the name, ticker symbol, and type almost never change.

Editing the asset class

Quicken uses the values in the Asset Class section to determine the asset allocation of your investment portfolio (see the box on page 350). Most of the time, you can skip this section entirely, because the asset allocation that Quicken downloads is usually just fine. For example, if a mutual fund covers numerous asset classes, Quicken automatically selects the Mixture option, and then fills in each class's percentage (to see them, click the Define button).

You may also skip editing the asset class if you want to use asset classes other than the ones Quicken provides. Quicken's asset class list isn't negotiable. Your only choices are Domestic Bonds, Global Bonds, Large Cap Stocks, Small Cap Stocks, International Stocks, Cash, and Other. If you want to include assets like real estate or precious metals, you can't use Quicken's asset classes. See page 349 to learn how to make your own asset categories.

Tip: To learn more about asset allocation, read the SEC's introduction to it at *www.sec.gov/investor/ pubs/assetallocation.htm*. The page includes a link to the Iowa Public Employees Retirement System's online calculator for determining asset allocation (*www.ipers.org/calcs/AssetAllocator.html*).

If you disagree with the asset class Quicken chooses, here's what to do:

1. **In the Edit Security Details dialog box, turn off the Download Asset Class Information checkbox.**

   Quicken doesn't try to go online when you click OK.

2. **If the security is a stock, bond, or other one-class investment, select the Single option, and then, in the Single drop-down list, choose the asset class. If the security invests in more than one asset class (like a mutual fund that covers stocks and bonds), select the Mixture option and then click Define.**

   The Single option also works for mutual funds that invest in a single asset class like a large-cap mutual fund.

   When you click the Define button, the Asset Class Mixture dialog box opens, as shown in Figure 12-9. In the cell for each asset class, type the percentage you want to assign. (You type the number and Quicken automatically adds the percentage symbol to the field.)

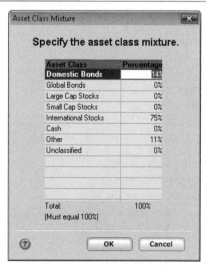

Figure 12-9:
You can't change which asset classes are listed in this dialog box. If a security doesn't include a particular asset class, set its percentage to zero.

Tip: One popular source for asset class allocations is *www.morningstar.com*. In the Quotes box near the top of the page, type the ticker for the security and click the right arrow. When the report for the security appears, scroll to the Asset Allocation section.

3. **When you're finished, click OK.**

   Quicken takes you back to the Edit Security Details dialog box so you can keep editing.

Editing tax-related details

The Tax Free checkbox and the Use Average Cost checkbox tell Quicken how to calculate a security's capital gains and total taxable income. Here's what the settings are for and when you should use them:

- **Tax Free.** If the security is exempt from taxes, like some municipal bonds are, turn on the Tax Free checkbox. Quicken removes the security's income and gains from Quicken's reports of taxable events (page 402). If the account that holds the security is tax-deferred, change the tax settings for the account, as described on page 272.

- **Use Average Cost.** Turn on this checkbox for the easiest way to calculate capital gains for the shares you sell. This setting tells Quicken to use the average purchase price of a security to calculate the cost basis when you sell, so it doesn't matter which shares you sell first. (The *cost basis* is how much you paid for a security, plus any commissions and fees for the purchase; it's used for tax reporting purposes.) The program turns this checkbox on automatically when you add a mutual fund because so many people reinvest the dividends and capital gains that mutual funds pay out; it's easier to use the average purchase price when you have a bazillion reinvestment purchases.

- **Back Load.** If a mutual fund charges a fee when you sell it, type the percentage in the Back Load box. Then, when you sell a share, Quicken calculates the back load and subtracts it from the proceeds of the sale. (You record a front-end fee when you purchase the shares, as described on page 354.)

Note: The IRS has lots of rules about calculating cost basis, mostly so you can't keep changing the method you use to reduce the taxes you pay. Keeping track of all these rules can be tricky, so if you want to change the Average Cost setting after you've sold some shares, it's a good idea to ask your accountant or financial advisor for help.

Categorizing Investments

You already know how useful categories are in keeping track of your spending and income. Similarly, Quicken gives you several ways to classify your investments. Besides asset classes, which you can't add to or change, you have two other *customizable* ways to look at your investments: *security type* and *investing goal*. Security

WORD TO THE WISE

Allocating Your Assets

Asset allocation isn't just a way to practice your math skills. How you spread your investment dollars across different types of investments (stocks, bonds, real estate, and so on) plays a big role in determining a portfolio's return and helping reduce the amount of risk involved. So what are these influential asset classes? As you can see in Figure 12-9, Quicken—with help from Value Line, an investment data and analysis provider—divvies up the investment universe into Domestic Bonds, Global Bonds, Large Cap Stocks, Small Cap Stocks, International Stocks, Cash, and a catch-all class called Other for investments like real estate, precious metals, or cash. Quicken's Asset Class Mixture dialog box includes a class called Unclassified, which shows you whether you've forgotten to assign part of the investment to a class. Your asset assignment is complete when Unclassified equals 0 percent.

Each asset class contributes a combination of return and risk based on decades' worth of performance data. For example, small cap stocks tend to deliver higher average annual returns, but the risk of a stomach-wrenching nose-dive in any given year is higher as well. On the other hand, domestic bonds deliver lower average annual returns but make up for that reduced return with less year-to-year volatility. Of course, these are just predictions—no one knows exactly how each kind of investment will perform.

Instead of trying to make a killing by investing everything in the next Wal-Mart, financial advisors (and savvy investors) consider good asset allocation the foundation of a successful portfolio. That means putting your money in several different asset classes so you won't lose everything if one goes downhill. By allocating dollars to various asset classes, your portfolio is more likely to grow steadily over the years with smaller drops during down markets. Page 403 has more info on Quicken Premier's asset allocation features.

types are like a more customizable version of asset classes, and investing goals help you remember why you invested in a particular security in the first place (to pay for retirement or a college education, for example). Once you apply these classification tools to your investments, you can use them to generate nifty reports, as explained in the box on page 352.

The Security Type list comes with the usual suspects (Stock, Mutual Fund, Bond, and so on), but you can add, edit, or delete any type on the list so that you can easily distinguish, for example, between large growth, large value, and large blend mutual funds. Or, if you invest in REITs and want to see how much of your portfolio's in real estate, you can add a Real Estate security type. Security types are like categories rather than tags: You can add only one to each investment.

The Investing Goal list lets you categorize your investments according to your reasoning for investing the money. This section shows you how to use both features.

Note: If you're anxious to start tracking your investment purchases and sales, skip this section for now, and jump to "Recording Investment Transactions" on page 353. Then come back later when you want to analyze and manage your portfolio.

Categorizing with security types

Quicken adds to the Security Type list as you download new investments, so you may already have a long list of types. You can add, edit, or delete the types in the list, and assign types to investments. For example, if you're a fan of Morningstar's style box (which breaks investments down into large, medium, and small companies that are growing, a good value, or a combination of the two), you can set up security types for each of Morningstar's nine style boxes.

Here are the steps for creating a new security type:

1. **Choose Investing → Security Type List.**

   This opens the Security Type List window.

2. **To create a new type, in the window's menu bar, click New.**

   The Set Up Security Type dialog box appears.

3. **Type the name for the new type, and then click OK.**

   For example, to create a new type for real estate, in the Type box, enter *Real Estate*.

Note: To edit a type, select it and then click Edit. In the Edit Security Type dialog box, type the new name and then click OK.

Here's how you apply a new security type or change the one that's already assigned:

1. **Press Ctrl+Y to open the Security List. Right-click a security and then click Edit.**

   The Edit Security Details dialog box opens.

2. **In the Type drop-down menu, choose the type you want and then click OK.**

   You won't notice any changes until you customize and run a report that uses Quicken's security types, as the box on page 352 explains. In Quicken, every security has to have a type. If the security doesn't fall into any of the types you use, choose Other.

Categorizing by investing goal

Quicken automatically populates the Investing Goal list with College Fund, Growth, High Risk, Income, and Low Risk. You can change the list to match your unique sets of goals. For example, you might change the list to College Fund, Retirement, and Bahamas, if you're investing some money for your kids' education, some for your retirement, and some in high-risk high-return investments so you can buy a sweet Nassau bungalow. Then, you can generate investment reports based on these goals, as the box on page 352 explains.

Slicing and Dicing Investment Reports

Quicken doesn't provide ready-made reports for reviewing your investments by security type or investing goal. But don't let that stop you from viewing your investments the way you want to. It's easy to tweak any built-in or custom investment report to show your holdings by either of these classifications.

Simply generate an investment report like Investment Performance (page 438). Then, in the report window, in the "Subtotal by" drop-down menu, choose Security Type or Investing Goal (or Asset Class, for that matter).

If you customize a report, you can not only subtotal by these classifications but also choose which security types or investing goals to include. Here's how:

1. Generate the investment report you want (page 439), like Portfolio Value or Investment Performance.

2. In the "Subtotal by" drop-down menu, choose Security Type or Investing Goal.

3. In the report's toolbar, click Customize.

4. In the Customize dialog box, click either the Security Types or Investing Goals tab.

5. Turn the security type or investing goal checkboxes on or off to tell Quicken which ones to include.

6. Click OK.

Quicken then updates the report so that you see the results subtotaled by either Security Type or Investing Goal.

Here's how you create an investing goal:

1. **Choose Investing → Investing Goal List.**

   The Investing Goal List window opens.

2. **To create a new goal, in the window's menu bar, click New.**

   In the Set Up Investing Goal dialog box, type the goal's name and then click OK.

Note: To edit a goal, select it, and then click Edit. In the Edit Investing Goal dialog box, type the new name, and then click OK.

Applying an investing goal to a security takes more steps than applying a security type. Here's what you do:

1. **Press Ctrl+Y to open the Security List. Right-click the security and then click Edit.**

   The Edit Security Details dialog box opens.

2. **At the bottom of the dialog box, click Other Info.**

   The Additional Security Information dialog box appears.

3. **In the Investing Goal drop-down menu, choose the goal you want to apply (you can pick only one). Click OK to close the dialog boxes.**

   For a new security, Quicken automatically fills in the Investing Goal box with *(none)*.

Note: In the Additional Security Information dialog box, the Comments field can hold notes and reminders about the security. The problem with the Comments field is that this information is usually out of sight—you can see your notes only by opening the Additional Security Information dialog box. You're better off adding to-do notes to a list that you check regularly, like the Task list in Microsoft Outlook or a sticky note on your wall.

Deleting security types and goals

You can delete an investing goal even if it's assigned to securities. In the Edit Investing Goal dialog box, right-click the goal and then choose Delete. If you haven't assigned the goal, a confirmation box appears telling you that you're about to delete the goal for good. Click OK and it's history. If you *have* assigned the goal, a message box warns you that the goal is in use and asks you if you're sure you want to delete it. Click Yes.

You can delete a security type *only if* it isn't assigned to any securities. Before you delete a type, you have to find the securities it's assigned to and reassign them.

To find securities assigned to a specific type, run the Portfolio Value report (page 439). In the report window's "Subtotal by" drop-down menu, choose Security Type. In the report, scroll to the type that you want to delete to see which securities are assigned to it. Edit each security (page 347) to change the type assigned to it. When the type is no longer applied to any securities, the Portfolio Value report's security type subtotal will be empty. Now you can delete that type: Choose Investing → Security Type. In the Security Type dialog box, right-click the type and then choose Delete.

Recording Investment Transactions

Setting up your investment accounts for online services so you can download transactions (as described in Chapter 6) saves you hours of data entry and head-scratching. If you've got online services up and running, go ahead and skip to "Downloading Investment Transactions," which starts on page 377. This section describes how to record the most common investment transactions in case you don't have Internet access, your financial institution doesn't work with Quicken, or you simply want to do it yourself.

Your starting point is the all-purpose Enter Transactions dialog box:

1. **In the Account Bar, click the investment account you want to work on.**

   The account's investment register appears.

2. **Above the register, click the Enter Transactions button.**

   The title of the dialog box that opens is "Buy - Shares Bought", but it's really the Enter Transactions dialog box. The title changes based on what you choose in the "Enter transaction" drop-down menu. From this dialog box, you can record any type of investment transaction, as you'll soon learn.

Tip: When the Enter Transactions dialog box opens, the Account box is grayed out. You can record transactions only for the account whose register you're in. If you want to record transactions for a different account, you have to close the dialog box, open the register for the account you want, and then click Enter Transactions again.

Quicken veterans often prefer to record transactions directly in the investment register. To use the register, in the Action field, choose a transaction type, as shown in Figure 12-10. The downside to recording investment transactions in the register is that you can choose only one transaction type. If you're recording end-of-year mutual fund distributions (which usually include dividends, short-term capital gains, and long-term capital gains), the Enter Transactions dialog box can handle all of those at once, as described on page 364.

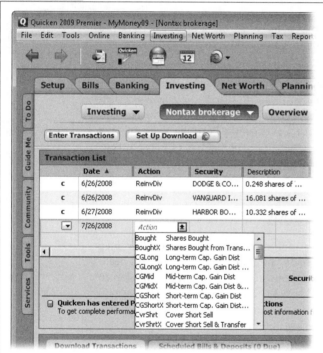

Figure 12-10:
In the investment register, each row shows fields for an investment transaction like Date, Action, Security, and Inv Amt (investment amount). You move around, select things, and fill in fields in this register just as you do in your checking account register.

Buying a Security

When you buy a security, whether it's shares of stock, a bond, or a mutual fund, you use cash from one of your accounts to pay for it. If the money comes from an account other than your investment account, then you don't have to create two transactions (one in the investment account and one in the cash account) to buy the security. When you record the purchase, just tell Quicken what you're buying, the number of shares, how much you paid, and the commission. Quicken calculates the cost of the purchase and then transfers the money from the cash account you specify.

Here's what to do when you buy a security:

1. **Open the register for the investment account that will hold the security, like your IRA when you're buying a mutual fund with this year's IRA contribution.**

   Click the investment account in the Account Bar or choose Investing → Investing Accounts and then choose the account you want to open. If the register doesn't appear, click the Transactions button below the main tabs.

2. **Above the register, click the Enter Transactions button.**

   In the "Enter transaction" drop-down menu, Quicken automatically selects "Buy - Shares Bought". The label also appears in the dialog box's title bar, as shown in Figure 12-11. "Buy - Shares Bought" is the perfect choice for recording purchases of stocks, mutual funds, or precious metals. Bonds have their own Bonds Bought transaction type, described on page 357.

Note: If you're recording purchases of precious metals in the "Buy - Shares Bought" dialog box, you have to translate the text box labels to fit your situation. In your mind, replace "Number of shares" with "Number of ounces or coins." Then, in the "Price paid" text box, type the price per ounce or per coin.

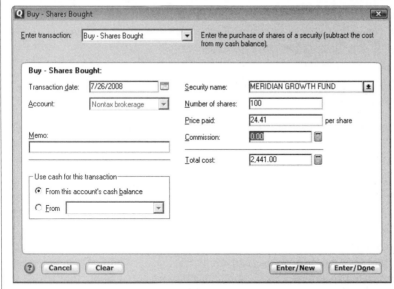

Figure 12-11:
Once you choose a transaction type from the Enter transaction drop-down menu, you can tab from field to field to record all the details.

3. **In the "Transaction date" box, enter the date you bought the security.**

   Entering the correct purchase date is crucial because it determines whether the capital gains are short or long (they're taxed differently) when you sell the investment.

4. **In the Security Name drop-down menu, choose the security you bought.**

   If the name's not on the list, at the bottom of the drop-down menu, click Add New Security to open the "Add Security to Quicken" dialog box (page 342). After you add the new security to your Security List, the dialog box closes, and you're back in the "Buy - Shares Bought" dialog box.

5. **In the "Number of shares" box, type the number of shares you purchased.**

   Quicken can track fractional shares to the accuracy of any brokerage. You can enter up to 12 digits in the "Number of shares" box, so the decimal places you can enter depend on the number of whole shares you purchase. For example, you can buy, say, 100.123456789 shares or 10000.1234567.

6. **Press Tab to skip to the "Price paid" box.**

   On many brokerage statements and orders, the price per share is rounded to the nearest penny, while the number of shares, commission, and total cost are exact. Skipping the "Price paid" box and entering the other values makes Quicken calculate the price per share for you.

7. **In the Commission box, type the broker's comission you paid to buy the security.**

   It's important that you record all the amounts that contribute to your cost basis (page 349), because that reduces your capital gains when you sell and the taxes you pay. The purchase amount comes from the price paid per share. You include all other fees like the commission *and* SEC charges in the Commission box.

8. **In the "Total cost" box, type the total for the purchase trasaction, including all fees and commissions.**

   If you don't enter a value in the "Price paid" box, simply enter the total cost from your statement or order in the "Total cost" box. Then, Quicken calculates the price per share so your transaction agrees with your financial institution.

   Another reason you might see a discrepancy when you buy fractional shares is if your financial institution calculates the number of shares to a higher degree of accuracy than Quicken (more than the 12 digits the program allows). If you can't make the number of shares match because of Quicken's restriction on share numbers, change the value in the "Total cost" field to match the financial institution's total. When you click another field or the Enter/Done button, the Recalculate Investment Transaction dialog box appears. Choose the "Price (recommended)" option and click OK. Quicken recalculates the price to make the totals match.

9. **If the cash for the purchase doesn't come from the account's cash balance, select the From option and then choose the account from which you withdrew money to buy the security.**

   Quicken automatically selects the "From this account's cash balance" option, which is what you want when you have cash in your investment account. If you select the From option, take care when you choose an account in the From drop-down menu: It lists *all* your accounts, including ones you probably wouldn't use to buy investments, like your house asset account and your car loan account.

10. **If you don't have any more transactions to record, click the Enter/Done button to close the dialog box.**

Voilà—you've recorded your purchase!

If you still have transactions to record, click the Enter/New button to save this transaction and start a new one.

Buying a Bond

Buying a bond is a lot like buying other types of securities, but the price you enter works differently, as the box on page 359 explains. You may also have to enter a value for interest that's accrued.

Note: Although Quicken has a special dialog box for buying bonds, you sell them as you would other securities. In the "Enter transaction" drop-down menu, choose "Sell - Shares Sold".

Here are the steps for buying bonds:

1. **In the Account Bar, click the investment account that will hold the bonds.**

   If the register doesn't appear, click the Transactions button below the main tabs.

2. **Above the register, click the Enter Transactions button, and then, in the "Enter transaction" drop-down menu, choose Bonds Bought.**

   The Enter Transactions dialog box takes on its Bonds Bought persona (that's Bonds, Bought Bonds), as shown in Figure 12-12.

3. **Fill in the "Transaction date" box and the "Security name" box as you would for a stock or mutual fund.**

   If the bond's name isn't on the list, click Add New Security at the bottom of the "Security name" drop-down menu to open the "Add Security to Quicken" dialog box (page 342). When you set up a new bond, add the *maturity date* (also known as the *call date*) to the bond's name, so you'll know when the bond matures. After you add the new bond to your Security List, the dialog box closes, and you're back in the Bonds Bought dialog box.

4. **In the "Number of bonds" box, type the number of bonds you purchased.**

   The number of bonds and their price don't follow the same rules as stocks and mutual funds. Your broker order may show a face amount of, say, $15,000. Because a bond's face value is $1,000 (see the box on page 359), the number of bonds is the face amount divided by 1,000, or 15 in this example.

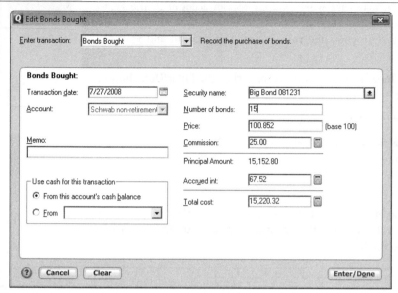

Figure 12-12:
When you choose a transaction type in the "Enter transaction" drop-down menu, the dialog box displays fields and labels that relate to that transaction type. For example, "Number of shares" changes to "Number of bonds", and the "Accrued int" field appears.

5. **In the "Price paid" box, enter the price** *per bond.*

   Bond price quotes are a percentage of the bond's face value (see the box on page 359). The label *(base 100)* to the right of the Price text box means that you can type a bond's price quote as is into the Price box.

6. **In the Commission box, type how much commission you paid to buy the bond.**

   Record the broker's commission and any additional fees in this box.

7. **In the "Accrued int" box, enter the amount of interest that has accrued on the bond but hasn't yet been paid.**

   If you purchase a bond from another investor after the bond's issue date, you have to pay the previous owner any interest that's accrued but hasn't been paid. Quicken records the accrued interest payment as a MiscEx (miscellaneous expense) transaction—see page 377.

8. **If you're paying for the bond purchase with money from another account, select the From option and then choose the account the money's coming from.**

   Quicken automatically selects the "From this account's cash balance" option, which is what you want when you have cash in your investment account.

9. **If you don't have any more transactions to record, click the Enter/Done button to close the dialog box.**

   If you have other transactions to record in this account, click the Enter/New button to save this transaction and start a new one.

A Bit about Bond Prices

Bonds have a face value of $1,000, which means that each one sells for $1,000 when it's first issued. For example, a $10,000 investment in a new bond issue buys 10 bonds.

Price quotes for bonds (*www.bondsonline.com* is one Web site with bond quotes) don't list value the way quotes for shares of stock do. Instead, bond quotes are shown as a *percentage* of their value, which makes for more compact notation. So if your bond was originally worth $1,000 and is now worth $1,008.52, that's 100.852 percent of its original value, and the price quote for that bond is 100.852. If you want to figure out a bond's current value based on a price quote, just multiply the quote by 10 (100.852 x 10 = $1,008.52).

When you record a bond purchase in Quicken, the Price box has the additional label *(base 100),* which simply means that Quicken wants you to enter bond prices as a percentage of the value, just like bond price quotes. So you can type bond quotes directly in the Price text box without worrying about the math.

Selling a Security

Recording the sale of a security is *almost* the same as recording its purchase. In fact, the "Sell - Shares Sold" dialog box has only two more features than the "Buy - Shares Bought" dialog box: The "Sell all shares in this account" checkbox and the Specify Lots button. Other than that, the only other differences are some slightly different labels.

Note: In the investment world, you can sell something you don't own, called a *short sale* (though you actually borrow the shares you sell). The box on page 362 explains how to record a short sale and the subsequent purchase you make to *cover* what you sold short.

Here are the steps for selling a security:

1. **Open the register for the investment account that holds the security and then, above the register, click Enter Transactions. In the "Enter transaction" drop-down menu, choose "Sell - Shares Sold".**

   The contents of the dialog box change to what you see in Figure 12-13.

2. **In the "Transaction date" box, enter the date you sold the security.**

   You need to know the sale date to figure out whether your capital gains are short or long, which determines how much tax you have to pay.

3. **In the "Security name" drop-down menu, choose the security you sold.**

   The only reason you wouldn't see the security's name is if you hid the security for some reason. In that case, close the dialog box. Then, open the Security List and unhide the security (page 344), and then start over at step 1.

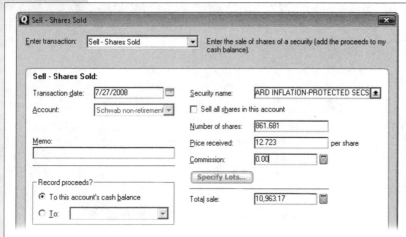

Figure 12-13:
If you turn on the "Sell all shares in this account" checkbox, Quicken fills in the "Number of shares" text box with the total number of shares you own (which might include partial shares). If you aren't selling all your shares, you can click the Specify Lots button to tell Quicken exactly which shares you want to sell.

4. **To sell all the shares in this account, turn on the "Sell all shares in this account" checkbox. To sell just some of your shares, in the "Number of shares" box, type the number of shares you want to sell.**

   If you reinvest dividends, then you end up owning fractions of shares. Those thousandths of a share continue to compound, and can eventually add up to big bucks. But until you sell your shares, they just seem inconvenient. Quicken takes some of the hassle out of dealing with these pesky fractional shares. When you turn on the "Sell all shares in this account" checkbox, Quicken automatically fills in the "Number of shares" text box with the number of whole and fractional shares you own in the account.

   Tip: If the "Sell all shares in this account" checkbox is grayed out, click the "Number of shares" text box, which (for some unknown reason) activates the checkbox.

   ---

5. **If you're selling only some of your shares held in a taxable account, *and* you want to control the capital gains you receive, click the Specify Lots button.**

   If you're selling a security in a tax-deferred account, you can ignore this button and simply type the number of shares into the "Number of shares" text box.

   Likewise, if you've set up a security to use the average cost of shares for simplicity (see page 349), this button is grayed out. Otherwise, when you click the Specify Lots button, Quicken opens the Specify Lots dialog box shown in Figure 12-14.

   The Specify Lots dialog box gives you ultimate control over the shares you sell. You can type numbers in the "Shares to sell" fields to specify exactly which whole and fractional shares you want to sell. If you don't click Specify Lots and the security isn't set to use the average cost, then Quicken sells the oldest shares first, which is the same thing as clicking First Shares In in the Specify Lots dialog box. Once you've specified which shares you want to sell, click OK to return to the "Sell - Shares Sold" dialog box.

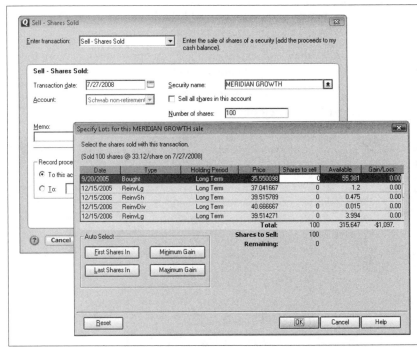

Figure 12-14:
The buttons in the Auto Select section automatically handle the most popular lot selection tasks for you. For example, if you click Minimum Gain, Quicken selects the most expensive shares you purchased to minimize your capital gains. Maximum Gain selects the least expensive shares to produce the largest capital gains.

6. **In the "Price received" box, type the price you received per share.**

   Someone pays you for a security you sell, so you fill in the "Price received" text box with the share price the buyer paid you. Or you can skip this field and enter the total transaction value in the "Total sale" field. Then, Quicken automatically calculates the share price.

7. **In the Commission box, type the amount of the commission you paid to sell the security.**

   Fill in the Commission box just like you do when you *buy* a security (page 356).

8. **If the "Total sale" value doesn't match the total cost of your sell transaction, edit the "Total sale" value.**

   Just like when you buy fractional shares, you can enter the "Total sale" value to match the total your financial institution came up with. If you change the "Total sale" value, then the Recalculate Investment Transaction dialog box appears. Choose the "Price (recommended)" option, and then click OK. Quicken recalculates the price per share to make the totals match.

9. If the cash is going somewhere other than the account's cash balance, in the "Record proceeds?" section, select the To option and then choose the account to which you're transferring money.

   Quicken automatically selects the "To this account's cash balance" option, which plunks the money in the account that held the shares and is often exactly what you want when you use the proceeds to buy something else.

10. After you record the details of a transaction, if you don't have any more transactions to record, click the Enter/Done button to close the dialog box.

    If you still have transactions to record in the account, click Enter/New to save this transaction and start a new one.

POWER USERS' CLINIC

Selling Short

Selling a security that you don't own is called a *short sale*. The process is ideally meant for a highly risk-tolerant and knowledgeable investor who borrows shares of a security and sells them to someone else. The investor hopes (*hope* is the key word here) to make money by purchasing shares later at a lower price to replace the ones he borrowed, which is called *covering* a short sale.

On the outside chance that you use this technique, you tell Quicken about short sales by choosing Short Sale in the "Enter transaction" drop-down menu. You enter the number of shares, price received, and commission as you would a regular sale. Quicken adds the proceeds of the sale to the your investment account's cash balance and keeps track of the shares that you sold short.

When you buy shares to cover the ones you borrowed, use the Cover Short Sale transaction type. The Cover Short Sale dialog box looks like the one for a regular purchase, except that Quicken subtracts the shares you covered from the ones you've shorted and subtracts the amount you paid for the shares from your account's balance. If you purchased the shares at a lower price than the ones you borrowed, Quicken calculates a capital gain on the sale. Talk to your accountant or tax advisor to find out whether the gains are short-term or long-term, because the IRS rules are—surprise!—complicated.

Recording and Reinvesting Income

Lots of investments pay dividends, which you can withdraw as cash to live on or reinvest to increase your nest egg. Many stocks pay cash dividends, and every once in a while you'll get a dividend in the form of additional shares of stock. Bonds pay interest on the money you lent to the issuer. And mutual funds distribute all kinds of income from the smorgasbord of securities they hold. Whether you use investment income as pocket money or reinvest it, Quicken's dialog boxes make it easy to record these transactions.

When you receive more than one type of income from an investment (which is almost always the case at the end of each year if you own mutual funds), using the "Reinvest - Income Reinvested" or "Inc - Income (Div, Int, etc.)" dialog box is much faster than adding each transaction individually. With your statement in

---

hand, you can type the dollar amount for each type of income in the appropriate Amount field (and type the corresponding number of shares in the Shares field if you're reinvesting).

The box on page 356 explains how to record stock dividends you receive. If you want to reinvest your investment income, here's how to record it:

1. **Open the register for the investment account that holds the security, and then, above the register, click Enter Transactions. In the "Enter transaction" drop-down menu, choose "Reinvest - Income Reinvested".**

   The dialog box changes to the one shown in Figure 12-15, so you can tell Quicken how much income you received, and how many shares that income bought.

Note: You can also display this dialog box from the investment account's register: Click the Action field in a blank transaction and then type *r*. When you press Tab or click away from the Action field, the "Reinvest - Income Reinvested" dialog box appears.

---

2. **In the Amount box for each type of distribution, type the dollar amount you received.**

   The dialog box has boxes for dividends, interest, short-term capital gains, mid-term capital gains, and long-term capital gains.

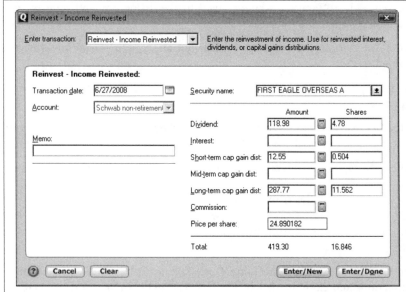

Figure 12-15:
As you type the dollars and number of shares you received of each type of distribution, Quicken calculates the total you reinvested, and the price per share. When you click Enter/Done, Quicken adds separate transactions for each type of income you received to the account's register.

3. In the corresponding Shares boxes, type the number of shares you bought with each distribution.

   Quicken calculates the price per share and fills in the "Price per share" box, and displays the total of all the Amount and Shares boxes in the Total row at the bottom of the dialog box.

4. **When you're done, click Enter/Done to create the reinvestment transactions and close the dialog box, or click Enter/New to create another transaction.**

   Quicken creates a separate transaction in the account register for each type of income distribution.

Recording cash dividends

Because the "Reinvest - Income Reinvested" dialog box is meant for income that you reinvest into more shares, it doesn't include a field for an account that receives the cash dividends. If you're transferring cash dividends you receive to another account, use the "Inc - Income (Div, Int, etc.)" transaction type. Its dialog box has a "Transfer account" field, which you set to the account that receives the cash.

Here's how you record income that you keep as cash:

1. **Open the register of the investment account that holds the security that paid the cash dividend, and then, above the register, click Enter Transactions. In the "Enter transaction" drop-down menu, choose "Inc - Income (Div, Int, etc.)".**

   Quicken adds a "Transfer account" field to the dialog box and removes the boxes for the number of reinvested shares.

2. **In the Amount box for each type of distribution, type the dollar amount you received.**

   The dialog box has fields for dividends, interest, and short-, mid-, and long-term capital gains.

3. **In the "Transfer account" drop-down menu, choose the account to which you want to transfer the cash dividend.**

   If the cash stays in the investment account, simply leave the "Transfer account" field blank. To transfer the cash to another account (your checking account, say), choose it from the drop-down menu. This field isn't available for any type of IRA account or brokerage accounts with linked checking accounts. For those, you transfer the money from the linked checking account to the account you want.

4. **When you're done, click the Enter/Done button to create the reinvestment transactions and close the dialog box, or click the Enter/New button to create another transaction.**

   Quicken creates a separate transaction in the account register for each type of cash distribution you receive.

Recording Stock Dividends

The other type of dividend that you see from time to time is a stock dividend. Instead of paying a dividend in cash, a company pays the shareholders by distributing more shares of stock.

For a stock dividend, in the "Enter transaction" drop-down menu, choose "Div - Stock Dividend (noncash)". Besides the security's name, the only thing you have to provide is the number of new shares you got for each share you own. If you receive .02 dividend shares per owned share, for example, in the "New shares issued" text box, type *.02*.

Recording a Stock Split

A *stock split* is an interesting phenomenon. It changes both the number of shares you own and the price of those shares, so the *value* of your investment is exactly the same after the split as it was before—only the number of shares you own changes. For example, a two-for-one stock split gives each investor *twice* the number of shares, each at *half* the original price. Companies often issue stock splits to keep the per-share price within reach of everyday investors. (For an example of what happens without stock splits, consider Berkshire Hathaway, a company that has grown for years without splitting its stock. At more than $100,000 a share, few investors have the funds to buy even one share.)

Although you'd think recording a stock split would just be a matter of telling Quicken the ratio (like two for one), the program makes you enter the number of new shares and the number of old shares. Here are the steps:

1. **Open the register for the investment account that holds the stock, and then, above the register, click Enter Transactions. In the "Enter transaction" drop-down menu, choose Stock Split.**

   The contents of the dialog box change to the boxes for a stock split. Choose the transaction date and the security as usual (page 355).

2. **In the "New shares" text box, type the number of shares you own *after* the stock split.**

   For example, if a stock splits two for one and you owned 200 shares, you now own 400 shares, so you enter *400*.

3. **In the "Old shares" text box, type the number of shares you owned *before* the split.**

   In this example, you'd enter *200*.

Note: The "Price after split" text box is optional. Because Quicken knows the number of new and old shares, it can do the math for the stock price after the split.

---

4. Click Enter/Done to record the split and close the dialog box, or click Enter/New to record another transaction.

That's all there is to it.

Handling Mergers, Acquisitions, and Spinoffs

A company spinning off a division seems unlikely in this age of mergers and acquisitions, but spinoffs occur all the time. If you own stock in a company that spins off another company, you typically receive shares in the new company on top of the ones you own in the parent company. On the other hand, if a company you've invested in buys another company, you usually receive additional shares of stock from the company you currently own. Quicken has transaction types in the "Enter transactions" drop-down menu for both spinoffs and acquisitions.

Recording corporate spinoffs

To record a spinoff, open the register for the investment account that holds the original security. Click the Enter Transactions button and, in the "Enter transactions" drop-down menu, choose Corporate Securities Spin-Off. Here's what you enter in each field:

- **Security name.** Choose the security you own.

- **New Company.** You guessed it—type the name of the new company that's been spun off.

- **New shares issued.** Type the number of shares you receive in the new company *for each share* you own of the old company, say, .12 shares in the new company for each share in the old.

- **Cost per old share.** Type the closing cost of the old company before the spinoff.

- **Cost per new share.** Type the price per share of the new shares you've received.

- Turn on the "This is a taxable spinoff" checkbox, if the spinoff is taxable (the old company can give you that info).

When you click Enter/Done, Quicken records *two* transactions in the investment account register. The first is a return of capital transaction (page 377), because the money for the spun-off shares comes from your original investment in the company. Quicken then adds the company to your Security List and records a purchase transaction for the shares in the new company using the numbers you entered in the "New shares issued" and "Cost per new share" boxes.

Recording corporate acquisitions

When one company acquires another, the parent company absorbs the other company completely. The shares of the acquired company disappear and you own shares in the company that's still around. To record an acquisition, open the register for the investment account that holds the security that's been acquired.

Click the Enter Transactions button and then, in the "Enter transactions" drop-down menu, choose "Corporate Acquisition (stock for stock)". Here's what you enter in each field shown in Figure 12-16:

- **Company acquired.** Choose the security you own for the company that's been acquired.

- **Acquiring company.** Type the name of the parent company that acquired the company you own shares in.

- **New shares issued.** Because the shares of the acquired company go away, type the number of shares you receive in the parent company *for each share* you owned of the acquired company. Say you've received 20 shares of the parent company for the 100 shares you owned of the acquired company. In that case, you'd type *.2* in the box (that's 20 divided by 100).

- **Cost per share of acquiring company.** Type the price per share of the parent company's stock.

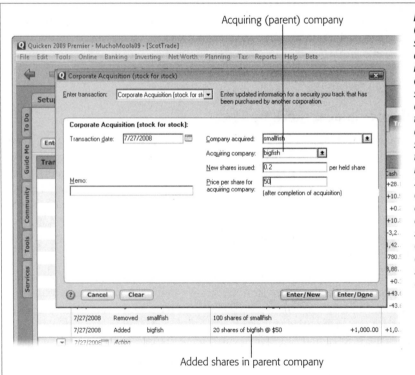

Figure 12-16:
Quicken removes the shares of the acquired company from your investment account. It calculates the number of shares in the parent company by multiplying the original shares you owned by the "New shares issued" value. In this example, 100 shares multiplied by .2 equals 20 shares in the parent company. The dollars added to your account are the number of new shares multiplied by the cost per share of the acquiring company: 20 shares at $50 per share equals $1,000.

When you click Enter/Done, Quicken records a transaction that removes the shares you owned from your account (page 376). Then, it adds the parent company to your Security list and records a transaction that adds the shares in the parent company using the numbers you entered in the "New shares issued" and "Cost per share of acquiring company" boxes.

Transferring Cash and Shares Between Accounts

When you want to buy a security, you may transfer money from a cash account (like checking or savings) *into* an investment account. You could also withdraw money *from* your investment accounts, for your retirement living expenses, say.

To record a cash transfer into an investment account, open the register for the investment account the money's going into. Then click the Enter Transactions button and, in the "Enter transactions" drop-down menu, choose "Cash Transferred into Account". You specify the account from which you're transferring the cash (your checking account, say) and the amount of the transfer.

If you're withdrawing money from your investment account, the process is the same except that you choose "Cash Transferred out of Account" to withdraw the money and then deposit it in a bank account. Specify the account that'll receive the transferred funds and the amount.

If you decide to switch to an ultra-discount broker, you may move your investments from your old broker to your new one, for example, from Merrill Lynch to ScotTrade. In that case, open the register for the account you're moving the shares out of. Then click the Enter Transactions button and, in the "Enter transactions" drop-down menu, choose Shares Transferred Between Accounts. Quicken removes the shares from the current investment account, and adds them to the investment account you specify.

Tracking Employee Stock Options

An employee stock option is noncash compensation that gives you the right to buy your company's stock at a fixed price. When your company gives you a stock option it's called a *grant*. You usually have to wait for a specified amount of time (called the *vesting schedule*) before you can *exercise* your stock option (purchase the shares at the option price). After you're vested in shares (meaning you've waited the specified amount of time), you can keep the option without buying any stock, buy the stock at the option price and sell it at the market price, or buy the stock and hold onto it.

When you record a stock option grant in Quicken, the program adds an option security to your Security List and tracks the vesting schedule for your stock options, so you know which options you can exercise. Quicken also keep track of the exercise price (the price you can buy the shares at) and the market price, so it can calculate your capital gains when you sell the shares.

This section explains how to track your stock options in Quicken, and what to do when you want to exercise your options.

Recording a stock option grant

The first transaction you record is the stock option grant that your employer gives you. Here are the steps:

1. **Create a new Standard Brokerage account for your options.**

   Page 335 explains how to create investing accounts.

2. **Open the register for the account you just created. Click the Enter Transactions button and, in the "Enter transaction" drop-down list, choose Grant Employee Stock Option.**

   The dialog box displays a "Transaction date" box and a Launch Wizard button.

3. **Type or choose the date of the stock option grant, and then click Launch Wizard.**

   If you don't already own the stock, you need to set up a new security. To do that, select the "A new stock" option, and then type the name and ticker symbol in (not surprisingly) the Name and Ticker Symbol boxes. Quicken creates a security for the stock. Click Next. (You set up a second security for the option in step 5.)

   If you already own shares in the stock, select the "A stock I already track" option and choose the stock from the drop-down list. Click Next.

4. **In the "Set Up an Employee Stock Option" screen, specify whether the stock option is for you or your spouse.**

   This screen appears only if you turned on the "I am married" option when you set up your account. By specifying the owner, Quicken can assign the gains from sales to the correct tax category when you exercise an option.

5. **Tell Quicken whether this grant is the first grant you've received for this stock or a new grant for an option you already have.**

   If this is your first grant, keep the "Create a new employee stock option" setting selected. Quicken automatically creates an option security and gives it a name that's the company name followed by the word "Option".

   If you receive another grant for the same option, select the "Create another grant for an option you already track" setting and then choose the stock option in the drop-down menu.

6. **In the "What day was the option granted?" screen, tell Quicken the date of the grant and then click Next.**

   Your employer sets the grant date. If you want to differentiate each grant with a number (if you expect to receive several options for the same stock, for instance), type the number in the Grant Number box.

7. In the "What type of employee stock option grant is this?" screen, select the appropriate setting for the kinds of option you received—nonqualified or qualified (ISO)—and then click Next.

Your choice determines how your stock options will be taxed. Ask your employer what kind of option you have.

8. **In the "Enter the shares and exercise price for Grant" screen, do just that.**

An option grant lets you purchase shares up to a maximum set by your employer. Type that maximum number in the "Number of Shares" box. The exercise price is the price your employer says you can purchase the shares at (regardless of the market price at the time).

9. **In the "What is the Vesting schedule?" screen, enter the number of months until the grant is fully vested. If you vest in a percentage of shares on a regular schedule, enter the percentage you receive in the first vest (20 percent, say) and the date. Then, enter the number of months between each additional vest.**

If the vesting schedule changes over time, you need to set up a separate grant for each schedule. Say you receive a grant of 100 shares on 2/1/2008 and are fully vested after four years (2/1/2012). You vest in 30 percent (30 shares) of the grant each year for the first two years, and then vest in 20 percent (20 shares) each year for the next two years. To track this schedule, set up one grant that vests 60 shares over 24 months with 50 percent at the end of the first year (2/1/2009), and another 50 percent 12 months later. Then, set up a second grant for 40 shares for the second part of the vesting schedule. So for the second grant, you enter *48* in the "How long from the Grant Date until you are fully vested" box. In the "First vest" box, type *20%*. In the "First vest" date box, type *2/1/2011*, because this vest occurs in the third year of the grant. Then, in the "then vest every _ month(s)" box, type *12*.

10. **If the grant expires, type the date in the "Yes, it expires on" box. Then click Next.**

Select No if the grant doesn't expire.

11. **In the "Please review your selections" screen, check that the numbers are correct. Click Next and then click Done.**

When you click Next, Quicken asks if you want to add another security and selects the No option. Simply click Done. Quicken adds transactions that show when you vest in shares to your investment account, as shown in Figure 12-17.

Exercising an employee stock option

When you exercise a stock option, you buy shares (up to the maximum that the grant allows) at the exercise price. You can sell the shares immediately at the going market price, but you'll pay ordinary income tax rates on the gain (the difference between the exercise price and the price you sell the shares at). If you buy the

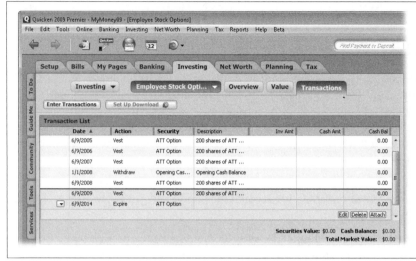

Figure 12-17:
When you set up a stock option grant, Quicken adds transactions to your investment account for every date that you vest in additional shares, even if the dates are in the future. If the grant also has an expiration date, Quicken adds another transaction to the register that shows when the grant expires.

shares and hold onto 'em, your cost basis becomes the fair market value on the day you bought the shares, so you pay capital gains tax only on any increase in the market value after you bought the shares. (In most cases, it's well worth holding onto the shares for a while.)

Here's how you exercise a stock option grant:

1. **Open the register for the account you created for your stock options. Click the Enter Transactions button and, in the "Enter transaction" drop-down list, choose Exercise Employee Stock Option.**

   The dialog box displays a "Transaction date" box and a Launch Wizard button.

2. **Type or choose the exercise date, and then click Launch Wizard.**

   Quicken asks for the exercise date and fills in the date you specified in the Exercise Employee Stock Option dialog box. If you hold onto the shares, your cost basis becomes the fair market value of the stock price on this date. Click Next.

3. **In the "Which grant?" screen, select the grant you want to exercise and then click Next.**

   If you have only one grant, Quicken selects that grant and shows the grant date, the exercise price, and the number of vested shares.

   If you have more than one grant for the same stock, click anywhere in the row for the grant you want to exercise.

4. **In the "What type of employee stock option grant is this?" screen, select the appropriate type—nonqualified or qualified (ISO)—and then click Next.**

   Your choice determines how much tax you'll have to pay. Ask your employer for the type.

5. In the "What type of transaction?" screen, select whether you want to exercise the stock option and immediately sell the shares ("Same-day Sale") or exercise the stock option and hold onto the shares ("Exercise and Hold"). Then click Next.

In most cases, you'll save a lot in capital gains tax by holding onto the shares. For nonqualified stock options, holding the stock changes your cost basis to the fair market value on the day you buy your shares. That way, you pay capital gains only on any increase from that price, not from the original exercise price. If you sell immediately, you pay the ordinary income tax rate on the difference between the exercise price and the market price.

For qualified stock options, you pay long-term capital gain rates if you sell your shares at least a year after exercising the option and at least two years after the option was granted.

6. Whether you're selling right away or holding onto the shares, in the next screen, enter the number of shares you're buying, the fair market price, and the commission. Then click Next.

The fair market price is typically the closing price on the day you buy the shares.

If you're holding onto the shares, the next screen asks you to choose the account where you want to hold the shares. If you're selling the shares, the next screen asks you to choose the investment account for the sale transaction and the account where you want to deposit the proceeds from the sale.

In either case, when you click Next, the screen that appears shows the transactions that Quicken will record. If you're buying and holding shares, Quicken adds an exercise transaction to show that you've exercised some of the shares in the grant. This transaction adds cash to your account to make up the difference between your purchase price and market price. Quicken also adds a purchase transaction. If you exercise the grant and sell the shares immediately, you'll see one additional transaction: the sale of the shares.

7. Click Done.

Quicken adds the transactions to your investment account.

Note: If your employer lowers the exercise price of one of your grants, use the Reprice Employee Stock Options transaction type. You choose the grant you want to reprice, and tell Quicken the date when the new price takes effect, the new price, and the investment account you use to track the grant.

Stock Purchase Plans

If your company sells shares to its employees at a discount (called an *employee stock purchase plan* or *ESPP*), you contribute money to the plan through payroll deductions. Your contributions accumulate from the initial offering date to the purchase date (the *grant period*). Then, on the buy date, the company uses your contributions to buy shares at a discount (sometimes as high as 15 percent). In Quicken, you record these purchases with the Bought ESPP Shares transaction type and sales of those shares with the Sold ESPP Shares transaction type. These transaction types differentiate your ESPP shares from any company stock you buy at an undiscounted price. That way, Quicken can track the different tax gains for your full-price and discounted shares. For example, when you sell ESPP shares, you may have to pay income tax on the discount amount as well as on any capital gains.

To get started, set up a Standard Brokerage account (page 333) for your ESPP shares. If you set up your paycheck in Quicken (page 192), you can add an after-tax paycheck deduction (page 192) to deposit the money into this investment account.

Buying ESPP shares

When you buy ESPP shares, Quicken adds a security dedicated to ESPP shares to the Security List. (Quicken tacks "-ESPP" onto the end of the security name for your company's stock, like *Google-ESPP*.) This way, Quicken can track your discounted ESPP shares separately from undiscounted shares you may own so that each security has its own price history.

Here's how you record the purchase ESPP shares:

1. **Open the register for the account you created for your ESPP shares. Click the Enter Transactions button and, in the "Enter transaction" drop-down list, choose Bought ESPP Shares.**

   The dialog box displays a "Transaction date" box and a Launch Wizard button.

2. **Type or choose the date of the ESPP purchase, and then click Launch Wizard.**

   The date that you choose is important, because it may affect how much income tax you pay when you sell the shares.

   When you click Launch Wizard, the Bought/Added ESPP Shares dialog box opens to the Easy Step tab. If this is your first ESPP purchase, you have to set up the ESPP security by selecting the "A new stock" option and typing the name and ticker symbol in the Name and Ticker Symbol boxes. Quicken creates a security with the security name you entered followed by "-ESPP". Click Next.

   If you already own shares in the stock, select the "A stock I already track" option and choose the stock from the drop-down list. Click Next.

3. **In the "Do you want to use money from a Quicken account to acquire these shares" screen, select the appropriate option and then click Next.**

   The "Yes, subtract from my cash balance in this account (Buy)" option is perfect when you've already transferred money into your ESPP account, using an after-tax paycheck deduction in your Quicken paycheck (page 198).

   To transfer money from another account, select the "Yes, subtract from another Quicken account (BuyX)" option, and choose the account in the drop-down list.

If you're adding shares you bought before you set up the ESPP account, select the "No, deposit the shares without affecting any cash balance (ShrsIn)" option. This adds the shares to your account without using cash in any account.

4. **After you click Next, the screen shown in Figure 12-18 appears. In the first section, enter the number of shares you bought, the price you paid per share, the date you bought the shares, and any commission or fees.**

   These boxes work like the boxes you see when you record a "Buy - Shares Bought" transaction (page 353).

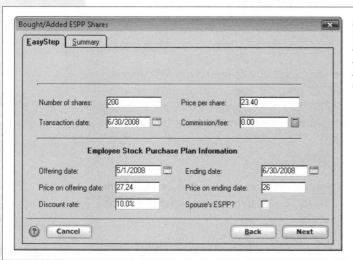

Figure 12-18:
Quicken tracks the price of ESPP shares separately from regular shares in the same company. This way, the regular shares and ESPP shares each have their own price history.

5. **In the Employee Stock Purchase Plan Information section, choose the starting and ending dates of your employer's offering period in the "Offering date" and "Ending date" boxes, respectively.**

   Employers often break ESPP benefits into different grant periods. The offering date is the first day of the ESPP purchase period, and the ending date is the last day of the purchase period.

6. **In the "Price on offering date" and "Price on ending date" boxes, type the fair market value of the shares on the first and last days of the purchase period.**

   You can get price quotes online or ask your employer for this info. ESPPs typically buy your shares using the lower of the two prices.

7. **In the "Discount rate" box, type the percentage discount your employer offers.**

   Quicken applies the discount to the lower of the offering and ending prices. If the purchase price it calculates differs from the amount you typed in the "Price per share" box, Quicken warns you. If your price is correct but different from the one Quicken comes up with (due to a rounding error, say) leave your "Price per share" value as it is.

8. **If this stock purchase is your spouse's ESPP plan, turn on the Spouse's ESPP checkbox.**

    This setting helps Quicken associate the proceeds from a sale to the correct tax category.

9. **Click Next, and then click Done.**

    The Summary tab opens, showing all the info you entered for this purchase. Double-check the number of shares, the price per share, and the total cost. If you find any discrepancies between these fields and your ESPP statement, change the values in the Summary tab's boxes. When you click Done, Quicken records the purchase in your investment account.

Selling ESPP shares

The income tax you pay depends on when you sell your shares. The rules for calculating the tax you owe are complicated, but the determining factor is whether you sell within 2 years of the offering date and 1 year of the purchase date. Quicken tracks your holding period and calculates the taxes you have to pay on both income and capital gains when you sell your shares.

Tip: Quicken's Capital Gains Estimator (page 403) can help you figure out the best time to sell your ESPP shares. The Estimator figures out the taxes you'll have to pay in different scenarios.

Here's how to record the sale of your ESPP shares:

1. **Open the register for the account you created for your ESPP shares. Click the Enter Transactions button and, in the "Enter transaction" drop-down list, choose Sold ESPP Shares.**

    The dialog box displays a "Transaction date" box and a Launch Wizard button.

2. **Type or choose the date of the ESPP sale and then click Launch Wizard.**

    When you click Launch Wizard, the Sold/Removed ESPP Shares dialog box opens to the Easy Step tab.

3. **In the "Which security?" drop-down list, choose the security you want to sell and then click Next.**

    For example, Microsoft shares that you bought through an ESPP show up as *Microsoft-ESPP*.

4. **In the "Do you want to record the proceeds of this transaction to a Quicken account" screen, select the appropriate option and then click Next.**

    The "Yes, add from my cash balance in this account (Sell)" option keeps the cash from the sale in your investment account.

To transfer money to another account, select the "Yes, add to another Quicken account (SellX)" option and then choose the account in the drop-down list. For example, if you want to transfer the proceeds to your checking account, choose it from the drop-down list.

If you're removing shares from the account, for example, to transfer them to another financial institution, select the "No, withdraw the shares without affecting any cash balance (ShrsOut)" option.

5. **After you click Next, an untitled screen appears. In the first section, enter the number of shares you bought, the price you received per share, the date you sold the shares, and any commission or fees you paid.**

These boxes work like the ones you see when you record a "Sell - Shares Sold" transaction (page 359).

6. **Choose the method you want Quicken to use to calculate your cost basis.**

Quicken automatically selects the Lot Identification option. Because the tax you pay depends on how long you've owned ESPP shares, the safest choice is to choose the first shares you bought. Keep the Lot Identification option selected and then click Specify Lots. In the Specify Lots dialog box, select the shares you want to sell. (See page 360 for details about the Specify Lots dialog box.)

Check with your accountant or tax advisor about the taxes you'll pay if you choose Average Cost.

7. **If this stock purchase is your spouse's ESPP plan, turn on the Spouse's ESPP check box.**

That way, Quicken associates the proceeds from a sale to the correct tax-related category.

8. **Click Next, and then click Done.**

The Summary tab shows all the info you entered for this sale. Double-check your numbers and change any values if necessary. When you click Done, Quicken records the sale in your investment account.

Recording Other Investment Transactions

Often, the hardest thing about recording transactions in Quicken is figuring out what *kind* of transaction to use. For example, your financial institution may notify you of a transaction, but you can't find anything by that name in Quicken. The following list describes the lesser-known types of transactions on the "Enter transaction" drop-down menu:

- **Add or remove shares without affecting your cash balance.** Sometimes you want to add shares to your account without using cash. For example, if you inherited 1,000 shares of stock from your grandfather, you don't need any money to buy the shares. After you hand over the stock certificates to your broker, you record this addition using the "Add - Shares Added" transaction type.

Similarly, when you donate shares of stock to a charity, you remove shares from the account and take a few additional steps to track the donation properly, as the box on page 378 explains.

Note: If you're adding shares that you've inherited from someone, your cost basis is based on the security price on the day of the person's death. When you choose the "Add - Shares Added" transaction type, in the "Price paid" box, type the closing price per share as of that date and choose that date in the "Date acquired" box.

- **Return of Capital.** Some investments act like loans. A bond, for example, is actually money you lend and receive payments for in return. If you hold the bond until it matures, you receive your original investment back (called the *principal* or *capital*). Investments in mortgage-backed securities and limited partnerships also return principal. This money isn't income or gains—it's *your* money. Record this kind of transaction with the "Return of Capital" entry, which reduces the cost basis of your investment.

- **Miscellaneous Expense.** This entry is for expenses that arise from time to time, like fees that your financial institution charges to handle your account. *Don't* use this entry to record the commissions you pay on trades—you record those as part of the trades themselves (page 356) because they increase your cost basis, which means you pay less capital gains tax.

- **Margin Interest Expense.** You're not likely to need this entry, unless you borrow money to buy investments (which makes you one of a small number of brave souls indeed).

Note: If you've diligently grown your portfolio into a substantial sum, borrowing against your investments instead of a credit card or home equity loan can be a good deal. Brokerages tend to offer competitive interest rates *and* the margin interest you pay is deductible against your investment income.

- **Corporate Name Change.** If a company changes its name, its security's name usually changes too. To change the name of the security for all of its transactions in your data file, choose the Corporate Name Change entry. Select the security, and in the "New security name" text box—you guessed it—type the new name.

Downloading Investment Transactions

Most of the time, downloading investment transactions is a piece of cake—and no different than downloading transactions into your checking or savings account (page 133). You give the downloaded transactions the once-over and then accept them into your account. Downloading investment transactions saves you even more time than downloading regular transactions does, because recording investment transactions manually involves typing more numbers, what with dollar values and fractional shares.

Donating Stocks to Charity

Donating to charity is a way to do good while avoiding the capital gains taxes you'd pay if you kept the proceeds from selling an investment. If you donate stock to a charity, you don't pay capital gains taxes on the proceeds. Plus, you receive a tax deduction for the total value of the stock you donated.

When you record a stock donation in Quicken, your first challenge is getting the shares out of your investment account without recording any capital gains. At the same time, you want Quicken to record your charitable contribution (the value of the stock as of the day you donated it) so that the tax deduction shows up in your Quicken tax reports (page 439).

Quicken doesn't have a single transaction type to handle a charitable stock donation, so it takes a little fancy footwork to record everything correctly. Here are the steps for recording a stock donation and the corresponding charitable contribution:

1. Open the register for the investment account that holds the donated shares.

2. To remove the donated shares from your investment account without changing the cash balance, click the Enter Transactions button and, in the Enter Transactions dialog box, choose the "Remove - Shares Removed" transaction type. Set the "Transaction date" box to the date you donated the stock. In the "Security name" drop-down list, choose the security you donated and, in the "Number of shares" box, type the number of shares you donated. If you want to give the charity your lowest cost shares (to avoid the most capital gains tax), click Specify Lots. In the Specify Lots dialog box, click Maximum Gain and then click OK. Click Enter/New.

3. To add the shares back into your investment account at the donation price (which means you won't have any capital gains when you "sell" the shares), in the "Enter transaction" drop-down menu,

choose "Add - Shares Added". Enter the same transaction date, security name, and number of shares as you did in step 2. Set the "Date acquired" to the donation date and, in the "Price paid" box, enter the closing price per share as of the donation date. Click Enter/New.

4. To set the value of your charitable contribution, record a sales transaction for the donated shares at the donation price: In the "Enter transaction" drop-down menu, choose "Sell - Shares Sold". Use the same transaction date, security name, number of shares that you entered in the last two steps, and enter the same price per share as you did in step 3. For example, if you're donating 100 shares valued at $50, set the "Number of shares" to *100* and the "Price received ___ per share" to *$50*. Leave the "To this account's cash balance" option selected. This transaction increases the investment account cash balance by the value of your charitable contribution, as shown in Figure 12-19. Click Enter/New.

5. Finally, record a check transaction for the amount of your charitable contribution. In the "Enter transaction" drop-down menu, choose Write Check. In the Payee field, type the name of the charity. In the Category drop-down menu, choose the category you use for charitable contributions (Quicken's built-in category is Charity). Type the value of your contribution in the Amount field. This transaction reduces your investment account balance back to where it was in step 2 and assigns the amount of your stock donation to the Charity category (or whatever category you chose instead) for your tax deduction. (You don't actually write a check to the charity; you've already donated the stock.) Now click Enter/Done because you are.

Recording all these transactions takes a bit of work, but hey—it's for a good cause.

Remove and add
shares to eliminate
capital gains

Sell shares to place dollars of
contribution in account

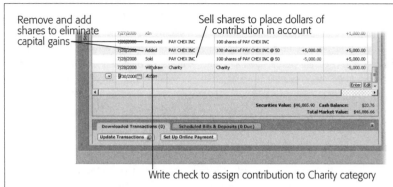

Figure 12-19:
*Recording a charitable
donation of stock requires
four Quicken transactions.
You remove the shares you
donate from your investment
account and then add them
back in at the donation price,
which eliminates any capital
gains. Then, you sell the
shares at the donation price
to show the dollar value of
your charitable contribution
in your investment account.
Finally, you write a check (in
Quicken only) for the amount
of the charitable contribution
so your tax deduction shows
up on Quicken's tax reports.*

Write check to assign contribution to Charity category

On the flip side, downloading investment transactions may lead to *placeholders*, which are Quicken's way of syncing your Quicken investment account with your broker's records. Placeholders, which are explained in detail on page 381, can be a help in the short term—and a huge headache from then on. Downloading can also create duplicate transactions if, for example, you manually record a transaction that Quicken doesn't match.

This section gives a quick review of downloading transactions. Then you'll learn how to get rid of placeholders and duplicate transactions.

The Download Process

Like their bank account register relatives, investment account registers display transactions in the top half of the window and tabs for downloaded and scheduled transactions in the bottom half. For the full details on downloading any kind of transactions, banking or investment, see Chapter 6.

If you included your investment accounts in One Step Update (page 141), then you can download *all* your transactions by clicking Update (the gold arrow chasing its tail) in the Quicken toolbar or by clicking the Update icon at the top of the Account bar. If you want to download and accept investment transactions for a particular account, follow these steps:

1. **Open the register for the investment account you want.**

   In the Account Bar, click the name of the investment account. If you see a screen other than the register (for example, if you viewed a different one the last time you looked), in the window's top-right corner, click the Transactions button to open the register.

Tip: If you've never downloaded transactions to this account, create a dummy transaction in the account as a precaution against unwanted placeholder transactions. It doesn't matter what security you pick or the number of shares or the price. Sometimes, the first time you download to an account, Quicken doesn't give you the option to reject the placeholder transactions it offers. By creating a fake transaction before you download, you trick Quicken into letting you reject its placeholders. Then, when you download transactions, you can tell the program you don't want placeholders. After that, you can delete the dummy transaction and fill in the old transactions to synch your account with your financial institution's.

2. **On the Downloaded Transactions tab, click Update Transactions.**

   If you don't use the Password Vault, type the password you received from your broker to access your investment account online in the Passwords box.

   If you use the Password Vault (page 144) to store your passwords, the Vault Password dialog box appears. Enter your vault password and then click OK. In the "Online Update for this account" dialog box, Quicken fills in your account password (displaying asterisks in place of the actual password) and then turns on the checkboxes to download your transactions.

   In the "Online Update for this account" dialog box, click Update Now. When Quicken and your financial institution are done talking, your downloaded transactions appear at the bottom of the register window.

3. **To add a downloaded transaction to the register, click the transaction's Accept button.**

   If you've already manually added a transaction in the register, select the corresponding transaction in the Downloaded Transactions tab and then click its Delete button.

   To accept *all* the downloaded transactions, click Accept All.

4. **If Quicken downloads a transaction with a security name that it hasn't used before, then the Matching Security dialog box opens, as shown in Figure 12-20. If you already own the security that Quicken is looking for, select the "Yes, Select from Quicken Security List" option, choose the matching security in the list and then click Done.**

   The Yes option comes in handy if you buy the same security from a different brokerage that assigns it a different name. You choose the name from the Matching Security list, so Quicken uses the security that's already in your Security List.

   If the security isn't in your Security List, select the No option and then click Done to add the security name that Quicken filled in to your Security List.

After you accept all the downloaded transactions, the "Adjust holdings account" dialog box appears if the number of shares that your financial institution says you have doesn't match the number of shares in Quicken. You don't have to accept the

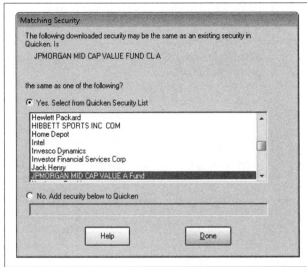

Figure 12-20:
Quicken displays all the securities in your data file, whether they're hidden or not. To scroll through the list, select the Yes option. If you don't find the security, select the No option and then click Done.

placeholders that Quicken suggests. In fact, as you'll learn in the next section, it's wise to figure out why the shares don't agree before you accept Quicken's placeholders, because placeholders can be tough to get rid of. The next section explains what this dialog box is all about, and what you should do in it.

Dealing with Placeholders

Sometimes, Quicken and your brokerage say you own different amounts of a given security. The difference is usually small (often less than a share), and can be caused by a dividend that you reinvested but forgot to record in Quicken, or rounding off fractional shares when your brokerage uses exact values. If you've had an account for years but are just starting to track it in Quicken, the placeholder discrepancy can be large.

If your financial institution and Quicken disagree on how many shares of a security you own, Quicken wants to create *placeholder* entries in your investment accounts. The placeholders represent positive or negative shares to make the two totals agree. Quicken also enters placeholders if you don't enter complete information about the securities you own, like if you set up a 401(k) account by specifying total amounts instead of the number of shares you own (page 336). The best approach to placeholders is to avoid them, because they make it so you can't use some of Quicken's investment features, like reporting your investment performance for the account with placeholders, which in turn affects a report for your entire portfolio. But avoiding them isn't always practical, especially if you have a long history with investments but a short history using Quicken.

The actual placeholder entries are simple: They contain only the security name and a number of shares, as shown in Figure 12-21. They're great for getting you up and running quickly, but eventually you'll need to provide the rest of the information.

Because placeholders are short on details, Quicken can't use them to calculate investment performance or produce accurate tax records. To calculate capital gains, for example, Quicken needs to know both the purchase price and the sales price of the security. But if you have placeholders in an account, the program can't do the math because it doesn't know the purchase price.

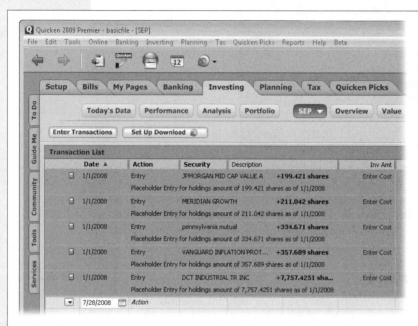

Figure 12-21:
Here are some placeholder entries. They show the security's name, the date purchased, and the number of shares. In the Inv Amt column, click Enter Cost to fill in the amount you originally paid to buy the shares.

Here are a few other situations that can make Quicken insert placeholders:

- **You create an account and enter only the securities you own without the price you paid.** For example, when you add an account without going online, Quicken asks how many shares you own but not how much you paid for them. After you enter the number of shares you own, Quicken creates a placeholder entry for those shares because it doesn't know how much you paid for them (like the ones in Figure 12-21).

- **You add an account and download transactions from your financial institution.** If you've had the account for a while, you may not be able to download your entire transaction history. (Some financial institutions keep only the last 3 to 6 months' worth of transactions online, so you can download only transactions that happened within that time frame.) For example, if you went off to Timbuktu for a few years and now that you're back you want to start downloading transactions again, some of the transactions that took place when you were away might not be available online anymore. Quicken creates placeholders in the account for the shares from missing transactions.

Tip: If you suspect that you have placeholder transactions, but you don't see them in the register, they might be hidden. To view them, choose Edit → Preferences → Quicken Program. In the "Select preference type" list, choose "Investment transactions". Turn on the "Show hidden transactions" checkbox, and then click OK. Now you see *all* your transactions.

Truth be told, you don't need Quicken's placeholders at all. You can create your own transactions to bring your investment accounts up to date. Whether you want to enter the investment's full history or an average cost simply click Enter Transactions above the investment account register and then record the missing transactions. If you want to use an average cost, in the "Price paid" box, type that average price per share.

Filling in missing transactions

If you plan to use Quicken to calculate your capital gains or your annual returns for your investments, you need a full history of when you acquired shares and how much you paid. But the program can't perform these calculations for an account that contains placeholders. You convert a placeholder to real shares by entering all the security's historical transactions (your original purchases and your reinvestments). With that information, Quicken can tell you your investment return and the capital gains you receive when you sell. If recreating a full history is impractical because you have decades' worth of transactions, simply add a transaction with the number of shares and an average cost.

Note: If the shares in your account are the result of years of buying additional lots and reinvesting dividends, adding one transaction (see page 382) for all those reinvestments doesn't provide enough info for meaningful performance reporting. The only way to have completely accurate records for both taxes and performance reports is to add individual transactions for each original purchase and each reinvestment.

Here are the steps for turning a placeholder into a history of transactions:

1. **Open the investment account that contains the placeholder(s).**

   In the Account Bar, click the account name. If you don't see the register, click the Transactions button.

2. **In the register, click the placeholder's Enter Cost link.**

   These links are easy to spot because they're the only blue text in the register. The Enter Missing Transactions dialog box opens.

3. **To start recording all the missing transactions, below the table of transactions, click Enter Missing Transaction.**

   Quicken opens the "Buy - Shares Bought" dialog box with the transaction date and security name already filled in, as shown in Figure 12-22.

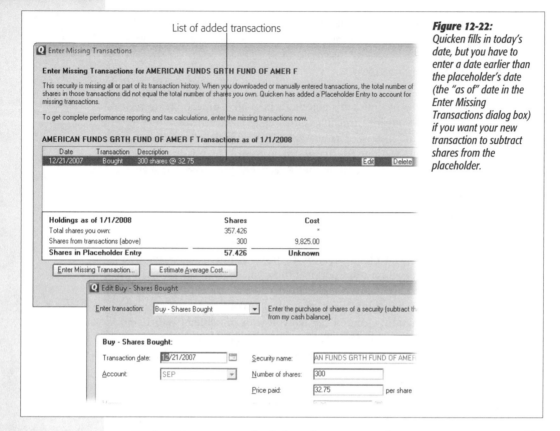

List of added transactions

Figure 12-22:
*Quicken fills in today's
date, but you have to
enter a date earlier than
the placeholder's date
(the "as of" date in the
Enter Missing
Transactions dialog box)
if you want your new
transaction to subtract
shares from the
placeholder.*

4. **In the "Enter transaction" drop-down menu, choose a transaction type like "Buy - Shares Bought" (which is the default) or "Reinvest - Income Reinvested".**

   Fill in the "Number of shares", "Price paid", and Commission text boxes as you would for a regular investment purchase (page 354).

5. **Click Enter/Done.**

   The transaction dialog box closes, and Quicken subtracts the shares from the placeholder. As you can see in Figure 12-22, the list in the Enter Missing transactions dialog box shows the missing transactions you've added so far. Each time you click Enter Missing Transaction and add another transaction, it appears in this list.

   Below the list, "Total shares you own" represents the number of original placeholder shares on the "as of" date (in Figure 12-22, this date is 1/1/2008). The value in the "Shares from transactions (above)" row is the number of shares you've accounted for by entering (or downloading) missing transactions that have a transaction date that's before the as-of date. "Shares in Placeholder Entry" shows the number of shares still in the placeholder transaction.

6. **Repeat steps 3 through 5 until you've entered all missing transactions.**

If you want to take a break, click Finish Later. When you're ready to continue, simply click the Enter Cost link in the register to pick up where you left off.

You know that you've entered all the missing transactions for the security when the "Shares in Placeholder Entry" value equals zero.

7. **Click Finish. You're done!**

Using average cost to complete your records

Rather than fill in every transaction that relates to the shares in a placeholder, you can give Quicken an average cost for shares if you don't have the transaction info, or you aren't willing to devote weeks to data entry. With this approach, your tax reports and investment performance reports won't be accurate, but you'll have your life back.

Warning: Switching a security from specific lots (which means you pick the exact shares you want to sell) to average cost means that you can't go back to picking specific lots for future sales (page 360). For tax reporting purposes, IRS regulations may not let you switch at all. Before you use the average cost approach, back up your Quicken data file in case you change your mind.

To use an average cost, follow these steps:

1. **In the investment account's register, click the placeholder's Enter Cost link.**

The Enter Missing Transactions dialog box opens.

2. **Click Estimate Average Cost.**

The Enter Missing Transactions dialog box displays boxes for entering the total amount you paid for your shares or the average price per share.

3. **Fill in either the Cost box or the Price/Share box.**

If you know the total amount you paid for your shares, in the Cost box, type that value. Quicken calculates the price per share by dividing the total cost by the number of shares. Conversely, if your financial institution provides the average cost you paid, type that in the Price/Share box, and Quicken calculates the total cost.

4. **Click OK.**

Back in the register, Quicken fills in the Inv. Amt field with the total amount you paid for the investment. However, the transaction still shows up as a placeholder entry, which means you can't see investment performance for that security, like annual return (page 400).

If you stumble across your missing paperwork later, you can fill in all the details of your purchase. In the investment register, double-click the placeholder transaction. In the Adjust Share Balance dialog box that opens, click Enter History to open the Enter Missing Transaction dialog box. Page 383 tells you what to do next.

Placeholders That Won't Go Away

If you download transactions and end up with a bazillion placeholders, the problem may be that you added shares to your Quicken account without transferring any cash to actually *buy* the shares. These transactions don't match up with the ones you download so you end up with placeholders for each transaction you download.

You're better off ignoring Quicken's placeholders (page 381) than replacing them with transactions. In the investment account register, double-click the existing transaction (not a placeholder) to open the Enter Transactions dialog box. Then, in the From drop-down menu, choose an account. If the cash came from an account that wasn't set up in Quicken at the time of the purchase, simply create a temporary account and then choose it the From drop-down menu. You don't have to worry about adding funds to it. Sure, the investment purchases take money out of the account and make the account balance negative. But after

you've edited your transactions to use that account, you can use the Update Cash Balance command (page 389) to set the balance to zero and then hide the account.

Placeholders can lead to some bizarre behavior. Because placeholders don't include a purchase price, they don't affect the cash balance in an investment account. But transactions that get linked to placeholders (as described on page 381) don't affect the cash balance either, which is a problem. If cash balances begin to go awry, the only solution is to delete the placeholder. Jot down the info about the original transaction linked to the placeholder (the number of shares, price, date, and so on), so you can re-record it after the placeholder and linked transaction are gone. Then, right-click the placeholder and, on the shortcut menu, choose Delete to get rid of the placeholder *and* any transactions linked to it. Now, you can re-record the transaction.

Resolving Duplicate Transactions

If you've only recently started downloading transactions or you recorded an investment transaction manually for some reason, Quicken may not match your recorded transactions with the ones it downloads. Maybe the date is slightly off or you used a different security name than your financial institution did. The simple solution is to delete one of the duplicates. To make sure your future purchases are listed under the same security name—the one your financial institution uses—delete the transaction you entered manually. (In the investment account's register, select the transaction you want to delete and then click the Delete button that appears to the right of the transaction's row.)

Another cause of duplicates is downloading transactions to your 401(k) account before you record the paycheck that deposits money in that 401(k). When you record your paycheck in Quicken (page 201), another deposit appears in the 401(k) account. The downloaded transactions include the deposit of money from your paycheck in the real world. The easiest fix is to enter your paycheck in Quicken *before* downloading 401(k) transactions. (If you already have duplicates, simply delete the downloaded transactions.)

Downloading Price Quotes

To track how your investments and net worth are doing, you have to keep your security prices up to date. Quicken can download current price quotes, so updated prices (and your recalculated net worth) are only a click away. If you want to see how your investments have done over time, you can also download price histories that go back up to 5 years.

Quicken has three ways to get price info:

- **Current price quotes.** If you're making big portfolio decisions and want up-to-date quotes, you can tell Quicken to grab price quotes immediately. Click the Investing tab and then click the Today's Data button. Right below Today's Data, click the Download Quotes button, shown in Figure 12-23. Quicken goes online right away and downloads quotes for every security on your watch list (page 394).

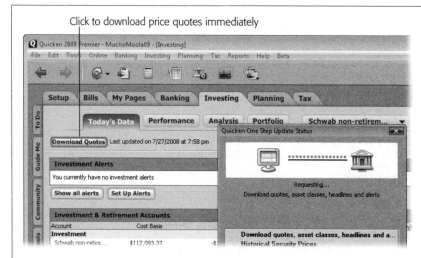

Click to download price quotes immediately

Figure 12-23:
If you click the Portfolio button to review your entire portfolio, choose Download Quotes in the Portfolio screen's menu bar.

- **Automatic price quote downloads.** The easiest way to keep price quotes up to date is to have Quicken take care of getting updated info. Choose Online → One Step Update. In the One Step Update dialog box, turn on the "Download quotes, asset classes, headlines, and alerts" checkbox. Then, Quicken downloads price quotes each time you go online. (If you don't set up One Step Update to download price quotes when you go online, Quicken downloads price quotes only when you tell it to, as explained in the previous step.)

- **Price histories.** If you want to know the investment return you've earned over the past 1, 3, and 5 years (page 400), price histories are a must. Quicken uses that information to calculate investment returns based on the changes in your investments' values over time. To get a price history for your securities, choose Investing → Online Activities → Download Historical Prices. Or click the Investing tab and then click the Portfolio button. Then in the Portfolio screen's menu bar, choose Download Historical Prices. In the Get Historical Prices dialog box, shown in Figure 12-24, choose the period you want (up to 5 years) and then click Update Now to go online and get the info you need.

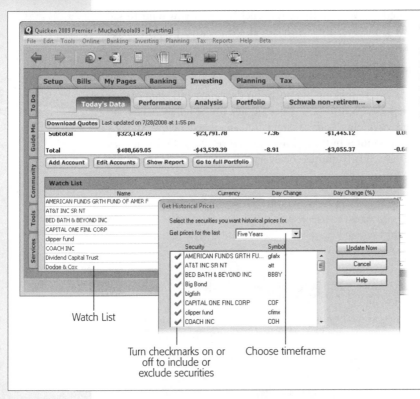

Figure 12-24:
The Get Historical Prices dialog box's list shows all the securities on your watch list. Turn checkmarks on or off to tell Quicken which price histories you want.

Watch List

Turn checkmarks on or off to include or exclude securities

Choose timeframe

Adjusting an Investment Account Balance

It's easy to bring your Quicken investment account balances into line with your brokerage and 401(k) statements. But why, you might wonder, would there be a difference? Two reasons:

- **You don't record investment transactions.** Perhaps you choose to forego recording investment transactions because you don't care about performance and you use your broker's paperwork to do your taxes. Or you've purchased an investment that doesn't lend itself to recording transactions (like a fund that isn't traded on an exchange, for example), so you want to update the value of the account when you receive your statement. See the box on page 390 to learn more about tracking these uncooperative investments.

- **The account balance is incorrect.** With reinvested dividends and purchases of fractional shares, your share balance may be off by a few hundredths of a share because you missed a reinvested dividend a few months back. Or the cash balance may be incorrect because you didn't record a cash dividend. If you want to update your Quicken investment account to match the 401(k) numbers from your employer, say, you can adjust *both* the cash and share balances.

If the discrepancy is more than a dollar, you're better off investigating to find the problem. To make sure your records are accurate and catch any errors your financial institution makes, look for a discrepancy between your records and your financial institution's. If you spot a mistake, and it turns out to be on your end, simply fix your error. If you spot a mistake your financial institution made, alert them immediately. If you just can't find the source of the problem, an updated cash balance is the answer.

Updating an Account's Cash Balance

If your account balance is off because you never bothered to add shares to the account, say, you can simply synch up the cash value in Quicken with your statement's ending balance. To update the cash balance in an investment account, follow these steps:

1. **Choose Investing → Investing Activities → Update Cash Balance.**

   The Update Cash Balance dialog box appears.

2. **In the "Enter the correct balance for this account" box, enter the cash balance from your statement.**

3. **Change the date text box—which may have a different label depending on the account you're in, such as "Adjust the balance as of this date" or "Adjust balance as of"—to the closing date on your account statement.**

   If your investment account has a linked checking or money market account, the cash balance is in that linked account, not the investment account. As an alternative to using the Update Cash Balance command, you can reconcile the linked cash account as you would your regular checking account. That way, you can make sure that Quicken and your institution's records agree.

4. **Click OK.**

   Quicken adds a miscellaneous income transaction to the register, as shown in Figure 12-25.

Updating an Account's Share Balance

The command for updating the share balance works much like the Update Cash Balance command (explained in the previous section). You can find it in two places. Either choose Investing → Investing Activities → Update Share Balance or, in the investment register, click "Enter transactions". In the dialog box that opens, in the "Enter transaction" drop-down menu, select "Adjust share balance". Then, follow these steps:

1. **In the Adjust Share Balance dialog box, in the "Security name" drop-down menu, choose the security you need to update.**

   If you're updating the account to match a paper statement, change the "Transaction date" box to the ending date on the statement.

Figure 12-25:
After you update an account's cash balance, the Cash Balance below the register equals the balance on your statement. Quicken automatically marks the miscellaneous income transaction as reconciled (the R in the first column), because your financial institution doesn't know anything about it and won't download a corresponding transaction.

Reconciled miscellaneous income transaction

Tracking Black Box Investments

Suppose you invest with money managers who trade securities more than you care to know. All you care about is how much your account is worth, and the performance the money managers deliver in exchange for their extravagant fees. Because you don't have transactions or price quotes to download, you have to trick Quicken into calculating performance for this kind of investment. Here's how:

1. Create an investment account for this investment.

2. Create a security (page 340) for the investment. You don't have to add a ticker symbol. When Quicken tells you it can't find data for the security, select the "Add manually" option. Choose a security type (page 351) and an asset class if you want to classify the investment.

3. Record a purchase transaction that buys a number of shares equal to the dollars you invested. (In the "Price paid" box, type *1*, which tells Quicken you bought those shares for $1 each. If you invested $10,000, type *10,000* in the "Number of shares" box.)

4. When you receive your statement, choose Investing → Security Details View. Choose the security from the drop-down list.

5. In the Security Detail View window's menu bar, choose Update → Edit Price History.

6. In the Price History dialog box, click New.

7. In the New Price For dialog box, put the ending date on your statement in the date box.

8. Fill in the Price box with the value that makes the account balance equal the statement balance. (Calculate the price by dividing the balance from your statement by the number of $1 "shares" you originally entered. For example, if you own 10,000 "shares" that are now worth $25,500, your new share price is $2.55.)

The Security Details View shows the percentage gain, as if this were a regular stock or mutual fund. Performance reports also show the annual returns.

2. **In the "Number of shares" text box, type the number of shares from your statement. Click Enter/Done.**

Quicken adds a placeholder entry to the register that makes the account show the right number of shares. (See page 383 if you decide to fill in actual transactions.)

Tracking 401(k) Holdings

When you're working on your 401(k) or 403(b) account in Quicken, above the account's register you see the Update 401(k) Holdings button. If you don't download transactions, click that button to bring Quicken in line with the statement you receive from your employer-sponsored retirement account. The first screen in the Update 401(k)/403(b) Account dialog box that appears shows the statement end date and asks whether your statement shows the shares you own and whether you took out a loan against the account. Change the "This statement ends" date to match your statement ending date. If you select the Yes option for the number of shares, the dialog box provides boxes for entering the amount you contributed and the number of shares purchased. The Update 401(k)/403(b) Account dialog box has text boxes for all of the events that may have occurred during the last period, as you can see in Figure 12-26.

If you decide to borrow against your 401(k), in the Account Bar, click the 401(k) account. Click the Overview tab. In the Account Attributes section, click Options and then choose "Create new loan" from the drop-down menu. Quicken creates a loan account and links it to your retirement account.

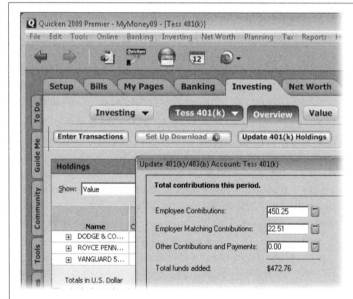

Figure 12-26:
Use the numbers from your 401(k) statement to fill in the Update 401(k)/403(b) Account dialog box. If your financial institution plays well with Quicken, it's a lot easier to just download the transactions (page 377).

Note: If you choose Investing → Investing Activities, you may notice that the menu lists a Track 401(k) option. This command doesn't have any magic powers. When you choose Investing → Investing Activities → Track 401(k), the Track My 401(k) dialog box opens displaying three choices. The "View an existing 401(k) account" option displays the account you ask it to (just like clicking the account in the Account Bar). The "Update an existing 401(k) account" option opens the Update 401(k)/403(b) Account dialog box as if you clicked Update 401(k) Holdings. And the "Set up a new account" option opens the 401(k)/403(b) Setup wizard as if you selected a 401(k)/403(b) account in the Account Setup wizard (page 57).

Evaluating Your Portfolio

Between investment reports and views, Quicken offers all kinds of ways to evaluate your portfolio. No more wondering whether your investments are paying off—you can easily see for yourself. This section tells you how to use Quicken's investment views, reports, and tools to track your portfolio.

Note: Quicken is great for tracking investments, but don't expect it to help you make decisions about the *merits* of the investments you own and what to buy or sell. The box on page 406 has info about another option for managing your portfolio that helps you do just that.

The Investing tab is home to a host of investment features and tracking tools. To get to it, simply click the Investing tab. Or, in the Account Bar, click the Investing heading.

Looking at Investment Values

Sometimes, all you want to know is how much money you have in your investment accounts. Perhaps you're anxious to cross the threshold of millionaire-hood, or perhaps waiting to reach the amount you plan to retire on. Here are the places you can find account and security values in Quicken:

- The **Investing section of the Account Bar** keeps investment account values in view. Quicken lists your non-retirement accounts ("investment accounts" in Quicken lingo) first, followed by your retirement accounts. The number in bold text below the last retirement account is the total value of your entire portfolio. The Account Bar doesn't show separate subtotals for your investment and retirement accounts.

- The **Investing tab's Today's Data screen** shows investment and retirement account totals separately. Click the Investing tab, and then click the Today's Data button. If you have any investment alerts (page 393), they appear at the top of the Today's Data screen. The Investment & Retirement Accounts section shows individual account values, the total value of all your investment accounts, and the total value of your retirement accounts. You can also see your cost basis and your gains or losses.

Note: If your cost basis is dismally close to the market value, the meager increase in value may not mean dogs are barking in your portfolio. When you reinvest dividends and capital gains to buy more shares, those transactions increase your cost basis, which is great for reducing the capital gains taxes you pay when you start withdrawing form an IRA. Your true performance is how much your portfolio has grown from the amount you originally contributed. See page 399 to learn how to find out how your portfolio is really doing.

GEM IN THE ROUGH

Investing Alerts

Most of the time, your portfolio can cruise along without your constant attention, but every so often, you may want to watch for a security whose price has dropped into your buy zone, soared past your "Sell! Sell! Sell!" point, or whose company has been acquired by Google. Instead of hovering hawk-like over your computer watching your investments, you can set up investment alerts that tell you when an event you're interested in happens.

Quicken has an investment alerts feature, but it may not notify you as quickly as you'd like. Even if you set up Quicken alerts using the "Urgent (pop up dialog box)" option (page 63) and an alert gets triggered, you see a pop-up message box the *next* time you launch Quicken—which might be too late for it to be helpful.

If you want to know about price changes right away, you can have Yahoo Finance send you emails when security prices rise or fall beyond the dollar values you specify, or prices change by percentages you set. On the Yahoo Finance home page (*http://finance.yahoo.com*), click the My Portfolios tab. After you add securities to a portfolio, in the menu bar above the portfolio, click Set Alert to create alerts for one or more securities in your portfolio. If you're always on the go, you can even tell Yahoo to send alerts to your mobile phone, as shown in Figure 12-27, so you won't miss a thing.

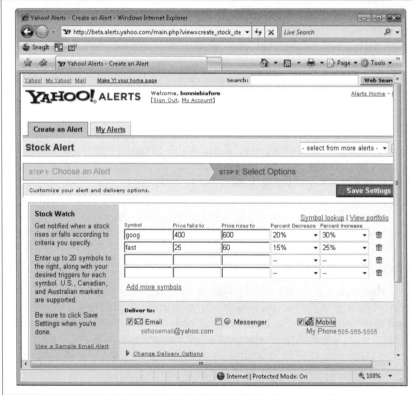

Figure 12-27:
You can set up Yahoo Finance alerts to email you, send instant messages to your Yahoo's Messenger account, or send text messages to your mobile phone. Turn on all three checkboxes to increase the chances that one of the methods gets through.

- The **Watch List** appears at the bottom of the Investing tab's Today's Data screen and shows each security you've added to the list (page 342 tells you how to add securities to your watch list) with the most recent price quote and the day's change both in dollars and as a percentage. You have to *look* at the watch list for it to be useful—something that's easy to forget to do. If you're the forgetful type, the box on page 393 tells you how to get alerted about investing tasks you may want to perform.

- The **Portfolio Value report** (choose Reports → Investing → Portfolio Value) initially shows the value of each investment you own. But you can customize it to group investments by account, so you see the market value of each security and the total market value for each account.

- The **Investing tab's Portfolio screen** can also show current values and a lot more. Click the Investing tab and then click the Portfolio button. The next section describes all the handy features the Portfolio screen offers.

Reviewing Your Portfolio

If you want to inspect your portfolio from every angle, the Investing tab's Portfolio screen is the place to be. (Click the Investing tab, and then click the Portfolio button.) Initially, the Portfolio page groups investments by account, as shown in Figure 12-28. You can group investments by other criteria, like investing goal, say, to review the investments you've earmarked for college education. Or if you're on a mission to find investments that aren't pulling their weight, you can tell Quicken to display info about your securities' average annual returns or the tax implications of selling each investment. This section tells you how to make these changes and more.

Changing your point of view

The Portfolio page comes with several views, which contain predefined columns of investment info. To change the columns you see, in the Show drop-down menu, choose a view like Historic Performance (shown in Figure 12-28).

Note: You don't have to use the Portfolio page views that Quicken provides—you can create up to nine custom views with exactly the fields you want to see. Page 502 tells you how to create your own view.

Here are the built-in Portfolio page views:

- The **Value** view is good for getting a warm and fuzzy—or possibly cold and terrifying—feeling. It shows you how much your investments are worth and how much their values have changed. You can review price quotes and the number of shares you own, and the market value and cost basis of each investment. This view displays your gain or loss since your original purchases, and the daily gain or loss, if you care about that sort of thing.

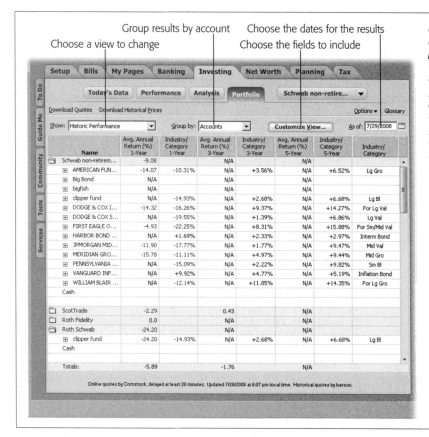

Choose a view to change
Group results by account
Choose the dates for the results
Choose the fields to include

Figure 12-28:
By changing the Portfolio page's groupings or the view it displays, you can use the page to review your account balances, investment performance, or the number of shares you owned on a specific date. Your wish is the Portfolio page's command.

Name	Avg. Annual Return (%) 1-Year	Industry/ Category 1-Year	Avg. Annual Return (%) 3-Year	Industry/ Category 3-Year	Avg. Annual Return (%) 5-Year	Industry/ Category 5-Year	Industry/ Category
Schwab non-retirem...	-9.08		N/A		N/A		
AMERICAN FUN...	-14.07	-10.31%	N/A	+3.56%	N/A	+6.52%	Lg Gro
Big Bond	N/A		N/A		N/A		
bigfish	N/A		N/A		N/A		
clipper fund	N/A	-14.93%	N/A	+2.68%	N/A	+6.68%	Lg Bl
DODGE & COX I...	-14.32	-16.26%	N/A	+9.37%	N/A	+14.27%	For Lg Val
DODGE & COX S...	N/A	-19.55%	N/A	+1.39%	N/A	+6.86%	Lg Val
FIRST EAGLE O...	-4.93	-22.25%	N/A	+8.31%	N/A	+15.88%	For Sm/Mid Val
HARBOR BOND ...	N/A	+1.69%	N/A	+2.33%	N/A	+2.97%	Interm Bond
JPMORGAN MID...	-11.90	-17.77%	N/A	+1.77%	N/A	+9.47%	Mid Val
MERIDIAN GRO...	-15.78	-11.11%	N/A	+4.97%	N/A	+9.44%	Mid Gro
PENNSYLVANIA ...	N/A	-15.09%	N/A	+2.22%	N/A	+9.82%	Sm Bl
VANGUARD INF...	N/A	+9.92%	N/A	+4.77%	N/A	+5.19%	Inflation Bond
WILLIAM BLAIR ...	N/A	-12.14%	N/A	+11.85%	N/A	+14.35%	For Lg Gro
Cash							
ScotTrade	-2.29		0.43		N/A		
Roth Fidelity	0.0		N/A		N/A		
Roth Schwab	-24.20		N/A		N/A		
clipper fund	-24.20	-14.93%	N/A	+2.68%	N/A	+6.68%	Lg Bl
Cash							
Totals:	-5.89		-1.76		N/A		

Online quotes by Comstock, delayed at least 20 minutes. Updated 7/28/2008 at 6:07 pm local time. Historical quotes by Iverson.

- The **Recent Performance** view isn't that helpful if you're a buy-and-hold investor. It shows your gain or loss over 1 month, 3 months, 12 months, and since you purchased your investments.

- **Historic Performance** is a good view for measuring how your investments are doing. It shows the average annual return for 1 year, 3 years, and 5 years. It also shows the average annual returns for each investment's industry or category, so you can see if your investment is keeping up with its peers. (To learn what average annual return represents, see page 400.)

- The **Fundamentals** view shows fields like dividend yield, P/E ratio (the price to earnings ratio, one measure of whether a stock is selling for a reasonable amount), and ROE (return on equity). If you use information like this to analyze investments, you can export it from Quicken to a spreadsheet for further study: Choose File → Print Portfolio. In the Print dialog box that appears, select the "Export to" option and then choose "tab-delimited (Excel compatible) disk file" from the drop-down list.

- The **Quotes** view simply shows quote info for each security—current price, opening price, closing price, and 52-week high and low, for example.

- The **Mutual Funds** view displays the type of fund (Large Growth, Mid Value, and so on) and Morningstar ratings. Then it lists the average annual returns, which show your mutual fund's performance based on when you purchased your shares. The performance results you see online won't match your results because they're based on owning a fund for whatever period the online results represent—1 year, 3 years, or 5 years, for example (as explained on page 400).

- The **Asset Allocation** view groups your investments by Quicken's asset classes (page 347), which are broad categories of investments. If an investment spans several classes, Quicken plops it in a group called Asset Mixture. A better approach for evaluating your investments is to use the "Group by" drop-down menu (explained below) to group your investments by security types or investing goals, both of which you get to define.

- The **Tax Implications** view is handy if you're trying to decide whether to sell an investment. It shows the net gain you'd receive after you pay taxes, the break-even price (the price that produces no gain or loss), the date when your gains switch from short-term to long-term (which are taxed at lower rates), and the number of days you'd have to wait to earn those long-term gains. When you first display this view, the tax implication columns are blank. To see values, click the + sign to the left of a security's name. Quicken then shows the tax implications of each lot you've purchased.

- If your company compensates you with stock options, the **Employee Stock Options** view shows you the market value of your options, and the number of shares granted, vested, and not yet vested.

To create a view that shows exactly what you want, click Customize View. In the Customize Current View dialog box, you can add, remove, and rearrange any of the columns as well as specify the accounts to include and the securities you want to see, as shown in Figure 12-29.

Group investments

You can also change how the Portfolio page groups your investments. In the "Group by" drop-down menu, choose from Accounts, Industry, Security, Security Type, Investing Goal, Asset Class, and Sector. If you group securities by account, for example, you can view the returns for individual investments as well as the overall returns for an account. If you want to see how much money you have in each security type, group by security type instead. Or group by investing goal to see whether the investments earmarked for a specific goal are delivering the results you want.

Change the date

In the "As of" date box, choose a date to see what your portfolio looked like on that day. Viewing your portfolio as of different dates is just the ticket when you want to find out when your Quicken records started to disagree with your statements. Type a statement date, and then compare the share values in Quicken to the

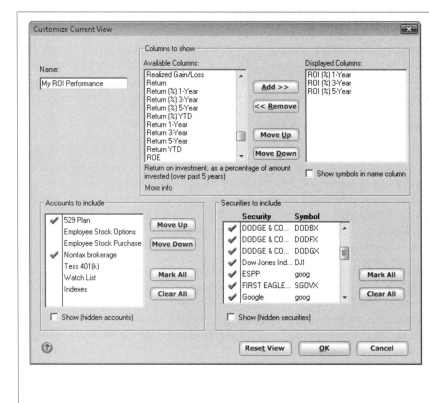

Figure 12-29:
In the Name box, type a name to identify the view you're creating like ROI for a return on investment view or Industry Comparisons for a view that shows your investments' performance compared to the corresponding industry. Select fields in the Available Columns list and click Add to include them in your view. Select fields in the Displayed Columns list and click Remove to get rid of them. Select a field and then click Move Up or Move Down to rearrange the order. In the "Accounts to include" and "Securities to include" lists, turn checkboxes on or off to include or exclude accounts and securities, for example, to include only the accounts you earmark for college savings.

statement. If they don't agree, type the date for the previous statement, and repeat the process until you find the discrepancy. (You start with recent statements and work backwards because you don't know when the discrepancy first appeared.)

Looking Over an Account

In addition to the Portfolio screen, which is perfect for reviewing your entire portfolio, you can review a single account in several ways. When you click an investment account in the Account Bar, Quicken displays that account on the Investing tab (the screen that appears is whatever one you last looked at for that account). Click the Transactions button to display the investment account's register, where you can enter transactions manually or download them. To review an investment account, click either of the following buttons:

• Click the **Overview** button when you want to edit the account's details (page 347). This screen shows the investments in the account, but the Portfolio screen (page 394) does that and more. The Investing Activity section at the bottom of the Overview screen shows deposits, withdrawals, interest, dividends, and any capital gains you've realized from selling investments.

• The **Value** button combines two types of graphs: a bar graph comparing the account's value to its cost basis over time, and pie charts of your asset allocation and allocation by security. Cost basis includes reinvested dividends and gains (page 362), so this graph doesn't show how your account is really doing. Typically, asset allocation and allocation by security is more useful when you apply it to an entire portfolio, which you'll learn how to do on page 403.

Reviewing Investing Activities

Investing activity falls into several categories: deposits, withdrawals, interest earned, dividends paid, capital gains realized, and unrealized gains or losses. Capital gains are also subdivided into short-term and long-term gains because they're each taxed at different rates. If you're saving aggressively for retirement, you can review investing activities to see how much you're socking away each quarter. If you're already retired, you can see whether your interest and dividends are enough to cover your expenses.

To review your investing activities, choose Reports → Investing → Investing Activity. Quicken initially sets the report's date range to "Year to date" and displays activities for all your investment accounts securities. To choose specific accounts you want to see in the report, in the report window's toolbar, click Customize. Then click the Accounts tab and turn off the checkboxes for the accounts you want to exclude.

Tip: You can review investing activity in one account without generating a report: Click the account in the Account Bar, and then click the Overview button and scroll to the Investing Activity section.

Reviewing Investment Transactions

Sometimes you want to review individual investment transactions, for example, to track down discrepancies between your Quicken records and your broker's. Quicken gives you several places to review your transactions. Here are your options and when to choose each one:

• The **account register** (click an investing account in the Account Bar and then click the Transactions button) lists all the transactions you've recorded or downloaded. If you're adding new transactions or want to edit a transaction to record the actual purchase or sale price, the register is your best bet.

• The **Security Detail View** window has a Transaction History section, which shows every transaction in every account for the selected security. If you suspect that you recorded a reinvested dividend in the wrong account, you can look through your all transactions for that security to see if the reinvestment is listed in the correct account. Choose Investing → Security Detail View and then select the security in the drop-down list.

- If you want to customize the transactions you see, to show only reinvested dividends, say, the **Investment Transactions report** is ideal. Choose Reports → Investing → Investment Transactions. The report initially shows every investment transaction you've made. In the report window's toolbar, click Customize and then modify the report settings (page 352) to show exactly what you want.

Reviewing Performance

Earning 4 percent a year on a savings account is darn good, but you expect more from your investments. A good way to review investment performance is by examining annual return, which you hope looks like a savings account on steroids. Quicken takes care of the performance calculations behind the scenes, as long as you hold up your end of the deal.

Here are the two things you have to do so that Quicken can calculate investment performance accurately:

- **Enter complete historical info.** Quicken's performance calculations are only as good as the data you've recorded. So if you've recorded or downloaded only part of your historical investment info, the performance Quicken calculates (in places like the Investment Performance report) isn't accurate—and the program lets you know by placing asterisks next to performance numbers that are based on placeholder entries, as shown in Figure 12-30.

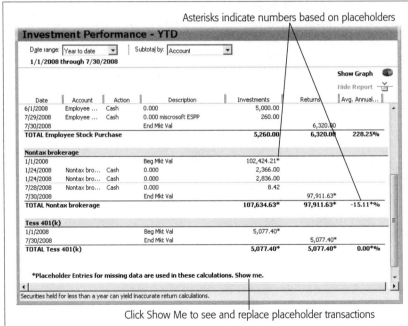

Figure 12-30:
Asterisks to the right of Cost Basis numbers indicate investments that have placeholder entries. When you expand a security (click the + to the right of the security's name), click the Placeholder entry in blue text to open the Enter Missing Transactions dialog box (page 384). At the bottom of the Investment Performance report, you'll see the text, "Placeholder Entries for missing data are used in these calculations. Show me." Click the "Show me" link to open the Resolve Placeholder Entries window.

• **Review performance over the correct time frame.** To get accurate performance values, you have to own a security for the entire reporting period (1 year, 3 years, or 5 years in Quicken). The Average Annual Return that you see on the Investing tab's Performance screen or in the Investment Performance report is your *real* rate of return (also called *internal rate of return* or *IRR*). Average Annual Return takes into account how much money you've invested (including dividends, interest, and capital gains you've reinvested) and when you invested it. It's the equivalent of the bank interest rate (compounded annually) that you'd need to earn to reach the dollar amount you have in a security or portfolio. The box below explains what can throw Quicken's performance numbers off. And the box on page 402 explains why Quicken's graph that compares your investments to financial indexes isn't all that helpful.

WORKAROUND WORKSHOP

When Performance Numbers Don't Perform

Because Average Annual Return takes the timing of purchases and sales into account, your return for an investment can be very different from the one reported in the news. Say you bought 100 shares of stock for $20 at the beginning of the year, and then you bought another 100 shares for $10 on June 1. At the end of the year, the stock made it to $30. The stock's annual return is 50 percent (it started at $20 and increased to $30, a 50 percent increase). However, *your* return is 200 percent, because you bought your shares at an average cost of $15, so the value doubled.

If you don't own a security for the entire reporting period, average annual returns can go haywire. Say you bought a stock on January 1 for $10. By July 30, it reached $12 (that's a straight 20 percent increase). However, using those same numbers, on July 30, the Investment Performance report for the year to date would report the average annual return at a bit less than 40 percent (37.08 percent, to be exact). What's up with that? Quicken assumes that the investment is going to keep up that pace of increase until the end of the year, which would mean increasing almost another 20 percent.

(That's why the straight 20 percent increase transforms into 37.08 percent.) This behavior can make Quicken turn small price changes into gigantic average annual returns, particularly when you run the Investment Performance report using the "Year to date" date range early in the year.

Performance results can be quirky for individual securities, especially if you sell them early in the year. Say that, in January, you sell one fund in your 401(k) with a small increase. Then you purchase a different fund, which decreases slightly over the entire year. Individually, the average annual return on the first fund is very high because of the way Quicken extrapolates performance over an entire year, as described in the previous paragraph. The average annual return on the second fund shows a small loss, because you owned the fund during most of the year and Quicken's performance mirrors the fund's true performance. By reporting the performance for your entire 401(k), you can eliminate Quicken's performance quirks and see the true performance of your 401(k).

The most reliable performance numbers come from reports that span one or more full years. Quicken's Investment Performance report is the best way to view performance, because you can customize the report so that it shows you meaningful numbers.

Here's what you do:

1. **Choose Reports → Investing → Investment Performance.**

   The Investment Performance report window opens with the date range set to "Year to date".

2. In the "Date range" drop-down list, choose Yearly, which sets the report to a full year.

A second box appears to the right of the "Date range" box and is automatically set to "Current year", which is what you want so that you can see this year's performance. This setting calculates what the average annual return would be if your investments ended the year at the price they are now, so it shows the percentage you've gained or lost so far this year, as shown in Figure 12-31.

3. To show the average annual return for your entire account or portfolio, in the "Subtotal by" drop-down list, choose "Don't subtotal".

The report shows a single average annual return for the entire portfolio. (If you want the average annual return for an account, you can subtotal by account.)

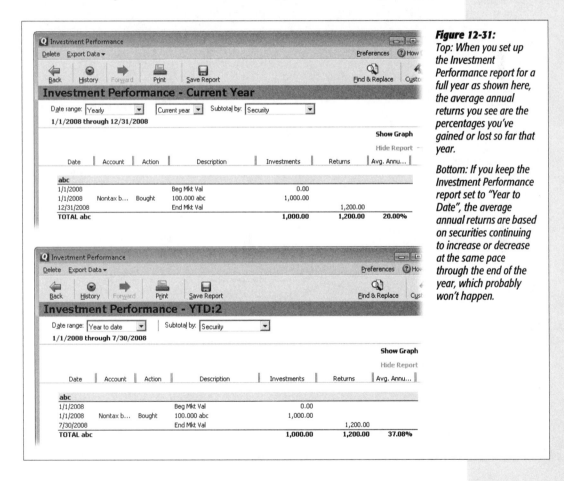

Figure 12-31:
Top: When you set up the Investment Performance report for a full year as shown here, the average annual returns you see are the percentages you've gained or lost so far that year.

Bottom: If you keep the Investment Performance report set to "Year to Date", the average annual returns are based on securities continuing to increase or decrease at the same pace through the end of the year, which probably won't happen.

GEM IN THE ROUGH

Comparing Apples and Oranges

If you click Performance on the Investing tab, you'll see a graph of your accounts' growth compared to the most popular indexes like the S&P 500 and Russell 2000, as shown in Figure 12-32. It's satisfying to see your accounts grow more than well-known indexes, but it's not the end of the world if they don't. For instance, your investment strategy may reduce the volatility of your portfolio in return for slightly lower growth. Besides, the comparison isn't accurate anyway, especially if you sank significant amounts of new money into investments during those 12 months, because the graph assumes that you owned everything since the beginning of the period.

Options above the graph let you choose which accounts and securities you want to see. If you select the Investment option, Quicken shows all your investment accounts. The Retirement option limits the accounts to those in the Retirement group (page 333). If you want to pick and choose accounts, select the Multiple Accounts option and then, in the drop-down menu, choose "Multiple Accounts". In the Customize dialog box, turn on the checkboxes for the accounts you want to include. If you want the graph to show the results for specific investments, click Choose Securities and then pick the ones you want to see.

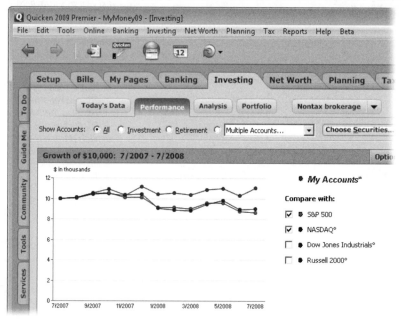

Figure 12-32:
Below the growth graph, you see your investment accounts. Quicken uses your historical transactions (not including placeholders) to calculate your average annual returns for the past 1-, 3-, and 5-year periods.

Reviewing Tax Information

The Investing report category (choose Reports → Investing) includes the Capital Gains report, which shows capitals gains you've realized from selling investments. If you're retired and living off your portfolio income, the Investment Income report shows the dividends, interest, *and* capital gains you've earned. The best way to get the information you need for your taxes, however, is to run one of Quicken's tax reports. For example, to gather *all* the numbers you need for your entire tax return—including your investment interest, dividends, and capital gains—run either the Tax Schedule report, which subtotals your tax info for each line item on each tax form and schedule, or the Tax Summary report (page 274), which subtotals tax info by the Quicken categories you use.

If your accountant or tax preparer asks you for your investment account balances, the Account Balances report is ideal. Choose Reports → Net Worth & Balances → Account Balances and Quicken generates a report that lists the balances for each account in Quicken.

If you run the Account Balances report after the first of the year, in the "Date range" drop-down list, choose "Last year" to show your account balances as of December 31 of the previous year. If you want to show only your investment accounts, in the report window's toolbar, click Customize. In the Customize dialog box that appears, click the Accounts tab. In the Select Account Group list, click Banking and then click Clear All. Finally, click Net Worth and then click Clear All. The report now lists only your investment accounts.

Estimating capital gains

If you use Quicken Premier, the Buy/Sell Preview feature is an easy way to see how much you'd pay in taxes if you sold an investment you own. You tell Quicken the security you want to sell, the number of shares, the date, and the price. Then Buy/Sell Preview calculates your gross proceeds from the sale and the federal tax you'd pay. (The sale date you choose determines whether it's a short-term or long-term gain.)

If you use Quicken's Tax planner, you can use the Capital Gains Estimator wizard (choose Investing → Capital Gains Estimator) to see how a sale would affect your taxes. Quicken lets you create up to three scenarios to play capital gains what-if games. This tool can also help you identify securities you can sell to offset your gains with losses. If you don't have cash to cover a big tax bill, you can use the Capital Gains Estimator to calculate the number of shares you need to sell to get the cash you need for taxes.

Reviewing Asset Allocation

One way to invest without losing sleep is to allocate your investments to stocks, bonds, real estate, and cash. By diversifying, you won't have to watch gut-wrenching ups and downs in your overall portfolio. Many financial professionals recommend a rough rule of thumb for asset allocation: the percentage of stocks in your portfolio should be your age subtracted from 100 (that's 45 percent for a 55-year-old, for example). But take this rule with a grain of salt because your marital status, health, risk tolerance, and other factors affect the proportions that make sense for you.

Quicken's asset allocation reports and graphs use the programs built-in asset classes (page 347) to show how your investments are distributed among those classes. (The box on page 350 explains the benefits of asset allocation.) If these asset classes cover your investments, choose Reports → Investing → Asset Allocation to see a pie chart and text report of your investments in each asset class that Quicken tracks.

If you use a different definition of asset classes, you can set those up with security types (page 350). To see your asset allocation by security type, choose Reports → Investing → Portfolio Value. In the "Subtotal by" drop-down list, choose Security Type. The pie chart at the top and the subtotaled tabular report below it both show the percentages of each security type in your portfolio. The pie chart legend shows the percentages of each asset class.

To evaluate your portfolio's asset allocation and lots more, you may want to try Morningstar.com's free Instant X-ray feature. This online portfolio tool slices and dices your portfolio more ways than a Ginzu knife. After you type in ticker symbols and the dollar amounts you have invested in each security, Instant X-ray shows your portfolio's asset allocation, its distribution over the Morningstar style boxes, and allocation by stock sectors and stock types, as shown in Figure 12-33. It also shows the fees and expenses you pay, the overall P/E (price to earnings) ratio of your entire portfolio, and your overall yield. To view an Instant X-ray of your investments, on *www.morningstar.com*, click the Portfolio tab. In the Portfolio Manager drop-down menu, choose Instant X-ray. If you subscribe to the site's Premium membership, you can save your portfolio and run the Instant X-ray any time you want.

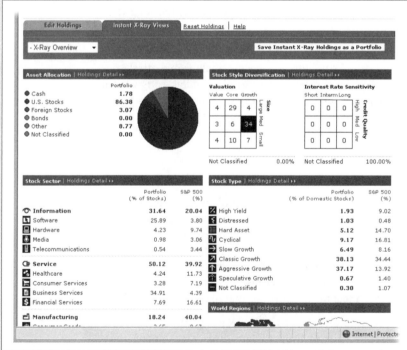

Figure 12-33:
For a free Instant X-ray, you have to enter the ticker symbols and dollar values for your investments each time. It's worth the effort, because the X-ray opens up all your mutual funds and gathers info about all their individual investments to produce its results.

Quicken's advanced portfolio tools

If you use Quicken Premier (page 5), you can see a pie chart of your actual asset allocation compared to a pie chart for your *target* allocation. Choose Investing → Asset Allocation Guide. In the Asset Allocation Guide, read about asset classes and recommended asset allocation percentages. Then, in the navigation bar on the left, click the "set your target allocation" link to tell Quicken the allocation you want to use. Next, click the "How do I monitor my asset allocation?" link to display the actual and target allocation pie charts. The legend in the Asset Allocation Guide window lists the percentage of your actual allocation in each class, the percentage you set in your target, and the difference between the two. If the Difference value is negative (meaning you have less in that class than you want to), then you should consider moving money into that asset class. If the Difference value is a large positive number, then you might want to reduce your investment in that asset class. (Of course, these are just guidelines. Most investors reallocate their portfolios every year or so, no matter what the allocations look like in between.)

If your current asset allocation is significantly different from your target, click Rebalance Portfolio (or choose Investing → Portfolio Rebalancer) to figure out what changes to make. The Portfolio Rebalancer window tells you how many dollars you need to add or subtract from an asset class to reach your target. If you double-click a pie slice in the Actual Asset Allocation pie chart, you can see the individual investments in that asset class. If you want to increase the money in that asset class, these are the securities you might want to buy. If you want to reduce the money in the class, consider selling some of your shares in these securities, especially the ones that take up a big slice of your portfolio. Then, use the proceeds to buy securities in the underfed asset class (or classes).

The Portfolio Analyzer wizard (choose Investing → Portfolio Analyzer) helps you evaluate your portfolio in several ways. It displays results and suggestions in the following categories:

- The **Performance** section shows your average annual returns from the year to date to the last 5-year period. It also shows your five best and five worst performers.

Tip: Just because an investment is one of your worst performers doesn't mean you should sell it. For example, the stock may be in a lull just before it shoots up. Similarly, your best performers could be overpriced, and you might want to sell them to lock in profits.

- The **Holdings** section shows pie charts and tables of your holdings. Use this section to look for securities that make up too much of your portfolio. If that security takes a huge hit, so does your portfolio. Diversifying your investments protects your portfolio from losses in a bad investment or a part of the stock market that's having an off year.

- The **Asset Allocation** view is the same one you see on the Analysis tab for your overall portfolio, as described on page 438.

• The **Risk Profile** section shows asset classes on a bar that ranges from low risk on the left to high risk (risk is measured by how much the return varies from year to year) on the right. Each asset class has its own combination of expected return and risk. Above this bar, you see your portfolio, positioned based on its risk.

• The **Tax Implications** section shows your capital gains and losses for the year, grouped by short-term, mid-term, and long-term.

POWER USERS' CLINIC

Using Portfolio Management Software

If you're a serious investor, Quicken's portfolio features may not satisfy you. For instance, say you want to track the performance of individual investments as well as your overall portfolio. Or perhaps you have more than one portfolio for different financial goals, each with its unique tax requirements. Quicken isn't designed to handle these kind of advanced portfolio-tracking maneuvers.

If you're looking for more powerful portfolio management software, Better Investing's Portfolio Manager or Investment Account Manager 2.0, both developed by Quant IX Software, Inc. (*www.quantixsoftware.com*), may be the answer. These programs are specifically for managing investments. They cost more than Quicken ($169 and $129, respectively), but if they help you make one portfolio improvement or prevent one tax gaffe, they can pay for themselves.

These programs can track an unlimited number of portfolios as well as the combined values of several portfolios. For example, you can set up a retirement portfolio, a nonretirement portfolio, and a college fund portfolio, and track them separately to see their individual performance, but also analyze them as a whole. And the programs handle securities that Quicken doesn't do a good job of tracking, like options. Both programs have great tools for making investment decisions, whether for improved performance or reduced tax consequences. And they provide dozens of portfolio reports that show more of what you want to know about your portfolio than you can coax out of Quicken.

If you already have investment transactions in Quicken, you can export your Quicken data to a .qif file (see Chapter 17), and then import it into Portfolio Manager or Investment Account Manager, which can also import transactions directly from financial institutions.

Planning with Quicken Tools

Whether you tend to scratch out your schedule on a napkin or prepare a minute-by-minute plan for your "spontaneous" vacation, the Quicken Planning menu has tools for you. The program's planning calculators are quick and easy to use. They ask for a few bits of info and then spit out a result like how much you have to save each year for retirement, what you can afford to pay in college costs, or whether it makes sense to refinance your mortgage. In this chapter, you'll learn how to fill in the fields and calculate different results.

But if only a thorough analysis will do, Quicken's planning wizards step you through planning for major goals like retiring, paying for your kid's college education, owning a home, or getting out of debt. These wizards ask for lots of financial details, but most of the steps and the info you give them are pretty straightforward. In fact, the planning wizards all work from the same financial details; once you've told Quicken about your planning assumptions, each wizard uses the same info, so you don't have to enter it over and over.

This chapter gives you an overview of these planning tools and what they can help you do. You'll learn the types of info you have to provide, how to enter and edit your financial details, and how to review the results. Once you know how to use the planning wizards, they can help you achieve the peace of mind that comes with knowing you're on track to reach your financial goals—or at least knowing what you have to change to reach them.

Note: The Planning menu has a few other tools, like ones that help you create savings plans, budgets, cash flow forecasts, and set savings goals. You can learn all about those in Chapter 11.

Telling Quicken About Yourself

If you're going to use Quicken's planning wizards, you can make less work for yourself by telling Quicken your basic assumptions *before* you work with a specific wizard like the Retirement Planner. Choose Planning → Planning Assumptions to open the "Planning assumptions" window, shown in Figure 13-1.

The various assumptions the program can track are listed on the left side of the window. To add assumptions to a section you haven't filled in before, display the section you want by clicking its name in the left-hand Assumptions list. Then click the blue link in that section (the word *here* in Figure 13-1, which is, alas, not in color) to open a dialog box with fields for you to enter the corresponding assumptions. To edit assumptions you've already entered, display the section you want and then click the Edit link at the section's top right. You don't have to fill out *every* section—if a section doesn't apply to you, skip it.

Note: Don't be surprised to see some assumptions filled in even if you haven't entered them yourself. Quicken automatically fills in some assumptions with info you've already given it in other parts of the program. For example, if you've created an investment account, Quicken adds the account and its market value to the Assumptions section dedicated to investments.

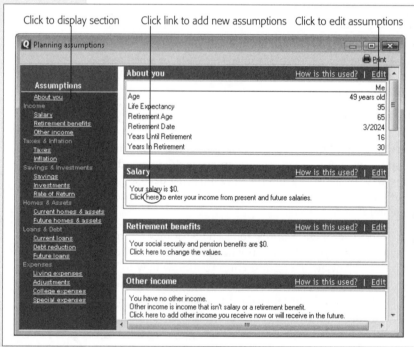

Click to display section   Click link to add new assumptions   Click to edit assumptions

Figure 13-1:
The "Planning assumptions" window shows all the assumptions sections on one long pane on the right, so you can scroll from section to section. To jump to a specific category, in the left navigation bar, click a section name—like "About you", "Salary", or "Current homes & assets"—and Quicken puts that section at the top of the right-hand pane.

The more you tell Quicken about your financial assumptions, the better the results you get from the planning wizards. Here are the different types of assumptions you can to provide:

• **Income** includes your salary, retirement benefits, and other income. Setting up a salary assumption isn't the same as setting up a scheduled paycheck (page 192), as Figure 13-2 shows. Retirement benefits include Social Security and pensions to which you're entitled. Set up any other income you might receive (like an inheritance or child support) in the "Other income" section of the Assumptions list.

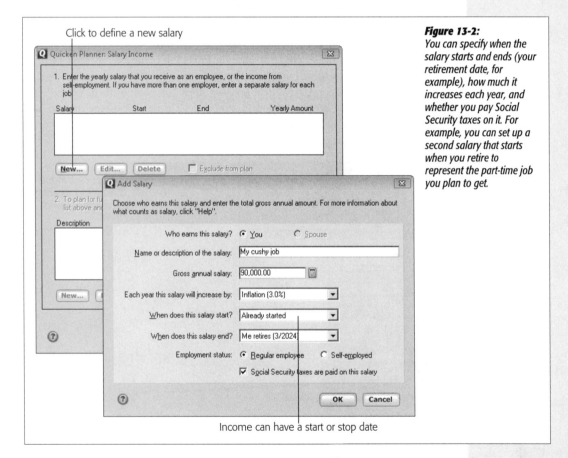

Click to define a new salary

Figure 13-2:
You can specify when the salary starts and ends (your retirement date, for example), how much it increases each year, and whether you pay Social Security taxes on it. For example, you can set up a second salary that starts when you retire to represent the part-time job you plan to get.

Income can have a start or stop date

• The assumptions in the **Taxes** section are the income tax rates you pay. Quicken can estimate the tax rate for you based on the state you live in and your annual income. For a more accurate value, select the "Tax returns" option and then enter your total income, and the federal and state taxes you paid. Quicken fills in the tax rate boxes with the appropriate percentages.

- Quicken automatically sets the **Inflation** rate planning assumption to 3 percent (compared to the 4 percent that the program assumes in its planning calculators, which are discussed later in this chapter). Skip this section unless you want to use a different inflation rate.

- **Savings & Investments** planning assumptions are, not surprisingly, your savings and investment accounts. Quicken already knows the accounts you've created and adds them to your plan. If you want to keep any accounts *out* of the plan, click either the Savings link or the Investment link. Then click the Edit link at the top-right of the section. To exclude an account, select it and then turn on the "Exclude from plan" checkbox. The text for that account turns gray to indicate that it isn't part of your plan.

  If you contribute to a savings or investment account, your 401(k) paycheck deductions, for example, you can include those contributions as part of your plan. To set up a contribution, select the account in the "Account name" list. In the "Contributions to <account>" section, click the New button. In the Add Contribution dialog box that appears, you can set up a percentage of your salary or a contribution that increases with inflation, as Figure 13-3 shows.

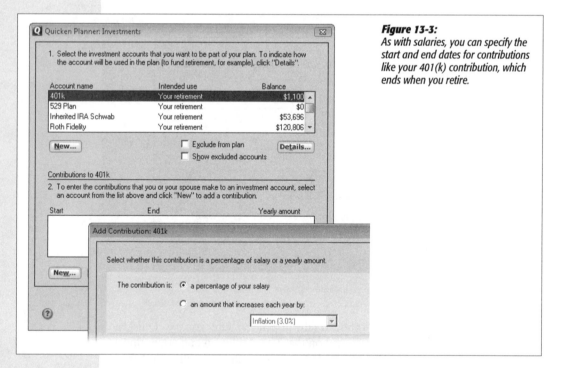

Figure 13-3:
As with salaries, you can specify the start and end dates for contributions like your 401(k) contribution, which ends when you retire.

In the Rate of Return part of the Savings & Investments section, you can specify the returns you expect to earn from your savings and investments. Quicken lets you set up different tax rates for before and after retirement, as well as for taxable and tax-deferred accounts. One shortcoming of Quicken's planning tools is that you can't set up different rates of return for different types of savings and investments. For example, you have to estimate the combined return you earn on your savings accounts and taxable investment accounts.

- The **Homes & Assets** section automatically includes all the house accounts and asset accounts you've created. If you want to exclude a house or asset from the plan (the house you plan to live in during retirement, say), you exclude it the same way you exclude a savings account (page 410). If you have your eye on another home or other assets, you can add them to the plan in the "Future homes & assets" section.

- The **Loans & Debt** section lists the loans you've set up in Quicken. If you plan to take out a loan in the future, you can add it in the "Future loans" section. If you have too much debt, you can set up a debt reduction plan (page 425). Otherwise, you can skip the "Debt reduction" section.

- The **Expenses** section shows your current living expenses and any changes in your expenses over time. You can use your Quicken data to fill in your yearly living expenses, or you can simply type a rough estimate. The Adjustments link lets you define major changes to your expenses, such as a decrease or increase when you retire. You can also set up college expenses or other special expenses with start and end dates.

When you reach the end of the list, you're ready to use the planning wizards, which are explained next. If you're up to your ears in debt, you'll want to work with the Debt Reduction Planner first—flip to page 425 to learn how.

Planning for Retirement

The Retirement Planner comes first on Quicken's Planning menu, and with good reason: Retirement could last 30, 35, even 40 years (yikes!), and you have to build a nest egg large enough to cover your expenses for that entire time. Quicken's Retirement Calculator and Retirement Planner can help you figure out how much to save and when you can afford to retire.

Quick Retirement Calculations

If you want to generate a rough retirement forecast, the Retirement Calculator is a good place to start. By typing in just a few values, you can figure out how much you have to save each year to retire in style. If you're already saving as much as you can, the Calculator can tell you how much annual income you'll end up with when you retire. You can also work backward from your retirement income and annual savings to see how much you need to have saved up by a particular age.

The Retirement Calculator squeezes everything you need into one dialog box, so you can quickly try out different scenarios until you find one you can live with. But the best approach to this calculator isn't starting at the top field and working your way down. This section shows you how to get the best results from the Retirement Calculator:

1. **Open the Retirement Calculator by choosing Planning → Financial Calculators → Retirement Calculator.**

   The Retirement Calculator dialog box opens. On the right side of the dialog box, you'll see that Quicken automatically sets the "Predicted inflation" box to *4.000%* (a conservative long-term average for inflation). If you're optimistic that inflation will remain lower than that, change the percentage in that box.

   The program also turns on the "Annual income in today's $" checkbox, which makes it easy to keep your numbers straight. This setting shows your annual retirement income in today's dollars so that you don't have to think about inflation when you estimate how much you want to live on decades in the future. For example, $50,000 a year today mushrooms into more than $160,000 after 30 years of 4 percent inflation. With this setting turned on, you can fill in the annual income you want based on what you spend today.

2. **If you want to increase your contribution each year to keep up with inflation, turn on the "Inflate contributions" checkbox.**

   Say you contribute $10,000 a year to your 401(k) from the time you're 30 until you retire at 65. After 35 years of 4 percent inflation, your annual contribution adjusted for inflation is worth about $2,500. By turning on the "Inflate contribution" checkbox, Quicken bases its calculations on the assumption that you'll contribute the inflation-adjusted equivalent of $10,000 every year.

Note: The Retirement Calculator doesn't let you increase your contribution by more than the inflation rate, even though most people can afford to save more as their incomes increase over time.

---

3. **In the Calculate For section, select what you want to calculate. In this example, select "Annual contribution".**

   Quicken automatically selects the "Annual retirement income" option, which calculates the annual amount you'll have to live on based on your current savings and your annual retirement contribution.

   If you know the annual income you want, select the "Annual contribution" option. This setting uses your current savings and the annual retirement income figure to calculate how much you have to contribute each year from now on.

   The "Current savings" option isn't that helpful. You tell Quicken how much you want to retire on and how much you plan to contribute each year, and it tells you how much money you need to have now. If you don't have that much, well, you have to select one of the other options to see how to adjust your retirement plan.

4. **Finally, tell Quicken your retirement info. First up, in the "Current savings" box, type your current retirement savings balance.**

Enter the total you've earmarked for retirement whether the money is in taxable or tax-deferred accounts like an IRA or 401(k).

5. **In the "Annual yield" box, type the annual return you expect your retirement savings to earn.**

Quicken automatically fills in *8.000%*, which is the return most financial planners recommend. If you're risk averse and invest in conservative securities like bonds, enter a lower percentage. If you think you can do better (consistently over several decades, mind you), type a higher number.

6. **If you selected the "Annual contribution" option, the "Annual contribution" value is already filled in. If you're calculating annual retirement income, type the annual amount you contribute to retirement funds.**

The "Annual contribution" calculation uses your current savings and the annual retirement income figure. But until you fill in the "Annual income after taxes" box, the "Annual contribution" value is completely off base, as you can see in Figure 13-4.

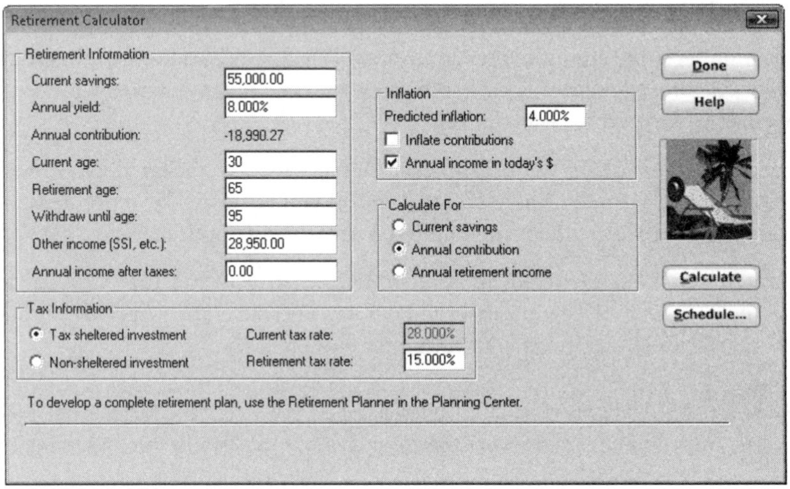

Figure 13-4:
If you're trying to calculate what your annual contribution should be and the "Annual income after taxes" figure is zero, as shown here, Quicken tells you that your annual contribution is a negative number. Obviously, spending money to save for retirement doesn't make any sense. This quirk is your clue that you haven't given the tool the values it needs to calculate the correct result. When you fill in the "Annual income after taxes" box, your contribution becomes a positive number, as you'd expect.

7. **In the "Current age" box, type your age.**

No cheating!

8. **In the "Retirement age" box, type the age you'd like to retire.**

   Quicken fills in 65. If you'd like to retire earlier, type that age instead. If your retirement plan doesn't work, you can come back and type a higher number indicating that you'll work and save for retirement longer.

9. **In the "Withdraw until age" box, type your best guess at your life expectancy.**

   Quicken fills in *85*, but the number you use depends on your health, your relatives, and your gender (on average, women live longer than men). If your older relatives are cycling cross-country in their late 80s, enter a number like *95* or *100*. Think twice before you type a number less than 85: Life expectancies continually increase and you don't want to run out of money prematurely.

10. **In the "Other income (SSI, etc.)" box, type the amount of annual income you expect to receive during retirement.**

    Type in your estimated annual social security, based on the age you plan to retire. (Check the most recent statement you received from the Social Security Administration to get this figure.) If you have a pension, add in the annual pension amount.

11. **If you selected the "Annual retirement income" option, Quicken calculates the "Annual income after taxes" value. If you're calculating the annual contribution you have to make, type your estimated annual retirement living expenses.**

    This number is the amount you plan to spend each year in retirement in today's dollars. Behind the scenes, Quicken figures out how much income you need to cover your living expenses *and* taxes.

12. **In the Tax Information section, Quicken selects the "Tax sheltered investment" option, which is usually what you want. But if you're saving for retirement in a taxable account, select the "Non-sheltered investment" option.**

    If you select "Non-sheltered investment", Quicken activates the "Current tax rate" box. Type your current income tax rate. The calculator uses this number to subtract taxes you pay on your retirement investments.

Tip: To get an idea of the value of tax-sheltered retirement accounts, select the "Non-sheltered investment" option. Your required annual contribution could *double* if you save for retirement in taxable accounts.

---

13. **Ready for results? Click the Calculate button on the right side of the dialog box.**

    Quicken fills in the value you chose to calculate—"Annual contribution" in this example.

14. **If you want to see a schedule of your contributions, your retirement savings balance, and how much you can withdraw each year of retirement, click the Schedule button.**

    Quicken opens a dialog box (Figure 13-5) with a table showing your results.

---

15. **If you don't like the results you get, change some or all of the values you entered, and then click Calculate again.**

For example, you can increase your annual contribution, decrease your annual retirement income, or postpone retirement. When you click Calculate, Quicken recalculates the results.

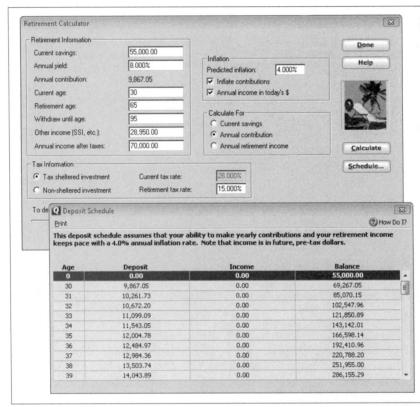

Figure 13-5:
If you turned on the "Inflate contributions" checkbox, each year's contribution increases for inflation, as shown here. The Income column is empty until the age you said you'd retire.

Retirement Planner

When you choose Planning → Retirement Planner, the My Retirement Plan window opens, which helps you figure out if you're on track to have enough money to make it through retirement. As you can see in Figure 13-6, it doesn't leave any stone unturned. Quicken uses information including your age and life expectancy, your estimates of inflation, investment returns, the assets you own, the contributions you make to retirement accounts, and the living expenses you expect during retirement. Even though it takes all these factors into account, the Retirement Planner has some shortcomings, as the box on page 416 explains.

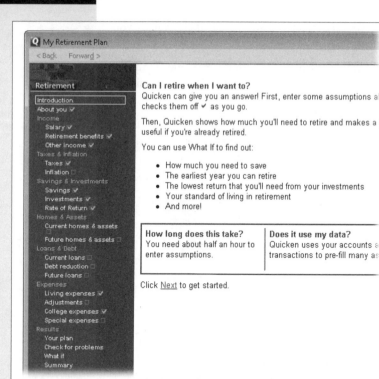

Figure 13-6:
The navigation bar on the left side of this window looks intimidating, but the Retirement Planner uses your Quicken data to fill in a lot of the info it needs. Quicken estimates that it'll take you 30 minutes to enter your assumptions. You can also stop any time you want. Quicken saves what you've entered, so you can come back to the planner later and start where you left off.

GEM IN THE ROUGH

Getting Good Results

The Quicken Retirement Planner isn't perfect. For one thing, you can't export the info you enter or the results that the tool produces. (You can at least print a report showing the results by clicking Print at the top-right of the window.)

The Retirement Planner produces a decent plan as long as you understand the tool's shortcomings and assumptions. For example, you can specify only two investment rates of return: before and after retirement (when your tax rate is probably lower). So, you have to estimate the overall return

for your *entire* retirement portfolio, rather than assigning returns to different types of investments (stocks and bonds, say). It's hard enough to come up with a realistic estimate for *one* kind of investment, let alone for a whole portfolio.

The planner also assumes that retirement begins when you start receiving your Social Security payments. If you plan to retire early and wait until later to receive Social Security, the results won't be accurate.

If you set up your planning assumptions ahead of time (page 408), you'll see orange checkmarks next to every assumption section you completed, as shown in Figure 13-7. If you didn't do your homework, you can enter your assumptions now (see page 409 for info about each section). When you've filled in the current screen, click the Next link on the right side of the window to continue with the next screen of assumptions.

When you're ready to look at your plan, click the "Your plan" link in the navigation bar. As you can see in Figure 13-7, top, the results show whether your plan is working. A green traffic signal at the top of the window means that your plan is working. If you don't get a green light, you can click Change Assumptions to pick different assumption values and see their results. Better yet, click Explore What Ifs to try different scenarios. With this feature, Quicken saves your current assumptions and lets you experiment with different assumptions until you find a set that works. Then, you can save the new assumptions to use from now on. Or you can throw away the scenarios you tried and go back to your original assumptions.

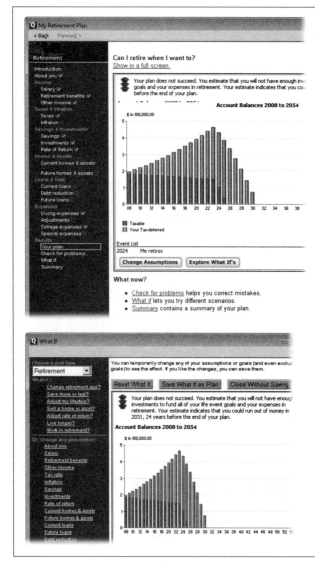

Figure 13-7:
Top: If your plan works, you'll see a green light in the traffic signal at the top of the screen. If it doesn't work, you can click Change Assumptions to try again. Or, you can click Explore What Ifs to experiment with different assumptions.

Bottom: In the What If window, you can change your assumptions, such as retirement age, life expectancy, or how long you work. If the changes you make do the trick, you can save the new scenario.

The What If window (Figure 13-7, bottom) lets you experiment with assumptions to find a solution. The "Choose a goal type" box is set to Retirement (it changes depending on which planning wizard you run), so the assumptions you can change include your retirement age, how much you save, how much you live on in retirement, and so on. Click one of the left-hand "What if I" links to change those retirement-related assumptions. The "Or, change my assumption" list includes *all* your planning assumptions. After you change an assumption, the What If window shows your new results.

If you find a plan that works, click the "Save What If as Plan" button. Quicken saves the new assumption values as your planning assumptions. To reset the assumptions to your original values, click Reset What If. To simply quit, click the Close Without Saving button.

Saving for College

Unlike retirement, most folks spend only a few years in college, but the price tag can be steep. A four-year stint at a top school can run $200,000 or more. If you've got one or more darlings to put through school, you have to start saving early. After all, you have fewer years to save for college than you do for retirement, and tuition payments arrive earlier in your career when you don't earn as much. Like Quicken's retirement planning tools, the College Calculator and College Planner can help you figure out how much you can afford to pay and how much you have to save to put your kiddos through the schools of their dreams.

Calculating College Costs

Quicken's College Calculator (Figure 13-8) is even easier to use than its retirement cousin. Enter some basic info about college expenses and your plan, and you can see how much you can afford in college costs each year, the current savings you'd need to cover specific costs, or how much you have to contribute each year to save the amount you want. The College Calculator fills in several boxes with the most common answers, so your data entry chores are short and sweet. This section walks you through the steps:

1. **To get started, choose Planning → Financial Calculators → College Calculator.**

   The College Calculator dialog box opens. The first fields to look at are in the bottom half of the dialog box. Quicken automatically sets the "Predicted inflation" box to *4.000%,* which is a safe long-term estimate, but you can change that percentage if you want.

2. **To increase your contribution each year to keep up with inflation, turn on the "Inflate contributions" checkbox.**

   If you're saving for college for 18 years or more, inflation can take a big bite out of your purchasing power. At 4 percent inflation, $1 today is worth about 49

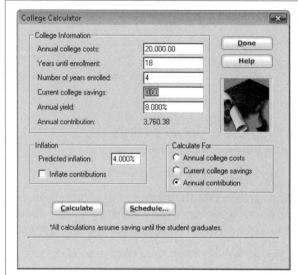

Figure 13-8:
The College Calculator assumes that you'll continue saving money toward college expenses until your child graduates, meaning that while your child is in college, you'll both contribute to and withdraw from the college nest egg. Quicken takes that into account in its calculations.

cents in 18 years, when your firstborn starts college. Turn on the "Inflate contribution" checkbox to increase each year's college savings by the inflation rate. If your first year's contribution is $1,000, the second year is $1,040, and so on.

3. **In the Calculate For section, select what you want to calculate. For this exercise, choose "Annual contribution".**

   Quicken automatically selects the "Annual contribution" option, which figures out how much you have to save each year to pay for the college expenses you're willing to cover.

   If you know how much you want to earmark each year for college savings, select the "Annual college costs" option. The calculator then figures out the college expenses you can cover for each school year.

   The "Current college savings" option calculates how much money you need to have right now based on the annual contribution you plan to make and the annual college costs you specify. If the answer doesn't match your college savings balance, you have to select one of the other options to try another scenario.

4. **Back at the top of the dialog box, in the "Annual college costs" box, type the expenses you're planning to pay for each school year.**

   You don't have to foot the *entire* bill. Your child could receive a scholarship (c'mon, full ride!), financial aid, fellowship, or take out a student loan and work part-time.

5. **If the numbers in the "Years until enrollment" box and "Number of years enrolled" boxes aren't what you want, change them.**

    Quicken fills in the "Years until enrollment" box with 18 years, which assumes that you start saving as soon as your child is born. If you're getting a head start or late start, type the number of years you expect to have before your kid starts college.

    Quicken fills in the "Number of years enrolled" box with 4. You may want to change this number, say, if you plan to pay for graduate school, too, or you think your young genius will get her sheepskin in fewer years.

6. **In the "Current college savings" box, type the amount you've already saved.**

    Enter your total college savings, whether the money is in a tax-advantaged account like a 529 Plan or a taxable account. The College Calculator doesn't take taxes into account. If you haven't started saving yet, jump to the next step.

7. **In the "Annual yield" box, type the annual return you expect your college savings to earn.**

    Quicken automatically fills in 8.0 percent, which may be too high, especially if you only have a few years until your child starts college.

8. **If you're calculating annual college costs, type the amount you plan to save each year in the "Annual contribution" box.**

    If you selected the "Annual contribution" option, as shown in Figure 13-8, the "Annual contribution" value is already filled in and you're done!

9. **To see a schedule of your contributions, your college savings balance, and how much you can withdraw for each year of school, click the Schedule button.**

    Quicken opens the Deposit Schedule dialog box, similar to the one for retirement (Figure 13-5).

If you don't like the results or you want to look at another scenario, change the values you want and then click Calculate.

College Planner

As you'd expect, the College Planner (Planning → College Planner) asks questions about the kids going to college, how much you expect college to cost (Figure 13-9), sources of funding, and the savings and investments you have earmarked to pay for it. As in the Retirement Planner, click a link in the left-hand navigation bar to fill in info or assumptions about college.

The Savings/Investments link opens a dialog box that asks the question all parents dread: How are you going to pay for this? If you have money set aside already, enter the amount or choose the accounts dedicated to college savings like 529 Plan accounts (page 52). After you fill in the amount you've already saved, Quicken calculates how much you have to save each month to save the rest.

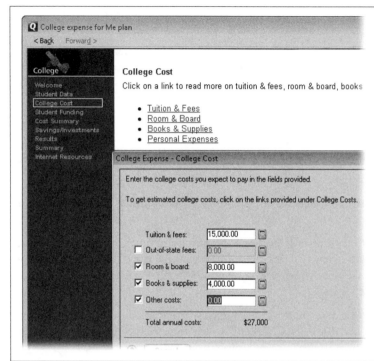

When you click the Results link, you see the same Results screen that appears in the other planning wizards. Regardless which planner you use, Quicken takes *all* your financial goals into account (retirement, college education, home purchase, and so on) and shows whether your plan succeeds.

The last link in the navigation bar is Internet Resources, which displays links to several valuable Web sites, including ones that help you find financial aid. Keep in mind that these sites probably pay Intuit to be listed here—so you'll want to do your own research, too—but they're good sites nonetheless.

Planning to Pay for a House

Quicken has several tools to help you plan for buying a house or refinancing the mortgage on a home you already own. The Loan Calculator simply figures out the payment you'll owe if you borrow a specific amount, or the total amount you can borrow given a specific monthly payment. If you don't know the answers to the questions the Loan Calculator poses (like the monthly payment you can afford or the total amount you're qualified to borrow), use the Home Purchase Planner instead. It helps you determine how much a lender is likely to let you borrow and the maximum monthly payment you'll have with such a loan. If you already own a home, you can use the Refinance Calculator to see whether you'd save money refinancing your mortgage. This section explains how to use all three of these tools.

Loan Calculator

The Loan Calculator can figure out two things: the amount you can borrow to have the monthly payment you specify or the monthly payment for a specific loan amount. If you know the highest monthly payment you want, regardless how much the lender is willing to lend, then calculate the amount you can borrow. On the other hand, if you just saw the house of your dreams and want to find out what the monthly payment would be, fill in the loan amount and calculate the payment. Here are the steps:

1. **Choose Planning → Financial Calculators → Loan Calculator.**

   The Loan Calculator dialog box opens.

2. **Skip down to the Calculate For section and select either "Loan amount" or "Payment per period".**

   Quicken automatically selects the "Payment per period" option, which calculates the monthly payment for the amount you're borrowing. With this option selected, the "Payment per period" field doesn't have a text box, but instead reads *CALCULATED*.

   If you select "Loan amount", the "Payment per period" field's text box appears and you see the word *CALCULATED* to the right of the "Loan amount" label instead.

3. **Back at the top of the dialog box, if you're calculating the payment, type the amount you want to borrow, as shown in Figure 13-10.**

   Type in the amount you plan to borrow, not the purchase price of the house. Your down payment decreases your loan amount. However, you can roll closing costs into your loan, which increases the loan amount.

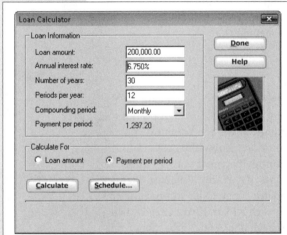

Figure 13-10:
The Loan Calculator fills in the "Number of years" box with 30 and the "Periods per year" box with 12, which is what you want for a 30-year mortgage that you pay monthly. If your loan's terms are different—it's a 15-year mortgage, say—change the value in the "Number of years" box.

4. **In the "Annual interest rate" box, type the interest rate on the loan.**

   Quicken fills in *8.000%*, so you have to change the rate to the one for your loan. Enter the loan's advertised annual interest rate, which you'll find somewhere on the good faith estimate the lender gives you. Don't use the *annual percentage rate* (APR), also called the *effective rate*, which you'll find on your loan disclosure agreement. It's the *real* rate you pay and is always a bit higher than the annual rate, because it includes origination fees and points you pay up front to get the mortgage, prepaid mortgage interest, mortgage insurance premiums, and other fees.

5. **If you don't have a 30-year loan with monthly payments, change the values in the "Number of years" and "Periods per year" boxes.**

   For example, if you're looking at a 15-year mortgage, type *15* in the "Number of years" box. Most loans have monthly payments, but you can change the value in the "Periods per year" box to match your payment schedule.

Note: The calculator also sets the "Compounding period" to *Monthly*, which is almost always correct. The only other choice is *Semi-annually*. If your loan compounds on a schedule other than those two options, the Loan Calculator won't give you accurate results.

---

6. **If you're calculating the loan amounts, type the monthly payment in the "Payment per period" box.**

   If you selected the "Payment per period" option, as shown in Figure 13-10, Quicken fills in the "Payment per period" value and you're done!

7. **To see a schedule of your principal and interest payments and remaining loan balance, click the Schedule button.**

   Quicken opens the Approximate Future Payment Schedule dialog box, which shows the principal and interest you pay in each payment (called an *amortization schedule*) and the amount you still owe.

To try out a different loan amount, interest rate, or payment, change the values you want and then click Calculate.

Tip: For the granddaddy of all mortgage calculators, HSH Associates offer the Homebuyer's Calculators program, which you can download for free. It includes calculators for mortgage qualification, amortization schedules, refinancing, comparing renting to buying, the effect of prepaying your mortgage, and more. Go to *www.hsh.com* and in the middle of the Web page, under Calculators, click the Homebuyer's Calculator Suite link. The sites *www.bankrate.com* and *www.dinkytown.com* also offer a plethora of calculators.

Refinance Calculator

Say you bought your house several years ago when mortgage rates were around 8 percent and now rates are closer to 6.5 percent. But you know that refinancing means paying another set of closing costs. The Refinance Calculator can tell you

---

whether refinancing your mortgage is worth the trouble and, if it is, when the savings would recoup the closing costs. Here's how to use this calculator:

1. **Choose Planning → Financial Calculators → Refinance Calculator.**

   The Refinance Calculator dialog box opens (Figure 13-11).

2. **In the "Current payment" box, type your current mortgage payment.**

   Type the *full* payment amount including escrow fees like homeowners' insurance premiums or property taxes. (In the next step Quicken subtracts the escrow amounts from the total payment to calculate your principal and interest payment.)

3. **In the "Impound/escrow amount" box, type your monthly escrow payment.**

   Type in the escrow payment that your lender collects for homeowner's insurance premiums, property taxes, private mortgage insurance, and so on. When you press Enter, Quicken calculates the amount that you pay in principal and interest each month.

4. **In the "Principal amount" box, type the amount you plan to borrow with the new loan.**

   If you plan to pay closing costs out of pocket when you refinance, the principal amount is approximately the remaining balance on your mortgage. If you plan to roll the closing costs into the new mortgage, add them to your current balance.

5. **If the new loan isn't a 30-year loan, change the value in the Years box.**

   If you've had your current mortgage for a while, you may not want to start over with another 30-year mortgage, so enter the length of the new mortgage.

6. **In the "Interest rate" box, type the interest rate on the loan.**

   Enter the loan's advertised annual rate, *not* the effective rate or annual percentage rate (APR) that you see on your loan disclosure agreement.

7. **In the Break Even Analysis section (Figure 13-11), type the closing costs for the new mortgage in the "Mortgage closing costs" box.**

   Closing costs include things like the application and origination fees, appraisal, credit check, and so on.

8. **If you're paying discount points to reduce your rate, in the "Mortgage points" box, type the percentage you're paying.**

   Mortgage points (also called *discount points*) are interest that you pay up front to get a lower interest rate on the loan.

9. **When everything looks good, click Calculate.**

   Quicken figures out how much money you'd save each month with the new mortgage.

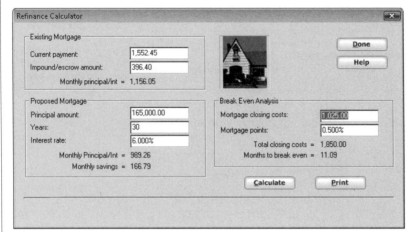

Figure 13-11:
In the Break Even Analysis section, the calculator shows how many months it will take for those monthly savings to pay back your closing costs. If you don't plan to live in the house that long, the refinance isn't worth it.

To evaluate a different loan amount, interest rate, or closing costs, change the values you want, and then click Calculate.

Home Purchase Planner

When you choose Planning → Home Purchase Planner, the "Can I afford that house?" window opens. Unlike the Loan Calculator, this planner helps you figure out how much lenders may let you borrow. You tell it about your income, existing debt, and the down payment you've saved to find out the maximum monthly payment and loan amount you're likely to qualify for.

The "How much house can I afford" screen (Figure 13-12) asks for the basic info a lender looks at: gross income, monthly loan and debt payments, and the down payment. You also fill in the mortgage rate for your loan. Click Calculate to find out what a lender may lend you. If you're still shopping for houses, you can stop the Home Purchase Planner right there because now you know the price range to look at. And when you finally buy your dream home, you can celebrate by telling Quicken about it so the program can add it to your overall financial plan. What could be more festive?

Planning to Reduce Debt

The Debt Reduction Planner (Planning → Debt Reduction) can help you figure out which debts to pay off first to minimize the interest you pay. If you want to see the planner's multimedia content (like pictures and videos), insert your Quicken CD into your CD drive when you launch the planner. You can skip these bells and whistles by clicking Next to move to the next screen.

The Debt Reduction Planner lists the debts you have in your Quicken data file: mortgages, credit cards, car loans, and so on. You may have to fill in details about each loan, like the minimum payment you have to make.

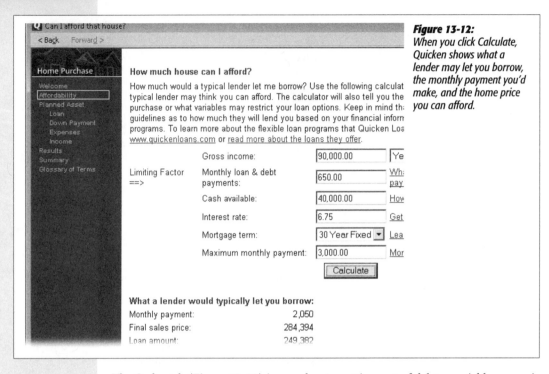

Figure 13-12:
When you click Calculate, Quicken shows what a lender may let you borrow, the monthly payment you'd make, and the home price you can afford.

The Order tab (Figure 13-13) is your key to getting out of debt as quickly as possible. It lists your debts in the order you should pay them off. It should come as no surprise that the one with the highest interest rate tops the list.

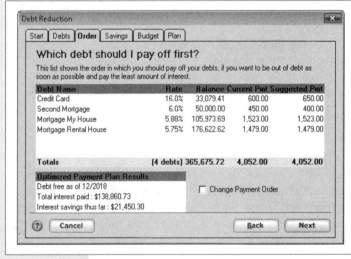

Figure 13-13:
The Debt Reduction Planner applies the minimum payment to each debt. Then it uses the money that's left over to reduce the balance on the debt with the highest interest rate.

If you have any money saved, you can use the Savings tab to see what would happen if you applied some of it to reducing your debt. The planner shows when you'll be free of debt and how much interest you'll save.

The Budget tab shows a few of your Quicken categories with the highest average monthly spending. You can calculate what would happen if you reduced your spending in those categories and used the savings to pay off your debt. However, you're better off working directly in your budget (Chapter 11) to find *all* the ways you can save.

The Plan tab tells you what you already know you need to do: Stop borrowing, make a one-time payment of savings to pay off your debt, and cut expenses.

Planning Other Major Expenditures

For any other major expenditures, you can use either the Savings Calculator or the Special Purchase Planner to figure out how to pay for it. The Savings Calculator is much like the College Calculator, and can figure out how much you can save, how much you need to contribute, or how much money you should have today to achieve your goal. It's helpful for getting a rough estimate of how much you need to save for a purchase, like a motorcycle, without dragging the rest of your financial plan into your calculations.

The Special Savings Planner helps when you're saving for something big, like a sailboat, or something that spans several years, like your sabbatical to Borneo. With this planner, you tell Quicken how much you plan to spend, when you plan to spend it, how you plan to pay for the purchase, and whether the cost might increase between now and the date you hand over the money. The planner takes this new expenditure into account and figures out whether your overall financial plan still works. It can set up a scheduled transaction for the monthly amount it calculates so you don't forget to put that money aside. This section explains how to use both savings tools.

Calculating Monthly Savings

If you're using a savings account to save for a goal like a nice vacation or a car, the Savings Calculator (Planning → Financial Calculators → Savings Calculator) can figure out how much you have to contribute today to earn enough to reach that goal, how much you have to contribute regularly, or how much you'll have at a given time based on your current balance. This calculator is similar to the College Calculator (page 418), but with different labels and slightly different fields. Here are the fields you fill in:

- **Calculate For.** Quicken automatically selects the "Ending savings balance" option, which uses your opening balance and regular contributions to calculate what you'll have at the end of the plan. If you want to figure out how much you need to save each period to end up with the final amount you need, select the

"Regular contribution" option. The "Opening savings balance" option shows you the amount you should have today based on the regular contribution you plan to make and the ending balance you want.

- **Opening savings balance.** If you already have money set aside for your purchase, type the amount in this box (which is equivalent to the "Current college savings" box on page 420). If you select the "Opening savings balance" option in the Calculate For section, Quicken calculates this value for you.

- **Annual yield.** Type the annual interest rate that your savings account pays or the annual return you expect to make on your investments.

- **Number of <periods>.** In the drop-down list, choose the period you want to use for your plan. Quicken automatically selects Years, but you can choose Weeks, Months, or Quarters for shorter-term goals. In the "Number of <periods>" box, type the number of periods in your plan. For a 3-year plan, you could either choose Years in the drop-down list and type *3* in the "Number of <periods>" box, or choose Months and type *36* in the "Number of <periods>" box.

- **Contribution each <period>.** Type the amount you plan to contribute each period. If you select the "Regular contribution" option in the Calculate For section, Quicken calculates this value for you.

- **Ending savings balance.** If you know how much money you want to save, type that amount here. If you select the "Ending savings balance" option in the Calculate For box, Quicken figures out how much you'll have at the end of your plan.

- **Predicted inflation.** Quicken automatically fills in *4.000%*, which is a good choice.

- **Inflate contributions.** If you plan to increase your contributions to keep up with inflation, turn on this checkbox.

- **Ending balance in today's $.** Turn on this checkbox to see your ending balance in today's dollars. Page 412 explains why this helps you estimate your savings.

Using the Special Purchase Planner

The Special Purchase Planner asks more questions than the Savings Calculator, but the interrogation is worth it if you're saving for something really big. Say you're planning to scrap your house and rebuild, and need savings and a loan to pay for the remodel. Or maybe you're taking 3 years off to build houses for Habitat for Humanity. Whatever your goal, this planner can figure out how much you have to save and borrow based on the details you provide. Here's what you do:

1. **Choose Planning → Special Purchase Planner. On the "What is it?" screen, click the Enter link to tell the planner about your purchase.**

   The Add Special Expense dialog box opens.

2. In the "Name or description" box, give your purchase a name like *Vacation, Sabbatical,* or *Car,* and then click Next.

You can also tell Quicken who gets the benefit of the expense (you, your spouse, one of your kids, or someone else who's part of your financial plan), but this doesn't affect the results.

3. On the "Enter the details about the amount and duration of the expense" screen, choose the date when the expense begins.

The planner automatically selects "Specific date". In the date box, choose the first date of the expense (the day you plan on starting that remodel, for example). If you've set up planning assumptions in the Retirement Planner or by choosing Planning → Planning Assumptions, you can also choose an assumption milestone like the date you retire.

4. If you're going to pay for your purchase for more than one year, select the "multiple-year expense" option, and then enter the number of years.

For example, if you're taking 3 years off, you fill in the "Specific date" box with the date those 3 years begin. Then, in the "years" box, type *3*. If you select the "multiple-year expense" option, the "Cost inflation rate" box appears. Select a rate to increase the purchase cost by between now and the beginning of the purchase.

5. In the "Expense amount" box, type what you expect the purchase to cost and then click Next.

If you select the "multiple-year expense" option, type the estimated cost *per year* for your purchase.

6. The next screen asks about how you're going to pay for your purchase. If you have money set aside already, click Choose Accounts. If not, skip to the next step.

The Choose Funding Accounts dialog box opens, as shown in Figure 13-14. The planner selects the "General expenses" option, which doesn't designate specific accounts for your current savings. If you don't use special accounts, leave this option selected. If you do, choose the "Specific accounts" option, as explained in Figure 13-14. Check that the amount and date are correct before you click OK.

7. If you're going to take out a loan to help pay for the purchase, in the "Amount from loans" box, type the amount you plan to borrow. Press Tab to move to the "Monthly savings target" box, which tells Quicken to recalculate the monthly value based on what you've entered so far. Click Done.

Before you click Done, the planner deducts the amount you've saved and the amount you plan to borrow from the purchase price. It then calculates the amount you have to save each month to reach your goal. When you click Done, the planner lists the purchase in the "What is it?" screen.

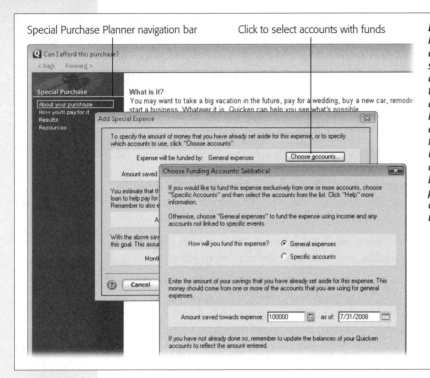

Special Purchase Planner navigation bar   Click to select accounts with funds

Figure 13-14:
*If you set up a special
account for your savings,
select the "Specific
accounts" option, and
the dialog box lists your
accounts (not shown
here). Click each
account you plan to use
for the purchase.
Unfortunately, you can't
designate part of the
balance for the
purchase–Quicken
assumes you want to
use the whole thing.*

8. **In the bottom-right corner of the window, click Next to move to the "How will you pay for it?" screen. Click the links in this screen to set up a scheduled transaction or loan if you're using them to pay for the purchase.**

   You may have thought that you told the planner this info in step 6. But this screen includes links to help you stick to the figures you entered in step 6. One is a Schedule link that you can click to set up a scheduled transaction (page 186) for your monthly savings. The other is an "Enter a future loan" link to set up a loan. See page 237 to learn about creating loans.

9. **Click Next to see the results.**

   The info Quicken displays—which looks like the results at the top of Figure 13-7—takes into account any other plans you've created, like your retirement or a house purchase. For example, your retirement plan may work on its own, but adding the special purchase to the mix shows you running out of money before you retire. See page 417 to learn how to revise your plan to make it work.

Creating Reports and Graphs

Quicken comes with all kinds of ready-made reports, perfect for getting a snap-shot of things like how much you spend, what you're worth, and what you need to prepare your tax return. Just click a few buttons, and in a jiffy you'll see what's up (or down) with your finances. This chapter tells you about the different types of reports Quicken offers, where to find them, and how to run them and print them.

And if the built-in reports don't suit your needs, you can customize them in lots of ways, and then save them for future use. If you're more into graphics than num-bers, you can also generate graphs of most of Quicken's reports. This chapter teaches you everything you need to know about customizing reports.

An Introduction to Quicken's Reports

Quicken reports come in all shapes and sizes, from quick snapshots of recent transactions to full-blown reports with lots of bells and whistles to reports that help you answer specific questions you're likely to ask. These reports are tucked in various spots throughout the program, so the information you want is always close at hand.

Probably the biggest challenge you'll face is figuring out which report to run. Each part of Quicken has its own built-in reports and graphs. You'll find information about specific reports in the chapters where they help the most. For example, "Where did I spend my money during the period...?" and the Budget reports are covered in Chapter 11, "Monitoring Spending and Saving." This section gives you an overview of the different types of reports you can generate, the categories of built-in reports, and where you can find details in other chapters.

From Quick to Comprehensive

As you work on your day-to-day financial tasks, you may want to peek at what you've done in the past. Say this month's electric bill seems higher than usual, and you want to see how much you've paid over the last several months. Or maybe you're on a mission to clean up your data file and want to see whether you still need some of the categories in the Category List. Quicken's minireports and QuickReports can gather up the info you need.

Quicken's reports can also help you look at your finances from a variety of angles, whether you're searching for missing checks or want to admire the progress you've made toward retirement. Built-in reports give you all kinds of different perspectives, and you can customize them to get just the point of view you want. You can also zoom in for a closer look: When you double-click an entry in a report, Quicken generates a QuickZoom report with more details about that entry.

This section describes each type of report—starting with built-in snapshots of transactions and lists and then moving on to in-depth reports you can customize to your heart's content—and where you find them in Quicken.

Minireports: Snapshots of income and spending

A *minireport* is a snapshot of your recent spending and income, usually by payee or category. If you want to see how much you've spent on groceries lately or with your buddies at Perfect Plumbing, you can produce a category or payee minireport right from your account register. For example, when you click a minireport icon (which looks like a dog-eared piece of paper) in a transaction's category field, a pop-up window appears, listing recent transactions in that category, as you can see in Figure 14-1.

Quicken scans all your accounts for transactions that match the selected payee or category. Initially, the minireport displays the shortest time period that has at least six matching transactions (up to 3 years). In the minireport window, you can click the down arrow to the right of the time period and select a different period, from as short as the last 30 days to as long as the last 3 years.

Quicken offers three kinds of minireports:

- **Category minireports.** In a register transaction, click a category field, and then click the minireport icon that appears at the right end of the field. The minireport shows up to six transactions for that category. In addition to the total for those transactions, the minireport calculates the average value of the transactions and the monthly average for the past several months.

- **Payee minireports.** A payee minireport works like its category cousin: In a register transaction, click a Payee field, and then click the minireport icon that appears at the right end of the field. The minireport shows up to six recent transactions along with their total and average, which is perfect for checking whether you're paying more or less than you have in the past.

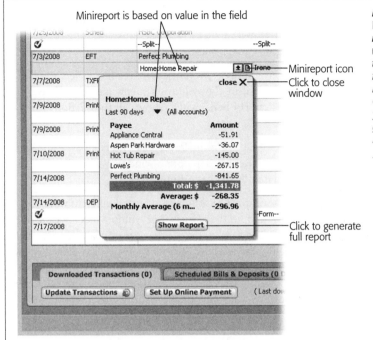

Minireport is based on value in the field

Minireport icon

Click to close window

Figure 14-1:
When you click the minireport icon in a transaction field, a pop-up window like this shows recent transactions for the value in that field, such as the Home:Home Repair category in a Category field. Click "close" to hide the report. If you click Show Report, Quicken generates a full-blown transaction report in a report window so that you can customize it (page 447).

Click to generate full report

- **Scheduled transaction minireports.** These reports show you the average value of several occurrences of a scheduled transaction. In the Scheduled Bills & Deposits window or on the Summary page of the Banking tab, simply position your cursor over a scheduled transaction. After a second or two, up pops a minireport showing the average of up to six recent transactions for the selected payee.

QuickReports for list items

A *QuickReport* is basically a transaction report for an item you select in a Quicken list, such as category, tag, memorized payee, or security. For example, if you want to compare your expenses to your spouse's, a tag QuickReport is the answer. Or if you want to check whether you're using a particular category, you can produce a QuickReport for that category. If the report comes up empty, you can delete that category.

You create QuickReports in a couple of different ways: In some windows, you click the dog-eared-page icon (yep, it looks just like the one you use to generate minireports in account registers), and in others you use the menu bar. Here's how to generate QuickReports for items on various Quicken lists:

- **Category List.** Choose Tools → Category List (or press Ctrl+C). In the Category List window, click the minireport icon to the left of the category you want to review. The QuickReport that appears shows the payees assigned to that category and the number of transactions for each one.

- **Tag List.** To view a tag QuickReport, choose Tools → Tag List or press Ctrl+L. In the Tag List window, click the minireport icon to the left of the tag, and Quicken generates a report showing all the transactions (or split transaction items) marked with that tag.

- **Memorized Payee List.** Choose Tools → Memorized Payee List. Select the memorized payee you want and then, in the window's menu bar, click Report. A window displaying a Payee Report opens, which shows all transactions for that payee for all dates in your data file.

- **Online Payee List.** Choose Online → Online Payee List. Select a payee and then, in the window's menu bar, click Report. Up pops a window with a Payee Report that spans all dates in your data file for that online payee.

- **Securities.** You can produce a security QuickReport in several different ways. One is to choose Investing → Security List. In the Security List window that appears, select the security you want to review and then, in the window's menu bar, click Report. If you're in the Security Detail View window (Investing → Security Detail View), choose the security you want and then, in the window's menu bar, click Report. Or choose Investing → Portfolio, right-click a security, and then choose Security Report from the shortcut menu. However you generate the security QuickReport, it shows you all transactions for that security for all dates in your data file.

EasyAnswer reports: Getting answers fast

With Quicken's *EasyAnswer reports*, it's a breeze to get the info you want—though there's no guarantee that the results will be easy to swallow (for instance, if you're spending way more than you earn). If you're new to Quicken or financial lingo in general, EasyAnswer reports were made for you—their plain-English names tell you exactly what they do. If you see the question you've been asking yourself, simply choose it from the Reports menu.

These reports are essentially precustomized versions of built-in reports and graphs, already set up to answer your questions. For some reports, you can choose a few additional settings to get more targeted information, such as payments to a specific payee within a particular timeframe. For example, with the "How much did I spend on…?" EasyAnswer report, you choose a category and a period, and the report tells you how much you spent.

To see the EasyAnswer reports, choose Reports → EasyAnswer. The EasyAnswer report category is at the bottom of the Reports & Graphs window. Click the name of the report to see what criteria you can change, as shown in Figure 14-2.

Regular and QuickZoom reports

When you know exactly how you want to see your financial information, you can use one of Quicken's built-in reports. Page 439 describes how to select a built-in report and generate it. Sometimes, a report shows you exactly what you're looking for out of the box. But if it doesn't, once you've generated a report, you can tweak and customize it in several ways (page 447).

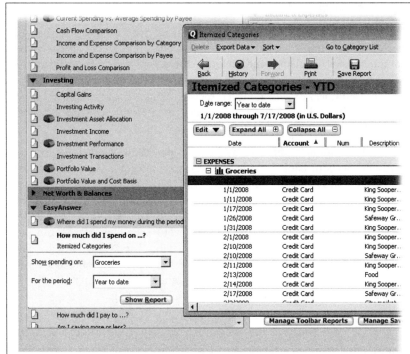

Figure 14-2:
When you click an EasyAnswer report's name, customization fields appear. Choose the criteria you want, such as a category or timeframe. Then, click Show Report to produce a tabular report. Click Show Graph (if it's available) to produce a graph.

From a report window, you can also drill down into the details with *QuickZoom reports*. For example, if you create a pie chart like the Asset Allocation graph, you can zoom in on the data by double-clicking a wedge to see a second graph of what makes up that wedge (the securities in that asset class, in this example). If you double-click one of the slices in the *second* graph, a report appears showing the details about that slice (that security's performance, in this example).

Tip: If you see a magnifying glass icon when you position your cursor over an entry in a report, that's your hint that you can double-click to QuickZoom for more details.

What QuickZoom shows you depends on where you start. For example, in a Budget report, double-clicking a category creates a QuickZoom report of all the transactions for that category. If you double-click one of those transactions, Quicken opens the register and highlights the transaction.

Categories of Reports

Intuit's done you the favor of rounding up the most commonly used reports and grouping them by category in the Reports menu. (When you position your cursor over a category, a submenu with report names appears.) This section gives you an overview of the different categories.

Keeping tabs on banking activity

The reports in the Banking category help you (not surprisingly) with banking activities. They pull info from your checking, savings, and credit card accounts. For example, the Reconciliation and Missing Checks reports help you with administrative tasks like comparing your Quicken records with your banks or finding missing check numbers in your Quicken register. Banking reports also show you payments, deposits, and transfers. Here's a quick overview of each type of Banking report:

- The **Banking Summary report, Cash Flow report,** and **"Cash Flow by Tag" report** all show your banking activity category by category. The Banking Summary report totals your income and expenses by category and also shows how much you transferred between accounts. The Cash Flow report is like the Banking Summary report without the transfers between accounts. It tells you whether you have enough income to cover your spending, so you can plan ahead to get through times when money is tight. The "Cash Flow by Tag" report shows income and expenses by tag, perfect when you want to see your finances by family member, rental property, and so on. Chapter 11 tells you how to use these reports to track your income and spending.

- The **Missing Checks report** is great if you're trying to find the checks you forgot to record in Quicken, though it shows *all* transactions in all your spending accounts, not just missing checks. See page 210 for more details.

- Run a **Reconciliation report** *before* reconciling if you want to check off the cleared transactions on paper as you reconcile. Then, when you reconcile an account (see Chapter 8), Quicken asks if you want to generate a new reconciliation report. When you run this report at that point, it shows the transactions you've reconciled and the ones still outstanding.

- The **Transaction report** doesn't have any fancy formatting. It's a workhorse report that lists all transactions in *all* accounts for the date range you choose and you can subtotal transactions by time periods, categories, tags, payees, accounts, or tax schedules. This can be handy if you want to look for transactions you recorded in the wrong account, tax deductions you may have missed, or you simply can't remember which built-in transaction report subtotals transactions the way you want.

Tracking spending

The reports and graphs in the Spending category give you detailed breakdowns of your income and expenses. These reports track your money based on who's paying you or whom you're paying (payee) as well as what you're buying (category). Among other things, you can compare current spending with average spending, see whether you're keeping to your budget, and spot other spending trends.

If you're perpetually short on cash or trying to squeeze more savings into your budget, knowing how you spend money is a great place to start. These reports and graphs get down to the smallest details and can be customized to include only the accounts, categories, payees, time periods, and transaction types you want to see. For example, the Itemized Categories report starts as a summary of income, expenses, and transfers for all your accounts, but you can drill down to individual transactions. (How did you manage to spend $300 at Starbucks last month?) Spending reports, such as Monthly Budget, can show you how you're doing compared to your budget. Chapter 11 gives the lowdown on tracking spending with these Quicken reports.

Tip: In a Spending report, to expand a category to see subcategories or transactions, click the + sign to the left of the category or subcategory's name. (This technique also works on other reports that start out showing summary values.) To collapse a category, click the – sign to the left of the category name. To hide or show all the categories at once, in the report window, click the Expand All or Collapse All button, respectively.

Making comparisons

The Comparison category has six reports to choose from, which all focus on tracking income and spending in different ways. For this reason, some of these reports are also in other categories, like the "Current Spending vs. Average Spending by Category" report, which also appears in the Spending category. And some take reports from other categories and add a comparison to another period. For example, if you want to create a budget, the "Income and Expense Comparison by Category" report shows your income and expenses for a given period (the last 12 months, say) compared to your income and expenses for the previous year. Flip to Chapter 11 for more information on these reports.

Keeping track of investments

The Investing category has reports for all sorts of tasks—from tax reporting to planning to gloating over your success. If you have *any* investments, you're bound to use almost every one of these reports at some point. Chapter 12 shows you how to put Quicken's investment reports to use. But these reports may fall short if you're trying to meticulously manage your investment portfolio.

Investment reports tackle two major activities: analyzing your investment portfolio and keeping track of investment transactions. Quicken is much better at tracking investments than at analyzing them, but the investment analysis reports have some benefits. Here's a quick rundown of the reports in this category:

- The **Capital Gains report** focuses on capital gains you receive from securities you sell.

- The **Investing Activity report** groups transactions into deposits and withdrawals; interest, dividends, and gains you received; and the change in market value of the securities you still own.

- The **Investment Asset Allocation report** may be the most helpful of Quicken's analysis reports. Allocating your investments to different asset classes is one way to control your portfolio's risk. For example, a portfolio of small-cap stocks is roller-coaster material, whereas a portfolio that includes large-cap stocks and bonds smoothes out the ride. The best way to see if your portfolio is diversified is to generate this report as a graph, as you can see in Figure 14-3.

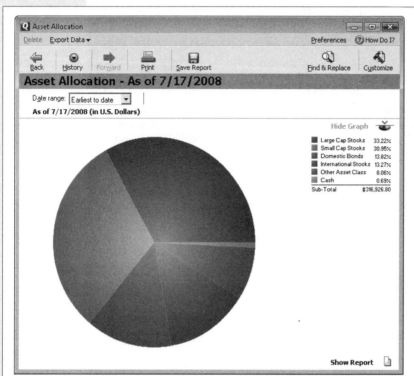

Figure 14-3:
To see your asset allocation as a pie chart, in the Reports & Graphs window, click the pie chart icon to the left of the report's name. If one of the slices in the Asset Allocation pie chart is ginormous, your allocation is probably out of whack. Check out the legend in the top-right corner to see your current percentages for each asset class. (Unfortunately, you can't change Quicken's list of asset classes.)

Tip: If you double-click one of the slices in the Investment Asset Allocation pie chart, Quicken creates a second pie chart that shows the allocation of securities *within* that asset class. If you double-click a slice in this second graph, you get a report showing that security's performance over time.

• The **Investment Income report** shows how much income you receive in dividends, interest, and capital gains. That's useful, come tax time, for finding out how much income you earned from investments, or whether your portfolio produces enough income for you to retire on.

• The **Investment Performance** report calculates the average annual return your portfolio earned during the period you choose. It uses the balance on the starting date, the present value of the portfolio, and the amount of time you're measuring to calculate this time-based return. For example, running this report for specific stocks you pick, and then running it again for your index mutual funds can tell you whether you're as good at picking stocks as you think you are.

• To get down and dirty with all your investment transactions, you can run the **Investment Transactions report** and customize it to show just the transactions you want. (Page 447 has info on customizing reports.)

- The **Portfolio Value report** simply shows how much each investment in your portfolio is worth.

- How much your portfolio is worth isn't as important as how much it's worth compared to how much you contributed. For example, if your portfolio is at $500,000 and you contributed $499,000, your investments haven't done much. Run the **"Portfolio Value and Cost Basis" report** to find out how much you deposited in each investment account you own, and how much each account is worth now.

Preparing tax paperwork

Even if you let your accountant do the dirty work come tax time, you still need to give her all your tax-related information. The Tax report category is a lifesaver when you want to gather this stuff up. You can generate reports specific to one tax form or pull all your tax-related transactions in one fell swoop, as long as your Quicken categories are linked to tax line items. (Chapter 10 describes how you set up your data file to track your tax-related transactions and how to use the built-in tax reports come tax time.)

Note: The Tax category is available in the Reports & Graphs window as long as you have the Tax feature turned on in the Setup Center (page 19). If you turn off the Tax checkbox in the Your Quicken section of the Setup tab, the Tax menu, Tax tab, and Tax report category all disappear.

Seeing what you own and owe

If you want to see whether you've mortgaged yourself to the hilt or enjoy reminders of your obscene wealth, the two reports in the Net Worth & Balances category are what you're looking for. The Account Balances report shows the balance in each of your Quicken accounts. At the bottom of the report is your Overall Total—your assets minus your liabilities—also known as your net worth (the net of what you own minus how much you've borrowed to own it). The Net Worth report lists all your asset accounts first, and then adds them up to show Total Assets (what you own). It then lists your liability accounts, and adds up what you owe. At the very bottom, the Overall Total is the same as the one on the Account Balances report. Chapter 9 explains how to put these reports to work.

Note: Turn to page 434 to learn all about EasyAnswer reports.

Running Reports

Finding the right report can be as easy as poking around in the Reports menu. But if you'd rather see all of Quicken's built-in and customizable reports in one window, the Reports & Graphs Center is the way to go.

When you choose Reports → Reports & Graphs Center (or click Reports on the Quicken Tool Bar), the Reports & Graphs window opens. It includes two clickable lists of reports: Quicken Standard Reports on the left and My Saved Reports on the right. The built-in reports are organized into the same categories as on the Reports menu. You can expand or collapse a category by clicking the black arrow to its left. If you store your customized reports in folders (page 457), then you can expand and collapse the My Saved Reports folders on the right side of the window in the same way.

Note: Throughout Quicken, you'll find ways to access reports that relate to the task at hand. For example, on the Banking tab, click Analysis & Reports to see income and expense reports. On the Investing tab, click Analysis to see an asset allocation report.

Generating Reports and Graphs

You can generate a report or graph in a few different ways. Here are your choices and why you might prefer each:

- **Reports menu.** When you know exactly which report you want and don't want to make any changes to it, the fastest method is to choose Reports, scroll to the appropriate category, and, on the submenu that appears, click the report's name, as shown in Figure 14-4. When you choose Reports → My Saved Reports & Graphs, your customized and saved reports (and report folders, if you've made any—see page 457) appear on the submenu.

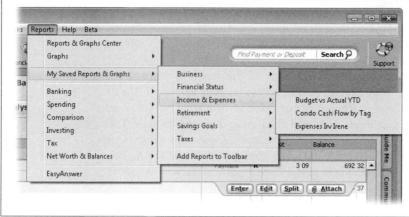

Figure 14-4:
To run a report you've customized, choose Reports → My Saved Reports & Graphs, and then click the report's name on the submenu. If you saved the report in a folder, scroll to the folder you created, and then, on the folder's submenu, click the report's name.

- **Quicken Tool Bar.** If you created a custom report that you run all the time, then you can add it to the Quicken Tool Bar for easy access; page 505 has the details.

- **Reports & Graphs Center.** This window (shown in Figure 14-5) gives you two ways to run a report or graph. Click the report or graph icon (the piece of paper or the pie chart, respectively) to run the report or graph as is. Or click the report's name to change its settings before you run it.

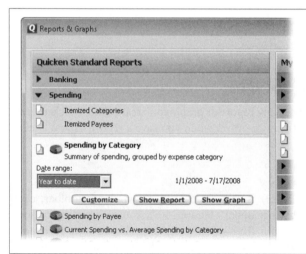

Figure 14-5:
Almost every report is also available as a graph and you can turn every graph into a report. In the Reports & Graphs Center, click either the report icon (the piece of paper) or graph icon (the pie chart)—or click Show Report or Show Graph—to run the report in that format. After you run a report, click the Show Graph link on the right side of the report's window to view the graph version of the report. (You won't see this link if there's no graph version of the report.) When you generate a graph, click Show Report to also display the graph as tabular data. Click Hide Graph or Hide Report to hide that format.

That's all there is to creating a report or graph. In the report's window, you can then save the report, print it, or click Customize to modify it (see page 447).

Note: Transactions for hidden accounts (page 64) don't automatically appear in reports. If you want to generate a report that includes transactions for a hidden account, customize the report (page 447). On the right side of the report window's toolbar, click Customize, and then, in the Customize dialog box, click the Account tab. Turn on the "Show (hidden accounts)" checkbox. That way, if you save the report, it'll always include hidden accounts, so you don't have to unhide those accounts everywhere in Quicken.

GEM IN THE ROUGH

Editing Transactions Within Reports

Every now and then, you generate a report and spot a mistake or see something suspicious, like a purchase assigned to the wrong category or a payment that ended up in the wrong account. Quicken gives you two handy ways to edit or inspect transactions.

- You can edit some transaction fields *directly in* reports. For example, select a single transaction, and then correct its payee or category. Or select one or more transactions (by Shift-clicking or Ctrl-clicking), and then add categories and memos. You can also modify one or more transactions in a report using the report window's Edit menu. Simply select the transaction(s) you want to change, and then, in the upper-left corner of the report (above the column

headings), click Edit. Then choose the task you want to perform: "Delete transaction(s)", "Recategorize transaction(s)", "Retag transaction(s)", "Rename payee(s)", or "Edit memo(s)". (The Edit button appears only when transactions are visible in the report; if all the categories in a report are collapsed, the Edit button disappears.)

- You can also fix errors in reports by jumping from a transaction in the report to the register where it lives. When you position your pointer over a transaction, it changes to a magnifying glass. Double-click the transaction to open its register with the transaction selected.

Tip: Want to feed report data to another program for fancy formatting or advanced calculations? Chapter 17 has the full scoop.

Printing Reports and Graphs

You can print or save a copy of any report or graph you create. And Quicken gives you a few different formats to choose from when you save a report, as you'll learn in the following sections.

Printing a Report

Telling Quicken to print a report is easy. In the report window's toolbar, click Print. In the Print dialog box that opens (Figure 14-6), you see printing options that you're probably familiar with from other programs. (If you want to change the contents of the report, like which columns appear, then you have to customize the report; see page 447.)

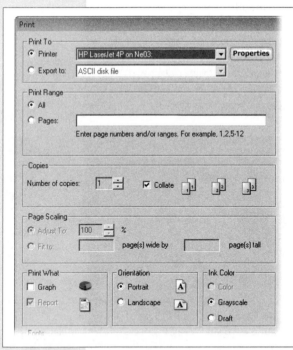

Figure 14-6:
To print, select the Printer option at the top of this dialog box, and then, in the Printer drop-down menu, choose the printer you want to use. You can also choose the page orientation, which pages to print, the number of copies, whether to print in color, and so on.

You can easily figure out most of the printing options. The Print dialog box even includes icons for portrait and landscape orientation, in case you forget which prints "the long way." Here are the options that aren't immediately obvious:

- **Pages.** In the Print Range section, the All option is selected initially, which prints every page of a report. If you want to print a page range, type the first page number, a hyphen, and the last page number in the range, for example, *1-6* to print pages 1 through 6. To print specific pages, separate each page number with a comma, for example, *2,4,8,10*. You can even combine page ranges and specific pages by separating the single pages and page ranges with a comma.

- **Collate.** In the Copies section, the Collate checkbox is turned on automatically when you choose a number of copies greater than one (click the up or down arrow next to the "Number of copies" box, or type a number in the box). This setting prints all the pages for the first copy before printing the pages for the second copy, and so on. If you want Quicken to print all copies of the first page followed by all copies of the second page, and so on, turn off the Collate checkbox.

- **Page Scaling.** If the preview on the right-hand side of the Print dialog box shows your report oozing past the edge of the page like your Aunt Hilda on a picnic bench, the "Page scaling" section has a solution. One way to rein in the report (not Aunt Hilda) is to shrink each page by a percentage. Select the "Adjust to" option and then type a number in the box, such as *80* for 80 percent of full size. The other approach is to select the "Fit to" option, and then tell Quicken how many pages wide and how many pages tall you want the report to be. The box on page 444 offers a few other tips for shrinking wide reports.

- **Ink Color.** When you print to a color printer, Quicken automatically selects the Color option. However, you can print a black-and-white report on a color printer by selecting the Grayscale option. When you print to a black and white (or grayscale) printer, Quicken automatically selects the Grayscale option. If you're rushing to give tax information to your accountant, select the Draft option to print more quickly by using a font built into your printer.

The Print dialog box's right side displays a preview of the report, as shown in Figure 14-7. Click the preview image to zoom in and see if the report or graph looks the way you want. For multipage reports, click the left and right arrows below the preview to look at different pages. The left and right arrow buttons that show a vertical line take you to the report's first page and last page, respectively.

Creating Print-Ready PDF Files

PDF ("portable document format") files are perfect if you want to send a financial snapshot that's hard for anyone to edit. For example, if you generate reports for loan applications, a PDF file ensures that a bank employee can't inadvertently change a value. (Anyone with Internet access can view a PDF by downloading Adobe's free Adobe Reader from *www.adobe.com*.)

Confusingly, printing to a PDF file doesn't actually mean that you print anything out on paper—at least not initially. You're really just saving the report in PDF format, but in Quicken this is called "printing" to a PDF. To create a PDF version of a report, do the following:

1. **After you run your report, in the report window's menu bar, choose Export Data → "Export to PDF format".**

   The Print dialog opens, with "Quicken PDF Printer" in the Printer text box.

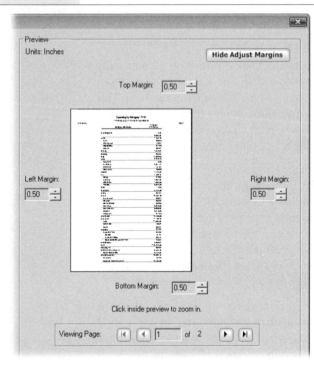

Figure 14-7:
If you want to adjust the margins, click the Adjust Margins button in the upper right (this figure shows the dialog box after that button's been clicked). Boxes appear along each margin so you can make your changes by using the arrow buttons or entering a new value in the boxes. Click Hide Adjust Margins when you're done.

WORKAROUND WORKSHOP

Fitting Reports on Paper

When your report has tons of columns, it's hard to squeeze it onto a single page of paper. Quicken automatically prints the columns that don't fit on additional pages, but trying to read multipage reports leads to paper rustling, grumbling, and ghastly taping accidents. Try these tricks for keeping your report on one page:

- Before you click Print, reduce the width of the report's columns. In the report window, drag the double vertical lines between column headings to the right to make columns narrower. Also, remove any columns you don't want (see page 452).

- In the Print dialog box, select the "Fit to" option, and enter *1* in both the "page(s) wide by" and "pages tall" text boxes.

- In the Print dialog box, choose Landscape page orientation. If the report *almost* fits on an 8.5" x 11" sheet of paper, switching to landscape orientation should do the trick.

Before you print, take a look at the preview on the dialog box's right-hand side to review your changes before committing them to paper and ink.

Tip: You can also print to PDF format by clicking Print in the report window's toolbar. Then, in the Print dialog box's Printer drop-down list, choose Quicken PDF Printer.

2. **Click Print.**

   The "Save to PDF File" dialog box opens.

3. **Choose a folder and a filename, and then click Save.**

   Quicken creates the PDF file in the folder you specified. Now, you can go ahead and print this puppy just like you would any other file. For example, right-click it in Windows Explorer, and choose "Open with Adobe Reader", and then choose File → Print.

Controlling How Reports Behave

Like other parts of Quicken, reports are willing to follow the guidelines you set. For example, you can set a standard date range you want the program to use unless you tell it otherwise. The following sections explain both your options for both graphs and reports as well as a few controls that only apply to reports.

Settings for Reports and Graphs

To reach Quicken's report preferences, choose Edit → Preferences → Quicken Program. In the Quicken Preferences dialog box's "Select preference type" list, choose "Reports and Graphs". Here are the report and graph preferences you can set, and why you may want to adjust them:

- **Default date range.** Quicken sets this box to "Year to date" unless you change it. In this drop-down menu, choose the time period that you use most often in reports, like "Year to date" or "Current month". Once you do that, Quicken will automatically use this date range for reports. (You can always change the date range for a specific report in its report window.)

- **Default comparison date range.** For reports that compare two periods, such as the "Has my spending changed in this category?" EasyAnswer report, choose the comparison date range you use most often. (Out of the box, this field is set to "Prior year period".) For example, set this preference to "Prior year period" to compare the date range for the report to the same period the previous year, as shown in Figure 14-8. If you set the "Default date range" to "Monthly", then you might set the "Default comparison date range" preference to "Last month".

Note: When you choose default date ranges, Quicken shows what the date ranges would be based on today's date. For example, on January 16, 2009, a default date range of "Month to date" would be January 1, 2009 to January 16, 2009.

The "Customizing reports and graphs" section has three settings:

- Quicken automatically selects the "Customizing creates new report or graph" option, which means that Quicken adds the original report you ran to the report history (page 449) when you make any changes to that report. (In a report window, click History to see a drop-down menu of reports you've run.) This option then adds each modification of the report or graph to the report history, so you can go back and re-run any version you want.

- Choose the "Customizing modifies current report or graph" option if you want only one version of the report or graph in your report history. (Because the report history stays tucked away unless you want to use it, there's little reason to choose this option.) As long as you don't save the modified report, the original is available the next time you choose it from the Reports menu.

- "Customize report/graph before creating". If you tweak every report you produce, turn on this checkbox to automatically open the Customize dialog box when you choose a report from the Reports menu.

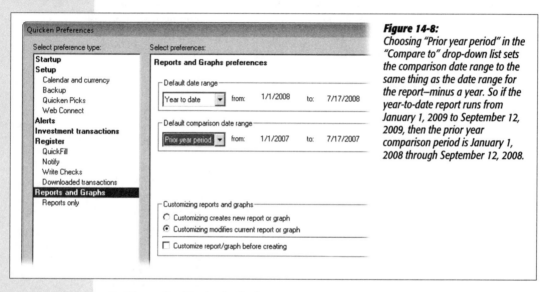

Figure 14-8:
Choosing "Prior year period" in the "Compare to" drop-down list sets the comparison date range to the same thing as the date range for the report—minus a year. So if the year-to-date report runs from January 1, 2009 to September 12, 2009, then the prior year comparison period is January 1, 2008 through September 12, 2008.

Settings for Reports Only

The Quicken Preferences dialog box has a few settings that apply only to reports. To see them, in the dialog box's left-hand "Select preference type" list, click "Reports only". These preferences control things like what reports look like, and are mostly innocuous:

- **Account display.** Quicken automatically selects the most concise option: displaying only account names in reports. Select the Description option to see account descriptions instead, or, to be completely sure which accounts you're looking at, select the Both option.

- **Category display.** Likewise, Quicken starts out showing category names, but you can change this preference to show category descriptions or both names and descriptions.

- **Use color in report.** If you prefer to see reports in black and white, turn off this checkbox. Keeping it turned on shows any shortfalls or investment losses in eye-catching red.

- **QuickZoom to investment forms.** This checkbox is turned on initially, which is what you usually want. With this setting, double-clicking an investment transaction in a report opens the corresponding investment dialog box. For example, double-clicking a dividend reinvestment transaction opens the "Edit Reinvest - Income Reinvested" dialog box filled in with the transaction's values, so you can review the transaction or edit it. If you turn this checkbox off, double-clicking an investment transaction in a report opens the investment account register instead, with the transaction selected. To open the corresponding dialog box, click the Edit button in the transaction's row.

- **Remind me to save reports.** Leave this checkbox turned on if you don't want to lose any new adjustments you make to reports. But if you've customized every report to meet your needs, you probably don't need a reminder to save reports, so turn this checkbox off.

- **Decimal places for prices and shares.** Quicken sets this preference to 3. If you reinvest dividends, you're likely to own infinitesimally small fractions of shares. The best setting for this preference is the number of decimal places for your most exacting financial institution. For example, if your Vanguard IRA reports prices and shares to six decimal places, type 6 in the box.

Customizing Reports

Before you know it, you're probably going to customize your reports. As you can see in Figure 14-9, a report window gives you lots of ways to customize reports, whether you're looking to nudge a column over, tweak the date range, or perform a major overhaul. You don't make your changes right in the report window like you do with a spreadsheet or text document. Instead, you tweak the report's settings in a dialog box, and let Quicken make the changes. It's a bit of a pain, but it gets the job done. Once you've created your masterpiece, you can save it (page 455) and avoid making the same tweaks the next time.

Here's where to find Quicken's report customization tools:

- **Reports & Graphs window.** If you choose Reports → Reports & Graphs Center, then you can make small changes to reports *before* you generate them. In the Reports & Graphs window (Figure 14-5), click a report's name, and then change the settings that appear. To open the Customize dialog box to make widespread changes, click the Customize button. Then click Show Report or Show Graph to generate the customized report or graph.

- **Customize icon.** After you've generated a report, at the right end of the report window's toolbar, click the Customize icon to open Quicken's most powerful customization tool—the Customize dialog box. The rest of this section explains how to use it to tweak reports.

- **Report window drop-down lists.** Below the report window's toolbar, you see drop-down menus for changing settings, such as the date range (and, depending on the report, which column to use for subtotaling the report's contents).

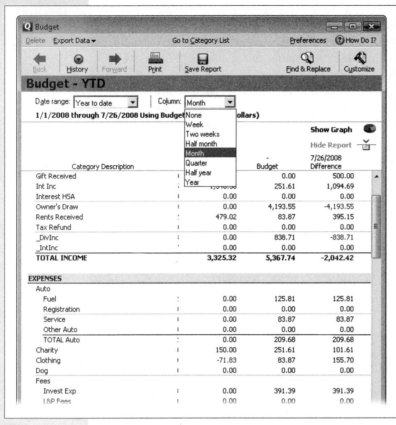

Figure 14-9:
Using a report window's drop-down menus, you can tweak the report by choosing different date ranges or columns. In the upper right corner, click the Customize icon to open a dialog box with even more options (page 452).

- **Report headings.** If a report has double vertical lines between column headings (like the ones in Figure 14-2 on page 435), you can drag them left or right to make a column narrower or wider, respectively.

Note: If Quicken doesn't let you customize a report quite the way you want, see Chapter 17 to learn how to export it to another program for fancy formatting, calculating, and other fine-tuning.

To save a customized report so you can run it later, in the report window's toolbar, click Save Report, and then type a name for the report. Quicken saves the report to the My Saved Reports folder. See page 455 for more on saving reports.

You have almost no control over reports' headers; Quicken automatically includes the report's date range and page numbers in the header. But you *can* change a report's title. Click the report's upper-right Customize icon to open the Customize dialog box. Click the Display tab, and then, in the Title text box, type your new title.

Fortunately, modifying a report doesn't mean you can't look at the original version. Quicken saves copies of every report that's run in a particular report window— including QuickZoom reports—in that window's *report history*. You can jump back to any report in the history, as shown in Figure 14-10.

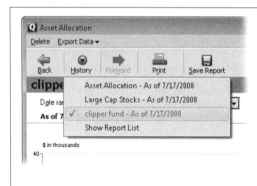

Figure 14-10:
When you click the round History icon, the drop-down menu lists the original report, along with edited and QuickZoom reports you ran in that report window. (If you have another report window open, it has its own history.) You can choose any report in the drop-down menu to view it, or click Back or Forward to move from report to report. The titles you see below the report window's toolbar tell you what each report shows, like the initial Asset Allocation report, the Large Cap Stocks QuickZoom report created by double-clicking the Large Cap slice of the Asset Allocation pie chart, and finally the QuickZoom report of the "clipper fund" mutual fund from your Security List (page 342).

Date Ranges

Different reports call for different date ranges. For example, tax reports often apply to the previous year, whereas a spending report might be for the current year to date. Because date ranges are the report settings you're most likely to change, Quicken gives you several places to set them:

- In the Reports & Graphs window, click a report's name to display a "Date range" drop-down menu.

- In a report window, below the report's title, you see a "Date range" drop-down menu.

- In the Customize dialog box, the "Date range" drop-down menu is at the very top of the dialog box.

Quicken has more than a dozen preset date ranges that are based on today's date. For example, if it's September 12, 2009, "Year to date" represents January 1 through September 12, 2009, and "Last month" covers August 1 through August 31, 2009. The "Date range" drop-down menus let you choose from several types of ranges:

- **Include all dates.** If you're trying to find a payee by searching through old credit card charges, choose "Include all dates". This period includes everything from the first date in your Quicken data file all the way up to and including today. (If you used the Copy command to remove older transactions—see page 479— "Include all dates" still goes back to the earliest date in the data file, but that's no longer the first date you started using Quicken.)

- **Durations.** Quicken includes three repeating periods: Monthly, Quarterly, and Yearly. If you choose one of these, then Quicken runs the report for the current month, quarter, or year, and displays an additional drop-down menu to specify which month, quarter, or year you want to see.

- **To-date durations.** You can choose from "Month to date", "Quarter to date", and "Year to date", which are particularly useful for budget-vs.-actual reports. "Earliest to date" is the same as "Include all dates". "Custom to date" lets you pick the starting date, and the report covers that date to today, which is perfect for things like reporting on job expenses since you started your new job.

- **Last periods.** You can choose periods from "Last month" to "Last 12 months". At tax time, "Last year" can come in handy, because it shows you the previous year's data.

- **Prior year period.** When you run a report that compares two periods, The "Compare to" drop-down list contains this additional choice. When you select "Prior year period", Quicken compares the first date range to the same date range in the previous year. For example, if you run a report on October 12, 2009 and the "Date range" is set to "Last month", the date range for the report is September 1, 2009 through September 30, 2009. The prior year period is September 1, 2008 through September 30, 2008.

If none of these date ranges are what you want, select "Custom dates" to open the Custom Date dialog box, where you can choose your own "from" and "to" dates.

Tip: Try to avoid *saving* reports that use custom dates. These dates don't change with the passage of time—and eventually you won't care how much you spent on tie-dye T-shirts in 1968. If you do save a report with custom dates, then you have to edit the dates every time you run it, which quickly grows tedious. The best solution is to choose one of the built-in date ranges, and then resave the report.

Subtotals

You can group and subtotal report results in several ways, depending on the report. For example, you might subtotal the Investment Performance report by account to see whether your stock picks are doing better than your 401(k) investments. Or, you can subtotal by security type, investing goal, or asset class to see which kinds of investments are living up to your expectations.

Note: Some reports, like Account Balances, have built-in subtotaling that you can't change. The Account Balances report subtotals your accounts by their use (Bank accounts, Asset accounts, and so on). The "Subtotal by" box simply doesn't appear in the report windows for these reports.

You can change your report's subtotal fields in two places:

- In the report's window, underneath the report's title, the "Subtotal by" drop-down menu offers several options specific to that report.

• In the Customize dialog box (which you open by clicking the report window's upper-right Customize button), click the Display tab. In the Headings section, look for the "Subtotal by" drop-down menu.

Figure 14-11 shows an example of how subtotaling can convey the information you need.

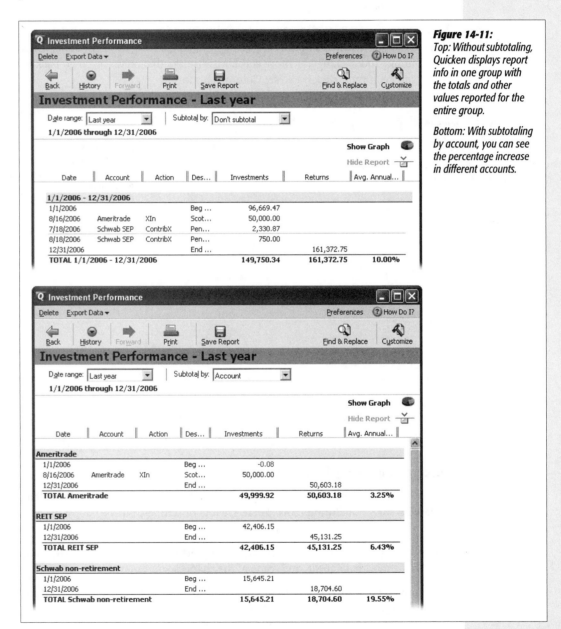

Figure 14-11:
Top: Without subtotaling, Quicken displays report info in one group with the totals and other values reported for the entire group.

Bottom: With subtotaling by account, you can see the percentage increase in different accounts.

Adding and Removing Columns

Each built-in report comes with a specific set of columns, all of which are initially displayed. In some reports, you can't change the columns at all, but in others you can choose which of the columns to hide or show. If the columns in a report are under your control, in the Customize dialog box, the Display tab includes a Show Columns section.

As you can see in Figure 14-12, on the right side of the Customize dialog box, checkmarks show which columns are visible. Clicking a turned-on checkbox hides that column, and clicking an empty checkbox displays that column. To go back to the original columns, click the Reset Columns button.

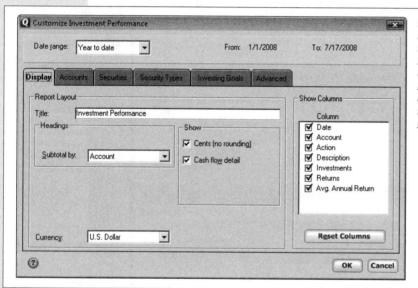

Figure 14-12:
In some reports, you can turn columns on or off by clicking their checkboxes. If you can't modify a report's columns, you don't see the Show Columns section.

Tip: On the Customize dialog box's Display tab, turn off the Cents checkbox to see amounts rounded to whole dollars.

Customizing Other Report Content

As you can see in Figure 14-13, the Customize dialog box includes several tabs that contain all sorts of tailoring tools. There are lots of settings, but you don't have to tweak all of them.

The settings you see depend on the type of report you're customizing. Here are some of the tabs that appear, and some of the changes you can make on each:

• **Accounts.** Choosing which accounts to include in a report helps you produce more targeted reports, like one that shows your retirement accounts separate from your spouse's. Turn accounts on and off by clicking them one at a time or by clicking Mark All or Clear All. Quicken hides accounts that you marked as Hidden in the Account List (see page 64). If you want to see info from hidden accounts, turn on the "Show (hidden accounts)" checkbox.

- **Categories.** You can choose individual categories, turn all categories on or off, or search for a specific category. You can also add additional criteria to look for transactions assigned to a specific payee, or ones that have categories and memos that contain specific text. For example, if you want to report on your income and expenses, you could fill in the "Category contains" box with the text you use to identify your categories (like your initials). If you use memos to identify those expenses, in the "Memo contains" box, you could type *Ski-Doo* to find all the payments you've made for your snowmobile.

- **Payees.** On this tab, you can turn payees on or off, and specify a category to report on, text in the payee name, or text in the Memo field.

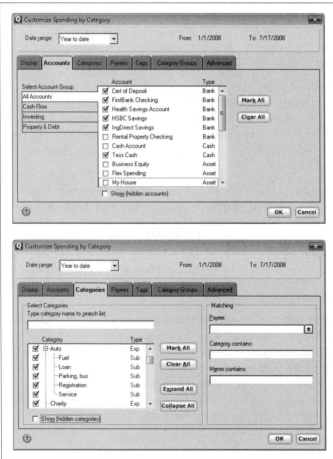

Figure 14-13:
Top: You'll probably want to choose which accounts to include in your reports. You can turn individual accounts on and off, or turn them all on or off with the Mark All and Clear All buttons, respectively.

Bottom: By picking specific categories, you can pinpoint trouble spots in your spending or find transactions.

- **Tags.** If you use tags, you can build reports that include specific tags (page 70), and specify a payee, text in the tag name, or text in the memo field.

- **Category Groups.** If you want to report on your finances at a very high level, you can choose the category groups (page 70) to include. For example, if you want a report of your bare-bones expenses, turn off all category groups except Mandatory Expenses.

- **Securities, Security Types, Investing Goals, and Actions.** If you run an Investment or Net Worth report, you may see tabs for Securities, Security Types, Investing Goals, and Actions. Select a tab and then choose the info you want to include. For example, to see all your transactions for a specific security, on the Securities tab, turn on that security's checkbox. Or, to limit a report to investments you made to pay your kid's college education, on the Investing Goals tab, turn off all the checkboxes except College Fund.

- **Advanced.** The Advanced tab is, well, advanced, but some of the settings come in handy more often than you'd expect. For example, if you want to look for uncleared transactions, turn off the "Newly cleared" and Reconciled checkboxes, but keep the "Not cleared" checkbox turned on. To change any report to a tax-related report, turn on the "Tax-related transactions only" checkbox.

The "Include unrealized gains" checkbox is good for what-if games with tax- or investment-related reports. (It appears on the Advanced tab only if it applies to a report.) Suppose you want to see how your taxes would be affected if you sold different stocks in your taxable investment account. Turning on this checkbox would show the capital gains you'd have if you sold stocks at their current prices.

The Transfers drop-down menu lets you choose whether to include transfers. The standard setting—"Exclude internal"—is ideal when you don't want to see transfers between accounts. For instance, if you just want to see income and expenses, leave this setting turned on so you don't see transfers between checking and savings, which are neither income nor expenses. If you use subcategories, you can create a high-level report by choosing "Hide all" in the Subcategories drop-down list.

Note: The "Show me change alerts for this report" checkbox is turned on automatically. With this setting, Quicken warns you when you try to run a saved report after you've created new categories, tags, accounts, or securities that may apply to the report. For example, if you've added categories since you customized your budget report, the saved report doesn't include the new categories. When you see the warning, you can run the report as is by choosing the "View the report as I saved it" option, and then clicking OK. To update the report settings, choose the "Go to the customize dialog box so I can add these items" option, and then click OK. Then, after you update the report settings, resave the report.

Sorting Reports

Quicken automatically sorts some reports, but the sort order isn't always obvious. Some reports let you choose your own sort order. If a report is sortable, the report window's menu bar includes the Sort command. Sort orders for reports are similar to the sort orders you can apply to an account register (page 92). The "Sort by" drop-down menu includes Account/Date, Date/Account, Account/Check#, Amount, Payee, Category, and Tag.

To change the sort order of a report, follow these steps:

1. **In the report's window, choose Sort.**

   A drop-down menu of sort options appears, with a checkmark next to the current sort order.

2. **Choose the sort order you want.**

   Quicken immediately sorts the report in that order.

You can also change the sort order by clicking Customize in the report's window, clicking the Customize dialog box's Display tab, and choosing from the "Sort by" drop-down menu.

Saving and Reusing Reports

Once you've customized a report, you can save it. You'll see the report in the Reports & Graphs window's My Saved Reports category as well as on the My Saved Reports & Graphs menu (page 440). If you're a prolific report-creator, you can create folders to organize your reports, like a Retirement folder for reports about your retirement savings or an Income & Expense folder for your budget and spending reports.

Later on, you can run a saved report again simply by choosing Reports → My Saved Reports & Graphs, and then picking the report's name (or the folder and then the report's name).

Note: If you modify one of Quicken's built-in reports, and then save it, the program doesn't overwrite the built-in report. It saves your customized report to "My Saved Reports & Graphs".

When you save a report, Quicken memorizes all your settings—like date range, accounts, categories, sort order, and so on—but not the data itself. For example, if you save a report whose date range is Monthly, the report shows info for June when you run it in June, and info for December when you run it in December.

Saving a report is easy:

1. **Run the report, and review it to make sure it has the info and formatting you want. Then, in the report window's toolbar, click Save Report.**

   Quicken opens the Save Report dialog box, shown in Figure 14-14.

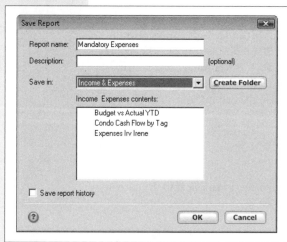

Figure 14-14:
Quicken sorts your saved reports alphabetically. To make sure your favorite reports are at the top of the customized reports list, put a letter A or two at the beginning of their names.

2. In the "Report name" box, type a name that conveys what the report does, like *Warrens Portfolio Performance.*

   If you plan to add the saved report to the Quicken Tool Bar (see page 505), make the name as brief and as meaningful as possible. The Description box accepts only 21 characters max, so it doesn't help you add much more info about the report.

3. **If you want to save the report to a certain folder, in the "Save in" drop-down menu, choose the folder you want.**

   If you're new to Quicken, you won't see any folders to choose from, but you can create your own by clicking the Create Folder button. If you don't choose a folder, the report shows up on the My Saved Reports & Graphs submenu below any folders you've created.

4. **Click OK to save the report.**

   If you notice later that you missed a setting, you can make the change, and then save the report again. If you go to save it with the same name, Quicken asks you to confirm that you want to replace the existing saved report.

Managing Customized Reports

You can build reports that do exactly what you want, but they're no help if you can't find 'em. A good naming system is the first step, but some organization goes a long way. In the Reports & Graphs Center, you can categorize, edit, or delete customized reports, and add reports to Quicken's Tool Bar for easy access.

Note: Adding your favorite reports, built-in and customized alike, to the Tool Bar means they're one click away at all times. Chapter 15 gives you the full scoop on adding reports—or report folders—to the Tool Bar.

In the Reports & Graphs Center (Reports → Reports & Graphs Center), at the bottom of the My Saved Reports pane, click Manage Saved Reports to open the Manage Saved Reports dialog box. Here's what it lets you do:

- **Create folder.** Folders make it easy to find the reports you want. For example, a Financial Status folder could hold reports that show your net worth or investment performance. A separate Income & Expenses folder could hold reports for your budget and targeted spending. And reports that you use to prepare your taxes could be in a Taxes folder. To make a folder, click "Create folder". In the "Create new report folder" dialog box, type a name for the folder, and then click OK.

Note: You don't have to save reports in folders. For example, you might want the graph that shows the meteoric rise in your savings to be on its own outside of any folder. In that case, simply don't select a folder when you save the graph (page 455).

- **Move to folder.** If you decide to reorganize your saved reports or you saved dozens of reports in a pre-folder version of Quicken (2005 or earlier), use the "Move to folder" command to reorganize them. Select the report you want to move, and then click "Move to folder". In the "Move to Report Folder" dialog box, shown in Figure 14-15, choose the report's new home, and then click OK.

Figure 14-15:
To delete a folder, you first have to remove all the reports stored in it. You can either delete the reports you don't use anymore, or move them to another folder.

- **Rename folder.** If you click a folder's name (the entries with a right or down arrow to the left of them), the "Rename folder" button comes to life. Click it, type the new name, and then click OK.

- **Edit.** This button doesn't do much. You can only edit a report's name and description. (To modify a report in other ways, run the report, and then click the Customize button. After you make the changes you want, resave the report.)

- **Delete.** Select a folder or report, and then click Delete, and it's history.

Part Four:
Quicken Power Tools

4

Backing Up and Protecting Your Quicken Data

Quicken makes tracking your finances easy. But all the convenient features in the world don't matter if you lose your data to a hard-drive crash or, worse, a thief. Quicken's ready to help. With a good backup routine, you can get back to work quickly. Passwords are the other half of keeping your data secure. If someone steals your computer *and* your data file, your money at the bank could soon follow. This chapter shows you how to implement both safeguards.

One more thing: Quicken data files, like houseplants, do better with proper care and feeding. As time passes and your Quicken skills blossom, your data files contain more transactions and financial information. Slogging through all that info slows Quicken down. You can help by buying a PC with a blazing-fast processor and ginormous hard drive—or by keeping your Quicken data file in neat, trimmed-down condition.

In fact, even if you have a computer that's the envy of your geek support group, there are plenty of good reasons to regularly maintain and archive your data file. For example, archiving your data file as of December 31 of each year lets you keep a copy of your file as it was when you prepared your tax return, which can be a huge help (if small comfort) in an IRS audit. (See the box on page 465 for more advice.) Or you can make a copy of your data file before you make significant (or experimental) changes to it.

Quicken provides several tools for protecting and cleaning up your data files. This chapter explains the subtle differences between each method—and the best times to use each one.

Backing Up and Restoring Data Files

Backing up your data file isn't the same as saving it. As you work on a data file, Quicken simply makes changes to the data file, so all you have saved is the current version of the file. When you back up, you save a copy of your data file in a different location (whether on the same computer or somewhere else, like on a CD). That way, if something happens to your saved copy, you can restore one of your backups instead.

Quicken gives you several ways to back up. But you may already back up *all* the information on your PC. If you're using, say, Windows Backup, then Quicken backups may seem pointless, given that your Quicken data is already getting backed up on a regular basis with all your other files.

Quicken backups are still useful, because they give you an extra layer of flexibility and protection. Suppose you're about to experiment with a Quicken feature, like downloading transactions or archiving your data; there's no sense backing up *everything* on your computer. You can back up only your Quicken data by running a Quicken *manual backup* (explained next). Then, if you don't like how the experiment goes, you can restore your data file from the backup. A Quicken backup is also a good idea if you've spent several hours getting your accounts, categories, and preferences just the way you want them, but your next Windows backup won't happen until 3:00 a.m. tomorrow. Just run a manual backup and sleep like a baby.

UP TO SPEED

Why Back Up?

You're probably reading this chapter so you'll be prepared if your PC's hard drive crashes. But keep in mind these other situations when backup files can be a real lifesaver:

- You delete your Quicken data file by mistake.

- You've assigned a password to your data file and now even *you* can't open it.

- Your data file won't open after being damaged by a power outage or power surge.

You can also use backups to easily move a Quicken data file from one computer to another if, say, you want to put it on your laptop before leaving on a business trip. Back up the data file on the first computer, copy the backup file to the second computer, and restore the backup file there.

Manual Backups

If you just spent several hours creating transactions, setting preferences, activating your bank accounts for online services, and customizing Quicken investment reports, you'll want to back up your data file right away. Manual backups are a great way to preserve all your hard work. Backing up to *removable media* (like CD, DVD, Zip disk, and so on) is a good option, since you can take the media out of your computer and store it somewhere else for safekeeping.

Here's what you do:

1. **Open the Quicken Backup dialog box (Figure 15-1) by choosing File → Backup or by pressing Ctrl+B.**

   At the top is the name of the data file you're backing up (*MyMoney09.QDF*, in the figure). The "Select the disk drive and path to the backup folder" box shows where Quicken will store your backup. Regardless which folder Quicken chooses, it's a good idea to create a dedicated folder for your Quicken backups and use it as described in the next step.

   The first time you back up your data file, Quicken automatically sets the backup location. If your computer has a floppy drive (A:), that's what Quicken picks. Even if you still have floppy disks, change this setting. In addition to holding only miniscule amounts of data, floppy disks tend to deteriorate over time, so you could lose your backup.

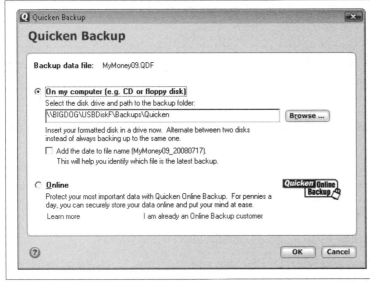

Figure 15-1:
You can also back up online. In the Quicken Backup dialog box, select the Online option if you want to pay Intuit to handle backing up and storing your data file via the Internet, as described in the box on page 469.

2. **To save the backup to a folder somewhere on your network (if you have one) or removable media, click Browse. In the Browse For Folder dialog box, choose the location you want, and then click OK.**

   Quicken will use this location every time you back up that file from now on (until you change it).

   If you want to store your backups in a folder that doesn't yet exist, in the Browse For Folder dialog box, click Make New Folder. A new folder appears in the folder list with its name selected so you can name it.

The only time you should save a backup to the same disk as the original file is when you're experimenting with Quicken's features, or saving your work until your computer-wide backup happens. (In other words, don't save the backup to your computer's main hard drive—usually called *C:.*) If that drive crashes, you lose the original *and* the backup. The rest of the time, your safest bet is to save the backup to a different disk drive, a CD, or other removable media to protect your data from hardware failure—and human error.

Tip: For the ultimate in backup protection, save your backups to several removable media (save to a different one each time) and store one of your backups offsite. For example, take a backup CD to your bank, and keep it in your safe deposit box. Then, if your house burns down, melting your computer *and* your removable media, you'll still be able to retrieve your electronic financial records.

---

3. **Turn on the "Add the date to file name" checkbox.**

   This setting lets you easily identify your last backup. For example, if you back up your *MyMoney09.qdf* file on September 10, 2009, the backup filename becomes *MyMoney09_20090910.qdf.*

   And there's another benefit to this setting: Because adding the date to the filename gives each backup a unique name, turning on this setting means that every backup creates a completely new set of files. (If you turn this checkbox off, each manual backup you perform uses the same filename, so it overwrites the previous one.) But all these backup files take up space, so if you back up to removable media with limited storage space (like CDs), keep a good supply on hand.

   The only downside to adding a date stamp to backup filenames is that your backup files multiply faster than fruit flies. So if you decide to date-stamp backup files, open your backup folder in Windows Explorer every so often and delete older backup files you no longer need.

4. **If you're backing up to removable media, insert it into your PC.**

   You can buy read-write DVDs (they cost less than $2 each and hold 4.7 gigabytes of storage, the equivalent of 500 Quicken data file backups). Or, for less than $20, you can buy a 2- or 4-gigabyte USB thumb drive (aka flash drive)—a nifty little storage stick that plugs into your computer.

5. **To begin the manual backup, click OK.**

   What happens next depends on your backup settings. If you turned on the "Add date to file name" checkbox, Quicken most likely displays a message telling you that your data has been backed up successfully. Click OK to close the message box and the Quicken Backup dialog box.

   If you selected your CD or DVD drive, you see a message that the backup is in progress. After Quicken finishes burning the backup to the CD or DVD, it opens a window that shows the files on the CD, as you can see in Figure 15-2.

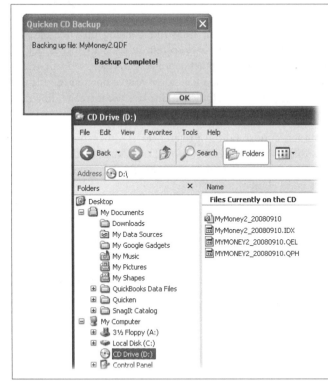

Quicken CD Backup

Backing up file: MyMoney2.QDF

Backup Complete!

OK

CD Drive (D:)

File   Edit   View   Favorites   Tools   Help

Back ▾   Search   Folders

Address D:\

Folders   ×   Name

Files Currently on the CD

Desktop
  My Documents
    Downloads   MyMoney2_20080910
    My Data Sources   MyMoney2_20080910.IDX
    My Google Gadgets   MYMONEY2_20080910.QEL
    My Music   MYMONEY2_20080910.QPH
    My Pictures
    My Shapes
    QuickBooks Data Files
    Quicken
    SnagIt Catalog
  My Computer
    3½ Floppy (A:)
    Local Disk (C:)
    CD Drive (D:)
    Control Panel

Figure 15-2:
*After you confirm that the backup files are on
the CD (like the MyMoney_20080910.qdf
filename you chose in step 3), close the CD drive
window. In the Quicken CD Backup message
box, click OK.*

If you've already created a backup file with the same name, Quicken asks if you
want to overwrite that file. Click Yes only if you are *absolutely* sure you don't
need the previous backup. To keep your previous backups, click Cancel. Then,
open the Quicken Backup dialog box again, and either type a new name for the
file, turn on the "Add date to file name" checkbox, or choose a different folder
for your backup.

FREQUENTLY ASKED QUESTION

When to Back Up

How often should I back up my data?

Good question. The answer is, "It depends." You should
back up whenever you wouldn't want to recreate the data
you'd lose if something happened (power outage, earth-
quake, alien invasion). If you hammer out tons of transactions each day, backing up daily is a great idea. And if
you've successfully completed a particularly gnarly Quicken
task, a midday backup couldn't hurt.

On the other hand, if you pay a few bills each month and
use your PC as a Post-it holder the rest of the time, a

monthly backup could do the trick. Of course, that monthly
backup may mean you back up your Quicken file every
time you use the program—which isn't a bad idea.

If you aren't sure which data you need to back up and how
often you should back it up, check out *Windows XP Home
Edition: The Missing Manual* or *Windows Vista: The Missing Manual* to learn how to use your operating system to
back up your data.

Backup Reminders

If you have trouble remembering important tasks like backing up your data or picking your kids up from school, Quicken backup reminders help ensure that at least *one* of your to-dos gets done. You can set a preference (page 491) that tells Quicken to remind you to back up your data file. After you've opened the file the number of times you set in the preference, Quicken displays the message shown in Figure 15-3 when you go to close the file.

To set up a backup reminder, choose Edit → Preferences → Quicken Program. In the Quicken Preferences dialog box, under Setup, click Backup. In the "Remind after running Quicken _ times" box, type the number of Quicken launches between reminders (3 is a good choice).

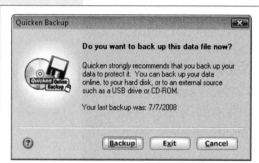

Figure 15-3:
To back up when you see this reminder, click Backup to open the Quicken Backup dialog box, and then just follow the instructions on page 463. If you didn't make many changes to the file, click Exit to close Quicken without backing up the file. And if you want to keep working in Quicken, click Cancel.

Automatic Backups

It's a horror story that happens in home offices every day: You try to open your data file, and Quicken begins to cough and wheeze (in its own computerized way). You grow nervous as you try to remember the last time you backed up your Quicken data—and then you remember that you never have! Don't panic: Quicken actually does some backing up behind the scenes, and restoring one of those files may get your data back. Automatic backups are still backup files, so you restore them like any other backup file (page 468).

Quicken's *automatic backup* feature creates a copy of your data file about once a week, and kicks in when you finish working with a data file: when you close the program by choosing File → Exit, open another data file, close the Quicken window, and so on. These copies are separate from backups you create manually or via a Quicken reminder. For example, if your data file is named *MyMoney* and you peek in Quicken's automatic backup folder, you'll see files like the ones in Figure 15-4.

Note: If you attach images to transactions (page 114), automatic backups have one big drawback: They don't back up your attached images. But manual backups and the ones Quicken reminds you about *do* back up attached images. So, to make sure that you're backing up your data file *and* your attached images, back up your data file regularly using Quicken backup, Windows backup, or some other backup program.

Out of the box, Quicken creates five automatic backup files, like *MyMoney1* through *MyMoney5,* in a special backup folder. In Windows Vista, Quicken creates a Backup subfolder in the *Documents\Quicken* folder. In Windows XP, the Backup subfolder is within *My Documents\Quicken.* Here's what Quicken does when it creates an automatic backup of a data file called *MyMoney:*

- Quicken renames all the *MyMoney4* files so they become *MyMoney5* files (including the .qdf, .idx, .qel, and .qph file extensions).

- *MyMoney3* files become *MyMoney4* files.

- *MyMoney2* files become *MyMoney3* files.

- *MyMoney1* files become *MyMoney2* files.

- And, finally, Quicken creates a copy of the current *MyMoney* files, and then names them *MyMoney1.* The cycle is complete until the next week.

Quicken includes a backup preference, "Maximum number of backup copies", so you can set the number of these automatic backups you want to keep (see page 491). You can keep up to nine, but if you'd rather conserve disk space, you can choose a number as low as one. If you have to restore your data file, start with the file with *1* in its name (the most recent). If that file doesn't get back the data you want, try restoring the next most recent file (the one with *2* in its name), and so on.

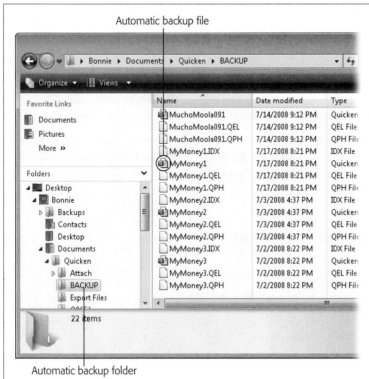

Automatic backup file

Automatic backup folder

Figure 15-4:
Automatic backup files add a single digit to the name of your Quicken data file, such as MyMoney1 and MyMoney2 in the figure. Don't let this window scare you. You can restore a backup file without ever opening this window by choosing File → Restore Backup File. The window shows several files with the same filename prefix (Money1 for example), because each Quicken data file is really several files with different extensions. However, the one that matters has Quicken QDF Data File in the Type column and the Quicken icon to the left of the filename (that's your data file, circled here). You can ignore the other files, because Quicken creates new ones if it doesn't find them (page 18).

TROUBLESHOOTING MOMENT

It's Always the Quiet Ones...

Hard disk crashes used to be dramatic events accompanied by impressive grinding noises. Hard disks today are smaller and run quietly—maybe a little *too* quietly. Even a massive hard drive crash can sneak up on you before you have time to back up.

If you hear your computer make *any* odd sounds—little chirps or squeaks, for instance—stop what you're doing and quickly back up your key files and any that you've worked

on recently. It's a good idea to keep a blank CD or a USB thumb drive near your computer for just such occasions.

If your computer crashes so badly that it won't reboot, a data recovery company can sometimes collect some of your data, but it'll cost you plenty. Backing up regularly is the best way to protect your data—and avoid paying to get it back.

Restoring Quicken Backups

The whole point of backing up your Quicken data is so that, after you've survived a hard drive crash, power outage, or natural disaster, you can take one of those backups and turn it into a working data file so you can work on your finances in Quicken again. As long as you follow the rules and restore one of the backup files you've made, it's a fairly simple process. If you *open* a backup file directly instead of restoring it, you dig yourself a deep hole. The box on page 471 explains why and how to pull yourself out.

To restore and start using a backup file, simply launch Quicken and proceed as follows:

Note: If you're restoring a backup file after a hard drive crash, you have to reinstall Windows and Quicken 2009 before you can complete these steps.

---

1. **If you backed up your data to removable media, put the disk containing your backup in the appropriate drive.**

   If you backed up to another hard drive on your computer or on a home network, make sure that you're connected to it. For example, if the backup file is on another desktop computer, connect it to your PC, and then turn on file sharing.

Note: For more about sharing files on different computers, see *Windows XP Home Edition: The Missing Manual* or *Windows Vista: The Missing Manual,* both by David Pogue.

---

2. Choose File → **Restore Backup File.**

   Quicken displays a submenu listing the backup copies you've made recently, as shown in Figure 15-5.

Backing Up Online

The Quicken Backup dialog box (Figure 15-1) includes an Online option. The "Learn more" link is a clue that Intuit charges for this service. If you're a computer whiz and you never miss a backup, you may prefer to keep your data (financial or otherwise) on your PC or removable media.

But online backups have a couple of advantages, particularly if you have a shaky grasp on how computers work. For one thing, you can specify the backup schedule you want. Using that schedule, the service automatically selects, encrypts, and sends your files to Intuit's data center, where certified geeks who live, eat, and breathe effective backup procedures protect your data from human error, computer problems, fire, theft, and so on.

The standard Online Backup service ($9.99 a year) covers up to 100 megabytes' worth of data files (a data file with several years of data can run 10 megabytes). If you're willing to pay more, you can sign up for higher levels of backup service. The Premium service ($49.99 a year) backs up any data on your computer up to 1 gigabyte (almost everyone

these days has more than a gigabyte of data). The Ultimate service backs up all your data up to 10 gigabytes for $149.99 a year.

But Quicken's Online Backup service isn't the only game in town. If the benefits of backing up online sound good, look at other services before you make your decision. For example, Carbonite (*www.carbonite.com*), a popular online backup service, offers unlimited storage space for $49.95 a year.

Regardless of your budget, online backup isn't a viable option if you have a dial-up Internet connection—it would take ages to back up even a single data file.

It's up to you to decide whether you want to send your sensitive financial information over the Internet. Quicken encrypts the data before sending it, and the data center has dedicated staff to protect it. But if you're uncomfortable with the whole idea of online backup, don't sign up.

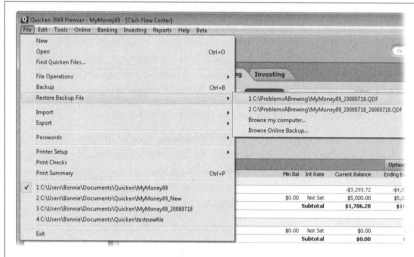

Figure 15-5:
If the backup file you want doesn't appear on the submenu, click "Browse my computer" or Browse Online Backup. In the Restore Quicken File dialog box that appears, Quicken initially opens the folder where you store backups of the current data file. If the backup file isn't in that folder, navigate to the folder or media that contains the backup you want to restore, select its filename, and then click OK.

3. If the backup that you want to restore is listed, click its name. Or choose "Browse my computer" or Browse Online Backup to choose another backup file.

When Quicken restores a backup file, it places the restored file in the same folder as the data file that's currently open. (This behavior can lead to big headaches if you open a data file stored in an unusual location, like a USB thumb drive. The box on page 438 explains how you can fix the problem.)

The restored file has the same name as the backup file it came from. For example, if the current data file is in *Documents\<your name>\Quicken*, the restored data file also appears in that folder. If the file was restored from a backup file named *MyMoney09_20080910*, you'll see *MyMoney09_20080910.QDF* in the *Documents\<your name>\Quicken* folder.

When you see the message that says your data has been restored successfully, you're ready to open the data file.

4. To open the data file, choose File → Open.

The Open Quicken File dialog box displays the folder that contains the current data file, which should also be the folder that contains the backup file you just restored. (The only time you have to navigate to a different folder is if you worked on another data file in between restoring a backup file and opening the restored file.)

5. In the Open Quicken File dialog box, select the restored data file and click OK.

The restored data file opens. If you save backup files with the date stamp in the name, your restored file name still has that date stamp. In that case, choose File → File Operations → Rename. In the Rename Quicken File dialog box, in the "New Name for Quicken File" box, type a new name that identifies it as a restored file. For example, remove the date stamp and add *_Restored* to the end of the filename. Later, when you're satisfied that you're up and running, you can rename the file again to remove the *_Restored* portion of the name.

6. Look the data file over and reenter any missing transactions.

If you entered transactions after your last backup, they won't be in the backup file. Look for things like a gap between the last check number in Quicken and the number on your next paper check, and then reenter any checks in between. Or just wait until you receive your next bank statement, and then add missing transactions as you reconcile your account.

7. Back up your recovered data file onto removable media or a different computer.

See page 462 for how to perform a manual backup.

Finding and recovering your data file gives you a chance to see how well (or poorly) your backup system works. If you think of anything that will make your life easier next time—buying more blank CDs, setting more frequent backup reminders, or using an online backup service—do it *now* before you forget.

The Perils of Opening Backup Files

Unlike most programs, Quicken creates backup files with the same file format (QDF) as regular data files. As a result, in Windows Explorer, backup files look just like regular Quicken data files. But Quicken treats them differently depending on whether you restore them or open them. Never open a backup file directly by double-clicking it in Windows Explorer. If you do that, Quicken obligingly opens the file, but opening a backup file in this way causes all sorts of problems.

First, *opening* a backup file instead of *restoring* it means that you're adding data to a backup file instead of a regular data file. It means that your working data file is now stored in a folder with backup files; this intermingling of data files and backup files is bound to get confusing down the road. And if you open a backup file that's stored somewhere other than your hard drive (for instance, an external drive connected to your laptop), Quicken then opens the file from that location from then on. So if you disconnect that external device, you won't be able to get to your working data file.

To make matters worse, if you open a backup file whose filename includes a date stamp (page 464), your next backup file adds *another* date stamp to the filename. For example, if the backup file you opened has a name like *MyMoney09_20080910.QDF*, the next backup you make becomes something like *MyMoney09_20080910_20081004.QDF*. In no time, you'll have a ginormous, unwieldy filename on your hands. At some point, even Quicken and Windows will tell you that the filename is too long.

Fortunately, the solution is easy: restore your backup file and then open the restored file. And if Quicken is opening a data file from the wrong location, you can move the file out of the oddball folder it's using. The trick is to create a Quicken copy (page 479) of the file and save it in the folder for your regular Quicken data files. (This technique works for moving a restored file out of your backup folder as well as for relocating your data file when you opened it from an unusual location, like a thumb drive or CD. Start with step 5 below to move a data file stored in the wrong place.)

If you've opened a backup file directly, you have to do some fancy Quicken footwork to recover from this quagmire:

1. With the backup file open in Quicken, choose File to find out which folder Quicken will use for the restored file, choose File. At the bottom of the File menu, look for the data file with a checkmark to the left of its name, as shown in Figure 15-5. Write down where the data file lives (in Figure 15-5, it's *C:\Users\Bonnie\Documents\Quicken*). That's where Quicken will restore your backup file.

2. Even though the backup file is open, go ahead and restore it (choose File → Restore Backup File, and then choose the backup's filename).

3. If you see a message about overwriting an existing file, simply click OK. When you see the message that the restore was successful, click OK.

4. Choose File → Open. In the Open Quicken File dialog box, select the restored or misplaced file and click OK.

5. Copy the file and move it to a different folder by choosing File → File Operations → Copy.

6. In the Copy File dialog box that appears, click Browse.

7. In the Copy Quicken File dialog box, navigate to the folder where you store your regular data files (*Documents\<your name>\Quicken*, for example). In the "File name" box, type a new name for the file. For example, if the restored and copied file is *MyMoney09_20080910Cpy*, change it to something like *MyMoney09_Restored*.

8. Click Save. Back in the Copy File dialog box, click OK.

9. In the File Copied Successfully dialog box, select the "New copy" option, and then click OK.

Quicken opens the restored, renamed, and relocated file, and you're ready to rock! Before you do anything else, create a backup of the reconstituted file, taking care to specify the backup folder you want to use (see step 2 on page 463).

Password Protection

You can never be too careful with your financial data. Quicken lets you assign a password to your data file, which you have to type before Quicken opens the file. (This password protects *only* your Quicken data, not everything else on your computer.) So if someone else uses your computer, they can't check out your account balances in Quicken. Considering the importance of your financial data, it's a good idea to set an operating system password (which you enter when you turn on your computer) *and* a Quicken data file password. That way, thieves have two hurdles to overcome before they get to your financial data.

Note: If you don't know how to set an operating system password, on the Windows taskbar, click the Start button, and then choose "Help and Support". In the Search box, type *create a password*.

Adding a Password to a File

If you already use a password to log in and out of Windows, you don't need a separate one for your Quicken data file. As long as you remember to log out of Windows whenever you get up from your computer, your Quicken data is protected along with all your other documents. But a Windows password *and* a Quicken password may deter less persistent crooks (really persistent and geeky ones can probably get in regardless of what you do). A Quicken password protects your data file as soon as you exit the program, so you don't have to remember to log off or shut down your PC.

Here's how to add a password to your Quicken data file:

1. **Open the Quicken data file that you want to protect. Then choose File → Passwords → File.**

   Quicken opens the Quicken File Password dialog box.

2. **In the New Password text box, type the password you want to use.**

   To hide your password from someone peeking over your shoulder, Quicken doesn't display the characters you type—you see asterisks instead. Quicken passwords can be up to 16 characters long and are case-sensitive. For example, *LiZarD980530* isn't the same as *lizard980530*.

3. **To make sure you typed the right combination of numbers, letters, and punctuation, type the password again in the Confirm Password box, as shown in Figure 15-6.**

4. **Click OK.**

   You're done. The next time you open your data file, Quicken opens the Quicken Password dialog box. In the Password box, type your password, and then click OK to access your records.

Figure 15-6:
Don't copy and paste the password from the New Password box to the Confirm Password box. If you made a typo in the New Password box, you won't be able to open your data file.

Changing a File Password

Someday, you might want to change the password on your data file (to one that your ex-husband doesn't know, perhaps). It doesn't hurt to change your password occasionally—every 6 months or so—just to make sure your data is safe. (The hard part is making sure you *remember* your new password; see the box on page 474 for advice.) To change your password, do the following:

1. **Choose File → Passwords → File.**

   The Quicken File Password dialog box appears.

2. **In the Old Password box, type the current password.**

   This is the password you used to open the file, and want to change.

3. **In the New Password box and again in the Confirm Password box, type your new password.**

   When you click OK, your new password is set. Use it the next time you open the file.

Adding a Password to Transactions

If you picked a great password for your Quicken data file, you may wonder why you'd want to add *another* password to some of the transactions in that file. Transaction passwords are a good way to prevent you from accidentally changing a previous year's records. If the IRS is auditing you, the last thing you need is to change or delete one of the transactions under investigation.

A transaction password doesn't stop you from making changes to transactions—you can make changes after you enter the password. The theory is that having to type a password first ensures that you *really* want to make the change.

When you create a transaction password, Quicken asks you to pick a date. The password applies to all transactions *before* that date. For example, once you've

Remembering Passwords

Passwords are double-edged swords: They keep crooks out of your data but, all too often, they keep *you* out as well. You've heard the advice: Create a password, write it down somewhere safe (not on a Post-it on your monitor!)—and then curse when you can't find it.

If you forget your Quicken data file password and need to get at your data, you've got two options. If you recently added the password to your data file, you can restore the last backup you made before you added the password. Your other option is to ask Intuit for help—but it'll cost you $9.95 for each data file and takes about 7 business days.

Keeping track of all the passwords you need nowadays is a challenge. You've probably got passwords for your work computer, your personal email account, and your home computer, among others. On top of all this, each organization has its own rules for passwords, from four digits to more than 12 characters including numbers, upper- and lower-case letters, and punctuation. People have resorted to keeping lists of passwords in all kinds of places: a text file

on your PC, in the address book on a cell phone, or even a paper notebook.

One way to keep track of your passwords yet still protect them from prying eyes is to use a code that's easy for you to remember, but hard for anyone else. For example, you might combine the name of your pet gecko with the digits for the date that you adopted him. You can tweak this combination of data into almost any format you need. For instance, you can capitalize some letters of the gecko's name or replace the number 1 with an exclamation point if you must include punctuation.

Then, wherever you document your passwords, you can use a *description* of the password format rather than the actual characters. For example, "name<punctuation> yyyymmdd" can remind you the password is Guy!20020605. That way, even if someone finds the scrap of paper where you wrote down the description, they won't know your actual password.

added all the transactions for 2008, you can apply a transaction password to all transactions before January 1, 2009. Here's how:

1. **Choose File → Passwords → Transaction.**

   Quicken opens the "Password to Modify Existing Transactions" dialog box.

2. **In the Password box and the Confirm Password box, type the password you want to use.**

   To make your life easier, you can use the same password that you set to protect your data file.

3. **In the Required For Dates Through box, select or type the date you want.**

   You have to enter that password to create, change, or delete any transactions dated *on or before* that date. So to protect the previous year, choose (or type) *12/31/* followed by the year.

4. **Click OK.**

   Once the transaction password is in place, and you create or modify a transaction dated earlier than the transaction password date, the Quicken Password dialog box appears. To complete the process, type the password, and then click OK. (Or, if the change was a mistake, click Cancel.)

Tip: Quicken gives you another way to protect your previous year's data *without* having to remember yet another password: At the end of each year, create a special end-of-the-year backup copy of your Quicken data file as explained next. Name it something like *MyMoney2008_EOY_Backup*.

Archiving and Compacting a File

Five years from now, you won't care how much you spent on that espresso you bought last Wednesday. So every once in a while, it's a good idea to clean up your Quicken data file and delete *really* old transactions you don't need to track anymore. This helps keep your data file to a reasonable size, and your hard drive uncluttered.

Some time after December 31 is a good time to clean up and organize all your Quicken data (see the box below for advice on when to clean), and the Year-End Copy command makes it easy. The command helps you create an *archive copy* (a copy for historical reference rather than data protection like backup copies) of your data file as of a specific date—perfect for freezing your data to show the IRS how you came up with the numbers you reported.

You can also use Year-End Copy to remove older transactions and clean up your data file, shrinking it by a third or more. To do this, you pick a date for the oldest transactions you want to keep. The Year-End Copy command doesn't delete *all* transactions before that date—it hangs on to investment transactions, regardless of how old they are so that you can evaluate your investment performance over time. Quicken also assumes you don't want to delete transactions until you've reconciled them (page 215), so it keeps uncleared transactions, too.

Note: If you don't reconcile regularly, the Copy command (page 479) is a more ruthless way to remove old transactions, because it lets you toss out *uncleared* transactions and investment transactions.

GEM IN THE ROUGH

It's All in the Timing

The Year-End Copy command sounds like a no-brainer: Mark your calendar, and at 11:59 p.m. on December 31, run it. But that may be the *worst* possible time to make a year-end copy. Creating a truly useful year-end archive is all about timing and patience.

You don't want to archive the previous year's transactions until you're done making changes to them. So at least wait until you've reconciled all your accounts through the end of

the year. It's also good to wait for year-end statements and W-2s from your employer, in case you have to adjust your earnings, deductions, or values in your 401(k) account. And you might want to recategorize transactions after you prepare your tax return. Strange as it seems, the best time to create a year-end copy of your Quicken data file could be as late as April.

You open the "Create a Year-End Copy" dialog box, shown in Figure 15-7, by choosing File → File Operations → Year-End Copy. The dialog box has several choices, but they really boil down to two tasks:

- **Create an archive file and leave your data file as is.** Select "Do nothing" if you want to make an archive copy of your data for tax records or so you can see all your transactions through the end of the calendar year. With an archive copy for every year, you can easily tell which file holds your 2008 info. When you choose this option, Quicken leaves your current data file alone, so you can still work on old transactions. But it creates an archive copy of your data file with transactions up to and including the date that you specify in the Archive Data File section (page 477).

- **Create an archive and slim down your data file.** Select "I only want transactions in my current data file starting with this date" to delete old transactions from your current data file. You pick the date, and then Quicken cleans out transactions from *before* that date. The archive data file that Quicken creates contains the transactions *up* to the date you set in the Archive Data File section. If you also want to keep a copy of your data file with *all* transactions intact, back up your data file before archiving.

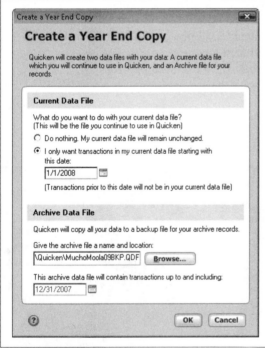

Figure 15-7:
The Year-End Copy command creates an archive copy of your current data file as of a date you pick. You can also tell it to clean out older transactions to shrink your current data file.

Cleaning Up Cash Accounts

Cash accounts don't include a command for reconciling (Chapter 8), because there's no statement to compare your cash spending to. But when you're cleaning up your Quicken data file, you need a way to reconcile old cash transactions, because the Year-End Copy command doesn't remove them otherwise. If you've got several years of cash purchases recorded, the prospect of manually changing the status of each transaction to Reconciled isn't pretty. Luckily, you can solve this problem with the Update Balance command (page 286).

When you update the balance in an account, Quicken marks as reconciled all the transactions earlier than the update date. Suppose you want the Year-End Copy to remove cash transactions up to the end of 2008. You can use the Update Balance command in each cash account (open the cash account register and then click Update Balance in the register's menu bar), and set the date to 12/31/2008. When you do, Quicken changes the value in the Clr field for all the cash transactions through 12/31/2008 to *R*, so you can delete those transactions using the Year-End Copy command.

Here's how you create a year-end copy of your data:

1. **With your data file open, choose File → File Operations → Year-End Copy.**

   Quicken opens the Year-End Copy dialog box, and automatically sets the dates to archive the previous year's transactions and remove them from the current data file. So if it's the middle of 2009, the program sets the "I only want transactions in my current data file starting with this date" to 1/1/2009. At the bottom of the dialog box, the "This archive data file will contain transactions up to and including" box shows 12/31/2008.

2. **In the Current Data File section, choose the option you want.**

   The "Do Nothing" option creates an archive copy, but leaves your current data file alone.

   The "I only want transactions in my current data file starting with this date" option creates a copy *and* cleans up your current data file. In the date box, fill in the earliest date for transactions you want to keep. Although Quicken automatically sets this date to January 1 of the current year (a popular choice because it gives you up to a full calendar year of data), you can change it to whatever date you want. For example, in 2009, if you want to keep up to 2 years' worth of transactions, type *1/1/2008*.

3. **In the Archive Data File section, in the "Give this archive file a name and location" text box, type the path and filename for your archive copy.**

   Quicken automatically chooses the folder that holds your current data file, and adds BKP to the filename. To make it easier to find your archive copy, change the filename prefix. For an archive of the 2008 calendar year, you might change *MyMoneyBKP.QDF* to *MyMoneyArchive08.QDF*.

If you want to store all your archive files in the same folder, click Browse. Then, in the Copy Quicken File dialog box that appears, click Browse Folders and then choose the folder you want. For instance, you might create a subfolder called Archives.

4. **In the "This archive data file will contain transactions up to and including" box, type the latest date for transactions in the archive file.**

To store last year's data, choose 12/31 of the previous calendar year. For example, in 2009, create an archive that includes 2008 by typing *12/31/2008*.

5. **Click OK.**

You'll see a dialog box showing Quicken's progress as it creates the archive copy. How long this takes depends on your computer's speed and free disk space, and the size of your data file. But hang in there; eventually, the File Copied Successfully dialog box appears, as shown in Figure 15-8.

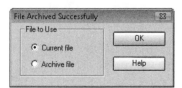

Figure 15-8:
Quicken gives you the "Archive file" option in the final step so you can add a password (see page 472) to the archive file. Archive files are historical records of your finances, and rewriting history isn't a good idea (even if Quicken makes it possible). So if you assign a password to the old file, close it as soon as you're done.

6. **Select the option for the file you want to open, and then click OK.**

Quicken automatically selects the Current File option, so in most cases, you just click OK. The program opens your current data file.

With your data file open—which is now leaner, if you removed old transactions—you're ready to get back to work.

TROUBLESHOOTING MOMENT

When Attachments Don't

If you attach check images and electronic bank statements to transactions and accounts (page 112), your data file can get huge. When you copy a data file that contains attachments like these, Quicken first copies your data, and then copies the attachments *only if* your backup media has enough room for all of the attachments.

If your backup media (CD, Zip disk, floppy disk, or external hard drive) runs out of space, Quicken won't copy any attachments—and won't even tell you that it's not copying them. Quicken *does* tell you if it can't fit a backup file on your backup media, but that doesn't change the fact that your data file isn't backed up. So it's always a good idea to check the available space before you make a backup or archive copy.

Quicken File Maintenance

File maintenance may sound like as much fun as cleaning crumbs out of the toaster, but it's important, and Quicken makes it simple. Your control center is the File Operations menu, where you can do things like copy a data file and tell Quicken which transactions to include, and rename and delete data files more easily than you can using Window's tools. The Validate command gives your data file a checkup and takes care of any problems it finds. This section explains how to use each command, and how to create a brand new data file.

Copying a File

The Copy command creates a new data file based on your current data file (and lets you choose which transactions to keep in the copy) without changing your current data file. If that sounds strikingly like the Year-End Copy command, you're right. But the Copy command can help you in ways that Year-End Copy never dreamed of. Here's what the Copy command can do:

- **Shrink your data file to a more manageable size.** You can create a copy of your data file that contains transactions going back as far as you want. The advantage of Copy over Year-End Copy is that you can tell Quicken not to keep uncleared transactions or old investment transactions (which Year-End Copy automatically keeps). For example, there's no need to keep transactions for mutual funds that you've already sold and paid capital gains tax on.

Tip: With the Copy command, you can't choose which accounts to clean up—it cleans them all—so you may be better off keeping all your investment transactions, including the old ones. For example, if you get rid of investment transactions, you may lose the info you need to figure out your cost basis on some of your investments.

- **Start (almost) from scratch.** With the Copy command, you can create a data file that has your categories, scheduled transactions, memorized payees, and other lists—but no transactions. This is great if you want to create a new data file but don't want to hassle with all the setup, like if you want to create a data file for your parents' finances that uses the same categories you know and love.

- **Create an archive file of any date range you want.** By choosing the starting and ending date for transactions, you can archive your data file between any two dates (like the dates of your marriage and divorce).

Here are the steps for copying a data file:

1. **Open the data file you want to copy, and then choose File → File Operations → Copy.**

   Quicken opens the Copy File dialog box, shown in Figure 15-9, and automatically sets values in all text boxes and checkboxes.

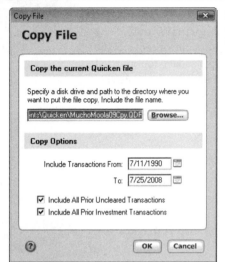

2. **In the "Copy the current Quicken file" text box, change the filename.**

Quicken automatically uses the same folder where the current data file is saved, and names your copy the same thing as the data file with *Cpy* added on. You can name the file whatever you want. If you're using the copy to create a data file for someone else, you might name it *BetsysDataFile*. If you're creating a squeaky-clean data file to use as a template, name it something like *DataFileTemplate.QDF*.

To store the copy in a different folder, click Browse, and then choose the folder.

3. **In the Include Transactions From text box, type the *earliest* date for transactions you want to keep in the file.**

For example, to create a file with a few years of transactions, you might type *1/1/2006*. If you want to create a file with no transactions, type today's date.

4. **In the To text box, type the *latest* date for transactions.**

To create a file that has transactions up to today, leave the date that Quicken filled in. If you want to create an archive up to the end of the previous year, type that date instead.

5. **To remove old uncleared transactions, turn off the Include All Prior Uncleared Transactions checkbox.**

Quicken automatically turns on this checkbox, so that the copy keeps transactions you haven't reconciled. But if you're using the Copy command to get rid of years of unreconciled cash transactions, turn off this checkbox. The program adds adjustment transactions to the accounts in the new data file to keep the balances as of the Include Transactions From date the same, even though the deleted transactions are gone. By doing that, your Quicken accounts still reconcile correctly.

6. **To remove old investment transactions, turn off the Include All Prior Investment Transactions checkbox.**

   Quicken automatically turns on this checkbox, keeping investment transactions regardless of their age. Turn off this checkbox only if you're *certain* you don't need investment transactions.

7. **Click OK.**

   Quicken begins copying your data file. The Quicken File Password dialog box opens.

8. **If you want to protect your file, fill in the New Password and Confirm Password boxes (page 472), and then click OK.**

   If you don't want to add a password, leave the boxes blank and click OK.

   The File Copied Successfully dialog box appears. It's almost identical to the one in Figure 15-8, but your options are "Original File" and "New copy".

9. **Choose the option for the file you want to open, and then click OK.**

   Quicken automatically selects the Original File option, so just click OK to continue using your data file.

   To open the copy you just created instead, choose the "New copy" option, and then click OK.

Tip: In addition to the Copy and Year-End Copy commands, you can also move Quicken data around by exporting it. Although people generally use exporting to transfer Quicken data to another program, you can also export data, one account at a time (as described on page 512), to try to fix a corrupted data file.

Creating a New Data File

If you want a new data file—for your parents' finances, say—you can create a new, blank data file. Here's how:

1. **Choose File → New.**

   The "Creating new file: Are you sure?" dialog box opens. Quicken automatically selects the New Quicken File option.

2. **Click OK.**

   The Create Quicken File dialog box opens.

3. **Select the folder for the file. Type a name in the "File name" box, and then click OK.**

   Quicken creates the new file, opens it, and displays the Setup tab. Now you're ready to start setting up your file. See page 19 for detailed instructions on the setup steps.

Renaming a File

You may not use the Rename command very often, but sometimes it's invaluable. For example, if you went along with Quicken's file naming suggestion and have a data file called *QDATA.QDF*, you can use the Rename command to change its name to something more meaningful, like *MarshaMoney.QDF*.

There are other ways to rename your Quicken data file (by right-clicking it in a Windows Explorer window and, from the shortcut menu, choosing Rename, for example), but the Rename command is the most dependable. Because a Quicken data file is actually a collection of several separate files, the Rename command takes care of renaming all of them. If you rename in Windows, you have to rename each one individually.

Note: If you've already changed the name of your .qdf file using some other method, and just realized that there are several related files that need renaming, too, don't worry. The easiest fix is to change the .qdf file's name back to what it was, and *then* use Quicken's Rename command. This solution is a lot easier than repeating the renaming process for all the other files in the data set.

To rename a file:

1. **Choose File → File Operations → Rename.**

   The Rename Quicken File dialog box opens.

2. **Choose the file you want to rename.**

   Quicken fills in the "File name" text box with the name of the file you pick.

3. **In the "New Name for Quicken File" box, type the new name you want. Click OK.**

   The program changes all of the filenames for you—but it doesn't rename backups or archive files that you've created from that data file.

Validating: Checking and Correcting Your Data File

Once in a great while, Quicken may act strangely. (OK, maybe more often than that.) For example, the numbers in an account register might be way off from what you'd expect. The cause of this weirdness could be a corrupt data file. That's the bad news. The good news is that the Validate command may be able to fix it.

Data files can get corrupted in lots of ways. Perhaps you worked through a thunderstorm and a power spike nibbled a chunk out of your data file, or the place on the disk drive where your data file sits has a tiny bad spot. Your data files could also suffer damage if you turn off your computer without shutting it down or if it crashes.

If categories are missing from transactions, reports don't show what they should, or Quicken behaves oddly, a damaged file could be to blame. That's where the

Validate command comes in. It analyzes your data file, tells you if it finds problems, and, to some extent, fixes problems it finds. To validate a file, follow these steps:

1. **First, make a copy of the file you want to check (page 479), and then choose File → File Operations → Validate.**

   Don't use the Validate command on your original data file. In some cases, Validate removes damaged data from the file, which could cause more problems than it solves.

2. **In the Validate Quicken File dialog box, choose the copy you just created, and then click OK.**

   A progress bar shows you how far along the validation is. If the command finds no problems, it lets you know that validation's complete. You can click OK, open your original data file, and continue working.

   If the validation process finds any problems—which is likely in a data file you've been using for a while—Quicken fixes them, documents the issues and repairs in a text file (called a *log file*), shown in Figure 15-10, and then tells you that it found some problems.

Figure 15-10:
Quicken opens the DATA_LOG.TXT file with Window's Notepad program, but you can open it with any text editing program you want.

3. **If you see the message box that says Quicken found data losses in your file, click Yes to view the log file.**

   Quicken describes the problems it finds in a text file called *DATA_LOG.TXT*, which it stores in the same folder as your data file.

Once Quicken completes its repairs, you can open your data file in any of the usual ways and get back to work. If the data file still acts funny when you open it, it may be time to contact Intuit's technical support. *Don't* delete that log file: The support technician is likely to ask for it to help you fix the problem.

Tip: Using a superpowered Validate command can sometimes help a file that won't validate otherwise. As with the regular Validate command, make a backup or copy of your data file and run the super-Validate on the copy. (If you attach encrypted images in your data file, you have to remove the encryption [page 117] before using the super-Validate command. If you don't, you won't be able to see your attached images in Quicken. If you've *already* run the super-Validate command with encrypted images attached, then you have to delete the encrypted images and reattach them.) To try a super-Validate, hold down the Ctrl and Shift keys while choosing File → File Operations → Validate. Quicken doesn't advertise this feature, because they would prefer that their technical support people walk you through it. However, if you're comfortable with experimenting, you can run the command on your own.

Customizing Quicken

Intuit does its best to make Quicken easy to use, but they can't please everyone. So, if certain things about the program drive you nuts, don't despair: You have lots of ways to customize Quicken so that it looks and acts more the way you want.

Quicken's *preferences* (called *options* in some other programs) are the settings that control how Quicken behaves and what it looks like. You can't control every single aspect of the program, but you can decide things like where the Account Bar appears, what Quicken does when you download transactions, and how often it backs up your data files.

Scattered throughout Quicken are tools that let you control what you see onscreen. The new Setup Center lets you choose the types of personal finance activities that Quicken displays. You can also customize the Account Bar and account registers to show accounts and transactions in different ways. Quicken 2009's My Pages tab is like your personal financial canvas. You can paint customized views of your finances, such as your net worth, your progress toward savings goals, what activities are coming up, and how well your investments are doing. Finally, for fast access to your favorite features, you can customize the Quicken Tool Bar to execute commands and generate reports with a single click.

This chapter teaches you how to make all these tweaks and more. You may not be able to make Quicken do *everything* you want, but some of these adjustments are likely just what you've been looking for.

Setting Preferences

Quicken's preferences let you control various aspects of the program's behavior and appearance. Lots of folks use Quicken for years without changing the preferences—even if they don't like the way the program behaves. In fact, aggravation may spur your first visit to the Quicken Preferences dialog box as you look for a way to stop Quicken from doing something annoying, like giving payees the wrong names.

As you gain experience and your needs change, you may want to adjust your preferences. Power users looking to speed up their Quicken sessions can troll the program's preferences for timesaving shortcuts they never knew existed.

Other chapters in this book include instructions for setting preferences related to the topics they cover. Whether you want to make a small adjustment or wholesale changes to the program's behavior, this section describes all your options. Just follow these steps when you're ready to start tweaking:

1. **To open the Quicken Preferences dialog box (Figure 16-1), choose Edit → Preferences → Quicken Program.**

   When you choose Edit → Preferences, you see two other menu choices: Customize Online Updates and Internet Connection Setup. Customize Online Updates primarily controls how Quicken and Quicken.com play together (page 143). Internet Connection Setup is where you tell Quicken how to go online (page 124).

2. **On the left side of the dialog box, from the "Select preference type" list, select a preference category.**

   The preferences in that category then appear in the "Select preferences" area on the right.

What Quicken Does on Startup

The Startup preferences tell Quicken what to display when you launch the program. By changing the "On startup open to" setting, you can head straight to your favorite financial task or account register every time you launch the program. For example, if you like to review your finances before diving into bookkeeping, you can add a custom view of your finances to My Pages (as described on page 502) and tell Quicken to display that on startup.

To choose a different view, or even a single account, in the "On startup open to" drop-down menu shown in Figure 16-1, choose the Quicken center or account you'd rather see. For example, if you use Quicken only as a checkbook, choose your checking account to start recording transactions, or Banking to see your checking, savings, and credit card accounts.

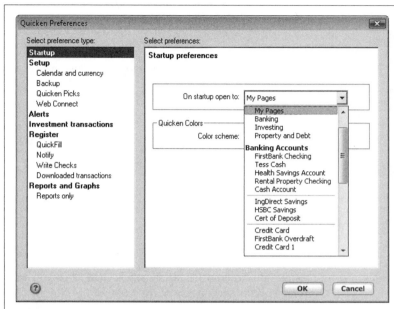

Figure 16-1:
If you have a question about a setting, click the question mark icon at the bottom-left corner of the dialog box. Quicken Help opens to the topic for the preferences you're looking at.

Note: When you create a data file, the program displays the Setup Center (page 19 in Chapter 1). The Overview page in the Setup Center has a Your Quicken section, which lets you choose what you see when you launch Quicken. Turn on checkboxes in the Show column to display the menus and tabs for different financial centers like Bills, Banking, and Investing. When you select an option in the Start On column, Quicken changes the "On startup open to" preference to the corresponding tab.

The other thing you can change here is the color scheme Quicken uses. Quicken's standard color scheme is soothing and unobtrusive, but if you aren't happy unless everything's purple—or green, or tan—you can change the program's background color.

Lights, Sound, Keyboard Action!

The Setup category is home to settings that control where the Account Bar appears, keyboard shortcuts, and sounds, as shown in Figure 16-2. Because confusing keyboard shortcuts and too much noise can drive you nuts, the Setup panel can have a big impact on your satisfaction with Quicken. This section explains all your setup options.

Account Bar and Side Bar display

With the Account Bar, all your Quicken account registers are one click away—and you can always see an overview of your financial situation. In the Account Bar Display section, select the option for the side of the screen you'd rather see the Account Bar on—left or right.

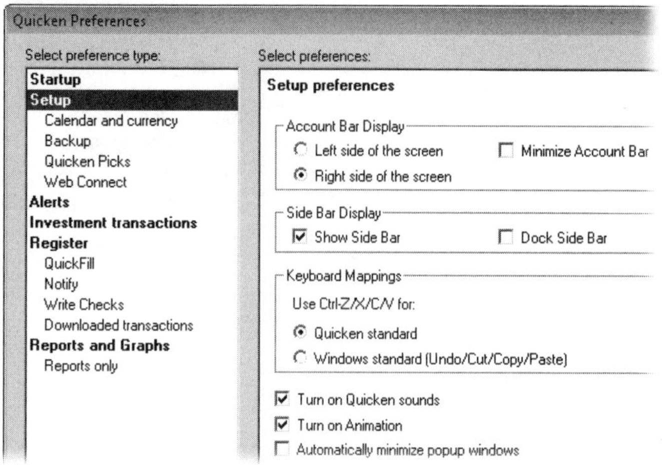

Figure 16-2:
If you can't stand Quicken's beeps, burps, and ka-chings, you're not alone. Simply turn off the "Turn on Quicken sounds" checkbox. Problem solved.

You can minimize and restore the Account Bar with a single click when you want more room in your Quicken window. (At the top of the Account Bar, simply click the – or + sign to the left of the word *Accounts* to minimize or restore it, respectively.) If you want the Account Bar to stay minimized until you want to see it, in the Quicken Preferences dialog box, turn on the Minimize Account Bar checkbox. With this setting, the Account Bar tucks itself away when you start Quicken; you have to click its + sign to display it.

Quicken 2009 sprouts more tabs than your Uncle Ernie grows mutant eyebrow hairs. The Side Bar (page 33) is another new flock of tabs, which, mercifully, you can turn off. If you know what financial tasks are on deck and don't need another way to get help or select tools, turn off the Show Side Bar checkbox. On the other hand, turn on the Show Side Bar and Dock Side Bar checkboxes to keep this panel in view at all times.

Keyboard mappings

If you're a speed demon with Windows programs, you've probably burned Ctrl+Z, Ctrl+X, Ctrl+C, and Ctrl+V into your muscle memory. But undo, cut, copy, and paste don't come up much in Quicken, so the program automatically chooses the "Quicken standard" keyboard mapping option, and assigns different meanings to these keyboard shortcuts, as shown in Table 16-1. If trying to remember two different meanings for the same keyboard shortcut is more than you can bear, choose the "Windows standard (Undo/Cut/Copy/Paste)" option. The far-right column in the table shows how to perform tasks if you switch to Windows standard keyboard mapping.

Tip: Keyboard shortcuts are the fastest way to perform tasks. To learn more Quicken keyboard shortcuts, see Appendix A.

Table 16-1. *Quicken and Windows Keyboard Mappings*

Keyboard Shortcut	Windows Command	What It Does in Quicken	Non-Keyboard Quicken Alternative
Ctrl+Z	Undo	Displays a QuickZoom report	Double-click a report entry
Ctrl+X	Cut	Jumps to the other end of the selected transfer transaction	Right-click the transfer transaction and, on the shortcut menu, choose "Go to matching transfer"
Ctrl+C	Copy	Display Category List	Choose Tools → Category List
Ctrl+V	Paste	Voids active transaction	Right-click the transaction and, on the shortcut menu, choose "Void transaction(s)"

Turning on sounds and animation

If your PC or laptop has speakers, you can't help but notice the odd noises that Quicken makes. If you prefer Brandenburg concertos without Quicken's percussion section chiming in, turn off the "Turn on Quicken sounds" checkbox (Figure 16-2).

Quicken comes with the "Turn on Animation" checkbox turned on. Simply turn the checkbox off if you don't require that level of handholding.

Tip: If you want Quicken's pop-up windows to minimize automatically whenever you click outside their boundaries, turn on the "Automatically minimize popup windows" checkbox. When you use this setting, the names of minimized windows appear along the bottom of the main Quicken window, so you still have to close them when you're done with them. With this checkbox turned off, you have to minimize or close any pop-up windows that appear.

Time and Money

For most people, Quicken's standard calendar and currency settings are just fine. Their year runs from January to December, and they deal only with U.S. dollars. But if your life is more complicated than that, in the "Select preference type" list, choose "Calendar and currency". Then you can tell Quicken to follow your fiscal year, and turn on the program's currency exchange feature. Here are your options:

- **Working calendar.** Quicken chooses the "Calendar year" option automatically. If you want to work with a fiscal year instead (for example, to track a home-based business), choose the "Fiscal year" option, and then pick the month when your fiscal year starts.

Tip: If you use Quicken to track your personal finances and a small business, it's best to create separate data files for your home and business finances. That way, you can set your personal data file to use the calendar year, and the business data file to use the company's fiscal year.

- **Multicurrency support.** If your income is in euros rather than dollars, or you travel the world spending money in dozens of currencies, turn on the "Multicurrency support" checkbox. Then, pick a currency for Quicken to use for all transactions, called your home currency, as the box below explains. With multicurrency support turned on, you can also record a single transaction in a foreign currency (purchases in euros at a Parisian boutique, say). In a transaction, you enter the amount you spent in the foreign currency and then select that currency from the Currency List, as described on page 90. If you have a bank account in another country (for example, where you deposit your paychecks from a Portugese summer job), you can specify a currency for that account when you create it (page 61).

UP TO SPEED

Currency Conversions

Windows Vista and Windows XP both come with Regional and Language Options, which control the language your computer uses as well as number formats, currency, times, and dates. Quicken ignores the rest of these options, but initially sets its *home currency* (the one it uses automatically for all transactions) to match the Windows currency.

To set the currency in Windows, choose Start → Control Panel → "Regional and Language Options", which opens the "Regional and Language Options" dialog box. (Depending on your Windows setup, you may have to choose Start → Settings → Control Panel → "Regional and Language Options", or, for Windows Vista, Start → Control Panel → Classic View → "Regional and Language Options".)

In the "Regional and Language Options" dialog box, click "Customize this format" in Windows Vista (or Customize in Windows XP). When the Customize Regional Options dialog box opens, click the Currency tab. You can set your preferred currency symbol, formatting for positive and negative numbers, decimal-point style, and whether you use a period or comma to separate thousands and millions. Click OK to close all the dialog boxes when you're done.

To specify a Quicken home currency that's different from the Windows currency, first turn on multicurrency support (above). Then, press Ctrl+Q or choose Tools → Currency List. In the Currency List window that appears, click the currency you want as your home currency. In the Currency List window's menu bar, click Home. You'll see a green checkmark in that currency's Home column to indicate that it's the currency Quicken will use automatically unless you tell it otherwise.

Backup Settings

If you use your computer for more than managing money, you probably (er, hopefully) run backup software, like Windows Backup, to protect *all* your data. That one backup procedure can help preserve your scathing letters to the editor, your Quicken data file, and pictures of your gecko.

So why should you care about Quicken's backup preferences? For one thing, your Quicken data file may change more often than your other information. Unless you're disciplined about backing up regularly, Quicken's backups provide extra insurance for your finances. And if you often mutter, "I should really back up my data today," but rarely follow through, Quicken's backup reminders could be just the nudge you need.

Tip: Another reason you might fall to your knees in gratitude for Quicken's backup copies is if you've forgotten the new password you set (page 472). As long as at least *one* of the Quicken backup copies doesn't have the new password assigned, you can open *that* data file, recreate the missing transactions, and you're set. And, oh yeah, be sure to assign a new password that you can *remember*.

Quicken's backup preferences control the program's backup reminders and how many automatic backup copies it keeps (page 466). Here are some guidelines for setting these preferences:

- **Remind after running Quicken _ times.** When you type a number in this box, Quicken reminds you to back up your data file after you've run the program that number of times. (The reminder appears when you tell Quicken to close.) The standard setting is 3, which means you get a backup reminder after three Quicken sessions. If you tend to slog through marathon Quicken sessions, entering dozens of transactions, set the reminder to 1 so you don't lose all your hard work.

   If only one or two transactions dribble in each time you run Quicken, set this preference to 5 or higher. You'll have backups that span a longer timeframe, but you still won't spend much time recreating lost transactions. (You can enter a number as high as 99, but that's not recommended.)

- **Maximum number of copies.** Quicken saves several sets of automatic backups (page 466) on your hard drive, so you can retrieve lost data. Quicken sets this preference to 5—the middle ground between safety and disk space conservation. To recover older files (and if you've got disk space to spare), choose a higher number (up to 9). To use less disk space, choose a number as low as 1. See page 467 to learn where Quicken stores these backups, and how it cycles through the copies.

- **Warn before overwriting old files.** Quicken turns on this checkbox automatically to make sure you don't accidentally overwrite backup files you want to keep. This preference applies to the backups you tell Quicken to make, *not* to the ones it makes automatically. Turn it off if you're satisfied that your Quicken and Windows backup routines are keeping your data safe, and you want Quicken to stop asking.

Note: Quicken Picks is a new feature for saving money. It's Intuit's version of coupon Web sites, such as *www.coupons.com*, that are popping up on the Web. To find Quicken Picks deals, click the far-right Quicken Picks tab in the main Quicken window and sign up for the service. (Read the fine print before signing up to make sure you're comfortable with how Intuit uses your Quicken data to suggest deals.) From then on, click "Take me to Quicken Picks" to open a browser window to the Quicken Picks Web site, where you can click the Categories or Stores tabs to see deals and discounts. If you don't want to use this service, in the Quicken Preferences dialog box's "Select preference type" list, click Quicken Picks and turn off the Enable Quicken Picks checkbox.

Web Connect

If some of your bank accounts use Web Connect to communicate with Quicken (page 126), the Web Connect preferences control how this feature works. If you want to save Web Connect data to a file on your computer, turn on the "Give me the option of saving to a file whenever I download Web Connect data" checkbox. With this setting turned on, you can reload the data into Quicken from that file if something goes wrong. Turning off this checkbox tells Quicken to load Web Connect data directly into your data file.

The program automatically turns on the "Keep Quicken open after Web Connect completes", which means you can keep working once you've downloaded transactions into your data file.

Alerts

The lone preference in this category tells Quicken which Quicken Calendar notes (page 316) you want to see in the list of alerts (page 508). For example, you can change the "Show calendar notes for" preference to "Next 14 days" to see your notes to yourself about what's coming up in the next 2 weeks. Or, if you're at the other end of the dependability spectrum, change it to "Last week" to see tasks you've missed.

Investment Transactions

Investment transaction preferences let you control how your investment register looks onscreen:

- **List display.** In the drop-down menu, choose One Line or Two Line to specify whether Quicken shows each transaction on one line or two in the investment register. Figure 16-3 shows what the One Line version looks like.

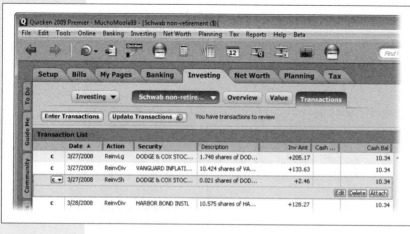

Figure 16-3:
Attention all laptop owners: If you want to conserve screen space, choose One Line, and Quicken shows each transaction on a single line—except the currently selected one, which expands to two lines so that it's easier to see.

- **Sort choice.** In this drop-down menu, you can choose Oldest First or Most Recent First to show your investment transactions from oldest to most recent, or vice versa. If you add new transactions frequently, stick with Oldest First, which Quicken chooses automatically. That way, your new transactions stay in view at the bottom of the list.

- **Show hidden transactions.** Quicken leaves this checkbox turned off, but you can turn it on if you want to see placeholder transactions or balance adjustments. If you notice an error and can't find its cause, turning on this checkbox can help you find the problem.

- **Show Attach button.** Quicken turns this checkbox on initially, so you see an Attach button in every investment transaction. If you attach trade confirmations or other documents to your investment transactions, keep this setting as is. In fact, the Attach button takes up so little room that you don't have much reason to turn it off.

Setting Register Behavior

You're pretty much stuck with the look and feel of your paper check register, but you can change the way the Quicken register looks and behaves. Because entering transactions in registers is such a big part of using Quicken, it pays to set the Register preferences to your liking. Most of these options are a matter of taste, but a few are worth special mention because they have a direct effect on your working speed. Here are the biggies:

- **Register fields.** Quicken displays the date in the first transaction field, but you can change that so the Num field comes first by turning off the "Show Date in first column" checkbox. If you don't plan to use tags (page 70) to categorize transactions, you can see more of the Category field by turning off the "Show Tag field" checkbox.

- **Use automatic categorization.** Quicken turns this preference on initially, with good reason: It tells the program to fill in the category automatically if the payee you type matches a company in the Quicken database. With this setting in place, choosing a category could be the exception rather than the norm. If you don't like Quicken's picks, just turn this checkbox off. You still won't have to assign categories very often after Quicken memorizes your payees.

- **Automatically place decimal point.** This setting can be a huge timesaver—once you get used to it. When you turn this checkbox on, Quicken positions the decimal point two places to the left when you type a number or enter a number using the pop-up calculator. You can fill in dollars and cents without having to type the decimal point. For example, if you enter *1578*, Quicken changes the value to *15.78*, as shown in Figure 16-4.

- **Show transaction toolbar.** This checkbox is turned on initially, which is why you see the Enter, Edit, Split, and Attach buttons for the selected transaction. If you're a right-clicking fiend and use the Transaction Edit menu (page 181)

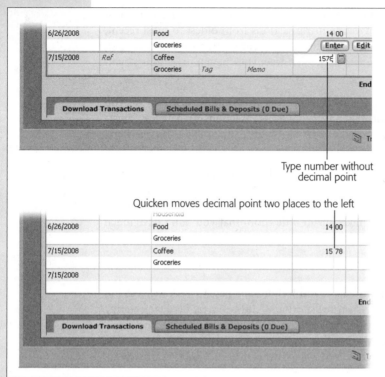

Figure 16-4:
Quicken places the decimal point (or rather, the line that represents the decimal point) when you save a transaction or click out of the value field. The only drawback with automatically placing the decimal point is that you have to enter two zeroes for values rounded to the nearest dollar.

instead of those buttons, you can hide them by turning this checkbox off. If you don't use attachments, you can eliminate the Attach button from the transaction toolbar by turning off the "Show Attach button" checkbox.

- **Display fonts.** Intuit finally figured out that baby boomers are growing older. By clicking Fonts, you can choose the font and font size that Quicken uses in the register and on lists. The standard setting is MS Sans Serif 8-point font. Give your eyes a break and choose 10 points or larger. (Keep in mind, a larger font size may increase the size of dialog boxes and other elements.)

- **Register colors.** If you've ever accidentally entered a check transaction in your credit card account or vice versa, you know how handy it would be to have a visual clue about which register you have open. Click Colors to open the Choose Register Colors dialog box. You can choose from seven pastel colors for account types like Spending, Savings, Credit, and Asset.

- **Remove memorized payees not used in last _ months.** The memorized payees feature (see page 202) alone is almost worth Quicken's purchase price. As soon as you type a memorized payee name in a transaction, Quicken fills in the amount, category, and memo for you. Unfortunately, as you buy stuff from more companies, the Memorized Payee list can get really long. The more names in the Memorized Payee list, the more characters you have to type before Quicken finds the matching payee and the more names you have to slog through in the payee drop-down menu.

To make Quicken take companies you haven't bought from recently off your Memorized Payee List, turn on this checkbox and type *14* in the box, as shown in Figure 16-5.

• **Keep register filters after Quicken closes.** You can filter (page 507) the transactions that appear in a register to see things like uncleared transactions for the past 2 years. Out of the box, each time you close the program, Quicken removes the filters you set during that session. When this checkbox is on, the filters are still in place the next time you run the program.

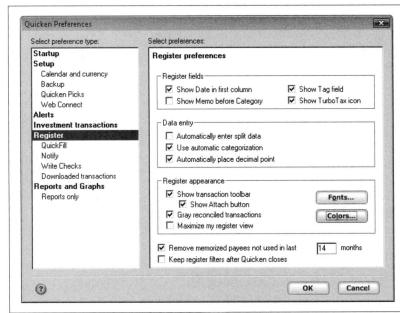

Figure 16-5:
Keeping 14 months' worth of memorized payees lets you pare down your memorized payee list without losing companies you pay only once a year.

Adjusting QuickFill

QuickFill (page 88) is one of Quicken's better efforts at speeding up data entry. Most of the time, it works surprisingly well. If you're happy with Quicken's fill-in assistance, you can bypass this panel altogether. But if transactions seem to take on a life of their own during data entry, modify these settings (shown in Figure 16-6) to tell QuickFill what you want:

• **Use Enter key to move between fields.** Out of the box, this checkbox is turned off, which means that you press Tab to move between fields, and Enter to record a transaction. If you'd rather press Enter to both move between fields and record transactions, turn this checkbox on. (Then, when you want to record the transaction immediately, you can either press Ctrl+Enter or click the onscreen Enter button.)

• **Recall memorized payees.** This checkbox is usually turned on—it tells Quick-Fill to fill in transaction fields with memorized payee values as soon as you leave the Payee field. If you turn this checkbox off, you effectively turn off QuickFill.

• **Provide drop-down lists on field entry.** With this checkbox turned on, Quicken automatically displays a drop-down menu as soon as you move to or click in a field. If you want to see drop-down menus only when you need them, turn this checkbox off, and leave the "Show buttons on QuickFill fields" checkbox on. That way, you can click a button when you want to see a field's drop-down menu.

• **Automatically memorize new payees.** Quicken comes with this checkbox turned on, which tells the program to save payees you use in transactions to the Memorized Payee List. If you want to memorize payees, you also have to keep the "Complete fields using previous entries" checkbox turned on.

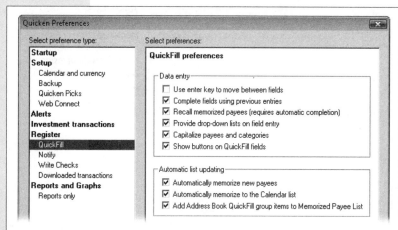

Figure 16-6:
"Complete fields using previous entries" and memorized payees go hand in hand: If you don't let Quicken memorize payees (by turning off the "Automatically memorize new payees" checkbox), QuickFill doesn't have any saved information to fill in. And if you turn off the "Complete fields using previous entries" checkbox, QuickFill can't use the memorized payee information it has saved.

Although "Automatically memorize new payees" ensures that QuickFill helps you fill in the next transaction with that payee, it can lead to an overpopulated Memorized Payee List. And then there are the vendors you'd rather not memorize—like the diner that gave you food poisoning. Rather than turn off this checkbox, you can keep your Memorized Payee List lean by deleting payees you don't want (page 205).

Remember, automatic memorization might prevent Quicken from memorizing the payees you *do* want it to remember. (The program stops memorizing new payees once your Memorized Payee List hits somewhere between 1,000 and 2,000 entries.)

Tip: If you turn off automatic memorization, you can still memorize payees as you add transactions by pressing Ctrl+M.

Getting Notifications

The Notify preferences tell Quicken when to warn or remind you about potential problems. Here are the settings and when you may want to use them:

• **When entering out-of-date transactions.** This setting warns you when you type a date that's more than 12 months different from today's date. It's a godsend during those first few weeks (or months) of every year, when you constantly type the wrong year.

- **Before changing existing transactions.** This option warns you when you try to save an existing transaction that you've changed, in case you changed it by mistake. If you know your way around Quicken and often change existing transactions (to add memos to downloaded transactions, say), turn this checkbox *off* to eliminate the frequent interruptions.

- **When entering uncategorized transactions.** Almost every transaction should have a category. This notification simply reminds you to do the right thing and supply one, so you should leave it on.

- **To run a reconcile report after reconcile.** You can turn off this checkbox without a second thought. Reconcile reports mostly tell you what you already know—which transactions have cleared, which haven't, and whether there's a discrepancy between your records and your bank's—so there's no point in running one every time you reconcile. But if you had to do some fancy footwork to reconcile your checking account one month, you can document that with a reconciliation report by choosing Reports → Banking → Reconciliation.

- **Warn if a check number is reused.** About the only time you intentionally use the same check number is when you're renumbering checks that you entered out of order. But this setting is a good way to let you know if your fingers slipped and you typed a number you've already entered, so keep it turned on.

Write Check Settings

The Write Checks preferences control the appearance of checks you write and print using the Write Checks window. (If you write paper checks by hand, skip this section.) Here are the few preferences you might want to change and why:

- **Allow entry of extra message on check.** If the company you're paying wants you to include your account or member number, you can type that information in the Write Checks window. If you turn on this checkbox, then Quicken includes a Message box in the check part of the Write Checks window, and prints the message you type there on the check.

- **Change date of checks to date when printed.** Quicken initially turns off this checkbox, which means that the date on the check is the date you type in the Write Checks window Date box, regardless of when you print the check. If your budget is tight and you consider postdating checks a critical cash management technique, this setting is ideal. But if you're a stickler for accuracy, turn this checkbox on so that checks always show the exact date you print them.

How Quicken Downloads Transactions

When you download transactions from your bank or credit card company into Quicken, you're at the mercy of somebody else's bizarre naming schemes (probably a computer's). After downloading, the first thing you do is pounce on the keyboard and rename the transactions so they'll actually help you remember what you did or bought. Quicken can help: It automatically creates *renaming rules* by "watching" you edit the transactions. The next time you download, Quicken substitutes your preferred payee names for you. Quicken's "Downloaded transactions" preferences affect how the program applies renaming rules. See page 146 for more information about renaming rules and the "Downloaded transactions" preferences.

Report and Graph Settings

Quicken wouldn't be much good if it couldn't produce a list of your tax-deductible expenses or a pie chart showing your investment diversification. In this category of preferences, you can specify the date range for reports and graphs you generate, and what to do when you customize a report. Chapter 14 provides the full scoop on how to use these settings.

Customizing What You See

The point of using Quicken is to manage your finances better, and make that management easier. But everyone has different areas of their finances that need work. If you're struggling to get out of debt, you want to watch your credit card balances and your spending closely, but investments probably aren't on your radar yet. On the other hand, if you're on your way to millionaire-hood, you probably pay more attention to net worth and investment performance than credit card bills.

You can tailor Quicken's tabs and the Account Bar to keep what's important to you in sight. The new My Pages tab (page 32) is where you can spotlight specific aspects of your financial life with custom views. You can also add your favorite commands or reports to the Quicken Tool Bar for easy access. And you can change the way the register looks, to make recording and reviewing transactions as easy as possible.

Displaying the Financial Features You Want

If you're an old hand at Quicken, you might not give one whit about the program's new navigation tools. Clicking an entry on the Quicken menu bar and then choosing a command is still the tried and true method for launching any feature you want. However, if you use only some of Quicken's features, you can clean up some clutter by turning off different financial areas (also known as centers or tabs).

The first thing you see when you create a new data file is the Setup Center (page 19). You can return to the Setup Center any time you want to turn financial centers on or off. Simply click the Setup tab below the Tool Bar and then click Overview.

On the Overview screen, the Your Quicken section is where you turn financial features on and off, as shown in Figure 16-7. The choices you make apply to every data file you work on. Here's how the Your Quicken settings work:

- **Show.** The checkboxes in this column control the tabs you see along the top of the window and the entries that appear in the Quicken menu bar. Turn off a checkbox to hide its tab and menu bar entries. Rental Property, Planning, Tax, and Quicken Picks are all turned off in Figure 16-7. Although a checkbox that's turned off looks like it's inactive (grayed out), you can click it to turn it back on.

Note: Unfortunately, Quicken's tabs are only so accommodating. You can't turn them off completely, for instance, if you prefer to use only the menu bar. And you can't shrink the amount of space they take up onscreen.

- **Start On.** Select one of the options in this column to tell Quicken what you want to see first whenever you start the program. For example, if you create a custom view (page 502) to summarize your financial status, select My Pages to display that view when Quicken starts. If you want to see an account register instead, you can use the "On startup open to" preference (page 486) to choose which one you want.

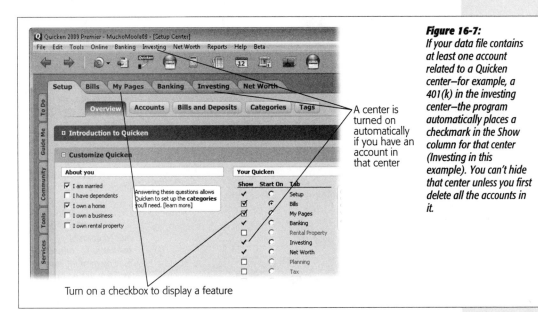

Turn on a checkbox to display a feature

A center is turned on automatically if you have an account in that center

Figure 16-7:
If your data file contains at least one account related to a Quicken center—for example, a 401(k) in the investing center—the program automatically places a checkmark in the Show column for that center (Investing in this example). You can't hide that center unless you first delete all the accounts in it.

Customizing the Account Bar

There's a lot to like about the Quicken Account Bar. In addition to providing an easy way to open any account register, it keeps your financial successes (or failures) where you can see them. Organizing the accounts in the Account Bar and choosing which accounts to include help you get a better picture of where you stand financially.

You customize the Account Bar in the Account List window, which you can get to in a couple of ways:

- At the bottom of the Account Bar, click Customize.

- Right-click the Account Bar and, from the shortcut menu, choose "Add/remove accounts from bar", "Rearrange accounts" or "Delete/hide accounts in Quicken".

- Press Ctrl+A.

The main changes you can make include specifying which accounts you see in the Account Bar and rearranging those accounts. Here's what you can do and why you might want to:

- **Show or hide accounts in the Account Bar.** The Account Bar initially shows all of your accounts. As the number of accounts grows, you can't see them all without scrolling. If you have an account that you rarely work with, like a 5-year CD, you can hide it in the Account Bar. In the Account List window, click the account you want to hide. When the account entry expands to show the account's checkboxes, turn on the "Hide this account in Account Bar" checkbox. When you do that, the account disappears from the Account Bar (as shown in Figure 16-8), but it's still visible in the Account List window, drop-down lists, and on the Quicken menu bar.

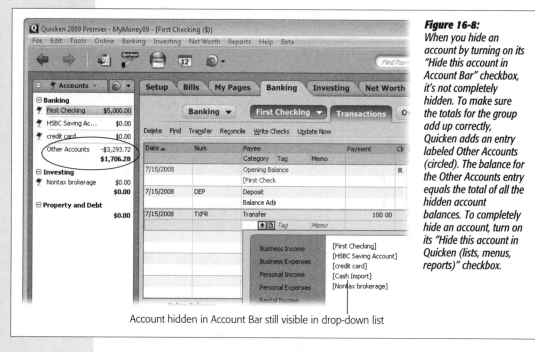

Figure 16-8:
When you hide an account by turning on its "Hide this account in Account Bar" checkbox, it's not completely hidden. To make sure the totals for the group add up correctly, Quicken adds an entry labeled Other Accounts (circled). The balance for the Other Accounts entry equals the total of all the hidden account balances. To completely hide an account, turn on its "Hide this account in Quicken (lists, menus, reports)" checkbox.

Account hidden in Account Bar still visible in drop-down list

- **Show or hide accounts in Quicken.** If, on the other hand, you have an old account that you no longer use, you can hide it completely. In this case, turn on the account's "Hide this account in Quicken (lists, menus, reports)" checkbox, and it won't appear anywhere except the Account List window (where you can unhide it).

- **Remove an account's balances from Account Bar totals.** Once in a while, you won't want an account's balance included in the Account Bar totals. For instance, you may want to omit the balances for your checking, petty cash, and credit card accounts (if you pay off the balance each month). By doing that, your net worth at the bottom of the Account Bar reflects assets and liabilities that don't change from day to day. Turn on an account's "Don't include this account in net worth total" checkbox to remove its balance from its group total.

Note: The Account Balances and Net Worth reports include the balances for *all* accounts, regardless of their "Don't include this account in net worth total" setting.

- **Change the order of accounts.** Quicken initially lists accounts in alphabetical order. To keep your most frequently used accounts at the top of each section, you can change the order in which accounts appear in the Account List and Account Bar. In the Account List window, click the name of the account you want to move, and then click the up arrow or down arrow to the left of the account's name.

- **Change an account's tab.** When you create accounts, Quicken associates them with one of the Quicken tabs (or centers) and a subgroup (which Quicken calls *used for*) within that tab. For example, new savings accounts are automatically assigned to be used for Savings in the Banking tab. But you can change an account's tab to better reflect its purpose. If you set up a separate checking account to pay rental property expenses, then you might want to keep that checking account in the Net Worth tab with your rental property assets rather than in the Banking tab, where Quicken puts it. To switch an account to another tab, select the account in the Account List window. Then click the "(change)" link to the right of the "Show in" label, as shown in Figure 16-9. In the Change Group dialog box, click the option for the new group.

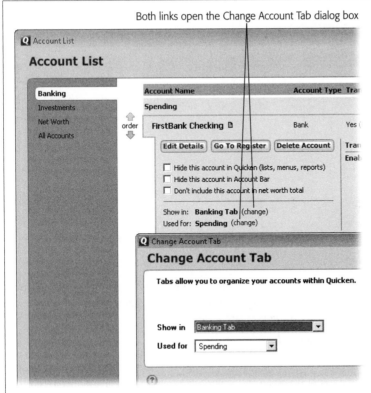

Both links open the Change Account Tab dialog box

Figure 16-9:
The Change Account Tab dialog box shows you that Quicken categorizes accounts by more than banking, investing, and net worth. For example, the Banking tab is divided into groups used for Spending, Savings, and Credit, whereas the Investing tab shows accounts used for Investment (for investment accounts not earmarked for retirement) or Retirement (for taxable and tax-favored accounts that you plan to use for retirement). The Net Worth tab splits accounts into groups used for assets and liabilities.

Creating Your Own Views

Quicken 2009 includes a tab called My Pages (Figure 16-10) where you can create custom views to show account information, reports, and other financial features you care about, such as net worth, scheduled transactions, and investment values. You can choose from dozens of views and reports, and tell Quicken the order in which you want them. You can even create more than one custom view. This section tells you how.

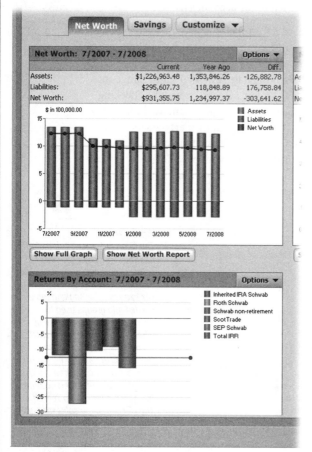

Figure 16-10:
The My Pages tab displays the view you were using when you last closed the program. To pick what you'll see the next time you launch the program, select your favorite custom view and then close Quicken. As long as you set the program's preferences so that it knows to start at My Pages (page 499), your custom view will be the first thing you see the next time you launch Quicken.

Creating a custom view

Creating a custom view is as simple as picking the things you want to see and putting them in the order you want. The hardest part is deciding what to include and what to leave out. Here's how you create a view:

1. **Click the My Pages tab.**

   If you haven't created any custom views, the My Pages tab displays a "Welcome to Your Pages" screen. If you already have custom views, it displays the last custom view you selected.

2. **At the top of the My Pages screen, click Customize and then choose "Create a new view" on the drop-down menu.**

In addition to opening the Customize View dialog box shown in Figure 16-11, Quicken adds a tab for the new view, named something like *View 2*, just below the main Quicken navigation tabs.

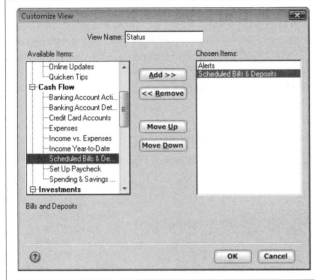

Figure 16-11:
After customizing a view, you may discover that some items are gluttons for space and push others out of sight. You could scroll down to see the out-of-sight items, but you may forget they're there. One fix is to create a separate view just for these space hogs. Or, if you've included Scheduled Bills & Deposits, for example, try turning off the "Show graph" and "Show calendar" checkboxes to regain a few inches of screen space.

3. **In the View Name box, type a descriptive name.**

For example, if the view includes your net worth, type *Net Worth*.

4. **To add items to the view, in the Available Items list, select an item or items, and then click Add.**

To remove items from the view, select them in the Chosen Items list and then click Remove. In both the Available Items and Chosen Items lists, you can Ctrl-click to select individual items or Shift-click to select several contiguous items.

5. **To reorder the items in the Chosen Items list, select an item and then click Move Up or Move Down until it's nestled where you want it.**

When your list of Chosen Items is all set, click OK to see how your new view looks.

Customizing a view

You can modify or delete custom views, or create new ones. Here are the commands on the Customize drop-down menu:

• **Customize this view.** Lets you modify the current view using the Customize View dialog box.

• **Create a new view.** Choose this command to make a new custom view.

• **Delete this view.** This command deletes the current view. A message box asks you to confirm your decision so you don't accidentally delete a view.

Customizing the Tool Bar

The Quicken Tool Bar runs along the top of the main Quicken window just below the menu bar and is the second-fastest way to access commands (after keyboard shortcuts). The Tool Bar comes with a built-in set of icons, but you can choose which ones to include. For example, if you don't use add-on services or Quicken.com, you can toss the Services and Quicken.com icons. Customizing the Tool Bar is similar to setting up a custom view (page 502): You choose the commands you want to include and the order in which they appear.

Here are the steps:

1. **Right-click the Tool Bar and then click Customize Tool Bar.**

   The Customize Toolbar dialog box opens, shown in Figure 16-12.

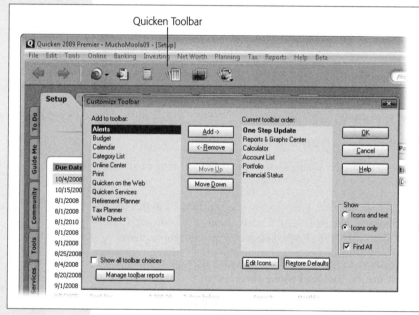

Quicken Toolbar

Figure 16-12:
Initially, Quicken selects the "Icons and text" option (on the dialog box's right-hand side), which shows icons and labels to identify what each icon represents. If you want to save screen space, select "Icons only", though you may have trouble picking the right command. To find out what an icon's for, point to it, and Quicken displays a ToolTip (a pop-up explanation).

2. **To remove an icon, on the right side of the dialog box, in the "Current toolbar order" list, select the command you want to remove and then click Remove.**

   The command disappears from the "Current toolbar order" list and shows up in the "Add to toolbar" list.

3. To add an icon, in the "Add to toolbar" list, select the command you want to add and then click Add.

   The "Add to toolbar" list may seem sparse at first. To see the dozens of commands you can add to the Tool Bar, turn on the "Show all toolbar choices" checkbox below the list.

4. To reorder the icons, select a command in the "Current toolbar order" list. Then click Move Up or Move Down to move the icon left or right on the Tool Bar.

   Moving an icon up in the list moves it to the left on the Tool Bar, and moving it down in the list moves it to the right.

5. If you want to remove the Search field from the Tool Bar, turn off the Find All checkbox.

   If you're used to pressing Ctrl+F to open the Find dialog box (page 175), then you may want to hide the Search box (page 173) and put more commands in the Tool Bar. Otherwise, the Search box is worth keeping around.

6. To change an icon's label or shortcut key, in the "Current toolbar order" list, select the icon you want to edit, and then click Edit Icons.

   In the Edit Toolbar Button dialog box, type a new label. To set a keyboard shortcut, type the letter you want to use. The keyboard shortcut becomes Alt+Shift+ that letter.

7. Click OK.

   The Tool Bar reflects the changes you made. If you want to restore the Tool Bar to its out-of-the-box condition, in the Customize Toolbar dialog box, click Restore Defaults. After you click OK again to confirm your decision, all the changes you made are gone forever.

Adding custom reports to the Tool Bar

If you customize reports and run them regularly, you can add them to the Tool Bar so you can get to them easily. Here's how:

1. Right-click the Tool Bar and then click Customize Toolbar. In the Customize Toolbar dialog box's bottom-left corner, click "Manage toolbar reports".

   The Manage Toolbar Reports dialog box opens. Initially, you see a list of the folders you've created within the My Saved Reports section (page 457).

2. To add an entire report folder to the Tool Bar, turn on the folder's checkbox.

   When you add a report folder to the Tool Bar, a small down arrow appears in the icon, as is the case with the Financial Status icon in Figure 16-13. Click the icon, and then, from the drop-down menu, choose the report you want.

3. **To add an individual report to the Tool Bar, click the arrow to the left of the folder's name.**

The folder expands to show the individual reports.

4. **Turn on the checkbox for the report you want to add to the Tool Bar.**

5. **Click OK to close the Manage Toolbar Reports dialog box and then click OK again to close the Customize Toolbar dialog box.**

The reports and folders you added show up on the Tool Bar.

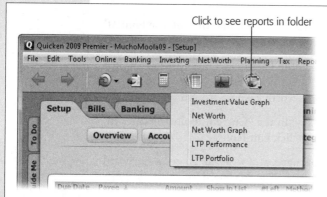

Click to see reports in folder

Figure 16-13:
If you turn on the checkbox for a folder of reports and then expand the folder, all the individual reports are grayed out. That's because you've already added them by adding the folder. You can't add individual reports to the Tool Bar if you've added the folder they're in.

Customizing the Register

You spend lots of time in account registers, so it's common sense to set up the registers the way you want. You can tell Quicken to show each transaction on one line or two, for instance, to mimic the number of lines you use in a paper register. You can also change the order of transactions, to focus on uncleared transactions, say.

Here's how to apply each of these customized views to a register:

• **One line or two.** Out of the box, Quicken uses two lines of the register to show each transaction. The date, check number, payee, and amount show up on the first line, and the longer entries for category, tag, and memo appear on the second line. To coax more transactions onto the screen at the same time, you can switch to one line per transaction. Immediately above the register, in the Register menu bar, choose View → "One-line display". Quicken squeezes all the fields (except for Memo) onto one line. To switch back to seeing memos again, choose View → "Two-line display".

• **Sort order.** The standard sort order for transactions is first by date and then by amount. Sorting by cleared status keeps you focused on transactions that aren't reconciled. To change to this sort order, choose View → "Sort by cleared status", which displays reconciled transactions first, followed by cleared transactions, and finally uncleared. (Because the register shows the bottom of the list, you usually see your uncleared transactions along with a few that have cleared.)

Other sort orders come in handy for troubleshooting. For example, to look for missing or duplicate check numbers, sort by check number. To spot missing monthly payments, sort by payee. You can also change the field Quicken sorts by without using the View menu; just click a column heading above the register to sort by that field.

Filtering Transactions

Filtering lets you focus on just the transactions you want to see. By applying a filter to an account register, you can look at specific types of transactions that fall within a certain date range. Here's how to put this feature to use:

1. **To display the filter boxes above the register, choose View → "Filter register view".**

   Quicken adds the View and Date Range boxes to the top of the register, as shown in Figure 16-14.

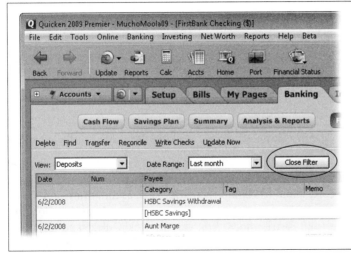

Figure 16-14:
When you apply a filter to a register, the same filter applies to that register the next time you open Quicken. To remove the filter, to the right of the Date Range box, click the Close Filter button.

2. **To show only a specific type of transaction, click the View box's down arrow, and then choose the type.**

   For example, to find transactions that you forgot to categorize, choose Uncategorized. Choosing Uncleared displays transactions that aren't reconciled or cleared at your bank. If you find uncleared transactions from several months in the past, check to see whether they're duplicates or whether someone hasn't cashed one of your checks. Choosing Payments or Deposits whittles the list down to money going out or money coming in, respectively. If you add flags to transactions to remind yourself of something, you can choose Flagged to quickly find those transactions.

3. **To restrict the dates that you see, in the Date Range drop-down menu, choose the period you want.**

   Your choices here are similar to the ones you pick in reports (page 449), for instance "Current month" or Last 12 Months. To pick specific dates, choose Custom.

Setting Up Alerts

If you hang a notepad around your neck so you can remember why you went upstairs, Quicken *alerts* might become your favorite feature. Alerts remind you about tasks you should perform or warn you when you need to take action. For example, scheduled transaction alerts remind you to make payments before exorbitant late fees kick in. Similarly, the credit card limit alert warns you *before* your card is turned down at a store. You can even be proactive by using the maximum balance alert to find out when to move some money into an account that pays interest.

You can set up alerts to pop up whenever you launch Quicken so that they're hard to miss. Alerts also appear in different financial centers, but a custom view on the My Pages tab (page 502) is another way to make them stand out. To tell Quicken which alerts you want to see, do the following:

1. **Choose Tools → Set Up Alerts.**

   The Alerts Center window opens.

2. **Expand an alert category (if necessary) by clicking the + sign to the left of its name.**

   Quicken groups alerts into three categories: Cash Flow, Investing, and General. Cash Flow alerts correspond to banking activities, such as minimum and maximum account balances. Investing alerts include reminders about downloading quotes or mutual fund distributions. You can also ask Quicken to alert you when stock prices and volumes hit high or low values. The most popular General alert is one that Quicken turns on automatically: "Scheduled bills or deposits", which reminds you when a payment or deposit is scheduled.

3. **Turn on the checkbox for the alert you want to set.**

   Quicken turns on the checkbox and displays the alert's settings, as shown in Figure 16-15.

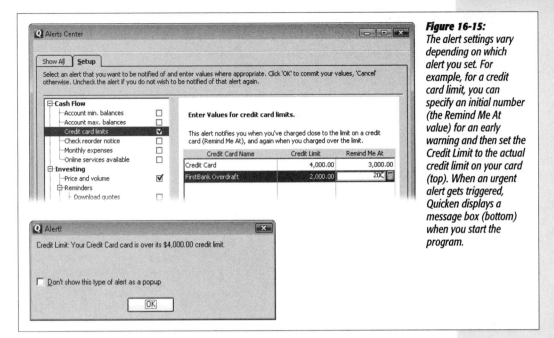

Figure 16-15:
The alert settings vary depending on which alert you set. For example, for a credit card limit, you can specify an initial number (the Remind Me At value) for an early warning and then set the Credit Limit to the actual credit limit on your card (top). When an urgent alert gets triggered, Quicken displays a message box (bottom) when you start the program.

4. **If you want Quicken to notify you about a triggered alert when you start the program, select the alert, and then select the "Urgent (pop up dialog box)" option at the bottom of the window.**

   With the "Urgent (pop up dialog box)" setting turned on, Quicken opens a message box showing the urgent alerts when you first launch Quicken (Figure 16-15, bottom). For less critical alerts, like a reminder to reorder checks, select the "Text in the alert list" option. This setting displays alerts in the Alerts Center and in the Alerts section of each financial center.

5. **In the "Keep the alert in the list for" drop-down list, choose "One week".**

   If you look at alerts regularly and take action, you can choose a short period, like "One month" or "One week". If you choose "One year", Quicken removes that alert from the list when a year has passed since it was triggered.

6. **After you've set all the alerts you want, click OK to close the Alerts Center window.**

   To see all the alerts that have been triggered, choose Tools → Show All Alerts.

Tip: If you want to add alerts to a custom view on the My Pages tab, in the Customize View dialog box (page 503), under the Overview heading, click Alerts, and then click Add.

Exporting and Importing

You probably appreciate the benefits of sharing information among different programs. Maybe you copy bullet points from a Word document for use in a Power-Point presentation. Or perhaps you're into downloading stats from *MLB.com* for an intense weekend of Excel analysis. (Anything to help the team.)

Quicken does the export and import dance, too. You can get data out of Quicken in several ways. For example, you can export a Quicken investment report, and then use Excel's powerful financial functions to analyze your portfolio. Or you might funnel data to other programs like Investment Account Manager, described on page 406.

On the other hand, Quicken is reluctant to import data. If your financial institutions offer downloadable transactions in the Quicken-friendly OFX (Open Financial Exchange) format, you can pipe those numbers right into Quicken, as Chapter 6 explains. If not, your ability to import data into Quicken is limited. This chapter does show you one fairly straightforward—albeit time-consuming—workaround.

Finally, you might want to transfer data from one Quicken data file to another. If you want to create a new data file to track your parents' finances, for instance, just export your category list and memorized payees to the new file. This chapter describes all these methods for getting data into and out of Quicken, and the benefits and drawbacks of each one.

Exporting Quicken Data

Quicken is a great personal finance program, but it can't do everything. When you're ready to liberate your data, you've got three options (detailed exporting instructions follow this list):

- **Copy and Paste.** Copying a Quicken report to the Windows Clipboard is easier than exporting data to move it to other programs—as long as the programs play well with copying and pasting. For example, pasting a Quicken report into an Excel spreadsheet takes fewer steps to get the same result as a tab-delimited export maneuver (described below). The only time exporting data wins out is when the other program doesn't let you paste data into it.

- **Export data to a QIF file.** Created as a way to transfer data to tech support folks, the Quicken Interchange File format morphed into a transaction download tool that's somewhat frail, but widely used. Beginning with Quicken 2005, Intuit started to limit how you could *import* QIF files. (See the box on page 519 for more detail.) However, there aren't any limits on *exporting* your Quicken data to QIF files, whether you want to export your categories and memorized payees in order to start a new data file, or use a QIF file to feed your investment transactions to another financial program.

- **Export reports.** You can export any Quicken report to a variety of file formats, the most useful of which is the *tab-delimited file* (that is, one where tab characters separate each item). This format is ideal when you want to export data to a spreadsheet program like Excel for esoteric calculations or to format a report in ways that Quicken can't handle. After you export the data, open the tab-delimited file in the other program, and then work on the data there. (Flip back to Chapter 14 if you need a refresher on Quicken's reports.)

Exporting Data to QIF Files

Many programs have come to rely on QIF files to get Quicken data. For example, if you decide to use a more powerful portfolio management tool, like Investment Account Manager (*www.quantixsoftware.com*), you can export your Quicken investment transactions to a QIF file, and then import them into the other program.

You also use QIF files to transfer memorized payees, account lists, category lists, security lists, and even transactions from one Quicken data file to another. For instance, if you want to create a new data file with no transactions, but you don't want to go to the trouble of recreating your custom categories, you can export that list without transactions and import it into another data file.

Regardless of where your data's going, here's how you export it from Quicken to a QIF file:

1. **Choose File → Export → QIF file.**

   Quicken opens the QIF Export dialog box, shown in Figure 17-1, and fills in the "QIF File to Export to" text box with the folder where you keep your Quicken data file.

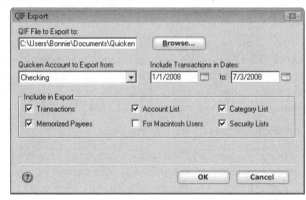

Figure 17-1:
In the QIF Export dialog box, you can choose the accounts you want to export, the date range of transactions, and the type of data you want to export. Your choice of accounts is limited to either one account or all the accounts in your data file (choose <All Accounts> from the drop-down list).

2. **Click Browse to navigate to another folder, and then choose a filename for the QIF file you're about to create.**

   You're telling Quicken where you want to save the soon-to-be created QIF file. In the "Export to QIF File" dialog box that opens, choose the folder where you want to save the file. To make it easier to find the files you want, create a folder dedicated to your exported files. To do this, in the "Export to QIF File" dialog box, click the Create New Folder icon, which looks like a manila folder. Then, type a name for the new folder. Once you've named the folder, double-click it to open it.

   In the "File name" text box, type a descriptive name for the QIF file. If you're exporting only lists, you might type a name like *MyMoneyLists*. When you click OK, you jump back to the QIF Export dialog box, where the "QIF File to Export to" text box shows the path and filename of the QIF export file you're about to create.

3. **If you want to export transactions, in the "Quicken Account to Export from" drop-down menu, select the account that contains the transactions you want to export.**

   If you want to export *all* your transactions, scroll to the top of the drop-down menu, and then choose <All Accounts>.

   If you're exporting only lists, not transactions, you can leave this box alone, since it has no effect on the lists Quicken exports.

4. **If you're exporting transactions, choose the date range in the "Include Transactions in Dates" boxes.**

   Quicken automatically sets the first date box to the earliest transaction date in your data file, and the "to" date box to today's date. To export transactions that occurred during a specific period, choose the first and last dates you're interested in. You can type the date in the box or click the calendar icon to the right of each date box. To move to the previous month, click the double arrows pointing to the left. Click the double arrows pointing to the right to move to the next month. Click a date to select it.

5. **To export transactions, in the "Include in Export" section, turn on the Transactions checkbox.**

   Because some Quicken for Windows accounts and transactions don't have a direct counterpart in Quicken for Macintosh, you can't import and export them seamlessly or completely. The For Macintosh Users checkbox exports only securities, security prices, and the last budget you saved. If you turn on the other checkboxes as well, you can transfer *lists*, but not transactions, to a Mac data file.

6. **To export lists, turn on the checkboxes for the lists you want.**

   The checkboxes are pretty self-explanatory. You turn on Account List to export accounts, Category List to export categories and tags, Memorized Payees to export the Memorized Payee List for Quick Fill, and Security Lists to export securities (along with their prices, price histories, security types, and investment goals).

   If you want to transfer your lists to a new data file *without* any transactions, simply turn on the checkboxes for lists, but leave the Transactions checkbox turned off.

7. **Click OK.**

   Quicken creates the QIF file, and then exports the data you specified to the location you chose in step 2. You can now use the file to import data into another program or another Quicken data file (page 516).

Exporting Report Data: Method 1

As you learned in Chapter 14, you can customize Quicken reports in lots of ways. But say you have in mind fancier formatting than Quicken offers. Or maybe you want to analyze your data in ways no amount of report customization can. The answer: Export your report, and then work on it in another program. Exporting reports is also handy if you want to get your data into a program that can't read QIF files. Quicken gives you two ways to export reports; the first method is a little quicker, and the second gives you a few more output options.

Method 1 goes like this:

1. **In Quicken, generate the report you want.**

   See Chapter 14 for the full scoop on generating and customizing reports.

2. **In the report window menu bar, choose Export Data, as shown in Figure 17-2.**

   The drop-down menu lets you choose between exporting a file Excel can read, copying to the Clipboard (page 182), or creating a PDF file. The PDF option creates a PDF of your report that you can print but not edit. It's a good choice if you want to email a copy of your report to someone who doesn't have Quicken.

3. **Choose "Report to Excel compatible format".**

   Quicken opens the "Create Excel compatible file" dialog box.

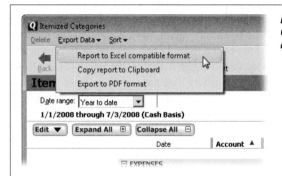

Figure 17-2:
Choose "Report to Excel compatible format" to create a tab-delimited file that Excel and many other programs can read.

4. **Navigate to the folder where you want to store the exported file. Type a name in the "File name" box, and then click Open.**

   Quicken automatically sets the "Files of type" box to "Tab delimited export files (*.TXT)". When you click OK, the program creates the file. You can now launch Excel or some other program, and then import the tab-delimited file (explained below).

Exporting Report Data: Method 2

Quicken gives you another way to create the ever popular tab-delimited file, plus a few other file types that you may occasionally need. Start by heading over to any report window's icon bar; click Print to open the Print dialog box. Turn on the "Export to" radio button, and then, from the drop-down menu, choose one of these three options:

- **ASCII disk file.** This format produces a text file that *looks* like your report, but because it uses space characters to align the data in columns, most programs have a hard time importing the info. No worries: Ninety-nine percent of the time you'll probably use the next option.

- **Tab-delimited (Excel-compatible) disk file.** Choosing this format produces a file with tab characters separating each value. Although the choice says "Excel compatible", lots of other programs can read files in this format, too.

- **.PRN (123-compatible) disk file.** Despite this format's convoluted name, it produces a plain old comma-delimited file, which works with relics like Lotus 1-2-3, as well as Excel and most other programs. Use this option if you're working with a program that for some reason doesn't handle tab-delimited files.

After you choose the file type, click Print, and Quicken opens the Create Disk File dialog box, where you can specify whatever filename you want to use, and then pick where you want to save the file.

Copying and Pasting Quicken Data

Quicken gives you an even easier way to export your transactions than the maneuvers described in the previous sections. That's right, the ol' reliable: copy and paste. Instead of creating a file in Quicken and opening it in another program, you can just copy the data and paste it into the other program. Any program that's on speaking terms with a data exchange system called OLE (short for "Object Linking and Embedding")—and that includes Word and Excel—gladly accepts copied transaction data from Quicken. Here's all you have to do:

1. **Launch the program you want to paste Quicken data into (such as Excel) and open a new file.**

   You can tell whether you can paste into that program by looking in the program's Edit menu for a Paste or Paste Special command. If you don't see one, read the program's Help topics for instructions. You might be out of luck.

2. **In Quicken, generate the report you want (see Chapter 14 for more on reports).**

3. **In the report window, choose Export Data → "Copy report to Clipboard".**

   Quicken doesn't do anything to show you that it's copied the data, but it has.

4. **In the other program's text or spreadsheet window, click where you want to put the Quicken report, and then choose Home → Paste → Paste (in Word 2007 and Excel 2007) or Edit → Paste (in Word 2003 or Excel 2003). Ctrl+V works in both Office 2003 and Office 2007.**

   The program pastes the data into the open file. As you can see in Figure 17-3, the result is the same as opening a tab-delimited file, but copying and pasting is a whole lot faster.

Now you can rearrange the data to your heart's content.

Importing Data into Quicken

When you need to get data *into* Quicken, you don't get nearly as many choices as you do when exporting. With that bit of cold water in your face, go ahead and choose File → Import, where you'll see three options:

- **TurboTax.** It's no surprise that Intuit lets you import data from its tax-preparation program, TurboTax. Part of the joy of using Quicken is decreasing the drudgery of tax returns, and TurboTax can read Quicken data. Then, after your return is en route to the IRS, you can import your TurboTax data *back* into Quicken to start planning for next year. Just choose File → Import → TurboTax, and then tell Quicken where your TurboTax file lives.

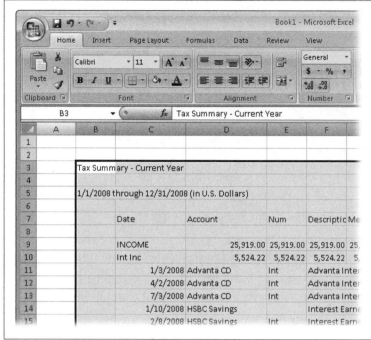

Figure 17-3:
When you open a tab-delimited file in another program, the data automatically shows up at the beginning of the file (in Excel, that means the spreadsheet's upper-left corner). But if you paste data into a text document or spreadsheet, then you can choose where you want to paste the data, as you can see here.

- **Web Connect File.** If your bank doesn't support direct downloads using Direct Connect or Express Web Connect, Web Connect is the next best thing (see page 126). You download OFX files (page 8), and then choose File → Import → Web Connect File to import them into Quicken.

- **QIF File.** Beginning with Quicken 2005, Intuit shut off QIF imports to most types of accounts. Due to these restrictions, you'll probably use QIF files mainly to copy lists from one Quicken file to another (as explained back on page 512). However, Quicken does still let you import transactions that are stored in QIF files into cash, asset, and liability accounts. If your financial institution hasn't upgraded to Quicken's OFX format for online financial services, the box on page 519 tells you how to import your bank's QIF files into other kinds of accounts.

Importing QIF Files

You can import QIF files only into cash, asset, and liability accounts. If you don't have a place to put imported transactions, create a cash account to store them in before you do any importing. You should also back up your Quicken data file, in case you import data to the wrong account, or make other changes you didn't want. Then follow these steps for importing a QIF file:

1. **Choose File → Import → QIF file.**

   Quicken opens the QIF Import dialog box, shown in Figure 17-4, which is almost identical to the QIF *Export* dialog box.

Figure 17-4:
The warning on the right reminds you that you can't just import QIF files into any ol' account. Your only options are cash, asset (including house and vehicle), and liability accounts.

2. **Click Browse to find the QIF file you want to import.**

   In the "Import from QIF File" dialog box that opens, navigate to the folder where the QIF file is saved, and then double-click the filename to select it.

3. **If you're importing transactions, in the "Quicken account to import into" drop-down menu, select the account where you want to put them.**

   If you're importing only lists, it doesn't matter what account you pick, so just leave this box set to whatever account appears automatically.

4. **To import transactions, in the "Include in import" section, turn on the Transactions checkbox.**

   Turn on the "Special handling for transfers" checkbox if you're importing transactions between Quicken accounts. By turning on this checkbox, you prevent duplicating transfer transactions when you import the transfers first from the account the money comes *from*, and then from the account the money goes *to*. Quicken imports the transfers from the first account. Then, when it sees the transfer when you import it from the second account, it knows to skip that transaction.

5. **To import lists, turn on the checkboxes for the lists you want.**

   Your choices are Account List, Category List, Memorized Payees, or Security Lists.

6. **Click Next.**

   If Quicken can't figure out how to handle data in the QIF file, a message box pops up asking you what you want it to do.

   After importing the data, the QIF Import dialog box tells you the QIF import was successful, and the number of items it imported.

Tip: If you import a QIF file you created by exporting data from another Quicken file, then you may see a message about a name being reserved for internal Quicken use. This message is harmless; simply click OK to continue. The message may reappear an annoying number of times, but it won't stop you from importing your data.

7. Click Done to close the QIF Import dialog box, or Go To Register to jump to the account you imported into.

Importing Transactions with QIF

My bank is a little behind the times, so all the transactions I download are in QIF format. How do I get these transactions into Quicken?

With Quicken 2005, Intuit stopped letting you use QIF files to import downloaded transactions into checking, savings, 401(k), and brokerage accounts. And with Quicken 2006, it stopped letting you import QIF files into credit card accounts.

The only accounts you *can* still import QIF files into are cash, asset, and liability accounts—and you can use this loophole to get information into your other accounts. How? By cutting and pasting transactions from a cash account to other kinds of accounts. It's not as convenient as automatic transaction downloads, but it ultimately imports your bank's QIF files into your checking, savings, or credit card accounts.

Here's how to get QIF files into your Quicken data file:

1. Import the QIF files from your bank into a cash account (see page 517).

2. In the cash account's register, select all the transactions you imported from the QIF file (by Shift-clicking or Ctrl-clicking).

3. In the register, right-click anywhere in a selected transaction, and then, on the shortcut menu, choose "Move transactions(s)".

4. In the Move Transaction(s) dialog box's "Move to account" drop-down menu, choose the account you want.

5. Click OK, and Quicken moves the transactions from your cash account into the account you chose.

You may have to do a little bit of cleanup after you move the transactions, as some information ends up in weird spots. For example, check numbers end up in the Ref field, so you have to copy and paste them to the Num field.

You may want to create a dedicated cash account for importing and moving downloaded transactions. This method makes it easier to spot transactions that don't belong there than if you import the data into an existing cash account, because the dedicated account contains only the transactions you've just imported, and should be empty after you've moved the transactions to the correct accounts.

Part Five:
Appendixes

5

Keyboard Shortcuts

You can do almost anything in Quicken by clicking something—the Tool Bar, a menu bar, a drop-down menu, or an onscreen button. But it takes time to mouse around from click to click, especially if your hand-eye coordination leaves something to be desired. Even if you spend only a few minutes a day with Quicken, keyboard shortcuts are your friends. They take you right where you want to go in a fraction of the time it takes to mouse there. This appendix lists Quicken's most useful keyboard shortcuts; the ones you should commit to memory are at the beginning of each section.

Note: For a *complete* list of Quicken's keyboard shortcuts, search the program's Help file (press F1 to open Help) for "keys" or "keyboard shortcuts."

Task Shortcuts

These keyboard shortcuts open the windows and dialog boxes you use to perform common tasks.

Task	Keyboard Shortcut
Open a file.	Ctrl+O
Back up a file.	Ctrl+B
Print the current page, transaction, or report.	Ctrl+P
Open the Quicken Help window to the section that covers the current window or dialog box.	F1
Open the Scheduled Bills & Deposits window.	Ctrl+J

Task	Keyboard Shortcut
Open the Account List window.	Ctrl+A
Open the Category List window.	Ctrl+C if "Quicken standard mapping" is turned on in Preferences; Shift+Ctrl+C if "Windows mapping" is turned on (page 488)
Open the Tag List window.	Ctrl+L
Open the Memorized Payee List window.	Ctrl+T
Open the Write Checks dialog box to a new check.	Ctrl+W
Open the Calendar window.	Ctrl+K
Open the Portfolio View window.	Ctrl+U
Open the Security List window.	Ctrl+Y
Open the Quicken Home window.	Alt+Home

Working with Transactions

Whether you're creating, editing, saving, or deleting transactions, keyboard shortcuts speed you right along.

Task	Keyboard Shortcut
Record the current transaction.	Ctrl+Enter for standard keyboard mapping; Enter, if the Tab key is set to move from field to field in Preferences (page 86); or Alt+T for either mapping
Select an item in a list, such as a category in a transaction drop-down menu.	Type one or more letters at the beginning of the item name
Memorize a transaction to the Memorized Payee List.	Ctrl+M
Find a transaction.	Ctrl+F
Go to a new transaction in the current register.	Ctrl+N or Ctrl+End
For a transfer between two accounts, go to the corresponding transaction in the other account.	Ctrl+X if "Quicken standard mapping" is turned on (page 488); no shortcut if you use Windows mapping (use the transaction Edit menu [page 181])
Void a transaction.	Ctrl+V if "Quicken standard mapping" is turned on (page 488); no shortcut if you use Windows mapping (use the transaction Edit menu [page 181])
Insert a transaction in the current register.	Ctrl+I (see page 183 for how to use this shortcut)
Delete the current transaction.	Ctrl+D
Recall a name and fill in the field (QuickFill).	Type the first few letters of the name, and then press Tab
Scroll in the QuickFill list.	Ctrl+up arrow or Ctrl+down arrow

Task	Keyboard Shortcut
Increase a check or other transaction number by one.	Press the + key when a Num field is selected
Decrease a check or other transaction number by one.	Press the – key when a Num field is selected
Open the Split Transaction window.	Ctrl+S
Cut a field in a register.	Shift+Del (Ctrl+X if you use Windows mapping)
Copy a field in a transaction.	Ctrl+Ins (Ctrl+C if you use Windows mapping)
Paste a copied field in a transaction.	Shift+Ins (Ctrl+V if you use Windows mapping)
Delete the character to the right of the insertion point.	Del
Delete the character to the left of the insertion point.	Backspace

Dates

When you're choosing the date for a transaction, you don't have to type the date or click the calendar icon. Here are some handy keyboard shortcuts for moving to the date you want when a date field is active.

Task	Keyboard Shortcut
Move to the next day.	+ key
Move to the previous day.	– key
Change the date back to today (Hint: That's T for "today").	T
Display the Date calendar.	Alt+down arrow
Choose the first day of the month (Hint: M like the first letter in "month").	M
Choose the last day of the month (Hint: H like the last letter in "month").	H
Choose the first day of the year (Hint: Y like the first letter in "year").	Y
Choose the last day of the year (Hint: R like the last letter in "year").	R
Go to a specific date. In the Go To Date dialog box, type or select the date then and click OK.	Ctrl+G

Tip: For shortcuts that move to the beginning or end of a period, such as M, pressing the key more than once jumps further forward or backward in time. For example, if it's June 14 and pressing M once moves to June 1, then pressing M two more times moves to April 1.

Moving Around in Quicken Windows

These shortcuts apply to windows and dialog boxes.

Task	Keyboard Shortcut
Move down one transaction or row in a register or report.	Down arrow
Move up one transaction or row in a register or report.	Up arrow
Move to the first transaction in a register or the first row in a report.	Ctrl+Home, or Home four times
Move to the last transaction in a register or report.	Ctrl+End, or End four times
Move to the next field in an account register transaction or in a dialog box.	Tab or Enter, depending on your preference setting (page 86)
Move to the previous field in an account register transaction or in a dialog box.	Shift+Tab
Move to the first field in a transaction.	Home twice
Move to the last field in a transaction.	End twice
Move to the beginning (left side) of the current field.	Home
Move to the end (right side) of the current field.	End
Move down one screen in a scrolling window.	Page Down
Move up one screen in a scrolling window.	Page Up
Choose the first transaction in a register window dated the *first* day of the same month as the current transaction. For example, if the current transaction is dated 4/20/2008, Ctrl+Page Up goes to the first transaction dated 4/1/2008. If you press this keyboard shortcut more than once, Quicken moves to the first day of the previous month (3/1/2008, in this example).	Ctrl+Page Up
Choose the first transaction in a register window dated the *last* day of the same month as the current transaction. For example, if the current transaction is dated 4/20/2008, Ctrl+Page Down goes to the first transaction dated 4/30/2008. If you press this keyboard shortcut more than once, Quicken moves to the last day of the next month (5/30/2008, in this example).	Ctrl+Page Down

Quicken Help

As you use Quicken to help reach your dream of becoming a millionaire (or what-ever your financial goals are), you're bound to run into some snags. Finding answers to Quicken questions isn't always easy, but you've got a few avenues to try.

Quicken Help, which you access within the program, is best when you're looking for step-by-step instructions. But it falls short when you're trying to learn what Quicken can do and how to apply those capabilities to your present predicament.

Quicken's Help is renowned for telling you what you already know; for example, "On the Category line, enter a category." (Gee, thanks.) Meanwhile, it remains obstinately silent on what you don't, like what to do about duplicate downloaded transactions: "Under most circumstances, your register entry would be recognized and the duplication problem would not occur." And Quicken 2009's Help feature doesn't even have an index, so you can't scan for topics that sound like what you're looking for. If you don't discover the magical search terms you need, you're out of luck. And searching doesn't find as many related topics as it used to in previous versions of the program.

Fortunately, the Quicken online forums can be a good source of answers to gnarly problems like how to allocate a refinanced loan to pay off an old mortgage. As you'll see in this appendix, you can find help in lots of ways—one of which is sure to suit your style.

Help for the Task at Hand

When you're in the middle of something and have no idea what an option or button does, you want an answer—fast. Although Quicken help isn't always helpful, you've got a couple of ways to find info directly related to what you're doing. Here are your options:

- **F1.** Pressing F1 is the one path to Quicken Help you can always count on. Whether you're looking at an account register, a dialog box, or a window, pressing F1 opens Quicken Help to the topic most relevant to the task at hand. For example, if the Write Checks window is active, pressing F1 displays the "Write a check" topic. Pressing F1 while you're staring at the Category List displays the "Tell me about categorizing transactions" topic, which includes some background as well as links to how-tos for category-related tasks. And pressing F1 when you're in your checking account register displays the "Tell me about using a cash flow register to track bills and income" topic.

- **Help icon.** At the bottom of most dialog boxes and in many windows, you'll find the Help icon, a red question mark in a gold circle. Like pressing F1, clicking this icon opens Quicken Help to the section about that dialog box or window. For example, if you click the Help icon at the bottom of the account register's Downloaded Transactions tab, the "Review and accept update cash flow transactions" topic appears.

> **Note:** If you have trouble displaying the Help window and the main Quicken window at the same time, see the box on page 530 for some tips.

- **How Do I?** Quicken windows that have a menu bar (like the Write Checks window and Memorized Payee List, but not the Account List or Category List) include the How Do I? command at the right ends of their menu bars. Look for the Help icon followed by the phrase, "How Do I?" Click it to open a Quicken Help window filled with links to how-to topics for that window, like the lower window in Figure B-1. Like other features in Quicken Help, the How Do I? command isn't as helpful as it used to be and it doesn't appear in as many places as it used to, either.

> **Note:** At the bottom of every Help topic, you'll see the question, "Did this Help topic give you the information you needed?" If the Help topic truly helped, let Intuit know by clicking Yes. If it didn't, click No and then take a minute to tell Intuit what you want to know by filling out the feedback window that appears. With feedback from folks like you, Quicken Help *may* become more helpful.

- **Guide Me.** Quicken 2009 includes yet another set of tabs, called the Sidebar (page 7), which cascades down the right side of the main Quicken window. (The Sidebar shows up on the left side instead if you move the Account Bar to the right side of the window.) The Guide Me tab includes instructions for working with what you see in the main Quicken window, like an account register or

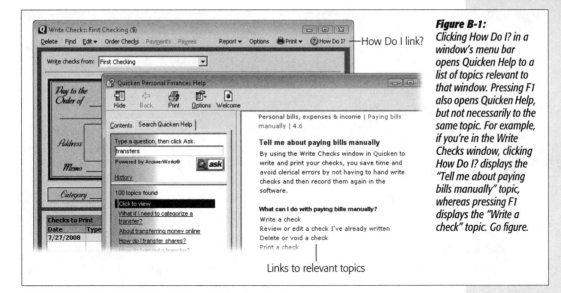

How Do I link?

Figure B-1:
Clicking How Do I? in a window's menu bar opens Quicken Help to a list of topics relevant to that window. Pressing F1 also opens Quicken Help, but not necessarily to the same topic. For example, if you're in the Write Checks window, clicking How Do I? displays the "Tell me about paying bills manually" topic, whereas pressing F1 displays the "Write a check" topic. Go figure.

Links to relevant topics

an Overview screen. To expand the Sidebar and get Quicken's guidance, simply click the Guide Me tab. To hide the Sidebar, click the – sign inside the square at the top of the Sidebar. See page 33 to learn what the Sidebar's other tabs do.

Tip: Out of the box, the Sidebar covers up some of the main window when it expands. If you want the Sidebar and the contents of the main window to display side by side, choose Edit → Preferences → Quicken Program. In the Quicken Preferences dialog box, click Setup in the "Select preference type" list and then turn on the Dock Side Bar checkbox.

Working with Quicken Help

Although you usually start out looking for a task-specific topic, you're likely to browse around after that. Quicken makes it easy to learn about things related to what you're working on. For example, in the Write Checks window, clicking How Do I? displays the "Tell me about paying bills manually" topic, as well as links to nine subtopics related to manual bill payments, such as "Write a check", "Delete or void a check", and so on.

You can also navigate Quicken Help topics to find exactly the information you want, or cure a case of insomnia. Start by pressing F1 or choosing Help → Quicken Help. The left pane of the Quicken Help window has two tabs, each of which gives you a different way of finding information and has its own pros and cons:

- **Contents.** The Contents tab is the better choice for help with a broad topic, like investing. To expand a topic, click the + sign in the square to its left. Then, expand the most likely topic at the next level until you find what you're looking for. When you see an entry preceded by a question mark (like the ones shown

WORKAROUND WORKSHOP

Resizing the Help Window

Sometimes the Help window refuses to yield the floor (or screen, in this case). In Quicken 2009, the Help window jumps into the background when you click anywhere in a dialog box or window, but it stays in the foreground if you click within the Quicken main window, for example, to add or edit transactions in a register. If you want to read the Help instructions *and* perform a task at the same time, an enormous monitor is the ideal solution. You'll have enough room to see the Quicken window and the Help window side by side. Simply drag the Help window to a spot where it isn't in the way. If you don't have a giant monitor, here are some other options:

- **Hide.** In the Help window's toolbar, click Hide, which reduces the window's width by hiding the left-hand pane with the Contents and Search Quicken Help tabs. All you see is the pane with the Help text.

When you want to find another topic, in the toolbar, click Show to display the other pane again.

- **Minimize.** In the Help window's top-right corner, click the Minimize button (the one with the under-score on it) to hide the window—and the instructions. When you're ready to read the next step, in the Windows taskbar, click the Quicken Personal Finances Help button (the one with a yellow question mark) to restore the window.

- **Resize panes and windows.** Drag the right side of the Help window to make it narrower (your cursor turns into a double-headed arrow). You can also drag the border between the left-hand search pane and the right-hand help text pane to see more of the Help text. Quicken wraps the contents in both panes to fit the new slimmer profile.

in Figure B-2), click it to display information or instructions related to that topic. If a summary topic on the right side of the Help window includes links, you can also click them to open the corresponding help topics.

- **Search.** The Search Quicken Help tab lets you type in more than one keyword, like "voiding checks". When you type in your keywords and click Ask, Quicken looks for topics that contain all the keywords you provided. The more keywords you type (between three and 10, say), the more likely Quicken is to find the topic that answers your question.

As you navigate from one help topic to another, in the Quicken Help window's icon bar, click Back to display previous topics or click Print to print the current topic.

Quicken Product and Customer Support

Choose Help → "Product and Customer Support" to open a window with links to all kinds of help—both free and for-fee. (Or choose the life-preserver icon at the main Quicken window's top-right corner to get to the same place.) Along with the Quicken Help topics you've seen (and perhaps given up on), you see links to a variety of online resources, support pages, and phone numbers. You can click the Quicken Technical Support Home Page link to access Intuit's support Web page. Or click the "Contact Intuit and Others" link to see lots of ways to reach folks who can help. At the bottom of the page, you see the phone number for Intuit's technical support.

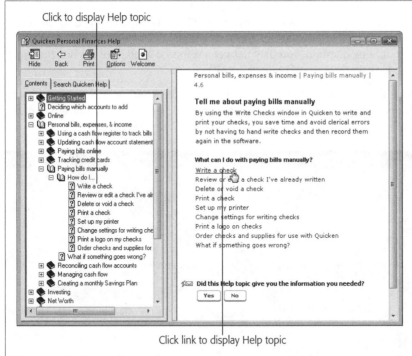

Click to display Help topic

Click link to display Help topic

Figure B-2:
To read more about a subtopic like "Write a check", point to it and then, when your cursor changes to a hand, click it. (You can easily spot subtopics because they're written in blue.) Most topics contain step-by-step instructions, but some provide descriptions of Quicken features.

Quicken phone support hooks you up with a human—sometimes for a price, depending on the topic. (See the "Contact Intuit and Others" page for a list of topics Intuit doesn't charge you for.) But there's no guarantee that an Intuit technical support person can solve your problem, particularly if it involves financial finesse in addition to Quicken handholding. Support fees can be steep, which adds extra stress to an already stressful situation. Before you resort to the telephone, consider using Intuit's email or chat support.

Intuit doesn't charge for email or chat support for the most recent version of Quicken (Quicken 2009), but they *do* charge if you're using an earlier version. Email support connects you to a human, though you have to wait for a response. Email support is great if you want to fire off a question and read the answer when you get home from work. Chat support occurs in real time. When you start a chat session, you type in your question and background information. Then, after a brief delay (usually a minute or so), a support person responds and you chat back and forth until you have your answer. One advantage to the chat service is that the technical support person emails you detailed instructions for resolving your problem—if you ask for them.

The Quicken Forums

Although the adage "You get what you pay for" is true *most* of the time, Quicken forums are helpful *and* free. Not only do Intuit employees prowl the forums and answer questions, but you're likely to get an answer from someone who's felt your pain and found a way through it. One downside to the forums is you usually don't get an immediate answer. And if you post a vague description of your problem or ask a rambling question, you may not get a response at all. (See the box below for tips on making the most of online forums.)

To visit the forums, choose Help → "Ask a Quicken User", which takes you to the Quicken Community Web site. In the browser window, click the link for the forum for your software ("Quicken for Windows", for example).

Each forum includes several high-level topics. You can navigate the forums by scanning the high-level topics, and then clicking the one that sounds the most like your problem to read the related posts. Many discussion titles are woefully vague—such as "Investments in Quicken," which has more than 4,000 related posts—so it's often faster to type a few words (like "account reconcile error" or "duplicate transactions") in the Search Community box at the top of the page and then click Search Community. When it's done searching, the page lists posts that contain the words you're looking for. You can search a specific topic or all topics, or limit posts to a date range. You can even look for posts from a specific person, if you know of someone whose answers tend be helpful.

Tip: If the forum search doesn't deliver helpful topics, consider searching Google using the same keywords. Google often does a better job of finding pertinent discussions in Quicken forums and in the Quicken knowledge base (an online database of support topics), as well as on a wide variety of other Web sites.

To post a question (or answer), you have to log into the forums. If you haven't registered, click the Free Registration link (in the Please Log In section) and then choose a name and password. After logging in, select one of the top-level topics. When you see the discussions within that topic, take some time to see if any of them answer your question. If not, at the top of the list, click "Start a New Discussion" and then fill out the form to post your question.

Installing Quicken

Quicken installations fall into two camps—fresh installations and upgrades from a previous version. Either way, Quicken installations don't give you many options. About all you get to decide is where to install the software, though you don't even *have* to do that. This simplicity may lull you into choosing options you'll later regret, such as upgrading Quicken instead of installing a second separate version. But don't worry; this appendix walks you through the installation process and explains which options you should choose and why.

Note: To run Quicken 2009, your computer has to use Windows 2000, Windows 2003, Windows XP, or Windows Vista.

Installing Quicken

The main thing you need to successfully install Quicken is a little common sense. This section tells you everything else you need to know. If you have a previous version of Quicken on your machine and run into trouble trying to install the new version, you'll have to perform a few extra steps, as explained in the box on page 534. If you want to install Quicken 2009 *in addition* to your current version to make sure you want to upgrade, see the box on page 537.

Here's how to do a fresh installation if you don't have any other versions of Quicken on your computer:

1. **As with most installations, it's a good idea to shut down any programs you have running, including your virus protection program. Then insert the Quicken CD.**

   Usually, the installation process starts on its own and the Quicken 2009 Install Wizard window appears.

   If the installation *doesn't* start automatically, use Windows Explorer to run the CD—in the Windows taskbar, click the Start button and then choose All Programs → Accessories → Windows Explorer. (That's *Windows* Explorer the search tool, not *Internet* Explorer the Web browser.) Look for the icon for the installation program, *install.exe,* and double-click it. (It looks like a tiny compact disc and it won't be inside any other folders.)

WORKAROUND WORKSHOP

Cleaning Up an Old Installation

Sometimes when you try to install a new version of Quicken, it gets tangled up with the one that's already on your computer. If the installation process start hiccupping and whining, you may have to clean up any existing Quicken folders and then run the installation with administrator privileges. That may sound intimidating, but the Quicken Web site tells you all the steps you have to perform.

To find these directions, go to *www.quicken.com* and then click Support. In the Support page Search box, type *install Windows Vista* (even if you don't use Windows Vista) and

then click Search. The topic "Unable to open, install, or uninstall Quicken on Microsoft Windows Vista" tells you how to clean up the Quicken folders that are causing trouble. The QcleanUI tool that you can download from this support topic cleans up leftover Quicken files and Windows registry entries. (This tool can also help if you have problems installing Quicken in another version of the Windows operating system.) The process isn't too complicated. When you're done, you can start with step 1 in the installation process (above).

---

2. **In the "Quicken 2009 - Install Wizard" window, click Next.**

   The License Agreement screen appears. Quicken's license agreement basically protects Intuit from lawsuits. For example, Intuit doesn't claim that the software is free of bugs and viruses, nor does it guarantee that using the program ensures correct tax returns.

3. **After you read the software agreement, choose the "I agree to the terms of the license agreement and acknowledge receipt of the Quicken Privacy Statement" option and then click Next.**

   To read the privacy statement, click the Quicken Privacy Statement link. You *have* to agree to the terms or you can't install Quicken.

4. **The Destination Folder screen appears. The wizard automatically chooses** *C:\ Program Files\Quicken* **as the place it'll install the program, which is fine for most people. If that location works for you, click Next.**

If you want to install to a different folder, click Change, choose the folder you want and then click OK. Then, click Next.

Note: If you install Quicken in a different folder, you may have to uninstall the program manually when you upgrade to the next version. See the box on page 539 for more info.

---

5. **The "Ready to Install the Program" screen appears. To begin the installation, click Install.**

The wizard tells you what installation task it's performing and displays a progress bar showing how far it's gotten. How long the process takes depends on your computer's age and health. If you're installing Quicken on a computer running Windows Vista, you're ready for the next step when the Install Wizard asks if you want to install the Quicken Billminder Gadget on your Vista Sidebar. On Windows XP computers, keep an eye on the Next button; when it becomes active, click it and then jump to step 7.

6. **Click Yes to install the Billminder Gadget on the Vista Sidebar, or click No if you don't want to use the Billminder.**

The Billminder is a handy tool that keeps financial tasks in plain sight so you won't forget them. If you click Yes, the Windows Sidebar dialog box opens; click Install. When the gadget appears on the sidebar, the "Quicken 2009 - Install Wizard" window displays the "Check for Quicken Updates" screen. If you click No to forego the Billminder's assistance, you hop straight to the "Check for Quicken Updates" screen.

7. **To make sure your software is completely up to date, connect to the Internet (if you're not connected already), and then, in the "Check for Quicken Updates" screen, click Get Update to start One Step Update.**

The version of Quicken that comes on the CD you buy isn't necessarily the latest and greatest. Intuit follows each new Quicken release with a few updates with bug fixes and additional enhancements, so you want to be sure to get any available updates. Updating Quicken also ensures that you have the latest information for online services.

Whenever there are updates to install (whether you're installing the program or opening after you've installed it), the One Step Update window appears and shows what it's updating, as shown in Figure C-1. If there aren't any updates, you see the Use Quicken Now button in the Quicken Update window, as described in the next step.

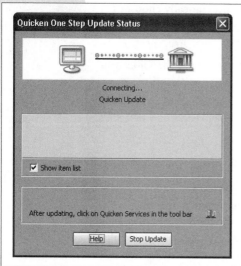

Figure C-1:
The One Step Update window shows you what it's updating in your version of Quicken. From now on, a window with updating instructions appears if a Quicken update is available.

8. **In the Quicken Update window, click Use Quicken Now if you're ready to get to work, or click Done if you'd rather launch Quicken later.**

    Congratulations—you're done installing Quicken! If you click Use Quicken Now, then the "Get Started with Quicken 2009" wizard cheerfully welcomes you to the program and helps you set things up. (See Chapter 1 for full details on the "Get Started with Quicken" wizard.)

Before you get too deep into Quicken, you might want to clean up some of the shortcuts that the installation dropped on your desktop. Most of these are offers for credit cards, savings accounts, credit reports, and a free month of Quicken Bill Pay. To delete a shortcut, right-click it, choose Delete and then confirm that you want to delete it. If you're interested in any of these offers, leave them there.

Quicken also adds a desktop shortcut for Quicken itself. If you like launching programs from the desktop, keep this shortcut. If not, you can delete the shortcut and launch Quicken from the Start menu or the Quick Launch toolbar, as described on page 15.

Upgrading Quicken

If you have an older version of Quicken on your computer and you're sure you want to use Quicken 2009, all you have to do is upgrade. Upgrading Quicken is as easy as installing the program in the first place. Here are the steps:

1. **Back up your data file to your hard disk or external media, as described on page 462.**

    Although Quicken makes a backup copy during the upgrade, you can't be too careful with your financial data. Creating your own backup is extra insurance in case something goes wrong.

Installing Two Versions of Quicken

Having multiple versions of Quicken installed on the same computer can come in handy. Say you've been running Quicken 2008 since it came out and you want to take Quicken 2009 for a test drive before you entrust your financial data to it.

Running two versions of Quicken takes a bit of planning, because the Quicken 2009 upgrade (page 536) uninstalls the previous version. And, to keep your data up to date until you make up your mind, you have to enter all your transactions into *both* versions. Here's how to convince Quicken 2009 and your previous version to run on the same computer with a minimum of sibling rivalry:

1. Before you install Quicken 2009, save a copy of your existing Quicken data file (page 462) and give it a name that indicates which version of the program it's attached to, like *MyMoneyQn2008.qdf.*

2. Begin installing Quicken 2009 as you would normally (step 1 on page 534).

3. When the "Quicken 2009 - Install Wizard" screen appears, press and hold Ctrl+Shift and then click the Next button. A message box warns you that the installer *won't* check for a previous version of Quicken, which means it'll leave your current version in place and install Quicken 2009. That's exactly what you want, so click OK to close the message box.

4. Choose the "I agree to the terms of the license agreement and acknowledge receipt of the Quicken Privacy Statement" option and then click Next.

5. To install two versions, you *have* to change the name of the installation folder to a folder for the *new* version (like *Quicken2009Test*, as shown in Figure C-2). If you forget this step, then you'll install Quicken 2009 over the older version.

6. The installation wizard steps you through the installation just like a new install.

To try the new version, launch it, open your *existing* Quicken data file and then follow the instructions for converting the data file to the new version (see page 24). As long as you made a copy of your data file (see step 1), go ahead and convert the copy. (You can always go back to your original file if you decide not to upgrade.) If you decide to use Quicken 2009, simply uninstall the previous version (page 539).

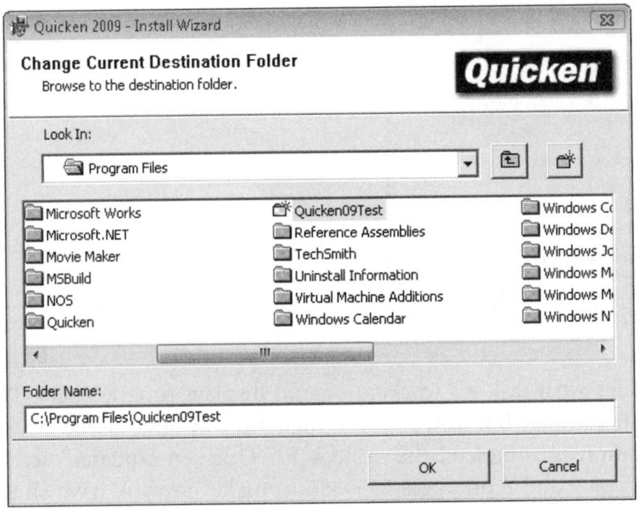

Figure C-2:
If you want to install Quicken 2009 alongside your previous version, you can't use C:\Program Files\Quicken, the default installation location. Simply modify the location by changing the folder to Quicken2009Test, for example. Then you can put Quicken 2009 through its paces to try it out and, if you don't like it, uninstall it (page 539). Then launch the previous version and open the backup copy of the data file you made with the previous version.

2. **Shut down any programs you have running, including your virus protection program, and then insert the Quicken CD into your CD drive.**

   Most of the time, the installation procedure starts on its own and the "Quicken 2009 - Install Wizard" window appears. (If it doesn't, launch the install program yourself, as described on page 534.)

3. **In the "Quicken 2009 - Install Wizard" window, click Next.**

   The License Agreement screen appears.

4. **After you read the software agreement, choose the "I agree to the terms of the license agreement and acknowledge receipt of the Quicken Privacy Statement" option and then click Next. (To read the privacy statement, click the Quicken Privacy Statement link.)**

   The Destination Folder screen appears. The wizard automatically chooses *C:\ Program Files\Quicken* as the place it'll install the program, which is fine for most people. If you want to install to a different folder, click Change and then choose the folder you want. When you're done, click Next.

5. **Now you get your first indication that you're upgrading. The "Ready to Install the Program" screen appears, telling you it's about to uninstall your previous version of Quicken and install Quicken 2008, as shown in Figure C-3.**

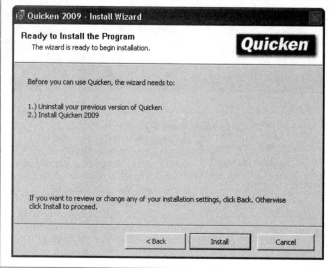

Figure C-3:
When you click Install, the wizard first removes the program files for your previous version of Quicken (don't worry—your data files remain intact) and then installs Quicken 2009.

6. **Click Install.**

   The wizard indicates what task it's working on and displays progress bars. The upgrade doesn't take long, but you have enough time to grab some coffee. When the installation is complete, the "Check for Quicken Updates" screen appears. Follow steps 7 and 8 on pages 535–536 to make sure you have all the available updates.

If you click Run Quicken when you're done upgrading, Quicken 2009 starts up and opens the "Get Started with Quicken 2009" dialog box. Chapter 1 describes how to convert an existing data file or create a brand-new one.

TROUBLESHOOTING MOMENT

When Quicken Won't Uninstall

If you installed a previous version of Quicken in a folder other than the one that the program suggests (*C:\Program Files\Quicken*), the Quicken 2009 Install wizard won't be able to find and uninstall it, so you have to uninstall it manually. To uninstall a program on a Windows Vista PC, choose Start → Control Panel → "Uninstall a program". To uninstall a program on a Windows XP PC, choose Start → Settings → Control Panel → "Add or Remove Programs". Select the older version of Quicken in the window that opens and then click Remove.

If you see an error message after you click Remove or have problems installing Quicken 2009, you'll need to run an uninstall program to remove the older version's files from your computer. Go to *www.quicken.com* and click Support. In the Search box, type *uninstall error 1638* and then click Search. The topic that appears outlines the steps for uninstalling and includes links to download the programs you need to clean out the prior version of Quicken.

Registering Quicken

At some point after you install or upgrade, the Product Registration window appears. You can click Register Later to postpone the inevitable, but eventually you'll have to register Quicken. For example, you have to register before you can use online banking or download financial transactions. If you decide to register later, you can do so at any time by choosing Help → Register Quicken.

There are two parts to Quicken registration, as the window shown in Figure C-4 explains: registering your software with Intuit so you can get program updates and free stock quotes, and registering with Quicken.com to take advantage of its online features or store information online.

Note: If you have trouble connecting to the Internet to register Quicken, the problem may be Quicken's Internet Connection settings. See page 124 to learn more about helping Quicken and your Internet connection communicate.

When you click Register Now, the registration window displays instructions for both parts of registration. Simply provide some basic information about yourself—like name, address, and email (required fields have red dots next to them; the rest are optional). If you feel like sharing, fill in the other text boxes and checkboxes to tell Intuit how you plan to use the software. Click Register when you're done. If you already have a Quicken.com ID, just click Finish and you're ready to use Quicken 2009.

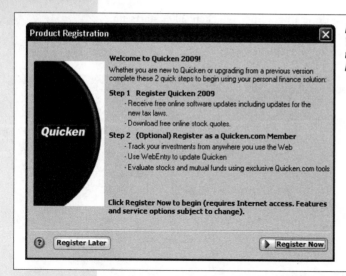

Figure C-4:
You need to be online to register, so be sure to connect to the Internet before you click Register Now.

If you don't have a Quicken.com ID, you see a screen for the second step of registration—setting up your Quicken.com member ID and password. You don't *have* to register for Quicken.com, especially if you plan to keep your financial data more secure by not storing it online. Just close the window and you're done. (If you decide to register for Quicken.com later, you can navigate to the registration site by clicking "Quicken.com" in the Quicken Tool Bar. Fill in the text boxes to create a Quicken.com member account and then click Finish to complete your registration.

Index

I

Colophon

Loranah Dimant, Rachel Monaghan, and Marlowe Shaeffer provided quality control for *Quicken 2009: The Missing Manual*. Ron Strauss wrote the index.

The cover of this book is based on a series design by David Freedman. Karen Montgomery produced the cover layout with Adobe InDesign CS using Adobe's Minion and Gill Sans fonts.

David Futato designed the interior layout, based on a series design by Phil Simpson. This book was converted by Abby Fox to FrameMaker 5.5.6. The text font is Adobe Minion; the heading font is Adobe Formata Condensed; and the code font is LucasFont's TheSans Mono Condensed. The illustrations that appear in the book were produced by Robert Romano and Jessamyn Read using Macromedia FreeHand MX and Adobe Photoshop CS.

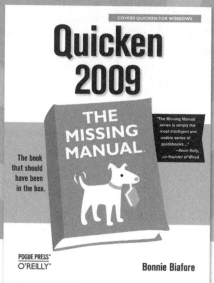